advance, but [illegible] warned Dublin Castle, & not even Birrell in London — one of them saying that it was better to let things come to a head! (But this may not be true) She expressed a very poor opinion of Sir John Simon, as unwilling to take off his coat to a political fight, and disliking his associates in such a fight.

Lady Barlow called, & gushed as usual.

# The Letters of Sidney and Beatrice Webb
## Volume III
## Pilgrimage 1912–1947

Lord Passfield and Mrs Sidney Webb

# The Letters of Sidney and Beatrice Webb

EDITED BY
NORMAN MACKENZIE

Volume III
Pilgrimage
1912–1947

Cambridge University Press
CAMBRIDGE LONDON NEW YORK MELBOURNE
PUBLISHED IN COOPERATION WITH
The London School of Economics and Political Science

Published by the Syndics of the Cambridge University Press
The Pitt Building, Trumpington Street, Cambridge CB2 1RP
Bentley House, 200 Euston Road, London NW1 2DB
32 East 57th Street, New York, NY 10022, USA
296 Beaconsfield Parade, Middle Park, Melbourne 3206, Australia



First published 1978



Printed in Great Britain
at the University Press, Cambridge

*Library of Congress Cataloguing in Publication Data* (*Revised*)

Passfield, Sidney James Webb, Baron, 1859–1947.

The Letters of Sidney and Beatrice Webb.

'Published in co-operation with the London School of Economics and Political Science.'

Includes indexes.

CONTENTS: v. 1. Apprenticeships, 1873–1892. – v. 2. Partnership, 1892–1912. – v. 3. Pilgrimage, 1912–1947.
I. Socialists – Great Britain – Correspondence.
I. Webb, Beatrice Potter, 1858–1943, joint author.
II. Mackenzie, Norman Ian. III. London School of Economics and Political Science. IV. Title.
HX243.P295 1978 335'.14'0922 77-1665

ISBN 0 521 21681 8 Volume I
ISBN 0 521 21682 6 Volume II
ISBN 0 521 21837 3 Volume III
ISBN 0 521 22015 7 Set

# Contents

# Introduction

The lives of Sidney and Beatrice Webb fell into three distinct phases, to which the three volumes of their letters correspond. The first was the period up to their marriage, which Beatrice described in *My Apprenticeship*. The second, from their marriage to the eve of the First World War, spanned the active years of middle life, in which their reputations were established in research, authorship and public affairs. This phase was covered in the second volume of Beatrice's autobiography, which she appropriately named *Our Partnership*. She had planned to complete the account of their careers in a third volume, to which she gave the provisional title of *Our Pilgrimage*. In June 1931 she worked out a timetable which envisaged a start on this work when she was 75, but age and ill-health overtook her before she was able to make a serious beginning. All that survives of her project are some preliminary drafts and a chapter which is headed 'The First Stage of the Pilgrim's Progress'. In place of her own edited selection from her diaries in these years the reader must turn to the extracts published by Dame Margaret Cole (up to 1932) and to the full text of the manuscript diary itself.

Beatrice's failure to complete the planned autobiography was due to several reasons. When she began work on *My Apprenticeship*, towards the end of the war, she was looking forward to a comfortable retirement, in which she and Sidney would devote themselves to the completion of their series of books on local government and in which she would have sufficient leisure to work up her diaries into publishable form. The purchase of their house at Passfield Corner as a permanent home in the country was part of that plan. It was disrupted by Sidney's unforeseen involvement in Labour politics, which began in 1916 when he became a member of the Labour executive and took a leading role in shaping the policy and organisation of the party. Though the Webbs managed to produce *A Constitution for the Socialist Commonwealth of Great Britain* and *The Decay of Capitalist Civilisation* in the aftermath of the war, the partnership was further disrupted by his election as M.P. for the Durham mining constituency of Seaham Harbour, which he held until he was elevated to the peerage as Lord Passfield in 1929. Secondly, a minority Labour Government was formed under Ramsay MacDonald early in 1924, and Sidney became a member of the Cabinet. Though Beatrice now spent much of her time in the country drafting *My Apprenticeship*, Sidney's official duties as President of the Board of Trade kept him in London – and even when Beatrice was in London she saw little of him, and much of her time was devoted to entertaining Labour politicians. This created another serious distraction, especially since Beatrice was the moving spirit in the Half-Circle Club, formed to provide a social focus for the wives of Labour men who suddenly found themselves thrust into the political milieu. In her diary entries which cover both the 1924 and 1929 Labour governments she described her demanding role as a Labour hostess. She suffered, moreover, from bouts of ill-health and depression, which delayed her work on her manuscripts. The most significant distraction was due to the change in her political outlook.

The 'Pilgrim's Progress' had led her steadily towards a new faith in old age. By the time the economic crisis in the summer of 1931 brought down the second MacDonald government Beatrice had become disillusioned with social democracy, and turned towards Soviet Communism, which she and Sidney were soon to hail as 'A New Civilisation'. Her conversion was ostensibly a rejection of the gradualist socialism to which the Webbs, as the main theoreticians of Fabianism, had given much of their lives. In *Our Partnership* she wrote that they had gone 'hopelessly wrong' in dismissing Marx's forecast of the breakdown of the capitalist system, and that the 'new social order' which had emerged in Russia was superior to the modified capitalism which had collapsed in 1931. Yet, in a profound sense, the new-found Soviet sympathies of the Webbs grew out of their earlier attitudes. They had always been collectivists who were attracted by the notion of national efficiency – what Beatrice came to call 'planned production for community consumption' – and by the idea of a caste of experts who would disinterestedly administer society for the common good. There had been a strong thread of elitism in their political assumptions, a legacy in part of their earlier exposure to the ideas of Comte and his conception of a Religion of Humanity directed by enlightened specialists. The Webbs found a contemporary embodiment of that creed and of Comte's 'Priests of Humanity' in the Soviet Communist Party. Shaw, visiting Russia before them, came to the same conclusion and reported that Lenin had established a Fabian state. When the Webbs themselves set off to the Soviet Union, before writing the vast compendium of *Soviet Communism* which was the last product of their partnership, Beatrice explicitly described it as a 'pilgrimage', and insisted that it was the goal to which they had been travelling throughout their lives.

Conversion was not simply a matter of intellectual conviction; it reflected a deep and unsatisfied spiritual hunger in Beatrice, and gave Sidney a lesser emotional satisfaction that collectivism worked in practice and on a large scale. For Beatrice, who called herself a 'religious agnostic', had rejected the forms of revealed religion without appeasing her craving for a faith. In Soviet Communism she found a secular creed which completed the shift from the service of God to the service of Man. In old age, she once said wryly, some people fell in love with their chauffeurs, and the Webbs had fallen in love with a social system.

It was this powerful commitment, which drained the remaining energies of the Webbs while it sustained their spirits, that made it impossible for Beatrice even to finish off *Our Partnership* let alone give herself to the planned third volume of autobiography. She had no regrets about this failure: on the contrary, she considered *Soviet Communism* a far better 'testament' to their life-work, ranking it with the founding of the London School of Economics, the Minority Report on the Poor Law and the launching of the *New Statesman* as one of their four 'children'.

In 1912, at the close of the second volume of these letters, the Webbs considered that their useful years were almost over. They did not foresee that they would remain in public life for nearly thirty years; as Shaw said long afterwards, in 1914 they ceased to be Fabians and became public personalities. The change led to a shift in the balance of the partnership from the close complementarity of the pre-war years. Sidney, as Beatrice had feared when she long ago sought to keep him out of Parliament, began to lead a more independent career, in which other priorities than their joint work pressed upon him. He was not a particularly happy or successful parliamentarian, but he felt needed by the Labour Party. Beatrice, by contrast, felt neglected, turning to autobiography in part as compensation for her separation from Sidney's working life, disliking her obligations as a politician's wife though she punctiliously fulfilled them, and more and more questioning the meaning of her long pilgrimage through life.

In 1938 Sidney suffered a stroke from which he never fully recovered; it left him able to read but not to write or engage in serious conversation. Beatrice, devoting herself to him, had also to cope with the difficulties of running a wartime home in the country, with worrying about money, and with her own increasing ill-health. During the last five years she showed little interest in politics apart from her obsession with the fate of the Soviet Union. She died in 1943. Sidney survived her by four years.

# A brief chronology

Only the main publications of Sidney and Beatrice Webb are listed below. A fuller bibliography is available in *Publications of Sidney and Beatrice Webb: An Interim Check List*, British Library of Political and Economic Science 1973.

1912 Beatrice joins I.L.P.; is elected to Fabian executive, becomes dominant figure in Fabian Society, sets up research department and promotes joint campaign of Fabians and I.L.P. for 'National Minimum'.

1913 Webbs plan and launch the *New Statesman*. Sidney and Beatrice Webb: *English Local Government V – The Story of the King's Highway*.

1914 Sidney joins War Emergency Workers Committee, and begins to collaborate with Arthur Henderson. Webbs commission Leonard Woolf to draft schemes for prevention of war and international government. Sidney Webb: Fabian Tract 176, *The War and the Workers*.

1916 Sidney becomes member of Labour Party Executive: opposes participation in Lloyd George coalition; begins to draft Labour's peace aims for party conference in January 1917: *Labour After The War*. Sidney Webb and Arnold Freeman: *Great Britain after the War*.

1917 Lloyd George appoints Beatrice to Reconstruction Committee, to consider post-war social problems: she revives her Poor Law proposals. Sidney collaborates with Henderson and MacDonald on new party organisation for Labour. Sidney Webb: *The Works Manager To-Day*. Fabian Tract 181, *When Peace Comes*.

1918 Sidney drafts *Labour and the New Social Order* as framework for Labour policy. Stands as Labour candidate for London University, coming second. Fabian intellectuals appointed to key positions on Labour Party Policy Advisory Committees. Beatrice, member of Committee on Women in Industry, produces minority report in favour of equal pay. Sidney Webb: Fabian Tract 183, *The Reform of the House of Lords*. Beatrice Webb: Fabian Tract 185, *The Abolition of the Poor Law*.

1919 Sidney is one of three members representing mineworkers on Sankey Commission on coalmines. Sidney comes top of poll for Labour Executive. Sidney Webb: Fabian Tracts 187, *The Teacher in Politics* and 188, *National Finances and a Levy on Capital*.

1920 Sidney nominated as Labour candidate for Seaham Harbour. Sidney and Beatrice Webb: *A Constitution for the Socialist Commonwealth of Great Britain; The Consumers' Co-operative Movement*.

1921 Beatrice forms Half-Circle Club for wives of Labour politicians. Sidney Webb: *The Story of the Durham Miners, 1662–1921*.

1922 Sidney elected for Seaham Harbour. Sidney and Beatrice Webb: *English Local Government IV – Statutory Authorities for Special Purposes; VI – English Prisons Under Local Government*.

1923 Webbs acquire Passfield Corner as country home. Sidney and Beatrice Webb: *The Decay of Capitalist Civilisation.*

1924 Sidney becomes President of Board of Trade in first Labour Government. Beatrice begins serious work on *My Apprenticeship.* Beatrice awarded honorary degree at University of Edinburgh. Sidney drafts Labour's election manifesto. Labour Party defeated.

1926 Webbs opposed to General Strike, and critical of intransigence of mine-workers union. Both Webbs awarded honorary degrees at University of Munich. Beatrice Webb: *My Apprenticeship.*

1927 Sidney and Beatrice Webb: *English Local Government VII–IX – English Poor Law History.*

1929 Labour becomes largest party and forms another minority government. J. R. MacDonald succeeds Webb in Seaham Harbour; Sidney becomes Lord Passfield and Colonial Secretary; Beatrice declines to use her title. Webbs move out of Grosvenor Road, temporarily taking flat in Whitehall Court, before moving to *pied-à-terre* in Victoria Street.

1930 Sidney responsible for White Paper on Palestine, evokes Zionist hostility.

1931 Beatrice begins to draft *Our Partnership.* Labour Government collapses in financial crisis and MacDonald defects to lead a coalition administration. Beatrice becomes friendly with Soviet Ambassador, Sokolnikov, and his wife.

1932 Webbs visit U.S.S.R. in May/June to collect material for their book. Sidney and Beatrice Webb: *Methods of Social Study.*

1933 Beatrice seriously ill with kidney complaint.

1934 Sidney revisits U.S.S.R. to check material.

1935 Sidney and Beatrice Webb: *Soviet Communism: A New Civilisation?*

1936 Political purges begin in U.S.S.R.; defended by Beatrice.

1937 'Retirement' party for Webbs at Passfield Corner, attended by many Potter relatives and political friends.

1938 Sidney, afflicted by stroke, becomes incapable of work. Fabian Society and new Fabian Research Bureau merged, Beatrice assumes honorary post as President.

1939–43 Beatrice Webb: *The Truth About Soviet Russia* (1942).

1943 Beatrice dies 30 April.

1947 Sidney dies 13 October. Webbs interred at Westminster Abbey 12 December.

*Posthumous publications*

1948 Beatrice Webb: *Our Partnership.*

1952 Beatrice Webb: *Diaries 1912–1924.*

1956 Beatrice Webb: *Diaries 1924–1932.*

1959 Beatrice Webb: *New Zealand Diary 1898.*

1963 Beatrice Webb: *American Diary 1898.*

1965 Beatrice Webb: *Australian Diary 1898.*

# Location codes

The following abbreviations are used in this volume to identify the location of letters.

| | |
|---|---|
| BEAV | Beaverbrook Library (House of Lords Record Office) |
| BEV | Beveridge Papers (BLPES) |
| BL | The British Library |
| BLHU | Baker Library, Harvard University |
| BLPES | The British Library of Political and Economic Science |
| BMJL | Brynmor Jones Library, University of Hull |
| BOD | The Bodleian Library, Oxford |
| BUL | Birmingham University Library |
| BWD | Beatrice Webb's Diary (BLPES) |
| EUL | Edinburgh University Library |
| FP | Fabian Papers, Nuffield College Library, Oxford |
| HL | House of Lords Record Office |
| HRCUT | Humanities Research Center, The University of Texas at Austin |
| HWUL | Herriot-Watt University Library |
| ISH | International Institute of Social History, Amsterdam |
| KCC | King's College Library, Cambridge |
| LP | Lansbury Papers |
| LPA | The Labour Party Archives |
| LSE | The London School of Economics and Political Science Papers (BLPES) |
| MMLMU | Mills Memorial Library, McMaster University |
| MUL | Manchester University Library |
| NH | Dr Henriette Noufflard (Halévy Papers) |
| NLNZ | National Library of New Zealand |
| NLS | National Library of Scotland |
| NLW | National Library of Wales |
| NUL | Newcastle University Library |
| PF | Sir Horace Plunkett Co-op Library, Oxford |
| PP | Passfield Papers (BLPES) |
| PRO | Public Record Office, London |
| RPD | R. Palme Dutt Papers |
| SP | Salter Papers |
| SU | Sussex University Library |
| UI | University of Illinois |
| UL | University of London Library |
| VWML | Vaughan Williams Memorial Library |
| WI | Weizmann Institute |
| WSL | Women's Service Library, City University |

# 1. New beginnings
## June 1912 – June 1914

When the Webbs returned from their trip around the world in the early summer of 1912 the mood of British politics was militant. There was labour unrest, the Irish problem was drifting towards violence and the extreme wing of the women's suffrage movement was resorting to arson, window-breaking and other forms of direct action. It seemed as though the crust of British constitutionalism had cracked during the dramatic struggle over the House of Lords in 1910–11. In this confused situation they found a somewhat demoralised Fabian Society. Another revolt against the domination of the Old Gang had been staged by a faction calling itself the Fabian Reform Committee. Bernard Shaw, writing to the absent Webbs on 29 March 1912 (PP) described his efforts to extract some coherence from the committee. 'It is', he said, 'the most difficult and uncertain body to work on imaginable. It runs about from week to week – a minute's speech is often enough to change the views of the majority on any point and another minute's speech to [turn] them back again.' The Society had been drifting all through the period when the Webbs had sapped its resources to support their Poor Law campaign; its political posture, moreover, was still complicated by its ambivalence towards both the I.L.P. and the Labour Party, by divided attitudes towards the suffragette movement and by a growing reaction against its doctrine of state collectivism.

The last of these disagreements was exemplified by the emergence of Guild Socialism, as an anti-bureaucratic form of collectivism based upon trade unionism. Guild Socialism, developed by S. G. Hobson and A. K. Orage in his weekly journal *The New Age*, was an intellectualised and romantic version of the concept of syndicalism, which was beginning to take hold among militant trade unionists – Tom Mann, making yet another of his conversions, became one of its chief protagonists – who were disillusioned by the inability of their moderate leaders to make much headway through Labour's tacit alliance with the Liberals. Many of the younger Fabians, especially some who had been active in the Poor Law campaign, were attracted to Guild Socialism; their leader was the young Oxford graduate G. D. H. Cole (1889–1959), whose enthusiasm for industrial action influenced the Oxford Fabians who were already displaying a rebellious temper. The new mood of militancy found a spokesman in the *Daily Herald*, launched by George Lansbury with the financial help of H. D. Harben, a wealthy Fabian.

There were many changes to which the returning Webbs had to adjust, and tactical questions which they had to answer. What, first of all, should they do about the remainder of their Poor Law campaign now that Lloyd George's social insurance schemes had, with Labour Party backing, effectively deflated that campaign? Should they endeavour to carry over their supporters into the Fabian Society? What role, secondly, did they intend to play in the Fabian Society themselves? Of the Old Gang, Wallas had long left, Bland was soon to die, Pease was ready to retire, Shaw felt that it was time to hand over to younger people if suitable new leaders could be found. Only Beatrice (with Sidney's far from enthusiastic acquiescence) was willing to throw herself actively into the Society's affairs, becoming a member of the executive for the first time after her return: for the next few years she was its effective leader. Thirdly, what line should they take towards Keir Hardie, MacDonald and the I.L.P., from which they had disdainfully kept their distance; and what should be their attitude towards the Labour Party in Parliament, now seemingly little more than a radical appendage of the Liberal government? Finally, how could the Webbs ensure the continuation of the social research which was their abiding concern, which they had fostered during the sittings of the Poor Law Commission and their subsequent campaign, and in which they saw the distinctive Fabian contribution to politics?

Before they made a new beginning they had to relax and catch up with events: Beatrice especially was exhausted by their travels. They went to stay in a rented rectory at Madehurst, near Arundel, and began to plan out their activities for the coming year. 'My nerves were all to pieces', Beatrice noted, 'and waves of depression and panic followed each other.' (BWD 5 September 12) But she felt that there was 'a clear call to leadership in the Labour and Socialist movement to which we feel we must respond'. (BWD 11 October 12) One step, long pondered and partly attempted in the founding of *The Crusade* as the organ of the Poor Law campaign, was the launching of a new political weekly. The Webbs felt they needed a means to speak directly to the amorphous constituency of reformers to whom they had appealed in their campaign: the greater the pressure within the Society to play a more direct role in politics the more the Webbs believed there was a need for a non-partisan journal of social reform – especially as they felt that the Labour Party was drifting into futility.

The new weekly paper was part of the plan to maintain contact with those who had supported the Poor Law campaign; the new approach to research was another. On Beatrice's suggestion in the summer of 1912 the Fabians appointed two committees of enquiry, one on Rural Problems (which published its report a year later) and the other, much more ambitious, a far-reaching discussion of the Control of Industry. The intention was to consider all possible forms of industrial organisation. Its very general terms of reference were an invitation to the young Guild Socialists to collaborate, despite their truculent and often ill-mannered posture towards the ageing Webbs. Beatrice, for all her misgivings and her prissiness, was generously tolerant to her young associates, criticising them in the privacy of her diary but publicly supporting them as energetic and originally-minded. Before long they dominated the committee and its successor, the Fabian Research Committee. Cole's chief ally, William Mellor (1888–1942) was appointed its secretary: he later became the editor of the *Daily Herald*. Beatrice was its chairman.

The Fabian Research Committee was to become both a focus for the Guild Socialist revolt in the Fabian Society – which narrowly escaped total capture in the next few years – and the most lively component of a society which was becoming increasingly routinised and uncertain of its role. The classical period of Fabianism was over. For the Webbs, as Beatrice repeatedly observed in her diary entries in this period, it also seemed that their personal career was ending in the shadow of approaching old age. Their hope, in this phase of the partnership, was to set the Society on a new course before they retired to the country to finish the series of books on local government planned long ago.

The Fabian Society had no chairman, the executive members rotating in this office for procedural purposes. Webb, however, was the *de facto* chairman of the Society from about 1888 to 1913, when Beatrice assumed much the same role, exercising a careful and continuing supervision over the Society's work and planning its policy statements. The Joint Committee of Fabians and the I.L.P. was to supervise a campaign for the National Minimum; the National Committee for the Prevention of Destitution survived but was soon to be wound up.

Albert Emil Davies (1875–1950) was a stockbroker, lecturer and author; for many years he was treasurer of the Fabian Society.

Madehurst Vicarage,
Arundel
18/6/12

[*Note at top of letter:*]
Is there anything that I am wanted
for *next week*? I want to know which
day, if any, I need to come up.

Dear Sanders

I propose to be present at the Conference with Group Secretaries on Thursday. Unfortunately I have failed to meet you, and I could not find out what was on the Agenda. If it is not inconsistent with the primary purpose of the meeting, I should like to put before them tentatively the proposal I intend to make to the Executive *viz*: that the Exec. should issue to the Society about September next as comprehensive a *scheme of work* as possible, which the Members, Groups and Local Societies should be urged to do this winter.

Such a scheme of work might fall under four heads, so as to cater for all tastes.

I. *Investigation and Study* (to be elaborated)
   (a) Emil Davies's Committees.
   (b) Local enquiries for Local Societies and Groups.

II. *Discussion* – by Groups and Local Societies, of definite problems submitted by Executive. I shall have one ready by August, *viz*: Syndicalism, in the form of a supplement to the August *Crusade*, of which the F.S. might take 1,000 copies at cost, and supply them for the purpose; *asking for criticisms and comments* with a view to turning it into a Fabian Tract. Reports from I(a) might be treated in same way.

III. *Political Work* Emphasise importance of definite work to increase Socialist and Labor members on Local Bodies, in cooperation with I.L.P. and Labor Party (e.g. Municipal and Metrop. Boroughs, County Councils, District Councils, P.L. Guardians) – ask for reports of action taken.

IV. *National Minimum Campaign* in October–December, conjointly with Joint Committee and National Committee: describe and urge active cooperation. Ask for reports of action taken.

It will not be suggested that all societies or members/groups can or will do all these things. But we want to put all before them so that each can do something. I suggest a special circular to (a) Members, (b) Secretaries to be issued early in September perhaps combined with an appeal for funds.

Will you please show this to Pease; and let me have a typed copy of I to IV, with any comments?

Sidney Webb

Have you addressed a *formal* letter to the Secretaries of the University Societies, formally asking them to bring the Summer School formally before their next members meeting; and formally inviting them to attend? They laid stress two years ago on the lack of this!

607 FP BEATRICE WEBB TO W. C. ANDERSON

William C. Anderson (1878–1919) was one of the abler leaders of the I.L.P.; he died in the influenza epidemic after the war. He was married to Mary MacArthur (1880–1921), an outstanding organiser of women workers.

Madehurst Vicarage
Arundel
27th June 1912

Dear Mr Anderson

I quite understand your difficulties. That is why I submitted to you the memorandum before bringing it formally before the Committee to-morrow. All I want is some sort of limitation of liability for my own Committee. During this winter I have to turn a difficult corner with my 3 or 4 thousand contributing members if I am to hand any of them over to the Fabian Society or I.L.P. next summer. Could you meet me at the Fabian office at 12.45 tomorrow? Mr Sanders and I are going to lunch at the London School of Economics, close to, and perhaps you could join us? We could then come to some arrangement about the exact form in which we would bring any proposal with regard to Finance for the Committee.

Would you telephone to the Fabian office to-morrow morning whether 12.45 or 1 o'clock would suit you?

Yours very truly
Mrs Sidney Webb

The Webbs wished to settle the wrangle with the Fabian Reform Committee and to clarify relations with the I.L.P., as a prelude to joint action with the I.L.P. on social policy. One of the demands of the Reform group had been for the exclusion of Fabians who belonged to the Liberal Party. Reginald Clifford Allen (1889–1939), later Lord Allen of Hurtwood, was a pacifist, a leading member of the I.L.P. and for a period after the war the effective controller of the *Daily Herald*. St John Ervine (1888–1972) was an Irish-born dramatist, critic and Fabian: among his books was a biography of Bernard Shaw.

Madehurst Vicarage
Arundel
*Private* 1/7/12

Dear Pease

I think that we – i.e. my wife – have arranged a compromise that will stop the wrangling in the F.S. (for the present at any rate); and in particular avoid a fight on 12 July.

Schloesser, Ervine and Clifford Allen have more or less agreed with us – subject to concurrence of their committee, and of course, of the Executive – on the basis of eliminating the negative and uniting the positive proposals. *We* want to maintain the freedom of the individual member. *They* want more effective support of the Labor Party.

What we have got them provisionally to agree to is

(a) All motions and amendments on the paper for 12 July to be withdrawn, without imputations.

(b) A motion such as I enclose to be moved – *they* insist that shall be by Mrs Webb – and (as *we* ought to urge, though this is not stipulated) seconded by one of themselves.

They personally agree to drop the idea of persecuting individual members, and silently to accept the position that the F.S. (subject to complying with the exact and literal requirements of the Labor Party constitution) cannot insist on its members, even on the Executive, not standing as Liberals, or supporting Liberals.

On the other hand, they want (and we have no reason to object to) a more active campaign of organisation and propaganda in support of the *Labor Party* (i.e. *not* the Labor Members in the House).

Instead of Schloesser or any other of them bringing the subject before a Member's meeting, they accept the idea of a *Committee* reporting on the subject.

The selection of such a Committee being invidious and opening up very awkward questions, they will accept, as the Committee, *the Members of the F.S. who happen to be on the Standing Committee of F.S. and I.L.P.* These are

| | |
|---|---|
| Mrs Webb | Miss Murby |
| Sharp | Anderson |
| Lloyd | Miss MacArthur? |
| Schloesser | |

with yourself and Sanders on the Standing Committee. Miss Murby is resigning and Mrs Webb proposes to move Mrs C. M. Wilson in her place. And as the I.L.P. want to *add* Innes, Mrs Webb wishes to propose to *add* Clifford Allen.

Such a Committee would be a very favorable one for the Exec. party, as it would include only Schloesser and Allen of the malcontents; whilst it would have (including you and Sanders) six of our Executive party, with Anderson, Miss MacArthur etc. also on our side in effect, and at any rate not eager for the F.S. to encroach on the I.L.P.

Please show this to Sanders, and to any other member of the Executive who comes in, other than Schloesser and Allen. Schloesser is to let you know on Wednesday morning what is the decision of their committee. If it is favorable (which they expect, and ?will secure), we suggest that you should send out on *Executive Agenda* the terms of the proposed resolution (as enclosed); so that members may be prepared for it.

I hope you and Sanders, and the Executive will agree to this (assuming that the malcontents agree). It will be a great gain to divert their energies from wrangling to work for the Labor Party. Exactly *how* the F.S. can organise such work, and how many members will give active assistance, we may leave to the Committee to discover and for experience to show. But it will be all to the good to have a private meeting in October, at which the Labor Party can be discussed, on a careful *constructive* report of suggested work, *without a motion on the paper* to leave the Labor party.

We can then explain in speeches the delicacy of the position; and also make a very necessary distinction between our support of the 'Labor Party'; and our agreeing with or endorsing the policy or action of the Labor Members in the House, individually or as a House of Commons 'party'.

Sidney Webb

## 609 FP BEATRICE WEBB TO EDWARD PEASE

Julius West, one of the paid workers of the Poor Law campaign, became secretary to the Fabian Research Committee; when he moved to the *New Statesman* he was replaced by William Mellor. Marion Phillips had worked for Beatrice as an investigator during the Royal Commission on the Poor Law. A leading member of the Fabian Reform Committee she became Chief Woman Officer to the Labour Party in 1918. On 3 September Beatrice went down to Newport for the Trades Union Congress. In the first entry in her diary since her return she noted that the left of earlier years 'the state socialists' were now on the defensive against the syndicalist faction, though the bulk of the delegates were 'the same stolid stupid folk they have always been, mainly occupied with their trade union work, their own eating, drinking and smoking, and their family happenings'. She felt, however, that there was one change. 'The ordinary trade unionist has got the National Minimum theory well-placed in his slow stupid head . . . And I think the idea of nationalising the great Public Services is just emerging out of the shibboleths of a minority into the settled intention of the majority.' (BWD 5 September 1912)

41 Grosvenor Road
Westminster Embankment
2nd September 1912

Dear Mr Pease

Here is a memo. which I want you to read and consider and when you have done so would you kindly send it to Mr Sanders with this letter.

I think we should try to make a big thing of this Report on the Control of Industry – something that the whole Society might feel proud of. There is a certain feeling among the younger folk that our tracts have been in the main concerned with useful reforms and the present capitalist system and that this work is practically exhausted; at any rate, we are faced with great lack of clearness of thought with regard to the ultimate aims of Socialism. And it would be to the interests of the Society to help to solve this big question in a way that would redound to its credit in the International Socialist Movement.

I should like to circulate some sort of memorandum to the whole Society so as to make the whole Society feel that they were taking part in the work. It would also serve as a sort of tract setting out the alternative ways of Control of Industry for discussion and investigation.

I am off to the Trade Union Congress this afternoon. I should be glad if you would pass it on to Sanders and if he and the new person taken on might be given to understand that the position would probably terminate in one year. Let me know what you and Pease think about it before I suggest it. The alternative I think, would be that clever Miss Sharp. But I consider that West has a prior claim if he desires to take up the work, and it would settle any question that might arise about desirable candidates. I am a little afraid that Marion Phillips has her eye on any position which would yield a £100 a year or something more!

Yours very truly
Mrs Sidney Webb

## 610 MMLMU BEATRICE WEBB TO BERTRAND RUSSELL

Now Bertrand and Alys Russell were separated, he maintained a flat in London to be near Lady Ottoline Morrell and commuted from his rooms at Trinity College, Cambridge.

41 Grosvenor Road
Westminster Embankment
Oct. 11th [1912]

My dear Bertrand

I was so sorry not to see you when you called the other day, and I feel that I cannot let your visit pass in silence.

Now don't be angry with me, if I ask you to put yourself in our place. Supposing you and Alys were living in absolute happiness and complete comradeship, and you became aware that Sidney had repudiated me, and that I was living on in a state of dark despair. Would you not, both of you, feel rather sore with Sidney?

I know nothing of the cause of your estrangement – all I know is that Alys wants us to be friends with you. And that is also my own instinct. I have always admired your very great intelligence and tho' I have sometimes had my doubts about the strength of your character, I have always felt its peculiar charm.

So don't think that I have withdrawn my friendship; and if, at any time, I can be of use to you, with or without your complete confidence let me know and come and see me. And now that I have expressed quite frankly what is in my mind come and see us, if you feel inclined, and talk about the world's affairs without reference to your and Alys' troubles.

We had a delightful time in the Far East and India – there are wonderful new outlooks in Human Purpose and Human Destiny, both in Japan and among the Hindus in India. We were wholly unable to appreciate China and found ourselves unsympathetic to Mohammedan India.

Now we are again immersed in British problems: but the memory of our travels is a constant refreshment. Why don't you go for a long holiday and complete change of thought?

Ever your friend

Beatrice Webb

### 611 FP BEATRICE WEBB TO EDWARD PEASE

The representation of the different socialist groups in Britain and their inability to agree, let alone unite, had for some years bothered the leadership of the Socialist International. The Bureau of the International, which had recently helped to heal the rift among the French socialists, sought a meeting in London in the autumn of 1912 to make a similar attempt in Britain. A second attempt was made by the chairman, the Belgian socialist Emile Vandervelde (1866–1938), in July 1913. On this occasion, at a meeting in the Fabian office, the Fabians, the I.L.P. and the British Socialist Party (the new name for Hyndman's Social Democratic Federation) agreed to form a United Socialist Council. A condition of the agreement was that the B.S.P. should renew the affiliation with the Labour Party that the S.D.F. had dropped. This was not so simple as it seemed: discussions dragged on. Beatrice and Sidney took a leading role in these negotiations, Beatrice becoming chairman of the standing joint committee. Though some headway was slowly made, the outbreak of war – reopening old divisions – prevented the intended merger.

41 Grosvenor Road
Westminster Embankment
9th November 1912

Dear Mr Pease

Sidney has been talking to me about the International Unity Conference which will come before the Standing Committee on Monday. I enclose some resolutions which he has drafted for me as possible resolutions to bring before that Conference when it meets. I do not propose to ask the Standing Committee to formally discuss them tomorrow but I have sent Anderson a copy and I send you a copy for consideration before I put them on the Agenda for some future meeting. I think that it will be very important for us to table some proposal – sufficiently detailed for a lengthy discussion and sufficiently on-coming to put us right with the International Socialist Bureau. It is far better for the others to object to our proposals rather than for us to be led to object to their proposals.

Sidney says that he has not seen the letter which has been drafted in answer to the International Bureau. To be quite frank I was not satisfied with the letter that was originally sent as I did not think it was sufficiently courteous to the B.S.P. but I have no right to make this criticism because, at the time, I could not think of any alternative. I say this because I may possibly ask that the letter which has been already drafted should be referred to one or two of us in order that it may be quite elaborately polite and friendly.

I know that you and Mr Sanders will laugh at my inexperience when I suggest that we might conceivably get at a Minimum of Joint Action not only in the B.S.P. but also with Syndicalist League!

Yours very sincerely
Mrs Sidney Webb

### 612 LP BEATRICE WEBB TO GEORGE LANSBURY

Lansbury, who had become an energetic supporter of the suffragettes, resigned his seat in Parliament to force a bye-election on the single issue of votes for women. His majority of 863 was turned into a defeat by 731. On 1 December Beatrice wrote that his defeat 'turned him into a wrecker of the Labour Party'. He had always had 'a sentimentally disruptive mind, forceful feeling, unguarded by reason . . . A strain of outraged vanity . . . will prevent his realising the folly of resigning his seat and add to his bitterness.'

Beatrice made no comment in her diary about the decision to join the I.L.P., which she and Sidney had often derided in private and disregarded in public. Yet it was a significant change. She had now clearly aligned herself with the left of the socialist movement for the first time.

41 Grosvenor Road
Westminster
[? November 1912]

My dear Mr Lansbury

We are very very sorry – for the last few days I have felt that I ought to have been down helping you – but I am working at the edge of my strengths, and you had almost more helpers than you could do with – (so [C.M.] Lloyd told me, who went down once or twice). Of course the Liberals 'turned' – and from their own standpoint, they had a right to do so. This I do not regret, as it is better to have a clear issue between them and us.

But the Bow election – *with all that led up to it*, deepens my depression as to the future of the Labour and Socialist movement in England. I do not know whether it is possible for us to arrest the 'liquidation', both of Socialism and of Trade Unionism. When you are rested – and rest you must – you and Mrs Lansbury ought to go away – we must have a long talk as to what can be done.

Meanwhile I have joined the I.L.P.: don't leave it, just as I am coming in!

Ever yours

Beatrice Webb

613 MMLMU BEATRICE WEBB TO BERTRAND RUSSELL

All through the autumn of 1912 the Webbs were preparing to launch the political and literary weekly they proposed to call *The Statesman* – a title changed at the last minute when Arthur Balfour pointed out there there was already a well-known Calcutta journal with that name. The *New Statesman*, Beatrice conceded, was the most risky of the Webb enterprises. It had little capital: Shaw, E. D. Simon, H. D. Harben and Edward Whitley put up £1,000 apiece: another £1,000 was collected in smaller donations. But Beatrice reflected that they had started the L.S.E. with no greater resources.

Shaw had been dubious about the venture from the outset.'My fear in the matter', he wrote to the Webbs on 10 July 1912 (PP) 'is that we are too old . . . on the 26th of this month I shall be 56. To depend on me for any part of the success of the enterprise is like entering a horse of 25 for the Derby . . . Unless you can find a team of young lions . . . and give them their heads, the job cannot be done.' He warned the Webbs of the strains involved: 'though you may have come through a tour round the world without coming to a judicial separation, you should think twice before you complicate such dangerous experiments with a joint editorship'. Shaw's doubt whether the Webbs could produce a commercially viable weekly was shared by H. W. Massingham, the experienced editor of the similar *Nation*. He, Beatrice noted, thought the paper would be 'the Webbs flavoured with a little Shaw and padded out with the contributions of a few cleverish but ignorant young men'. (BWD 11 January 1913)

The new weekly, in fact, was well-planned. 'We are too old to make a failure of this business – now we have undertaken it we must see it through to a big success', Beatrice wrote to Shaw on 19 February 1913 (HRCUT). 'We have got to get the full advantage of being amateurs at the job. Fleet Street has got into such a rut that it needs some amateurs to pull journalism into the open.' Its editor was to be Clifford Sharp, who had gained experience running *The Crusade*. Sidney, writing to Beatrice on 7 December (PP) thought him 'weak, timid and slow' but wisely thought they would be unwise to 'nurse' him and that he should be given a chance to make something of the venture. He was to be supported by an able group. The literary editor was John Collings Squire (1884–1950), the City column was to be written by the Fabian stockbroker Emil Davies, and the drama critic was Desmond MacCarthy (1877–1952), who held this post until after the Second World War. Julius West became the company secretary, working from the offices of the National Committee for the Prevention of Destitution. The initial subscriptions (2,000 were needed to ensure survival) were collected by mailing a prospectus to over 20,000 possible readers, whose names were culled from the membership of the Poor Law campaign supporters, members of the Fabian Society, people associated with Shaw and Granville-Barker at the Court Theatre and similar special constituencies. The Webbs were to contribute regularly; so was Shaw, though the trouble with Shaw's articles that ran on until he separated from the paper three years later began when he refused to put his signature to his perverse contributions. It was, Beatrice ruefully observed, his name that was needed to sell the paper not his nonsense. The paper was also to carry regular supplements prepared by the Fabian researchers and other specialists on special topics.

41 Grosvenor Road
Westminster Embankment
Dec. 11th [1912]

My dear Bertie

I did not answer your little note because I felt we had exhausted the question – we have cleared the air of any constraint or misunderstanding – and all else could be impertinence.

I send you now our latest venture, which may interest you. It is to come out in the Spring. I hope you will someday be a contributor on your own questions. Could you suggest to us any clever young man – more or less of our way of thinking – who might be willing to be connected with the paper? We want to make it representative of the best type of sane collectivism.

I enclose you also an article by me on the relation between Efficiency and Self-government to show you the trend of our thoughts on social and political questions.

Affectionately yours
Beatrice Webb

614 NH BEATRICE WEBB TO ÉLIE HALÉVY

Sharp was sent off with £50 to visit Paris, Berlin and Vienna before the first issue of the *New Statesman* appeared: from Vienna he reported to Beatrice that a major war was inevitable within a year.

41 Grosvenor Road
Westminster Embankment
18.12.12

Dear Monsieur Halévy

There is one thing in particular that my wife and I want to talk over with you when you come, and that is the new weekly journal described in the printed prospectus sent herewith. At last, after many demands and temptations, we have succumbed to starting a paper! It is to be a first-class sixpenny on the lines of *The Spectator* or *The Nation*, but with its own basis of a sane and practical Collectivism. Bernard Shaw is one of the little group of proprietors, and is to write a good deal, whilst we shall watch over the editing, and also write.

Now, could we persuade you to write for *The Statesman*, as it is to be called? We should like occasional reviews of *important* French books on economics or politics; occasional articles or letters on 'movements' or tendencies in France, whether economic, political, religious or social; and so on. We shall pay everyone a fixed rate of a guinea a column (of 550 words), and contributions may be two or three columns each.

But I have a further favor to ask. The able young man who is to be Editor – Mr Clifford Sharp – will be visiting Paris in January, just to get a general idea of what is being said and thought there, and to see all sorts of people. I shall venture to give him a note of introduction to you; in the hope that, if he is fortunate enough to find you in Paris, you will talk to him a little, and perhaps introduce him to others.

With salutations from my wife; and to Madame Halévy.

Yours very truly

Sidney Webb

615 KCC BEATRICE WEBB TO MRS CHARLES ASHBEE

Mrs Ashbee was the wife of the progressive architect and designer Charles Robert Ashbee (1863–1942) who founded the Guild of Handicraft.

41 Grosvenor Road
Westminster Embankment
Jan. 15th 1913

Dear Mrs Ashbee

You may have seen from *The Crusade* of January that after a most successful campaign this autumn, we are damping down the propagandist activities of the National Committee for the Prevention of Destitution, at any rate for this year. We are not therefore asking for any renewal of subscriptions to the National Committee.

My husband and I are turning our efforts into the establishment of a first-class weekly journal, which will be wholly non-Party, and which will concentrate public attention on constructive social reform whilst aiming at excellence as a political and literary journal.

Now would you be so very kind as to transfer your subscription for this year from the National Committee and augment it to one guinea? This will mean that you will be getting a 'Sixpenny Weekly' for the guinea instead of a 'Penny Monthly' for 10/0. During the year you will be able to sample the wit of G.B.S. and the wisdom of the Webbs!

In starting this new Weekly, my husband and I and one or two friends are making ourselves liable for a very big expenditure and our pecuniary loss will in any case be considerable. But the present disorder and chaos of thought and feeling within the Progressive Movement seem to us so dangerous that we are willing both to give our work and to risk our money trying to remedy it. In asking the members of the National Committee to subscribe prior to issue, and if possible, to get others to subscribe, we think we are offering a very good bargain. Perhaps we are not fair judges of this! But however this may be, there is no doubt that a long list of subscribers would enable us to get advertisements, and in that way would diminish the loss on the first year's issue. I should be grateful if you would return the Subscribers Form filled in and if you would let me know whether you could help me in getting other subscribers.

Yours very truly

Beatrice Webb

## 616 HRCUT SIDNEY WEBB TO GEORGE BERNARD SHAW

Frederick Whelen, a member of the Fabian executive for a number of years, had been the founder of the Stage Society which gave private performances of advanced or uncommercial plays.

41 Grosvenor Road
Westminster Embankment
4.2.13

Dear Shaw

Thanks to [Granville] Barker's kindness, we are getting the Kingsway Theatre list (described by West as apparently nearly all 'Fabians and Aristocrats'): we shall probably get a Stage Society list of members from Whelen: and we shall get from Somerset House lists of the shareholders in the Liverpool Repertory Theatre Company Limited (and possibly others). We shall probably have (after dropping duplicates) several thousands (possibly 5,000 or more) of people interested in the drama, and largely in Shaw.

Now it is rather a pity, with such a list, which will cost £25 to circularise, not to do it as effectively as possible. It seems a shame merely to send them a letter signed by Sidney Webb.

Will you spend 10 minutes in *cutting down your Fabian letter*, so that it could be sent to these people?

The first page, with slight omissions, seems to me to do. A brief par., as to the width of interests – literary, artistic, dramatic – that the new weekly will serve, and your connection with it – should be substituted for the second page.

Yours

Sidney Webb

The cold, which made me uncomfortable, grumpy and stupid, did not survive its merciless treatment.

617 BLHU BEATRICE WEBB TO H. S. FOXWELL

The Webbs had maintained an uneasy acquaintance with Herbert Foxwell, professor of political economy at University College, London, for many years. The enclosure was Volume v of the local government history, *The Story of the King's Highway*.

41 Grosvenor Road
Westminster Embankment
18th February 1913

Dear Professor Foxwell

I quite understand that you do not care to support a newspaper with which you disagree so fundamentally as you do with Collectivist views. By the way, we are *not* in favour of Institutionalism – on the contrary, if you can generalise on the subject, we prefer Home Treatment; though we think it is a matter to be determined according to the special disease or incapacity. But broadly speaking you are quite right in your estimate of our views: we *are in favour of State Action* – more local than central.

My husband tells me that he has written to you not knowing that I had already written to you about our Thursday afternoons. Pray do not answer his note.

We send you our latest bit of historical research completed in a whirlwind of other work. We have still three or four volumes practically finished but requiring some months of detailed corrections, and expansion, and press corrections. It is annoying that our present life makes it so difficult to complete our historical work. However we shall do it if we live another 10 or 15 years.

Always yours sincerely

Beatrice Webb

(Mrs Sidney Webb)

## 618 HRCUT SIDNEY WEBB TO GEORGE BERNARD SHAW

George Radford was appointed to sell advertising space in the *New Statesman*, charging for it in guineas and accounting for it in pounds less fifteen per cent.

41 Grosvenor Road
Westminster Embankment
27.2.13

Dear Shaw

What can you properly do for the *New Statesman* with Constable's? I think you control your own advertising, as we do with Longmans.

*We* don't pay for *any* advertisements, in the press; but I don't feel I can be asking Longman to advertise extensively in our journal, without enabling him to include the Webb books in his list! Their omission would be very marked; and moreover, it must be a good advertising medium for both of us.

Hence I propose to authorise him to spend £20 in the course of the year (we can't afford more) on condition that this is exclusively to cover the space he takes for our books in his lists in the *New Statesman*. I shall consult Radford *how much* he can importune Longman for. What would be magnificent would be to get him to take 52 columns for the year! We don't want *special* advertisements of Webb books (or for that matter Shaw books); as it would be better not to seem to make it a 'Kept' paper – but, rather, publishers lists week after week, in some of which we appear.

Can you do anything of the sort with Constable? It is urgent, as Radford will be immediately approaching them.

Yours

Sidney Webb

Don't forget the letter we want from you – the envelopes are waiting.

## 619 PF SIDNEY WEBB TO HORACE PLUNKETT

George William Russell (1867–1935), the Irish poet who was known as 'AE', was editor of the *Irish Homestead*. T. W. Rolleston (1857–1920) was a man of letters and journalist. George Birmingham was the pseudonym of James Owen Hannay (1865–1950), an Anglican clergyman and humorous Irish novelist. The *New Statesman* supplement on Ireland appeared in the issue of 12 July 1913.

41 Grosvenor Road
Westminster Embankment
28.2.13

My dear Plunkett

We very much want your help for an enterprise that may be as useful to Ireland as it will to us and to England. You will have heard of our newest enterprise, a new sixpenny weekly journal, on the lines of the *Nation* or the *Spectator*, but from our own particular political and economic standpoint.

One of the original features of the *New Statesman* will be an occasional supplement *on a subject*; and the first of these will be on Ireland – to be called, perhaps, The Awakening of Ireland, and to appear at the beginning of July.

For this (16 pages) we want half a dozen brilliant and well informed articles of anything between 500 and 2,000 words each, on all the different aspects of Irish Life and Thought – giving rather the go by to the common political rut, and describing, fairly and critically, the present situation in regard to such matters as the Co-operative Movement, the Gaelic Movement, the Catholic Church, the real life and feeling of Ulster, the state and requirements of Education, Irish contemporary literature, and (as it is important to appreciate it exactly, and to point out its proper developments under Home Rule) the Local Government, and, as far as may be necessary, the Central Government in its administrative and economic aspects.

We think that such a Supplement, ably done by really competent people, would be of great use in putting the English people into a better state of mind about Ireland; and I cannot help thinking that it might be useful in Ireland, as helping to put a new spirit into the internal politics of that country.

Now we want you to be so very kind as to get us the right people, whom you know so well – we should like George Russell, T. W. Rolleston, John Hone – above all we should like George Birmingham, whose books and whose play have secured him such a hold on the reading public. Would he, do you think, consent to give us the very great assistance of an article on Irish Local Government, or Central Government, or whatever aspect of it he thought best?

We should want the articles by the end of *May*, if possible, so as to get all things ready (because these Supplements are to be more than journalism).

Of course the articles will be paid for. We are to have a regular rate of 2 guineas for two columns (i.e. for about 1,100 words): and they may be either signed; or if preferred by any contributor, unsigned.

I need hardly say that we should be delighted to welcome such contributors also to our weekly issue, which begins 12 April. We are starting under extraordinarily promising chances – over 850 people, in all ranks and of all views have *already*, six weeks before issue, subscribed for a year, and paid their money.

Yours very truly

Sidney Webb

Within a few weeks the Webbs realised that Shaw was trailing his coat in his unsigned articles for the *New Statesman*: 'the articles and notes that he sends', Beatrice observed on 25 May 1913, 'are hopelessly out of keeping with our tone and our methods'. The first serious clash came when Shaw used the occasion of a general strike in Belgium on a franchise issue to write a sweeping attack on political strikes. Sharp published Shaw's comments as an unsigned letter to which Sidney wrote an unsigned reply.

Helmuth von Moltke (1800–1891) was chief of the Prussian and then German Imperial general staffs, and directed the military campaigns which led to German unification.

41 Grosvenor Road
Westminster Embankment
22.4.13

Dear Shaw

Beatrice and I have tried our best to agree with your article. But we cannot make anything out of it without entirely rewriting it.

It must be remembered that, however useful it may be to drive home a single point, *any* article on the General Strike will be understood as *an all-round judgment* on such a device.

Now, it seems to me that there are circumstances in which a very widespread strike (such as those which have become known as General Strikes) would be a very potent engine, *by way of a political demonstration*; and might well be the only available engine (e.g. if electoral rights or opportunities are denied or nullified). The poorer the strikers were, and the more they voluntarily suffered, the more effective would be the demonstration.

When you used to throw back cheques in editors' faces, because they did something that you did not like, you chose this suicidal course because it *was* effective as a demonstration, and because it was the only way open to you. That you suffered by it was just what made it effective. Your friends often predicted that you would starve – but you did not.

On the narrow point, I don't believe that even an absolutely universal strike of all *wage earners* would instantly fail *from want of food*. (There are many other reasons for disbelieving in the possibility of its occurrence, or of its success.) There *is* food in the country – before resorting to human corpses – enough to last several weeks. (We could eat all the oxen, sheep and, for that matter, also the remaining horses!) If the price of food went up, every ship on the sea would instantly be diverted by wireless telegraphy towards our ports, in order to get the higher prices. (You must remember that there are nearly 4 million adults *employed* who are not manual working wage earners, besides the Army and Navy, so that there could be no absolute standstill even in a universal working-class strike.)

As a matter of fact, the argument is peculiarly irrelevant to the Belgian

General Strike, because so many of the workmen are *also* small agriculturists. (The Antwerp dock-laborers, on days when they get no dock work, simply stay at home and grow cabbages. I don't know what a small holder would find to dig up to eat in April; but such people *do* store their harvest – I have seen it.) This, of course, does not affect your theoretic argument but it *is* relevant to the question of what the article (occasioned by the Belgian General Strike – with its lengthy preparations in stores of food, supplies laid in by the Co-operative Societies and so on) says on the mere shortage of food.

There is much to be said for a 'science' of striking – we want a Moltke of striking – and therefore for a selecting of points to attack. But, remember, even here, you have to make the whole working class solid in refusing to become blacklegs – (this is where your 'fancy' strikes of retainers of the rich have their ludicrous side). This means, in practice, that you must have a great swing on; i.e. that there must be a *big* strike on, almost a 'General' strike, *in order merely to ensure that the trades struck will not be blacklegged.*

In fact, what has to be secured is that there *shall* be a Universal Strike, insofar as the *minds* of the working classes are concerned, manifested in a universal refusal to blackleg the *particular* trades who are chosen to come out on strike, and in a universal willingness to support them with funds. *Then*, the trades to come out could be chosen with a view to the dynamic effect of stopping these particular industries – the best point of attack would be the trades currently yielding *the highest profits.*

All this the German trade unions seem to be working out, much more intellectually than we are doing. It may be that the employers would reply by a general lockout – this they *would* do, if what was demanded was such an increase of wages as would, in their judgment, make their future business quite unprofitable.

But if the object is merely franchise or any other political change, which does not destroy business profits, the employers would put pressure on the Government to concede it.

Of course, things don't, in England, come to that extremity. Anything like a widespread strike, in protest against a Bill in Parliament, *would in my opinion, be at once successful.* If you could have induced the trade union leaders to have a General Strike against the Insurance Bill, and if only their two million members had struck – a smaller proportion than are now on strike in Belgium – the Bill would have withdrawn in a week. If such a strike were to break out now, in favor of Woman's Suffrage, Asquith would bring in a Bill this very session. So great a *demonstration* of working-class solidarity of opinion would, in England, be instantly irresistible *in the political arena.* But we never can get it! The workingmen do not want anything political with sufficient conviction and unanimity to go on strike for it!

We may have to try to get it, as against a Tory Reaction; or compulsory military service; or such like. Hyde Park meetings are played out.

Now, if *you* like to say, in your own name, whatever you like to the contrary, pray do so – it will be brilliant! But strikes would be regarded as peculiarly *our* subject; and *we* should be regarded as specially responsible for anything editorial on the point – just as you would be for anything on the Censorship.

I did not suggest to Sharp the excision of the sentence as to the General Strike, nor was I aware of it until it was done. But I told him I quite agreed with his action. To put it on the lowest ground, if we cannot agree among ourselves on any point, we must not dogmatise on it editorially. This is why signed articles are sometimes indispensable.

It is always worth arguing with you, because there emerges a residual product of agreement when (as you would say) your logic has penetrated my accumulated pedantry! Tell me on Friday (when we come to lunch) what you think about it.

Yours

Sidney Webb

621 VWML BEATRICE WEBB TO CECIL SHARP

Cecil James Sharp (1859–1924), the collector of English folk songs and dances, founded the English Folk Dance Society in 1911. He was one of a number of Fabians who felt that the Society, under pressure from its left wing and with the belated acquiescence of the Webbs, was swinging away from political independence to a closer commitment to the Labour Party.

41 Grosvenor Road
Westminster Embankment
7th May 1913

Dear Mr Cecil Sharp

I venture to write on behalf of the Fabian Executive to beg you to reconsider your decision to withdraw from the Fabian Society. This Society is hard at work at permeation and also at research, as the forwarded documents will show you. But it was felt that we had to take some part in the organisation of a Labour Party, as perhaps the most potent instrument for permeating working-class opinion. I admit all the deficiencies of the Labour Party. But incidentally its establishment has had the effect of bringing about a forward movement both in trade unionism and in Co-operation. Moreover the very fact of its existence means that the Liberal Party is more anxious to take up Collectivist measures.

All these questions of policy are extraordinarily difficult and no way is a perfect way. But it will be very difficult to go forward unless those who are in general sympathy with the Socialist ideal but who have not the time to take part in the work will give their moral and financial support to those who are actually in the battle field.

Are you ever in the neighbourhood of Westminster? If so, we should so much like to see you here to lunch. We want you to help us to improve the *New Statesman*. We have hardly as yet touched on all your questions for lack of anyone to direct us.

Yours very truly
Mrs Sidney Webb

622 MUL SIDNEY WEBB TO E. D. SIMON

By May it was clear that the new weekly was off to a reasonable start though, as Beatrice noted on 25 May, there was 'conflicting criticism – the paper is dull; it is mere brilliant writing and there is not enough solid information; the political articles are good but the literature "rot"; the literary side is excellent but the political articles not sufficiently constructive'. The difficulty with Shaw, however, was increasing. By July Beatrice had decided that he had 'injured the *New Statesman* by his connection with it; we have the disadvantage of his eccentric and iconoclastic stuff without the advantage of his name'. (BWD 5 July 13) Clifford Sharp reacted even more strongly to what Beatrice called Shaw's 'intense vanity and intellectual egotism', believing it was better to lose Shaw as a contributor than to continue on these unsatisfactory terms. To Sharp's credit he was willing to publish Shaw's blistering tract 'Commonsense about the War' as a *New Statesman* supplement on 14 November 1914, though the paper as well as Shaw was vilified for shameful lack of patriotism.

41 Grosvenor Road
Westminster Embankment
19.5.13

Dear Simon

We are glad you approve, on the whole, of the paper. The 'Bluebook Monthly' promises to be both attractive and useful. I think Sharp is quite to be trusted for politics.

As to the 'literature', we must be tolerant. I find that this part of the paper is greatly admired by many people, and Squire is very highly thought of. I think him very clever and a very charming fellow. But my own taste in 'literature' is apparently limited, and I don't always appreciate what he does! One has to remember that the 'new generation knocking at the door' has to be welcomed and encouraged, even if their elders don't appreciate them!

I study the *Nation* and the *Spectator* carefully – with a view to learning what other people do – and I find lots of the 'literature' there to be, shall I say? 'beyond me'. I find I simply pass it over: whereas in the *New Statesman* I expect *every column* to be exactly what I like and consider good. This is doubtless a good critical attitude, but I try to remember that *if* every column did seem to me exactly right, the sum total would not commend itself to anyone not named Webb!

This does not mean that your criticism is not useful (and valid). Pray continue to express it whenever you feel like it, because it all tends to *inform* the Editor, and keep him up to the mark.

The Directors' meeting will be next Friday at 3. I am trying to get presented then some statistics.

We got back Saturday night from a lovely week's walk in the Wicklow mountains.

Yours

Sidney Webb

623 HRCUT SIDNEY WEBB TO GEORGE BERNARD SHAW

Several members of the Liberal government, including Lloyd George and the attorney-general, Sir Rufus Isaacs (1860–1935), were involved in the Marconi scandal. They had speculated in the shares of a company associated with the parent Marconi company to which a government contract had been given. Godfrey Isaacs, the brother of Sir Rufus, brought a criminal libel action against Cecil Edward Chesterton (1879–1918) and Hilaire Belloc (1870–1953) for allegations of corruption – with anti-semitic undertones – which they made in the *Eye-Witness*, which they edited. Chesterton had been a prominent Fabian and Belloc a Liberal M.P. before turning to 'Distributivist' politics. Both were intemperate social critics. Shaw wrote a fiery article for the *New Statesman* defending Chesterton. Sharp, believing that Shaw was wrong about the facts and the law, rewrote the article. Webb sent this explanatory letter to Shaw but he was not mollified and from this time wrote less often for the paper.

In March 1912 Frederick Pethick-Lawrence (1871–1961) and his wife, both prominent in the women's suffrage movement, together with Emmeline Pankhurst, had been charged with conspiracy and sentenced to short terms of imprisonment. Pethick-Lawrence joined the Labour Party in 1922, became a peer and was Secretary of State for India in 1945. Sir Walter Phillimore (1845–1929), the father of Webb's friend and L.C.C. colleague from Deptford, was the judge in the Pethwick-Lawrence case.

41 Grosvenor Road
Westminster Embankment
13.6.13

Dear Shaw

As it will be convenient all round to have the legal point made clear, I spent an hour this afternoon in looking it up (as to Liability for Costs).

Of course in all *civil* proceedings the defendant may be ordered to pay the costs, whether the Plaintiff is the Crown or any possible person. This is true of Libel Actions as of others.

But Libel is one of those things for which one may be proceeded against either civilly (for damages and costs) or criminally (for punishment of fine or imprisonment). A criminal action is taken in the name of the King, by any person who chooses to do so (called the prosecutor); and the prosecutor has to incur his own costs. He may, and usually is, repaid these out of the County Rate (primarily).

Until lately, it was quite at the option of the prosecutor whether to take action for Libel civilly (for damages and costs), or criminally (for punishment). Then it was provided that (as some protection to newspapers) he could only proceed criminally on getting leave from the Court (Judge or Master in Chambers is, I think, the expression). [*Footnote*] N.B. This was the course taken by Godfrey Isaacs against Chesterton.

When the Crown itself chooses to take criminal proceedings, these are taken by the Public Prosecutor (as in the case of Pethick-Lawrence). Ninety-nine criminal cases out of a hundred are left to the private prosecutor.

Now as to the sentence to pay costs, when the defendant has been convicted in a criminal trial. The law was confused and scattered. Apparently the prisoner could always be ordered to pay the costs of the prosecution in Treason, all Felonies, and a good many misdemeanours. All sorts of particular statutes had added offence after offence for which this could be done.

For instance (and this is exactly Chesterton's case) it was specially enacted in 1842 (6 and 7 Vic.c.96.sec.8) that where, in a criminal trial for libel the defendant pleaded justification – which involves of course, heavy costs – he might, on conviction, as part of his sentence, be ordered to repay to the prosecutor the costs to which the latter had thereby been put.

Thus, Chesterton might have been ordered to pay to Isaacs the costs in a similar case anytime since 1842. The Act of 1908 made not a particle of difference to his case.

What the Act of 1908 (c.15) did was (i) to codify all the scattered provisions as to costs in criminal cases; (ii) to substitute a general provision enabling costs to be part of the sentence on *all* criminal offences, instead of on Treason, all Felonies and some misdemeanours chosen haphazard.

It did one thing more, which does not concern Chesterton, but may perhaps have hit Pethick-Lawrence. By an accidental omission, the Act of 1842 (cited above) as to award of costs in criminal libel when justification was pleaded, did not enable the Judge to order costs to be paid to the Crown, *when the Crown had instituted the proceedings*, but only to a private prosecutor. It seems that in some other offences the Crown found itself under a similar disability. Hence, in the Codifying Act of 1908, no distinction was made between criminal proceedings in which there was a private prosecutor, and those in which there was not.

Pethick-Lawrence was sentenced to imprisonment and to pay the costs of the prosecution. This *may* have been one of the cases in which the sentence to pay costs *to the Crown* could not have been given prior to the 1908 Act. But of this I cannot be sure. (Of course the mere fact that it was stated to be under the 1908 Act does not prove that it was a new liability, because *all* proceedings are now under that Act, which repealed all the previous law.)

I don't see that the 1908 Act was a bad one, or any particular attack on Liberty. The Judge has to take into account the costs that he orders the prisoner to pay, in estimating the fine or imprisonment that he awards. I think, as a general principle, those who commit offences ought to pay the cost to which the nation is put, as part of the sentence – rather than put the cost on the ratepayers. If rich men break the law, it is hard that the ratepayers should be put to expense without opportunity to recoupment.

This might be otherwise if you were right in your supposition that the defendant who could not pay such costs might thereby be imprisoned for life! There is no such power. The Judge may order imprisonment until a *fine* is paid (Phillimore did this); but *not* until the costs are paid. The remedy of the Crown in Lawrence's case, as it is the remedy of Godfrey Isaacs in Chesterton's case, is simply to (i) go to execution, seize the defendant's property by the Court Bailiff, and after the statutory days, have it sold by auction; and (ii) do as the Public Prosecutor is actually doing in Lawrence's case, present a petition in bankruptcy, and get all or enough of the defendant's property vested in the Trustee in Bankruptcy to enable the creditors (including the Public Prosecutor and the L.C.C. which had had to find some of the costs meanwhile out of the rates) to be paid. (I suppose that, theoretically, *if it could be proved that the defendant had means, and refused to pay*, he might be had up for Contempt of Court, and committed to prison for a definite term for the contempt: but this is another story!)

Yours

Sidney Webb

624 BL BEATRICE WEBB TO GEORGE BERNARD SHAW

Shaw's speech 'The Case for Equality' – delivered to the annual dinner of the National Liberal Club on 1 May 1913, was one of the most coherent statements of his eccentric brand of socialism. The reference is probably to J. A. Hobson (1858–1940), the economist and journalist, rather than to the Fabian, Sam Hobson.

As Beatrice noted on 12 July relations with Shaw had become strained. 'For the last year or so we have found it increasingly difficult to discuss with him; he no longer tries to meet another person's points – he merely orates and all his talk revolves around persons and not ideas.' In his writings, she added, the literary quality 'is not distinguished enough to carry the poor and petulant reasoning, the lack of accuracy, logic and dignity'. Shaw's relationship to his wife Charlotte, moreover, had been affected by his infatuation with the actress Mrs Patrick Campbell (1865–1940), a revival, Beatrice thought, of his former habit of 'rather cruel philanderings with all kinds of odd females'.

41 Grosvenor Road
Westminster Embankment
17th June 1913

My dear G.B.S.

Ever so many thanks for letting us see your case for Equality. The force of your statement against Inequality is tremendous. And we are much interested in certain new points which had not struck us before. I like the paragraph about Idolatry. One argument about equality of income which we have stuck into our article, partly at your suggestions, you have not included. Assuming that the great bulk of production is accomplished by compulsory or voluntary organisations of consumers or for that matter of producers, it is desirable to make provision for personal production and consumption. This can best be done by leaving a margin of personal income, over and above the necessaries of life, to each individual so as to create eccentric demands for new commodities.

We are still not convinced by your biological argument though I notice that Hobson valued it highly! We do not think you prove your initial position that personal attraction leads to good breeding. Moreover even if it did so you rather give your case away by your admissions about the Brownings [Robert and Elizabeth]. Unless you are going to make marriage a much less permanent arrangement than it is, many other considerations besides the sort of personal attraction which is felt in a walk down Piccadilly will come into the decision, and come in increasingly with greater deliberation and greater foresight. With equal incomes men will certainly prefer an economical housekeeper! However, this is too big a question to discuss in a letter. One incidental advantage from starting the *New Statesman* is that you and we are apparently going to exchange our thoughts much more than we have done for the past 15 years. Perhaps 'the Webbs' and Shaw are both alike getting a bit ossified: but I hope we still have sufficient elasticity to exchange the product of our respective minds: for I believe they are extraordinarily complementary. At least that is our opinion.

Ever yours

Beatrice Webb

625 LSE SIDNEY WEBB TO B. M. HEADICAR

Though Webb was no longer chairman of L.S.E. he continued to take a close interest in its affairs, especially in the development of the Library. A few typical letters to Headicar have been included from the considerable number of such notes which survive.

41 Grosvenor Road
Westminster Embankment
21.6.13

Dear Mr Headicar

1) See enclosed as to things on India. I think you might write a careful letter, stating what you have out of the list, and asking for a complete set; and to be put on their list for the future.

2) It appears that the subscription for Parliamentary Papers does not include *all* that the Government publishes. The Departments have other

things not presented to Parliament, which they individually dispose of. I think you should write a letter to these Departments. i) asking to be put on their list to receive all their publications; ii) saying that the Treasury sanctioned our being put on the list for all

the Parliamentary papers.

etc. etc.

The Departments concerned are

Board of Education (especially their Special Reports)
L.G.B. (especially their medical reports)
W.O.
Admiralty
Public Record Office?
Board of Agriculture
Road Board

There may be others.

Sidney Webb

626 PP BEATRICE WEBB TO LADY BETTY BALFOUR

Beatrice had been on close terms with Arthur Balfour's sister-in-Law, Betty, for some years: she subsequently decided that the presumed intimacy had been one-sided and that it had merely suited the Balfour family to be friendly while A. J. Balfour was on good terms with the Webbs. She was more hurt by this discovery than by other social snubs she received.

The supplement in the *New Statesman* of 1 November 1913 was called 'The Awakening of Women'. Charlotte Perkins (1880–1935), was a notable American writer on social topics. She wrote on 'The Arrested Development of Women'. Jane Harrison (1850–1928) was an outstanding classical scholar and one of the pioneers of the higher education of women. B. L. Hutchins was a Girton graduate and Fabian, and editor of *Women's Industrial News*. Adelaide Anderson (1863–1936), another Girton graduate, who was one of the first women factory inspectors, wrote on 'Women in Public Administration'. Her article was called 'New Types of Subordinate Women Brain Workers'. Mrs W. L. Courtney was Beatrice's sister Kate. Mrs Millicent Fawcett wrote on 'The Remedy of Political Emancipation' and Maud Reeves on 'Exclusions'. Eleanor Cecil (1868–1959) was married to the Conservative leader Lord Robert Cecil. Ruth Cavendish-Bentinck (1867–1953), was a progressive Tory who gave money to some Webb projects. The wealthy Fabian H. D. Harben was providing funds for the militant wing of the suffrage movement, led by Christabel Pankhurst, who wrote the article on 'Militancy'. The Fabian summer school was held at Barrow House, near Keswick.

Arthur James Cook (1883–1931) became secretary of the Mineworkers' Federation of Great Britain in 1924 and a leading figure in the coal and general strikes of 1926. *The Miners' Next Step* was drafted by Noah Ablett, leader of the Unofficial Reform Committee which pressed syndicalist policies. W. Arthur Colegate, a civil servant who married into a wealthy family and became a Tory M.P., had been assistant secretary of the National Committee for the Prevention of Destitution.

In June 1913 there was a bye-election in Leicester, a two-member constituency in which Ramsay MacDonald held one of the seats. Not wishing to endanger the relationship with the Liberals which gave MacDonald a clear run the Labour Party did not put up a candidate: but the British Socialist Party did and he ran a bad third. In August, at Chesterfield, Labour did not contest the bye-election when a miner was run as a 'Lib-Lab'. In mid-July Beatrice commented that the Labour Party in Parliament 'has, in fact, not justified its existence either by character or intelligence'. She thought the movement as a whole was 'in a state of disruption. There is more evil speaking and suspicion than there has ever been before and there is less enthusiasm'. (BWD 5 July 13) MacDonald did, in fact, have some inconclusive contacts with Lloyd George on the possibility of a coalition with the Liberals.

The report of the Fabian Committee on the Control of Industry, drafted by Sidney, was submitted to the Society in October. It set out a scheme of four working groups – Associations of Consumers, Associations of Producers, Associations of Wage-earners and Public Services.

Innisfield, Ropley, Hants
August 22nd 1913

Dearest Betty

I have been meaning to write to you for some time – partly to get some of your news – partly to beg you to write me something for the Woman's Supplement of the *New Statesman*, to appear early in the winter. I have got articles from Mrs Gilman, Miss Jane Harrison, Miss B. L. Hutchins, Miss Anderson (the Factory Inspector) Mrs W. L. Courtney, Mrs Fawcett, Mrs W. P. Reeves – come, or coming immediately. I want one from you on *Motherhood* showing how it will not be adversely affected by suffrage and general enlightenment. *I* think of doing one on 'Marriage as a Partnership'. I am not going to have one on Prostitution – I cannot find anyone to do a short article, and I think if we have that subject at all it ought to be a supplement by itself.

Christabel Pankhurst is, I think, going to do the article on 'The Meaning of Militancy'. H. D. Harben, who is a director of the *New Statesman*, was very anxious to have her – thinks her the greatest woman on earth, and so on – and one has to respect the wishes of one's co-directors. So do – dear lady – get to work and write me 2,000 words on the Motherhood of free women! I think of writing to ask Lady Robert Cecil to do the final article on the affect of the awakening of women on the progress of the race – do you think she would do it? The articles I have got in are very good – I think the Supplement will be a good one. I wonder what you thought of the Rural Reform Supplement?

We had a satisfactory but tiring time at the Fabian Summer School. I took the chair six days running, for 5 hours a day – and we had some first rate technical discussions on all the alternatives to the capitalist management of industry – with a conference of about 70 Co-operators, trade unionists, municipal experts and civil servants – and the leader of the

South Wales Syndicalists – the man who wrote 'The Miners Next Step' – the revolutionary pamphlet that created such a stir during the last miners' strike. The conference was supplied each day with expert memoranda from the exponents of the different movements, taken as read, and discussed both in detail and on the general principles. This week was extraordinarily successful, as we were all living together and got to know one another's points of view. The week after we had a meeting of the N.A.C. [National Administrative Committee] of the I.L.P. with their organisers to meet the Fabian Executive. The I.L.P. is in a state of dire depression, owing to the quarrels within the Labour Party, and J. R. MacDonald's somewhat tortuous policy with regard to the Liberal Party. None of his party seem to know whether he really intends to play for some eventual fusion with Cabinet Office for himself, or whether he is going to maintain the independence – Leicester looks like the former policy, Chesterfield the latter. I doubt whether he knows himself. Like J. Burns he is really converted to the standpoint of the ordinary mild Whig governing-class man – but his position as leader of the Labour Party and a certain shame at going back on it, makes him stand out fitfully against his own change of opinion. He finds the Liberal Ministers and M.P.s pleasanter and more sympathetic company than the stodgy dull T.U. Labour M.P., or the erratic, querulous Socialist-Labour man. The British governing class is extraordinarily clever in winning over the abler revolutionary elements! Imagine a German Social-Democratic leader playing golf with the German Prime Minister! That aloofness from his opponents was the strength of Parnell, and his tradition of non-intercourse. The desire to enjoy the amenities of the House of Commons is the weakness of the Labour members – if they are going to pose as a Party.

We are hard at work down here drafting the Report of the Fabian Control of Industry Committee, from the material that has been collected during the last year. Directly that is finished – or rather before it is finished – the Fabian Research Department is starting an enquiry into the working of Industrial Insurance – both under the Act, and also the Life Insurance of the Prudential and other companies. All our predictions about the Health Insurance are coming true – it looks as if we were in for a big national disaster in the insolvency of a large number of the Approved Societies. One secretary of a P.H. Approved Society told me that their Society would have exhausted the whole reserve value of their members in 9 months! There is a real panic setting in among the secretaries of the Friendly Societies and T.U. Approved Societies. The miners and trade unions have wisely kept out of the whole thing – and are drawing their sick pay from any approved society that has accepted them as members. What will the Government do, I wonder, when they are faced with *varying degrees of insolvency*: they cannot make up all the deficits, and it will be impossible to increase contributions or decrease benefits in particular societies, without producing a state of chaos – all the good lives will clear out, and the Societies will soon be unable to pay even a minimum of benefits.

What a task the Conservative Party will have to clear up the muddle – and what a bill to pay! Perhaps the Fabian Society will bring some light on the question.

By the way, Colegate has lost his wife – she died suddenly of heart disease – I feel remorseful of having disliked the poor little woman so much!

Goodnight – dear lady – write me that article and send me a letter of news.

Ever yours

Beatrice Webb

627 FP SIDNEY WEBB TO EDWARD PEASE

Pease, who had received a substantial legacy, decided to retire from the paid secretaryship of the Fabian Society at the end of 1913, a new post of Honorary Secretary being created for him. He was succeeded by W. S. Sanders. The membership was then 2,804 in the parent London society and about 1,300 in the 39 provincial and 11 university societies. The publishing programme was going quietly but steadily, some 20 tracts appearing between 1911 and 1914. In the past year Pease had been the target of personal attacks by the younger rebels: G. D. H. Cole, who had a bent for satirical doggerel, spared neither Pease nor the Webbs. In the autumn the Webbs had inaugurated the long-lasting series of Fabian Autumn Lectures, with six talks on the nature of socialism. They had yielded a profit of £250 from an average attendance of 600 at the Kingsway Hall. Pease's seat on the Labour Party executive went at first to Sanders, but his withdrawal after the outbreak of the war opened the way for Webb to take the Fabian seat on the Labour Party executive. This change had important consequences for it put Webb for the first time into a position among the Labour leadership.

41 Grosvenor Road
Westminster Embankment
2.12.13

Dear Pease

I think you have decided aright – not because what people will think, but in view of the situation, individual and collective. I do not believe that anyone ignores the value of your services, now as well as in the past; and I am sure everyone will want you to continue them somehow.

I think the Society's present trouble is almost wholly financial – otherwise it is healthier than often before! It is certainly a gratifying thought that your unswerving devotion and selflessness has kept it alive so long, and now leaves it in many respects stronger than ever. I don't think you need have any hesitation in looking back with approval on the choice you made a quarter of a century ago to give your life to it. It has been well spent.

I don't myself see any reason to regret our F.S. policy throughout. We did right, even when the results did not follow that we expected.

Yours

Sidney Webb

I agree that it is best to announce *after* this week.

628 PP SIDNEY TO BEATRICE

The Fabian committee on the Control of Industry was preparing a report on Co-operation. Part I was on 'Co-operative Production and Profit-Sharing'; Part II, which appeared on 30 May 1914, was entitled 'The Co-operative Movement'.

Beatrice had gone to Edinburgh as one of the Fabian delegates to the Labour Party conference. It was, she noted, 'a personal triumph for J. R. MacDonald ... with his romantic figure, charming voice and clever dialectics ... he is superior to all his would-be competitors'. (BWD 6 February 14) Sanders, she added on 12 February, had told her that on the Labour executive – apart from MacDonald, Snowden, Arthur Henderson and Keir Hardie – the members were simply ordinary workmen 'who neither know nor care about anything but the interests of their respective trade unions and a comfortable life for themselves ... MacDonald ... does not want anything done in particular; he honestly disapproves of nearly all the planks in the ostensible party programme ... he remains the Parnell of the Labour Party – but a Parnell who does not believe in his cause'. Beatrice felt that the socialists in the party were 'bolstering up a fraud – pretending, to the outside world, that these respectable but reactionary trade union officials are the leaders of the social revolution ... by belonging to the Labour Party they are ... hampered in the old Fabian policy of the permeation of all parties, this policy demanding that socialists should be free to work inside all social sets and political parties. But to go back on the creation of a Labour Party would be to admit failure'.

In 1913 Philip Snowden had persuaded the I.L.P. conference to accept proportional representation on the grounds that it would increase Labour representation in Parliament: in 1914 the Labour Party conference rejected both proportional representation and the alternative vote.

41 Grosvenor Road
Westminster Embankment
30.1.14

Dear One

This goes to you at Edinburgh, where I hope you will not be quite tired out – I have nothing to report except that I seem to be making little headway against the mass of things to be done. Yesterday I had the table left standing in the drawing room, and began again at 2.30. Except for tea, I did not look up until the gong suddenly sounded for dinner!

Here are a few letters – Halévy sends useful minor corrections of French Productives, but says it reads all right as a whole. Albert Ball writes from Brussels a general approval of the Italian bit, but has no materials with him for detailed revision. So on Sunday and Monday I must finish that job off for the printer – as Sharp *may* want to issue it 7 February instead of 14 February.

I enclose a further bit of the Insurance Report – containing *the proposals* as far as I can put them together yet – which you might show to Dr Mackenzie if there is time (or leave them with him).

The crushing vote against P.R. and also against the Alternative vote, shows how rightly MacDonald estimates the position – and also how little 'advanced' are the mass of the delegates, and how little equipped with any programme of change. I think you will have to make the I.L.P. realise that *their* business is still mainly educational and propagandist among the rank and file, and the T.U. executives and officials. You will have to stand up against a movement to *come out* of the Labor Party, as utterly unsatisfactory.

Now there is only one more day, and you will be with me once more, to keep up my courage and be my inspiration. Dear one, it is only our love that keeps us either well or productive, as it gives us happiness. We have a great treasure and therefore we owe much – we owe to the world all we have and can. Good night.

Sidney

629 FP BEATRICE WEBB TO W. S. SANDERS

The situation in Ireland was drifting towards violence: the militant Home Rulers in Dublin were beginning to form para-military groups, as were the passionate opponents of Home Rule organised in the Ulster Volunteers. After Asquith had moved the second reading of his Home Rule Bill on 9 March 1914 it became clear that a section of the army might refuse to 'coerce Ulster'. On 20 March officers of the cavalry brigade stationed at the Curragh, with support from some infantry regiments, made it known that they would not obey an order to move north against any outbreak in Ulster. With a growing risk of a European war, the government in effect surrendered to this threat of mutiny, giving an ambiguous assurance that the army would not be asked to enforce a Home Rule Bill in Ulster: it was widely believed that George V had condoned the military pressure on the Cabinet.

41 Grosvenor Road
[? March 1914]

Dear Mr Sanders

Would it not be possible for the Labour Party Exec. to bring before the Conference on the 7th a strong resolution about the action of the Officers and the Court. I think we have got to make a Devil of a row or else we shall be back in the 17th century again and all our share and the woman's share will go by the board. If J. R. MacDonald knows his business he will sail straight into an anti-Court-army agitation. It would be a horrid nuisance, but the only chance of preventing a barren battle over the Crown is to make a big row now and frighten Buckingham Palace.

Could not the *Trade Unions* and I.L.P. organise a public meeting in Hyde Park on April 4th?

Ever yours

Beatrice Webb

630 BL BEATRICE WEBB TO GEORGE BERNARD SHAW

Beatrice gave Shaw the full version of the report on Co-operation which had appeared in the *New Statesman* on 30 May.

Beatrice was worried about the future of the *New Statesman* which was fast using up its initial capital and needed more money from its backers – a situation that persisted for almost twenty years, when it became self-supporting and ultimately rather profitable. She was equally concerned about the Fabian Society and the Fabian Research Department. 'We do not seem to be securing competent successors to take over the leadership', she noted on 3 May 1914. 'The successive groups or individuals who have aimed at taking over the leadership have not had the combined conduct, brains and faith to enable them to do it.' Though Cole was 'the ablest newcomer since H. G. Wells', she considered him intolerant, impatient and impractical. The root of the problem, she considered, lay in the fact that the Fabian Society had very little to offer an ambitious young man except unpaid work and a humble type of leadership.

John Leslie Palmer (1885–1944) wrote a number of books on the theatre.

41 Grosvenor Road
Westminster Embankment
13th June 1914

My dear G.B.S.

If you are really reading the Report on Consumers' Co-operation you might as well glance over the remainder of it which was not published and part of which was not even printed. The Belgium Co-operators have distinguished themselves for their communistic use of the Co-operative funds and the Swiss Co-operators for their inclusion of all classes within the Co-operative Movement and their extraordinarily good arrangements with their employees.

I am so glad you are really going to turn your big brain onto problems arising out of the future Socialist organisation. The Fabians have practically cleared up on the problems of the transitional stage and worked out the national *minimum* of civilised life which makes the transition possible. But no Socialists have yet worked out Socialism, Sidney and I will do our best to work out the distribution of *Power* among persons and classes of persons. You must work out the distribution of wealth – or of the pleasure of consumption and the effect of this on such eternal institutions as the Family, religion etc. The great crime of the Capitalist systems has been to combine a plethora of both in the hands of a tiny sector, whilst leaving the bulk of the people without either Power or Enjoyment of wealth. I agree with you that there need not be, perhaps ought not to be, *any* connection between the possession of power and the possession of wealth. If you could completely divorce one from the other I am not sure that the bulk of men would not prefer to be without power over the lives of others, might even prefer, during their wealth-producing lives, to be under the direction of others – in order to retain more mental energy over for the enjoyment of life – in the consumption [of] their share of wealth?

I am afraid you and we will have to remain in harness within the Socialist Movement for some years longer. If we could safely steer the Fabians into a unified socialist party, and leave it provided with a philosophy and a programme, and a research department, and an organ issuing out of the research department, we could comfortably retire into our old age. Your presence at the Research Dept. Conference at Barrow House and the International, will be a help towards this – and the issue of six definitive articles in the *New Statesman* and in the principal Socialist organs on the Continent would be another big step forward. I think we have to try and keep the *N.S.* as the organ of the young intellectual Fabians and the embodiment of new knowledge on Economic and Political facts. But of course this may not be possible, unless we can push way on during this year.

Always yours affectionately

Beatrice Webb

By the way could you tell your servant to send me back the book on Prostitution? I am sending back Palmer on Restoration drama.

B.

# 2. The earthquake

## July 1914 – February 1916

All through the last week of the Fabian summer school in July 1914, Beatrice noted four years later (BWD insert August 1918), 'there had been the rumblings of the approaching earthquake without our awakening to the meaning of it'. Sidney, she added, had refused to believe in the probability of war, and she confessed that the Webbs 'had never interested' themselves in European politics and 'had known nothing of the diplomatic world'. On their few visits to Europe they had 'gone merely as tourists seeking recreation'. Suddenly, after an exhausting week at Keswick discussing the Control of Industry and coping with the ill-mannered rowdyism of Cole and his fellow-rebels, and after another week reviewing industrial assurance, Beatrice realised that the 'hideous business' was upon them. 'Ulsterites, Suffragettes, Guild Socialists and rebels of all sorts and degrees may be swept out of mind and sight.' (BWD 31 July 1914)

The Webbs were confused by the war. Many of their Liberal and Socialist friends were pacifists or opposed to a war of capitalist powers; the Webbs themselves had admired much in modern Germany. 'We may live to regret' the 'backing up of the Slav against the Teuton', Beatrice noted on 5 August. The issues were so 'blurred and indistinct' that she was 'quite uncertain who ought to win from the standpoint of the world's freedom and man's spiritual development. The best result would be that every nation should be soundly beaten and no one victorious. That might bring us all to reason'. In a few weeks, as Beatrice's letter to Gilbert Murray and Sidney's memorandum to Professor Steffan show, the Webbs had worked out a reasonable position for themselves, but they were still unsure what to do once the war had disrupted their normal routine of life. On 10 August Beatrice observed that 'we shall do very little in the next months but sit on committees'. She was emotionally distressed by what she called 'that horrible Hell a few hundred miles away'. (BWD 25 August 1914) For most of the war, indeed, she was in a miserable state of depression and poor health: after a serious breakdown in 1916, when she feared that she had cancer, she was not able to tackle any work consistently for some years.

The situation in the Labour Party was dramatically changed by the war. Most of the I.L.P. and some Labour M.P.s were opposed to it. But the majority of the Parliamentary Labour Party and the Labour Party executive decided to support it. MacDonald, though not an out-and-out pacifist, disapproved of the foreign policy which led to the war and disliked the idea of leading a party committed to winning it: on 5 August he resigned in favour of Arthur Henderson (1863–1938), secretary of the party from 1911 to 1933. An emergency Labour conference called for that day, intended originally as a protest for peace, set up the War Emergency Workers Committee, representing all sections of the Labour, socialist and trade union movement. Its purpose was to protect living and working conditions. This was an important step. In the first place it helped to maintain contact between the pro-war and anti-war elements in the party, on issues on which they were broadly in agreement, thus reducing the chances of the kind of disastrous split which occurred in other socialist parties. Secondly, it provided a forum where Labour policy could be developed during the war years. Thirdly, and also significantly, it brought Sidney Webb, as one of its members, into a close personal and political association with Arthur Henderson, who was its chairman. Meeting two or three times a week they came to understand and respect each other in a way that had never been the case with Webb and MacDonald. Before long Sidney was drafting the pamphlet *The War and the Workers*, and he was increasingly consulted and employed as a policy draftsman by Henderson: as the war years passed Webb became one of the inner group which Henderson set up to prepare a party policy and to plan its reorganisation after the war.

### 631 LPA SIDNEY WEBB TO J. S. MIDDLETON

James Smith Middleton (1878–1962), assistant secretary of the Labour Party from 1903 and secretary 1935–45, was the secretary of the War Emergency Workers' Committee. Its immediate anxiety was about employment, for on the outbreak of war it was assumed that Britain's commitment would be predominantly naval; no one foresaw a long war of attrition and a large army supported by a vast munitions industry. Looking back on this period at the end of the war Beatrice thought that later events had shown the prescience of the Minority Report of the Poor Law Commission in its proposals for unemployment: 'maintenance under training (in this case in the Army) with the organisation of production and the state of the labour market by the government, according to national needs'.

41 Grosvenor Road
Westminster Embankment
14.8.14

Dear Mr Middleton

It is reported to me from Deptford that the Admiralty's Victualling Yard there is working its men 12 hours a day, instead of 8 hours – refraining from taking on additional men, of whom there are many unemployed able to do the work.

Also that the War Office orders for *tinware* in Deptford are all given to some firms, which are working desperate overtime, whilst none are given to another similar firm in the district (A. and G. Scott) which is working very short time, and may presently have to shut down. The latter firm happens to be the one in which the conditions of employment are most favorable to the workers.

Yours very truly
Sidney Webb

### 632 LPA SIDNEY WEBB TO ARTHUR HENDERSON

Less than a month after the war began the Trades Union Congress proclaimed an 'industrial truce', but Webb and other members of the W.E.W.C. were determined to see that hard-won trade union rights and practices were not whittled away under the mantle of the emergency.

41 Grosvenor Road
Westminster Embankment
21.8.14

Dear Mr Henderson

You will have had brought to your notice the question of insisting on Trade Union rates of wages on Government work now undertaken. I see no reason for any relaxation of this rule, wherever it is a question of men being *hired* to execute work for wages at all.

I want to draw your attention to the Treasurer's Letter of 4 November 1912 (enclosed) laying down the principle on the advice of the Official Advisory Committee on the Fair Wages Resolutions, that they are to apply to work done by quasi-public authorities *to which Government Grants are made* (as by the Road Board, the Development Commissioners, etc.).

I think you may like to refer to this deliberate Government decision, in connection with any grants for works now undertaken to keep up the volume of employment.

Of course, this does *not* apply (and in my judgment ought not to apply) to 'Relief Works' – that is, works started to employ the unemployed. Here the men are not hired at wages; they are not set to work at their several trades; consequently there can be no question of each of them getting his own particular trade union rate. When a mixed crowd of unemployed men have to be put to work, just to help them from idleness, on some common task of digging, what they receive can only be deemed *relief*, not wages; and must be based on subsistence of all alike.

I would, if I had my way, start so many real public works, *to be carried out for wages in the ordinary way*, that there should be no great mass of unemployed – only sporadic cases. But if the Government won't or can't do this, we must come to relief allowances for training or on Relief works.

Yours truly

Sidney Webb

## 633 PP BEATRICE WEBB TO MARY PLAYNE

On 25 August Beatrice noted in her diary: 'capacity for work destroyed by anxiety and restless searching for more news . . . We are going away for ten days . . . to walk ourselves into a quieter state of mind. Sidney has been drafting memoranda for government departments and resolutions for Labour meetings. I have been drifting between letter writing and reading successive editions of the papers.' Louis Meinertzhagen was the youngest son of Beatrice's sister Georgina, who died that autumn. The letter was written from Seaford in Sussex.

Seaford
Aug. 29th 1914

Dearest Mary

We are here with the Louis Meinertzhagens for the Sunday; and we are going for ten days walking over the Downs before starting on our author's work. For the last fortnight we have been immersed in this unemployment and distress business – attending committees and drafting instructions etc. and consulting with all and sundry. On Monday Haldane dined alone with us and we had a long talk about the relation of the collapse in the city to unemployment in all our staple industries. This was followed up by a most interesting meeting at dinner on Friday night of Haldane with Lloyd George, Grey, Isaacs (Lord Reading), Montague (the Financial Secretary of the Treasury) and ourselves. All these ministers were very grave and all had lost any conventional discretion and aloofness, and all were working at the top of their energies. Grey was especially 'human' – terribly concerned about the fact of the war and that he had been unable to prevent it – eager for intimate discussion and sympathy. (He is usually a cold self-centred person.) Lloyd George really is a brick – he is so devoid of self-consciousness and pedantry (so extraordinarily alert in intelligence and cheery and calm). Our special mission was to make the Cabinet realise the connection between the collapse of the Remittance market and the unemployment of millions of men and women in large centres of population: (incidentally I think we have done Fred Huth and Co. a good turn!) I think Lloyd George is prepared to back up the great Accepting Houses if this will solve the question of international trade. We also talked about all the plans of preventing [*illegible word*] duties. About the War Haldane was grave, tho' I think confident we should pull through. He does not believe the Russians can get to Berlin, even if they continue victorious, for another 2 months and by that time the Germans may be in possession of the north of France and its ports if not between us and Paris. But the Cabinet is determined to fight the thing to a finish even if it takes 2 years or more. Of course the financial situation is serious as Germany has so arranged apparently with methodical foresight that she owes us, on balance, some 200 millions, so that her merchants are actually flush of money and need no moratorium. Haldane remarked that we should all have to live on 50% of our incomes before the war was over! All the fringes of our living will have to go to provide the necessaries of the poorer classes.

Louis and his wife are pleasant young people and he has intellectual and moral distinction. But like Stafford Cripps it is a pity he has married so young, and to a young person with a very low standard of effort and a very high standard of comfort! He takes far too little exercise and dawdles about with her. She is not able, and has no training for any kind of work. She has been brought up simply to be a 'nice girl' and is a very enervating companion. Still they are very happy together and perhaps she may improve. But it is a handicap for Louis if he is to be a director of the world's affairs. I think the 'nice girl' ought once for all to be abolished – she is worse than a nuisance, she is an insidious parasite not only on men's incomes but on their characters and intellects.

How are you getting on? Any letter you write will be forwarded.

Ever yours

Beatrice Webb

634 PP SIDNEY WEBB TO MR DIXSON [*retained copy*]

The addressee is not known.

41 Grosvenor Road
Westminster Embankment
29.9.14

Dear Mr Dixson,

You ask me what have I 'to say to the dear old lady who cannot get out or the other type of old lady who lives upon an income that is not earned though it is at the same time limited – her only way of giving help is to make garments'.

This raises the question whether, because these old ladies wish to indulge their feelings and satisfy their uneasy consciences, they are justified in *doing an injury* to unseen seamstresses of different sorts who are now being thrown out of work literally by thousands.

I don't think that *any* self-indulgent craving justifies an injury. The mere fact that these old ladies prefer to do needlework does not seem to mend matters.

In the first place they certainly must not cause the nation's substance to be wasted. It is literally true that the garments so made often cost more out of pocket for material in small parts, cutting out, packing, carriage, handling, than they could be bought for made up wholesale. The handiwork of the old ladies is not only usually horribly inefficient; it is not only thrown away; it is positively levying a tax on us!

In the second place they need not do the injury to the seamstress. Let them (i) confine themselves to luxuries that the W.O. or inc [*sic*] soldier would not anyhow buy; or (ii) give away the garments to people so poor as to have no 'effective demand'.

That is, if the garments have any utility at all, which is often not the case (literally).

Sidney Webb

635 PP BEATRICE WEBB TO BETTY BALFOUR

Beatrice was appointed to the central committee which was promoting local committees to administer relief for 'distress arising out of the war'. The report on 'State and Municipal Enterprise' appeared in the *New Statesman* on 8 May 1915.

41 Grosvenor Road
Westminster Embankment
3rd October 1914

My dear Betty

At the last meeting of the London Advisory Committee we were asked to sanction weekly cheques to the London mayors for distribution in money and food. We started off with a cheque of £100 for Battersea. The Labour man and I, together with one or two representatives of the C.O.S., vehemently protested against the policy: but the payment was sanctioned. Another £100 was proposed for St Pancras, whereupon I insisted that if we were going to distribute money we ought to do it systematically; allocating our grant to each Borough according to the carefully prepared report of the L.G.B. [Local Government Board] Intelligence Department as to the relative amount of unemployment and distress in the 29 London Boroughs. Taking £100 for Battersea as the standard we ought to give St Pancras £300 and Shoreditch £350. This caused a panic and the whole question was adjourned and I was asked to bring up resolutions defining an alternative policy. Here are the Resolutions and also a memorandum which we have drafted to send to a few friends connected with this business of the Prince of Wales's Fund. If you think that either Mr Gerald Balfour or Mr Balfour would be interested would you let them see these documents. I don't want to bore anyone with this question unless they are really interested in it. Of course it seems a small matter compared to the war but as we are in for a long period of dislocated trade it seems to be worth while not to begin a policy of demoralisation. So far as I hear from our two parties in the Cabinet Committee, one in favour of constructive measures and the other preferring the easier policy of doles to keep the Local Representative Committees satisfied – Masterman is the leader of the Doles party and H. Samuel of the constructive schemes policy – so I hear.

We are trying to struggle back to our own work – a long report on State and Municipal industry which will be a supplement to the *New Statesman*. Shall we come down to lunch next Saturday? and from whither shall we walk to Fisher's Hill? I see another Cecil is dead: it is all very horrible and if disease breaks out – as it surely must very soon – the slaughter of our finest men will be the natural calamity of the century.

Ever yours sincerely
Beatrice Webb

636 BWD BEATRICE WEBB TO GILBERT MURRAY

[*Beatrice inserted a copy of this letter in her diary for 14 October 1914 with the following comment:*] 'We were asked by Professor Gilbert Murray to sign the manifesto in reply to that of the German Intellectuals affirming the rightness of the British Government to declare war on Germany. This was my reply.'

Dear Professor Murray

We were so sorry to have given you the trouble of sending a telegram: we thought the printed statement and your letter was in the nature of a circular which would be replied to only in case of acquiescence – so we did not trouble you with any answer.

We have both of us a rooted disinclination to sign statements on questions about which we have no special information or enlightenment. It was largely this feeling that made us refrain from taking sides in the South African War – much to the disgust of many of our fellow Socialists. Speaking for myself this feeling of hesitation is increased by a suspicion that great catastrophes like the present war are brought about by the whole state of public opinion among all the nations concerned. I quite agree that in this case Germany is the ostensible aggressor just as we were in the case of the South African war. But so long as the public opinion of the German and the British Empire (and of the old Boer states, by the way) believes in the material interests being the purpose of a nation's life, and physical force being the method by which this purpose is fulfilled, wars are inevitable with all their attendant brutalization and suffering. How to end this state of things I don't know, and I feel personally quite helpless in face of it. I am not sure whether the best solution of the present gigantic struggle would not be the complete collapse of all the parties concerned. Fortunately I am not called upon to take any decision. It looks to me as if it is not unlikely that the war may be terminated, not by men and iron, but by disease and famine. I admit this is a very unsatisfactory state of mind – but you will understand that it makes any signing of statements or manifestoes practically impossible. Of course if our signatures were of any use to our country we should give them whatever our scruples might be. But as we are of no account on all these questions of international relations and have neither knowledge or philosophy about them we feel inclined to be scrupulous.

It would be an immense pleasure to see you some day and talk it all over with you. I always feel that you have both the philosophy and the knowledge which we lack.

Always yours sincerely

Mrs Sidney Webb

### 637 BWD SIDNEY WEBB TO GUSTAV STEFFAN

Professor Steffan of Gothenburg University in Sweden, who had met the Webbs when he was in England doing research on agricultural history, had asked Sidney's opinion about the war. Steffan was later expelled from the Swedish Social Democratic Party for pro-German views. This copy was retained in Beatrice's diary.

Do not believe any statement that 'the whole United Kingdom – nay, the whole British Empire from Canada to India – is not whole-heartedly in favour of fighting out this war to the bitter end. I have never in all my life seen England so much united in feeling. The Labour Party, the Irish Party, the Party of Ulster are all of them as steadfastly supporting the Government as the Liberal and Radical Party and the Unionist or Conservative Party. All these political parties are helping the recruiting, and supplying men and money freely.

The recruiting for our additional army has been unexampled in its success. Only five weeks ago was the call made for half a million men. Already over 300,000 medically picked, stalwart young men are enrolled; and they are still coming in at the rate of three army corps per week. Within less than eight weeks, the whole half million will have been enrolled, put into uniform, equipped and armed and taken into camp for training. I do not think there has ever been, in all the history of the world, so extensive and so rapid a purely voluntary recruiting. How quickly the men can be made into efficient infantry, cavalry and artillery I do not pretend to say; nor yet how soon they can be adequately provided with trained officers and non-commissioned officers, guns, transport and horses. But the unprecedented success of the recruiting, drawn from all social classes, without compulsion and without money bounties, is evidence of the solidarity of the nation, and of its determination.

No less extraordinary has been the enthusiastic support in men, money and material given by India; by the great self-governing dominions of Canada, Australia, New Zealand, South Africa and Newfoundland, and by the smaller Colonies. Already more than 100,000 fully equipped men – two-thirds of them trained soldiers – are on their way, and some have already arrived in England on their way to the front. The Empire is unanimous. We shall carry on the fight, if necessary, for as many years as we did, a century ago, against Napoleon; and with much more unity of spirit.

What is it that has swept away in an hour the growing movement in favour of Peace, the entire 'class-conscious struggle' so far as it ever existed in England, the very real growth of Internationalism which would have shown itself in an unprecedentedly large English delegation to the International Socialist Congress at Vienna? I need hardly say that England believes most fervently that it is at war in a righteous cause – (i) in fulfilment of its plighted word to maintain the neutrality of Belgium, and incidentally, therefore, in protection of the independence of all the smaller States of Europe; (ii) in defence of our ally, France, which has been reluctantly forced into war and had its territory actually invaded before taking any aggressive action, and to which we had a special moral obligation, in that it has concentrated its fleet in the Mediterranean in order to enable England to concentrate hers in the North Sea; and (iii) virtually in defence of the British Empire and of England itself against the aggression which the Prussian military class disdained to hide.

But it is a feature of the present world war that every one of the six Great Powers and three smaller Kingdoms that are engaged in it sincerely believes itself to have a righteous cause, and even to have some special justification for going to war! The strength and reality of this national feeling in such case is shown by the behaviour of the Socialist Parties in the several countries. In France and Belgium their leaders have actually joined the Ministry, in Germany they are wholly supporting the Government, and even sending missions to Italy to induce that country to join them; from Russia and Austria, as from Servia, Montenegro and Japan I have no news, but I believe the position to be essentially the same; whilst in England the great Labour Party, together with two out of the three Socialist organisations which are comparatively small, are equally supporting the Government.

My own belief is that this war, like the smaller Transvaal War of fifteen years ago, had, as a result of evil thoughts, gradually become inevitable. It is the outcome of long continued national pride and ambition, coupled with a belief in irresistible power, and a willingness to use that power ruthlessly in pursuit of national aims. Doubtless each nation views the position from its own angle.

To us in England it seems that (i) Germany, under Prussian leadership, has grown so powerful and so wealthy, that an opinion has become widespread, not only through the military class but also largely through the professors and business men, that it could, if it chose, make itself the dominant power in the world; (ii) that as it possessed the power to make itself dominant, it had a right to this position, or at least to the 'place in the sun' from which the existence of the British Empire, Russia, France and the United States seemed to exclude it; (iii) that this moral right to take whatever it needed for the fulfilment of its national ambitions was strengthened by a conviction that England and France, in particular, were morally and intellectually unworthy of their great positions, and ought therefore to be removed from an influence in the world to which they had no just claim; (iv) that England, especially, was effete, and had, indeed, only acquired its Empire by the chronological accident of no other rival being at the time ready to contest the matter – and (v) that Germany, filled with these feelings, could not imagine that England (in an unholy alliance with Russia, France and Japan) was not purposely thwarting the expansion of Germany at all points, and only watching, indeed, for a favourable opportunity to destroy her power and invade her territory.

I believe that Germany was wholly mistaken in its apprehension of an attack by England. If Russia and France had desired such an attack England would not have helped them. The English people would never have allowed any Ministry to engage in such an attack. I do not say this in any spirit of self-righteousness. It happens that England has nothing to gain from anything but peace. It desires none of Germany's possessions. It believes that every increase in Germany's wealth and economic prosperity, in itself conduces to the increase in the wealth and economic prosperity of other nations, including most of all England itself. The more manufacturing and trading is done by one country, the more will be done by other countries.

But it is true that the British Empire stands in the way of Germany's aspiration to become the dominant power in the world, and stands, in particular, in the way of Germany's seizure of tropical or other Colonies. There are three great world powers, the very existence of which Germany feels to be antagonistic to the fulfilment of its ambitions. The United States, the unassailable, guards, with its Monroe Doctrine, the whole Continent of North and South America. Russia, the unconquerable, dominates all Northern Asia. It is what seems to every Prussian, the swollen, unwieldy and unorganised British Empire which is Germany's nearest obstacle.

With this spirit and this belief becoming dominant in Prussia, a conflict was, sooner or later, inevitable. On a much smaller scale an analogous growth of power and state of mind in the Transvaal Republic (dragging with it the 'Austria' of the Orange Free State) made inevitable the Boer War. It so happened that, by official insolence and blundering, in all that led up to that war, England put itself superficially in the wrong. We are more fortunate this time in our Ministers and officials, and are able, with assurance, to believe that our country has been, even in superficial matters, scrupulously in the right. But whether or not this had been the case, I fear that the clash of Germany's ambitions, aspirations and natural self-complacency, with the very position of the British Empire in the world – remembering how very imperfectly human nature is yet moralised, and how prone it is to take whenever it feels the power to take – made a life and death struggle inevitable.

[Sidney Webb]

### 638 MMLMU BEATRICE WEBB TO BERTRAND RUSSELL

Russell believed that Grey's foreign policy had been one of the factors making for war; he also disliked and distrusted Russian autocracy. He would have wished Britain to remain neutral. During the autumn of 1914 he joined Edmund D. Morel (1873–1924), Phillip Snowden, Charles Trevelyan, Ramsay MacDonald and Norman Angell (1874–1967) in founding the Union of Democratic Control to campaign for greater control over foreign policy and for open diplomacy. Morel had achieved some notoriety by his exposure of Belgian atrocities in the Congo; Angell's book *The Great Illusion* (1910) was a forceful criticism of great power politics. Other key figures in the U.D.C. were Charles

Roden Buxton, a Liberal M.P. who became an adviser on international affairs on joining the Labour Party after the war, and Arthur Ponsonby (1871–1946), later Lord Ponsonby, another Liberal M.P. who went over to Labour in 1922. Liberal pacifists such as Trevelyan, Buxton and Ponsonby formed an influential group in the post-war Labour Party, providing it with much of its ministerial material and a core of monied and middle-class intellectuals whose general disposition was to the left.

41 Grosvenor Road
Westminster Embankment
Oct. 14 [1914]

My dear Bertie

I hear you are sometimes in London. Do come and see us? We have been very much interested in your articles in the *Labour Leader*. We are disinclined to sign anything about the war for, or against. It is one of those huge catastrophies which arise when evil thoughts prevail – and I don't feel personally, able to fix the responsibility on any particular persons or facts – at any rate – in my present state of ignorance. One can only go on working for what one thinks right in the internal organisation of one's own country about which one does know and one has definite principles – I mean relatively to other people!

Ever

Beatrice Webb

Let us know when you will be up in London next.

## 639 SU BEATRICE WEBB TO LEONARD WOOLF

Leonard Woolf (1880–1969), former civil servant in Ceylon and the husband of Virginia Stephen (1882–1941) was one of the radical intellectuals whom the Webbs encouraged. Though better known as a member of the Bloomsbury set, Woolf became an active and important member of the Fabian Society and maintained a lifelong association with the Webbs. After throwing up his post as a civil servant on his marriage, much of his time was devoted to caring for his semi-invalid wife, and he worked mainly as a free-lance writer.

The Fabian Research Department, tackling the fourth part of the scheme to study the Control of Industry, had now begun to survey the professions. 'In our work on trade unions we omitted the professional organisation of brainworkers and only referred to it in a note as requiring investigation', Beatrice wrote. (BWD 14 February 15) 'It was only when the Syndicalists and Guild Socialists claimed, for the normal working trade unions, complete control over the organisation of industry, that we insisted that we must enquire into the self-government claimed and exercised by organisations of brainworkers, such as the lawyers, the medical men, the teachers and the civil engineers.' The Fabian group was in fact setting itself a formidable agenda: Beatrice at this time made one of her wistful remarks about the Webbs retiring to a life of research and pleasant companionship, but like similar comments made at intervals through their career this private hope was the victim of the partnership's energetic promotion of its public purposes.

41 Grosvenor Road
Westminster Embankment
23rd November 1914

Dear Mr Woolf

You were kind enough to say that you would help with the Report on Professional organisation. I wonder whether you would undertake a comparative statement of the organisation of the legal profession in England, America and as many of the continental countries as you can get hold of? I ask this with some hesitation as it is extraordinarily difficult to determine how much of the actual facts about the legal profession we shall embody in our Report. But what is clear is that we shall require them for any generalisation that we make about the control of the legal service by the persons who exercise it and their power of determining the entry into their profession, the etiquette which governs it, and the selection of those members of the profession who become salaried officials of the State. It seems to me that in this study of professional organisation we have discovered a new field and one likely to be very illuminating from the standpoint of alternatives to the capitalist system. It is quite clear to me that in the case of a profession like Engineering or Auditing the direct and indirect professional control is considerable and that this professional control necessarily excludes any crude application of a democracy of manual working producers, on the one hand, and, on the other, supplies the complement of control by political democracy. It is a grave misfortune that Civil Servants have no professional organisation with its development of professional technique and its etiquette of independence from external pressure. It seems to me that professional organisation is the only safeguard against the intrigue and secretiveness of Government departments. What I should like to do would be to show you the little we have on the legal profession and to talk over the points which ought to be discovered and discussed. What days are you in London and could we arrange to meet at the Fabian office and talk the matter over?

I am sorry to say I have not got your Wimbledon address: I hope this will reach you.

Always yours sincerely
Beatrice Webb
(Mrs Sidney Webb)

640 SU BEATRICE WEBB TO LEONARD WOOLF

This proposal was the impetus which carried Woolf into a lifetime concern with international organisation and peace.

41 Grosvenor Road
Westminster Embankment
16th December 1914

Dear Mr Woolf

I think my husband spoke to you the other night about the possibility of an enquiry – with a view to constructive proposals – into the whole arrangements of international control over Foreign Policy, Armaments and methods of warfare. I enclose you a letter from Joseph Rowntree. He has for some time subscribed a £100 – first to the National Committee for the Prevention of Destitution, and for the last two years to the Fabian Research Department. He now wishes his £100 to be used definitely for a study on Internationalism. I think it would be extraordinarily valuable if the Fabian Society as the intellectual leader of the Socialist and Labour movement did a thoroughly fine piece of work on this subject.

Now it has occurred to my husband and myself that you might perhaps be willing to undertake the executive part of this enquiry and to serve as Secretary to a small Committee of the Fabian Research Department. If you are inclined to do so we should propose to the Fabian Society to use £50 of the £100 as a fee to cover out of pocket expenses and to provide a small remuneration for the drudgery entailed. I realise the inadequacy of the payment regarded as payment – but we cannot afford more: it just prevents the work from being an additional expense to anyone who undertakes it for love! (I think we ought to be able to complete the work in about 3 months from the time of starting.) Would you consider this fee sufficient to warrant you giving up a good deal of time to the work? I think the remainder of the £100 would be required for printing, typing and postage. Of course we have not consulted any members of the Fabian Executive, but we should like to know before making a definite proposal to the Fabian Executive whether you would be inclined to undertake the work. The Report might be published by the Fabian Research Department with your name attached as the Author.

Perhaps you might write me a letter which I could show to Sanders and perhaps read to the Executive.

Yours very truly

Beatrice Webb
(Mrs Sidney Webb)

P.S. By the way I suppose you have noted this decision of the General Council of the Bar – I hope you will be able to complete the study on the organisation of the Law before we begin that on International Peace? I shall be able to send you in a week or so my draft report on Organisation in the Engineering Industry. I have an idea that we might publish these Reports as a separate volume on Professional Organisation: they will be too long and detailed to include in our main Report; and as there is no work on Professional Organisation it would be most desirable that they should be published as a companion volume to our trade union studies.

B.W.

641 SU SIDNEY WEBB TO LEONARD WOOLF

Woolf had submitted an outline of the policy document on international peace which, when approved, he was to develop into the *New Statesman* supplement of 10 July 1915, 'Suggestions for the Prevention of War'; and a Fabian book, published as *International Government* in 1916. Webb's letter anticipates much of the discussion which led to post-war attempts to regulate and arbitrate international differences, and to the League of Nations.

41 Grosvenor Road
Westminster Embankment
21.1.15

Dear Mr Woolf

My wife and I have thought over your very suggestive Memorandum. On consideration, having in view the peculiarities of committees, we think you would do well (i) *not to present alternatives* to them; (ii) not spontaneously to *open up* any suggested lines other than that which may be deemed by you the best. We may, with advantage, listen to criticisms and suggestions from the Committee, for the sake of getting new ideas and fresh light. But it would not be wise to dazzle the Committee with many suggestions; nor put them under the necessity of choosing.

We suggest that you would do well not to commit yourself to dealing *historically* with any part of your work. You will not need to hamper yourself with enumeration of everything that has happened, nor yet with any chronological sequence.

We think, too, that you had better confine yourself strictly to what could be put in the Terms of Peace (including of course, a Congress and Treaty) – to the exclusion of 'what can be done in the future to lessen the frequency of wars', an endless task!

What is needed is to arrive at a strictly practical suggestion, or rather alternative suggestions, explained and supported by accounts of *what has been tried with useful results*; and of past experiments and analogies suggestive of any new expedients we can devise. This points to an analytic form (of course with historical illustrations).

The question really is twofold (a) By what expedients or machinery to secure permanent compliance with the terms of the Treaty of Peace; and (b) How to arrange for the settlement, without war, of future issues, or how to provide for changes in the terms of the Treaty. The expedients in the past seem to have been

(i) Negotiation and Agreement
(ii) Arbitration

(iii) International Law
(iv) International Guarantees

Much has been done by these means; and it would be well to set forth succinctly how much. But the lack has always been in an ultimate sanction other than war. Attempts towards such a sanction have been

(a) Embargo on shipping
(b) Blockade and stoppage of trade, (also post and passenger intercourse)
(c) Refusal of loans
(d) Export duties
(e) Coercion by the guaranteeing powers, 'Concert of Europe', etc.

Could we not move to a supersession of national conflicts on the same lines as those on which we have superseded personal and municipal conflicts, viz. by an overriding law, made by a superior authority interpreted by a tribunal with power to *fine*, and enforced by all the power of the Superior Authority? Why should not the Council of all the Powers *impose* the Treaty of Peace on the world as a law, constitute a permanent tribunal to try all issues between nations with power to fine heavily, and pledge all the signatories to contribute their share towards the sanction enforcing the tribunal's decision (e.g. by embargo, non-intercourse, by export duties to be imposed and accounted for to realise the fine – even if an international police force is yet to come).

One of the terms of the Treaty of Peace might be partial disarmament – what is practicable? The manufacture of war vessels, armourplate, cannon, shells, military rifles might be everywhere

(a) taken out of capitalist hands;
(b) made the exclusive prerogative of the Supreme Authority or Supernational Council, which should allow the several Governments to purchase up to an agreed maximum quota according to population, area, trade etc.

Another of the Terms of the Peace Treaty, or of the Congress discussions might be a change in the Content and forms of Diplomacy (Treaty of Vienna *did* deal with this). We might *remove* from diplomatic relations some of the things dealt with – by settling them by law. We might also change the forms by (1) insisting on much more publication of correspondence to the world, (2) by requiring some things, e.g. treaties, statements of claim on other nations, complaints before the Supernational Tribunal etc., to be made only by vote of the Legislature.

This would enable a brief discussion of 'Popular Control of Diplomacy' – what it means, and where it amounts to a fallacy.

As to 'Pacifism', insofar as this means an improvement in the *righteousness* of peoples – a coming to right and reasonable thinking among men – this seems to us quite outside the scope of the present enquiry. Changes in the minds of men take place only gradually and slowly. The present enquiry concerns what can be put into the Terms of Peace, perhaps within 12 months. We want to devise means to avoid war *in a world containing unrighteous* persons, and perhaps even unrighteous nations.

I have run on just to submit ideas to you. But I return to my first point, viz: that the Memo. for you to submit to the Committee had better be confined to a very brief and decisive statement of the points *that you propose to deal with*, on which you would like to hear the suggestions of the Committee.

Mrs Webb begs me to remind you that she has arranged to be at the Fabian Common Room on Monday next, 24th inst. from 4 to 6 p.m.

Yours

Sidney Webb

642 SU BEATRICE WEBB TO LEONARD WOOLF

The Webbs were on good terms with W. C. Anderson and his wife, Mary MacArthur – Beatrice thought him 'a most conciliatory and agreeable colleague' and her 'the most remarkable woman in the Labour world'. (BWD 14 February 15) The composition of the committee showed the division among the Fabians on the war issue. Sharp was pro-war, and was soon to be released from the *New Statesman* for intelligence work in Scandinavia; Clifford Allen was a fanatical pacifist and the public champion of conscientious objectors; Ensor believed in the punishment and dismemberment of Germany; Sidney Webb favoured a peace settlement under supranational control; W. S. Sanders was also about to join the intelligence service.

At the Fabian annual general meeting on 14 May, Cole and other Guild Socialists made an attempt to restrict the Society's role to research, to deny membership to Liberals and to take over the executive. This failed. 'Cole', Beatrice noted on 15 May, 'disgraced himself . . . by an ill-tempered and tactless argument and then, when the vote went against him, by a silly display of temper.' He denounced his opponents as 'bloody fools' and, with Mellor and other acolytes, resigned from the Fabian Society. This, Beatrice added, was 'the old story of H. G. Wells and J. R. MacDonald. It is all the more amazing to us as we are honestly anxious to find successors and if these rebellious youths and maidens had only refrained from asking for a public execution of the old people we would have gladly stepped down from our position as soon as they had secured some sort of respect from the members at large'.

41 Grosvenor Road
Westminster Embankment
21st January 1915

Dear Mr Woolf

The Fabian Research Department Executive confirmed the decision of the Fabian Society so that you may consider that you are now authorised to go ahead with the work of enquiry with a view to the Report on International Peace. I don't know whether you took away the enclosed memo but perhaps you might as well have it. The proposal is that the essay should be published over your name and that you alone will be responsible for its contents. It is possible that the Committee might add its own Resolutions. But I gather that the members of the two Executives would prefer to issue a separate tract on the question of policy after they have your publication to discuss – possibly at meetings of the Society during next Autumn. I think it would be desirable to get your book published in the summer if you could get it done by that time. We appointed a Committee of about 14 persons including the three officials of the Research Department and Clifford Sharp, Clifford Allen and R. C. Ensor, etc. and we are asking W. C. Anderson, the Chairman of the Labour Party, who is a member of the Fabian Society to join the Committee. It was agreed that you should meet this Committee and discuss the scope of your Report and that if possible your suggestion should be circulated prior to this meeting so that the individual members of the Committee might make suggestions for your consideration. It remains to be seen whether you get anything out of them, but they are representative of various phases of opinion and some of them have a knowledge of sources.

I am so glad you have been able to undertake this work as I think it is extraordinarily important to give the Labour and Socialist Party some material to think about and I hope your Report will be extensively circulated in the Labour world. As we shall be circularising the trade union movement for Cole and Mellor's series of monographs on the organisation of the various industries we shall be able to include a circular giving the particulars of your Report and perhaps letting Labour organisations have it at cost price.

Yours very truly

Beatrice Webb

(Mrs Sidney Webb)

643 LSE SIDNEY WEBB TO B. M. HEADICAR

Hedley Le Bas (1868–1926) was a publisher and later a director of the *New Statesman*.

41 Grosvenor Road,
Westminster Embankment
9.2.15

Dear Mr Headicar

*Hedley Le Bas*

whose address will be given in *Who's Who* doubtless, is said to be managing the Recruiting Posters for the W.O. Would it not be worth sending him a flattering letter, saying that you were making a special collection of war matter, and that a full set of his admirable posters ought to be preserved, *and asking him to send you a set*.!

Sidney Webb

Possibly the Director may know him. He is the Caxton Publishing Co. and a candidate for parliament.

P.S. I find I want *at once* in connection with work for the Fabian Research Department, practically all the *current* bluebooks about local Government in England and Wales, i.e. the last Annual Reports and statistics of L.G.B.
Local Taxation Returns
Registrar General of Births and Receiver of Metropolitan Police
Gas Company Returns or Statistics
Water Returns or Statistics
Tramway Returns or Statistics
Allotments and Smallholdings
Housing
Infant Protection
B. of Education
School Statistics of all sorts
Lunacy (Board of Control of Lunacy)
Customs Report for Old Age Pension
Board of Trade as to Street Traffic
Road Board
Poor Law Statistics

This is a large order! I wonder whether you have not many of these *among your duplicates*. If so, I should be grateful if you would sort out a pile, and *lend* them to me for a time. It is only the bluebooks published in 1914–15 or 1913, that would be of use.

644 NLS BEATRICE WEBB [*Draft letter to the press*]

This undated draft is in the Haldane Papers.

[? Early 1915]

Sir

We desire to express through your columns the grave concern we feel as to the national consequences of the present landslide with which we are threatened in the matter of education and child labour. It is a strange contradiction that at a time when Britain is making unparalleled sacrifices of her manhood in defence of all she holds dear we should tolerate simultaneously an attack on the best interests of the children for whom in a large measure these sacrifices are made. If to our lot has fallen the heat and stress of battle to them will fall the onerous and exacting duties of rebuilding the nation. The children of today are the citizens of tomorrow, and the omens point to their task being no light one. To fit them for it by every means in our power is a sacred obligation we owe to the dead. The lives given in Britain's cause will be given in vain unless we rear a strong, healthy, and efficient generation to gather in the fruits of a lasting and honourable peace.

It seems to us deplorable therefore that this happier future for which we pray should be prejudiced by any weakening of our educational system or a relaxation of the safeguards which protect the employment of children. Such a policy in our opinion cannot be justified on the grounds either of national economy or war emergency. Half-educated, overworked children when they grow to manhood and womanhood cannot sustain worthily the obligations of an Imperial race. Great though the need for the conservation of our national resources at this time public retrenchments must be inspired by a spirit of wise expediency and intelligent discrimination between essentials and non-essentials.

Educational economies so far as they are concerned with bricks and mortar have our hearty approval.

The South African camp schools during the Boer War proved what could be done under a sailcloth with enthusiasm as a directing force. Many administrative charges can doubtless be reduced by reorganisation of work. We feel no less strongly, however, that all economies in the matter of personnel (which destroy the essential efficiency of education) together with proposals to exclude infants from school age to facilitate the employment of children of eleven are fraught with real national peril. In view of the support given to these proposals by Chambers of Commerce, War Agricultural Committees, and Educational Authorities the danger is no chimera.

There is a lack of imagination in all this which goes to the root of a great national failing. Britain's apathy about education has proved the Achilles' heel through which time over and again she has been wounded in this war. From German morality and German standards the British people recoil in horror. But from German educational efficiency we have all much to learn and indeed may have much to fear if we elect deliberately to fall behind in the race. Scientific method is still in its infancy and there will be no place in the new world for any race loose-end in method and slipshod in practice which allows the younger generation to grow up half-trained and half-equipped to struggle with the heavy obligations of modern citizenship. The error if we make it is bound to cost us dear. We may rest assured it is one of which our enemies will not be guilty.

We are satisfied that the danger of the present tendencies is a very real one. It can only be combated by a quickened sense of public opinion brought to bear on educational and civic authorities both centrally and locally. It is to this end we make the present appeal. We would urge our fellow countrymen to realise all that is at stake in this matter and not jeopardise through short-sightedness during the stress of war the whole future of Britain for which so many brave lives daily are being yielded up.

Beatrice Webb

645 PP SIDNEY WEBB TO GRAHAM WALLAS

Wallas had become a member of the London University Senate on his appointment as professor of political science.

41 Grosvenor Road,
Westminster Embankment
12.3.15

Dear Wallas

With reference to your letter of some weeks ago (as to your position on the Senate etc.), I have had an opportunity of some talk with Reeves over the M.Sc. degree. He clings to the idea of asking for a deputation, and I think this should be allowed (preparatory to making the best of it, if that is the outcome).

We discussed generally the position as to Academic Council and Senate business, and the need for constant watchfulness against the interests of the Economic Faculty and the School being ignored or misunderstood, in the general play of the hand, often at the instance of other Faculties and Schools.

Reeves spontaneously expressed himself very desirous of constant consultation with you, and much regretted that you so seldom confide in him.

Now, what it seemed to me that the situation required was a *fixed regular* mutual consultation, however brief. I have found the fixing of a regular interview of the greatest value. Hewins and I met once a week regularly for years. Clifford Sharp and I meet regularly every Tuesday without fail. No matter how often I may happen to see him any week, the Tuesday appointment always stands. This is of the greatest value as an administrative device. The regular meeting becomes easy. There is no sense of obligation to find topics. The mere opportunity for mutually exchanging ideas is invaluable.

I suggested it to Reeves and he cordially welcomed it. I gather the Academic Council agenda is issued Friday night. I learn that he and you have no opportunity of meeting on Saturday, Sunday or Monday, so that habitually there is no chance for consultation before Monday afternoon's meeting. This seems bad.

You go, I gather from Highgate to S.K. [South Kensington] on Monday afternoon nearly every week. Could you not start an hour earlier, and go by way of the School? I asked Reeves if he could always have a quarter of an hour's talk with you at 3 p.m. each Monday, and he warmly and gladly agreed. I hope you won't think this an unreasonable inroad on your time. I am sure it will tend to save you much subsequent time and worry.

Of course, I don't think your business on the Senate is to be a mere delegate of the Faculty, or the School, or retained solely to work for the advantage of either of them. I had the same problem on the L.C.C., where I was conscious of being interested solely in London, and not really *caring* for any separate or peculiar interest of Deptford. But my conclusion was that, in a representative body, the member has two distinct duties, neither of which he ought to neglect, or even to subordinate. He must play the hand as a whole. At the same time, he is there to *make felt* in the assembly (a) the needs, (b) the interests, and (c) the power, or potential force for disruption, of the constituency that he represents.

A difficulty arises when he feels a real clash. Fortunately life, even on a representative body, is not all tragic moments! Normally what happens is that it is positively for the good of the whole, and useful to the play of the hand, that the (a), (b) and (c) of each constituent part should be quite effectively and vividly brought to the front – not as antagonistic to the whole, but because the maximum development of the whole can only occur by the very full, if not always the maximum development of each part.

I think that very frequent meetings and consultations with one's constituents are a duty of the perfect representative. It was a besetting error of myself that I hated and avoided them at Deptford all I could. I don't say you have the same fault, but I am sure you would find the fixed, regular gossip with Reeves of great use in more ways than one. I hope you won't mind my suggesting it; and that you will go in next Monday and see him!

Sidney Webb

## 646 SU BEATRICE WEBB TO LEONARD WOOLF

Virginia Woolf attempted suicide in September 1913 after completing *The Voyage Out*. Publication was delayed; she had a serious relapse in the spring of 1915 when the novel was published. Leonard Woolf's novel *The Village in the Jungle* appeared in 1913 and *The Wise Virgins* came out a year later.

41 Grosvenor Road
Westminster Embankment
March 16th [1915]

My dear Mr Woolf

I am so grieved to hear of your trouble: I hope your anxiety will not be too long drawn out. I will mention the state of things to my colleagues on the Committee and let you know the result. I myself should certainly wish you to go on – at your leisure, with the work, as there is no one else whom I should care to trust the job to, even if you had not already begun it. And

I cannot believe that it will be good for you to give up thinking about outside things however anxious and saddened you may be by your wife's illness. In that sort of trouble I have always found it restful and comforting to work on some impersonal problem. But I gather from your letter that you do not contemplate anything but delay and that I think the committee will be willing to accept, as the lesser evil to losing your services. I will let you know directly I have heard from the Chairman.

By the way I have just finished your two novels – I was immensely interested in both – my husband prefers the Ceylon tale. I, on the whole, find myself more interested in *The Wise Virgins*. I am presenting them both to Fabian Club room.

Ever yours sincerely

Beatrice Webb

647 KCC BEATRICE WEBB TO JOHN MAYNARD KEYNES

John Maynard Keynes (1883–1946), the outstanding economist of the inter-war years, divided his time between teaching in Cambridge and the financial and official worlds of London. He became the chief Treasury representative at the Versailles Conference in 1919, resigning in protest at the terms of settlement and publishing his dissent in his influential tract, *The Economic Consequences of the Peace*, 1919.

41 Grosvenor Road
Westminster Embankment
23rd April 1915

Dear Mr Keynes

We should very much like to have some talk with you if you have any spare time when you are in London. I wonder whether you would come to lunch one day, 1.30? – almost any day except Tuesday suits us.

We have been very much interested to hear your somewhat alarming prophecy of the level of prices at the conclusion of the war, and we should also like to discuss with you the results of an investigation by L. S. Woolf and a little Committee of the Fabian Society into the possibility of a Supernational Law for the prevention of war.

I understand that Mrs Keynes is not in London, otherwise it would be a great additional pleasure to see her.

Yours very truly

Mrs Sidney Webb

648 SU SIDNEY WEBB TO LEONARD WOOLF

Woolf's draft was the basis of Part I of *International Government* and Sidney was now suggesting that Woolf should move on to what became Part II. The third part ('The Supernational Authority That Will Prevent War') was jointly written by Woolf and Webb.

The Hobson mentioned was J. A. Hobson; Richard E. Cross was the solicitor to the Rowntree family. The so-called 'Bryce Committee' (Lord Bryce attended some meetings) was started by G. Lowes Dickinson in the first weeks of the war to study international organisation; in its report in 1915 it proposed a union of states agreeing to arbitration and sanctions against violators of an international code. The meeting at Barrow House, near Keswick, was to bring together the Fabian group and some of the Bryce Committee members to discuss Woolf's memorandum. Shaw, Beatrice noted on 5 June, as usual scintillated 'perversely brilliant criticism and paradoxical proposals'. After the meeting some of the group went walking together in the Lake District.

This meeting in 1915 played an important part in shaping Labour's peace aims. In 1915, moreover, a League of Nations Society was founded by Lowes Dickinson and Beatrice's two brothers-in-law, Leonard Courtney and Alfred Cripps; this was distinct from the League of Free Nations Association, formed in 1917, which supported the war and backed President Wilson's concept of the League – though the two groups later amalgamated.

41 Grosvenor Road
Westminster Embankment
25.5.15

My dear Woolf

We have just ended a most successful, and I think, fruitful conference, in which your Memo. and the draft scheme has been very generally approved. Lowes Dickinson, Hobson, Cross and Wallas from the Bryce Committee were very helpful; and I think we have gone far to convert them to the Scheme. They will all join our Committee to take part in the final discussions. We think that it will be well to publish, if we can, in a *New Statesman* Supplement in July sometime. We should therefore be glad if you would finally correct and complete your Memo. at your early convenience.

I have diligently picked up ideas from the discussions which I want to submit to, and discuss with you for the Amendment of our Scheme.

First, as to nomenclature. The names that most commended themselves were 'International High Court' and 'International Council'.

Secondly, various people of weight strongly advised our respecting the firmly-rooted prejudice of the smaller States in favor of equality of votes. Of course, the small States cannot be given really equal power with the Great Powers. But I am much disposed to try to avoid the arithmetical apportionment of votes by some system of classification – our plan of Councils for America and the Eight Great Powers, and our making the latter an unobtrusive 'Upper House' may suffice.

(3) I think our suggested additional article (extra par. to sec.h(4) on p.4) will have to be dropped, as Ensor advised; or at least curtailed. As it stands it would allow a three-fourths majority to partition Spain among them!

(4) The most important point made on behalf of the Bryce Committee was that the function of the Supernational Legislature *in legislation* called for a quite different set of representatives, a quite different state of mind, and a quite different relation to the Constituent Governments, from its proposed function *in composing intractable disputes* (our h(1)(2)(3)(4) on p.3).

My feeling is that this objection is valid. Our Legislature, in legislating, must directly represent the views of the several Governments – in fact, the Governments will be instructing their delegates hourly by telephone! This would not be a good body to mediate in an intractable dispute. But the two projects can, as it seems to me, easily be combined. When the dispute is brought before the International Council (as in h(1)) the Council must anyhow refer it to some Commission of Enquiry.

Can we not expand the words 'after examination' into 'refer it to the Council of Mediation', whose report shall be presented to the International Council, and be by it ratified:

In this way the Bryce 'Council of Mediation' would become only one of the organs of our International Council.

When we get back ten days hence, I propose to revise the draft and send it to you for consideration and discussion.

We think it would later be very desirable (i) to expand your Memo. into a book; (ii) to have a bigger Conference in London on it in the Autumn; and (iii) to continue the work by investigating all the non-governmental International structure – there are *220* such associations actually affiliated to a Union of International Association at Brussels, which has held two Congresses, and publishes a Journal and an annual. We ought to make this known, and describe this new and growing international issue.

Hoping that Mrs Woolf is better. I am.

Yours

Sidney Webb

649 PP SIDNEY WEBB TO EDWARD PEASE

On his retirement Pease began to write *The History of the Fabian Society* (1916). The manuscript (BLPES) contains interesting but sometimes inaccurate marginal comments by Shaw; the following letter by Webb differs from both Shaw and Pease on a few important points. Tract 6, *The True Radical Programme* was written by Shaw in 1887, under the nominal auspices of the Fabian Parliamentary League.

Gilbert Slater (1864–1938) was an economic historian and early Fabian who became Principal of Ruskin College, Oxford, 1909–15.

This letter should be read with those in Volume I for the autumn of 1891 which deal with the Newcastle Conference.

41 Grosvenor Road
Westminster Embankment
4.6.15

Dear Pease

We only got back last night from a week's tramp over the Cumberland hills.

As far as I remember the story is as under.

I began in 1886 or 1887 probably 1887 to try to make the Liberal Party realise that it ought to have a programme apart from Ireland. We had a Fabian Tract criticising 'the Nottingham Programme' (they meant to have no programme, and I think we invented the phrase). In the summer of 1888 I wrote a pamphlet, printed at my own expense, called 'Wanted a Programme, an appeal to the Liberal Party' – which I sent out to a thousand leading Liberals all over the country – using the *Star* that year in the same sense. (You should get, or consult at the School of Economics, an orange-covered sensational pamphlet published three years ago by the Anti-Socialist League called *Great Socialist Conspiracy Revealed*, which reprints my pamphlet of 1888, and says all subsequent legislation is derived from it!)

Then, during 1889–90 (or perhaps also during 1888) I got resolutions moved at many Liberal Associations to the same effect, and sent up to headquarters – Shaw got E. J. Beale the Liberal candidate, to move one in Holborn. Gilbert Slater moved one in South Devon. We got them mentioned in the *Star*. When the National Liberal Federation met at Newcastle in 1891, it was found that its Executive Committee, evidently with Gladstone's unwilling acquiescence, had expanded the Nottingham resolutions of 1886 (or 1887) into a much fuller list of measures (yet not so very much after all!) This we magnified and exaggerated into 'the Newcastle Programme'; and when the 1892 General Election yielded a bare 40 majority, I ascribed the fact that there was a majority at all to there being a social programme. I think I wrote an article for the *Contemporary Review* about June 1892 to this effect.

We tried the same sort of game in 1894 ('To your Tents, O Israel'); but Lord Rosebery and Sir W. Harcourt refused to respond even as much as Gladstone had done – and the Liberal *débâcle* of 1895 was the result.

I forget who co-operated in getting resolutions passed in 1887–91 except Shaw and (as I happen accidentally to remember) Gilbert Slater; but doubtless Graham Wallas was in it, and a dozen others.

I certainly had no hand in drawing up the resolutions which the Executive Committee of the N.L.F. submitted at Newcastle; and was in no way consulted. All that is true is that I wrote a programme in 1888 in the *Star*; and circulated it to Liberals; and then organised the passing of resolutions calling for a programme on those lines. The Newcastle resolutions were quite poor and feeble, in reality; but they were made to sound well!

Sidney Webb

650 PP BEATRICE WEBB TO MARY PLAYNE

The 'two other Fabians', on the walking trip, were John Squire and the popular historian Philip Guedalla (1889–1944). The 'eminent American' was Jane Addams, the social reformer and feminist whom the Webbs had met in Chicago in 1899. She was on an extended 'peace' mission on behalf of the Hague Conference of Women, representing the neutral countries, and she visited Germany, Austria, Italy, France and Britain. She gave Beatrice the impression that Germany felt strong enough to consider peace proposals before the winter. In an undated letter to Kate Courtney (late 1915 or early 1916 PP) Beatrice expanded her attitude to peace negotiations 'I should like the representatives of peoples to behave exactly as well-bred kindly individuals do towards each other when they are opposed to each other. I never could understand what was gained by boasting or angry silence. I would always negotiate, day by day, as a matter of course. That does not mean that I feel certain that Peace should be made on the terms that would be accepted by the Germans. Upon that count I have no opinion, and perhaps, if the whole of the facts were before me, I should *not* agree with you and Leonard as to what Peace is desirable or even admissible as an alternative to continuing the daily slaughter. *The conditions under which people live are infinitely more important than millions of premature deaths.* Death is the event of least importance.'

In mid-June the Webbs were upset by Haldane's enforced resignation from the Cabinet as a result of demagogic attacks on his presumed 'pro-German' affinities.

Dr Thomas Faulder was married to Julia Cripps, the elder daughter of Beatrice's sister Blanche; Harry Cripps was Blanche's youngest son. William Playne was Mary's only son. Frederick Cripps was the third child of Beatrice's sister Theresa.

41 Grosvenor Road
Westminster Embankment
[8 June 1915]

Dearest Mary

We have just returned from a delightful fortnight in the Lakes – the first five days at the Fabian country house on Derwent Water conferring about the possibility of setting up machinery for preventing War(!) and the rest of the time walking over mountains with G.B.S. and two other Fabians.

The results of the conference and three months work on the subject by L. S. Woolf will appear in July as a supplement to the *New Statesman*. We thought it would be useful – at any rate to the Labour and socialist movement – to give a historical and analytic account of what machinery had or did exist and where it had succeeded and failed; with a scheme carefully worked out in detail as to what could be done in constructing a supernational authority if the Powers are sufficiently disgusted with the slaughter and loss to be ready to do it. I can't help hoping that the terrible losses and exhaustion to all the combatants and the loss and inconvenience to the now-combatants will bring about some desire for an International authority and possibly International sanctions to enforce that authority. Otherwise it looks as if Western Civilization were going to exterminate itself by a long series of barbarous wars. London is full of camp-rumours about the reason for the Coalition government: but they are so contradictory that they are not worth repeating. It is said we have lost another battleship at the Dardanelles – the *Agamemnon* – and that we may be forced to retire but Winston seems to contradict this today. I hear from American travellers that the Germans are far more confident of winning than they were in the winter and that they expect to keep Belgium and levy an [indemnity] on the other allies. The same eminent American says that if once they lose this confidence they will collapse because their internal credit depends on their certainty of recoupment. I hear also that the U.S. will probably come in and help with finance and munitions. Certainly public opinion in governing circles in London is far more alarmed than it was 2 months ago – and this accounts for a part of our losses owing to lack of munitions – all very depressing and horrible. Tom reports that we have lost 60,000 in France [and] Flanders alone during May (I hear this is correct) and I am told 50,000 on the Dardanelles – killed and wounded. A good many people estimate our losses at 500,000.

Harry Cripps I hear, goes back to the front in about 3 weeks time. Where are Bill and Fred Cripps? When are you coming to London? It would be so delightful to see you.

Ever yours

Beatrice Webb

651 BL SIDNEY WEBB TO GEORGE BERNARD SHAW

The vicarage at Penalt in the Wye Valley was close to Beatrice's old home at The Argoed.

Shaw's perversity had brought his differences with Clifford Sharp to breaking point. On 5 October 1916 he wrote a long letter (PP) complaining about Sharp's editorial support for Asquith and saying that the *New Statesman* should either 'attack the big national idols' or make sufficient money to obviate the need for subsidies. Shaw broke his connection with the paper on 13 October.

The British Socialist Party had split into pro- and anti-war factions. H. M. Hyndman, F. H. Gorle and Victor Fisher were the leading figures in the 'patriotic' faction, Fisher soon forming the British Workers National League; some of the anti-war group broke away to reclaim the original title of the Social Democratic Federation. A substantial part of the B.S.P. joined with the loose alliance of 'revolutionary' groups that formed the Communist Party of Great Britain after the war.

Arthur Henderson, now leading the Labour Party, had entered the Asquith coalition as President of the Board of Education: two other Labour men, William Brace and G. H. Roberts, were appointed to junior posts. In October 1916 Henderson, who was in effect the liaison between the Cabinet and the Labour movement, became Paymaster-General.

Penalt Vicarage
Monmouth
18.8.15

Dear Shaw

This place remains quite unchanged in 18 years – no new house anywhere, no advance in visible civilisation (except a telegraph wire, an afternoon post, Old Age Pensions, and a voluntary District Nurse) – still only an underpaid woman as the teacher of 60 or 70 children – no looking after the infants or children physically. The 80 or 90 families have gone on growing their meagre subsistence, and producing annually two or three young men and two or three young women who have drifted away into productive activity elsewhere.

Chatfield reigns at The Argoed, a hale old man farming the estate – the Pelhams at Moorcroft as before – and no one else.

Your draft (returned herewith) seems to us unobjectionable and to have the right tone.

But who is the Socialist Party in England? Not only the I.L.P. but also the B.S.P. is in the hands of an extreme Pacifist Executive. The only body which could adopt such a Reply to the German Socialists, and speak for the English socialists, is the British section of the International.

It seems to me that what you ought to do with it is to send it to W. S. Sanders (who will now be back at 25 Tothill Street), and consult him as to whether it could be adopted by the British Section. He might get it manifolded, and then see what support could be got for it. We could then circulate it to the members of the Fabian Executive individually (omitting Clifford Allen, who is too violently Pacifist for anything), so as to be able to get their signatures *individually* (this seems to be the best form, as we could then get Hyndman, Gorle, Victor Fisher and other members of the B.S.P. *individually* also, and possibly some members of the I.L.P. individually – it being hopeless to get their executives as such).

I confess I do not see very much importance in issuing such a manifesto at this juncture; but if the others agree (as above) I would sign it. Possibly Sanders will say that the British Section will do nothing corporatively (partly because the I.L.P. and B.S.P. representatives on it would refuse, partly because A. Henderson, being now a Cabinet Minister would refuse); but that some of them would sign individually. Hence it would be all a matter of individual signatures.

I am rather afraid that very few of them all would consent to sign, even as individuals; but on that Sanders would be able to advise.

As to Military Service, the difficulty is that any proper system that we could advocate *takes time to mature*; and the pressure (and danger) is of an immediate measure, which is really useless for its professed purpose, and dangerous ultimately.

What could be advocated is Compulsory Training of all youth, from 14 to 21, not in military drill only, but in *everything* needed for citizenship (including drill and the use of arms) – not of the physically fit only, but of everyone, *especially* those who are below par physically. This should be done, as we proposed ten years ago, by Universal Half-Time (extension of present Factory Act Half-Time from 12/13 to 14/21), and devotion of the time thus set free from industrial servitude to real organised half-time training by the Local Education Authorities. Then, let the War Office and Admiralty continue their voluntary army and navy, paying the full rate of wages. Those who did not enlist should be compulsorily enrolled as Territorials, giving no more time to drill and camp than heretofore.

But this plan (a) costs much money, in greatly increased Education rates; (b) yields nothing for the purposes of the present war – and is therefore out of the question at present.

If I were in power, and were driven by either urgent military needs, or political pressure, to do something drastic, I should decree *Universal submission* to the National Need – not young men for the trenches only, but everyone for what he was fitted; and not persons only but also property and possessions – everything to be placed at the disposal of the Government against a mere receipt in paper – and then let the Government Departments *organise* what they could in each branch, preparing plans for Munitions, Aircraft, Ships, Transport and what not, with the materials in persons, things and cash thus placed at their disposal. The real crux is obviously not lack of fighting men, not even of munitions, but of organising ability and determination. And half a million additional food for powder won't augment this.

Yours

Sidney Webb

By the way, why omit Japan? The World Congress (to which you now admit Russia) ought certainly to include (a) all the belligerent states, (b) all other European states, (c) the U.S.

Pease had sent the draft of his Fabian history for the Webbs to read.

41 Grosvenor Road
Westminster Embankment
20th October 1915

Dear Mr Pease

I have read through your M.S. with very great interest – you have really made a domestic chronicle entertaining and useful, even, I think, from the point of view of a national historian.

I have one or two suggestions. I rather object to the last four lines of your little Preface. No one likes to be definitely committed to statements about themselves – flattering or otherwise, and yours are usually flattering as far as the critics you have chosen are concerned. I think I should omit those lines. In chapter 1, page 13, you say that Co-operation has succeeded. But the particular type of Co-operative advocated by Mill was a complete failure. I suggest that you alter this because I remember Marshall telling me that the whole of his economic thought had been influenced by Mill's faith in Co-operative Production and that he still held to that faith as the ideal towards which we should work – which accounts, I think, for Marshall's failure to influence economics. Chapter 4, page 4, is it wise to single out two of the original essayists for world fame? Your readers will assume that it is Shaw and Webb whom you designate. But there are many students in America who would give Graham Wallas a higher place than the Webbs for instance! I should leave it vague. Page 7. I doubt the wisdom of your reference to the Oxford gentleman. Moreover, the Suffragettes were not among the leaders of the Syndicalist movement as implied in your sentence – also Gild Socialists object to being called Syndicalists. In your last chapter you mention socialist unity and you say it has been deferred until after the war. But ought not you to mention the War Emergency Workers National Committee which is none the less significant because it has been a quite unconscious manifestation of Socialist Unity? It is certainly remarkable that all sections of the Labour and Socialist Movement including three Socialist societies and also the Co-operative Movement are here combined with a larger number of Trade Unions than are represented by the Trade Union Congress. I think it quite possible that this Committee will become the germ of a United Socialist Party. Anyhow it ought to be mentioned in connection with Socialist Unity even if you dismiss it as a mere ad hoc and temporary body.

Yours very truly
Beatrice Webb
(Mrs Sidney Webb)

I shall have a lot of detailed suggestions to make, when I can find time, in a day or two. But it is very good.

SW

Archibald Fenner Brockway (b. 1888) was an I.L.P. journalist, then editing the *Labour Leader*: he later became general secretary of the I.L.P. and, as a Labour peer after 1945 became a specialist in colonial policy. In November 1914 he founded the No-Conscription Fellowship, one of whose publications is the subject of this letter.

On 26 April Beatrice realised that her friendship with Betty Balfour – 'quite the most fascinating woman I have ever known' – was to be a casualty of the war and that the long and agreeable association with Arthur Balfour, now Foreign Secretary, was also at an end. Betty Balfour called at Grosvenor Road about the time of this letter but Beatrice felt the strain between them was such that they were unlikely to meet socially again: in fact, the relationship was resumed in a casual and distant manner some years after the war. Beatrice was hurt by the breaking of a tie she had valued and consoled herself with the thought that 'there can be no real friendship between persons inspired by radically different social ideals and whose life is rooted in altogether different traditions and circumstances'.

41 Grosvenor Road
Westminster Embankment
October 28th, 1915

Dearest Betty

I am glad to get your letter – glad to think that you still find it pleasant to write to me.

I was much interested in your vivid reactions from the anti-conscriptionist pamphlet. If I had had the task of drafting it, it would have been differently phrased – but with the substance of it I entirely agree. Frankly, I don't think your criticisms of its statements and arguments are valid. For instance, you are, I think, mistaken in asserting that there never has been an idea of Industrial Conscription. In the first place industrial conscription is implied in military conscription and is actually in force in all continental countries – the trenches being the alternative to recalcitrant work. But in England the conscriptionists, both in and out of Parliament (more especially Lloyd George) have affirmed it as a *distinct and additional proposal* apart from the implication of it. So far as I have read the speeches and statements, one of the main objects has been to get a sufficient supply of labour, under military discipline, for munition work.

Then you say that the British property owners are contributing more in taxation towards the war than the continental property owners – a quite correct statement. But it is exactly because the continental governments can use conscription as a method of getting both a cheap army and cheap munition workers, that they are able to save the property owners, even the very small and insufficient contribution imposed in England.

The feeling against conscription among thoughtful working men is intense. They feel that it is indescribably mean of the governing class to use the war to carry out a social revolution in their own favour. I think in this accusation they are wrong. I don't believe that even Milner and Curzon have any deliberate intention of cheating the people out of their freedom on the plea of patriotism. I believe that the conscriptionist lacks imagination. He fails to see that in asking the workman to give up his personal freedom to take work or to leave it, he is asking him to give up all that makes his daily life endurable. I think the workman would make the sacrifice if he saw that the property owner was willing to do likewise. But what secures, to you and to me, our freedom of action is our income from private property – a far greater freedom than is possessed by the manual worker. The workman thinks that if the property-owning class really believed this country to be in danger, they would be willing, during the period of the war, to pool all incomes over and above subsistence.

You say that motor-cars cannot be used in Flanders owing to the mud(!) That is no reason why labour and material should be used *here* – when both the labour (especially mechanics like chauffeurs) and the price of the material is needed for munitions. In using one hour of a man's or woman's work the income spender is abolishing the equivalent amount of output of munitions or exports.

However, it is difficult to carry on an argument by letter writing. But try to be charitable! After all those who take the view of the writer of the pamphlet (that is, all the committee whose names appear on the title page) are unquestionably British (in spite of your scepticism!); and they have as good a record for public-spirited and self-sacrificing work and possibly a far greater knowledge of industrial conditions than some of their critics!

I hope this unruly scrawl won't make you even more angry and contemptuous of its writer than you are of the writer of the pamphlet! I have always felt that this war will be the parting of the ways for many of us – but we are confronted with a class war far more bitter than anything we have yet experienced – just as this war has been more horrible than any previous racial war. And what is going to bring this class war about, is not real bad intentions but simply a misunderstanding of each other's position and each other's motives.

Always yours affectionately
Beatrice Webb

654 NUL SIDNEY WEBB TO C. P. TREVELYAN

41 Grosvenor Road
Westminster Embankment
18.11.15

Dear Trevelyan

Would it not be well for a question to be asked – *not* by a Labour Member – about the need for a woman member of a Munitions Tribunal where women are concerned? Quite dreadful cases come up (indecent assaults by foremen e.g.), when the girls insist on leaving, and the firm refuses consent, and denies them a leaving certificate. The Women's Unions feel very keenly about it. There is nothing about it in the Government Bill, to be introduced at the end of next week – unless the great Glasgow strike delays it (what a suppression of news!) – I have seen the Bill (a bad one). Enclosed a question.

Yours

Sidney Webb

655 HRCUT BEATRICE WEBB TO EDWARD PEASE

41 Grosvenor Road
Westminster Embankment
29th December 1915

Dear Mr Pease

So far as I can remember, my first experience of the Fabian Society was at a lecture by Mrs Annie Besant at the Eleusis Club about 1887–88 – a couple of years before I knew Sidney. At that lecture I remember seeing G.B.S. and Sydney Olivier, and I think Graham Wallas – Sidney failed to get in owing to the crowd. The lecture did not impress me, and delayed my adhesion to Socialism until I came across its sanest representative. The subject of the lecture was, unfortunately, 'the Nationalisation of Railways' and, to me a daughter of a railway administrator, Mrs Besant's wholesale inaccuracies were distinctly discouraging. I remember the lecture on 'the Quintessence of Ibsenism' – I should think that was my second experience of the Fabian Society. I came across Sidney because my cousin, Margaret Harkness, told me that he was the only man who could give me all the facts about the history of working-class organisation in the early part of the 19th century.

Always yours

Beatrice Webb
(Mrs Sidney Webb)

656 SU BEATRICE WEBB TO LEONARD WOOLF

41 Grosvenor Road
Westminster Embankment
25th February 1916

Dear Mr Woolf

Very many thanks for letting us see the Basis. I am afraid we have a rooted objection to signing anything about the war – either about the causes or its proper settlement. We both feel that we know very little about the technique of foreign affairs: more especially about any such generalisations as the principle of nationality and the right of economic expansion. Are the allies prepared to apply the principle of nationality? What about India, Egypt, Corea, as well as all the sub-races in Russia and the colonies of Italy and France? Then again, what exactly is meant by 'the demand of the Central Powers for economic expansion', with reference to peace terms? If this economic expansion is to be quite independent of political protectorates or 'spheres of influence', it can only refer to some such internal question as tariffs or port dues? Now all such methods of taxation must be left to local parliaments, and whatever arrangements were made in this respect in the terms of peace they might all or any of them be upset at the very next sessions of the parliaments of sovereign states and self-governing colonies. Does anyone suggest that control over national taxation is to be transferred to the international tribunal? If not, the term 'economic expansion' is meaningless unless there is behind it some notion of political power such as the demand of Japan for some control over Chinese appointments. But, of course, the originators of the Basis may see their way clear through these difficulties: we do not.

It is most disheartening to feel, as we do, that nothing can be done, at the present time, by popular agitation or popular discussion to settle the detailed terms of peace, or even the broad principles upon which it should be based. We can only hope that other people are right in their more optimistic view.

Thanks very much for promising to send me the book on Democracy.

Always yours

Beatrice Webb
(Mrs Sidney Webb)

# 3. The turning point
## October 1916 – July 1917

By the end of 1915 Beatrice was lapsing into a deep depression. 'I exist in a state of chronic weakness brought about by continuous sleeplessness.' (BWD 12 October 15) In 1916 Sidney joined the Labour Party Executive when W. S. Sanders went to the War Office for intelligence duties; Pease returned from retirement to serve as caretaker secretary to the Fabian Society for the remainder of the war.

The ambiguities which marked Labour's attitude to the war – at the party conference in Bristol there was a vote for continued support of the war yet a warm welcome to MacDonald and Snowden – were reflected within the Fabian Society and in Beatrice's own attitude. She still encouraged Cole and his colleagues, most of whom were anti-war and seeking ways of avoiding military service; the reorganised Fabian Research Department, controlled by the Guild Socialists, was providing information and advice to trade unions, and its monthly circular was strongly biased to militant defence of trade union standards; and at the same time Beatrice was thinking of ways in which all this work could be linked more formally to the Labour Party machine. The group changed its name to 'Labour Research Department' in 1918.

The crisis of the war came in the summer of 1916, when the long battle of the Somme with its dreadful casualties showed that there would be no early or easy victory. Beatrice had already broken down in June, fearing that she had cancer. This anxiety, she wrote in her diary in June 1919, was 'the opening phase of a breakdown which lasted, in an acute form, for six months, and from which I did not recover for over two years. Partly war neurosis, partly too persistent work to keep myself from brooding over the horrors of the war, partly I think from general discouragement arising out of our unpopularity with all sections of the political and official world . . . the breakdown proved to be the turning point from middle to old age. I now feel that I am packing up so that I may be ready to depart when the day comes'.

Beatrice spent much of the summer and autumn away in the country, staying with her sister Mary at Longfords and taking a seaside rest at Margate. At the end of the year she reflected on her attitude to the war. 'I want a peace in which none of the great belligerents gain anything whatsoever. I want all of them to feel that the war has been a hideous calamity without any compensating advantages – a gigantic and wicked folly from which no good can come . . . I should like the propertied classes of all the belligerents to be mulcted and the working classes to suffer sufficiently to make them revolutionary. The only indemnity should be paid to Belgium and the only state I would sweep away would be Turkey, and that, if possible, without giving anything to Russia. On this basis of universal loss and humiliation I would build the new League of Nations with the U.S.A. as one of the guarantors.' (BWD 2 December 16)

These comments were written on the eve of the collapse of the Asquith government and the formation of a new coalition under the premiership of Lloyd George. On 7 December Sidney and other members of the Labour Party executive had a private meeting with Lloyd George. Sidney, Beatrice noted on 8 December, thought Lloyd George was 'at his worst – evasive in his statement of policy and cynical in his offer of places in the government'. When the executive voted 18 to 12 in favour of accepting the offer Sidney was one of the minority. He did not accept the argument that participation would give the Labour Party a say in the terms of peace and he felt that Labour had failed to exact any price for its support of Lloyd George. He believed that the officeholders would be 'a mere tool in the hands of men who have been the hardened oppressors of their class'.

At the end of the year Beatrice bought a typewriter and began copying and editing extracts from her diaries to make 'A Book of My Life'. It would, she reflected, be no more tiring than endless reading, 'hardly more so than my desperate attempt at Longfords to knit soldiers' socks. And it is more interesting to me than either, and perhaps more useful'. (BWD 3 January 17) This work gradually developed into the first volume of autobiography, *My Apprenticeship*, at which she worked on and off for another six years.

## 657 PP SIDNEY TO BEATRICE

Miles Malleson (1888–1969) was an actor who dabbled in left-wing politics.

S. K. Ratcliffe (1868–1958) was a lecturer and journalist who maintained a loose association with the *New Statesman* for the next thirty years.

Richard Henry Tawney (1886–1962) was a radical Christian and his distinguished career as an economic historian showed his concern with religious ideologies and ethical codes. He had been introduced to the Webbs during the Royal Commission on the Poor Law, by Thomas Jones (1870–1955), who had worked as an investigator for the Commission and went on from an academic career to become assistant secretary to the War Cabinet and the confidant of Lloyd George. Jones was a key figure in Whitehall from 1916 until his retirement in 1930. Tawney was badly wounded in an action he described in *The Attack*. In 1919 he was appointed reader in economic history at L.S.E., professor in 1931. He remained a close associate of the Webbs and drafted a number of policy documents for the Labour Party.

41 Grosvenor Road
Westminster Embankment
31.10.16

Dearest

Here is a batch of mixed reading – Miles Malleson is a pacifist crank, and his two plays have been seized under the Defence of the Realm Act. I don't know whether they are worth reading.

Shaw's card is interesting. I have replied, pointing out that the F.S. still goes on functioning as before, and that its receipts from subscriptions have hardly fallen off. I will send him further particulars, when I get them. But his drift will not be uncongenial to you.

By the way I find I have *your* fountain pen as well as my own. As it will go safely with this envelope I enclose it.

I found Julia and Tom [Faulder] quite happily settled here. He has received no orders as to his 'light duty', and is in fact doing nothing. She has gone off to see Harry [Cripps]. Tom agrees that you have nothing to do but rest and eat, and that you will get well, so long as you are not 'bored' by Margate.

Sharp and Squire had no news of any sort – except that the Roumanian check was due entirely to the non-arrival of sufficient Russian troops and munitions, owing, apparently, to nothing more serious than failure of coordination, the Russian Generals on the Eastern Front having themselves annexed what had been meant for the Dobrudsha. Sharp thought that the Germans were now 'held up' and would get no further, but Ensor was pessimistic and expected them soon to enter Bucharest. At Salonika the English are in greater strength than the French, and the latter are not increasing their forces there, rather the contrary; and the result was that the Allies had neither men nor transport enough to advance into Bulgaria; and were not expected to.

I enclose a cutting as to a grave accident to Willis Bund; who must come to an end sometime!

Guedalla had told Sharp that the Government Offices were seriously disorganised by having taken in so many women and parted with so many managing people; and that it was now the Army itself that needed 'combing out'.

Sharp is moving into the house which Ratcliffe has been occupying, only a few hundred yards away from his present one; and expects to get in within a week or so. He was quite cheerful about the *New Statesman*, and did not need any article from me this week – which is very convenient.

Lloyd came to lunch in very good form. He expects to rejoin his Depot – at Cleethorpes – in a fortnight; and was still uncertain about getting or accepting a home job. He had just heard that Tawney had been ordered to join the Depot (the same one) in 10 days; but he said this could hardly happen as Tawney could only just hobble on sticks, and would not be well for months. He was shot through the liver.

Now dear one I must take this to the post, or it may not be there to greet you before you sally out for your ante-prandial promenade. It is good to think of you enjoying today's sunshine, and preparing for a good night's rest. Perhaps a little self-hypnotism – some kind of auto-suggestion – is needed to persuade you that you *are* going to have a good night!

Goodbye until tomorrow.

Sidney

'The Coming Educational Revolution' appeared in the *Contemporary Review* for November and December 1916. Webb spoke on 'Labour' on 3 November and Shaw on 'Religion' on 1 December in the Fabian autumn lecture series.

Anna Barlow, who was the wife of Sir John Barlow (1857–1932), was unsuccessful Liberal candidate for High Peak in 1922 and Labour candidate for Ilkeston in 1924.

Alice Green had been much concerned over the arrest and execution of Sir Roger Casement (1864–1916) after the Irish rebellion at Easter 1916, and had tried to involve Shaw in his defence. Sir John Simon (1873–1954), a prominent Liberal lawyer, was Home Secretary 1915–16 and Foreign Secretary 1931–35. He was an Asquith supporter and an opponent of Lloyd George.

Sir Warren Fisher (1879–1948), a senior official in the Treasury, became its permanent secretary and head of the civil service from 1919 to 1939. Hubert Hall (1857–1944) was a senior official in the Public Record Office and a noted archivist.

41 Grosvenor Road
Westminster Embankment
1.11.16

Dear One

I send the *Contemporary Review* with the first half of my article – also various other things, including the *Christian Commonwealth* with full report of Shaw's lecture.

I went round to Mrs Green yesterday, as she had been so pressing. She apparently only wanted to gossip, and she imparted very little. She said the London police knew of the projected Dublin rebellion in advance, but never warned Dublin Castle, and not even Birrell in London – one of them saying that it was better to let things come to a head! (But this may not be true.) She expressed a very poor opinion of Sir John Simon, as unwilling to take off his coat to a political fight, and disliking his associates in such a fight.

Lady Barlow called, 'gushed' as usual. She said that American Quakers were quite unaware of the hardships of the Conscientious Objectors' or the Pacifist feelings here. She had not been ordered by the W.O. not to talk of *these* things, and so she had done so freely in Quaker circles. She had heard both presidential candidates, and was of course strongly for [Woodrow] Wilson.

The Faulders brought a brace of grouse, which we began yesterday: and [Sir Hickman] Bacon sent a brace of pheasants – so we are set up with game!

I will set to work tomorrow on my lecture, and do what I can to prepare it. I think I can do quite a good lecture, with a little trouble.

Vaughan Nash was quite friendly today at the Development Commission and asked me what the Parliamentary Committee [of the T.U.C.]

could mean by proposing to the Employers Parliamentary Federation a Three Years Truce, which must necessarily mean Compulsory Arbitration. I told him it was only a foolish Congress resolution which the Parliamentary Committee had sent on formally, but which did not really mean anything. Yet the Parliamentary Committee is so queer that I don't know what they might not agree to.

It rained in buckets last night, and I did not sleep very well, it may have been the rain, or it may have been the loneliness! But in three days I shall be with you again – to find you I hope distinctly a further stage nearer health.

I discussed your case with Tom at some length, and he agreed that our diagnosis was quite right, and that rest and food, *continued for some time*, were what was wanted.

By the way, [Hubert] Hall said today that the British harvest was the *worst* since 1879; and that the potato disease was the most serious since 1846 (Irish famine) – due to the continuous wet weather.

No more news as to pensions organisation, but Middleton thinks Warren Fisher will come up top after all!

I put in the *Labor After the War* drafts on Demobilisation and Unemployment, which get interminably delayed, but will get passed at last somehow.

Goodbye, dear, I have no more time.

Sidney

659 PP SIDNEY TO BEATRICE

Sidney, working closely with Henderson, played a significant part in drafting Labour's peace aims, and post-war policy. In October he persuaded the Labour Party executive to draft a series of resolutions for the party conference due in January 1917 as the basis for *Labour After The War*, which he hoped would provide 'an impressive and consistent programme'. (To Beatrice 11 October 16 PP) A. K. Bulley was a well-to-do Liverpool merchant and Fabian who provided financial support for the Fabian Research Department. Robin Page Arnot (b. 1890) was Cole's closest associate in the Fabian Research Department; later, he and other members of the newly-formed Communist Party 'captured' the Labour Research Department. John Hodge (1855–1937), the leader of the Iron and Steel Trades Confederation, became the first Minister of Labour when Lloyd George's coalition was formed in 1916. Miss Mactaggart was a most competent administrator who was secretary of the L.S.E.

41 Grosvenor Road
Westminster Embankment
2.11.16

My own dear One

Your letter did not arrive until 11 o'clock – I missed it. But I am very glad to hear you are still progressing. I have realised that you were suffering, but I thought it better not to make too much of it, as I did not want to enlarge it psychologically! I was always pressing you to rest and eat.

I have spent the morning preparing my lecture for tomorrow in considerable detail. Tomorrow I shall be busy all day with Labour Party Executive and Research Department Executive.

I enclose Cole's memo. for this afternoon's Group meeting. It comes to nothing – it is clear he can't make up his mind.

The trade union leaders are hopeless. Yesterday I spent two hours (on *Labor after the War*) struggling with their complacent stupidity and apathy, and with the real desire of some of them to prevent anything being published that would 'arouse expectation', and lead to anything beyond what the Government is conceding. Bowerman does not believe there will be any serious labour difficulties or unemployment after the War; and has really no desire to get anything done. They fail altogether to realise the three-quarters of the whole who are outside trade unionism, or the low-paid laborers and women, or the incapacity and disorganisation of the trade unions themselves. (I did not get angry, and we are on the best of terms; but we have to adjourn and adjourn, and these leaders – who insist on being on the committee – can't come to meetings!)

I send an invitation from Bulley, which you had better answer (in the negative). By the way, he sent £100 yesterday to the Research Department, on no more invitation than the circular enclosing the Annual Report. Cole and Arnot are also pleased at having secured the adhesion of Hodge and the Steelsmelters to their trade union survey.

At the School I asked for Reeves, but he had gone home early with a touch of fever. Miss Mactaggart was radiant at the London and North Western Railway having at last joined the Railway Section, to the extent of £200 a year. She expects now to get back the Great Eastern and Great Northern presently. The general fees are now only £140 behind last year.

By the way, in the *Labour Leader*, posted to you today, there is an account of a meeting of the United Socialist Council, at which it was decided to appoint a Committee on Peace! This makes it clear that the F.S. could not join without promptly having to withdraw, as we certainly could not agree with the others on an immediate Peace Manifesto. I am glad that the matter is thus decided.

Nominations for the Labour Party Executive have to go in by 16 December. If the I.L.P. continue to nominate two, and if the B.S.P. nominates one, the F.S. nominee (myself) may very probably be ousted. Nothing has transpired yet, and Pease doubts whether they will go so far as to eject me.

Now I must go off to the Group Meeting at 5 p.m. to discuss Cole's way of maintaining Standard Rates. Dear One, goodbye until tomorrow. I hope you will continue to have warm sunny days. Don't try to do too much. I shall be with you in 48 hours or less.

Sidney

John Fischer Williams (1870–1947) became the British legal adviser on the Reparations Commission and, in 1936, the British member of the Permanent Court of Arbitration at The Hague. Sylvia Pankhurst moved into left-wing politics in London's East End as her sister Christabel became leader of the militant suffragettes. The group around her paper became one of the components of the post-war Communist Party. Arnold Freeman (1885–1972), anthroposophist, Fabian and warden of the Sheffield Educational Settlement, was joint author with Webb of the booklet *Great Britain After The War*, published in 1916.

Monica Ewer, secretary of the National Guilds League, was the wife of the Labour journalist, W. N. Ewer. Margaret Postgate, daughter of Professor J. P. Postgate, who taught classics at Cambridge and Liverpool, married G. D. H. Cole in 1918: she later edited works by the Webbs and wrote a biography of Beatrice. *Towards Social Democracy*, by Sidney Webb, was published by the Fabian Society in 1916. Mabel Atkinson, journalist and lecturer on economics, was an active Fabian: after an unsuccessful marriage she emigrated to South Africa in 1926.

41 Grosvenor Road
Westminster Embankment
8.11.16

Dearest

Mary has sent a telegram to Arthur saying that there is nothing to report. Her Dr Simons is unavailable, so Tom sent her to a Dr Waring in Wimpole St. She went there this morning, and he said he was *not sure*, and that she was to come again on Monday. She says she thinks he means that it is 'the old complaint'.

Tom is now at Millbank Hospital all the morning and afternoon, and Julia at Golden Square for about five hours a day.

I enclose some letters for you to answer. The one from 'Marjorie Williams' is from Mrs Fischer Williams, the wife of the barrister who is now employed at the Home Office.

Also an amusing review of 'Great Britain After the War', by Sylvia Pankhurst in *The Women's Dreadnought*. She is an amazingly incompetent person – cannot even understand what some of the things mean!

I also put in The *Christian Commonwealth* with a report of my lecture – also a review of *Great Britain After the War*.

These two reviews might be posted to

Arnold Freeman
4 Oakbrook Road
Sheffield

or you might keep them for me.

It is quite clear that you must stay where you are for another fortnight. Let me know whether you want me to bring anything on Saturday when I shall be glad to come as usual. I find I live in a rush during the four days of the week, looking forward to the three days that I am able to spend with you.

Arnot has had a blow! After the Committee had appointed Miss Winter as assistant at £100, she finally decides to remain at the Ministry of Munitions. He has now two alternatives *viz.* Mrs Ewer, who is temporarily appointed by the National Council of Civil Liberty; and Miss Postgate, daughter of the professor, who is a first-class Classic, now an assistant mistress at St Paul's School for Girls at £160, but wants to leave teaching: and has been a volunteer in the office two days a week, and will not be free until Xmas. Cole is away, so I said he must be consulted, but that we must not *persuade* anyone to come to us. Probably Mrs Ewer will get it, though Arnot evidently thinks Miss Postgate the better worker. (But I warned him that we did not want too expensive an article.)

By the way, we sold 50 or 60 of the shilling *Towards Social Democracy* on Friday, because I advertised it in my lecture. Miss Atkinson was full of praise of the lecture.

Now goodbye dear one, I must rush off to give my fifth lecture on Commercial War. Until Saturday.

Sidney

### 661 PP SIDNEY TO BEATRICE

Beatrice's nephew Stephen Hobhouse had become a Quaker, given up his civil service career and renounced his inheritance. Though he would have been medically exempt from military service he chose to make a stand as a conscientious objector. After a series of convictions he was court-martialled and his case became a *cause célèbre*. His mother, Margaret Hobhouse – 'with all her energy and unscrupulous wit', Beatrice remarked – eventually used influence to secure his release. He later collaborated with Fenner Brockway on the Fabian prison enquiry, based on the experiences of wartime conscientious objectors. Joseph Alan Kaye (1895–1919) was assistant secretary of the Fabian Research Department. His claim for exemption from conscription on political grounds was rejected; he committed suicide after the war.

Although the Webbs supported the war they helped several of their young associates (such as Cole and Kaye) to escape military service on the grounds that their work for the trade union movement qualified as work of national importance. Eduard Bernstein (1850–1932) was the leader of the moderate wing of the German Social Democratic Party. He had spent years of exile in London and was well-known to the Fabian set. Ernst Schnattner was the son of Bernstein's wife by her first marriage. George Augustus Moore (1852–1933), best known for his novel *Esther Waters* (1894), published *The Brook Kerith* in 1916.

41 Grosvenor Road
Westminster Embankment
15.11.16

Dearest

I was glad to get your cheery letter. Maggie says she has written you about Mary; she has to go into a nursing home shortly, for a tentative operation – if it turns out to be tubercular, little will be done; if more malignant a thorough operation. Stephen is to be court-martialled today, and both the Courtneys have gone down to Warminster to be present, and use any influence they can (see a par. in *Times* today). Maggie says he has refused to be medically examined, so she has been unable to get him off on that ground.

Kaye has done his fortnight's gaol – says it was not at all bad! He has now seen the Military Representative at Oxford, who will not oppose his exemption conditional on his continuing to do research in the Department! Cole consulted me as to what was to be done: and I said we must stand by Kaye. I therefore wrote a letter to Kaye for him to present, virtually offering him continued employment in the Department on existing terms. Cole said he personally felt bound to Kaye, but as he had engaged Miss Postgate (after Xmas) he had not then contemplated the Department having Kaye as well. I said that the Department had better temporarily afford both, to enable the work to be got on with; and I reminded Cole of the need for finishing both the Railway and the Piecework pamphlets, which he and Arnot agreed to do their best to complete.

Schnattner, Bernstein's stepson, telephoned to me: and came to see me today, bringing report of a speech of Bernstein in the Reichstag, which he was anxious the *N.S.* should reproduce. There is not really much in it, but I have written a note on it, which Squire may insert.

I have done an article on the new Pensions Bill which seems to me likely to prove a fiasco. It does not seem really to unify much; and its chief effect is to oust the Chelsea Hospital Commissioners from awarding disability pensions. I am not sure whether the Statutory [Pensions] Committee is *much* interfered with. The House may demand greater unification.

I send the *Christian Commonwealth*, for Wallas's lecture and review of Lodge, and of *The Brook Kerith* – also the agenda of Labour Party Conference, so far as the branch resolutions are concerned.

Pease says they sold about £2 of literature on Friday, and that tickets are still selling daily.

Dearest, goodbye.

Sidney Webb

662 PP SIDNEY TO BEATRICE

The Earl of Derby (1865–1948) was Director of Recruiting 1915–16; his voluntary scheme was a transition to conscription. He became Secretary of State for

War in December 1916. Sir Auckland Campbell Geddes (1879–1954), a professor of anatomy and an honorary brigadier-general, was Director of Recruiting and in 1916, he became Minister of National Service and later British ambassador in Washington. Emile Vandervelde, leader of the Socialist International, spent part of the war in Britain.

41 Grosvenor Road
Westminster Embankment
16.11.16

Dearest

It is evidently the more bracing weather that picks you up! However, once you are up you will be able to stand even warm weather.

Lady whose husband died last year, now living alone wishes to SELL her beautiful HOME of nearly 30 years. Picturesque, creeper-clad, 10-roomed House (lounge hall): two cottages; 8 acres (including paddocks): winter and summer tennis courts, golf, rock gardens, all perfect order: stabling, garage; spring water; gas. East Grinstead neighbourhood; £20,500 Freehold. Rent £120. No agents – Box Z.452. *The Times*

This advertisement might almost be the Turners Hill house – but for the death last year, and the golf. It indicates just about what the place might fetch as a maximum.

I think it represents just about the place I should like to be able to retire to, when we have to give up a London residence. However, how much money will be left no one knows!

The joint meeting to hear Lord Derby and General Geddes was very flat. I cannot say it did not go off well, because the bulk of the people were resolved to accept and approve everything without question. First of all the Ministers (Henderson with them) came just an hour late, without sending any message. We sat and smoked, and sent messengers to find out why they did not come, and had just resolved to separate at 4 p.m., when they arrived. Lord Derby with his bluff, hearty, intimate manner – really very insolent – made a perfunctory apology (they had gone to another Conference with engineers at Ministry of Munitions, which had dragged on – no explanation of why they did not telephone or send across). Then General Geddes, an able but insincere man, explained 'Substitution' (of 'C' for 'general service' men), trying to prove there was no 'industrial conscription'. Questions followed (I asked what about Wages), but I had to leave at 5 (for my lecture) before he replied.

I suggest that these T.U. leaders become helpless when they *act together*. Each in and for *his own Union* is much more sturdy, and even more competent, than when they are acting together for their own class as such.

I believe I am sleeping as badly as you do! But there is only one more night – tomorrow I shall be with you for three days. We can get better together!

Vandervelde, by the way, is the President of the Students' Union this year; and gives his address on 8 November after a dinner in the Refectory to which I felt obliged to consent to go. The School seems to go on very successfully, but I have not yet seen Reeves (who is there for several days per week).

Lloyd was in the Common Room – looking very well and fat – he has to go before his Medical Board in a fortnight – his future still uncertain. He had seen Tawney, who is recovering slowly in the Bishop's Palace at Cuddesdon; and expects to be wholly discharged from the Army, when he will resume W.E.A. work – Lloyd is coming here for lunch next Tuesday.

I hear there are to be 1,000 additional Labor Exchanges opened on Demobilisation so as to have one in every big village. This is doubtless the wise way to get the aggregate increase that we have asked for. Perhaps this expansion will be permanent.

Now dearest goodbye till tomorrow.

Sidney

663 UL BEATRICE WEBB TO MARY BOOTH

Charles Booth died in November 1916: though Beatrice had never resumed a close friendship with the Booths after the estrangement at the time of her marriage she had seen them from time to time.

41 Grosvenor Road
Westminster Embankment
24/11/1916

One line of sympathy, dear Mary – I had a very rich affection and constant admiration for Charles. Knowing how terribly I should feel the loss of my own mate, I can feel for my old friend in her sorrow. But you have had a glorious life together – a creative life both in children and in pioneer work for this world. And he has died as he would have wished to die – in harness to the last.

Sidney sends his remembrances and desires me to add his tribute of admiration for the great man's life.

Ever yours affectionately
Beatrice Webb

Tell Antonia to let me know how you are and do not yourself trouble to answer this note.

664 PP SIDNEY TO BEATRICE

The Labour Party conference took place in the shadow of the war crisis which had made Lloyd George prime minister. Henderson was now one of the inner War Cabinet of five and there were five other Labour men in the government. The conference voted by 1,849,000 to 307,000 to approve entry into coalition, but the mood of the delegates was restless and suspicious. The government, Beatrice noted on 12 December 1916, 'is a brilliant improvisation – reactionary in composition and undemocratic in form. For the first time (since Cromwell) we have a dictatorship by one, or possibly by three men: for the first time we see called to high office distinguished experts not in Parliament; for the first time we behold Labour leaders in open alliance with Tory chieftains; for the first time a Cabinet has been created, not by a party political organisation . . . not by the will of the House of Commons, but by a powerful combination of newspaper proprietors'. In some ways she thought it was a change for the better. Asquith and his Whig colleagues 'hated state intervention . . . This government will be boldly and even brutally interventionist . . . The British ruling class is really far more concerned for their prestige as the leading members of a ruling race than for their interests as property owners within their own country'.

William Gillies (1885–1958) was the head of the international department of the Labour Party. George Barnes, general secretary of the Amalgamated Society of Engineers, had just been made Minister of Pensions: he resigned from the Labour Party when the coalition broke up at the end of the war. W. J. Davis, M.P. was an official of the Brassfounders Union. Charles Renolds, managing director of a chain manufacturing firm, was a progressive industrialist who had supported the Webb's Poor Law campaign and was an advocate of modern managerial methods.

Victoria Hotel
Manchester
23/1/17

Dear One

I got your letter this morning, and was glad and I am sorry you did not get mine (which I posted early on Sunday).

I had a friendly and confidential talk with MacDonald, over a cup of tea. He said the trade unions were now a terrible incubus on the Labor Party, but that it had been inevitable to have them. Only by them could the Party have got mass, and money (the Labor Party has now actually £20,000 in hand). He said that the present organisation of the party failed totally to represent the rank and file; and he looked more and more to the Trades Councils and similar local bodies. He said Scotland and South Wales were strongly with him. He had just had a very nasty time at a meeting at Nuneaton, where he had been fiercely assaulted and nearly ducked in the canal. He admitted that there was no prospect of a pacifist reaction when the war is over, as happened after the Boer War and Crimean War; but thought that the people would come to hold that the I.L.P. had been much more right than had been thought at the time.

In the evening I carried off Gillies to the 'Pictures', to see the Tank films! They are very much like the Somme pictures that we saw – rather better. The Tanks are not very prominent but a *few* films show them effectually. But they come out much the same as in the *Sphere* illustrations.

Today Charles Renolds came to the Conference (I sent him a platform ticket) and carried me off to lunch at the Reform Club (merely a sandwich and coffee), to discuss further his piecework and Workshop Committee. I am introducing him to G. Barnes M.P. and W. J. Davis.

At the conference we have had a bitter and very eloquent debate on the Coalition. Henderson made an impressive speech, with simplicity and earnestness. Snowden this afternoon made a diabolically clever speech, full of the strongest points, but disfigured by too much bitterness. Clynes replied, ably, but also bitterly. The vote is a foregone conclusion as it is understood that the Miners support the Coalition by a block vote: they are very hostile to the I.L.P. as such.

I will write to Pease sending Woolf's letter, and suggesting that we should go on. And I will write to Rosie.

Mrs Anderson began to chaff me about the trade union articles of which she did not detect the authorship until the very last. I hear that Arnot says they are by a man named Duncan, and that they betray acquaintance with the materials collected by the Fabian Research Department.

I don't know what I shall do this evening – the hotel is uncomfortable. But perhaps I will write my article in the Commercial Room – I am glad you have been having so many people to see. We shall be together again in three days. Goodnight.

Sidney

665 PP SIDNEY TO BEATRICE

Clifford Sharp was called up but withdrawn from military service and sent on an intelligence mission to Stockholm: John Squire became acting editor of the *New Statesman*. Arthur Greenwood (1881–1954) moved from workers' education into Labour Party work, becoming an M.P. in 1922. He was Minister of Health in 1929–31; later he was Deputy Leader of the Labour Party and held posts in the War Cabinet and the post-war Labour government. G. H. Wardle, acting chairman of the Labour Party, was a right-wing trade unionist. Lord Northcliffe (1865–1922), the founder of the *Daily Mail* and owner of *The Times*, had played a key role in the intrigues which led to Asquith's replacement by Lloyd George. David Kirkwood (1872–1967) was the leader of the Clyde Workers' Committee who, with other militant shop-stewards, had been deported from the Clyde in March 1915 without charge or hearing, after the engineering workers had struck in protest against dilution. This issue gave the conference a chance to react against the erosion of trade union standards. Henderson was placed in a difficult position, for a matter of civil liberties was fused with trade union anxieties. J. T. Brownlie (1865–1938) was president of the Amalgamated Society of Engineers (and then of the Amalgamated Engineering Union) 1913–20.

[Manchester]
24.1.17

Dearest

The post is evidently unreliable. Fortunately I wrote my article last night, and posted it at the main office at 9 this morning. I shall try to send a second letter this afternoon with a note or two. I have asked Squire to write or telephone to you the *hour* of Sharp's hearing on Friday, as I had better attend myself. I shall therefore return on Friday morning by the 10.40 due 3.40 at Euston and soon after 4 at home, to see once more my dear wife.

Cole, along with whom I dined yesterday, told me definitely that H. G. Wells *had* written *The Times* 'Reconstruction' articles, in conjunction with Denis Page, who signed them D.P. He said that Wells had now said he would advocate National Guilds, but would have nothing to do with Cole and Mellor. Cole said he was sorry that Wells was taking it up, and that he (Cole) hated the name of National Guilds. It seems to me that Cole is retreating more and more to mere trade unionism of the older type.

Lady Barlow is attending the Conference; as she says taking notes for Sir John, who wants an uncensored report. Today Tawney has come, looking very well. He has taken a flat at Hampstead – we ought to ask him and his wife. Greenwood is also here today – the W.E.A. have a meeting this afternoon at which I will look in.

This morning, at the opening of the Conference, Wardle read a telegram from Lloyd George congratulating Henderson on yesterday's great majority. It stupefied the I.L.P. part of the Conference who burst into uncontrolled laughter and asked where the telegram from Northcliffe was!

But the sensation this morning was David Kirkwood, the Clyde deportee. It had been arranged that he should second the resolution on Trade Union Conditions. When he rose there was an unparalleled ovation. He gave a bitter account of his deportation; and concluded dramatically with the announcement that he was going back to his home and defied the Government to stop him. At this the conference rose, and cheered and cheered; and called for Henderson – who eventually rose. He explained that the Government had acted constantly in close touch with the elected Executive and District Committee of the A.S.E.: described how Kirkwood repudiated rudely both Brownlie (Chairman of A.S.E.) and himself; and how some of the shops refused to meet them; how the Clyde Workers Committee said 'You'll not get your meeting with Lloyd George on Christmas Day'. The deportation was done without his being consulted. He did his best to modify the action. He proposed to the conference to elect a small committee to investigate, and promised all official aid. Brownlie followed. Neither of them dealt with the administrative act of deportation.

This very heated scene is really all to the good. It is the touch of passion that puts a stiffening into the resolutions.

Goodbye dearest. I must post this at the midday interval.

Yours

Sidney

On 17 February 1917 the Reconstruction Committee, which had been a small group of civil servants, was reorganised by Lloyd George and its membership enlarged. It was to co-ordinate thinking about post-war social problems with other government agencies and to consider what further enquiries should be made in connection with reconstruction. Lloyd George was the nominal chairman: the vice-chairman was Edwin Samuel Montagu (1879–1924), who had been Minister of Munitions under Asquith and served as Secretary of State for India in the Lloyd George coalition, 1917–22. Beatrice's old friend Vaughan Nash was secretary of the committee, working with Sir Maurice Bonham-Carter (1880–1960) who was married to Asquith's daughter Violet. Other members were: Philip Kerr (1882–1940), later Marquess of Lothian, who was the founder and editor of the *Round Table*; W. G. S. Adams (1874–1966) was Gladstone Professor of Political Theory and Institutions at Oxford 1912–33. He served as private secretary to Lloyd George 1916–27, and later became Warden of All Souls; the Tory M.P. John W. Hills (1867–1938), who had supported the Poor Law campaign; and Sir Leslie Scott (1869–1950) who became Lord Justice Scott. On the Labour side, apart from Beatrice Webb, there was Arthur Greenwood as assistant secretary, J. R. Clynes (1869–1949); and J. H. Thomas (1874–1949), secretary of the railwaymen's union. Clynes and Thomas became Cabinet ministers in 1924. B. Seebohm Rowntree (1871–1954), the social investigator, and Thomas Jones, now serving as Lloyd George's personal contact man with the civil service and public personalities, were also appointed. On 25 February at Beatrice's invitation, Jones lunched with the Webbs and R. H. Tawney at Grosvenor Road: he noted in his diary that 'Mrs Webb is full of interest in Reconstruction and eager to begin devouring reports'.

41 Grosvenor Road
Westminster Embankment
26th February 1917

Dear Mr Beveridge

I wonder whether you have time from the consideration of food problems to come and spend a quiet evening here for a talk about demobilisation etc. ? As I dare say you know, I have been put on the new Reconstruction Committee which the P.M. has set up to supervise and consider the work of the other Committees, and I should very much like your counsel on certain points. I wish you were on this Committee!

We were glad to see Mr Tawney yesterday and to find that he is not seriously altered by his terrible experience. It will be interesting to see what effect the war has on all our friends who have been through it.

Always yours sincerely
Beatrice Webb
(Mrs Sidney Webb)

667 LSE SIDNEY WEBB TO WILLIAM PEMBER REEVES

Lawrence R. Dicksee had taught accounting and business organisation at L.S.E. from 1902, becoming professor in 1914. Sir Robert Blair (1859–1935) was the chief education officer of the L.C.C. 1904–24, and especially interested in science and technical education.

41 Grosvenor Road
Westminster Embankment
11.3.17

Dear Director

I have got to know that the L.C.C. is excogitating a great scheme of Commercial Education for 'After the War'; and I have accordingly been seeing L.C.C. people about it. From what they tell me, the feeling towards the School is quite friendly; and what they are mainly dealing with is Commercial Education in the Secondary Schools and Evening Institutes.

But they tell me they want to put out to the public a complete scheme for London, including Higher Commercial. They tell me they would be glad if the University would 'play up' and 'get a move on' – not to do anything now, or even to arrange anything definitely; but to enable the L.C.C. to advertise a complete scheme presently, as under consideration. Some of them would like a little alteration in the B.Sc. degree, so as to enable it to be taken by more concentration on 'Commercial' subjects.

As regards instruction I find that the idea is to leave all the higher work to the School (with which a good deal of satisfaction is expressed); but our friends at the L.C.C. ask for a move on our part. They tell me that it would not be wise to let the enquiry go on further without our 'advertising' ourselves and our intentions for 'After the War'. The enquiry has indicated to them that this and that ought to be provided; and it is put to me that, *if we do not say we are going to provide it*, it will be difficult to prevent some aspiring Polytechnic or Institute from proposing to do it.

I have cross-examined some of these people (e.g. some of the Inspectors and organisers of Commercial Education, as well as others), about what is felt to be wanted to complete our scheme.

It comes, essentially, to three separate expansions (for which, as I pointed out, neither lecturers, nor students, nor funds are at present in sight!)

There is a demand for a great many more separate courses on Commerce – both on the Imports and Exports, Products and Consumption *of particular regions* of which about a dozen were named (e.g. South America, India etc); and also courses on the *principal commodities*, their sources, conditions of production or manufacture, destinations and purposes; such as Textiles, Metals, Foodstuffs, Coal etc. to the number of ten or fifteen.

With these courses, there is asked for a comprehensive one on the *Customs Tariffs of the World*, their several kinds and classifications.

I pointed out how much we had already done in this way in courses and lecturers from time to time.

But apparently what is asked for is the addition to the yearly programme of, possibly, 3 sets of 60 lectures each, or even more!

The second line concerns Accountancy, in which the excellence of Dicksee's work is fully admitted. All that can be suggested here is the addition of some interesting and highly specialised short courses on *Cost Accounts* for (a) manufacturers generally (factory bookkeeping); (b) builders, including estimating; (c) printers; and (d) solicitors. I am doubtful whether we could get competent people to give these, or what the demand would be; but it is worth thinking about.

The third line in which the L.C.C. really want help is in training their teachers; and on this, it seems uncertain what they would be willing to do. They are very much impressed with our success with the Irish teachers, and it seems possible that they would give some whole time Scholarships to selected teachers each year (for a whole session).

Two other ideas have turned up, one a course for *Managers* of Factories; and another a course on *Shipowning and Shipbroking*. It seems to be thought, also, that we might go ahead now on Fire Insurance.

I thought I had better put to you the result of my enquiries, just for what it may be worth. Of course, it is absolutely impossible to take any steps, or make any arrangements now. Moreover, we could not make such additions (even when we find the men) without a definite promise of funds.

But the situation seems to be that the L.C.C. *is not afraid* of talking about greatly increased expenditure on Commercial Education after the war. It is preparing greatly to increase its grants!

I think, on the whole, that the School would do well to put in a proposition very promptly; not definitely committing ourselves to anything; but indicating how much more we were willing to do if funds were provided. I am told that this ought to be in the hands of Sir Robert Blair *before Easter*.

Now, as I have this in my mind, after all my conversations with these people, some of whom sought me out in the first instance, I have ventured to jot down roughly, the sort of memo that it might be useful to send them. I will let you have it in a day or two, when it is typed – when I should like to talk it over with you, as you could improve on it in the light of your own thinking about these things.

Yours

Sidney Webb

668 PP BEATRICE WEBB TO G. D. H. COLE

Beatrice was seeking to put the Fabian Research Department under the joint control of the Fabian Society, the Labour Party and the T.U.C., serving as a research service to all three while retaining a separate identity. The Labour Party and trade union leaders were suspicious of Cole and other militant members of the National Guilds League, who were associated with the most radical elements in the trade union movement; and Cole sent a rude reply to this letter, saying that 'I cannot write temperately of Fabians'. If, he added, 'I find myself secretary of a "group of the Fabian Society" it is from the basest financial motive and without any feeling of obligation to or friendship for the Fabian Society which to be candid I detest'. Confessing that he wanted to split off the F.R.D. 'as soon as it is strong enough to stand the strain', he insisted that he was entitled to do so without seeking the formal sanction of the Fabian executive.

41 Grosvenor Road
Westminster Embankment SW
14th March 1917

Dear Mr Cole

I think it would be well if I could have a talk with you and some of the other members of the Fabian Research Department who are anxious for a change of name – perhaps some afternoon next week? Meanwhile perhaps you will consider the following observations; which I jot down as they occur to me.

The Fabian Research Department is still a Group of the Fabian Society, and I imagine it would need the consent of the Fabian Executive to change its name. But passing over this 'legality' there remains the fact that the Department is at present dependent on Fabians and the Fabian Executive for the larger part of its income and the use of cheap, and convenient offices, with a hall. Moreover, certain members of the Fabian Society feel that they started the Department, and that they have put a great deal of work into its publications. Very naturally they do not care for these assets to be transferred away from the Fabian Society.

On the other hand, the National Guildsmen and their friends are the most active workers in the Department at the present time, and it is to their energy and persistence that the Department owes its present advantageous connection with the trade union movement. I can quite understand that, now that they are beginning to produce reports and books, they do not see why their efforts should redound to the credit of the Fabian Society, with whose traditions and policy they are out of sympathy. The present valuable collection of trade union material has been largely their work; though, of course, some Fabians have helped to get the trade unions to send their reports to the Research Department.

Now the problem before us is how to reconcile these two apparently conflicting claims? Assuming that the labour movement were to start its own Research Department under the auspices of a Joint Committee in order to organise a Department of the labour movement as a whole. From the Fabian point of view this would have the advantage of vacating the offices of the Research Department, which would then be free for specifically Fabian developments. The National Guildsmen and their friends could then make their own terms with the Joint Committee of the labour movement.

The other alternative would be to create something of the nature of the Workers' Educational Association – an organisation made up of trade unions etc. on the one hand, and of independent intellectuals on the other. The Research Department material might be handed over to such a federal body, or be left in the Research Department as might be thought convenient. In that case there would be no need to interfere with the name of the Fabian Research Department or its future activities, as all the publications contributed by non-Fabians could be issued in the name of the new federal organisation – exactly as the *Labour Year Book* is now issued by the Joint Publishing Committee. If the new organisation had a separate and distinct name, the word 'Fabian' would not appear on the title page – and it is this appearance of the word 'Fabian' which I imagine is annoying to non-Fabians? The Fabians remaining in the Research Department could continue to publish their reports through the Fabian Society or the Fabian Research Department – if they preferred to do this – or they could give these reports to the new organisation for publication. The National Guildsmen could then decide whether they preferred to join the new organisation, or to form a constituent unit of it, or whether they found it more convenient to remain in the Fabian Research Department.

Personally, I am very anxious to see a separate and distinct organisation for research and publication purposes for the benefit of the trade unions and the labour movement, in which all sects of Socialists can combine. What is important, is, to find some way in which non-manual working 'intellectuals' can place their services for the use of the labour movement, and share in its counsels in responsible positions. The difficulty, of course, is to get the right constitution and the right name for any such organisation, and to secure the confidence and goodwill of organised Labour. It is very difficult to foresee what will be the cleavages of opinion in the labour movement during the next four or five years. I am inclined to think that the cleavages which were apparent before the war may be swept away, and that we may find ourselves redistributed in new groups taking different lines on particular questions.

Always yours

Beatrice Webb

669 NLW BEATRICE WEBB TO THOMAS JONES

Beatrice had started worrying about the powers and procedures of the Reconstruction Committee in a manner which recalled her early moves on the Royal Commission on the Poor Law. It was clear that Montagu from the outset did not intend the committee to take a vigorous initiative: he had planned little more than a revision of the work of the committee's predecessor. On 22 February 1917 Beatrice sensed that the committee was little more than a piece of window-dressing and that it was unlikely to accomplish anything unless some of its members tried to animate it. She wrote to Jones on 27 March suggesting that like-minded members of the committee should meet 'by ones and twos or threes and fours, so as to concert action. Otherwise I am afraid that meeting after meeting will go by without things happening that we wish to happen': she reminded Jones that as a Fabian he was technically a member of the Labour Party. She wrote again on 6 June complaining that no progress was being made.

Hydro Hotel [?]
Sunday [? May 1917]

Dear Mr Jones

I have read and re-read Mr Montagu's memo on Procedure without getting any clear idea as to its meaning. But it seems to me of the utmost importance that the R.C. should not lightly agree to it. Would it be possible for some of us to meet to discuss it before the meeting of the R.C.? I shall be back on Saturday afternoon and I shall be free on Sunday – we could meet in the morning or at lunch or for evening supper – if you could arrange a meeting at Grosvenor Road?

One thing is clear – he wants to give the go-by to the Reconstruction Committee as a whole. The Committee is to be shorn of all powers of initiative: it is not to carry out its reference which expressly includes deciding on the subjects to be dealt with, deciding on the methods of dealing with them, and advising the War Cabinet as to results. All those functions are to be carried out by Mr Montagu himself, after consulting with such members of the committee as he himself selects. Beyond his own decisions there are vague references to the Panels – tho' even here it remains in doubt whether these bodies are to act as individuals or as committees. The Reconstruction Committee itself is to be strictly limited to a veto on schemes put before it – either by Mr Montagu or by the Panels. But it is by no means clear whether the Panels are to have any powers of initiative – or whether they also are not to be limited to accepting or rejecting a modifying scheme submitted *on the initiative* of the Vice-Chairman?

Frankly I do not see that the R.C. could accept this purely passive function – it would be better that it should be relieved of the responsibility and that Mr Montagu, Mr V. Nash and Sir M. Bonham Carter (who, I hear, is to be appointed secretary) should be appointed to R.C. They might then consult any of us as private individuals when they thought fit to do so. I should be quite prepared to help [with] my advice – but I should be relieved of all personal responsibility and of a good deal of worry.

What do you feel about it – what do Mr Kerr and Prof. Adams think?

I have no secretary down here so I can only send you this scrawl – which I hope you will be able to read.

Ever yours

Beatrice Webb

I should be delighted to see Mr Kerr and Prof. Adams at 41 Grosvenor Road for lunch or supper.

BW

By midsummer Beatrice had realised that Montagu was lazy and that the staff of the Reconstruction Committee lacked energy or direction. At Easter some of the members had protested at inaction, forcing the Committee to set up separate panels for Education, Local Government, Labour and Industry. Beatrice sat on the last three of these panels. She produced a memorandum on Poor Law reform: 'I seized my opportunity to get on with the Minority Report'. (BWD 31 July 1917) She thought the committee, at once too pretentious and too powerless, unlikely to survive the summer. 'I am inclined to recommend that it should be definitely discharged with gracious thanks from the P.M. for its services. That would leave the new Minister with a free hand to choose his amateur advisers – if he wants any – and, *what is of the utmost importance, to select his own staff.*' She had enjoyed her work on the committee and liked her colleagues but she felt that 'the machinery had grit in it from the start'. Dr Christopher Addison (1869–1951), who had been professor of anatomy at Sheffield, was a Liberal M.P. appointed as Minister of Reconstruction in September 1917. The committee was dissolved but the work of the panels went on: one outcome of its work was the idea of a Ministry of Health; another was the Machinery of Government Committee, which reviewed the pattern of the civil service.

41 Grosvenor Road
Westminster Embankment
Sunday [8 July 1917]

Dear Mr Jones

I will see whether we could change the day to Monday 16th – but will you keep yourself disengaged for the 12th and the 16th and do the lecture dates suit you? I think some of us must get together and work out a programme for the autumn, otherwise we shall be at Xmas with very little done either in respect of the pressing problems or with regard to the larger aspects of Reconstruction.

There are 3 questions which must be grappled with within the next few months

(1) Commercial policy – an alternative to [Board of Trade?] litter of reactionary reports, which will probably get published if we have no alternative policy.

(2) Emergency legislature: which of the powers under the D. of R.A. [Defence of the Realm Act] ought to be retained?

(3) Finance and taxation. We are deciding on great expenditure on housing, education, health. How is this expenditure and the huge war debt to be met? If we leave it to the Treasury *no* expenditure will be provided for except the interest on the War debt.

The R.C. with Montagu, V. Nash and B.C. [Bonham Carter] is a quite hopeless piece of machinery. I suppose one must let the matter simmer at present. But before the autumn something must be done, or else we must rely on doing work outside the R.C. and trying to get it adopted as a finished product by the R.C. or by its sub-committees.

Ever yours

Beatrice Webb

# 4. The new Labour Party

## August 1917 – December 1923

After the first Russian revolution in February 1917 the Labour Party's relationship with the Lloyd George government was severely strained, and the Labour movement itself was subjected to divisive stresses. Arthur Henderson was sent to Petrograd as a member of the War Cabinet to review the situation. While he was there he decided that it would be sensible for the Labour Party to support the proposed international socialist conference to consider war aims. This was first proposed by the neutral Scandinavian and Dutch socialists and supported by the new Russian government headed by the socialist lawyer Alexander Kerensky (1881–1970). The Labour Party, meanwhile, had been divided on the matter. The pro-war elements were unwilling to meet with socialists from Germany and Austria and were afraid that the conference might strengthen the demand for a negotiated peace; the pacifists saw the meeting as a means to that end. It was agreed to hold a special Labour conference on 10 August to discuss the issue. Henderson, on his return, was in a very difficult position. After initially appearing to encourage Henderson to support the conference Lloyd George reversed himself under pressure from Tory and Liberal members of his Cabinet.

A series of complicated discussions ensued. It appeared that the government was unwilling to issue passports to Labour delegates if the party insisted on participating in the conference at Stockholm. On 7 August Henderson told Lloyd George that he would resign if passports were withheld. At this point Lloyd George seemed to be unwilling formally to prohibit Labour participation but, by procrastinating on the passport issue, he was hoping to give the Labour conference time to reject the proposal to go to Stockholm. If the decision favoured Stockholm, Lloyd George would, as an alternative, then be able to claim that Henderson was under the control of revolutionary sympathisers who wanted a negotiated peace.

The question of the Kerensky telegram was complicated and obscure, though there is no doubt that it was a typical Lloyd George deceit. On 3 August, Henderson telegraphed to Tereshchenko in Petrograd asking for an assurance that any decision at Stockholm should be regard as 'a party concern', not binding on socialists who were in government. On 9 August Tereshchenko replied, giving that assurance, and the Russian *chargé d'affaires* in London repeated this assurance to Lloyd George. To judge from Henderson's note to Lloyd George, written at noon on 10 August after he had finished his opening speech to the conference, it was this telegram that Webb refers to as coming from Kerensky. Henderson did not see the text, sent to him by hand at the conference, before he spoke. That afternoon the conference voted by 1,846,000 to 550,000 in favour of Stockholm. Meanwhile Lloyd George leaked another (probably spurious) telegram to the press; it purported to come from Kerensky and apparently repudiated Stockholm. Henderson, accused of suppressing this telegram, flatly denied in the subsequent parliamentary debate on 13 August that he had ever received it and claimed that he was told of it only when he was waiting in an ante-room at Downing Street for the interview with the Prime Minister that led to his immediate resignation from the government. On 13 August Kerensky also denied that he had sent such a telegram. The only evidence produced by Lloyd George was a telegram supposedly sent by the French socialist leader Albert Thomas (1878–1932) indicating that Kerensky did not want the conference to take place.

Lloyd George, by intrigue and innuendo, had destroyed what he now called 'a fraternising conference with the enemy', and followed this up by abusing Henderson and casting doubts on the patriotism of the Labour Party. The duplicity was not without effect. When the Labour conference reconvened on 21 August the miners union and some others had changed sides. Though there was still a bare majority of five thousand votes for Stockholm, the refusal of passports settled the matter. George Barnes took Henderson's place in the War Cabinet.

This breach between Lloyd George and most of the Labour Party had important long-term effects. First, it helped to unite the Labour Party: the issue created some common ground between the pacifists and the pro-war elements. Secondly, it released Henderson both from the collective responsibility of the Cabinet and from his official duties, turned him into an embittered opponent of Lloyd George and enabled him to devote his energies to building up the Labour Party for post-war political battles. Thirdly, it made Labour concentrate upon its own plans for the post-war world, rather than attempt to influence the Lloyd George government and operate essentially as an appendage of the Liberal Party. Finally, it brought Henderson, Webb and MacDonald together to consider the future of party organisation and policy. Early in September Henderson began holding informal meetings to plan Labour's new structure and plan its electoral strategy. Webb had already drafted *Labour's War Aims*, released to the August party conference and approved by another party conference in December. Thomas Jones noted in his diary on 30 October 1917 that he had attended a meeting at which Henderson, Webb, Tawney, Cole, Greenwood and others had discussed 'the programme of the new Labour Party'. Henderson was tolerantly willing to collaborate with the young Labour intellectuals and in the next two years he used them as the party's informal civil service: at long last it seemed that the clever young acolytes of the Webb partnership might become the brains trust of the Labour movement.

The modern Labour Party in fact dates from the autumn of 1917: its constitution and the main shape of its policy – both of which at last clearly distinguished it from the Liberals – were determined in the first months after Henderson asserted himself and became the architect of Labour's future. By the end of September 1917 he had made up his mind on some crucial points. Though Labour was to maintain the federal structure which represented the small socialist societies, the I.L.P. and the trade unions there was to be a distinct national Labour Party, with local branches in the constituencies enrolling individual members for the first time, contesting a large number of seats and offering a comprehensive programme. The details were referred to a sub-committee consisting of Henderson, MacDonald, Webb, Purdy, Hutchinson, W. C. Robinson, G. J. Wardle and Egerton Wake (1871–1929), an I.L.P. pacifist who became the party's national agent after 1919. The proposals put before the party executive on 16 October included what became known as

'Clause IV', the formal commitment to a socialist objective; several variants were considered but it was Webb's draft that was preferred. This read: 'To secure for the producers by hand or brain the full fruits of their industry, and the most equitable distribution thereof that may be possible, upon the basis of the Common Ownership of the Means of Production and the best obtainable system of popular administration and control of each industry or service'. The draft notably left open the debate between those who favoured municipal ownership, state socialists and nationalisers, Guild Socialists and Co-operators. At the time the phrases which were calculated to appeal to middle-class socialists and professional workers seemed to weigh more heavily with the committee than the ambiguities about the appropriate form of public ownership.

Henderson had to prepare the way for this far-reaching change by negotiations with sectional interests, both regional and trade union. At another Labour conference, in Nottingham in January 1918, Beatrice noted that Henderson was still anxious lest the unions, especially the miners and cotton workers, should reject the new model which seemed to threaten their domination of the political wing of the movement. (BWD 21 January 18) Despite a powerful speech by Henderson, refuting fears that the party would be manipulated by left-wing intellectuals, the proposals were referred back by a narrow majority. Before the conference reconvened in London on 25 February 1918 Henderson had changed the proposals to increase the trade union membership of the national executive, to give the Parliamentary Labour Party (then dominated by trade union members) a voice in policy-making, and to bind Labour candidates to accept the party's electoral programme. At this meeting the I.L.P. opposed the new version, objecting to the undivided or 'block' vote of the unions at the conference and to the election of the executive by the conference as a whole, rather than permitting each section to choose their own representatives – a method which protected the socialist societies. The new version, however, was adopted. Between the conferences Beatrice noted that Asquith was making overtures to the Labour leaders: the Liberals, she wrote, 'have always taken us up when they are in opposition and have always dropped us when they are in office. The policy of permeation is played out and Labour and socialism must either be in control or in whole-hearted opposition'. (BWD 31 January 18)

### 671 PP SIDNEY TO BEATRICE

John McGurk (1874–1944), of the Lancashire and Cheshire miners, was on the Labour Party executive. Ben Turner (1863–1942) was president of the National Union of Textile Workers. He became M.P. for Bately in 1922. In 1928, as chairman of the T.U.C., he signed a document calling for industrial peace. The co-signatory was Sir Alfred Mond (1868–1930), later Lord Melchett, the founder of Imperial Chemical Industries. The document became known as the 'Mond–Turner' agreement. William Cornforth Robinson (1861–1931) was General Secretary of the Amalgamated Association of Beamers, Twisters and Drawers. He later became Labour M.P. for Elland. William H. Hutchinson was a Guild Socialist who was on the executive of the Amalgamated Society of Engineers. William Frank Purdy (1872–1929) was the current chairman of the Labour Party and an official of the Shipwrights Union. Frederick Edwin Smith (1872–1930), late Earl of Birkenhead, and a notable barrister, was conservative in temper. Attorney-General in 1915, he became Lord Chancellor in 1919.

41 Grosvenor Road
Westminster Embankment
13.8.17

Dearest

Here are letters, and the Wick. I had a wearisome journey up, train full and late; and all to little profit. When I got to the meeting, I found that Henderson was to speak for an hour and be followed by the P.M. – all the M.P.s naturally absent, and we adjourned until 7 p.m. when I shall attend, unless telephoned to by Middleton that it is put off till tomorrow.

All those present (McGurk and Carter, miners: Ben Turner and Robinson, textiles, and Hutchinson, Engineers) were furious and fierce – the only significant one being McGurk, because he had been against the Conference. He said that he should stand firmly for the Conference decision, now that it had been given. Before I could mention 'victimisation', they declared that anyone taking Henderson's place would be a blackleg. They were full of abuse of Lloyd George's trickeries. Hutchinson declared that no responsible T.U. leader could now say with any confidence that his members were for continuing the war, the feeling had quite changed since a year ago. Purdy, the Chairman, was there, but he went away promptly, so I don't know his feelings.

It appears that Henderson was only handed Lloyd George's letter enclosing the Kerensky telegram *when he sat down.* Finding it only confirmed what he had said, he naturally did not read it. As Middleton says, it would have suited him exactly to have read it in his speech, because it distinctly agreed to issue passports to the Congress and the Russian delegation, (who arrived at 9 p.m. on Friday from Rome) were indignant even at Kerensky's partial repudiation; and whilst issuing their statement went straight to the Russian Embassy and had a telegram sent to Kerensky asking him what he meant by it (!) to which they have naturally not (yet) received a reply.

It appears that the Attorney-General (F. E. Smith) had given an opinion that the Common Law against communicating with the enemy actually prevented the issue of passports (?) (perhaps to any but the King's agents); and that this opinion was communicated to all the Labour Ministers (on their giving a dinner to Cresswell); whereupon *they* unanimously begged that it should not be known, lest it should infuriate the Labour Party Conference, and make it vote for going to Stockholm!

Middleton says that Henderson's only difficulty is that if he gave the whole story, the Government would fall at once. There is one telegram to him which would ruin them. Apparently he has been very badly treated by them ever since he returned from Russia two or three weeks ago – actually one (at least) Cabinet held from which he was excluded, whilst Barnes was present.

I think there is every sign that the Executive will stand by Henderson, and also the conference: but the bulk of the Labour M.P.s, like the Labour Ministers, may be against him. The question is what *these* will do; and this must depend mainly on Henderson's own line.

It appears that the whole of the Terms of Peace resolutions will be reprinted and circulated again as the Agenda for the adjourned Conference – more publicity!

Dear one, I don't stop to add more, in order to ensure catching the post. Goodnight.

Sidney

Emily has already gone.

672 HL BEATRICE WEBB TO HERBERT SAMUEL

Beatrice, now a member of the Machinery of Government Committee, was happy to be working again with Robert Morant and R. B. Haldane, 'discovering the land of Whitehall for the future Labour Cabinet'. (BWD 14 November 17)

41 Grosvenor Road
Westminster Embankment
27th October 1917

Dear Mr Samuel

Here are the questions which I have drafted but not submitted to my Committee. I formulated them partly to clear my own mind as to the character of the information that was needed if the Committee was to fulfil the whole of its reference, but also to give to personal friends in the Civil Service or having an intimate knowledge of the Civil Service. You will see that they are typed on different pages, and I do not necessarily give them all to any one individual. I send them all to you as your great knowledge of government work would enable you to give me hints on any one or all the subjects, and you also might be interested in knowing what is the sort of things that I think ought to be investigated. It would be very interesting if we might meet and have a talk about it, more especially if you would send me notes in the meanwhile which would raise other points. Perhaps you would come and dine with us some night later on? In any case, I shall look forward to your short memorandum on Cabinet offices.

I do not know whether our very small and humble committee will be able to do more than to make some suggestions to prevent overlapping and possibly to organise a Central Department of Research connected with the Intelligence Department of the various government departments. But I am quite certain that if we are going to rely on government machinery, as seems likely, for the performance of one service after another, we must overhaul government offices. We have put too little thought into the construction of government departments and we have hardly become aware of certain typical diseases which affect the bureaucrat.

Personally I rely a great deal on the creation of Advisory Committees on a statutory basis without any statutory powers to obstruct or delay Government (as in the case of the Council for India) but with definite statutory powers to undertake enquiries and to publish reports to be laid before Parliament. For instance, I think that the new Ministry of Health ought to have an Advisory Committee of medical men nominated by the profession in one or other of its aspects and with the statutory duty of reporting on any questions of public health – the reports to be published and laid before Parliament if so desired by the Advisory Council. In the same way I think our Local Health Authority ought to be provided with a Local Medical Committee to which would be given the power of reporting on public health administration, their report to be circulated to all ratepayers. Similar provisions ought to be made for the Teachers with regard to the Board of Education and the Local Education Authority, whilst Advisory Committees of Engineers, Architects and Accountants ought to be attached to the appropriate government departments.

I am convinced that the Inland Revenue Office, for instance, and the Exchequer and Audit Department would be enormously improved in efficiency if there were attached to them Advisory Committees of Accountants with statutory powers of reporting on methods of audit or methods of assessing taxes.

Then there are other types of Advisory Committees which I think would be useful, on the lines of the Engineering Standards Committee, for the invention of technical contrivances. Here you need a somewhat different constitution representing not only the producers of the service but also the consumers of the service. The only Advisory Committee which I think perfectly useless is a big nondescript body called in by a government department not really to advise them or to criticise them, but to 'cover their operations'.

Do send me any remarks, however casual, that may occur to you on my questions.

Always yours sincerely

Beatrice Webb

(Mrs Sidney Webb)

One enclosure

673 BEV BEATRICE WEBB TO WILLIAM BEVERIDGE

The panel on Local Government was now working as a sub-committee of the Ministry of Reconstruction: Beatrice was collaborating with J. H. Thomas. Though she later disliked and despised him, at this time she thought him 'one of the ablest of the trade union leaders and one of the most statesmanlike of their parliamentary representatives'. (BWD 3 October 17) She was delighted that she and Lord George Hamilton, with whom she had been at odds when he had chaired the Royal Commission on the Poor Law, had been able quickly to agree on a report 'embodying all the conclusions of the Minority Report'. The achievement of this agreement was, she thought, 'my masterpiece'. (BWD n.d. 18) She conceded that 'I have learnt committee manners'. (BWD 11 December 17) The report, however, was squashed and a reform of the Poor Law again delayed.

41 Grosvenor Road
Westminster Embankment 1
7th November 1917

Dear Mr Beveridge

I venture to send you, in strict confidence, the memorandum which Mr Thomas and I are circulating to the Reorganisation of Local Government Committee dealing with the problem of the Able-bodied. If you have time to look it through and give me your opinion and any suggestions I should be very grateful. I send you a previous memorandum dealing with the other classes on the basis of our unanimous decision to abolish the Boards of Guardians, transfer the Poor Law Services to the County Councils and County Borough Councils, and, as regards specialised institutions, put them under the specialised Committees of the County Councils and County Borough Councils.

You will be glad to hear that the Committee is, on the whole, most promising, and Lord George Hamilton and I are working hand in hand for the abolition of the Poor Law and the breaking up of its services among the specialised Committees of the Local Authority. This, of course, is confidential information.

Always yours

Beatrice Webb
(Mrs Sidney Webb)

Enclosures

674 MUL SIDNEY WEBB TO E. D. SIMON

Willard Straight (1880–1918), the wealthy American diplomat and journalist, launched the *New Republic* as an American analogue to the *New Statesman*. The novelist Arnold Bennett (1867–1931) was a director of the *New Statesman* and a regular contributor to it.

41 Grosvenor Road
Westminster Embankment
30.11.17

Dear Simon

The advertisement of the *New Republic* is certainly very attractive – but also costly!

They have done very well – but at unlimited cost. It was said that Willard Straight and his friends put down £100,000 capital to start the paper; and after three years of quite exceptionally favourable times for them, they are still running at a heavy loss. The *New Statesman*, which has consumed in less than five years only some £14,000 capital does not come out of the comparison so badly, I think, from the financial standpoint.

Numbers, advertisement prices, and cash transactions are all bigger in America than here; and with more than twice the population to appeal to, very cheap postage rates, and practically no rival, it is only natural that the *New Republic* should stand better than the *New Statesman*.

If each subscription means a loss of $3 a year, when they had some 15,000 to 18,000 circulation, they were losing from £9,000 to £11,000 a year in July 1916. Even for the current year, after the immense boom they have had – a supreme piece of good luck – they still admit a loss on the year, of $1 per subscriber; apparently some 30,000 = £6,000.

Now I believe we might have had as big a result (alike in circulation, and in loss!) if we had been prepared to spend anything like such sums. I go further. I have not the least doubt that another £20,000 judiciously expended would have wiped out all our current loss of £2,000 a year, and turned it into a net profit. I think this could still be done. But I never had the audacity to propose such an expenditure of other people's money. We are running the paper with a crippled office staff and overworked writers, without relief or 'understudy'; incessantly dependent on my writing; not paying either me or Bennett; unable to pay for special information; unable to launch out into schemes for increasing circulation or advertisements – all in a perpetual struggle to keep down the deficit.

The *New Republic* has pursued the diametrically opposite policy of always getting the very best, spending the very utmost, and working with the greatest ease and elbowroom. It has not yet paid the owners financially, in stopping the loss, but it has got a large circulation and an international influence, and has no doubt created a saleable property.

It seems to me that, in newspapers as in the speed of steamers and trains, any increase beyond the commonplace *costs quite disproportionately much* to achieve – but is then doubtless worth all it costs in monopoly value. The question is, whether the owners can go in for the larger policy?

There is no doubt we are coming to a specially critical time. We *could* increase our circulation and get more advertisements if we could spend more – but it would mean increasing the present deficit for a time, and of course, there is no certainty of *financial* success in the present adverse times.

I like to have your incitements and monitions but *I* can't do any more!

Yours

Sidney Webb

675 LPA SIDNEY WEBB TO J. S. MIDDLETON

The formation of a local Labour Party in Westminster was based on the new model rules but the move was made in advance of the approval of the new constitution. Unofficially, quite a number of 'local' Labour parties had been formed around the country, enrolling individual members – catering partly to those who, because of the anti-war stand by the I.L.P., felt unable to join the Labour Party by way of membership of the I.L.P. The anomaly of double membership persisted in various forms. It was possible for a member to be counted four times – as an affiliated trade unionist, member of the Labour Party, member of the I.L.P. and member of the Fabian Society. Such double counting applied especially to the most active individuals in the movement. The Royal Arsenal Co-operative Society, the only one to affiliate directly to the Labour Party, provided a fifth means of enrolment for socialists living in south-east London.

41 Grosvenor Road
Westminster Embankment
7 Dec/17

Dear Middleton

I beg to apply for affiliation to the Labour Party for the Westminster Local Labour Party, and I enclose cheque for 15/- which I gather is the minimum under the rules.

The Association was formed at a meeting on 29 November called by the enclosed circular which was addressed to all the Trade Union, Socialist and Co-operative organisations that could be discovered in Westminster City (2 new constituencies), nearly 60 in number. Delegates attended from many of them, and declared that their Societies joined; but in order to get the adhesions on a precise footing the enclosed second circular has been sent out, asking for the numbers of their members for their nominations to the General Committee.

The Labour Party draft Model Rules were provisionally adopted, and a provisional Executive Committee and Officers were appointed by the Meeting – the President being Mr Henderson; the Treasurer Mrs Sidney Webb; and the Executive including representatives of the National Union of General Workers, the Railway Clerks Association, the National Union of Clerks and the Postmen's Federation – these to hold office until the Annual Meeting in April.

Yours truly

Sidney Webb

## 676 KCC SIDNEY WEBB TO J. M. KEYNES

Webb wished the Labour Party to contest the university seats, in which the electors consisted solely of graduates, as a sign that it was a truly national party and to demonstrate that it had a place for 'brainworkers' as well as trade unionists and ideologues. He wrote to Thomas Jones on 27 January 1918 (NLW). 'It seems as if no better person than myself is likely to be found willing to stand as a Labour candidate for London University . . . it is important to get something of the sort under way quickly'. Webb in fact did rather well in the first post-war election, running second with 2,141 votes to the 2,810 cast for the Unionist and the 2,000 odd votes distributed among three other candidates. Beatrice felt that he was disappointed not to win. 'I think he had been looking forward to a spell in Parliament – wanted to test his powers as a parliamentarian . . . But he hates taking the plunge from the dignified and detached position of a disinterested helper into rivalry with colleagues for prized positions . . . He cannot bring himself even to hint that he has a claim to a winnable constituency.' (BWD 22 December 18) Keynes, courted by the Webbs in this period, was much less sympathetic to their position than they inferred: his letters show a determination to keep himself free of any public commitment to Labour.

41 Grosvenor Road
Westminster Embankment
14.1.18

Dear Keynes

I don't know whether Desmond McCarthy has done as he intended, and approached you about your allowing yourself to be nominated as the Labour Candidate for Cambridge University.

The Labour Party wishes to run a candidate for each University election, just to emphasise that it is not a workman's party, and that it claims support of all classes as a national party.

I think this is a good idea, and with the Alternative Vote or Proportional Representation it can do the Liberal Candidate no harm.

You are, of course, most usefully and busily employed in the government service; but, I assume, not as a member of the permanent civil service; and those temporarily serving are presumably not debarred from standing for Parliament. Some of them, of course, are actually M.P.s. Anyhow, a university candidature is very unobjectionable, as there are no meetings and nothing beyond the issue of an Address, which the government will post free of charge.

I venture to hope you will not dismiss the idea. If you do not peremptorily do so, some Cambridge people will put in hand a requisition to you, which we are sure would be very numerously signed by the younger men.

Of course, we are not expecting you to be returned! But you would certainly poll a very respectable minority; and it would do a great deal of good to the atmosphere!

The Labour Party's 'War Aims' are known to you. I enclose a new draft 'Report on Reconstruction'. But no Labour Candidate need commit himself to anything in particular.

Yours very truly
Sidney Webb

677 LPA SIDNEY WEBB TO ARTHUR HENDERSON

Dr Alfred Cox (1866–1954) was medical secretary of the British Medical Association 1912–32.

41 Grosvenor Road
Westminster Embankment
5.2.18

Dear Henderson

My wife has been seeing Dr Cox, Secretary of the British Medical Association, on other matters; and she finds that this Association, which considers itself *the* Trade Union of doctors, is somewhat offended that the Labour Party should have received a deputation from the State Medical Association.

The B.M.A. has therefore asked you to receive a deputation from itself; and my wife suggests that, however inconvenient, it may not [be] desirable to refuse.

It was explained to Dr Cox that the Labour Party could not practically have anyone on its Advisory Committees who was not an avowed supporter of the Labour Party; and that it was under no obligation to put its political opponents on its Committees – not being itself the Government. But the B.M.A. is, of course, a very influential body all over the country, and must not be offended.

We suggest that if it is possible to let the B.M.A. appear and make its suggestion, it would be a good thing. The deputation could then be asked whether there was any member of the B.M.A. whom they could suggest as being a supporter of the Labour Party, who could, if thought fit, be invited to serve on the proposed Advisory Committee.

I send this merely for your information as you are no doubt dealing with the matter.

Yours

Sidney Webb

## 678 PP SIDNEY TO BEATRICE

Sidney was one of a Labour delegation (which included Henderson, MacDonald, Will Thorne, John McGurk and Charles Bowerman) which went to Paris to meet the French socialists and discuss the final arrangements for an inter-Allied socialist conference to be held in London on 20 February. Part of the agenda was a consideration of the war aims statement recently approved by the Labour Party. Léon Jouhaux (1879–1954) was for many years secretary of the Confédération Générale du Travail and did much to create the International Labour Office; Albert Thomas, a leading member of the French Socialist Party, became the first Director of the I.L.O.

Beatrice noted that the trade unionists in the party 'spent most of their time eating and drinking . . . It makes one despair of the Labour Party as an organ of government. These men are not only incapable of doing the work themselves; they are not fit judges of other men's capacity. It is a mere lucky chance that they have Sidney at their disposal'. (BWD 19 February 1918) H. D. Harben was working for a British government agency in Paris.

Hotel de Calais
Rue des Capucines, Paris
16.2.18

Dearest

I got no further chance to write yesterday; and I doubt when you will receive this. We spent yesterday afternoon in a vain attempt to see Jouhaux and the Confédération Générale du Travail, travelling out to Belleville (say Stratford) but finding that, by their usual muddling, these were not assembled. Then we came back and dined quietly at the hotel – after which I went off with MacDonald and McGurk to meet the French Party Executive at 8.30. Various delegates turned up – Italian (one section) independent Trentino, a Bosnian and so on. Three-quarters of an hour late the first Frenchman arrived, and we began an hour late! Then came protests and declarations; and at last we got to the African Colonies and spent an hour or more debating. At 11.15 they said we must stop, in order to get home; and a little Committee (including me) was appointed, but only for 11.30 this morning to draft. We walked home at midnight.

We are going to lunch with Albert Thomas (we don't know yet where or when!) At 2.30 we are to meet the Executive again: and probably another late sitting tonight.

Fortunately the weather is beautiful but cold.

The three trade unionists got here late last night. They slept at Folkestone, and heard the firing in the Channel!

We expect at this moment, to leave here Sunday night, and get home Monday late afternoon – perhaps much the same time as you! I will telegraph to Emily. But we may be delayed again.

There is really a great disposition to agree: and we have great hopes we shall be able to bring off the Inter-Allied Conference some time next week. But the delays are endless.

Paris has *lots* of food, no restrictions on meat, butter, sugar: but no confectionery to be sold, no milk after the morning, very few cigarettes to be bought. Many badly crippled soldiers, and widows in mourning. All shops shut at 7 p.m. and streets deserted in the evening but not very dark.

We are going now to Harben's office to try to secure our passports for return.

I was cold last night, alone, and only slept a few hours. It is horridly uncomfortable, but we are certainly doing good – and it had to be done.

Now dearest goodbye. You may find this at home when you arrive, before me. It would be hopeless to send it to Boscombe, where I hope you have had a pleasant time this weather.

Sidney

## 679 NLW BEATRICE WEBB TO THOMAS JONES

Jones had been considered but not accepted as Principal of the University College at Cardiff. Beatrice had developed a scheme for reorganising the civil service based upon a pattern of fourteen ministries and a strong Cabinet secretariat. At this point she thought that if Labour were to form a government Sidney would become secretary to the Cabinet.

41 Grosvenor Road
Westminster Embankment, S.W.1
26th February 1918

Dear Mr Jones

We were so sorry to see that the Cardiff business has not gone quite straight – at least if you desired it to do so. We want you, of course, for other work!

I wonder whether you could get me a memorandum by Sir Auckland Geddes on National Registration, which I understand has been circulated to some of the Ministers? I am now writing a memorandum on the function of Registration in the work of Government, for the Machinery of Government Committee, and also for a Local Government Board Departmental Committee on National Registration. It would be a great advantage if I could see what Sir Auckland Geddes is proposing so as not to run counter to his purpose. The worst of all these different Committees and Ministers is that we may quite unwittingly be mutually obstructing by proposing conflicting ways of doing the same job. When I have read the memorandum I could suggest to the Chairman of the Local Government Committee that we consult with Sir Auckland Geddes before drawing up a Report. I would, of course, regard the memorandum as strictly confidential.

We decided at the last meeting of the Machinery of Government Committee to ask you and Professor Adams to come and talk to us about a Prime Minister's Department. I suppose you have been supplied with the printed memorandum on the Allocation of Services among fourteen separate Departments? It will be most interesting and helpful to discuss the question with you and Professor Adams.

Always yours sincerely
Beatrice Webb

## 680 PP BEATRICE WEBB TO LADY COURTNEY

Richard von Kühlmann (1873–1948) was Counsellor at the German embassy in London 1909–14, and German Foreign Secretary 1917–18.

On the day that this letter was written the Webbs dined with Haldane to meet Lloyd George, supposedly to discuss Beatrice's ideas about the machinery of government. There was no such discussion, Beatrice complaining that 'the low standard of intellect and conduct of the little Welsh conjurer is so obvious and withal he is so pleasant and lively that official deference and personal respect fade into an atmosphere of agreeable low company . . . intimate camaraderie with a fellow adventurer'. (BWD 1 March 1918) Lloyd George, she thought, was feeling out the prospects of some electoral deal with the Labour Party. The letter was presumably written after the dinner for, without revealing the source, it repeats the substance of the conversation as noted in Beatrice's diary.

41 Grosvenor Road
Westminster Embankment
28th February 1918

Dearest Kate

We were glad to get your letter. So far as the immediate purpose of Inter-Allied agreement is concerned both the Paris visit and the London Conference were a great success. You have probably seen the *Daily Chronicle* and Sidney's two articles – the one yesterday summarised the results of the London Conference. He is somewhat exhausted, as during the Paris visit he had not only to be a responsible delegate but to act as courier and interpreter to the entire party – not one of them speaking a word of French.

We are all very gloomy in London and the foreign delegates were even more gloomy. The position seems to be this. There is a much better chance than ever before of a cynical peace at the expense of Russia and for the defeat of revolutionary tendencies. In fact, I believe there are *pour parlers* going on through a special diplomat who has come straight from Kühlmann. Such a peace would entail a complete sanction of Germany's conquests in the East and a promise of economic 'friendship', whilst Germany would evacuate Belgium and France and be 'accommodating' about Alsace Lorraine. The two obstacles to such a peace are the *quid pro quo* to the British Empire and Wilson's 'mania' for democratic equity in the settlement. If such a peace were to be proposed the British democrats and pacifists would be puzzled to know whether they wanted it or not.

A democratic peace is further off than ever. Germany is said to be intoxicated by her prospects of having Russia as a dependency and the world power such an extension of territory and influence offers her. Such a peace would 'right' the German Government with her own people and justify militarism. On the other hand, such a peace would seem to entail the continuance of conscription and armaments for the other countries.

But if such a peace is declined then we are in for a terrible prolongation of the war and it is doubtful whether in the end we should not have to accept Germany's terms.

The U.S. is reported to be becoming more and more bellicose and is only fearing the weak will of her allies.

Ever yours affectionately
Beatrice Webb

A number of Fabian intellectuals – Cole, Tawney, Woolf, the historian Arnold Toynbee (1888–1975), J. J. Mallon (1875–1961), Warden of Toynbee Hall, and C. Delisle Burns (1879–1942) – had moved into the Labour offices at 1 Victoria Street and were busy setting up a series of policy centres called Advisory Committees, drafting policy statements and preparing leaflets. The Fabian Research Department was converted into the Labour Research Department, moving into the Labour headquarters on 1 July 1918, providing research and information under four heads – trade unions, Co-operatives, trades councils and labour parties – in return for a payment of £150 a year.

Fabians were chairmen and secretaries of almost all the Advisory Committees. *International:* Webb and Woolf. *Trade and Finance:* J. A. Hobson and G. D. H. Cole. *Industrial:* W. F. Purdy and J. J. Mallon. *Machinery of Government:* MacDonald and Beatrice Webb. *Public Health:* W. C. Anderson and G. P. Blizzard. *Rural:* F. E. Green and M. I. Cole. *Drink:* J. H. Thomas and E. R. Pease. *Education:* H. W. Goldstone. *Local Government:* F. W. Jowett. G. D. H. Cole was made co-ordinating secretary for the whole cluster. Only Purdy and Thomas were outside the Fabian orbit.

With their young associates holding such key positions in policy-drafting, and with a round of lunches, dinners, committees and introductions, the Webbs were now back in the political swim, getting on well with the Labour Party leaders, patronising the young and influencing policy and organisation. Sidney's main published contribution was *Labour and the New Social Order* – which Beatrice described as 'the Webb programme' – setting out the framework of Labour policy for many years to come. *Empire and Commerce in Africa* was written by Woolf under a contract with the Fabian Society and it was published in 1919.

41 Grosvenor Road
Westminster Embankment
11.3.18

Dear Woolf

Your letter of 24 February has remained unanswered through press of work.

I am afraid it is hopeless to get a Committee at this moment to sit and consider abstract alternative ways of Colonial exploitation. It is, as you say, too vague, and we have none of us practical knowledge.

As to the development of a Foreign Affairs Department of the Labour Party, this is contemplated in the form of an Advisory Committee on Foreign Relations, in connection with the Labour Intelligence Department.

I think it might be well if you would furnish Pease with a general report as to how your book is progressing, so that he may be in a position to say we have not neglected to enquire!

Yours

Sidney Webb

682 NLW BEATRICE WEBB TO THOMAS JONES

Shaw's satirical play about the ladylike brothel-keeper was still refused by the censor. The actor–manager Charles Charrington was a long-time friend of Shaw and had been a member of the Fabian executive before the war. Sir Maurice Hankey (1877–1963), later Lord Hankey, was secretary to the Committee of Imperial Defence 1911–38, and to the Cabinet 1919–38.

41 Grosvenor Road
Westminster Embankment, S.W.1
13th March 1918

Dear Mr Jones

I have been asked by Mr Charrington to see whether it would be possible to get the Prime Minister to consent to a deputation to put before him the desirability of the production of *Mrs Warren's Profession*. For your consideration I enclose the petition to the Lord Chamberlain with regard to it, together with a list of signatories. You will note how many M.O.H. are in favour of it, though no doubt the M.P.s will seem more important to you! I understand that the Lord Chamberlain is still obdurate and there seems nothing for it but to appeal to the Prime Minister.

Perhaps you will send me back the enclosure.

We had a most interesting afternoon with Sir Maurice Hankey, who seems to be an ideal personage for the position he occupies.

Always yours sincerely
Beatrice Webb

[*Enclosed list*]
Bishop of Lincoln, Bishop of Winchester, Bishop of Kensington, Mr G. N. Barnes, Lord Selborne, J. W. Hills, M.P., H. W. Goldstone, A. F. Whyte, All leading Actors and Authors, About 30 leading Medical Officers of Health.

683 KCC BEATRICE WEBB TO J. M. KEYNES

Beatrice had sent Keynes a copy of her scheme for reorganising the central government. J. W. Nixon had been the treasurer of the Fabian Research Department.

41 Grosvenor Road
Westminster Embankment, S.W.1
14th March 1918

Dear Mr Keynes

Very many thanks for your most interesting letter, with its valuable comments on the memorandum. I fully agree with you that it is most important to increase the prestige of the Treasury: in fact that seems to be one of the objects of our little Committee. But the present organisation into divisions having jurisdiction over special Departments seems to have been responsible for the loss of prestige by the Treasury. The principal clerk dealing with a group of Departments seems to get possessed by the assumption that it is the business of the Treasury to check all expenditure, and that it is somewhat immaterial what expenditure he checks. It has never occurred to any Treasury official that efficiency may demand an increase of expenditure in certain directions. I understand, for instance, that it has not occurred to a Treasury official to insist on higher salaries for particular kinds of work – a very usual recommendation of efficiency experts called in to advise private enterprise. Nor has it occurred to any Treasury official to advise the extension of a Department in order to increase its profitableness, e.g. the Post Office.

That, of course, raises the question whether the activities of the Department of Finance ought to be purely negative – whether there ought to be any bias in favour of either more or less expenditure. Why should there be any bias on the part of a financial expert in favour either of more or less expenditure? If every Treasury official is against public expenditure *per se*, he very naturally offends one school of thought, and a school of thought which may become the dominant school of thought – with the unfortunate result that his advice on purely technical financial questions is regarded with suspicion and is apt to be ignored. For instance, the strong opposition to Old Age Pensions put up by the Treasury rendered their objection to the financial basis of Lloyd George's National Insurance Bill suspect and prevented their criticism being attended to. Why should a Treasury official allow his administration to be dominated by a particular theory with regard to the relation of public and private expenditure any more than an official of the Education Department should insist on carrying out his own theory as to the relation of voluntary schools to council schools? However, I do not wish to drag you into a controversy. Perhaps some day we may meet and talk the matter over.

By the way, I understand that there is to be a Treasury Committee on the Cost of Living. I do not know whether the Treasury has fixed on a Secretary, but there is a hard-working and able official in the Statistical Branch of the Unemployment Insurance Department of the Ministry of Labour – J. W. Nixon – who would very much like to undertake the work. He is known to Professor Bowley and Sir William Ashley. I venture to mention his name as it is so hard now to get efficient secretaries for Departmental Committees. Pray regard this suggestion as confidential.

Yours sincerely

Beatrice Webb
(Mrs Sidney Webb)

Pray forgive this hastily dictated letter.

BW

684 NLW BEATRICE WEBB TO THOMAS JONES

The German offensive on 21 March had broken the British Fifth Army in France. Though the offensive was halted after heavy fighting, for a week or more the German advances threatened to become a decisive victory.

41 Grosvenor Road
Westminster Embankment, S.W.1
3rd April 1918

Dear Mr Jones

I send you a memorandum by me, which is being circulated to the Machinery of Government Committee, bearing on the relationship of the Ministry of Labour to the Ministry of Munitions, Admiralty, etc., and answering objections which have been made before our Committee to a single Ministry dealing with all questions relation to employment. Would it be possible for you to circulate to the Machinery of Government Committee any additional memoranda relating to the Ministry of Labour and the other Departments? For instance, you said something about a dispute between the Ministry of National Service and the Ministry of Labour with regard to the Employment Exchanges, and the Machinery of Government Committee would very much like to read the arguments for or against the transfer of the Employment Exchanges to the Ministry of National Service.

As at present advised it seems to me that there can only be one Ministry of Employment – but which of the present organisations ought to swallow the other is, of course, another matter. It would be quite impossible to separate the Employment Exchanges from Unemployment Insurance on the one hand and from demobilisation on the other. If the War Cabinet is in any difficulty about the matter why not refer it to the Machinery of Government Committee for quick decision?

I am glad to think that matters are looking better on the Western Front than they did when you had supper here ten days ago.

Yours sincerely
Beatrice Webb

685 HWUL SIDNEY WEBB TO SIR ROBERT BLAIR

41 Grosvenor Road
Westminster Embankment
9.4.18

Dear Sir Robert

Your letter of 23 February, enclosing scheme on the Teaching of Modern History in the highest classes, was put aside for reply – for which I never found time!

I agree entirely with the idea, and have little to criticise in the details, I am not sure that the *Position of Women* ought not to come in! I am inclined to doubt whether *Sea Power* is a good subject; but it might be put as *The Influence on the World of Overseas Communications* (or 'The Ocean as the Larger Part of the World'). It is the sea in peace, not the sea in war, that is the most important.

But the main difficulty lies with *the mass* of the teachers, whom you cannot get to take in such an idea by a mere Circular, or enable them to carry it out by mere incitement or order. They need to be *shown* what to do, and how to do it. This means, a 'Normal Course' on the subject as a whole – object, method of drawing up syllabus, how to get up the several subjects, how to lecture, what 'objects' to show in connection with each lecture, how to 'follow up' each lecture by essays or class visits etc. I confess that I itch to show them how to do it! But this, of course, is mere delusion of the amateur. You certainly need such a Normal Course.

Thanks for showing me the scheme.

Yours

Sidney Webb

686 PP BEATRICE WEBB TO LADY COURTNEY

Leonard Courtney died on 11 May 1918. Though Beatrice had not greatly cared for her brother-in-law in the first years of his marriage to her sister she wrote after his death that he 'was one of those rare natures that grow in breadth of vision and warmth of sympathy with old age . . . a noble man . . . of exquisite tastes in literature, in nature, in music, in art'. (BWD n.d. May 1918) But she felt that he had no intellectual distinction, subtlety or originality, 'an impossible person to talk to except on the trivialities of life'. Paul Hobhouse had been killed in France.

41 Grosvenor Road
Westminster Embankment
Monday [13 May 1918]

Dearest Kate

It was a great shock to get your news this morning. I thought that he would pull through this attack.

You will feel his loss terribly – as I shall the loss of Sidney. But you too have had a gloriously happy and fruitful life together and Leonard had in all human probability to go before you. And with his dependence on you it is best he should. He has been a noble force in public life and an inspiration to his friends and to the two families that have centred round him. To the Potter family he has certainly been a spiritual father. I am so glad Sidney and I had that happy time with you both at Bude and Wynhoe and watched him in his ideal old age with his physical and mental vigour almost unimpaired. I am glad Maggie and Henry will be with you – their sorrow is both less and greater than yours – less because Paul was not part and parcel of their most intimate life – greater because unlike Leonard's life, Paul's had not born its fruit. And there was so much promise in his nature. It is kind of you to tell us not to come back. We will not do so as we both need the rest in order to be able to get on with somewhat harassing work. The times are so tragic and the future is so menacing that one feels that one has to keep one's old body as fit as possible so that one may pull one's weight. We shall be back on the 27th. I hope Maggie will let me know how you are and what are your immediate plans.

Ever yours affectionately

Beatrice Webb

687 NLW BEATRICE WEBB TO THOMAS JONES

The Committee on Women in Industry was set up to determine whether the Government had carried out its pledge that where women 'dilutees' did men's work they were to be paid men's wages. Beatrice concluded that the pledge had not been implemented. Unable to convince any of her colleagues she submitted a minority report which went beyond the Government's record to discuss the general principles of equal pay. This report was published by the Fabian Society under the title: *The Wages of Men and Women – Should they be Equal?*

A typist mistakenly sent the invitation to be chairman to all members of the committee, all of whom accepted. The chairman in fact was Richard Atkin (1867–1944), later Lord Atkin and a distinguished judge.

Longfords
Minchinhampton
Aug 28 [1918]

Dear Mr Jones

I received a telegram yesterday from the P.M. asking me to be chairman of a committee to investigate and report on the ratio to be established between men's and women's wages. I accepted though I doubt whether I am the best person for the task. I should be so grateful if you could let me know who are likely to be my colleagues and who will be secretary? So much of the success of the committee will depend on the secretary – whether he knows the sources of information and whether he will work with a woman chairman with cordiality. I suppose he will be someone from the Ministry of Labor? Of course they have some very good men there – Butler or Reid – though these two may be too big for the job. Could you also let me know anything as to the speed that is desired in getting the report. It will be necessary to take some evidence not only to inform our own minds but also to satisfy public opinion that the committee has not prejudged the question.

The above will be my address until Sunday morning's post: we leave for London early on Monday morning and we shall be there for lunch. If you are in London could you come to lunch either on Monday or on Tuesday.

Sidney goes to Derby on Tuesday morning but I shall be at home. Forgive my amateur typing, but it is better than my handwriting.

Ever yours

Beatrice Webb

688 PP SIDNEY TO BEATRICE

Beatrice was concerned about the prospects for the post-war world. 'Burdened with a huge public debt, living under the shadow of swollen government departments, with a working class seething with discontent, and a ruling class with all its traditions and standards topsy-turvy, with civil servants suspecting business men and business men conspiring to protect their profits, and all alike abusing the politicians, no citizen knows what is going to happen to himself and his children, or to his own social circle, or to the State or to the Empire. All that he does know is that the old order is seriously threatened with dissolution without any new order being in sight.' (BWD 4 November 1918) On November 11 she asked: 'How soon will the tide of revolution catch up with the tide of victory?'

The Labour rally at the Albert Hall was large and tumultuous but, Beatrice noted, its size 'did not redeem it from political, intellectual and spiritual failure'. (BWD 17 November 1918) She thought the platform 'weak and divided in aim, every speech was interrupted by irreverent and spiteful remarks, by rowdy singing and red flag waving'. The rowdiness led the trustees of the Albert Hall to cancel a letting for a *Daily Herald* demonstration on the following Saturday. The electricians then pulled the fuses and announced that no power would be supplied for any gatherings at the Albert Hall: the government intervened to persuade the trustees to change their minds.

Queens Hotel
Birmingham
[? 11 Nov 1918]

Dear One

Birmingham is 'Mafeking'; so I suppose is London. The streets are crowded with shouting people: the hotel full and uncomfortable. There is perpetual noise in my bedroom – the maid says it is in all – from the water-pipes. So it is not a place for you to come to!

I got a Box for Thursday night's Labour Demonstration at the Albert Hall, which will be a sight. There are apparently 8 seats, so you might send about tickets, retaining one (or two) for yourself in case you care to go.

I am now sitting down to tea and eggs before starting out to my meeting, which will be as it will be. Some strange things are going to happen in the nation, what I don't know; but we are supremely fortunate in having our love and ourselves.

Sidney

689 BUL SIDNEY WEBB TO SIR OLIVER LODGE

Lloyd George had decided to combine a 'khaki' and a 'coupon' election to profit from the euphoria of peace, hoping to secure a parliament dominated by supporters of his coalition. The seven Labour ministers wished to remain in the government and profit from the coupon. At a special Labour conference on 14 November the vote was 2,117,000 in favour of leaving the coalition and 810,000 against. Four of the Labour ministers (Barnes, Roberts, Wardle and Parker) left the party and remained as temporary 'Labour' supporters of Lloyd George; the other three (Clynes, Hodge and Walsh) reluctantly accepted the party call to resign.

Labour ran 361 candidates, polled 22 per cent of the vote and won 61 seats, running ahead of the Asquith Liberals in 79 other constituencies. But the hysteria of the election had cost MacDonald, Snowden and other I.L.P. anti-war candidates their seats. Henderson, who had given up his safe seat at Barnard Castle to fight a London marginal, was also defeated. The strengthened party, about to become the official opposition, was thus unfortunately deprived at a critical moment of its main leaders in the House of Commons.

The enclosed letter follows: it was published in the *New Statesman* of 23 November 1918.

41 Grosvenor Road
Westminster Embankment
26.11.18

Dear Sir Oliver

The P.M. is a man of 'push', and is, I believe, sincerely desirous of social reform. But can you trust him, without 'H.M. Opposition', to be *able* to withstand the pressure of an essentially reactionary majority, largely in the hands of capitalists who are frankly out for making large incomes by combinations to raise prices (or maintain them higher than need be) to the consumer? Or can you believe that he can get through the House of Lords, without a very specific mandate, anything that touches land or hereditary privilege?

I by no means ostracise Lloyd George: he may be a great force for progress, but he can only get forward on the lines that his associates permit. My wife and I have done every job we could get for the Government during the war (as before); and we have seen the P.M. privately more than once during these four years.

Unfortunately, as we think, he has put himself in the hands of a majority which won't let him go *our* way, even if he wished to do so! It is as though a very pushful and successful commercial traveller attached himself to a great firm which insisted on selling only certain kinds of wares. His pushfulness would not sell any other kind, because he would not be allowed to propose them!

But there is a very grave constitutional issue at stake. Are we electors, or are we not, to be allowed to pronounce on *which* general lines we want the Government and legislation to be carried on? The idea of a universal Coalition, eliminating all contests, except against 'freak' candidates, looks uncommonly like a negation of Democracy. The electors are done out of their right to *choose* between one policy and another; naturally the

M.P.'s like it – in fact, it might almost be called a conspiracy of the sitting members to maintain their seats without having to face the electors.

If I go to Parliament – which I don't particularly wish to do, and which is scarcely credible; though I must say the amount of support I have got makes me sometimes believe I shall get in – I shall go as a free and unpledged man – not like the Coalition candidates pledged to support the Government through thick and thin; and on the other hand, bound by no pledge or understanding to *oppose* the Government. I certainly should do nothing to 'block' any measure, however little I liked its method or details; and I should be as willing to support (and to try to improve) a Government measure as any other – in fact, much more willing, because it would be much more likely to become law! I believe the Labour Members will all take this line, to the best of their ability. But they flatly refuse to go pledged to support the Government, even if this refusal costs them their seats. I cannot doubt that they are right.

One other point. I believe this country is going through a period of grave peril, industrially. There is an ugly temper abroad (not in the Labour Party and, in fact, in revolt against the constitutional parliamentarianism of the Labour Party). The best safeguard against 'Bolshevism' is a strong Labour Party in Parliament, voicing the discontent and bringing to light the grievances of the masses. That is why the attempt of the Coalition Party to extinguish the Labour Party, or suppress its independence, or to make it dwindle into a handful of members, seems to me about the most dangerous thing to do. Imagine the outcry there would be against a 'packed Parliament', and the impetus this would give to 'direct action'. If you *want* a Bolshevist revolution in this country, the surest way to get it is to succeed in eliminating or discrediting the Labour Party! It is not too much to say that the survival of any popular respect for Parliamentary institutions *depends* on there continuing to be a strong and independent Parliamentary Labour Party, functioning as 'H.M. Opposition'.

I enclose a letter which I sent to a constituent, and you may have missed in the *New Statesman*. It gives the explanation of why the Labour Party refused to extend its membership of the Coalition beyond the term for which it entered it (for the prosecution of the war).

With kindest regards from Mrs Webb, I am

Yours very truly

Sidney Webb

[*Copy of letter to 'some electors of London University'*]

Dear Sir

I am much obliged for your frank letter. Of course, I should be very sorry to lose your support, but my own election matters little. What I am concerned about is that the action of the Labour Party Conference should be so misunderstood, and, as I think, misjudged.

First, on the constitutional point. The whole object of an election is to consult the electorate, and ascertain their opinions and desires, not upon details, but upon the general lines on which the government and legislation are to be carried on. This we hold to be indispensable to give that consciousness of consent, which is the basis of British government. But the only way in which the electorate can express itself is by *choosing* between rival policies advocated by competing candidates.

What Mr Lloyd George is avowedly asking to do is to have *no* rival policies submitted to the electorate for its decision; and as far as practicable, no competing candidates. If he had his way, the General Election would be an election without contests, a series of uncontested nominations arrived at by mutual agreement in London.

Approaches were made to the Labour Party on these lines. We refused to countenance what we regarded as a negation of democracy. Unless a choice of policies and of candidates is presented to the electorate, how can it express any opinion at all? The whole basis of consent, which gives the strength to our Government, would be destroyed. The people would not have consented because they would not have voted at all! The eight million women who have been most seriously, many of them, considering how to vote, would find themselves cheated. So would the soldiers. An uncontested election is, from the standpoint of democracy, no election at all.

Fortunately, the Labour Party, and now, as I gather, Mr Asquith's Liberal Party, refuses to enter into the compact to dispense with contests, and with the submission of policies to the electorate; and to the extent to which these two sections can effectively put candidates into the field, the rights of the electorate will be preserved. But over a large part of the country the Coalition Compact will apparently supersede any real consultation of the electors.

It seems to me that this Coalition Compact, now exposed to all, ought to enable us to understand better the reason why the Labour Party Conference refused to renew the permission (given only for the prosecution of the war) to Labour Party Members of Parliament to hold office in a Ministry dominated by persons of quite opposite policies and opinions than those of Labour members. There may have been good reason to allow Labour members to enter into a Coalition Ministry so long as the prosecution of the war was the overwhelmingly dominant issue, *on which all the members of the Ministry were agreed as to policy*, and compared with which all other issues, on which they differed, sank into relative insignificance. But when a proposal is made to renew the Coalition, for purposes not of war, but of the Reconstruction in Peace – and when it was made quite clear that the other members of the Government were not prepared to adopt, even in the broadest outline, the principles and policy of Reconstruction which the Labour Party has worked out during the last two years, and in which it believes; but were intending, as we sufficiently ascertained, to carry out Reconstruction in nearly every department upon quite contrary principles, and with very different policies – which we believe to be economically unsound and morally wrong – the Labour Party rank and file up and down the country had a sound instinct in rejecting it; and in preferring that the rival principles and policies should be frankly submitted to the electorate for its decision. The Labour Party will do its best to put the issues to the electors, and take their decision. Unfortunately, Mr Lloyd George and his Coalition (which is insisting, mind you, on an absolutely rigid promise from every one of its candidates to vote for every Government measure whatever it is) has so far refused to disclose to the public the lines on which these measures are to be framed. But we know a good deal about it.

Finally, and this is the most serious point. We shall have to face a time of grave industrial unrest, and serious trials to the millions of wage-earners. Some of them are already excited by the events on the Continent. Others are very much disillusioned with Parliamentary Government. I put it to you, what is likely to be the effect on their minds of a Parliament from which, if Mr Lloyd George has his way, every sort of opposition, and every kind of independent Labour representation unpledged to support the Government through thick and thin, is excluded? What confidence will Labor have in a packed Parliament? What authority will they feel that they have given at a general election from which, as far as possible, all genuine contest is eliminated? It seems to me that those who are afraid of 'Bolshevism' would be well-advised not to teach the British workmen to give up the House of Commons as a hopeless institution, removed completely out of their reach. The best antidote to an outbreak of Workmen's and Soldier's Councils seems to me to be a strong and effective, and entirely independent Labour Party in Parliament. I venture to suggest that the constitutional historian of the future will hold that, in this issue, it is the Labour Party which has chosen the wiser, as well as the manlier and the franker course. We believe in consulting the electorate, and in not hindering its choice. I stand myself on this line.

Yours very truly

Sidney Webb

690 LSE SIDNEY WEBB TO WILLIAM PEMBER REEVES

Sir Ernest Cassel (1852–1921), financier and philanthropist, provided £150,000 with which L.S.E. was able to establish a faculty of commerce and offer the B.Com. degree. Blanche Patch became Bernard Shaw's secretary until his death.

41 Grosvenor Road
Westminster Embankment
29.11.18

Dear Director

I was sorry yesterday to find you indisposed. I hope you are better.

1) Enclosed from Manchester College of Technology may interest you – keep it. We ought to have something of the sort at the School when money comes in.

2) I think, by the way, that I *have* got a pretty big sum to throw into your City scheme very shortly from Commerce. I think the donor will ask for the establishment of a distinct Faculty as well as a degree; but he will centre it at the School. More anon.

3) I hope you will tell Headicar to take on the proposed library lady (Miss Patch) *at once full time, until 31 December*. It is only a matter of four or five weeks at £3 a week; and I am sure it would pay in keeping the staff in health and contentment.

Yours
Sidney Webb

691 SU SIDNEY WEBB TO LEONARD WOOLF

William Adamson (1863–1936), a Scots miner, was chairman of the Parliamentary Labour Party from 1917 to 1921. He had, Beatrice noted on 14 January after lunching with him, 'an instinctive suspicion of all intellectuals and enthusiasts'.

41 Grosvenor Road
Westminster Embankment
10.4.19

Dear Woolf

Adamson, the Leader of the Parliamentary Labour Party, asked me today to furnish him privately with notes for his speech next week, when Lloyd George relates what he has done at Paris.

It is worth while to help him to this, not only for its own sake, but also to encourage him to make use of the Advisory Committees etc. But I am incapable of doing it and also have absolutely no time.

If you could possibly do this for him it would be most valuable.

What seems to me required is a series of succinct notes on each of the points that Lloyd George is likely to touch on, with any appropriate comments that the Labour Party ought to make, from your point of view.

If you would be so good as to do this, please accompany it with any of the memos on subjects that the Advisory Committee has prepared – these *by themselves* would not do, as he could not use them but they might usefully illustrate your notes – and send them to him at the H. of C. as soon as you can, saying you sent them at my request.

I should be grateful if you would send me a card, or a telephone message, saying you could do this. But I hope to be at the International Advisory Committee on Monday.

Yours

Sidney Webb

692 PP SIDNEY TO BEATRICE

In late February 1919 the Webbs again dined privately at Haldane's to meet Lloyd George. Beatrice took the opportunity of telling the Prime Minister about her minority report on equal pay. But Lloyd George wanted to discuss the membership of a royal commission on the mining industry. In January the miners' union had threatened to strike for higher wages, shorter hours and nationalisation. It seemed likely that this strike would be backed by the railwaymen and transport workers. Lloyd George had offered a commission of enquiry if the strike were called off. Sidney counselled the miners' leader Robert Smillie (1857–1940) to accept on certain conditions – especially the right of the miners to choose their own members of the commission. Under the repeated threat of a strike Lloyd George appointed three colliery owners, three other employers, three miners and three experts chosen by the union. These three were Webb, Tawney and Leo Chiozza-Money (1870–1944), a Liberal Fabian. The chairman of the commission, which began sitting on 3 March, was Sir John Sankey (1866–1948), a judge who later joined the Labour Party and in 1929 became Lord Chancellor.

Herbert Smith (1863–1938), a Yorkshire miner, was president of the Mineworkers' Federation of Great Britain in 1921; Sir Alan Smith was a solicitor who was chairman of the Engineering and Allied Employers National Federation, and had replaced Sir Thomas Royden, a shipping magnate, on the Commission; Frank Hodges (1887–1947) was the secretary of the M.E.G.B. in 1918.

On 12 March Beatrice noted that Sidney was 'enjoying himself hugely'. The significance of the proceedings, she thought, lay in 'the precedent set for similar state trials of the organisation of each industry by a court made up, half of the prosecuting proletariat, half of the capitalist defendants, with power to call for all accounts and all documents and to search out the most secret ways of the profitmaking craft'. On 20 March the Sankey Commission rushed out an interim report conceding higher wages and a seven-hour day. This proposal was accepted by the miners. On the next report, appearing on 23 June and dealing with questions of nationalisation and control, there was no agreement. The chairman produced one plan, the six Labour members another, five of the six employers a third version, and the fourth came from Sir Arthur Duckham (1879–1952), a consulting engineer who had been in charge of aircraft production during the war. All the plans favoured nationalisation of the unmined coal; only Sankey and the Labour members went so far as public ownership of the industry in any form. Lloyd George seized on these variants to claim that there was no majority for any course of action.

Dr Ethel Bentham was a Labour M.P. and a member of the Labour executive.

41 Grosvenor Road
Westminster Embankment
22.4.19

Dear One

It is a quarter past 10, and I have only just finished dinner! I met Tawney and Money and Herbert Smith, with Cole and Arnot at 4 p.m. at 25 Tothill St to concert our action; and the Commission met at 5 p.m. We sat until nearly 9.30! We had spent a couple of hours arranging the evidence – nothing from the Mineowners – when Alan Smith, who had sat quiet, started to break up the Commission. We had asked for the Mineowners Scheme for Unification; and he began to discuss the Chairman's Report, on the lines of suggesting that if the Mineowners were to be restricted to Nationalisation or Unification (in whatever form) it was evidently a prejudged issue, and they might as well resign. Sankey got very angry with him, and after an hour's wrangle, we separated into two sides. Sankey came into our side, and said that he had been aware that Alan Smith intended to break up the Commission, and that it was for the Commission not to give the Mineowners an excuse for withdrawing. Herbert Smith said the Miners were only on day-to-day contracts; and if the Commission broke up there would be a strike in three days (Smillie and Hodges were away). Sankey then went into the others, and argued with them for an hour or so – we waiting meanwhile and being given tea and biscuits. Eventually we were called together, and it appeared that he had patched things up, temporarily, with difficulty – the Mineowners to meet their clients tomorrow to consider what to do. We meet at 11 at the Kings Robing Room, when we shall hear half-a-dozen economists, including Wallas perhaps (his statement is not in, and Tawney has gone off to see him about it, and get him as right as he can).

I *think* the Commission will go on, including the Mineowners; or *perhaps* even if they withdraw.

We shall probably not sit on Mondays and Saturdays; and take an additional fortnight, bringing us to the week before Whitsunday – which suits me pretty well.

I enclose my Statement of Evidence, which seems all right – also Cole's, which is ingenious and interesting.

As to the Local Government Conference, Arnot said there were up to just before Easter about 90 delegates notified – this is not so bad. I could not consult about speakers, etc.

The Lloyds called in the afternoon, bringing the corrected proofs of his introductions for each section, very well done, I think. He has to start for Paris this week, so cannot see Morant; but he is to write him, sending proofs, and asking him to depute someone to see Arnot about them. Mrs Lloyd hopes to be able to join him at Paris soon, as his secretary, if she can get a passport.

Dr Ethel Bentham had called.

I travelled up first class with *nine* in the compartment – an American officer, and Australian ditto, an English ditto, an Italian person of official status with his wife, with three others – the whole train packed, and a quarter of an hour late.

Now this is all for tonight, as it is 11 p.m., and I doubt whether you can get this by the afternoon post. I have remembered to tell Emily about the beds for Monday. I like to think you are probably already asleep. Good-night.

Sidney

693 PP SIDNEY TO BEATRICE

Arthur Cecil Pigou (1877–1959) became professor of political economy at Cambridge in 1908. The leading exponent of Marshall's economic theories, he showed a marked social sympathy which was reflected in his standard work, *The Economics of Welfare*, 1912. Sir William Ashley, whom the Webbs had known for forty years, was professor of commerce at Birmingham University. Sir Arthur Balfour (1873–1957), later Lord Riverdale, was a Sheffield industrialist who was active in public affairs. Sir Arthur Steel-Maitland was now chairman of the L.S.E. W. P. Reeves was resigning the post of Director at L.S.E.

At this time Beatrice was drafting *A Constitution for the Socialist Commonwealth of Great Britain.*

41 Grosvenor Road
Westminster Embankment
23.4.19

Dear One

We had an uneventful morning at the Commission with Pigou and Ashley, who took up all the time from 11 a.m. to 2 p.m. when we adjourned for lunch, and did not resume – leaving the afternoon for the Mineowners to confer with all the rest of them, who are gathered in London. Tomorrow we have another private session in the morning and a public one at 2 p.m. for the rest of the economists, though we shall hardly get through more than two or three – the others will presumably be taken on Friday. Pigou and Ashley count on the whole to our side, and we had only a little friendly questioning. No one could make much out of them. There is very general disapproval and blame of Alan Smith, as having wantonly tried to break up the Commission – I mean he is much disliked by Balfour and Duckham. The Coalowners have said nothing, but I think they personally dislike him.

Steel-Maitland is coming to see me tonight at 6 to 7. He seems to hesitate about Keynes, whose brilliancy he admits, but of whom he for some reason disapproves as Director. I shall hear about it tonight.

I managed to write an article this morning between 9 and 10.30 a.m. on the Economics of Nationalisation, which does very well to keep the idea going.

Now I must send this off to ensure your getting it tomorrow morning, when perhaps I shall get another little welcome note from my B.

Yours

Sidney

694 BEV SIDNEY WEBB TO SIR WILLIAM BEVERIDGE

At the end of April Sidney 'had to undertake the unpleasant duty of telling an old friend that the time had come for him to resign'. (BWD 29 April 1919) Reeves, who had an imperious manner, had caused discontent among the L.S.E. staff and come to an 'open break' with the school secretary, Miss Mactaggart. Reeves tried to cling to the post, bitterly resenting Sidney's refusal to let old friendship sway his judgement. Sidney's first choice for his successor was J. M. Keynes; hence the reference in his letter to Beatrice on 23 April 1919. He was unaware that Keynes disliked the Webbs and had no intention of being inveigled into any of their ventures. William Beveridge was among three possible successors on the final list: on 4 May Sidney wrote to ask if he were interested in the post. On 23 June Beatrice noted that Beveridge 'has his defects – he is not the sweetest-tempered of men and has a certain narrowness of outlook. But he is a good administrator, an initiator of both ideas and plans and a man who will concentrate his energies on the School'. The judgement proved correct. Though the Webbs did not care for Beveridge personally, disapproved of his indiscreetly close relationship with Mrs Janet Mair, who became a dominating secretary of the L.S.E., and were uneasy when Beveridge adopted autocratic attitudes towards the staff, they respected his energetic promotion of the L.S.E. in the ensuing fifteen years.

41 Grosvenor Road
Westminster Embankment
17.5.19

Dear Beveridge

I don't want to hurry you, or to imply anything either way. But you ought to be reminded that time is running on; and it may be found necessary for the Chairman and his colleagues at the School of Economics to come to a decision as between possible candidates. No date is yet fixed, even implicitly; but I am a little anxious lest some one may presently be fixed upon without your name being responsibly considered.

The fact that Reeves will be released at the end of this month in itself leads to pressure for some decision, although the actual carrying on is not difficult of arrangement. Moreover, the Senate approval has to be obtained: and this makes a *June* decision imperative – hence we must be getting on.

Ever

Sidney Webb

695 SU BEATRICE WEBB TO LEONARD WOOLF

Henry Noel Brailsford (1873–1958) was a distinguished socialist journalist. *A League of Nations*, published in 1917, helped create a climate of opinion and is said to have greatly influenced Woodrow Wilson. He was a brilliant editor of the I.L.P.'s *New Leader* 1922–26. His anti-imperialist book, *The War of Steel and Gold*, appeared in 1914.

41 Grosvenor Road
Westminster Embankment
29th May 1919

Dear Mr Woolf

Could you give me any references to books or pamphlets containing apt quotations from business sources demonstrating the close connection between the greed of markets and the arming of nations and the outbreak of war? I have got plenty of quotations from German books proving the connection in German policy between the development of the export trade and world power. But I have got nothing specific or authentic from British or French sources. I need this material for use in our chapter on the Failure of the Capitalist System. When will your book be published? I shall want to quote from that. But in general, I think I had better avoid quotations from admittedly pacifist authors. For instance, I looked at Brailsford's book on *The War of Steel and Gold* and I find that it is general denunciation, which is not much use for my purpose. One wants to convict the financial imperialists out of their own mouths.

Always yours

Beatrice Webb
(Mrs Sidney Webb)

696 KCC SIDNEY WEBB TO J. M. KEYNES

At the beginning of June, feeling that the Allies were devastating Europe by the proposed Treaty of Versailles, Keynes threw up his post as Treasury representative on the Supreme Economic Council and other committees involved in drafting the peace settlement. Three days after this letter from Webb he began to write his indictment of Versailles, *The Economic Consequences of the Peace*.

Sir George Murray (1886–1947) was a civil servant who was secretary to the Post Office 1914–1934. Philippa Fawcett, the daughter of Henry and Millicent Fawcett, was a Newnham graduate in mathematics who became an assistant education officer in the L.C.C. in 1905.

Keynes was no more interested in becoming head of the faculty of commerce at L.S.E. than in becoming its Director. He was cutting down his academic commitments at Cambridge to give himself time to make money in the City.

41 Grosvenor Road
Westminster Embankment
20.6.19

My dear Keynes

We are naturally in the dark; but my wife and I venture to offer our heartiest congratulations *and* sympathies on your withdrawal from what we suspect was a horrid atmosphere – whilst expressing very great appreciation of the devotion and ability with which you so long grappled with a thankless task, as we hear. What an exhibition it has been of a vulgar greed and passion, which seems as senseless and shortsighted as it is otherwise deplorable!

However, we do not know all the facts, and I try to suspend judgement.

What impels me to write is another matter. You may remember that I am one of the trustees of Sir Ernest Cassel's gift of half a million, part of which is to endow a Faculty of Commerce at the University of London, which will be centred at the London School of Economics (the new Director of which will be, assuming ratification in the next four weeks by the University Senate etc., Sir William Beveridge KCB). The other trustees are Asquith, Balfour, Haldane, Herbert Fisher, Sir George Murray and Miss Philippa Fawcett.

The formal institution of the new Faculty goes slowly, owing to complications of University machinery etc. But at the trustees' meeting last night there was a unanimous desire expressed, so far as the new Chair of Banking and Currency is concerned (exact title not settled) to 'short-circuit' the matter; and to get *you* at once to accept the appointment at £1,000 a year, plus 10% contributed to the University Superannuation Fund. (This latter is on a Life Assurance basis; the beneficiary contributing also 5% of the salary, and the two sums (i.e. £150 a year) being used as premiums for an endowment policy payable at death or at 60, the policy being handed over to the beneficiary on any prior retirement.) The Trustees expressed the very cordial hope that you would see your way to take up this work. They believe that there is a really big opportunity to make the Chair of supreme use, in a way that no professorship in the subject has ever yet been in this country; with the quickened appreciation of the importance of finance, the new willingness both in the City and in the civil service to learn, and the chance of setting the standard for other universities (meaning particularly those in the industrial centres), and attracting post-graduate students.

It is not possible, as you will understand, to make you formally the offer of the new University Chair that is to be established. But I was asked to write or see you at once, and to say that you could be immediately appointed definitely to do the work – the desire was that you should begin next session (October) lecturing at the School of Economics on the terms named.

I think you will understand that it will be quite within the capacity of those concerned to ensure the carrying out of their intentions with regard to the University Chair. In the meantime the Governors of the School of Economics would make the appointment and assume the liability, at the Trustees' request; and you would be formally recognised as a university teacher, member of Faculty and Board of Studies and so on. It is only the formal creation of a London University Professorship that has to be postponed.

You would, of course, be the head of the department of Banking and Currency, with freedom to map out what should be done, and to initiate developments. There will presumably be an Assistant Professor (or Lecturer or Reader), who would work under you, and on whom would devolve the bulk of the junior tuition; and there should, I assume, be also courses from time to time on special subjects, by whatever 'experts' can be found who can express themselves intelligibly(!). But all this we should look to you to advise on.

Foxwell, as you know, has lectured in London on the subject – with most admirable success, and to everybody's satisfaction – for a score of years. But the University Senate won't believe that he is not too old, and has definitely refused to continue him. We may still be able to have his services for some lecturing. He has kept his classes together with great success; but under all sorts of difficulties. Now I hope there is the chance of a great bound forward. The banking world is at last much more sympathetic; and with the concurrence of King's College, the School of Economics will come forward to meet them.

I need hardly say that all that I write is in confidence, and must not be divulged; but Foxwell would tell you all about the School of Economics, and you are of course free to consult him and anyone else in confidence as to the proposal itself.

Yours very truly

Sidney Webb

697 PP SIDNEY TO BEATRICE [*incomplete*]

The victorious Allies were supporting anti-Bolshevik armies still engaged in the Russian civil war and the British had landed a force at Archangel. In the Labour movement there was a growing demand for 'direct action' to stop intervention and, at the least, to stop the shipment of supplies to White armies. There was, moreover, a marked drift towards the use of industrial action for other political ends, such as the ending of conscription, or the demand of the miners for nationalisation. The issue dominated the Labour Party Conference which Sidney was attending in Southport. Beatrice was at Longfords.

[Southport]
[22.6.19]

At the [Labour] Executive Committee we had a long discussion about 'Direct Action', which Robert Williams and the I.L.P. members are agitating for in the country at great demonstrations, and to which Henderson violently objects, with the majority of the Executive. We stand to our view that it is not our business; that it is solely for the trade unions to decide whether or not they will ballot for a 24-hours strike against intervention in Russia etc.; and that we as a party do not advise it, as our business is for Parliamentary action. I think it will all go off in smoke and 'hot air'. We are, however, to receive Jouhaux and another delegate from the Confédération Générale du Travail tomorrow on the subject. The real inwardness of the situation is that the French and Swedish (and perhaps the Italian) *officials* would much prefer the English to refuse, and give them an excuse to their own members!

I have now seen the *Morning Post* and *The Times* on the Coal Commission Report. The former is wholly abusive, and finishes up with an appeal to the Duke of Northumberland to fight the Schemes to the death! *The Times* is much more half-hearted, and evidently expects legislation.

I have also seen the *Herald* which, according to what is to be expected from it, omits all names except those of the Miners Federation.

I have a nice personal letter from Cooper, the Durham Coalowner – on the Commission, which I enclose (I have answered it).

But I must now close to catch the post. Goodbye Dear One.

Sidney

698 PP SIDNEY TO BEATRICE

The estimate was for the redecoration of Grosvenor Road. Henderson's eldest son, David, had been killed in 1916; the two other sons, Arthur and Will, both became Labour M.P.s.

The request from Rowntree was for a series of lectures.

Prince of Wales Hotel
Southport
23.6.19

Dear One

I enclose Sims' estimate which comes to £185, and seems a sufficiently great difference to warrant preferring him.

I see the *Manchester Guardian* and *Daily News* accept Sankey's Report as the inevitable basis for early legislation, but without much warmth – as is natural! I have not yet seen *The Times*, but I expect it to take the same line. The Labour Party is well satisfied, and such miners' leaders as I have seen. Hodges is radiant: he has brought a nice-looking, simple wife. There are lots of wives and children here. Henderson's two sons are also here – the second just demobilised from being a captain in the artillery; he is going to Cambridge next October, and proposes to become a barrister. Ramsay MacDonald is here, in his usual form. He says the Socialists all over Europe, whilst hot against the Peace Treaty, are also indignant with the Germans, and wish to take a 'European' attitude about the peace terms, rather than a pro-German one, protesting against the Treaty on the grounds that it does not rebuild the economic life of the world, and provide for general industrial reconstruction. This is his usual good sense in council and in criticism. It is a pity he is not more constructive.

Today it is cold here, and windy and cheerless, and I am dispirited at being away from my dear counsellor and companion. But I am glad to think that she is probably resting and comfortable, walking in the woods and on the common. I hope Mary is well.

P.S. I hardly know what to say to the enclosed from Seebohm Rowntree. If it were £30 for three Fridays and Saturdays it might be worth earning the money. But if it is only £10 *for the three*, it is not good enough. I don't know what to answer, and shall wait until I see you.

S [Sidney Webb]

699 PP SIDNEY TO BEATRICE

Among foreign delegates expected at the Labour conference were Jean Longuet (1876–1938), the grandson of Karl Marx and the leader of the minority wing of the French Socialist Party; and Camille Huysmans (1871–1968), the Flemish socialist, who had been secretary of the International Socialist Bureau since 1905.

Sidney came top of the poll for the Labour executive: his work on the Sankey Commission had earned him much trade union support.

Prince of Wales Hotel
Southport
25/6/19

Dear One

I am sure it is just as well that the typewriter has refused to work! It will throw you more into the open air, and into the companionship of the family, both of which may be what you need!

As to the two estimates, I don't know that there is much to choose between them. The notice as to possible rises of wages, etc. will apply to both.

Our foreigners did not arrive until 10 last night, so we have not yet met them. Longuet and another are rumoured to have been stopped at Folkestone somehow, and to have returned to Paris – cause unknown. I have not seen anyone to ask this morning.

Now we are at the beginning of the Conference, the Executive seated in bright electric light on the stage of a gigantic theatre, the delegates forming the audience, and nearly filling the hall, being in darkened light. This is the only place here big enough for us; and it has been lent to us free of charge for the three days, with organ performance thrown in, just for the sake of the advertisement (and the delegates' possible patronage in the evening). McGurk, the Chairman, is reading his dull speech. No one can foresee what the conference will do, or whether it will amount to anything at all (as seems most probable). Whether we shall get the delegates to increase the party's revenue is not quite sure – the Miners having decided to approve the increase by 1d., but to disapprove the abolition of grants to candidates (which cost 1d. at present). On the other hand the Textiles have disapproved the increase of the contribution. I told Henderson if they both acted strictly on their mandates, they would cancel each other in both cases; and leave the smaller Unions to carry what the Executive desires.

I have invited Huysmans to come to us anytime on Saturday or Sunday next, *if he can*. He expects to be detained here until Saturday, and he may have to go straight home, without any time in London. He is quite cheerful about his own prospects. He seems to have recovered the support both of Vandervelde and the *Partie Ouvriere*, and has been unanimously chosen to head the list of party candidates for his constituency, which ensures his re-election (in October); and he has become connected with a big Flemish newspaper at Antwerp, for which he writes. He is, however, gloomy as to the state of Belgium.

Last night old Ashton, the ex-Secretary of the Miners' Federation, got hold of me and asked most affectionately after *you*, telling me that he had known you before I had, and that he had never been able to accept your repeated invitation, as whenever he was in London, he had no minute to spare!

Smillie is the hero of this Conference. When he rose this morning (to support Robert Williams' desire for some kind of favor to 'Direct Action') the whole conference cheered uproariously and at length. It is a great pity he cannot be got into the Executive Committee, and, indeed, the House of Commons so that he might share responsibility; and also so that the support he receives should be behind the Executive, instead of being always a separative influence, and sometimes a disuniting one.

On the whole I think an election will have become almost inevitable in the Autumn. The feeling in favor of 'doing something' to stop the Government is certainly growing; and there *will* be strikes, I think. But, anyhow, the Labour Party will do well to prepare for an Election, and to believe in it.

Hodges told me last night that I was to get the full 600 votes of the miners for the Executive Committee – which doubtless secures my election. Miss MacArthur has not yet arrived, and maybe delayed until too late, which militates against her chance, although I think she will get in as there are finally only 6 candidates for 4 seats (but the other new candidate is the textile nominee).

I shall be glad to get home on Friday night. I do not get good sleep here, though I eat carefully. And I can't get on with rearrangements at the School whilst I am away, or proceed with other work. I do not forget, also, that you are struggling on alone with the book; and we must try to get our joint efforts concentrated on it. The fact is that I miss both the companionship and the inspiration – the eleven becomes suddenly only one when it is severed – and I want to come home.

Sidney

700 BEV SIDNEY WEBB TO SIR WILLIAM BEVERIDGE

Thomas Fisher Unwin (1848–1935), the founder of the publishing firm, was married to Jane, the daughter of Richard Cobden (1804–65), the great spokesman for Free Trade. She offered her father's old home at Dunsford, near Midhurst, as a country retreat for L.S.E. staff and students. The gift was accepted but there were recurring problems. The house was not greatly used; it cost the School money and above all Mrs Unwin remained possessively fretful about the condition of the house and the behaviour of the students who used it. Though in 1922 the Webbs seriously considered building a cottage for their retirement in the grounds, the gift was eventually renounced in exchange for a financial donation to L.S.E.

Bryan's Ground
Presteign
Radnorshire
1.8.19

Dear Beveridge

(1) Please consider what to do about Headicar. At the urgent request of Reeves, the Council of Management was urged, and it agreed, to raise his salary from £300 to £450 (which is *none* too much for the post, and the increase does not equal his increased cost of living since 1914). But we did not take into consideration what has now happened, *viz* a request from the new School of Librarianship at University College that he should give there a course on Librarianship (2 hours a week) for £100 a year. *It is desirable* that he should accept this, and relinquish the course he gave at the School for nothing, largely for the instruction of his own staff, and a few outsiders.

I should say, unhesitatingly, let him have the extra money; but two things need consideration, (1) it may be a precedent for other 'full time' people to ask to be allowed to do work outside for money; (2) Miss Mactaggart may not be pleased at his getting altogether £550 to her £600: I know she thinks she is worth more than he is by £200! Headicar is so good and ungrasping that he would (I am sure) be willing to forego the extra pay(!), but we ought not to take advantage of his sweetness.

Altogether I don't know what to advise. How would it be to propose to ask him to surrender to the School *half* this 'outside' earning?

(2) The other matter is a bigger thing. Fisher Unwin, the publisher (or his wife) is the owner of a Victorian mansion with 150 acres of free-

hold land $1\frac{1}{2}$ miles from Midhurst, which was the home of Richard Cobden. *He has practically offered this to me for the School as a gift.* The difficulty is (a) there is no endowment, and though some 100 acres is let to a farmer the rent – say £100 a year or so – would not suffice for taxes, upkeep etc.; (b) I believe the house, though in good structural repair, and inhabited up to three years ago, is unfurnished. He does not want the matter talked about until finally settled. Now, a country house, in charming grounds and pleasant country, would be a most valuable adjunct. The Fabian Society found no difficulty in making pay Barrow House on Derwentwater, including a rent of £200 a year, and the purchase of much furniture. I am told that Swanwick is easily made to pay; and that Jordans is now booked for parties months ahead. My idea is that we could run 'reading parties', 'weekends' and 'Summer Schools' nearly all the year round, with great educational advantage to our own students and others. Some of the professors would like to go there from time to time, especially if we let them (as Directors) go there free of charge.

I have written out a scheme (enclosed), which incorporates what I gather are the donor's desires with my own ideas of the ends the gift *might* be made to serve. I propose to submit this to the donor presently, when I hear from you and Steel-Maitland. (The donor would give a considerable nucleus of the proposed Library, with busts, pictures and other memorials of Cobden.)

I should, of course, propose to run the place by a separate Committee, and to appoint a permanent Housekeeper (a capable woman director). We might have to raise a couple of thousand pounds to furnish the house – we might borrow this and repay annually – and we should have to make a few hundreds a year out of it to pay the Housekeeper and other expenses. But the demand for such places is very great.

Would there be any objection (from political Tariff Reformers) to accepting a Cobdenite Memorial? We ought to be able to overcome this. After all, we are all Free Traders as an ideal(!); and Cobden actually negotiated a Reciprocity Treaty! You may talk it over with Miss Mactaggart and Sir Arthur Steel-Maitland, to whom I have written.

Yours

Sidney Webb

### 701 MMLMU BEATRICE WEBB TO BERTRAND RUSSELL

Major C. H. Douglas (1879–1952) was an engineer who became a currency reformer and founder of the Social Credit movement. He had some influence on Labour intellectuals, especially the Guild Socialists in their final phase. A. K. Orage swung his weekly *New Age* behind Douglas, publishing his *Economic Democracy* in general form between June and August 1919. Douglas later became a neo-fascist and anti-semite.

Russell had run for Lord Rector of Glasgow University against Gilbert Murray, as a Liberal, and Andrew Bonar Law (1858–1923) as a Conservative. Bonar Law won, Russell coming last with a mere eighty votes.

41 Grosvenor Road
Westminster Embankment
28th October 1919

My dear Bertrand

I send you under separate cover, the whole series of articles of Major Douglas, in which he describes his new scheme for organising industry and the philosophy which underlies it. Neither Sidney nor I can understand the one or the other. But perhaps your keener and more subtle intellect may fathom his meaning. His philosophical position seems a strange jumble of separate propositions with regard to the facts and social expediency. As for his scheme, I cannot visualise it, and his use of economic and commercial terms is bewildering. However, if such an able man as Orage has been enthused by it, there must be something in it, and it is exactly this something that I want to get at. But at the present time I have not the remotest idea what it is.

If you feel inclined to bring the articles back and to discuss it some Sunday afternoon before we meet on the 19th or 20th (I have not heard which day Orage has selected) we should be very glad to see you.

I am sorry you did not get a better vote for Glasgow University; but the university students of Scotland are almost as bad as university graduates, in fact I think they are worse. You would have done better at Oxford, the home of lost causes.

Always yours

Beatrice Webb

P.S. I have just got a letter from Orage saying that he and Douglas will come on the 19th, so I will expect you then in any case (7.30 – morning dress).

[*Note by Russell on letter*]
The W's asked me to lunch to meet Douglas and Orage, and undertook to adopt whatever opinion I formed of Douglas's scheme as their own. I thought the scheme fallacious and told Douglas so. The W's accepted my judgement.

702 MUL SIDNEY WEBB TO E. D. SIMON

The trade union book had been revised and brought up to date. The Webbs had always sought ways of producing cheap versions of their work. The success of this venture led them to make a practice of producing subscription editions. They ran off 19,000 copies at five shillings and the income was sufficient to cover the whole cost, making the receipts from the 3,000 copies sold commercially a windfall profit.

41 Grosvenor Road
Westminster Embankment
8.11.19

Dear Simon

1) There will be a *Statesman* Board meeting at 2.30, and Annual General Meeting at 3 p.m. on *Friday, 28 November*. I hope this will suit you.

2) I am grateful for your invitation to stay (at Lawnhurst) for the night of 2 December when I am to lecture at the Technical College – which I am doing, honestly, because they offered me £20 for it. We are hard up this year, and exceeding our income – which must be happening to thousands living on investments – so that I have to earn whatever honest pennies offer themselves, though very eager to get time for thinking and writing before the end for me comes.

3) We are just reprinting revising and bringing down to date our *History of Trade Unionism* which will sell for 21/- net; and as a corollary of that high price, I am arranging to let individual trade unionists, applying now, have the book on cheaper paper for 4/- paper cover or 5/- plain cloth! I have to take a risk; but *if* they take several thousands, I can do that without loss. If they take more, I should make a little profit, even at that price, but the object is to enable them to get the book. This transaction we keep dark about, as regards the public and the booksellers; otherwise it might spoil the sale of the good edition, which may be ready in January.

4) What an unexpected Labour triumph at the Municipal Elections. I hope you will like the new Council better than the old, and will find it more efficient.

Yours

Sidney Webb

703 MUL SIDNEY WEBB TO E. D. SIMON

Simon had responded to what seemed a hint for financial help in Webb's letter of 8 November by offering money to support their research. From this time there is a recurring concern about money in the Webb letters. Though they were comfortably off, and in the next few years were able to maintain a modest London home and a country cottage, they felt that they were living up to their income and that they must watch their expenditure carefully. Despite legends of their parsimony they in fact entertained a great deal; their considerable research costs approximately balanced the income from their books over a period of years.

41 Grosvenor Road
Westminster Embankment
17.11.19

My dear Simon

My wife and I are much touched at your most generous offer, and very grateful to you. But we do not really need it at present. We regard our dividends as our salary, and we have the inestimable privilege of choosing our work! This year we have had to sell out (only £450 which you won't think much) to make both ends meet; but this is not serious as our expenses included some outlay in the nature of capital, which will not recur. We shall have a heavy printer's bill for the new edition of the *History of Trade Unionism* continued down to date, but that will be remunerative in the long run; and we expect the trade unionists will pay cash down for enough copies that we are letting them have at 5/- instead of a guinea(!) to go a long way to meet that. And we hope to let our house for three months in the Spring to rich Americans – we retiring to a cottage to write more.

Altogether, we can pull through. What I meant by my remark was that it seemed to 'pay' me to earn a few pounds where I could easily do so, in part recoupment of our secretarial and similar expenses.

I have refused to write for the daily newspapers under £25 for an article; which prevents me from being importuned except occasionally by the *Daily News*, *Morning Post* and *Observer*! But of course, I write for nothing for the Labour people.

I quite appreciate what you have in your mind as to the danger or waste of frittering away one's time and energy over matters not primarily important. On the other hand, it is essential (a) not to get out of touch with the 'movements' which one seeks to influence; (b) to acquire the confidence of their people by sharing in their trivial work and helping them; and (c) to get information by taking places on government committees etc. All the more reason, you may say, for not digressing further in order merely to make money! That is true; but the making of money by writing or lecturing on one's own subjects is itself part of the propaganda; and is counted to me for merit by the labour movement, and by one's personal followers. The articles and lectures gain adhesions.

But we have to be on our guard against too much dispersion of thought and energy; and we do strive, accordingly, to reserve time for thought and more concentrated writing. It would not be good to concentrate wholly in that way. It is, for instance, not profitable (for us at least) to spend more than a few hours a day at our main task; or to waste the rest of the day in what is called amusement!

You are so kind that I say frankly that I would turn to you if any financial emergency did threaten to suspend our work; and lay the position candidly before you. For the moment our investments are good; and our nominal gross income is *below* the level to which I apprehend much additional taxation. (We should, of course, lose by any heavy 'Capital Levy'; but not much, I imagine, in income, if the Income Tax were reduced.)

I repeat, that we are both most grateful for your very magnificent offer; and if we do not accept it, the very fact of our being on such terms with you (that you could make the offer, and that we should be willing to accept it were it needed) is, in itself, a great pleasure to me.

Yours very truly

Sidney Webb

704 PP SIDNEY WEBB TO LUJO BRENTANO

Most socialists were angered by the punitive terms of the Versailles settlement and showed strong sympathy with the civilian population in Germany which was suffering an economic blockade. 'My thought and feeling goes out to Germany in her heroic struggle to reconstruct her political and social machinery', Beatrice wrote. 'The future of the civilised world depends on her success.' (BWD 14 January 1919) The international socialist conference planned for February was put off to a summer meeting in Geneva.

41 Grosvenor Road
Westminster Embankment
15th December 1919

My dear Professor Brentano

It is extremely kind of you to let us have the proceedings of the Bavarian Socialisation Commission. Do you require it back again? It will probably reach us in a few posts after the receipt of your letter.

My husband and I are very distressed about the retention of the German prisoners in France. The difficulty is that it is impracticable to compel the British Government to take any strong measures against the French. I think we have returned all our prisoners? The behaviour of the French is, of course, detestable and our Government has its responsibility. But then our Government is quite out of our own control – i.e. the Labour and Socialist control. The Government is losing ground rapidly in the constituencies, but there is at present no alternative to Lloyd George, and I am very much afraid that owing to the financial weakness of the Labour Party and difficulties arising from its constitution based on Trade Unionism, it will hardly come into power at the next election. The situation all over the world is most gloomy and most of us feel that the British Empire is in an unwholesome state – what with Ireland, India and Egypt. The only hope is in the U.S.A., but that seems rather an uncertain one at the present time.

The International Socialist Congress will probably be put off from February to July or August. But my husband and I will certainly be there and we hope that we may meet you. I should like to make an excursion into Germany: but we are getting old, and we have a lot of work to complete.

We are making arrangements for the translation of our new edition of the *History of Trade Unionism* – the latter part of which may interest you.

Pray let us have any interesting information about Germany and any articles that you write which you think relevant to propaganda in England.

We should, in particular, like all schemes of socialisation or any reports on the working of those that have been adopted.

Always yours sincerely

Beatrice Webb

(Mrs Sidney Webb)

705 PP BEATRICE WEBB TO GRAHAM WALLAS

Margaret Whetham was the granddaughter of Beatrice's eldest sister Lawrencina Holt: her mother Catherine was married to the Cambridge scientist Sir William C. Dampier-(Whetham). May was the only daughter of Graham and Audrey Wallas: a Newnham student, she subsequently taught French and Italian at L.S.E.

41 Grosvenor Road
Westminster Embankment
5th March 1920

My dear Graham,

You have never called for your umbrella: shall I send it to the School? Let us know by telephone (Victoria: 7413).

I think I told you that Sidney and I are writing an elaborate report for the Fabian Society on the constitution of the Socialist State in Great Britain, and making novel proposals alike for the national government and for the conduct of industries and services. We are just finishing the preliminary part giving a necessarily cursory description of democratic organisation as it at present exists – consumers, producers and citizens. I wonder whether you are too busy to go through both this Part I, and later on Part II, giving our proposals? If not, I should be very grateful if I might send you Part I in a few days as I want your criticisms of our description. We are going to take it down to the Shaws on the 13th so it would be convenient if you could let us have Part I back again by Saturday week. We could send it to you tomorrow if you would 'phone through.

By the way, Margaret Whetham was delighted with May and May's kindness in making her acquaintance. She says she was the most interesting girl at Newnham. It would be very kind of May if she would see something of her, as I believe she is very melancholy, partly because of her domestic trouble about her mother who I think I told you was in a mental home.

With love to Audrey

Always yours

Beatrice Webb

706 NLW BEATRICE WEBB TO THOMAS JONES

Robert Morant died suddenly of septic pneumonia in mid-March. The Webbs had always had a high opinion of him: 'with all his faults – and he had some grave ones – he remains one of the biggest minds and one of the most attractive personalities I have known . . . as a brilliant and devoted public servant and also as a true friend'. (BWD 18 March 1920)

The Webbs had first met Sir John Anderson (1882–1958), later Viscount Waverley, in India. He was secretary to the Ministry of Shipping 1917–19 and later a prominent Conservative statesman, becoming Home Secretary in the Second World War. Sir Aubrey Symonds (1874–1931) was second secretary of the Ministry of Health 1919–25, and he became Permanent Secretary to the Board of Education in 1925.

On 18 March, after receiving a reply from Jones that reassured her and seeing 'Symonds' sinister expression' at the Morant memorial service Beatrice concluded 'that this calamity to Morant's work will be avoided'.

41 Grosvenor Road
Westminster Embankment
16 March 1920

PRIVATE

Dear Mr Tom Jones

Sidney and I are very much concerned about Sir Robert Morant's death, not only from a personal point of view – and he was one of our best friends – but also from the standpoint of the reorganisation of Local Government in relation to health. I wonder whether it would be possible to get Sir John Anderson as Permanent Head of the Ministry of Health? That is really the only chance of preventing the Ministry of Health from relapsing into a Poor Law Board, which might suit the Labour Party excellently, but would not suit the people of England! And as I do not think the Labour Party will come into power for some time, I prefer to think of the people of England. Seriously, it would be really fatal if Symonds were to be made Permanent Head. I worked with him for three months on the Machinery of Government Committee and he was by conviction a complete reactionary, almost as bad as Kershaw who stopped all the housing saying that there was 'too much reconstruction about'. When he was not openly reactionary he was so shifty and tortuous that it was almost as bad.

If the P.M.'s new party is to have any kind of success it will have to build itself up on National Health as an alternative to the more thorough policy of Socialism. We must at least get a minimum of health even for Capitalism!

Always yours

Beatrice Webb

## 707 MUL BEATRICE WEBB TO PERCY REDFERN

Percy Redfern (1875–1958) was a socialist journalist who joined the Co-operative Wholesale Society in Manchester in 1899, becoming editor of its magazine *The Wheatsheaf* which, by 1920, had a circulation of over 500,000. He wrote the first of his two histories of the C.W.S. in 1913.

41 Grosvenor Road
Westminster Embankment
22nd March 1920

Dear Mr Redfern

It is a very long time since we have seen you or heard from you. When are you coming to London again? We shall be away this week but we expect to be in London during April. After that our plans are uncertain.

We are revising our supplement on the Co-operative Movement which the Labour Research Department is going to issue in a book. If you happen to have a copy by you it would be extremely kind if you would go through it and give us any suggestions for revision. If you have not a copy I will send you one, though they are scarce. In particular I wish you would give us your confidential views as to the right organisation of labour within the Co-operative Movement. Are you a believer in the Employment Union – the A.U.C.E. or do you hold by the decision of the Trades Union Congress that Co-operative employees must be organised in unions extending to other forms of industry? And what about the brainworkers? I cannot make out that there is any adequate organisation of the brainworking employees to protect their freedom and to counteract the bad features of bureaucracy. I have a great faith in the future of professional organisations of brainworkers as a way of curbing the secrecy and favouritism of an hierarchical government of industry. I wish you would give us your frank views, not so much for the Co-operative supplement as for a Report we are writing for the International Socialist Bureau, on the general question of Socialisation.

I send you, under separate cover, a copy of our *History of Trade Unionism*. I have not seen that it has been reviewed in the *Co-operative News*. I wonder who is doing it?

Always yours sincerely
Beatrice Webb
(Mrs Sidney Webb)

## 708 PP SIDNEY TO BEATRICE

Webb was much respected by the miners for his work on their behalf on the Sankey Commission. In August 1919 he was approached by some of the lodges in the Durham constituency of Seaham Harbour to accept nomination as parliamentary candidate. Though he thought of refusing Beatrice encouraged him. She believed that he could not play a significant role in the Labour Party unless he had a seat in Parliament and was thus eligible to sit in a Labour Cabinet. Sidney nevertheless declined to accept until he knew the wishes of the powerful Durham Miners Association. After a delay of five months he accepted nomination and offered to meet all his election expenses. A week later he received a letter from the D.M.A. to say that Seaham was 'a miners' constituency' and that it should be represented by a miner. Sidney then withdrew, but his supporters persisted.

In May it was agreed that he and Beatrice should spend two weeks touring the division and addressing meetings. At the end of the fortnight 'on approval' he was to abide by the decision of the selection conference.

41 Grosvenor Road
Westminster Embankment
14.5.20

Dear One

Here are some letters of no great interest.

It is good to think of you having this perfect weather. I only hope you will be comfortable enough to be able to sleep well. If you will simply rest these days, it will really save time.

I have just received Clark's bill for *History of Trade Unionism*. Including everything, it is £3,168, (of which £3,000 has been paid to them) which includes £111 paid for carriage of parcels and £21.10.6 for despatching and packing them. So that the free delivery of the 19,000 that we agreed to deliver (assuming that the last 500 to W.E.A. [Workers Educational Association] is not included nor the 1,000 they have still in hand) is less than 2d. per copy all round, taking large and small together. We have already received just upon £3,800; we have about £110 due to us; and have still to dispose of about 1,000, which will yield £225 – making a total of £4,135, besides the receipts from Longman, which will by January next (assuming all sold by then), be £1,500, with the American sheets in addition (£225 received, and some £300 to come). *Altogether* we ought eventually to receive some £6,000, for what will have cost us about £3,200 – so that we shall be able to print very freely this year and next, without drawing on our own income. The enclosed letter from the Seaham Secretary indicates that it is my proposal (to hold meetings) that the forthcoming Conference will accept, and I am to hear by Tuesday what arrangements have been made – so that [Egerton] Wake was probably premature.

Here is the Morant Circular, which I have ordered to be struck off.

Now goodbye dearest until Sunday evening.Give my love to Rosie with all proper apologies.

Sidney

709 PP SIDNEY TO BEATRICE

In June W. S. Sanders resigned as secretary of the Fabian Society to work for the League of Nations in Geneva. He was succeeded by F. W. Galton, who had been the first research secretary to the Webbs after their marriage: they were aware that he was amiable, lazy and pettifoggingly dull, lacking in ideas and enthusiasm, but they seem to have made no real effort to find an alternative to him. He had a depressing effect on the Society, which barely survived his period of office.

Both Henderson and MacDonald had been out of Parliament in this critical period in the development of the Labour Party: it was, in effect, being led from outside the House of Commons. Henderson got back at a bye-election in Widnes in September 1919 but MacDonald could not find a seat. He spent much of his time trying to stop revolutionary elements in the I.L P. dragging it into the Third International and blocking attempts to pull the Labour Party under Communist influence.

41 Grosvenor Road
Westminster Embankment
15.5.20

Dear One

What a lucky chance to have such weather. It is good to think of you getting about in the sun and warmth; I hope not walking too many hours in the day.

I enclose the second batch of proofs for you to look at and bring back with you – also some letters.

Last night we had a pleasant and entirely harmonious Annual Meeting of the F.S. – about fifty present – not more than half-a-dozen members of the Executive, and mostly women members – not a very 'vital' assembly – Sanders by the way, told me that he had a very nice letter from Shaw.

Henderson's son told me yesterday that a Committee of the Parliamentary Labour Party had decided to recommend that J. R. MacDonald be 'asked to give the Party the benefit of his knowledge and experience'; and it is suggested that he should be given the very first chance of getting back to Parliament. It remains to be seen whether this is adopted, and how much it means.

I find it very difficult to go on working in your absence – all sorts of little difficulties raise obstructions, and the jobs don't get completed. However, there is only tomorrow now. Mrs Green came in suddenly yesterday evening, and wanted to talk, as I could not stay then she is coming after lunch today. She returns to Ireland tomorrow morning, so you will not see her. She seemed just the same as ever – much pleased by the *New Statesman* taking a more extreme line (as she thinks it is).

Now goodbye dearest until tomorrow.

Sidney

### 710 SU SIDNEY WEBB TO LEONARD WOOLF

On 31 May Woolf wrote to Webb to say that he had been asked by the Seven Universities Democratic Association to stand as their candidate at the next election. (He had been first approached by the Association in 1918.) He sought an assurance that as a member of the Labour Party he would not be opposed by a Labour nominee. On the strength of Webb's letter Woolf stood unsuccessfully in 1922.

[41 Grosvenor Road]
1/6/20

My dear Woolf

No one can give such a *guarantee*. But you may be quite sure that nothing will be done from Headquarters directly or indirectly to put up a candidate against you (assuming you *allow* yourself to be called Labour Candidate, *as Hobson did* without disavowal; *whatever the S.U.D.A. itself chooses to call you* – you should make this clear to their Committee). The only uncertainty is whether somebody might not start up within the constituency calling himself Labour Candidate. He would not be encouraged or endorsed by Headquarters, and would doubtless be strongly discouraged; unless, indeed, there should arise, within the universities, an organised Labour Party, *co nominee*, which affiliated to Headquarters, and chose a candidate according to the Party Constitution. *Then* it might be impossible to refuse endorsement.

I tell you this only as a theoretical possibility. There is no sign of it. I completely disbelieve in its possibility.

You may certainly proceed in confidence.

Sidney Webb

711 PP SIDNEY WEBB TO R. J. HERRON

R. J. Herron was a Congregational minister and secretary of the Seaham Harbour Labour Party. He became Webb's election agent. 'I am much impressed' Sidney wrote to Beatrice on 3 December 1920, 'by his devotion and philanthropy . . . the place would be helpless and hopeless without him.' This letter of acceptance is included as an example of other formal letters to Webb's local party and constituents which have been omitted.

41 Grosvenor Road
Westminster, S.W.1
20th July 1920

Dear Mr Herron

I have your letter of the 12th instant, informing me that, at the Selection Conference of the Seaham Divisional Labour Party held at the Murton Miners' Hall on the 10th instant, I was unanimously chosen as the Prospective Candidate at the Parliamentary Election for the Division. I have since received a letter from the Executive Committee of the Labour Party stating that my prospective candidature had been definitely endorsed in accordance with the Constitution and Rules. I accept this candidature as for the next Parliamentary Election in the constituency, whenever it may occur.

How the Candidature arose

As you know, this position was not of my seeking. It is now just upon a year ago that I began to receive requests from organisations in the Seaham

Division that I would permit my name to be put forward. I held off for a long time, and suggested the choice of some one connected with the local industry. When the requests were renewed, actually from the Miners' Lodges themselves, as well as from Trade Union Branches and other bodies representing different sections of the community, I preferred to visit the constituency and address more than a dozen meetings in the various districts, in order that every one might have an opportunity of judging whether my candidature would be the one most generally acceptable. The evidence then afforded to me, together with the decision now given, leaves me no excuse for doubt. To an invitation emanating from the Lodges of the Durham Miners' Association, and very nearly every other Trade Union and Labour organisation in the Division; joined in by leading members of the Co-operative and Friendly Societies; supported by Ministers of Religion of various denominations and by electors of all classes – by shopkeepers, professional men, officials and teachers as well as by wage-earners, and by women as well as men; and conveyed to me as the unanimous decision of the Divisional Labour Party – I have no right to oppose my own reluctance to assume a new responsibility. In accepting the position I thank all concerned for the honour of their confidence.

## A Grave Crisis

The General Election, for which we must immediately prepare, will be one of supreme importance to every household. We are living in critical times. The present apparent prosperity is very largely fictitious. We have a Cabinet that has shown itself intellectually bankrupt, and unable to find any effective or consistent policy, whether on the Social Reconstruction that it promised for this country, or on the Restoration of Europe on which our own prosperity depends. Meanwhile the cost of living continues to rise; the shortage of houses becomes week by week actually greater and more acute, and the misery of overcrowding more widespread. We have failed to reinstate in employment many thousands of the men who fought in our defence. Moreover, there are signs of short time, workmen are being turned off in various industries, and I hear ominous threats of coming reductions of wages. The reason why practically nothing is being done by the Government to avert these evils, is that the Cabinet Ministers are seriously divided among themselves, about both home and foreign affairs, whilst the majority of the members of the House of Commons refuse to allow any interference with capitalist profit making.

## Administrative Paralysis

The result is a paralysis of administration from which the whole nation is suffering. All the public business is in arrear. The necessary decisions are not taken. To give only one example, I count it nothing short of a scandal that, more than eighteen months after the Armistice, the development of the great industry of coal-mining should be still paralysed by the uncertainty in which the Government leaves the matter. It is this uncertainty that hinders an adequate re-equipment of the more backward mines, obstructs the much-needed increase of cottages, and prevents fresh developments for the advance of the industry. This is not a grievance of the miners alone. Because the Cabinet and the House of Commons cannot bring themselves to accept the 'Nationalisation' proposed by the Miners' Federation, or even the recommendations of the Chairman of the Coal Industry Commission, and cannot find any other acceptable plan, the whole industry is made to suffer, the output of coal is far less than it would be if capital expenditure on the mines had not been suspended, the price to the consumer is needlessly increased, the export trade is restricted, the supply of cottages for the miners' families is arrested, and the very serious overcrowding continues to depress the vitality and raise the death-rate.

## Housing

Do the women of the Seaham Division realise why it is that the babies in the mining districts continue to die at so high a rate? It is partly because the Cabinet Ministers cannot make up their minds to take the action that would, as they know, result in a great improvement in the housing and the sanitation of the mining villages. There are a hundred other reforms equally held back by the failure of the Government and Parliament to cope with the nation's pressing business.

## The present Members of Parliament are to blame

Unfortunately, the great majority of the present members of the House of Commons do not insist on the nation's work being done. They do not suffer in their own persons from the delay. They are naturally not eager for the reforms that might interfere with the profits of themselves or their friends. In fact, the Cabinet is actually prevented by the present House of Commons, no less than by the House of Lords, from even attempting to fulfil its promises of Social Reconstruction.

## The Labour Party

This is why the coming General Election is of such great importance to every man and every woman. Not until we elect quite a different House of Commons, can we get even the beginning of the New Social Order to which we aspire. I see no hope of deliverance in the Unionist or Conservative or Coalition members, who are definitely committed to opposition to what I believe to be the ideals and desires of the great mass of hard-working folk in this country, whether their labour is by hand or by brain. Nor can I put more faith in the 'free' or 'independent' remnant of the once-triumphant Liberals. Their present leaders, unwilling to carry forward to the new issues the reforming zeal of the Liberalism of the past, have to-day apparently no other policy on Home Affairs than a drastic reduction of public expenditure. This can only mean a calamitous restriction of the work in Housing, Education, Public Health, and the Provision for Maternity and Infancy, Sickness, Unemployment, and Old Age; services that it is vitally important to develop rather than diminish. The only Party before the country which has worked out a definite programme of Social Reconstruction at home (set forth in detail in the pamphlet Labour and the New Social Order), and has outlined a comprehensive policy for the peaceful restoration of Europe, is the Labour Party, to which I have belonged ever since it was established. It is upon such a policy of Peace and Social Reconstruction – to be explained at the meetings that I hope to address in every part of the constituency – that I shall ask for the votes of the men and women of the Seaham Division.

### A Partnership in Work

A Parliamentary Candidature is of the nature of a partnership which cannot be successful unless the burden is duly shared between the candidate and his supporters. You may count on my doing my part without stint, although I must warn you that my work in London will compel me to concentrate my meetings in the Division in successive visits of a few weeks each. Those who have pressed me to stand – the members of the Miners' Lodges and other Trade Union Branches, women's societies, the Divisional Labour Party, and all the various bodies concerned – will, I am sure, not fail in their part of organising every separate local centre, and getting into communication with every elector.

### An Appeal for Citizenship

But it is no narrow faction fight in which we shall be engaged. The Labour Party is not, as is so often ignorantly asserted, a Party of Labourers; but a Party into which are welcomed all workers by hand or by brain whatever their occupation or position, who accept its principles and agree with its proposals. It is not so much our rights that we claim, as an opportunity for every one to fulfil the duties of citizenship. Our appeal must not be to the miners only, or to those only who work for wages, or even to those only who are suffering or discontented. In every district there are men and women in other circumstances who feel as deeply as we do the evils that we deplore; who are more and more coming to recognise that the principles we expound are really akin to those by which they themselves live; and that only along the lines of such a policy as we advocate can any honest solution of the nation's social problems be found. To all such men and women in the Seaham Division, irrespective of creed or class or position, I shall appeal for an unprejudiced consideration of my proposals; confident that if they find themselves in general agreement with those views, they will not be deterred, either by partizanship or by party labels, from giving their votes for the candidate who expresses them. What must be weighed are principles, not those who are but their exponents, or those who carry the flag. I venture confidently to hope that, if at this crisis in the nation's history we can put the principles and policy of the Labour Party effectively before all the electors of the Seaham Division, we cannot fail to find among these men and women an overwhelming majority of supporters.

Looking forward to being soon with you at Seaham

I am

Yours sincerely

Sidney Webb

712 UI BEATRICE WEBB TO H. G. WELLS

'We are reconciled to H. G. Wells', Beatrice noted on 29 November 1920. She found him 'fat and prosperous and immensely self-complacent . . . I am too near the end of life to keep up a vendetta with any human being'. Wells had sent her his *Outline of History*, which had already appeared in serial form. (His modern-dress version of the Book of Job, *The Undying Fire*, had been published in 1919.) When Sidney read it five months later he wrote to Beatrice that 'with all its shortcomings it is a great achievement, nobly planned and patiently executed with great ability and courage'. (2 February 1921 PP)

Leo Kamenev (1883–1936), one of the Bolshevik leaders and editor of *Pravda*, had visited England and met the Webbs with Leonid Krassin (1970–1926), who had negotiated the Brest-Litovsk treaty and was in London 1920–21 as a plenipotentiary attempting to arrange an Anglo-Soviet commercial agreement. One week of the Fabian summer school at Godalming was set aside for a meeting of foreign socialists. Some of those invited could not get passports and others were refused British visas: the Webbs had great difficulty in bringing off the meeting – several omitted letters deal with the arrangements – and less than ten of the fifty invited actually arrived. Those who did come were amazed when they found that the Webbs had invited Kamenev and Krassin to speak. In August the Webbs had been among the British delegates to the meeting of the Second International in Geneva, which made Beatrice feel 'depressed and disheartened' at the general feeling that the Soviet regime was 'a huge and disastrous failure if not an actual menace'. (BWD 20 August 1920) Their continued absence on holiday meant that the Webbs missed the formation of the Councils of Action of the trade union movement to block British intervention in the Russo-Polish war.

41 Grosvenor Road
Westminster Embankment
Sept 8th 1920

Dear Mr Wells

I was really very much gratified to get the great work direct from you – not merely on account of its value, but also as a token of 'mutuality' in regard for each other's work – a regard that has been constant on my part.

The book is a great achievement and this very morning, when I saw the announcement of its publication, I have decided to order it. I have resisted the temptation to read it in instalments as I have always regretted being enticed into reading *The Undying Fire* in morsels. You take so many things in your stride, that, unless one watches you marching on and on and on towards your chosen end, one loses half the meaning of your message.

Do you and Mrs Wells often come to London? If so would you come to dinner with us some day and meet Kamenev and Krassin (if I can get them here)? We had an hour's oration from each of them – one in French, the other in German – at a little private meeting of Fabians and Krassin struck me as a remarkable personality – quite the most remarkable Russian I have ever met. His account of Soviet industrial organisation as it was and as he wished it to be, is that of the most rigid form of state socialism; the dominant note being 'Working to a Plan' conceived by scientific men and applied without any regard for personal freedom or group autonomy. The sinister aspect is the military caste based on creed and supported by millions of peasants incapable of democracy. One wonders whether the world having got rid of theology is drifting into an era of creed wars between the Whites and the Reds? With kind remembrances to Mrs Wells.

Always yours sincerely
Beatrice Webb

713 SU BEATRICE WEBB TO LEONARD WOOLF

The book Beatrice mentions may have been Virginia Woolf's novel *Night and Day*, published in October 1919. The letter cannot be precisely dated.

41 Grosvenor Road
Westminster Embankment
[?Autumn 1920]

My dear Mr Woolf

I have just read your wife's book – will you tell her that she has won the admiration of an old woman. She has made the novel the form in which to present the most subtle criticism of character and the most poetic appreciation of nature – the whole harmonized by charming kindliness towards weary humanity. I wish I could see something of her; but I gather that she does not feel strong enough to come across new friends – do tell her that I shall now watch for her recovery with anxiety because I realise that she has an extraordinarily valuable instrument in her spiritual insight and literary gift – it would be a sin against humanity if it were lost to the world through continued ill health. *She must make herself well.*

Here is the syllabus of the Fabian Conference. I will retain a single room for you – of course the F.R.D. will pay your expenses up as its representative. Arnot will not be there as he is too busy with his Labor and Socialist amalgamation.

Always yours

Beatrice Webb

714 PP SIDNEY TO BEATRICE

The Webbs energetically made themselves known in Seaham, Beatrice going up to join Sidney early in December for a series of fifty lectures in the mining villages. They had also decided to write a brief *Story of the Durham Miners 1662–1921*, to be published by the Fabian Society.

In November the long-expected strike of the miners had begun and Beatrice noted that the men had nothing to do but 'listen to the Gospel as preached by Sidney'. She was enraged by the folly of the mineowners. 'When Ireland is being treated with savage brutality, when Central Europe is slowly dying, both catastrophes being deliberately brought about by the Lloyd George government, it is tragically absurd to be destroying the national wealth for the sake of a 2/- increase per day.' (BWD 21 October 1920)

Peter Lee (1864–1935), was a leading figure in the Durham Miners Association, and in 1933 became President of the Miners' Federation of Great Britain. He was first elected to Durham County Council in 1909, and became its chairman in 1919 when the Labour Party secured a majority.

Grand Hotel
West Hartlepool
28 Nov 1920

Dear One

I got your postcard and letter together this morning. I have ratified the Birmingham F.S. engagement for 3 March, though I am appalled at the idea of a Town Hall meeting for my little self. They will lose on it what they made over G.B.S.!

I fear you had a damp and muddy walk yesterday. It set in feebly raining here, and the huge crowds of football enthusiasts who filled all the trains made the streets frightfully muddy. But at least it was not cold. I worked all morning, after taking a little walk, and left at 1.30 for (a) meeting of Divisional Executive – some 20 enthusiastic people – (b) lecture in Herron's chapel, to audience of about 75 (filling the little hall, and quite a satisfactory meeting). Peter Lee, the aged miner Chairman of Durham County Council, presided, and told the audience he remembered you and me in Newcastle 30 years ago, studying trade unionism.

Very satisfactory talks with Herron who gave me tea and supper. Got home at a quarter to eleven!

Note that *your* meeting at Thompson Memorial Hall, Monk-Wearmouth (quarter of an hour from Roker Hotel) is on Wednesday, 15 December, 7.30 Religion. This subject has excited the interest of the teachers; and they very much want you to give it *to them alone*, in Seaham Harbour about 4.30 or 5 p.m. the same day you lecture on Co-operation. Seaham Colliery at 7 p.m. Tuesday 14 December. Herron wondered whether you would be equal to this, if he provided a car to take you home. The places are close together. What do you think?

Herron is very optimistic but does not conceal the fact that there are difficulties, inside the miners' Lodges, and in local weaknesses of organisation which he says time is gradually overcoming. I do not think they are yet getting much local revenue (as some of the Lodges still won't pay, saying they already pay to Durham). Now dear one I must close in order to go for a walk! I look for your letters.

Sidney

### 715 PP SIDNEY TO BEATRICE

E. Hayward, elected as a Liberal in 1918, was beaten into third place by Sidney in 1922; the Conservative, T. A. Bradford, came second.

On 29 November Beatrice spent an evening with Maud Reeves, noting that their old friendship was 'not impaired as was the friendship with her husband by the curious deterioration in intellect and character . . . due to his pathological vanity'. Maud Reeves, like a number of Beatrice's acquaintances, had become a spiritualist after losing a son in the war.

Grand Hotel
West Hartlepool
1.12.20

Dear One

Last night I went out to Wingate, a horrid place, with unpaved roads, deep in mud and pools of water into which I splashed in the dark. We have practically no organisation there, but a few faithful supporters. The Miners Hall is a former chapel, ugly and squalid to the last degree. There gathered 80 or so men, nearly all miners, but with the secretary of the Co-operative Society and a few shopkeepers. I gave quite a good lecture on Nationalisation to an attentive audience who were, I think, appreciative but very dead. The Chairman was to have been the President of the Miners Lodge, and he came and sat at the head; but he had only just got home from Durham, and seemed dead tired; so he refused to speak, and made a more zealous supporter act as Chairman. A few questions followed, and I made another speech intended to stir them to political activity, with, I fear, little success. No literature on sale. Then we issued into pouring rain; and I had nearly an hour to wait for my train. There was a whispered colloquy, and thereupon the secretary of the Co-operative Society took me home for a cup of coffee. He and his wife were sound for Labour, he said: he had 2,500 members with 4 Branches and a turnover of a quarter of a million (£2 per week each). We chatted by the fire very pleasantly, until it was time to catch my train, which got me to the hotel by 10.30 p.m.

Tonight I take a taxicab to get to Kelloe where the meeting is bound to be even smaller.

I learnt from the Co-operative Secretary that Hayward is a nice speaker, a 'gentleman' in behaviour, and quite popular, so that it will not be at all an easy job to oust him. However, the miners are likely to go fairly solidly for Labour when the time comes.

This morning is fine and sunny, so after writing some letters, I took the train to the old Hartlepool, thus saving miles of tramp by dock walls; and spent an hour or more walking up and down the esplanade in the sun and wind – as you would have advised!

This letter from Boni and Liveright, the American publisher, is not promising, and if we get a doubtful financial report through Emil Davies presently, as is quite probable, I should not be inclined to go on with him.

Longman writes me direct, approving the Circular; and asking for 3,000 without Fabian Bookshop for distribution among his booksellers. This I have ordered. He reports that he has only 380 left of *History of Trade Unionism*; and *of these* 250 were intended for New York; so he will want the copies now ordered by the New Year. He has still 1,200 left of *Socialist Constitution* (out of 3,000).

Dear One, I was delighted to get your letter with its cheery news. Can we, perhaps get Mrs Reeves back into Fabian activities, so long as they remain in London, which may probably now be indefinitely? She might put the Women's Group on its feet again, with its own set of activities and lecturing.

I think hotel bedrooms must have been the scenes of the greatest loneliness and unhappiness in all the world. I am exceptionally fortunate; but if I were not – if I was seeking a situation, or vainly striving for something, or not knowing where to turn, I think a hotel bedroom would be the worst possible place. Do people commit suicide in hotel bedrooms more than elsewhere?

But now this is my sixth day out of nine. In three more days I shall have you again to tell me what to do and see that I do it. I will come to meet your train at Sunderland (make sure whether it is 9.50 *or* 10 a.m. from Kings Cross: there is some uncertainty). Goodbye, dear one.

Sidney

## 716 PP SIDNEY TO BEATRICE

Beatrice was away in Manchester collecting material for *The Consumers Co-operative Movement* which appeared in 1921.

The *New Statesman* had survived the war but it was in difficulties, both circulation and advertising being too low to meet rising costs. Hedley Le Bas was called in as a consultant. At this meeting he submitted his report to the Board; he joined the Board himself in March 1921 and remained a director until his death in

1926. The Webbs had drifted away from the *New Statesman*, Sidney still attended Board meetings and wrote occasional articles but he felt out of sympathy with Sharp, who was anti-Labour and had become a hanger-on of the Asquith set.

Tom Sykes was a Primitive Methodist minister who served on the Newcastle Circuit 1908–17, and from 1917 being 'without pastoral charge' he was serving as a Connexional Evangelist and was in a good position to furnish Sidney with introductions.

41 Grosvenor Road
Westminster Embankment
7.1.21

Dear One

I have nothing to send you today, except love – I went to the *Statesman* Board meeting, only [Arnold] Bennett and [H. D.] Harben present, to receive Sir Hedley Le Bas and hear his suggestions. He is a strong, cordial, able personality, evidently of great experience, and very zealous to help. He says it is a fine property, sure to pull through. He advises (I) publication of circulation and advertising it to advertisers, (II) putting up advertisement rates; (III) getting cheaper paper, of equally good appearance mixed with wood pulp instead of 'pure', by which the cost of paper could be halved; (IV) possibly getting a cheaper printer; (V) going on with the canvassing scheme; (VI) urging the existing subscribers to get others: and (VII) looking out for another journal to share publishing expenses.

He thinks these things might save £2,000 a year, and at the same time increase receipts.

Meanwhile the deficit this year is £4,000, and Sharp doubts whether he can get through to April without further subsidy. Unfortunately Whitley couldn't attend, whom he was going to ask for a cheque: and Harben said he could give nothing whatever. I left Bennett with Sharp considering. I said they should draw up a careful statement of ways and means up to 31 March, and see whether any payments could be deferred until the April renewals came in.

I went to the Primitive Methodist Head Quarters and bought their Yearbook, which gives me half a dozen useful addresses in the Seaham Division. That part of the world is their very strongest District. There are 5 'Stations' in, or on the edge of Seaham; with about 1,500 Church Members in the Division. I don't at present see any central person whom I can get at, so that Henderson's introduction of Rev. Tom Sykes was a godsend.

As I walked home my eye caught the Evening Star – Venus – and I thought of the last time I noticed it in connection with you, on my Ober Ammergau trip in August 1890, when I wrote to you about it, 30½ years ago! I think it has been a beneficent star.

Dear One, Goodnight.

Sidney

Patrick and Leonard Dobbs were the sons of Beatrice's sister Rosie and her second husband George Dobbs, now working for a travel agency in Switzerland.
Walter Rathenau (1867–1922), German industrialist, writer and politician, was Minister of Reconstruction in 1921, Foreign Secretary in 1922, when he was assassinated. William Lionel Hichens (1874–1940) was a businessman who had been one of Lord Milner's 'kindergarten' in South Africa and had an enlightened attitude to labour problems.

41 Grosvenor Road
Westminster Embankment
13.1.21

Dear One

You write cheerily; but I am afraid you are doing too much. I hope Miss Schmidt is returning with you, so as to be with you on the journey. It will be good to have you safe here again, where you can take your time over the work. There is no hurry!

Pat arrived late last night – we had saved a supper for him. He did not tell me, but *The Times* today has half a column mostly about him and Leonard, their exploits in the ski-ing competition at Wengen, which you must look for in the copy posted herewith. It will please the family – Pat has now gone out shopping, and will be here for lunch and dinner.

Rathenau stayed 1½ hours; a well-dressed, able, fluent talker, rather the sort of man one would assume Lionel Hichens to be, giving the impression of being a university lecturer turned business administrator (I don't know whether he is that). He was elaborately polite and flattering; most regretful at not meeting you, unable to stay over Sunday; said he had followed our work for 20 years, the F.S. was the most important of all societies, and so on.

For the rest he orated almost continuously; said the years to come would be worse than the war; that ruined Central Europe would inevitably depress British wages, and lead to political reaction and complete cessation of progress. When I tried to get to practical remedies, he said there were none; that no people learnt except by bitter experience; that England and France must inevitably find out by years of suffering; that there was no chance of any wisdom being listened to, and so on.

The one thing I gathered was that the relatively low cost of labour in Germany would presently enable its manufacturers to undersell all British and American competitors in the neutral markets, and entirely supersede us there – in which I don't in the least believe.

He talked so incessantly himself, in a way not to be interrupted, that the conversation was almost useless.

As to the *New Statesman*, Sharp (who could not come Tuesday) writes that they need £1,500 to carry them through to April next! Which is awkward with Glynn Williams and Simon away, and Harben out of the running. I dare say they can do with less, and that Arnold Bennett and Whitley will help – I agree with you that it is no longer particularly our affair, though beyond making clear to Sharp that we have no more to give, I don't propose to betray that feeling.

I lunched with Beveridge, who is in great form and good spirits. The receipts from fees and other tuition payments will justify his estimate for the session of £20,000. But he can get no definite promise of additional grants yet; and is being driven to contemplate a loan to enable him to start the new building in April. I am still in hopes that McCormick and [Robert] Blair can arrange something. The place is apparently going on well. (It certainly looks odd to see 15 couples waltzing in the Hall after lunch, to the Herbert Spencer piano.) Beveridge wants you to go there Thursday afternoon next to help a small committee to choose a new lady for Dunford House – for which the deed was duly signed 26 November; and there is a good deal of forward booking.

The Labour Party will get its Unemployment Report in time, as we have set Greenwood to write it out of existing material (Cole had done a good Advisory Committee Report, and Tawney another on the Education side).

I could not sleep well last night, and, am evidently needing my dear companion back again. But I am much more anxious about her, and can only beg her again to be careful not to crowd in too much!

Sidney

718 PP SIDNEY TO BEATRICE

Margaret Hobhouse was dying of cancer of the lung: Eleanor was her second daughter.

Graham Wallas had published *Human Nature in Politics* in 1908 and *The Great Society* in 1914.

41 Grosvenor Road
Westminster Embankment
31.1.21

Dearest

I fear you will only get my letter by second post this morning: I took it to the District Office, but realised too late that I had only put 2d. stamp on it! Your own letter this morning made me feel ashamed of my momentary absent-mindedness, which may have given you a disappointment.

Eleanor rang up this morning with a strange message from Maggie that she could not see you this afternoon as she was to have an injection. She thanked you much for your cheering letter.

When I explained that you were at Leeds, Eleanor was confused – it may have been merely one of her own blunders. I asked her how her mother was, and she said 'Better'.

As to the Shaws, Charlotte now writes that her sister is ill, and wants to see her, so she will be away for the 5/7 February – the weekend you have already declined – and expects us for the following weekend. I have written explaining we will come Sunday morning 13th.

Yesterday I met Mr Justice Sankey in the street, and he was particularly cordial and interested, so I asked him whether he would not come to dinner with us alone in a week or two, when you were returned – which he very cordially accepted, leaving you to fix the date. Haldane said he had become very pro-Labour, passing straight from Conservatism.

In the evening I read right through Wallas's *Human Nature in Politics* and *The Great Society*. I thought very highly of them, notably the former, for originality, insight, excellence of form, and even wisdom (all of which made me realise how inadequately I had appreciated them). But then a feeling came over me about their essential futility. I thought of the phrase 'ineffectual archangel'. This, of course, is what makes me impatient with them and unappreciative. It is not fair on them or on him, because analysis is anyhow useful, even if it is not accompanied by practical proposals. But it is curious that it should be he who reproaches the Utilitarians and Radicals for their failure to make their projects and methods such as would appeal to, and be workable by, the average sensual man; who himself is unable to suggest any way by which what he regards as inevitable and desirable Democracy should be made to work as he would like it to work. The answer to him is that Democracy *does* work; and if its roughnesses and crudities shock him, the shock ought to lead him, not to repine, or to forget the positive results, but merely to wish to effect improvements. And the odd thing is that this is what actually happens in him personally, though not in his books. The books leave the impression of querulous discontent with Democracy itself – and that is why they are so popular in academic America! They would go down better in England if they each ended up with a hopeful chapter suggesting positive minor reforms in democratic machinery.

Goodbye dear one: don't work too hard, and spare yourself as much as you can.

Sidney

719 PP SIDNEY WEBB TO GRAHAM WALLAS

After much industrial unrest, which the government feared might be leading to a revolutionary crisis, the miners were locked out and another bitter dispute began. On 8 April the railway and transport workers voted for a sympathetic strike but after confused negotiations they withdrew their support on 15 April, known thereafter as 'Black Friday'. The miners, who remained on strike until June, were forced to go back on a basis of local terms rather than any national agreement. Beatrice thought this 'catastrophic anti-climax' showed that 'the leaders clearly funked it': it demonstrated, she added, that they were unfit to govern, and 'not even equal to their own extremely limited business of collective bargaining'. (BWD 16 April 1921)

Roker Hotel, Sunderland } To 25 April only

21.4.21

Dear Wallas

Thanks for your letter about *The Story of the Durham Miners*, which is no more than it professes to be!

I am a little amused at your regret that the book does not contain several other things.

We have done our very best to set forth the economics of trade unionism, and how far its demands are consistent with the community's other interests, in our *Industrial Democracy*, in which a good many pages are devoted to this question – pages which I do not think have been refuted in the 23 years that have elapsed. I could hardly discuss the point in this little story (which was, of course, written before the outbreak of the present trouble).

And as to the relation of trade unionism to the Government, well have we not done our own little best in *A Constitution for the Socialist Commonwealth*? This, too, I could hardly have repeated in the little Durham story.

Now, I don't bother my head about *judging* J. H. Thomas and other men, I leave that, so to speak, 'to their Maker'. The 'cosmic processes', as it seems to me, take little account of what men's consciences tell them, if they tell them (or us) anything significant. Their psychology, indeed, is one of the factors: and a queer make-up it is! As I know next to nothing about the facts, I just let it pass, without thinking about it.

We, at least, have done our best to make constructive proposals of definite character. That is our way of criticising G. D. H. Cole!

I shall get home on Monday.

Yours

Sidney Webb

### 720 SU SIDNEY WEBB TO LEONARD WOOLF

Leonard Woolf's book was probably *Socialism and Co-operation*, which he published early in 1921. The Webbs had recently spent two weeks in Paris and Brussels. Beatrice was depressed by France. 'The socialist and labour movement broken down beyond immediate repair; all the other sections of opinion looking to German money [reparations] for their salvation and no public spirit or public morality anywhere apparent.' (BWD 19 May 1921)

41 Grosvenor Road
Westminster Embankment
16.5.21

Dear Woolf

Thanks for your book, which we have read with much interest. Your emphasis on the certainty of continuance for a long time of the perverted psychology due to Capitalism, and on the need for changing it, strikes me as true and useful. And, of course, your demonstration (as against the Marxians, Syndicalists and Guildsmen) of the necessity of vesting ownership and control in the community of consumers is very welcome to us. All this (which is the main thesis of the book) seems to us very useful.

But we should say that you underrate the necessary *complexity* of the organisation required in the modern community. We had tried in our book of last July to work out this complexity. Though you make one long quotation from this book, I do not feel sure that you have had time to read it through, so I send you a copy, in which I think you will find (with some things with which you may not agree) a great deal of coincidence.

One important difference between us is that you make *the* essential difference, between the Co-operative Movement and State and Municipal enterprise, that between industrial and political functions. We make *the* essential difference that between voluntary and obligatory association. I neither think nor desire that the Co-operative Movement as we know it can ever become legally obligatory, as this would involve a statutory constitution and area, and statutory powers and contributions. We want to preserve as much as we can of *voluntary* association in the Socialist State; and hence our long-continued advocacy, both of the Co-operative Movement and trade unionism (for which we were, thirty years ago, denounced by nearly all who then called themselves Socialists). But just as trade unions cannot become legal monopolists and State organs without losing their present character of voluntary organs of defence and resistance against the employing community, so it seems to me that Co-operative Societies could not become bodies in which membership was legally obligatory, with monopolist powers (as you seem to suggest they should become for railways, coal etc.), without losing much of what is advantageous, notably in their freedom, which is bound up with their voluntary nature.

Moreover, when one considers how vast is already the domain of municipal services (in the U.K. already administering twenty or thirty times the amount of capital employed by the whole Co-operative Movement); and the unlikelihood of the railways, postal services, forests, coal-mines, oil, etc. being handed over to a congeries of Co-operative Societies – to say nothing of steamship lines, the smelting of ore etc. – I am compelled to believe that national and municipal government will be the owners and controllers of these big, national industries, rather than Co-operative societies endowed with statutory monopolies, as you seem to suggest.

You assume a necessary continuance of the *unity* of the government organs. You will see that we contemplate a separation – first between the 'Political' and the 'Social' Parliament; and secondly between control and administration, the latter being undertaken by National Boards *ad hoc* (under the Social Parliament), and by Committees of Management *ad hoc* (under the Town Councils).

I hope we may have a chance of talking all this over with you one day – we have just returned from a hasty inspection of French and Belgian Co-operation, which we find much less imbued with the conception of furnishing *an alternative form* of industrial administration to Capitalism than our own movement.

Yours

Sidney Webb

721 NLS SIDNEY WEBB TO R. B. HALDANE

Haldane had maintained a close interest in philosophy throughout his career as a lawyer and politician. In 1921 he published *The Reign of Relativity*. John Kemp had been his collaborator in translating Schopenhauer's *The World as Will and Idea* in 1883–86.

Dunford
Midhurst } to 18 June only

13.6.21

Dear Haldane

We are very grateful for your magnificent volume which Beatrice hopes to study at leisure – it is a tough morsel for such simple folk as ourselves, who (John Kemp was once provoked into declaring) 'care only for processes in time'! I have already skimmed right through it, in my journalistic curiosity, which does not preclude a real reading later on. I will not pretend to discuss it, and will only congratulate you on completing so gigantic a task. I humbly accept my inability to understand Einstein, along with the rest of the universe in which my 'self-awareness' seems to find itself; but I am not foolish enough to deprecate, even in thought, the patient efforts of those who successively refine our long series of approximations to a comprehension of the nature of things.

However, I will venture on one remark – not by way of criticism, so much as of emphasis and speculation. On page 421 you give a definition of Democracy, 'that is to say the rule of those who have been selected to be directly responsible to the citizens as a whole, and to conform to the general will of the nation, in the sense in which that will was interpreted in the chapter on the State'. When I turn back to p. 367–8 I see that the general will is to be interpreted by Ministers *fresh from an election*, not according to the letter of the voting (of course); not even according to its essence or contemporary *meaning* (!) because it 'may be undergoing rapid and yet silent modification'. The voters 'may not really have intended to give a *final* decision'. (Certainly, I should say, never a *final* decision.) But then you add, they may 'have meant that the Ministers in effect chosen should decide for them'(!) The reason of the discrepancy is just 'the manifold nature of the mind of the individual voter'.

Now, I don't make the common crude objection to this doctrine. But I observe that Ministers to whom one could safely trust such an interpretation must be, not merely honest and candid, but also singularly free from innate acquired prejudices, prepossessions and partialities; and (what is even more important) ought to be required to live in a social environment which did not bias them powerfully, even if unconsciously, in a direction different from that in which the general will was pressing.

In short, no Ministry that I have ever known could be safely trusted to make correctly so delicate an interpretation. Moreover, even this can only apply to a newly-elected Ministry. If you try to give [it] as a definition of Democracy for three years out of every five, it amounts to still less.

I don't say I can suggest a more 'democratic' definition that could be strictly construed. But I suggest that the root of the difficulty is to be found in what you call 'the manifold nature of the individual voter'; and in your implicit assumption that there is no conceivable device for eliciting or registering the general will other than one gigantic election to settle all things in one vote. But already we have several elections concurrently, Parish, District, Borough and County Councils; Trade Unions or Professional Associations and Co-operative Societies; as well as Parliament.

You will have to come round to our idea of having at least two Parliaments, so as to represent eight or ten different aspects of the life of the individual voter. I don't see why we should continue to be fettered by Ptolemaic conceptions of sovereignty in society, when even Copernican conceptions of the cosmos are superseded.

However, enough of this attempt to grasp the infinite.

We go to Labour Party Conference for next week, and return to London (to greet the General Election) on 24 June.

Yours

Sidney Webb

722 NH BEATRICE WEBB TO ÉLIE HALÉVY

The Halévys had spent three weeks at Dunford. The Webbs went on to the Labour Party conference at Brighton. There they heard speculation about the possibility of Labour being strong enough to form a government by 1924, though needing to bring in 'non-party' sympathisers such as Haldane and Beatrice's brother-in-law Alfred Cripps. Some recruits of this type would be required because there were no lawyers in the Labour Party sufficiently eminent to provide a Labour administration with the necessary Law Officers. The conference, Beatrice recorded, was gloomy in the shadow of the miners' defeat. The first of a series of attempts to affiliate the Communist Party was defeated by 4,115,000 to 224,000. The Labour Party, however, had as yet no rules under which Communists could be prevented as attending as delegates from other affiliated organisations.

41 Grosvenor Road
Westminster Embankment
27th June 1921

My dear Professor Halévy

How nice of you to write to us about those pleasant days at Dunford. It was very pleasant having you and Madame Halévy there: seeing each other in London is always such a hurried and incomplete method of social intercourse – a few days in the country together gives one an opportunity of good long talks.

The Brighton Conference was, of course, depressed because all the unions have run dry and are looking towards the future with considerable consternation. But the spirit was amazingly united and in a sense determined, with a swing forward towards political action. The Englishman does not really like anything else. In his heart of hearts, he is a political animal. The Communists were almost negligible and I think that you are mistaken in attributing to Bolshevism the determination of the miners to hold out for better terms. That stubbornness has always been a characteristic of the miners: they never know when they are beaten. Time after time they have held out long after the case was hopeless.

With kindest remembrances to Madame Halévy

Yours sincerely

Beatrice Webb
(Mrs Sidney Webb)

### 723 LP BEATRICE WEBB TO ARTHUR GREENWOOD

The Labour Research Department had become a useful information service to trade unions but there was growing strain with the Labour Party. When the majority of the L.R.D. staff joined the Communist Party (the Coles excepted) and became openly hostile to the party officials and executive the L.R.D. was given notice to quit the party offices. Beatrice sought a compromise. 'Will the little group of Guild Socialists-cum-Communists have the sense to accept some sort of terms or will they go out into the wilderness and become permanently out of touch with the whole of the labour movement except the little clique of rabid revolutionaries?' she asked. (BWD 12 July 1921) By October the situation was exacerbated when the Coles announced that the L.R.D. was to receive £6,000 a year from the Russian Trade Delegation to study capitalist enterprise. The Department, Beatrice noted sadly on 7 October, 'a promising child of ours – ends in a lunatic asylum'. In December the L.R.D. changed its Russian sponsor to Arcos (the trading organisation representing the Russian Co-operatives). This trouble came after an earlier episode in November 1920 when the Soviet sympathisers on the *Daily Herald* had engaged in a fantastic operation to get a £75,000 subsidy from the Russians by selling some of the Tsarist jewellery in London.

Beatrice noted on 24 December that of the old group which she had gathered together in the original Fabian Research Department some had gone to the *Daily Herald*, the spokesman for the extreme left of the movement and not yet the official Labour paper, some had become Christians or been converted to Social Credit, others had joined the Communist Party. The Webbs were now building a different group of young collaborators, such as Woolf, Tawney and Harold J. Laski (1893–1950), who had returned from Harvard after the war to begin a distinguished career as a teacher of political science at L.S.E. and as an active Labour politician and theorist.

41 Grosvenor Road
Westminster Embankment
4th July 1921

Dear Mr Greenwood

Could you dine here on Thursday at 8 o'clock and meet Josiah Wedgewood and his wife? And would Mrs Greenwood come with you?

I enclose you a copy of a memorandum by me on the future of the Research Department. The Labour Research Department executive appointed a small Sub-Committee of Cole and the staff to draft a report on the future of the Department assuming that it comes to no arrangement with the Joint Council, and I was asked to draft a report embodying some views which I had expressed. I should like to talk the matter over with you. Personally I do not much care what happens to the balance of the funds and even the material, except that I do not want any quarrelling about it, or any overt hostility to the Labour Party, or from the Labour Party to the young people of the Research Department. We must try and finish up the business in a reputable way without leaving any soreness on either side.

Always yours

Beatrice Webb
(Mrs Sidney Webb)

724 LSE SIDNEY WEBB TO JANET MAIR

Mrs Mair was married to William Beveridge's cousin. On 14 May 1922 Beatrice described her behaviour as the new secretary of L.S.E. as 'ambitious and domineering'. She was bothered about the gossip about her and Beveridge who had what she described as 'an official relationship combined with more than sufficient sympathy and cousinly affection'.

L.S.E. decided on the motto *Felix Qui Potuit Rerum Cognoscere Causas*. It was an institutional joke that the beaver made a suitable emblem for an academic institution since it worked hard for half the year and hibernated for the other half.

Roker Hotel
Sunderland
13.10.21

Dear Mrs Mair

Note that from tomorrow morning my address will be as above until 31 October.

I am sorry to be unable to confer as to the 'Coat of Arms'. My desire was to ascertain exactly what it was that was felt to be needed, and what for. I believe that (apart from the Royal Arms, and from attempt to get goods on false pretences) anyone is legally free to adopt and use any device or crest he pleases. The grant of the College of Heralds is superfluous, and only an occasion for levying fees; and the grant of a 'Coat of Arms' to an institution is rather meaningless and anachronistic. Moreover a '*Coat of Arms*' in the literal sense seems to be not at all the sort of thing useful for the badge or crest or device of a boat, a flag, a jacket, a button, or anything of the sort.

If what is wanted is a device for practical use, why not let us simply adopt a figure of the beaver in a shield-like frame, without calling it a

'Coat of Arms'; with any motto thought appropriate (which, I urge, should be in the English language).

If, however, it is really seriously desired to go through the farce of paying the College of Heralds twenty or fifty guineas (which does not go into the poor Exchequer!), I will not object.

Yours

Sidney Webb

725 SU BEATRICE WEBB TO LEONARD WOOLF

The money left by Henry Atkinson, an old Fabian, was used in part to support the work of the Society's Local Government Bureau. Herman Finer (1898–1969) was an L.S.E. graduate who was appointed lecturer in public administration at the School in 1920 and later became a professor there.

41 Grosvenor Road
Westminster Embankment
26th June 1922

Dear Mr Woolf

Here is a letter from Redfern, which you might consider. I think it would be a good thing for the Fabian Society to get a tract by him, and we might or might not include it in the set prepared for the Conferences next autumn and winter. When do you think we had better have those conferences? Galton suggests they should be in the late autumn or early winter, as we shall have the King's Hall lectures for this year beginning on 30th October.

Are you in London, and if so could you come to lunch some day next week and have a talk? How do you like Sidney's two pamphlets: are they what you want? And how are the others shaping?

I also wanted to talk to you about other research. I daresay you have heard that Sidney and Pease have been left something over £2,000 – probably about £3,000, by an old member of the Fabian Society for the promotion of socialism? They both think that the best use of this money would be publication and research. We are sending a young lecturer of the School of Economics, Mr Finer, to Germany this summer to complete a study of the new National Economic Council representing economic interests of one kind or another, and we want to find some person who would go to Italy and investigate all the latest development of Co-operative and trade union production. But a more ambitious proposal is to send somebody to Russia – nominally to investigate the Co-operative Societies, but actually to supplement documentary research into the Soviet system of government and its later developments. Of course I do not know whether that would be practicable at the present time, seeing that the Soviet Government is likely to become more intolerant, if anything happens to Lenin, to make investigation or even sojourn almost impracticable to foreigners. But if it were possible, is there the remotest chance of your being able to do it? And what do you consider the cost would be? There must be a mass of information which is get-at-able outside Russia, but even a rapid visit would give the atmosphere of the place.

Always yours sincerely

Beatrice Webb

(Mrs Sidney Webb)

726 PP SIDNEY TO BEATRICE

Beatrice was somewhat anxious lest Sidney overwork in the election campaign caused by the break-up of the coalition and Lloyd George's replacement by Bonar Law. In the winter Sidney had collapsed and lost consciousness while on a walk near Hastings. It seems probable from the symptoms noted by Beatrice that he had suffered a slight stroke. In the summer of 1922 he had a minor nervous breakdown. Beatrice worried about her own health, fearing that she might die and leave Sidney a semi-invalid. Though he recovered his capacity for routine work from this time he seemed to lack imaginative energy and became more dependent upon the initiative of others.

When in Seaham Sidney took lodgings in Maureen Terrace, the street in which R. J. Herron lived. Sir Chettur Sankaran Nair (1857–1934) was an Indian jurist who was a member of the India Council at this time. William Whiteley (1889–1955), leader of the Durham miners, won Blaydon by two-to-one majority; he became Labour Chief Whip 1942–55. Benjamin Spoor (1878–1928), who became the Labour Chief Whip in 1924, did equally well at Bishop Auckland. Sidney preferred to hire a car from Meek rather than to hurtle around in Herron's sidecar.

32 Maureen Terrace
Seaham Harbour
30.10.22

Dearest

I found both your letters at breakfast, and they cheered me up. I am very glad you did not go to Dunford in the cold and wet. Here it is sunny and bright, and not unduly cold in the day; but with constant liability to short showers of hail and rain; and of course an East wind.

I have written politely to Sir S. Nair explaining why I think he had better go elsewhere.

We are getting under way here, with a dozen meetings fixed for this week – the delivery of the Election Address begun – canvassing being started (Herron thinks he can canvass practically the entire electorate); and apparently complete unanimity among the Miners Lodges, and other elements belonging to Labour. I go to Blaydon for Whitely (Durham Miners) on Sunday 5 November, and have offered to go to Bishop Auckland for Spoor on Sunday 12 November, so you will be left alone these days! But these lodgings will suit you very well. The view is quite charming and your bedroom looks comfortable. Mrs Candlish cooks well, and is very anxious to make you happy. I am proposing a common meal of fish and (your own) eggs for tomorrow at 5 p.m., as I have to hurry off to Trimdon; and you and Mrs Bolton [Ivy Schmidt] will have come a journey. But for other days you will make your own arrangements.

I hope to meet you at Sunderland tomorrow, but Meek's car will be there anyhow. Try to bring the *MAP*: 8 copies of *Hist. of Liquor Licensing*; my penknife, if you find it; and above all yourself in good health and spirits, full of love for your lover; and of wise judgement and management for our common task and duty – now goodbye until tomorrow.

Sidney

At Murton (3,000 electors) the Miners Lodge has 80 regular collectors of some subscription from house to house. 74 of them agreed to canvass systematically for me, and have taken canvass books.

727 UI SIDNEY WEBB TO H. G. WELLS

Tawney objected to Wells and preferred Russell, declaring that Wells was a cad and Russell a gentleman. Such a distinction, Beatrice remarked in a long diary entry on the permissive post-war mood, was 'hardly relevant if it is sexual morality which is to be the test'. (BWD 10 July 1922) Once Wells decided to stand as Labour candidate in London University Beatrice invited him and his wife to meet some of the party leaders. 'When he sat by me I could not help reflecting that in some ways he is an unclean beast . . . He is no longer agreeable company; he is deteriorating intellectually . . . never tries to discuss as he used to do, and never listens seriously to anything that is said.'

On polling day, 15 November, Sidney was swept in with a large majority. In the country as a whole Labour fought 414 seats, increasing its parliamentary representation from 75 to 142, and doubling its popular vote to over four million, only one million less than the Tories and more than both the two Liberal groups combined. The main gains were in the North-East, Yorkshire and Scotland. The election brought back MacDonald, Snowden and other pacifists defeated in 1918, a significant group of radical I.L.P. members from Clydeside, and a number of middle-class intellectuals, formerly Liberal, who had moved into the Labour Party. By a narrow majority (in a contest so ridden with intrigue that the facts are still disputed) MacDonald was again made party leader. Labour was now unmistakably the official opposition and the alternative government.

41 Grosvenor Road
Westminster Embankment
28.11.22

Dear Wells

We can't make a defeat into a victory; but I think the L.U. [London University] vote, taken as a whole, is much better than in 1918. I only got some 750 more than you, with all the advantage of having no Liberal against me. Many electors hung back until the last minute then, and told me they only voted for me because there was no Liberal. I don't suppose I got 1,000 Labour Party votes, and you have done 50 per cent better. Still, I wish you had been elected, if only to enliven the House out of its deadly ruts of ancient respectability.

What you did most effectually was to help the Labour cause in the constituencies (one great reason for University candidatures). Your speech at Manchester was just what was needed; delivered where it would be most valuable; and precisely well timed. There was no equally effective stroke during the whole contest.

Mrs Webb joins in congratulations in this sense; and also in the regrets!

Yours

Sidney Webb

## 728 PP BEATRICE WEBB TO FRIENDS OF SEAHAM

This letter is characteristic of a long series which Beatrice, in a new role as the wife of an M.P., addressed to the women of Seaham Labour Party. They are unusual in their length and in the conscious attempt to use such letters as a means of political education. A number of these letters over the next seven years have been included: more are in the Passfield Papers. In one or two cases they were drafted by Sidney. Though Beatrice disliked constituency work both she and Sidney were punctilious about their obligations to Seaham electors and party workers. 'I am haunted', she wrote on 23 November 1922, 'by the vision of those pit villages, and those strained faces of the miners and their wives listening to our words. Can we get into an intimate and sincere relation to them, so that we may understand their lives?'

41 Grosvenor Road
Westminster, S.W.1
December 1922

Dear Friends

I am delighted to hear from Mrs Boyle that you would like a letter from me to be read at your next meeting.

My husband has already discovered that one of the difficulties of being a Member of Parliament is that you see so little of your electors. The life of a Member of Parliament in London is so entirely different from the life of the miner or agricultural labourer, the doctor or the teacher in the country. The Member is compelled to live in London in order to attend Parliament, and even when Parliament is not in session in order to keep in touch with Government Departments about the multifarious business in which his constituency is interested. He has to be perpetually thinking about all sorts of subjects from foreign treaties to the sugar tax, from the problem of unemployment to that of housing. If he has his own professional work to do, as well as representing his constituents in Parliament, it is not possible for him to spend much time in his constituency. That is why I think it may be useful both to you and to my husband, if I write you a monthly letter.

I think it may interest you to know exactly where we live and how we live, before I begin to talk to you about public questions. Ever since our marriage – thirty years ago – we have lived in a little house on the Westminster Embankment. In front of our house is the River Thames, at a point where the river is about four times as broad as the Wear at Sunderland. But there is very little shipping on it; it is only a great expanse of water, and only occasionally a barge swings up or down the river, or one of Lord Londonderry's steamers brings coal from Seaham Harbour to the Londonderry wharf at Vauxhall. I often wonder whether there are any of our friends at work on those steamers. Our house is only five minutes walk from the Houses of Parliament, which is very convenient now for my husband, because he can come back to his own home for his meals when the House is in session.

My husband and I live a very regular life. Every morning at eight o'clock punctually we have each one cup of coffee and bread and butter on a tray in our workroom; we read our letters and skim through the *Times* and the *Herald* newspapers, and then we get to work, and work steadily until our midday meal at one o'clock. In the first place there are the letters to attend to. I suppose my husband gets about twenty letters a day. Since he has been Member for Seaham there are always about five or six from the Seaham Division on all sorts of subject – from persons who cannot get their pensions paid or have failed to get compensation for some accident, or who want employment, or who have some grievance about the action of some Government Department or Local Authority. These letters generally mean that my husband has to write to some Government Department to get the necessary information, or go himself to enquire about the case; and then to write and explain matters to his correspondent. But there are other letters from working men or other students who want to know what books to read, or otherwise to be helped in their studies; or from Americans, Japanese, and other foreigners who want information; or from members or officials of the Labour Party. When these letters have been attended to we set to work on the book that we happen to be writing. Writing books is very hard work. You have first to discover all the facts, and get the information; then you have to make up your mind as to what it is right and useful to propose; and then you have got to state it in a way that other people can understand and be interested in it. In the course of the last thirty years we have written about twenty books. I am afraid you would find most of them very dull and difficult reading. But there is one of them by my husband that might interest you – *The History of the Durham Miners* – and if there is any member of the Women's Section who would like this little book I will gladly send it to her. In the afternoon there is other work to do. When Parliament is sitting my husband has to be in the House of Commons from 2.30 to late at night. When Parliament is not sitting there are committees to attend at the Labour Party Office, or students to see or lectures to give, for my husband is a Professor of London University. But we generally manage to get a walk in the afternoon; and most evenings we sit quietly at home and read all the books and newspapers that have to be read in order to know about things.

Now I want to tell you something about public affairs. The two questions which have most interested us during the last month, and which are being most talked about in London, are unemployment, on the one hand, and on the other the determination of France to invade Germany and take possession of some of her coalfields and forests. Unfortunately these two questions are closely connected one with the other. The unemployment of British workers is largely the result of the Peace of Versailles which ruined Germany, and indeed most of Europe, so that we cannot sell much of our coal, or of our manufactured commodities because there are so few people in Germany or in Austria or in Russia able to buy them. I am afraid that the action of France which will still further ruin Germany will make it still harder for the workers of England to find employment or to get proper wages. That is why Mr Bonar Law, who unfortunately is as responsible as Mr Lloyd George for the bad features of the Treaty of Versailles, has now repented; and has broken with France, at least so far as to refuse to give his consent to the invasion of Germany or to let England take part in it. But everybody hears in London that France will persist, and that in a few weeks – perhaps in a few days – the French soldiers will have seized the coalfields and manufactories of the Rhineland in order to take the coal and wood for use in France without any payment.

Meanwhile the British unemployed – and there are still $1\frac{1}{2}$ million unemployed wage-earners – are trying to draw public attention to their terrible distress. On Sunday afternoon I attended a great demonstration in Trafalgar Square, a quarter of an hour's walk from this house. The open space was packed with masses of unemployed working men, all of whom had marched from different parts of London. It was impressive to see these great processions, with the banners of the different trade unions, surging into Trafalgar Square from the east and the west and the north and the south. They were mostly young men, and they looked very wretched tramping in the mud – and underfed and hopeless. In the centre of the Square there rises up the Nelson monument, and from the base of this monument some twenty feet above the ground, George Lansbury and other Labour Leaders spoke to the unemployed and told them to go on agitating and demonstrating until the Government consented to listen to them. But I am afraid that Mr Bonar Law and the Conservative majority in Parliament, have made up their minds to sit tight and do nothing. They say that there will sooner or later be an improvement in trade and that in a few months the numbers unemployed will be diminished, perhaps by one-half. Meanwhile these men and women – some of them boys and girls just out of school – are becoming demoralised by idleness and lack of proper food, warm clothes and decent housing. Conservative and Liberal Members of Parliament talk glibly about unemployed persons being 'unemployable'. But keeping men idle on insufficient food, and crowding whole families into one or two rooms, is exactly the way to make the unemployed 'unemployable'.

My husband and I are coming up to Seaham for Easter week, when Parliament will not be sitting. If possible I should like to meet the members of the Dawdon Women's Section some afternoon in that week.

Yours very sincerely

Beatrice Webb

## 729 PP SIDNEY TO BEATRICE

Relations between the Second and Third Internationals was a continuing problem during the first years of the peace, both between the various socialist parties and between the factions within them. The Vienna or 'Two-and-a-Half' International to which the I.L.P. had now affiliated, together with the Austrians, Swiss, and parts of the French and German movement, was an attempt to form a single grouping open to both social-democrats and communists. After complex manoeuvres, the situation was eased when the two wings of the German party reunited and made it possible to consider a fusion between the Vienna and Second Internationals. The International Federation of Trade Unions called a World Peace Conference in Amsterdam, to which it invited delegates from trade unions, socialist parties, women's and peace societies. The occasion was used for a meeting between the Vienna and Second Internationals: this arranged a further conference in Hamburg in May 1923 when a new Labour and Socialist International was formed. Peter Jelles Tröelstra (1860–1930) had been leader of the Dutch Socialist Party since 1894.

Weltfriedenskongress
Veranstaltet vom Internationalen Gewerkschaftsbund
Im Dierentuin
Haag (Holland)
10–15 Dezember 1922
11th Dec (Monday) 1922

Dearest

It is raining here, intermittently, and warm, so that I have never even undone your rug. The Congress is the strangest agglomeration of 600 delegates from 24 countries, representing a total membership (so it declares) of 14 millions – ranging from Radek and other Russian Bolshevists up to Willoughby Dickinson, the Dean of Worcester (Moore Ede) and Lady Parmoor (whom I have not yet seen, and who may have gone home). There are 8 British Labour MPs, but MacDonald returns tonight. The arrangements are all characteristically loose and time-wasting, but very good-humoured, and fundamentally sensible for a mere mass demonstration. Yesterday afternoon we began (very late) in a vast hall filled by a huge crowd of delegates and visitors with an oration by J. H. Thomas, who is Chairman; addresses of welcome from all the Dutch bodies: double translation of every one of them, interspersed with excellent singing of [a] Dutch cantata by a great amateur chorus. This consumed all the session. In the evening I attended (from 8 to 12) a meeting of the Second International Executive to receive a deputation of seven (Adler, etc.) from the Vienna 2½ International – speeches all translated once at least – ending in agreement (resolution to be instantly published all over the Socialist world) for reunion [*sidenote inserted:* prompt invitation by Tröelstra of us all to dinner tomorrow]; appointment of joint Committee to summon a united International Socialist and Labour Congress (assuming exclusion of the Russian Third International) to meet probably in April in or after Easter Week. So there is another foreign engagement; I hope for *both* of us!

I saw Miss Jane Addams this morning; she is coming to London for Christmas Week. I warmly invited her to come to 41 Grosvenor Road if she could spare us the time. I have shaken hands with, been introduced to, or spontaneously greeted heaps of people, some of whom I remembered, and others not. I have so far done my best not to eat too much, which is made difficult by the practical impossibility of getting anything but a heavy meal, and yet fostered by the fact that these heavy meals are appallingly dear, usually seven to ten shillings each. On the other hand, bed and breakfast at the very good Hotel are only to be charged to us at 5 gilders (or about 8/9). I was kept up until midnight yesterday, but I then slept straight through until this morning light about 6.30 a.m., so that is all right. My cold is nearly gone.

I am inclined to think I can return by Wednesday's night's boat, arriving Thursday morning. I will let you know. I have not yet learnt the post, but I fear you will not get my letter of Sunday until Tuesday, so that this one may perhaps follow on it quickly.

Today I lunched with Willoughby Dickinson and the Dean of Worcester (Moore Ede). Dickinson deplored the strife between Liberal and Labour, but admitted that the Liberal leaders made it inevitable, together with the local elections.

Goodnight.

Sidney

730 PP SIDNEY TO BEATRICE

Karl Radek (1885–1939) left the German Social Democratic Party to become a Leninist in 1917. From 1920 to 1924 he was secretary of the Communist International. Later he was tried as a Trotskyist. Friedrich Adler (1879–1960) was the secretary of the Austrian Social Democratic Party 1911–24 and became secretary of the new International 1923–40. Sir George Paish (1867–1953) was editor of the *Statist*. He was an early advocate of a League of Nations, publishing a book on it in 1918. Mrs Rollo Russell was married to Bertrand Russell's uncle; Mary Sheepshanks was an I.L.P. pacifist and a friend of MacDonald; Isabella Ford, a cousin of Edward Pease, had been present at the founding of the Fabian Society in 1884 and thereafter remained active for advanced causes in Leeds. Margaret Bondfield (1873–1953), the organiser for the General and Municipal Workers Union, became the first woman to enter the Cabinet on becoming Minister of Labour in 1929. J. W. Bowen was the general secretary of the Union of Public Employees and a member of the T.U.C. general council; R. J. Davies was Labour M.P. for West Houghton and a member of the Labour Party executive. Miss Ruider may be a mistake for Miss Maude Royden, a well-known Quaker and member of the Fight the Famine Council formed in January 1919 to campaign against the continuing blockade of Germany.

Grand Hotel Central
Lange Poten
's-Gravenhage
Tuesday 12th Dec/22

Dear One

It seems likely that I may arrive home before this letter reaches you. I am proposing to cross tomorrow night, and may be home about 10 a.m. on Thursday. I have so telegraphed you this morning, in order to stop possible letters ( I have as yet received none). Yesterday I had tea with Sir George Paish, Mrs Rollo Russel, Miss Sheepshanks (who has spent a year travelling all over South America), Miss Isabella Ford and MacDonald.

In the evening as there was nothing to do, a party of us went to a concert (festivals of the National School of Singing), with Henderson, Gillies, Miss Bondfield, Bowen and R. J. Davies. I had no sooner laid my head on the pillow than I fell asleep, and woke only with the morning light! But it is all rather futile and boresome, because it is mere declamation and vague emotional oratory, with the General Strike against any outbreak of war in the background. At the luncheon interval, a small party of us are going to Scheveningen for a walk along the sea front; returning in time for the afternoon session. Tonight I am dining with Second and the Vienna Internationals, at Tröelstra's invitation. A great 'Commission' of sixty is apparently going to be appointed to prepare resolutions for Friday. I could have got on this, but am not really wanted; and I devoted myself to securing representation (in the quota from Great Britain) for the non-Labour elements of whom Pethick-Lawrence and Miss [?Ruider] (for the Fight the Famine Council) were arranged for (most of the other notables are going away).

I think the Congress has been successful in propagandist value, and in increasing international acquaintanceship. I am sorry to be away from the House tomorrow when I gather there may be a discussion on the mining industry. But I should not have spoken (as the miners would have had the preference), and I hope there will be no division. Radek has just spoken, pouring scorn on the Conference for its absurd reliance on a General Strike on the outbreak of war; pointing out that this meant the Social Revolution, which could not be undertaken on any precise date foreseen in advance. He scoffed at the strange composition of the Congress to which middle-class Liberal pacifists had been invited, but not the Societies as such. He declared that only the 'United Front' of the working class was of any use: that to fight war was also to fight the bourgeoisie; that the differences between the Socialists and the bourgeoisie were much greater than between the Socialists and the Communists. He suggested that, to be practical, the Congress should decide on a universal week of propaganda for peace, ending with a 24 hours universal strike, just to impress the Governments. (He and some Russian Co-operators had secured visas, but five other Bolshevists had been stopped at Berlin by refusal of Dutch visa.) To him followed Vandervelde (great excitement and applause) who theatrically welcomed Radek's transformation into mildness when he wanted to inveigle the Western Socialists into union. But would Radek's government give Georgia its freedom, and amnesty the Social Revolutionaries? He said the Conference of Premiers at London had broken up, under conditions of which he was most [*word omitted*] and that of Lausanne was continuing under circumstances of which he was even more apprehensive. He and the French Socialists stood for Reparations, but if it meant reducing the German workmen to slavery, they were against it. The only remedy was the International, which he was glad to say was now at last reunited. A magnificent oration, but containing very little. This ended the day. The Commission is not yet appointed as the 'Bureau' will consider it tonight.

Dear one, goodnight. I feel I have had enough of it, and too much because you are not here for companionship. But it would have been terribly tiring for you – the heat, the smoke, the noise – outside, the cold wind today, and the difficulty of eating. Goodnight, if this reaches you before I arrive, expect me one morning about 10 a.m. But I think I shall cross tomorrow (Wednesday) night.

Sidney

731 MUL SIDNEY WEBB TO E. D. SIMON

The Liberal weekly, the *Nation*, was controlled by the Rowntree family. A combination of financial difficulties and a growing disagreement between the proprietors and the editor, H. W. Massingham – increasingly opposed to Lloyd George and favourably disposed towards the Labour Party – led to a situation when it seemed that the weekly review would be closed if new backers could not be found. After protracted negotiations the weekly came under the control of the 'Oxford Summer School' group of Liberals, which included J. M. Keynes and Walter Layton (1884–1966) editor of the *Economist* 1922–38. Massingham then resigned. At the same time the new owners were privately negotiating with Clifford Sharp who, to the displeasure of the Webbs, had swung the *New Statesman* into a Liberal orbit. They discussed a plan to merge the two weeklies, very similar in character, with Sharp as the editor. Sharp put two propositions to Webb. Either Webb should sell out and permit the merger; or he should find sufficient money to ensure the survival of the *New Statesman* on its own.

Webb, after the initial shock, was disposed to sell. Under Sharp, Beatrice noted, the paper 'had ceased to be of use to us'. (BWD 11 January 1923) Moreover, Sidney's position had changed. When the Webbs launched their weekly in 1913, Beatrice remarked, permeation 'was still a conceivable policy'. The Webbs, like the Fabian Society, were now firmly committed to Labour, and they saw no point in retaining links with the paper if it became overtly Liberal in its politics. Two of the *New Statesman* directors, Glynne Williams and Edward Whitley, were opposed to the sale: they offered to underwrite the continuing deficit. Williams became chairman and Whitley vice-chairman of the Board. The curious structure of the *New Statesman* company, devised by Webb, ensured that the paper was controlled by the owners of a small number of management shares, irrespective of the much larger holdings of ordinary shares. Williams, Whitley, the Webbs and Shaw held a comfortable majority of the crucial shares. Arnold Bennett and E. D. Simon, both disposed to the amalgamation with the *Nation*, were now relieved from making any further subsidies.

41 Grosvenor Road
Westminster Embankment
3 Jan/23

Dear Simon

Sharp told me yesterday of the project – of course I don't like it. Whatever Sharp may think, it means the end of the purpose for which *I* projected the N.S. in 1913. But that has already been very largely determined by the course of events in particular by (a) Sharp's own gradual 'liberalisation'; and (b) the failure of the Labour or Socialist side to find continuously the necessary subventions. Hence I am resigned to such a change; and do not resent it at all.

I can see no way of keeping the *N.S.* going on Labour and Socialist money. Hence, when a chance comes along to turn it into a profitable venture by absorbing its chief rival, and running it on lines which commend themselves to you and most of the others, I feel that I have no right to stand in the way. It will still be doing useful work; not quite with the effect that *I* should wish, but nevertheless good in itself.

Whitley (whom I saw by coincidence yesterday, and who turns out to be the largest shareholder of you all) takes a somewhat stronger objection to the paper becoming 'Liberal' as it inevitably must, (though, of course, of the 'Manchester' variety). He intended at once to consult with Glynne Williams to see if some means could not be concerted to go on as at present. On the other hand, I gather now from Sharp that Glynne Williams had concurred with him as to the advantage of his plan. And I don't think Whitley could see his way to the necessary money without you and the others.

As to the date of the necessary Board meeting, as it must be before you leave for S. Africa on the 11th, and I *must* imperatively leave London for Newcastle (bye-election) at 9.50 a.m. *that morning*, there is no time to lose. I fear it must inconvenience most of us, but there seems no alternative to a meeting on either 5, 6, 7, 8, 9, 10 January. I urged Sharp to telephone or telegraph this morning to arrange for this – assuming that he heard this morning that his own conditions were provisionally accepted by W. T. Layton and Co.

If it goes through as you project, I feel that I must get out of the concern (my position as chairman of the Labour Party makes that necessary to me). I have never had a penny for all the work I have put in for the paper these nine years – nothing, of course, for superintendence, which I never wished – and no cash for writing, of which I have done a lot, at times, when needed, to my own loss. The ordinary contributors' rates for my writing have been credited to me in shares, which (with the £300 put in by Mrs Webb and myself in cash) now come to something like £1,750.

On the other hand I don't like making any terms for myself which do not extend to other dissentients such as Whiteley, on the one hand; and Bernard Shaw, and Bulley on the other. (There is also Harben, from whom no one has heard for a year or so.)

It looks as if about half the nominal capital (apart from Glynne Williams) were 'dissentient' – not so much to the scheme itself, which for myself I feel I have no moral right to obstruct, as to remaining in the new concern.

What would you propose to do about this aspect of the case? The one alternative which (at least in my own case) seems negative is retaining an interest either (a) in any form permanently; *or* (even temporarily) (b) dependent on profits.

I hope I have made it clear that I have not the slightest ill feeling about the matter; and that I am cordially desirous only of making the best arrangement for (a) the paper, and (b) all concerned.

Yours, most warmly and cordially

Sidney Webb

732 MUL SIDNEY WEBB TO E. D. SIMON

41 Grosvenor Road
Westminster Embankment
5.1.23

Dear Simon

Your invitation to the *N.S.* Board to dinner at the Berkeley on Wed 10 January at 7.30 (including Mrs Webb) is a welcome opportunity for a general talk, which will, I am sure, be warmly responded to. Sharp tells me that Layton and Co. may by that time have been able to formulate a definite proposal.

I confess that I see considerable difficulties if (as I anticipate) it is intended to change, materially, the composition of the Board, to say nothing of the policy of the paper, as regards its attitude to political parties.

Whitley, who is the largest shareholder, is very strongly opposed. Bernard Shaw, to whom Massingham has now appealed personally, is equally opposed; and though he has stood very aloof since the first year, he has a considerable holding. In fact, the Management Shares are held as under:

| | | | |
|---|---|---|---|
| Whitley | 64 | Simon | 49 |
| S. and B. Webb | 37 | Bennett | 26 |
| Shaw | 16 | Le Bas | — |
| | 117 | | 75 |
| Harben | 15 | Glynne Williams | 46 |
| Bulley | 6 | | |
| | 138 | | |

This, in effect, puts a serious responsibility on *me*: if only to consider the interests of our original colleagues.

It may, of course, turn out that not so much change is involved as they fear and expect. Moreover, I must emphasise (a) the possible financial advantage of any proposal; and (b) the necessity of considering the contingencies involved in rejecting it.

Nevertheless, apart from my own feelings, I have to regard the matter as one of trusteeship. Apart from Glynne Williams (who is not quite in the same intellectual or party position as my wife and myself, Whitely, Shaw, Harben and Bulley) there is a total of a little under £12,000 (nominal) capital at stake *among these*.

But we must await the definite proposal. At present I am quite in the dark on many important points.

Yours very truly

Sidney Webb

733 HRCUT SIDNEY WEBB TO EDWARD PEASE

After Massingham had been eased out of the *Nation* he made an attempt to launch a new left-wing weekly, with support from H. G. Wells and Harold J. Laski, but nothing came of the plan. He worked briefly for the *Spectator* before his death in 1924. The *Nation* in fact survived for another seven years: it was then absorbed by the *New Statesman*.

John Lawrence Le Breton Hammond (1872–1949), journalist and historian, wrote a number of books on economic history with his wife Barbara.

Pease had a scheme to underwrite a biography of Robert Owen. In 1900 Sara Hall had left money to the Fabians to further the ideas of Owen, but for more than twenty years these funds had been blocked by an unsympathetic solicitor: the Fabian Society had only just come into the income of £300 per year.

(2–9 February at Hotel Alexandra, Lyme Regis)
41 Grosvenor Road
Westminster Embankment
1.2.23

Dear Pease

The dissolution of the *Nation* at the end of March leaves available for paid work (and needing jobs) various useful people; unless Massingham succeeds in starting on a new paper.

First and foremost is J. L. Hammond, the very able and erudite author of *The Village Labourer*, *The Town Labourer* and *The Skilled Labourer*, three admirable monographs on the beginning of the 19th century, derived from the unpublished material in the Public Record Office. We think most highly of him (and his wife who collaborates).

Is he not exactly the man to write your Life of Robert Owen? He is sympathetic; knows more about the social and industrial history of the period than anyone; is probably about to join the F.S.; and would almost certainly jump at the chance. He would be certain to produce not only a good book, but also one that would sell and have both reputation and influence.

If you want to read one book of his, and have not yet done so, I advise your getting his middle one (*The Town Labourer*) which is, I think, the best.

Another man left stranded is L. S. Woolf, who has, as you will remember done two books successfully for the F.S.; and endless unpaid service for the Labour Party and the Co-operative movement. We should much like to get him to do a book on Russian Bolshevism (he knows Russian, and is well acquainted with Russian literature). This would be a big job, involving visiting Geneva (where the International Labour Office has a mass of material), and Moscow, nominally to study Co-operation there. Would you be disposed to spend out of the Atkinson Fund, say £250 for expenses and a fee of £250, the latter recoverable from royalties before he got anything out of them? I don't know whether, or when, Woolf would undertake it.

Yours

Sidney Webb

734 PP SIDNEY TO BEATRICE

The Webbs had gone to Lyme Regis for a rest. Sidney returned to London to take his seat in Parliament on the Tuesday. The Parliamentary Labour Party was to caucus at Caxton Hall.

Reginald McKenna (1863–1943) had been in the pre-war Liberal Cabinets at the Admiralty, Home Office and the Exchequer. He lost his seat in 1918 when he supported the Asquith Liberals. In 1919 he became chairman of the Midland Bank. J. A. Spender, the outstanding Liberal journalist of the time, wrote biographies of Campbell-Bannerman and Asquith. Robert Brand (1878–1963), later Lord Brand, had been one of Milner's 'kindergarten' in South Africa, becoming a leading financial specialist and heading British missions overseas. Sir Patrick Hastings (1880–1952) was a brilliant advocate who was elected as a Labour M.P. in 1922 and became Attorney-General in MacDonald's 1924 government. Sir Herbert Lawrence (1861–1943), soldier and banker, had been the chief of the general staff in 1918.

41 Grosvenor Road
Westminster Embankment
10.2.23

Dearest

It seems clear that I must stay until Monday morning: there is a train arriving 9.50, which *may* leave me time to come here on my way to Caxton Hall.

Last night's dinner was on the whole useful and interesting. The house very gorgeous inside; the dinner costly and stylish, but short. Present: McKenna, his wife; Grey, Spender, Brand: MacDonald, Hastings, Snowden, Lawrence and Webb. I sat between McKenna and Spender, and talked almost exclusively with the latter. He had been in France, and knew practically nothing about the *Nation* episode.

After dinner, Grey made an attempt to talk Foreign Affairs, which MacDonald politely avoided; and we settled down to discuss the Capital

Levy. McKenna objected to it, (a) as fatal to credit facilities; (b) as dependent on mere estimates of values: (c) as not being in much of its working superior to an Extra Income Tax on Unearned Income; (d) as being objectionable because a 'new tax', whereas old taxes gradually became harmless and painless. Brand was mostly silent, but allowed it to be seen that he simply hated the whole thing. Grey and Spender were concerned at the violence with which the press and the bankers and business men would oppose and denounce it. MacDonald sat silent; and Snowden did not intervene much. Lawrence and Hastings and I fought McKenna. He finally admitted that there need be no disturbance of credit if the Government (where the business man could or would not pay in cash or Government stock) contented itself with taking it by instalments, *without insisting* on a *mortgage or charge*, and simply claiming as creditors.

His final rally was his asserted objection to mere estimates of value (as in Death Duties).

It was noteworthy that not anyone of them had taken the trouble to read the Labour Party pamphlet or any book on the subject whatever. It was quite clear that, whilst finding intellectual reasons for their objection, they really objected to increased taxation of the rich – as they *said*, because (a) the wealth was in the hands of those who knew how to use it best (!); and (b) because more was saved out of large than out of small incomes. Grey and Spender refused (when I challenged them) to admit that a big shifting of taxation from the mass to the wealthy, whatever form it might take, was part of the Liberal policy. (Nor do I believe it is; yet their candidates often say so.)

Incidentally McKenna expatiated on the American debt bargain, approving the agreement as the best thing we could get, but saying that our policy ought to be to pay all that we had to pay by buying gold and shipping it to America, where it would upset their prices and business terribly, and teach them within a few years to let us off altogether. He declared axiomatically that all considerable international payments were absolutely *impossible*; though no business man in England anymore than in America or France could believe it.

I was struck by the vigour and brightness, yet narrowness, of McKenna; and with the sulkiness and stubborn silence of Brand (who, by the way seemed to think McKenna flashy and superficial! Mrs McKenna seemed very charming; much interested; and more sympathetic to Labour than he was. Her eldest son (13) and another are at Summerfields, Oxford, which is, I think, where Dick Russell is going.

Now I must start as the Hendersons are going by the 3.55 train. Goodbye, dear one

Sidney

I hope you got my letter this afternoon

In August 1920, while attending the international socialist conference at Geneva, Beatrice had talked to the wives of several Labour leaders about their loneliness and social isolation in London. On her return, with the help of Mrs Clynes and in the face of opposition from MacDonald and others, she organised the Half-Circle Club for the wives of Labour politicians and trade union leaders. It soon had over 150 members who met regularly (usually once a month), sometimes at Grosvenor Road. Its aim was both to provide a meeting place for these women and, to some extent, to prepare them for the adjustment to life in London Society. The latter purpose laid Beatrice open to criticism as a *grande dame* coaching her social inferiors in the graces and problems of social life, but the club was popular and met a real need.

In the spring of 1923 Lady Warwick asked the Labour Party if it was interested in using Easton Lodge, her large house in Essex, as a conference centre. She had already made it available for weekend meetings. (Wells lived next door at Easton Glebe.) A working party which included MacDonald, Henderson and the Webbs went down to Easton to find that Lady Warwick had leaked the visit to the press and the group was pestered by photographers. The publicity was unfortunate, giving the impression that Labour was being corrupted by the prospect of luxurious living. Beatrice, who admired Lady Warwick's public spirit and energetic support of socialism, rightly anticipated that the plan would not work.

THE HALF-CIRCLE CLUB

41 Grosvenor Road
Westminster Embankment, S.W.1
25th April 1923

My dear Mrs Wells

I send you the enclosed card in the hopes that you and H.G. will be able to come to this gathering. I suppose you would not come and lunch here and go on to the Chelsea sights afterwards?

I have not heard whether the parties at Easton Lodge have been a success or not, except the one which Henderson chaperoned, which I gather that he and the others much enjoyed. But I have been so busy with various matters that I have not had time to go round to the Labour Party office and find out what is happening with regard to Easton Lodge. I gather that all the arrangements are in the hands of one of the staff under the direction of Mr Henderson.

You will see from the enclosed circular that the H.C.C. is proposing to go to Easton Lodge for the weekend of July 7th. What is suggested is that the executive, together with any husbands who are able to attend, should stay for the weekend, asking the members to come down for a picnic in the woods and tea afterwards at Easton Lodge. We should all bring our lunch so that there would be the least possible bother over the arrangements. I hope that you and H.G. and your sons will be there. I should imagine if the day were fine we should have about 200 – perhaps even more, as I think there is a good deal of curiosity about Easton Lodge. Would you be inclined to put up any of the executive in case all decided to come, which would make too large a party I think for Easton Lodge? Also there is the Entertainments Committee, some of whom I should like to have there in order to consult about various matters. It would, of course, be very nice if the Bernard Shaws could be there as your guests. I understand that the following week-end, July 14th, the women members of the Labour Party executive are proposing to have a small conference of Labour M.Ps. and women organisers to discuss the whole question of women's interests in Parliament. Here again they would no doubt be very grateful for extra accommodation for the M.Ps. and if you were going to be there and had your rooms vacant I might suggest one or two of the M.Ps. as your guests. We shall not be there, as I hope to be in the country at that time. Also I think the women members of the executive had better run the party and not be bothered with mere wives.

I should like to hear what your impression is about all these arrangements. We still remember with pleasure our evening at your house.

Always yours

Beatrice Webb
(Mrs Sidney Webb)

736 NH BEATRICE WEBB TO ÉLIE HALÉVY

Harry Gosling (1861–1930), a former docker, was president of the Transport Workers Federation: he became Minister of Transport in 1924. Stanley Baldwin (1867–1947) was Chancellor of the Exchequer in 1922–23, in the latter year succeeding Bonar Law as Prime Minister.

With Sidney's advent to Parliament Beatrice became busy as a hostess again, giving political lunches and promoting the Half-Circle Club. 'I have always had some such double life to lead', she noted on 11 May 1923, 'literary work on the one hand, and some cause to advance by social intercourse'. Sidney was enjoying his first taste of the parliamentary life: his relations with MacDonald, Beatrice remarked, were 'unexpectedly cordial'. (BWD 30 May 1923) The Webbs had spent ten days in Hamburg as part of the British delegation to the founding conference of the new International.

Lord Robert Cecil (1864–1958), the son of the Marquess of Salisbury, became Viscount Cecil in 1923, and President of the League of Nations Union 1923–45. He held several offices in Conservative governments: in 1923 he became Lord Privy Seal, and in 1924 Chancellor of the Duchy of Lancaster.

41 Grosvenor Road
Westminster Embankment
1st June 1923

My dear M. Halévy

We are really most grateful to you for sending us the third volume of your great History. I am taking down both volumes to the country to read during our holidays – in the present whirl of Parliamentary work and entertaining – I have to keep open house for the Labour Members – combined with my own literary work, I simply have not got the capacity to read anything worth reading. Sidney, however, did read the other volume and was immensely delighted with it, and will I am sure enjoy this one even more, as the period becomes exciting from the standpoint of democratic development. I was delighted to see such an admirable review in the Literary Supplement of *The Times* of the former volume.

We have just returned from the Hamburg International Socialist Congress. It was pitiful to see the depression of the Germans. Though of course they were extremely polite and accommodating to the British delegation they did not care to talk to us, they were too sore and 'down and out'. There is no doubt prosperity among the peasants. But Hamburg is a dead city, and Gosling, the General Secretary of the Transport Workers, who knows the port well, told me, after a trip round it in a tug which he chartered himself, that it was 'as on Sunday' and that there was hardly any trade going on except a little with the U.S.A. and England. But no internal trade. The feeling against France is, of course, intense; and the outlook for the whole of Europe seems to me to be unprecedentedly black.

The present Government is a stronger one than the last owing to the inclusion of McKenna and Lord Robert Cecil – also there is a general feeling that Baldwin is a more determined and on the whole abler man than Bonar Law, though not nearly so clever a Parliamentarian. The Liberal Party is going to pieces more rapidly than ever: the hatred of Lloyd George being the dominant feeling among the Independent Liberals, whilst the National Liberals are breaking away into Conservativism on the one hand and slinking back into the official Liberal ranks on the other. The Parliamentary Labour Party is going very well – barring a few indiscretions in the way of singing revolutionary songs in the Lobby. J. R. MacDonald is proving a far better leader than I should have expected and there is more intercourse among the members and participation in the work of the Party than I should have thought possible a year ago. But of course the inherent difficulty of social reconstruction in the present international circumstances is immense, and all the forces of reaction are consolidating, in Great Britain as elsewhere, against any change in the existing order. Whether we in England will pull through to another and a better kind of civilisation is still open to question.

With kindest remembrances to Madame Halévy

Yours very sincerely

Beatrice Webb

(Mrs Sidney Webb)

## 737 BMJL BEATRICE WEBB TO HAROLD J. LASKI

In 1922, Wilfred Paling was elected for Doncaster, Tom Smith for Pontefract and Tom Williams for the Don Valley. All three held various posts in Labour governments.

Sir Oswald Mosley was born in 1896. His wife Cynthia was the daughter of Lord Curzon (1859–1925), recently Foreign Secretary and passed over for the succession to Bonar Law on the grounds that the prime minister could no longer sit in the House of Lords. Mosley was elected to Parliament as a Conservative, but at the time of this letter he was about to join the Labour Party in which, for a few years, he was regarded as a possible successor to MacDonald as leader. Handsome, rich and an excellent speaker, Beatrice considered that he was 'the most brilliant man in the House of Commons'. (BWD 8 June 1923) She thought he combined great charm with 'solid qualities of character, aristocratic refinement with democratic opinions'. She sensed, however, 'some weak spot which will be revealed in a time of stress – exactly at the moment when you need support – by letting you or your cause down or sweeping it out of the way'.

41 Grosvenor Road
Westminster Embankment
14th June 1923

Dear Mr Laski

I am asking three Labour Members whom I do not think you know – a trio of young men representing Yorkshire constituencies – Paling, Tom Smith and Tom Williams, to lunch at the School of Economics on Wednesday 27th. If you can will you reserve yourself and ask Mr Finer if he could do so likewise, as they are very eager to learn and I should like to introduce them to you both. I may ask one or two more so I shall engage a table for the party.

By the way we had Oswald Mosley to dine here the other night. What a perfect person – almost too perfect for this wicked world. And his wife seems a charming creature – more American than English aristocrat and quite ready that her husband should join the Labour Party. But whether he will get through the eye of the needle of great wealth I do not know. Perhaps you can expedite the change as I believe you know him. We have got Patrick Hastings to take the Chair for you in the autumn course, and we shall try to get Mosley for Tawney if the Bishop of Manchester refuses, as I expect he will. In that case perhaps for Bertrand Russell.

Always yours
Beatrice Webb
(Mrs Sidney Webb)

## 738 PP BEATRICE WEBB TO FRIENDS OF SEAHAM

It was at the Labour Party conference in 1923 that Webb used, in his chairman's address, the phrase by which he is best remembered: 'the inevitability of gradualness'. It was not intended, as it is customarily interpreted, as an approving gloss upon the Fabian policy of step-by-step social change. It was in fact a summary of his argument, based upon the steady increase in Labour representation in Parliament, that Labour would before long be in a position to form a government.

James Maxton (1885–1946) was a schoolteacher who was elected as an I.L.P. member for Bridgeton, Glasgow: he became the chairman and main leader of the I.L.P. in the inter-war years. John Wheatley (1869–1930), a former miner, was M.P. for Shettleston and, as Minister of Housing in 1924, one of the successes of the first Labour government. Campbell Stephen (1884–1947) was the M.P. for Camlachie 1922–31, and was again elected on the I.L.P. ticket in 1935. George Buchanan (1890–1955), one of the leaders of the Clydeside shop-stewards during the war, became Minister of Pensions in 1947–48 and chairman of the National Assistance Board.

Thomas Burt (1837–1922), a miner from Morpeth, was elected as Liberal M.P. in 1874.

41 Grosvenor Road
Westminster S.W.1
23rd July 1923

Dear Friends

I am afraid that my letter this month will not reach you in time for your July meeting. But I had to insist on my husband going away with me into the country for a week's complete rest. What with the Labour Party Conference, long hours in Parliament, and, be it added, the stifling heat, he was thoroughly tired out. I am glad to tell you he soon got quite fit for his work until the end of the session.

During the last month the three events which have interested me most are the Labour Party Annual Conference, the Prime Minister's statement about the French occupation of the Ruhr district of Germany, and the suspension of the four Scottish Members owing to their defiance of the Speaker's ruling.

I will first deal with the Labour Party Conference over which my husband presided. I wonder how much you know about the constitution and business of this Annual Conference of the Labour Party? The Conference consists of the elected representatives of the national Trade Unions, the local Labour Parties and three Socialist organisations – the I.L.P., the Fabian Society and the Social Democratic Federation – with a total membership of nearly four million men and women. Among all these different bodies the Miners' Federation of Great Britain, with its membership of nearly a million and its consequent voting power, stands out preeminent, the largest of the other Unions being the great organisations of the railway workers, the cotton operatives, the engineers and shipbuilders and the general labourers. This annual Conference elects an executive of 23 members and at its first meeting this executive selects a Chairman. It so happens that last year they chose my husband to be Chairman of the Executive. That is why he presided at the Annual Conference held in

London three weeks ago. It is this Executive which carries on the whole business of the Labour Party throughout the year; meeting for two or three days each month, appointing various committees to carry out the detailed business, and to recommend policy. But all the work done by this executive and its committees has to be reviewed by the Annual Conference from which it receives its orders for the following year. The Labour Party Conference stands, in fact, to the Labour Party in the same position as Parliament stands to the country; and the Labour Party Executive is the Cabinet of the British Labour Movement.

How can I describe to you all the business which is transacted by this great Conference of some eight hundred delegates from all parts of Britain? If I were to send you the agenda you would be puzzled by the multitude of questions which come up for decision, from foreign policy to housing, from the government of the British Commonwealth of Nations to workmen's compensation. But each year there are one or two subjects which absorb most of the interest of the Conference. This year the two predominant subjects, which were always coming up for discussion in one form or another, were, first, the important question whether or not the Labour Party should accept the Communist Party as one of its constituent bodies, and secondly, foreign affairs, more especially the French occupation of the Ruhr.

I do not think that you have many Communists in the Seaham Division? The miners are a hard-headed lot, and though they have always been in the forefront of Labour politics – did they not elect the first Labour man to Parliament? – they have always refused to be carried away by this or that new craze. But in the crowded slums of Glasgow, Manchester and London there have arisen little groups of exasperated men and women who wanted to persuade the members of the Labour Party to accept the doctrines and follow the example of the Russian Communists and the present Soviet Government of Russia. I have not the time or the space to tell you what I think about Bolshevism. But the theory and practice of the Russian Soviet Government is wholly inconsistent with the theory and practice of British Socialism. We British Socialists believe in political and industrial democracy: we do not believe in revolution through the dictatorship of a minority. We object altogether to dictatorships, whether they be of King or Pope, of Lords or Labourers, or Soldiers or Sailors. The British Labour Party has, however, never condemned the Russian Revolution; and the whole British Labour movement has vehemently objected to, and we think prevented, the intervention of the British Cabinet to upset the Soviet Government. We fully realise that owing to the abominable despotism of the Czar, and the absence of any representative institutions, it may well be that the only way in which any change could be made in Russia was by violent revolution. But unfortunately when once you begin with violence it is difficult to stop being violent: when once you set up any form of autocracy, whether it be government by an individual autocrat or by a militant minority – experience proves that it is extremely difficult to introduce government of the people, by the people for the people. Hence the British Labour movement does not consider that any British organisation which like the Communist Party, denies democracy, has any right to be part and parcel of the British Labour Party. Also the Communists are never tired of telling us that they will only join the Labour Party in order to upset its peaceful policy and to advocate and practise violence in getting hold of the government of the country. If you have read my husband's address to the Conference you will see how dangerous it would be for organised Labour in Great Britain to follow the example of the Russian Bolsheviks, and to attempt to seize the Government by force. What would happen in England is that the powerful associations of capitalists, having the money and the opportunity, would do as the capitalists have done in the United States of America and in Italy: they would shoot down the workers, and would establish a reign of terror in every industrial district. But the fundamental reason why the Labour Party Conference refused to accept the Communist Party as a constituent body was that the Labour Party actually disapproves of violence: it thinks it not only stupid but wicked. Hence we were content when the Labour Party Conference decided by a majority of two million votes not to admit the Communist Party to its counsels. Whenever the Communists of Great Britain cease to preach violence and become honest democrats we shall gladly welcome them as comrades.

From the standpoint of national prosperity the second question rousing discussion at the Conference was the more important. How best could the Labour Party bring pressure to bear on France to stop the illegal and iniquitous military occupation of the Ruhr District of Germany? Here again the Labour Party showed its abhorrence of any form of tyrannical conduct and illegal violence. In my last letter I described the terrible results of the seizure of the richest province of Germany by the French army. Every day matters grow worse; not only in the Ruhr district but in the whole of Germany. Any day you may read in the newspapers of hunger riots in the great towns of Germany, and of desperate attempts by the adherents to the ex-Emperor to re-establish a Dictatorship of the Proletariat. When millions of men, women and children are starving, anything may happen. Some people say that the French Government actually wants to bring about chaos in Germany in order to ruin the German nation and to prevent it from recovering its prosperity and its strength. But the British nation have everything to lose by this policy. Until Germany and Austria recover their prosperity there will never be the old market for our coal, our ships, our machinery, and our cotton cloth; and we shall continue to have hundreds of thousands of unemployed existing, day after day, on the miserable dole. It is only fair to acknowledge that the present Prime Minister seems to be aware of this fact and to be doing his best to persuade the French Government to withdraw from the Ruhr. Hence Mr Ramsay MacDonald, after listening to the statement of the Prime Minister, promised the support of the Labour Party in this wise policy. It is significant that the British Cabinet is beginning to be nervous about the menace of French militarism. We are told that the French have a great fleet of aeroplanes and that these aeroplanes are stationed on the north coast so that they can be used against Great Britain. That is why we are building large fleets of aeroplanes ourselves; that is why we cannot take off the tax on tea. Is it not a horrid throught that the result of the Great War has been to make France as dangerous to us to-day as Germany was before 1914?

Now about the four Scottish Members who have been suspended from attendance in Parliament. This trouble arose out of the insolent jeers of some Tory Members during the speech of the Labour Member for the Bridgetown Division of Glasgow. Mr Maxton was objecting to the reduction of the Public Health vote for milk for infants; he was describing in eloquent and vivid words how the cutting down of public expenditure on medical treatment and proper nourishment of children and babies had increased the death rate in the slums of Glasgow – that more infants were actually dying or being permanently diseased by this mistaken economy. Thereupon some Tory Member – it was thought the representative of the City of London – cried 'Hear, Hear!' an interruption which Mr Maxton and other Labour Members not unreasonably resented as callous rejoicing over the death of the little ones. 'Murderer' shouted Mr Maxton. When he was asked by the Speaker to withdraw this unparliamentary epithet he refused, and in this refusal he was supported by three other Scottish Members, Messrs Wheatley, Campbell Stephen and Buchanan, all of whom defied the Chair. Mr Ramsay MacDonald and other leaders of the Party tried to persuade our comrades to apologise for this defiance of the Speaker's ruling, and Mr MacDonald still thinks that they made a mistake in not doing so. I agree with our leader: I think it is not wise to bandy ugly words with the Tories, however insulting they may be: it is better to treat their ill-manners with silent contempt and go straight forward with argument and statement of fact. But when Labour men are jeered at because they try to compel the House of Commons to realise all the preventable death and disease caused by the neglect and starvation of the children in the slums, it is not altogether surprising that they lose control of their tempers and obstinately refuse to conform even to right and necessary rules of procedure. What some of them say is that it is only by these violent scenes that they can open the eyes of public opinion to these terrible tragedies of working class life.

I leave London the end of July and my husband joins me in the country when Parliament rises. During the Parliamentary recess we shall pay a brief visit to the Irish Free State so as to enable my husband to better understand the working of the new form of government. Perhaps I shall have something to tell you about Ireland in my next letter. But I am afraid I shall not be able to write to you again until September. Meanwhile, best wishes to you all

Your sincere friend

Beatrice Webb

(Mrs Sidney Webb)

739 LPA BEATRICE WEBB TO ARTHUR GREENWOOD

G. D. H. Cole resigned from the L.R.D. early in 1924 when it was clear that it had fallen completely under the control of the Communist Party.

41 Grosvenor Road
Westminster Embankment
27th July 1923

*Private*

My dear Mr Greenwood

As I shall not be seeing you again before I leave London on Monday I had better report about what I hear with regard to the Labour Research Department. I saw Hutchinson just after he had left the meeting of the Executive of the L.R.D., and I understand from him that Arnot and his party in the L.R.D. are likely to prevail over the Coles with regard to keeping the L.R.D. going in its present form – that is so far as income permits. Hutchinson told me – though he was not very clear on the matter – that the income from Trade Unions is about £1,500 a year and at present shows no signs of diminishing – at any rate at any rapid rate. On the other hand the Arcos subsidy of thousands terminates in October, though it is conceivable that they may get a small subsidy for work done for Arcos. But this is not at all certain. I gather that the representatives of the trade unions on the Trade Union Council and in the membership, are critical and think that they get very little value from the money they give. But they will not 'do a man out of his job', and they will refuse, Hutchinson thinks, to dismiss Arnot, and without this no alteration can be made. So I do not think that Cole will come along with any definite offer about the L.R.D. What he may be prepared to do is to bring over what he himself possesses in the L.R.D., and to refuse to give the L.R.D. the help of his name and his influence with the Trade Unions such as it is. I am inclined to think that they are, in fact, drawing a considerable income from trade unions and even individuals who are quite unaware that they are still unconnected with the Labour Party. I know a friend of ours sent them £100 not long ago thinking we were still concerned with the organisation, and only a few days ago Galton reported that a member had sent them in £5 for the L.R.D.

thinking it was still part of the Fabian Society. He returned the money to the donor and told him exactly the position of the L.R.D. with regard to the Labour Party and Fabian Society, leaving it to him whether to send it or not.

It may be desirable some time or other to clear the matter up at any rate with the trade unions, and of course if Cole would help to do that it would be a great advantage. However, I write all this for your and Mr Henderson's information, seeing that I spoke to Mr Henderson and you about it. Perhaps you would show him this letter or tell him about it, as I may not be seeing him again until the autumn.

How glad you will be to get away with Mrs Greenwood for a holiday. I hope it will be a good one.

Always yours

Beatrice Webb
(Mrs Sidney Webb)

### 740 PP SIDNEY TO BEATRICE

After the Webbs abandoned their plan to build a cottage at Dunford they began to look seriously for a country home. They assumed that Sidney would at most sit in one more Parliament and that they would then retire to the life of reading and research that Beatrice enjoyed. They also planned to leave such a house after their deaths for use as a retreat by L.S.E. staff and students. At the end of July they placed an advertisement in the *New Statesman* which was picked up in other papers as an item of gossip.

> Mr and Mrs Sidney Webb require a building site of an acre or more within a radius of 50 (or 75) miles of London in any direction (south preferred); preferably with a habitable cottage which could be developed. It must be relatively high with a pretty view; and above all completely isolated from houses harbouring cocks or dogs. Anyone knowing of such a site is begged to inform Mr Webb, 41 Grosvenor Road, Westminster.

Among those who replied was Edward Pease, offering a neighbouring plot to his own house at Limpsfield, where the Oliviers and other Fabians had settled. In August, while Sidney was at the Fabian summer school at Hindhead, he found Waterside Copse, near Liphook. It was high up, not large, and capable of extension. It was some distance from the road and it was necessary to install a water supply and a generating plant for electricity. The Webbs paid £1,750 for the property and over eight acres of hayfields and woodland. 'Happy hours Sidney and I spend in discussing alterations and possible extensions, and if we keep our health and strength we can hope for a happy old age under our own oak tree.' (BWD 31 August 1923)

Beveridge had completed the arrangement, which involved the consent of the Charity Commissioners, to return Dunford to Mrs Fisher Unwin in exchange for a cash settlement.

41 Grosvenor Road
Westminster Embankment
31.7.23

Dear One

Here are some unimportant letters. The *Westminster Gazette* had a third of a column on its front page, with the *N.S.* Advertisement in full: and the result is about a couple of dozen letters offering houses and land from Hereford and Norfolk down to Dover! Some of them seem quite eligible. I will bring them all with me on Thursday. I am sending the slip to Auctioneers in Berkshire today; and will send to some in Hampshire, Dorsetshire and Wiltshire tomorrow, so as to have the whole range of choice.

Beveridge telephones that Unwin's solicitor offers £7,250; and he has ascertained privately that the Charity Commissioners will approve – so that will go through. There will doubtless be still lots of trouble over details but that he must get through. He will then be able to *complete* the London building, which will be a very good thing.

The carpets and furniture have been taken away today, so that it looks more desolate than ever – the desolation began when I came home last night, and found you gone! Today it is uncomfortable; and I shall be glad when Thursday comes.

I hear the *Daily News* has a further paragraph about our demand for a cottage; the *Westminster Gazette* sent to ask whether we had had letters! Various M.P.'s asked me about it. So we shall receive some more letters presently.

There was great trouble at the House this afternoon about removing the Suspension but Baldwin, MacDonald and Asquith – so I am told – were very impressive; and the motion was ultimately carried without a division. I was busily engaged elsewhere. And must now post this to ensure arriving tomorrow.

Goodnight dear one

Sidney

### 741 BL BEATRICE WEBB TO GEORGE BERNARD SHAW

Mary Playne died of cancer in October. Beatrice Ross (known variously as 'Bichy' or 'Bice') was her secretary companion. Elizabeth Durning Russell was the second daughter of Beatrice's sister Lawrencina Holt. Lion Phillimore was an old friend, the widow of Sidney's fellow L.C.C. member in Deptford. She lived abroad between the wars.

Longfords
Minchinhampton
Sept 20th [1923]

My dear GBS

We were so glad to hear that you were again in England: Birmingham will be exciting – I see that *Joan* is to be acted this winter? Those latter acts we want to hear directly we meet again.

I am back here watching my poor dear sister dying of cancer of the lung – that is the third sister to die of cancer. But she was first operated on 15 years ago and again 5 years ago and except for a recent loss of memory she has had no illness until this last stage of the complaint. Her son and his wife are not over dutyful and are away in Scotland so I felt I must come down both for her sake and that of her devoted companion. I have to go back to London the middle of next week but may return here unless the end comes quickly – I hope it will, as she is wretched and weary though not in great pain. Sidney is in London and very well.

We thoroughly enjoyed our time with Lion Phillimore – a comfortable home, good cooking and a private sitting-room with a fire – motor drives out to hills and her agreeable companionship. She was [?writing] hard at [?Paul] and very full of all her reading – also arranging and paying for a big social party before the meeting of the Senate at which, all sides were to foregather. She talks of settling permanently in Ireland, living near Dublin in the winter and her place on the coast in the summer (I forget the name) – but I tried to dissuade her – she would weary of her fellow Celts after a time – she is too used to the variety of English life. We saw Æ. He struck me as depressed and worked out – not really knowing what to be at in Ireland and grasping at shadowy Ideals – I doubt the success of the *Irish* [?*Statesman*] inspite of your brilliant send off. Plunkett says he has £10,000 a year for 3 years guaranteed.

Betty Russell has Graves disease – which is curable if taken in time – she was down on her luck and they are bent on selling Bryan's Ground. We have possession of our cottage – which is nowhere near to Portsmouth Rd – the end of next week. Love to Charlotte.

Ever yours

Beatrice Webb

742 PP SIDNEY WEBB TO JANET MAIR

41 Grosvenor Road
Westminster Embankment
14.10.23

Dear Mrs Mair

I notice that Fire Insurance is a big item. I believe you could save 16 per cent of this by offering to pay seven years premiums down (they insure for 7 years in return for 6 years premiums). (I did this seven years ago; but am now only renewing annually – the School is, unlike me, immortal!) This might at least be thought of if you want to dispose of too big a surplus.

Yours

Sidney Webb

743 PP SIDNEY TO BEATRICE

Beatrice had spent ten days with Sidney at Seaham, where the Webbs had launched a circulating library among the women's sections of the Labour Party. Baldwin had come out strongly for Protection and an election seemed likely in the near future.

Beatrice, hoping to get into the cottage (which they had renamed Passfield Corner) on 21 November, intended to settle down seriously to the writing of *My Apprenticeship*, on which she had worked at intervals for some years. Charles Zueblin, American Fabian, municipal reformer and an old acquaintance of the Webbs, was offering to give a lecture at Shotton, one of the mining villages in the Seaham constituency.

J. Bainbridge was the Liberal candidate opposing Ben Spoor at Bishop Auckland: the reference may be to a joint meeting of several opposing candidates in the area.

32 Maureen Terrace
Seaham Harbour
28.10.23

Dear One

Here am I, on Sunday morning, a beautiful day, after a very stormy night – so noisy that I seem scarcely to have slept – but quite well; and pleased to be writing to my dearest. I am hoping that you, too, are enjoying the morning, in your own home, recovered from your ten days discomfort and exertions, and finding all well.

Yesterday I had a very good little meeting at Wheatley Hill, all very pleasant and enthusiastic some 50 present, including all the leaders of the Lodge, but, of course, none but miners. Half-a-dozen youthful I.L.P.'ers asked questions in a Communist direction, but without malice towards me. I warned them of the probable election, and of the Party's poverty, and that it would have to be done entirely on a voluntary basis. Then I came back to a good dinner of steak and onions (!), and wrote letters after tea till post time. Bainbridge came in, lame and weak, brought with his sons in a car to settle as to tonight's South Shields meeting, and was very pleasant. I had a quiet talk with Herron about the election arrangements. He quite desires the addressing done in London as before. He proposes to try to get the whole series of meetings arranged in advance, so as to print all on one poster, to be exhibited everywhere, and so save money – and so on.

I had a telegram from Zueblin late yesterday, which I handed to Herron to deal with; offering choice of 4 dates in November for Shotton, his agent (Christy) to be consulted as to fee. Herron is to write him thereon. I rather doubt whether this will come off, but this is for the Shotton miners to settle.

Last night it blew so hard that I could do nothing but think of my dear wife, and my great happiness and good fortune in life, and perhaps also the obligation that it put me under, more than ever, to remember the millions less fortunate, and deprived, unnecessarily, of the opportunities and happiness that might be so much more evenly shared, and thereby actually increased for all. My own particular way is not to be always thinking of that obligation, but to make it the base of life and work, so that merely in doing what is habitual we may be fulfilling it, perhaps even more effectively than by always having it in mind as a motive–I am amused to think that this, too, is a sort of 'Economy' and 'Efficiency', for which we are reproached; but all the same, it is my way.

Now, dear one, goodbye for the present. Don't work too hard, or think too much about the furnishing. There is time; and the difference between one thing and anyther – never so great as it seems – is always rather uncertain in net result.

Sidney

744 NLNZ SIDNEY WEBB TO WILLIAM PEMBER REEVES

It is not clear whether Reeves sent a monetary gift to the Webbs or a contribution to Sidney's election expenses. The Asquith and Lloyd George factions had come together again.

41 Grosvenor Road
Westminster Embankment
14.11.23

My dear Reeves

How very generous and kindly of you! I gratefully accept, not only because the gift is a welcome addition to strained resources, but even more because of the friendliness of the act, which my wife and I heartily appreciate. I have largely drifted out of the things we so long did in common, because of new responsibilities – not the House only, but the Party itself, involves great work. I have not broken down, however: indeed, people tell me I am better than I was two years ago – as I hope you are also. I go down to Seaham on Monday for a very strenuous fortnight of meetings. A great majority is, like other possessions, a great responsibility – one always feels bound in honor to maintain it unimpaired, even though a few thousands less would make no difference!

I predict the defeat of the Government by the loss of 40 to 50 seats net –

about half (net) to Labour and half to united Liberalism, for which the sudden re-emergence of this particular issue (due to the machinations of Hewins, and Amery and Lloyd George) is a quite unforeseen windfall. What *then* will happen is obscure.

With kind regards from my wife, and from us both to Mrs Reeves. I am

Yours very truly

Sidney Webb

## 745 PP SIDNEY TO BEATRICE

On the previous day Beatrice had reported that she had met Sanders and Galton at the Fabian office and that they thought Labour would get only 120 seats.

32 Maureen Terrace
Seaham Harbour
20/11/23

Dear One

Your letter was most welcome. All is well here. Decision of Liberals *not* to run a candidate. Herron working hard at organisation, with apparently no dissensions, and none but the usual difficulties. I found my last night's meeting fixed for Easington, where I had the usual very cordial meeting, (but not very full). Great determination to increase the vote and the majority.

Weather cold, but mostly fine, with occasional sharp showers.

I enclose some specimen Election Letters sent by Clark to me by post. The first batch ought to reach the Committee Room tonight. I slept the night through and am quite well.

I don't see how the pessimistic views of Sanders and Galton can be sustained. It looks to me as if the Free Trade defections from the Unionist ranks can hardly fail to sweep away their present majority. The only thing at issue is how this loss of 40 to 80 seats by the Unionists will be shared in gains by Liberals and Labour. I cannot believe that Liberalism will, *in addition*, displace Labour Members (as Sanders thinks). Labour is not likely to be less than 150 and maybe 185. Liberalism is not likely to be more than 165 or less than 130. I admit the horrid possibility of Liberalism just beating Labour; but I don't believe it.

Goodbye, dear one, I hope this will reach you at Passfield tomorrow. But there is a smash on the line south of York, and no London papers have arrived yet, so that there maybe delay. I hope you won't find many 'skeletons in the corner'.

Yours

Sidney

On polling day, 6 December, the Conservatives came back as the largest party with 258 seats, but they were outnumbered by the combined Labour (191) and Liberal (158) members. Webb was returned again with a very substantial majority. William Alexander Robson (b. 1895), a graduate of L.S.E., barrister and specialist in political administration, was for some years editor of the Fabian local government bulletin. He was a prominent Fabian and member of the Labour Party. He held the chair of public administration in London University 1947–62. He was a close associate of the Webbs in the later part of their lives.

41 Grosvenor Road
Westminster Embankment
16.12.23

Dear Robson

The one thing that neither I, nor anyone else could write now is 'What a Labour Government would do'! (I see your letter is to my wife, but she is too busy for anything; and the same objection also applies.)

But do you want such a 'political' article at all? I had not thought of such a thing. Are you sure that such a lead on central government *policy* is the right thing to give? After all, the task of the Councillor is to work the law as it is. Your object is to show him how to get the most out of it, irrespective of legislative or even administrative changes at Whitehall.

But even an article on these lines would not be for *me* to do now. How do I know that my fate may not be to be Minister?

Yours

Sidney Webb

# 5. The first Labour government

## December 1923 – December 1924

The Labour leaders had not expected to form a government and the possibility had not been seriously discussed. The decision rested with Asquith and Lloyd George, whose Liberal factions were now uneasily reunited, whether to permit Baldwin to continue or to put Labour in – there being no likelihood of Labour agreeing to a coalition with the Liberals. Baldwin himself believed it would be wise to give Labour a taste of office, thus strengthening the hand of the constitutionalists in the party; and the Liberals disliked Baldwin's protectionist trade policies so much that they preferred to support a minority Labour government, believing that after a few difficult months Labour would be unable to continue and that the Liberals might slip in without another election.

The situation, however, was unclear for several days. On Sunday 9 December Henderson lunched with the Webbs at Grosvenor Road. He told them that he favoured taking office, if the chance offered, with Liberal support for a moderate programme. Webb thought that no guarantees should be offered to the Liberals and that Labour should run the risk of defeat and press forward with its own policies. On the next day Henderson, MacDonald – who had only just returned from his Welsh constituency – Clynes, Thomas and Snowden lunched with the Webbs. They all, Beatrice noted, had 'cold feet' at the idea of office but agreed that MacDonald could not refuse if asked by the King to form a Cabinet. 'But what happens to the first Labour Cabinet – acting merely as a stop-gap government – is not really of much importance', Beatrice remarked. A spell of office would be 'like a scouting expedition in the world of administration – a testing of men and measures before they are actually called to exercise majority power'. (BWD 12 December 1923) 'Unanimous that moderation and honesty were our safety', MacDonald noted in his diary.

Though it was not then certain that MacDonald would become prime minister, for the formal vote in which Labour and Liberals combined to force Baldwin's resignation came only on 21 January, the complicated business of forming a Labour government for the first time went on all through the Christmas recess. MacDonald isolated himself by going off to his Lossiemouth home. Before he went (in fact, immediately on reaching London and before the meeting at Grosvenor Road) he saw R. B. Haldane, who had left the Liberals in 1922, and offered him whatever post he might choose, including the leadership of the House of Commons, Chancellor of the Exchequer, Defence and Education. Haldane elected to become Lord Chancellor. He also had a considerable influence on MacDonald's other choices.

MacDonald did not deal so simply with Henderson. There was no doubt that Henderson was entitled to high office: he had sat in the wartime Cabinets of Asquith and Lloyd George, and been chairman of the Labour Party during the war, its secretary for twelve years, and its chief whip in the previous Parliament. But he had lost his seat at the election; and MacDonald, expecting another contest within the year, thought he would devote his energies to refurbishing the party machine for the contest. MacDonald, who always had difficulties in his personal relations with Henderson, certainly gave Webb the impression that he was trying to keep Henderson out; and he apparently considered him for the Colonial Office, Ministry of Health and the War Office – as well as for the chairmanship of the Committee of Ways and Means – before he finally offered him the senior post of Home Secretary. Henderson and other senior colleagues undoubtedly felt that MacDonald had failed fully to consult them. It was hard for MacDonald to please his party. He was also pestered by aspirant Labour M.P.s who felt they were entitled to government posts and were put out when he included a number of ex-Liberals who had only recently come over to Labour. Beatrice's brother-in-law, Alfred Cripps, who became Lord Parmoor in 1914, had drifted away from his old Tory allegiance. He became the leader of the House of Lords as a non-party member of MacDonald's Cabinet; it was so difficult to fill the legal posts that one of them had to be given to a Conservative.

Beatrice was uneasy about the outcome. She thought it absurd that Labour should try to govern as a minority in Parliament and in the country dependent upon Liberal favours: she would have preferred to see a Liberal–Tory coalition confronted by a vigorous Labour opposition. She was, moreover, afraid that if Sidney took office they would be unable to carry out their plan of peacefully retiring to Passfield.

### 747 PRO SIDNEY WEBB TO RAMSAY MACDONALD

On New Year's Eve 1923 Sidney received a letter from MacDonald asking if he would become Minister of Labour, with a special responsibility for dealing with the continuingly high level of unemployment. If Webb accepted, MacDonald said, he was to plan what he wanted to do: 'As little legislation as you can do with, please, though you will need some . . . I should in the ordinary way be inclined to offer you another office, but Labour and the Foreign Office are the two arduous and most important jobs we have to face'. MacDonald also proposed Margaret Bondfield as Sidney's Parliamentary Secretary, and suggested he should go and see Sir Allan Smith, permanent secretary of the Ministry of Labour.

Sidney's reaction, as recorded by Beatrice, was positive. The post, he told her, 'just suits me – it is an unpretentious office with a low salary and no social duties'. He was, Beatrice added, 'naively excited', and said: 'If anyone had prophesied a year ago that J.R.M. would be prime minister and would invite me to be in his Cabinet, I should have thought the first extraordinarily unlikely, but the two combined a sheer impossibility'. (BWD 3 January 1924) Beatrice realised that she would have to make her contribution, not least as a hostess – though she hoped to keep out of Society and Court functions on the plea of old age and delicate health. Only by limiting a commitment that she found distasteful could she hope to complete the first volume of her autobiography.

Passfield Corner
Liphook
31.12.23

Telegram to Sidney Webb
Passfield until Wednesday *night*

Dear MacDonald

I only received your letter this morning; and have at once telegraphed to you. 'Cordially agree to your letter in order to facilitate your progress in arrangements.' I have no papers here; but will go home on Thursday morning to begin to think out things. Your suggestion for the Parliamentary Secretaryship is very welcome to me. I propose to wait a bit before acting on your suggestion with regard to Sir Allan Smith, who will, I think, be willing to deal with me; as I, of course, shall with him.

Within the next four months (to which I prefer to limit my vision!) I see at present 4 subjects of first-rate importance; *viz.*

Unemployment *Benefit* revision (needs a very early Bill, but no money from Treasury, except possibly some slight increase in the well-secured overdraft).

Schemes of *employment* and training. This needs no legislation (probably) except in connection with a loan, which the Treasury must be willing to raise gradually as required; and no very obvious charge on revenue immediately, beyond such interest as becomes payable. But it does involve the friendly concurrence of the Chancellor of the Exchequer, Minister of Health and President of the Board of Trade, as well as the Foreign Secretary, for credits; works by local authorities; housing, railway works, etc. The Unemployment Grants Committee (jointly representing these offices?) will need invigorating.

Trade Boards. To make the delayed awards, and restore the administration. International Labour Office – to ratify the conventions that are still open.

Disputes. These may be difficult, but not immediate. Mines Nationalisation Board may be the only way to avert a stoppage. The Home Secretary should be in agreement.

Apart from the Minister's own departmental administration, I venture to suggest that *Schemes of Employment* call for joint action among Ministers, to such extent as to call for a continuous committee of the Cabinet.

In the nature of things, not so very much can be put into actual operation in the first few weeks. We ought to elaborate and publish – much more effectively than has been usual – far-reaching plans for grappling with the problem, even on a ten years basis. Housing, for instance, should certainly be so dealt with; and with it dilution and training of building operatives, by agreement with the building trades unions (which could be got on practicable terms). But this means cordial co-operation by the Minister of Health, who ˹ought to work out˺ the plan with the Minister of

Labour and President of Board of Trade. Putting modesty aside, I see my way to all this; but it cannot be done by any one Minister, even to the extent of a publishable plan. I don't know how much you can stipulate for in offering the posts but I am very much more concerned at the possibility of finding *some* indispensable Minister obstinate, not against this or that colleague only, but against the Cabinet itself!

But I will not trouble you more at the moment.

Sidney Webb

748 PP SIDNEY TO BEATRICE

The Labour Party had now moved its offices to Eccleston Square. Frederick William Jowett (1864–1944), an outstanding I.L.P. leader from Bradford, was a pioneer of municipal enterprise and welfare: he became First Commissioner of Works. Alban Gordon wrote *Social Insurance: What it is and what it might be*, published by the Fabian Society in 1924. Dr Knowles (1870–1926) taught economic history at L.S.E. Kendals was Lion Phillimore's Hertfordshire house.

41 Grosvenor Road
Westminster
3.1.24

Dear One

Here I am, safely arrived, and sitting in the dining-room, after finding all in order. No important letters, some sent herewith. I went off after lunch to Eccleston Square, and found only Henderson. He very discontented with MacDonald's reticence, not apparently made aware of anything; and keenly apprehensive that J. R. M., with his imperfect knowledge of the several men (owing to his absence and lack of close contact), will make all the wrong selections. Henderson evidently expects high office in spite of absence from Parliament; and wants some place compatible with continued attention to Eccleston Square. He assumed that Haldane would accept Admiralty (though Henderson wished to have him at India Office, which would comply with statutory requirement). He viewed with alarm any creation of an outsider as peer on the ground that John Hodge had a prior claim, and that the T.U. must not feel slighted. He said there was only *one* Deputy Speaker place at £2,500 (the Chairman of Committees being also Chairman of Ways and Means) as we had originally supposed; and thought the second was only an Assistant at £100. The Government Whip had reminded him that both had to be elected straight away after the Speaker, as otherwise there was no one to relieve the latter; had asked whether we would oppose the re-election of the present two (who are both returned to the new Parliament). Henderson said that it had always been understood that they changed with the Government; and assumed that he would have to reply that we would support their re-election on the understanding that they resigned with the Government. He did not much favour Jowett for either post, though he admitted the difficulties.

Altogether he was full of regret for the loss of three weeks in holiday. He and Mrs H. had spent a night with the Snowdens and said it was a slap-up mansion, costing he believed some £3,500. Philip quite assumed that he would be Chancellor, whether with or without warrant – Henderson, by the way, suggested that I should go to the Board of Trade, as I certainly ought to have one of the first grade places. I said that it was plain from the fact that J. R. M. had asked me to enquire about Unemployment that I might expect one of the three places dealing with that subject; but that it would be all the same to me what grade of place I had.

I failed to see Greenwood (who was away for the day); or Middleton (who had gone to his father who was worse). Egerton Wake has gone home to Barrow, rather better and relieved to hear that the more alarming symptoms at first suspected were now declared non-existent: but he has to go slow for some time.

By the way Henderson and Mrs H. had been staying at Kendals. I had brought away the cheque for £100 for your party, which Henderson proposed to put into his Special Private fund; and to pay from it any bill you presented. Or he would simply hand you the cheque. Lion [Phillimore] had written offering J. R. M. the ensuing weekends for consultation, but had got no reply.

Then I went to Galton, who was cheery as usual. Alban Gordon has written (and had typed) a good little book on the Health Insurance position, which it is hoped that *you* will look through and report on to next Publishing Committee. Galton suggests publishing it as a half-crown volume. He had no political news, and I gave him none. I saw Miss Dawson, who said that acceptances were pouring in, and only three refusals. She is sending to the Buxton list of clerics, to Galton's list of Fabian or sympathetic Civil Servants or [?exes.], and to her two assistants.

Beveridge called here at 5.30 – the School is going ahead at nearly all points, and he is very contented. Mrs Knowles's [husband] died yesterday, but he does not expect her to resign. However, she has subsided. The Fisher Unwins are querulous about the proposed scheme for Charity Commissioners, but they have been seen about it, and say it is all right, and that they will deal with them. So we expect to send in the suggested scheme in 10 days or so. This does not delay the building, as this money would anyhow not be wanted for months.

Beveridge was not disposed to talk much about Unemployment problem.

He says there is no probable opening for Pat [Dobbs] at the School.

Now dear one this is all the news, except that I am very lonely in this room without you. Come back in good heart on Saturday.

Yours

Sidney

## 749 PRO SIDNEY WEBB TO RAMSAY MACDONALD

On 17 and 18 January Webb saw MacDonald, who told him that some senior colleagues had objected that Webb was being offered a 'Cinderella' post and felt that he should be given one with higher status. These meetings followed a private dinner given by Haldane on 14 December, attended by the Labour Front Bench. At this dinner MacDonald was at pains to point out that it was not a meeting of the future Cabinet: several of those present were still uncertain whether they were to be offered any post at all. Finally Webb became President of the Board of Trade and it was Tom Shaw who went to the Ministry of Labour. The only other prominent Fabian in the government was Sydney Olivier, who accepted the India Office and a peerage. As 'a veteran of the movement', he told MacDonald, he was prepared 'to be used up anywhere'.

When the government was finally formed only three of its members had previously held office and only two, Henderson and Haldane, had Cabinet experience. The first Cabinet met at 4 p.m. on 23 January 1924.

41 Grosvenor Road
Westminster Embankment
17.1.24

Dear MacDonald

As you have scant time for personal discussion, I have put down thoughts on the *size* of the Cabinet, for your consideration.

As for my job, I hope I made it clear that I much *prefer* your original proposal to any later suggestion. You will find the office of 'higher status' more valuable as something to give elsewhere.

But I think you should make some definite arrangements for Labour, Health, Transport and the Board of Trade (as regards 'credits' and 'trade facilities') to *work together* for unemployment, as a committee or otherwise. The C.O.; the Treasury; and to a lesser degree all other departments would have to co-operate on particular points; but *I* would not have them actually on the committee.

I should like to annex the lady (as P.M.G. [Paymaster-General]) as an additional Under-Secretary for training and women. But I recognise that you may not have the place to spare.

Yours

Sidney Webb

## 750 PP BEATRICE WEBB TO FRIENDS OF SEAHAM

Stephen Walsh (1859–1929), a former miner and M.P. for Ince, had held a minor post in the wartime coalition and in 1924 became Parliamentary Secretary to the Local Government Board; Vernon Hartshorn (1872–1931), president of the South Wales Miners' Federation, M.P. for Ogmore, became Postmaster-General ; Josiah Wedgwood (1872–1943), former Liberal and a Single-Tax enthusiast, became Chancellor of the Duchy of Lancaster. Lord Parmoor married his second wife, Marian, in 1919.

41 Grosvenor Road
Westminster, S.W.1
22nd January 1924

Dear Friends

In my December letter, written two days after the declaration of the Poll, I promised to tell you about the development of the political situation in the first month of the New Year.

The prospect of a Labour Government was a shocker of the first magnitude. It shocked London Society; it shocked the owners of great estates; it shocked lodging-house keepers in seaside resorts; it shocked the better paid clerks in the counting houses of our great cities; it even shocked the proverbial 'man in the street' and many a worthy citizen on the top of a bus. Further, it has sent an ugly thrill through all the governments of Europe; more especially those governments occupying the territories and persecuting the peoples of their defeated enemies. This consciousness of shock was deepened and broadened by the loud shouters of the capitalist press. The *Daily Mail* and the *Daily Express*, the *Evening News* and the *Morning Post* raved night and morning about the red ruin which would come first on Great Britain, and afterwards on the whole world, through the horrible spectre of Ramsay MacDonald seated cross-legged and in his shirt sleeves, with the red cap of Liberty on his head, in the Cabinet Room at 10 Downing Street – Henderson, Clynes, Thomas and Snowden – those grim ogres of democracy crouching by his side, with the wily Webb somewhere in the shadows. It was this terrible troupe, half-comic, half-tragic that was to preside over the destiny of the British Empire in the dark hour of its dissolution. Was there ever such an absurd exhibition of political hysteria?

But let us admit straightaway that the coming of a Labour Government, like a bolt from the blue, *is* a rather shocking fact even to the intelligent citizen, whether he be Conservative, Liberal or Labour in opinion. For we must always remember that political democracy is assumed to provide an executive government which is supported by a majority of the representatives of the people; and that these representatives are assumed to be elected by the majority of the men and women who record their vote at the polling booth. Now it is as clear as noonday that Mr MacDonald and his fellow members of the Labour Party are less than one-third of the members of the present House of Commons. Moreover, these 193 Labour Members have been elected by less than one-third of the voters at the recent general election. Thus the Labour Government represents neither a majority of the members of Parliament nor a majority of voters in the country. And yet the House of Commons decided on January 21st by 329 to 256 votes to turn out the Conservative Government, knowing full well that by so doing they were placing a Labour Government in Office. For King George had no option in the matter. If a Prime

Minister resigns his office because he is deliberately and decisively defeated in the House of Commons, the King is practically compelled, by the British Constitution, to send for the Leader of the next largest party – the party which always bears the honourable title of His Majesty's Opposition. The King's Government must be carried on: if His Majesty's Government goes out, His Majesty's Opposition comes in.

It is certainly odd that none of us foresaw that if the Conservatives were defeated at the polls a Labour Government would probably rule in Great Britain. Most people thought that one of two events would prevent this chain of circumstances. Mr Asquith and his 150 followers might refuse to upset the Conservative Government – in which case Mr Baldwin would continue in office. Or MacDonald, after consulting with his 190 followers, might decline to take office on the ground that he had not an independent majority in the House of Commons. In that case Mr Asquith might be sent for; and, with the support of the Conservative Party, might rule in Mr MacDonald's stead. What I propose to explain in this letter is why neither of these events happened: why the Liberals insisted on turning out Mr Baldwin, and why Mr MacDonald agreed to take over the reins of government.

The action of Mr Asquith and his followers can be easily explained and justified. The re-united Liberal Party came back from the general election supremely disappointed and depressed. In spite of having more candidates and heaps more money than the Labour Party, in spite of Mr Lloyd George's fervent eloquence, Sir John Simon's polished periods, and Mr Winston Churchill's masterpieces of rhetoric, the Liberals found themselves after the election the smallest party in the new Parliament and compelled to accept a subordinate position either to the Conservative Party or to the Labour Party. They were in fact on the horns of a dilemma. The one outstanding verdict of the general election was the defeat of Fiscal Protection and of the Government which had proposed it. Up and down the country every Liberal Leader had been denouncing this Government as 'pre-eminent in vacillation and impotence both at home and abroad'. 'There is one theory' (I quote Mr Asquith's words in the House of Commons) 'which will not hold water for a moment: and that is, that we were sent here to maintain the present Government in office.' Hence the Liberal Party could hardly refuse to vote for Mr Clynes's Amendment to the Address – 'That Your Majesty's present advisers have not the confidence of this House'. That meant, as I have already shown, the placing of His Majesty's Opposition on the Treasury Bench. But His Majesty's Opposition was, in substance and form, a Socialist Party, and some Liberal Leaders, including Mr Churchill, had denounced Socialism as The Enemy – far more dangerous to the national welfare than any conceivable Protective Tariff. There is only one escape from this dilemma. Mr Asquith and Mr Lloyd George could say, and have said that though they turn out

His Majesty's Government and put in His Majesty's Opposition they do not intend to maintain in power any government that is Socialist in practice as well as in theory. But will Mr MacDonald's Cabinet, either by administration or by legislation bring into being the Socialist Commonwealth? 'Wait and see' is once again Mr Asquith's attitude.

Here I come to the central question raised in my letter; the crucial point round which all other matters revolve. Ought Mr MacDonald to have accepted the King's invitation to form a Cabinet and thus become responsible for the Government of Great Britain and her Dominions? This is a heart-searching question; not merely for the present Prime Minister and his colleagues but also for every member of the Labour Party. Indeed the twenty-one thousand men and women who voted for my husband on the 6th December have a quite peculiar responsibility. For by so doing they have not only sent a Labour man to Parliament but they have, by sending my husband, actually helped to make up the first Labour Cabinet. I hope, dear friends, that you feel satisfied with the result of the Seaham election. I trust that you feel more completely easy in your minds than I do! I confess that when a few days after the election it became apparent that the Labour Leaders would have to decide whether or not to take office, I whispered to my husband 'Better not'. For it is no use deceiving ourselves about the dangers and risks of this gigantic task. The Labour Cabinet starts with a heavy handicap. The business of government, especially of a government so world-wide as that of Great Britain, is enormously complicated. To carry on this extensive and intricate administration without a majority in the House of Commons, and with practically no representation in the House of Lords, needed immense pluck and determination. But what was the alternative? His Majesty's Government had been decisively beaten at the polls on an issue which they had deliberately put before the country, and Mr Baldwin had said that he would stand or fall on the verdict of the electors. If the verdict went against the Government His Majesty's Opposition were entitled, and even required, to take their place. Thus if Mr MacDonald had refused to accept office he would have justified the taunt of the capitalist press that Labour was 'unfit to govern'. He would, in effect, have said to the King, 'I regret that owing to the incapacity of the members of the Labour Party I am unable to carry out the work of government'. Then the King would have turned to Mr Asquith, the Leader of the Liberal Party, and would have said, 'Though you have fewer followers than Mr MacDonald, these followers are apparently superior in capacity, and therefore I command you to form a Cabinet and to carry on until you think fit to have a dissolution'.

You will agree with me that, confronted with this alternative, it was quite impossible and would, in fact, have been a betrayal not only of the Labour Party but of the whole community of workers for Mr MacDonald and the other Labour Leaders to refuse, on the defeat of the Conservative

Party, to take over the government of the country. 'Here was a critical situation', he writes in the *Socialist Review* for this month (an article which, by the way, you ought to read), 'a government had to be formed and some pressing things had to be done. Obviously the duty of the Party was to leave its tents and come out and serve the nation as it believed it could.' 'It is not a moment for elation', said the new Prime Minister on the night of his appointment. 'It is a terrible responsibility. We shall have to do our best to face it. Fail or succeed, I can say this – that no government responsible for the affairs of this country will more honestly try to serve. I am very proud of the Labour Party; and it will be a great inspiration to every workman and workwoman in the country to work and to sacrifice to do their party honour and to enable it to succeed.'

One word about Labour's first Cabinet. Some friends are surprised to see that there are Peers in the Cabinet. One of the reasons given by the capitalist press against Labour taking office was the fact – and it was a true fact – that there were no declared Labour men in the House of Lords. And yet, according to the present British Constitution, it is not possible to govern without representation in the House of Lords. First, there must be a Lord Chancellor and he must be a Member of the Cabinet. Further, according to statute, one of the principal government departments to be represented in the House of Lords in order that the members of this House may ask questions and get information about the government of the country. We may dislike having an Upper House, we may dislike still more having an Upper House which is hereditary. But so long as it is by law established we have, unless we are anarchists, to accept this institution until we can amend or abolish it by Act of Parliament. Confronted with this difficulty, Mr MacDonald has, I think, taken a wise course. He picked out from among the Peers three who were sympathetic to the Labour Party. There was Lord Haldane, an old friend of ours, who, as perhaps some of you will remember, came and spoke for my husband in Seaham Harbour in the first year of his candidature. There is Lord Chelmsford who, though nominally a Conservative, has spent his life in non-political public service – first as Governor in Australia, and then as Viceroy of India. About Lord Parmoor I can speak with even greater knowledge, for his first wife was my sister, and his second wife is my friend. Though originally a Conservative Member of Parliament, he became during the War closely identified with Mr MacDonald and the cause of a democratic and beneficent peace, and he has, for the last two or three years, acted as a sort of informal representative of the Labour Party in the House of Lords. Besides these existing Peers, the King, on the advice of the Labour Prime Minister, will raise to the Peerage two trusted members of the Labour Party. There is Sir Sydney Olivier, who some forty years ago was resident clerk with my husband in the Colonial Office, and like my husband, was one of the founders of the Fabian Society. He has remained a Socialist right through a successful civil service career, part of the time as Governor of Jamaica, and finally as Assistant-Controller and Auditor-General. There is Brigadier-General Thomson, who becomes Secretary of State for Air in the House of Lords – a distinguished soldier and diplomatist who was so disgusted with the Treaty of Versailles that he joined the Labour Party in 1919 and has fought two elections as a Labour Party candidate.

Except for these five Peers the remainder of the twenty members of the Labour Cabinet are all well-known Labour Men. We are all delighted that Mr Henderson has accepted office as Home Secretary, and it will be one of the first objects of the Labour Party to find him a safe seat. Leading representatives of the great trade union movement, like Mr Clynes and Mr Thomas, Mr Walsh and Mr Hartshorn, are reinforced by socialist intellectuals like Mr Philip Snowden and my husband; and a group of accomplished and devoted men who left the Liberal Party during the War and joined the Labour Party because they felt that their spiritual home was with the party of the workers – Mr Noel Buxton, Mr C. P. Trevelyan, Colonel Wedgwood – find their place in the first Labour Administration. But all the twenty Members of the Cabinet, whether they be working-class or middle-class by birth and training, have one characteristic in common – they none of them belong to the idle rich, they are none of them profiteers, they have all lived strenuous lives, mostly in the public service. These characteristics, combined with their common faith in the principles of the Labour Party, will, I believe, weld them together against the hostile forces by which they are surrounded and will enable them, not indeed to bring about the Socialist Commonwealth, but, as the new Prime Minister has happily phrased it, 'To build a new road' so that future Labour Governments may progress towards a society founded on the principles of Liberty, Equality and Fraternity.

Thus, when the Liberals ask whether the new Labour Cabinet will bring about Socialism, the answer is not 'Wait and see' but my husband's dictum, 'The Inevitability of Gradualness'. We of the Labour Party believe that we can only proceed step by step, and that each step forward can only be taken with the consent of the people. On the very first day of its existence the Cabinet set to work energetically on the most pressing problems – the promotion of peace in Europe, the improvement of trade, the housing of the people, and the provision for the unemployed and ex-Service men. In my next letter I hope to tell you something about my husband's work as President of the Board of Trade.

As I write this last sentence, I see before me a box of beautiful flowers from my best friends in Seaham – the members of the Women's Section of the Local Labour Party. How delightful of you to remember that January 22nd, the day on which my husband becomes a Cabinet Minister, was also my birthday – alas! my sixty-sixth birthday; which reminds me that I am an old woman, though I am glad to say I do not feel like one!

Always sincerely yours
Beatrice Webb

751 PP SIDNEY WEBB TO CHARLES WRIGHT

Sir Charles Theodore Wright (1862–1940) was the secretary of the London Library 1893–1940 and the brother of Sir Almroth Wright (1861–1947), the distinguished bacteriologist.

Board of Trade
Great George Street, S.W.1
31st January 1924

*Private*

Dear Mr Wright

Many thanks for your letter so kindly expressed. I need hardly say that I am still in the process of learning where I am and what this Department is like!

I do not know how long it is since you left the Department, but I can easily understand that you find your present climate more congenial. I had a letter from your brother the other day, and I feel almost abashed to realised how many of my contemporaries have retired whilst I am beginning a new career! I need hardly say that the whole thing has been utterly unexpected, not only to myself but to our Party. We should much have preferred to have had the advantage of deferring the responsibility for a few more years; but, when it became apparent that we should be put to the forced alternative of acceptance or refusal, it became at once evident that refusal would have been suicidal, and hence all consideration of the risks and perils, and dangers, and trouble of accepting office necessarily fell away. It is a great adventure; and – if you will forgive the irreverence – I am still young enough to feel that it is 'a great lark', amid the irresistible onward sweep of cosmic forces. My wife has already reminded me, apropos of going into Parliament, that I have the great advantage, psychologically, of being able to feel that I have got my career behind me, which is a characteristic observation of the Faithful Wife.

Yours very truly
Sidney Webb

752 PP SIDNEY TO BEATRICE

Miss Kearley was the secretary–companion of Beatrice's sister, Catherine Courtney. Miss Piercy was Beatrice's new secretary. Sir Esmé Howard (1863–1939) was appointed ambassador to the United States in 1924 at a time when relations between London and Washington were strained.

Beatrice's diary entries at this time show that she was worried whether sudden elevation would turn the heads of some of the new Cabinet ministers. The pretentious aspirations of some of their wives, and the left-wing criticism of ministerial salaries added to her anxieties. Of the additional £3,500 that Sidney was now to receive, she proposed to devote £500 to additional costs of entertainment and the rest to extending Passfield Corner. In March she refused to attend a reception at Buckingham Palace: 'there is not the slightest reason why the *wives* and *daughters* should be dragged into smart society, with the inevitable "dressing up" and extravagant expenditure'. (BWD 3 March 1924) She thought it better for the good of the party's soul if the Government were turned out in the summer, 'otherwise we shall go rotten'. MacDonald had already shown that he was susceptible to what on another occasion she called 'the aristocratic embrace'. 'Deep down in his heart', she wrote, 'he prefers the company of Tory aristocrats and the Liberal capitalists to that of the trade union officials and the I.L.P. agitators. It may be human nature but it is not good comradeship; it is not even successful politics.' His attitude, she added on 15 March, was 'another form of the famous policy of permeation, far more Machiavellian than that of the Webbs' and bound to lead to trouble with the I.L.P. 'Yet as a political performer he has shown himself a consummate artist. We had never realised that he had genius in this direction.'

Board of Trade
Great George Street, S.W.1
12.2.24

Dear One

See among the enclosed a note from Miss Kearley as to Kate's *influenza*!

Your notes this morning were a joy. I did not have a very good night, but only heard several strikings of the hour. I am afraid you will find the cottage cold, as you will be tempted to economise labour in fires! But I hope tomorrow Jessie will be about.

Last night's reception was in every way most successful: large, convenient range of rooms; abundance of people, certainly 1,500, and probably a couple of thousand; three-quarters of the Cabinet present, and many M.P.; with the usual Half-Circle faces. The Scottish members were the only noticeable absentees. The P.M. came late (10 p.m.) after a dinner somewhere. Everybody jubilant, many enquiries after you. Alys Russell, Lion Phillimore, Mrs Cavendish Bentinck, Mrs H. G. Wells (he still in Portugal); the Laskis, Mrs Virginia Crawford etc. etc. etc.; (*The Times* reports of all the Party receptions make a queer contrast).

The P.M.'s speech was very cautious and restrained, in a House at first hostile, then cold, and finally I think sympathetic – that is so far as the Conservatives were concerned. But you will read it. I had to come out before it was over to attend to pressing business (possible dockers' strike, which I hope and expect will not happen).

I finish this in haste. Goodnight, dearest. I will speed off Miss Piercy tomorrow. (When I have to see Sir Esmé Howard at 11.30 a.m.) Cabinet tomorrow at 9.30 p.m.!

Yours

Sidney Webb

753 PP BEATRICE TO SIDNEY

Beatrice, who needed a rest, had gone with her sister Catherine Courtney to stay at Lady Warwick's house, Easton Lodge. The visit gave her an opportunity to decide about a proposed arrangement whereby the Labour Party would pay £300 a year to cover the rates and other outgoings and, in return, individual guests would be able to stay at the house for two guineas a week, or less for a weekend. This was yet another of the Countess of Warwick's schemes, as her own finances dwindled, for saving her house and helping the Labour Party at the same time. There was, Beatrice commented, 'a grave disadvantage in having the Countess on the premises' and she felt that 'all this magnificence is altogether out of keeping with the peculiar position of the Labour Party – a party which is apt and, in a sense, compelled to promise much and perform little'. (BWD 7 April 1924) She felt thc scheme should be wound up, her sister agreeing that such surroundings must either be 'repugnant or demoralising'. (BWD 9 April 1924) The Ways and Means Committee was debating a Bill validating a series of charges and levies left over from wartime legislation; the milk clause dealt with charges on licences to sell milk.

Scott was Henderson's personal assistant at Labour Party head office. Miss Dawson was probably the L.S.E. housekeeper at Dunford who apparently considered the offer of a similar post at Easton Lodge.

[Easton Lodge]
[8 April 1924]

Dearest One

I was so glad to get your long and interesting letter. I see you got your bill except the milk clause – which I suppose you did not expect to win. *The Times* does not expect the Government to consider the defeat – in the rent restriction bill – as important, but I have not noticed what exactly it means in respect of the Bill itself.

Kate is thoroughly enjoying herself and thinks, that, on balance, the Labor Party could not avoid trying the experiment of 'socialising' this place. My own feeling is that the chances are against the success of the experiment – but it had better be tried. I doubt whether sufficient number of guests will be found of a desirable character to justify the expenditure on it. However £300 is not a big sum and if they got 500 persons as boarding guests and had galas down here it would not seem much to pay for the privilege. The trouble will be (1) the outré magnificence of the place which is out of keeping with Labor Party creed, *viz.* the great amount of service lavished on garden, etc. (2) the dominant and arbitrary personality of the Countess – who really is a good sort but *too* dominant to make it possible to feel free – one always feels that one is 'on sufferance' here and must not offend her susceptibilities. *We* shall not come again and I fancy that other persons have felt likewise or in other ways the constraint and have not come again. There is nothing one can complain about but only a feeling of malaise and apology. For humble folk the very magnificence of the place produces the same effect. 'They do not feel sure' as Scott said to me, 'that they are behaving in the right way' in her presence and the presence of her servants.

However time will prove whether it is feasible and desirable. I am glad I came here because I now know exactly what it is like and what are the possibilities and the limitations. And I am heartily glad I stopped Miss Dawson having anything to do with it.

Beatrice

I come back Thursday 9th

754 PP SIDNEY TO BEATRICE

Ernest Thurtle (1884–1954) was elected for Shoreditch in 1923 and held junior post in the Labour governments of 1924 and 1929 and in the wartime coalition. Walter Ayles was elected for North Bristol in 1923: he was a leading member of the I.L.P. and treasurer of the 'No more War' movement.

The Labour government was already having difficulties with the left-wing of the party, and especially with the vociferous Clydeside group which claimed MacDonald owed his election as leader to their support and felt betrayed by him. John Wheatley, the spokesman for the left in the Cabinet, developed an ambitious and creditable public housing policy. When Labour took office there was much concern about possession-orders against laggard tenants (over 21,000 in less than a year) and evictions (almost 5,000 in Clydeside alone in the past year). A Labour back-bencher, Benjamin Gardner, promoted a Bill to cut rent increases, but it languished in committee for two months before Wheatley brought in a measure to prevent eviction when arrears of rent were due to unemployment or when the landlord desired possession for himself and did not offer alternative accommodation. Asquith tried to substitute payment of rent as part of poor relief. W. H. R. Pringle, on behalf of the Liberals, then talked out Wheatley's Bill. The Government was confused and the matter was raised again on 7 April when a muddled amendment drafted by the Government was defeated 221 to 212; it eventually accepted the Prevention of Evictions Bill which had been introduced by Sir John Simon on 26 March.

Sir George Gillett, Labour M.P. for Finsbury 1923–31, was one of the few members who defected with Ramsay MacDonald in August 1931.

Senator R. V. Wilson was member of the Australian Senate for South Australia and Senator Allan McDougall represented New South Wales.

Sir James Stephenson (1873–1926) was managing director of John Walker, the whiskey distillers, and was a key figure in munitions supply during the war. He was chairman of the Exhibition Board which was responsible for the British Empire Exhibition at Wembley in 1924. Sir Charles Hobhouse (1862–1941) was for many years a Liberal M.P. and his last office was as Postmaster-General in 1915.

41 Grosvenor Road
Westminster
3.4.24

Dear One

Today I am rather tired and excited, after being up all night over the Army Annual Bill. We began it at 11 p.m. and went on until after 5 a.m., when we succeeded in getting it all through without amendment. Our own party behaved disgracefully – Lansbury, Thurtle, Ayles, and Maxton concerting to move successive amendments, from abolition of the death penalty down to allowing recruits to record on enlistment whether or not they were willing to be used in aid of the Civil Power to maintain order! They gave us no time to draft carefully worded concessions; and we had to decide to call for a report as to what on these lines could be done without destroying army discipline, and to promise to decide later. This did not in the least appease them, and they insisted on moving all their amendments, in which they were supported by irresponsible and conscientious Liberals – the result being that we were only able to stave off the most destructive of their proposals by majorities of 50 or 60, *furnished mainly by the Unionists* in conjunction with the Ministers, their Parliamentary Secretaries and a certain number of the faithful. The Unionists behaved well in sitting up with us to 'save the Army', instead of going to bed and leaving the Government to be defeated by its own tail. MacDonald was away (at National Gallery Centenary Dinner) and was paired. Clynes (in charge) was very disgusted.

Before that we had had a storm over Wheatley's Bill to prevent evictions, which Asquith declared against, and which the Unionists cut up in argument. I found on enquiry that MacDonald had contemplated the probability of going to defeat on this, partly because of the electioneering appeal, but mainly, I suspect, as the only way of convincing the Clyde brigade, which had insisted on it, that it could not be carried. As it turned out, the Speaker (privately) refused the closure, and Pringle (who did not want the Liberals to be recorded as voting with the Unionists against it) talked out the Bill for that sitting. Then, in private members' time (8.15 to 11 p.m.) a Unionist moved a resolution denouncing the Capital Levy, which Pethick-Lawrence and Gillett very ably expounded and defended, but where we were voted down by some 320 to 160.

So it was a pretty exciting day from 3 p.m. to 5 a.m. I went home quietly to dinner at 8.30 and only came back about 10 p.m., prepared for my all-night sitting (which, this year, I found intolerably boresome). I went to bed for 2½ hours at 6 a.m. in broad daylight, and slept uneasily. This morning I did business at the office from 10.30 to 12.30, incidentally receiving Sir Charles Hobhouse, who wants to be officially sent to a forthcoming Milan Exhibition.

Then I went to a great Australian lunch (Senators Wilson, MacDougall etc.) of a couple of hundred, when I responded, along with Sir James Stephenson, for the British Empire Exhibition, making quite a suitable speech, and then rushing back to the House for Questions and a Cabinet Committee. Presently I shall go home to dinner and not return, unless I am sent for; and go to bed by 10 p.m. if I can.

Henderson said that at a little committee on Easton Lodge, they had decided *not* to employ Miss Dawson for it, in view of your memo. pointing out that she needed (besides expenses) a temporary coadjutor, and that a contribution ought to be made to her salary. Henderson has appointed his own secretary, Scott, to do the whole work from 33 Ecc. Square, as Henderson's removal to H.O. [Home Office] left Scott some free time.

Tomorrow I shall find you for lunch, to which I will come at 1 p.m. if I can leave the House. Dear One, I have missed you sadly, even amid rather distracting days. It is not good for me to be without you.

Sidney

A Cabinet is fixed for 11 a.m. on Saturday, 26 April: and I may have to return from Seaham on Friday.

## 755 BEAV BEATRICE WEBB TO JOHN ST LOE STRACHEY

John St Loe Strachey (1860–1927), journalist and author, was editor of the *Spectator* 1898–1925.

Beatrice disliked Ethel Snowden for her snobbishness: 'every "class-conscious" Labour man or woman listens for the echoes of Ethel – climbing, climbing, climbing, night and day! out of the Labour world into that of plutocrats and aristocrats'. (BWD 8 February 1924)

Strachey's son, John Strachey (1901–1963) had begun his career by writing for the *Spectator* but joined the Labour Party in October 1923 and moved to the I.L.P.'s weekly *New Leader*. He resigned from the Labour Party in 1931; he then became the leading English populariser of Marxism, but broke with his Communist associates in 1939, returning to the Labour Party to hold Cabinet office in the post-1945 governments.

41 Grosvenor Road
Westminster Embankment
9th May 1924

My dear Mr St Loe Strachey

It would have been a great pleasure to write anything for the *Spectator* at your request. But alas! I have no gift for occasional articles on subjects about which I have not thought, and have no special knowledge. Certainly the King and Labour is a matter about which I have little or no opinion – except that I have the warmest respect for the present King and Queen for undertaking such a tedious task. But owing to my age I have not thought it necessary to be presented at Court, like some of the other

Cabinet Ministers' wives, so I am afraid that I have not even seen the outside of the Court Circle and cannot in the least describe what is or should be the relation between the King and his Labour Ministers. I suggest Mrs Philip Snowden would write the article admirably.

We were so glad to make the acquaintance of your son. I suppose if we had a son he would be a Conservative – it is a very wholesome instinct on the part of young people to react against the opinions of their immediate elders, as it brings fresh blood into each political party and keeps it from degenerating into a hereditary sect.

With kindest regards from my husband, and many thanks to you for thinking of me as a possible contributor.

Yours very sincerely

Beatrice Webb

(Mrs Sidney Webb)

756 PP SIDNEY TO BEATRICE

W. Lunn was Labour M.P. for Rothwell 1918–42.

Ramsay MacDonald, who was well-travelled and well-informed about the world, was Foreign Secretary as well as Prime Minister. His most immediate problems were those of German reparations and the French occupation of the Ruhr – both legacies of the Treaty of Versailles which he had vehemently opposed: by August he had engineered the Dawes Plan, the first important negotiated settlement in Europe after the war. On taking office he recognised the Soviet regime and Arthur Ponsonby, as Under-Secretary for Foreign Affairs, was negotiating a commercial treaty with the Soviet government, and a wider treaty which included a settlement of the debts repudiated by the Russians after the revolution – an acceptable settlement being the condition of a British loan to Russia. The general treaty, strongly opposed by both Liberals and Tories, was to lead to the fall of the MacDonald government.

41 Grosvenor Road

Westminster

28.5.24

Dear One

I posted some things to you this morning, and now send a letter.

Last night I dined with Kitty Dobbs, and stayed with her until past 9 p.m. before going back to the House. She seemed quite satisfactory in health and conduct, and apparently interested in things. I have asked Pat (who is to be alone in London next Sunday) to come in during the afternoon (as I am uncertain about lunch). Rosie and Kitty go to Cambridge for the weekend. Rosie's address is 18 Cromwell Crescent Earl's Court S.W.

Today I had to waste 3 hours at Wembley, in attendance on the King and Queen, and the Italians. Lunn called for me in a car at 12.30 and got to the Government Pavilion at 1.20 p.m. The Royal Party, due to arrive there at 1.30, was late, having naturally dawdled over the immense exhibition where they had been tramping about since 11.30. I am quite satisfied that *we* need not go to see this show, big and interesting as it is. We did not get lunch until 2, at tables of eight. I was at neither the King's nor the Queen's table, as there were so many royalties, dukes etc.; but at the next table with the Italian Count and Countess di Campello in waiting (who cordially invited me to Rome and gave me their address there) and Colonial High Commissioners. As soon as the party rose, I went to the King and asked to be excused for House of Commons, which of course he graciously accorded, and asked how tomorrow's division would go. He said no one wishes the Government turned out. So Lunn and I got back by 3.30 p.m.

I hope you have this brilliant hot weather, which will suit Bryan's Ground, but is tiring in London. Thomas is reported as proceeding satisfactorily. Mrs Thomas also. You will be interested to hear that it was at the Evening Court that she caught a severe chill, and nearly collapsed then and there that evening; and had to be carried away prematurely. Lunn says that there is intense feeling in the Party throughout the Country against participation in these Court functions; and great resentment against Mrs Snowden. The Spanish Socialist Professor and his wife, who came before, are again in London, and I have asked them for Sunday afternoon.

Now dear one I must close, as it is nearly post time; and I have to go to the P.M. for a little conference on the Russian negotiations (which look like proving abortive).

Sidney

757 PP SIDNEY TO BEATRICE

Beatrice was staying for a month to rest and as company for Betty Russell at her cottage, Bryan's Ground, in Radnorshire, and had asked for weekly papers to keep in touch. E. M. H. Lloyd, Professor of Economics at Sheffield, was employed in the Overseas Trade Department.

On 25 May Beatrice had noted: 'It looks as if an election now would just about finish up the Liberals as a separate party. Sidney sees many advantages in such an election and has always favoured going to the country in June . . . he has the satisfaction of feeling that Fabianism is justified – that slowly attained, incomplete and mixed communal control is all that is either practicable or desirable, and that the rival policies of revolutionary action or "workers' control" or anti-socialism or fiscal "protection" are all on the down-grade and cannot be put into force . . . Where I think the Labour leaders have been at fault – and we are among them – is in implying . . . that the prevention of unemployment was an easy and rapid task instead of being a difficult and slow business involving many complicated transactions and far more control of capitalist enterprise than anyone has yet worked out'.

Sidney complained about the expense of entertaining Seaham constituents –

the lunch mentioned cost £1.7.0 – and added that it was 'fortunate that Seaham visitors are few and far between!'. (To Beatrice PP 6 June 1924)

41 Grosvenor Road
Westminster
5.6.24

Dear One

I have asked Miss Piercy to send you in a batch the weekly papers that I have omitted to post hitherto. I am sorry I forgot them; also Hansard for yesterday for Wheatley's speech, which sounded better than it reads. It was very successful for its purpose; and we almost expect to get the Money Resolution at 8.15 tonight without a division. I may have to speak about 10 p.m. tonight on a foolish Unionist motion about 'Imperial Trade' (owing to absence of J. H. Thomas); and then again after 11 p.m. when we hope to get the third reading of the tiresome War Charges Validity Bill – which Snowden told me yesterday that he had never expected to get passed: the Treasury is pleased at my getting it through intact.

I lunched at the Club again today, when there were over a dozen present, including Ted Lloyd and a guest; several from Eccleston Square; Galton and an Italian guest, and others whom I did not know. It secures universal approval, but I expect much use of it will be of slow growth. Tomorrow I have to entertain at the House an Easington doctor and three others – expensive, but worthwhile as he was doubtfully a supporter a year ago!

It looks as if we were about to enfranchise all women at 21 on the same terms as men, that is, mere residence. I don't think this likely to be bad for the Labour Party, but it will add on the average, 7,000 to each electorate – probably making Seaham up to 50,000 (Burnley is more than that already, and Coventry already 60,000: these will be raised to about 60,000 and 70,000 respectively). Henderson presses for the Alternative Vote, which the Liberals *think* would benefit them, but it is not by any means clear that they would gain on balance.

Here is Miss Gibson's account for typing your letters: it works out exactly at 2d. each, as it happens. The weather continues very unpropitious and does not bode well for next week.

You need not fear that I shall become attached to office! It is altogether too onerous and distracting, and involves too many personal interviews and consultations which I do not enjoy – as well as the chance of being much harassed by attacks in the House, which I have hitherto practically escaped. I should be quite pleased to go out now, because I think it would be best for us – or in November, as I now predict.

But I must now close to ensure the post. Goodbye

Sidney

I enclose by the way a critical comment on the Board of Trade estimates – nothing very serious, and of course *we* are not to blame.

758 EUL BEATRICE WEBB TO CHARLES SAROLEA

Dr Charles Sarolea (1870–1953), Professor of French at the University of Edinburgh 1918–31, published his *Impressions of Soviet Russia* in 1924.

41 Grosvenor Road
Westminster Embankment
16th June 1924

My dear Dr Sarolea

It is most kind of you to send us your book and I shall value it greatly as an addition to the books I have on Russia. I had already read it, though I do not possess it, and I was very much interested in your experiences of that very doubtful 'Paradise'! My husband and I have always been against the Soviet System, and have regarded it as a repetition of Russian autocracy based on a creed – a very Eastern conception. But some interesting experiments may be the result, though I am afraid the conclusions will be more negative than positive. But I altogether doubt your suggestions that they have much direct application to the present conditions in this country.

By the way, my husband and I have never been State Socialists as you seem to imply in some passage of your book – we have always advocated municipal and co-operative organisation as preferable to nationalisation for any but one or two industries.

With many thanks for your kindness in thinking of us

Yours very truly

Beatrice Webb
(Mrs Sidney Webb)

759 PP BEATRICE WEBB TO FRIENDS OF SEAHAM

41 Grosvenor Road
Westminster, S.W.1
June 25th 1924

Dear Friends

For one whole month I have been out of London, right away in mid-Wales living in a gardener's cottage in a beautiful garden surrounded by mountains and moors. My excuse for deserting my husband was the illness of a beloved niece who begged me to come and stay with her and cheer her up. I am glad to say that, owing to my presence – so she tells me – she is on the road to complete recovery. So my excuse turned out to be a good one! But if I must be frank with you – and I try to tell you the truth in these letters – I was heartily glad to get out of London. For, as Mrs Wilkinson and Mrs McIntosh will have told you, London is a terribly noisy place, with its crowded streets and continuous roar of traffic. Even more distracting are the innumerable people I have to see when I am in London: journalists, professors and students from all parts of the world; members of the British Labour Party from all the counties of Great Britain; not to mention my husband's colleagues in Parliament and on the Treasury Bench, and, most welcome of all, an occasional visitor from Seaham. During the Whitsun holidays, I am glad to say, my husband was with me and we had a delightful time, writing letters and reading in the mornings; taking our midday-meal with my niece in her charming house; and then roaming through woods and over hills in the afternoon and evening.

But I was haunted by one troublesome question – how was I to write my monthly letter to Seaham? Whilst I had been revelling in the silence and beauty of the countryside, all sorts of interesting events had happened in London. The Labour Government had been within an ace of defeat on a vital issue, which would have meant a general election. When that crisis was over, Mr Wheatley had introduced his great housing scheme to remedy the worst evil of the present day, the lack of houses for working men and their families. The trouble was that I knew little or nothing about either of these events. And yet I could not disappoint my friends at Seaham. That letter *had* to be written; and it would never do to put you off with nonsense made up out of my own ignorance. Suddenly the very evening before my husband joined me I had an inspiration; and I think that you will agree that it was a brilliant idea. 'Why not interview Sidney?' I asked myself. My Seaham friends will much prefer to hear direct from the President of the Board of Trade what has happened to the Labour Government than from his unknowing wife! And he never refuses to answer my questions if I put these questions in the right way and at the right time.

So I waited patiently until after breakfast on the third day of his holiday. 'Now,' said I, 'supposing you just tell me what has been happening while I have been away.'

'You want me first to explain, I suppose, how it was that the Labour Government came near defeat on May 22nd/29th,' said he, settling down comfortably in his armchair by the fire, for it was raining hard and very cold.

'The occasion was the vote for the expenses of the Ministry of Labour, which include the employment exchanges and the administration of unemployment insurance,' he continued in his placid way. 'You know that it is a privilege of the opposition to select which of all the votes shall be put down for consideration in a particular day, so that the opposition may raise a discussion on any one of the government departments whenever it chooses. The Unionists therefore asked that the Minister of Labour's Vote should be taken on the 22nd May, because they wanted to make a big attack on the Government for not having done more for the unemployed. It was really very comical to hear how the Unionists, who had when in office with a big majority done so little for the unemployed, one after another denounced the Minister of Labour, Mr Tom Shaw, and his colleagues in the Cabinet, after only sixteen weeks of office, and supported only by a minority of the House of Commons, for having "broken their pledges" to the electors, because there are still men and women out of work! It was in vain that Shaw demonstrated that during the three months of the Labour Government, and owing at least partly to the Government's policy, the number of men and women out of work had actually gone down by a quarter of a million; that the various schemes of the Government were already finding employment at wages for a larger number than had ever been found work before, and larger by twenty per cent than under the late Government; that other schemes were in hand, but could not have been got going in so short a time; that various hampering restrictions on the employment provided with Government help by Local Authorities had been removed; and that women's training schemes, formerly suspended, had been again set going. But this was not all. The Labour Government, in its anxiety to prevent unemployment, had aided public utility works, like the Seaham Harbour Dock. For those for whom work at wages could not yet be found, the Minister of Labour had removed the cruel 'gap', which deprived them for weeks at a time of any Unemployment Benefit. Finally, he was actually pressing on the House of Commons the provision not only of an increase in the amount of this maintenance, especially for fathers of families, but also asking that it should be continuous as long as unemployment lasted.'

'The plain truth is,' continued the Member for Seaham with a note of indignation in his voice, 'this attack on the Government was a put-up job. Several Members admitted privately that no previous Government had done so much for the unemployed in so short a time. But in order to make the public think that the Labour Government had failed, the outcry about "broken pledges" was kept up for two successive Thursdays, and made much of in the capitalist newspapers. As if the Labour Party had ever pledged itself to remedy the whole unemployment trouble, without a majority of the House of Commons, and within the space of sixteen weeks!'

'What made the matter serious was not the Unionist Party's attack – which its members made with tongue in cheek, so absurd was it felt to be – but the desire of some of the Liberals to join with them in defeating the Government. What was actually moved was a resolution to refuse part of the salary of the Minister of Labour – a most unfair proceeding as Mr Tom Shaw was certainly not to blame, and everyone privately admitted that he had done all he could. If this motion had been carried, it would have been a vote of censure upon the Government as a whole; and the Prime Minister would have had immediately either to resign, or to ask the King to dissolve Parliament. He would, of course, have done the latter, and as it would have been highly unconstitutional for the King to have done other than consent, we should then have had an immediate general election. On realising this, the Liberals "funked". They know that they will lose a lot of seats when the election comes; and accordingly they wish to put it off. Hence, on the second day of the debate, after a brilliant speech from the Prime Minister, Mr Asquith, acting as leader of the Liberals, told his followers to vote with the Government. Most of them did so, amid the jeers of the Unionists; and so it was clear that the motion to reduce Mr Shaw's salary would be defeated. But many of the Liberals refused to obey Mr Asquith's directions. Some actually voted with the Unionists, and still more (including Mr Lloyd George) abstained from voting. Hence the division was exciting; and in the end the Government won by a small majority.'

'Now tell me about Mr Wheatley's Housing Bill,' I asked, 'for it is no use being kept in office unless you get something done for the people.'

'That is exactly what we have all been feeling,' my husband answered. 'Unless we can get a big move onward we would rather go out of office. What seemed to the Labour Ministry the most urgently needed of all legislative reforms was a new Housing Act. The very serious overcrowding nearly everywhere prevalent is our gravest social problem; whilst it is in a big programme of house-building, with all the decorating and furnishing which additional houses involve, that we see the most extensive provision of employment for the unemployed. But this has meant a huge task for the Minister of Health, Mr Wheatley, and also for the other Ministers. We have been almost continuously working at the plan for the last three months'.

'Now the Cabinet saw at once that there must be no more tinkering at the problem, but that a bold, complete and far-reaching programme was required. The nation needs at least two millions of additional houses, not for sale to people who could afford to purchase them, but to be let to the wage-earners at rents within their means. To get these two million houses built will require more bricks than are now being produced, and more bricklayers and plasterers than are now available. In order to secure these requisites, a long-term programme must be arranged, and sufficient money provided. This is the plan that Mr Wheatley eloquently explained to an appreciative House of Commons on the 2nd of June. His Bill, which we defy either the Unionists or the Liberals to vote against, provides for a government subsidy that will enable every Town and District Council, without any undue burden on the local rates, to start building working-class houses at once, and to go on building continuously for fifteen years, by which time the whole shortage ought to have been made up. These houses are to be let at rents carefully fixed so as to be within the means of wage-earning families. And most important of all, power is sought by a separate Bill to enable the Minister of Health and the President of the

Board of Trade to prevent all profiteering in bricks and other building material, and to take over, in case of need, the land, buildings, machinery and stocks of anyone who seeks to hold up prices or refuses to supply what is required.'

'That is where you, as President of the Board of Trade, come in' I observe. 'But tell me, is there the remotest chance that either the Liberal Party or the Tory Party in the House of Commons will vote for this large public expenditure on providing homes for the people and this determined attempt to stop profiteering on the part of the capitalists?' I asked.

'Well, we have just got to wait and see' said my husband. 'What is certain is that on these two Bills there is going to be a big Parliamentary struggle. They constitute the first bit of the Labour Party's social programme. If passed into law they will give us, not only houses for the homeless, but also work at wages for hundreds of thousands of unemployed. But such a big housing scheme will cost money, and will thus stand in the way of a reduction of the present income tax and supertax on the wealthy. And of course any provision of houses in abundance so that there is one available for each newly married couple will bring down the scarcity rents of existing houses, a fact which houseowners resent. For both these reasons our two Bills will be strenuously opposed by half the House of Commons. But the Labour Party will do its utmost to pass them into law before the end of the present session: and if they are defeated, we shall have to carry the campaign to the country, and rally public opinion to our support. So, after all, we may have a general election either at the end of the summer session or when Parliament reassembles in the autumn, perhaps at the end of November.'

Such was the report of the Member for Seaham of what had been happening to the Labour Government in May and June. I trust that you have been as much interested as I was. There is, however, another event, not in London but at Durham, which has delighted me: the magnificent success of the Durham Gala. From all accounts, I gather that the women of the County of Durham have had out and away the biggest success in the United Kingdom in this great labour demonstration. The citizens of that ancient city, dominated by its cathedral and its castle, I wonder what they thought as they watched the never-ending procession of ten thousand Labour women with their green and white flags flying, wending their way through the narrow streets to the great meeting where they were addressed by the Labour Members for the County? It is needless to tell you that my husband would have liked to be there himself. But he had been working night and day since Easter, and I insisted that he must have a complete rest for those few free days at Whitsun.

Now good-bye dear friends. I propose to delay writing my next letter until the rising of Parliament early in August so that I may try and sum up the work of the Labour Government during its first Parliamentary session.

Your sincere friend
Beatrice Webb

760 PP SIDNEY TO BEATRICE

Over the next few years Beatrice had some difficulty with the domestic staff at Passfield Corner – a difficulty exacerbated by her own ill-health and neurotic suspicions about their honesty and morality. This attempt to find a naval pensioner as gardener failed. A couple named Oliver were employed for a time as gardener and housekeeper; two sisters, Jessie and Annie Smith, stayed with them as maids for many years.

41 Grosvenor Road
Westminster
30.6.24

Dear One

The drive to the station was certainly pleasanter than a dusty walk; and it deprived me of excuse for being tired!

At the P.M.'s, the most important matter was Egypt, whence the news is bad. The Egyptian Parliament has gone most extremely nationalist about the Soudan, from which the British cannot withdraw. There may be serious riots in Cairo and Khartoum: movements of troops; and conceivably a new 'little war' with Egypt. Parmoor apparently made a rather rigid speech in the Lords last week, which caused the Egyptian Parliament to boil over (he had not consulted the P.M., who has failed to see him since). The P.M. made a serious reply to a question today. The Government must maintain the administration of the Soudan, though making all possible concessions as to forms and details. If we withdrew, all the information is that there would immediately be massacres and civil war, as the Arab Sheiks simply will not stand the Egyptian officials, and will not submit to an Egyptian army. We have never promised to withdraw from the Soudan, and the House would never stand it.

Haden Guest has had columns in the *Daily Mail* and similar papers, with photo of self and wife, as probable Ambassador to Moscow, for which there is apparently no basis whatever, except his extreme desire to get some paid appointment – Thomas says that lots of Labour members have applied to him for Colonial Governorships, including the most unlikely people!

I see that Mrs Noel Buxton was presented at the last Court, but no other Labour woman.

As to end of session, Spoor and Henderson do not see how it *can* be before 15 August; but the Unionists are offering co-operation to get it over by 8 August, it may happen. There are signs of a steadily increasing divergence between Lloyd George and the official Liberal Party.

I think, on reflection, that you have made, and will make Passfield Corner perfectly charming, and a perfect honeymoon bower for our old days. I only hope you won't overstrain yourself by doing too much. I can't yet find the Naval Employment Agency: there is no such organisation in the current Telephone Book under any title whatever. But I am still enquiring, and will write presently somewhere. I have been given an address to reach a similar committee at Portsmouth.

Now goodnight dear one as I must post this in time.

Sidney

761 PP SIDNEY TO BEATRICE

Beatrice had gone to Edinburgh to receive an honorary degree from the university. A. V. Alexander (1885–1965), the Co-operative leader, was M.P. for Hillsborough and Parliamentary Secretary to the Board of Trade. In 1929, and again during the wartime coalition, he was First Lord of the Admiralty. Emmanuel Shinwell (b. 1884) was M.P. for Linlithgow 1922–24. In 1935 he became M.P. for Seaham and a Cabinet minister in the 1945 Labour government; William Graham (1887–1932), the I.L.P. journalist, was Financial Secretary to the Treasury in 1924 and President of the Board of Trade in 1929. The Bill amending the Insurance Act made modest increases in the rate of unemployment assistance and liberalised some conditions of benefit. The Labour left continually sought to write in amendments, such as that proposing benefit to persons thrown out of work by a strike in which they were not involved. The government was also in great difficulties about plans for public works and other measures to relieve unemployment.

Walter Leaf (1852–1927) was a classical scholar who became a director and then chairman of the Westminster Bank and, in 1919, chairman of the Institute of Bankers.

Sir Herbert Read (1863–1949) was assistant under-secretary at the Colonial Office responsible for Africa.

At the Lewes bye-election on 9 July, in a three-cornered contest, Labour polled 2,700 against 6,100 for the Liberal and 9,600 for the Tory. At Holland-with-Boston, a large rural seat in Lincolnshire, Hugh Dalton was beaten by 800 votes in a three-cornered election on 1 August.

41 Grosvenor Road
Westminster
10.7.24

Dear One

Your letter was very welcome. It has been, and is terribly hot here. Last night, having virtuously abstained from going to the Trinity House dinner, in order to let Alexander (and the Attorney-General), go, my two little Bills never came near coming on! The entire time was spent in wrangling over clauses in Shaw's Unemployment Insurance Bill, which failed, by a long way, to get completed by midnight when (by agreement beforehand) we adjourned. The business is getting increasingly into arrear. Tonight they are to attack us on Reparation Claims, but Graham is the objective, as it is the stinginess of the Treasury which is mainly complained of, and Alexander is to help him. So I am absolved, though I shall be there also. Alexander is quite humanly desirous of doing as much as he can be allowed – and I am very willing to allow him (and Shinwell and Lunn) all the opportunities that I can.

Lunn, by the way, said that the Wembley Authorities would no doubt jump at the chance of being attentive to you; and I am to let him know exactly when you propose to go.

This afternoon Dr Leaf, of the Westminster Bank, came to see me about a small matter at the House; and we had a very friendly talk for an hour, about current accounts, the virtually public management of banking, stabilisation, the Bank Rate and so on.

I had lunch at the Parliamentary Labour Club: about a score lunching four from Eccleston Square, Dr Brend (who is at Ministry of Pensions) Sir Herbert Read of the C.O. and Mrs Green of Colchester, the friend or relative of [Ben] Keeling. I talked to Gillies about coming to see us one day, which he was eager to do. He *may* have to be at Geneva all September at the League of Nations Assembly, to which Henderson is to accompany MacDonald. What day in August could you propose?

I looked in at Olivier's party at the India Office – very large, gorgeous with Oriental costumes, and highly successful. There were any number of humble Labour people – half-a-dozen from Deptford – but not too many Labour M.P.s. Olivier was in kneebreeches and stockings, with orders etc., very handsome. Bands of music of Indian regiments played in the upper galleries; attendants carried out trays of ices, coffee etc. The main crowd was in the great covered interior court, circulating into the tiers of corridors which formed galleries around – an ideal place for a first-class reception. Mrs O'Donnell, whom we met so often at Allahabad, was there, effusively greeting me.

The Lewes result is only 50–50, but not a failure. I only hope Dalton pulls off the Holland Division.

Now dear one I must close to ensure the post. I will come tomorrow by the 4.50 p.m. and probably taxi up, as I shall be very tired.

Sidney

## 762 PP SIDNEY TO BEATRICE

MacDonald was increasingly distrusted by and distant from his ministerial colleagues and the Labour backbenchers. Sidney, however, thought him 'head and shoulders above the rest of the Cabinet' (BWD 4 July 1924) and 'the very best available leader... quite irreplaceable either in Parliament or in the country'. (BWD 30 August 1924)

On 24 March MacDonald had accepted a £30,000 gift from an old friend, Alexander Grant, a self-made Scot who ran the McVitie and Price Biscuit Co. In May Grant was made a baronet. The honour was in fact for genuine acts of philanthropy; MacDonald's action made it seem that there was an implicit connection between the private loan and the public honour. Coming so soon after the 'sale' of honours by Lloyd George, MacDonald's naive disregard for appearances and his inept handling of the matter aroused much criticism. On 13 September he stated that he had not received the capital sum and that it had merely been invested in his name to provide an income which would enable him to have his own motor: the capital was to revert to Grant or to his son after MacDonald's death. Early in 1925 he gave up the car and returned the shares. R. B. Haldane wrote to Beatrice on 17 September (PP) to say that the episode 'rubs the gilt off the gingerbread' and hastened the disintegration of the government. 'MacDonald has done very well indeed. But he is not a good man of business . . . Anyhow it is well worthwhile to have had him and his party in control during these months.'

The Monday lunches at 10 Downing Street were attended by Thomas, Henderson, Clynes, Snowden and Webb, with Ben Spoor as Chief Whip. They served more as a party caucus than as an inner Cabinet: some ministers were apparently unaware that these lunches took place.

Arthur Ponsonby (1871–1946), later Lord Ponsonby, had begun his political career as private secretary to Campbell-Bannerman. A Liberal M.P. 1908–18, and a lifelong pacifist, he became a Labour M.P. in 1922, Under-Secretary for Foreign Affairs in 1924 and Minister of Transport in 1929.

41 Grosvenor Road
Westminster Embankment
28.9.24

Dear One

I found all right here – thanks to your care – we had (as I telephoned) a very successful day yesterday, all going off perfectly. (Two plain clothes policemen accompanied the P.M. as a matter of regular course: travelling in the next compartment, and following in a car wherever his car went.) His reception was royal, cheering crowds, groups outside the carriage door at each stopping station, most enthusiastic huge meeting and every sign of popularity (in the Party, and within our particular strata). You will read his speech ere this, which must be counted very successful. It sounded the right note, full of warning to the Liberals. What he had not time for was a description of the position if the Treaty were rejected.

We had practically no talk going as we thought it right not to distract his attention. Returning (he dropped off at Aylesbury, with his bodyguard, to drive to Chequers), we had a rather gay meal together, and some free talk. He had no more and no other things to say about the political position than we know: he would not be certain what the Liberals would decide, or what their procedure would be; or even whether we could practically escape remaining in office after an election producing no essential change.

He said there would have to be changes if we stayed in: he could not continue to hold double office: he would not mention any names (naturally). Altogether he was very civil and quite friendly; but not in the least intimate, even with Ponsonby, who evidently gets no nearer to him than I do. He suddenly asked me whether I had heard much of the motor car (!), and I told him of the universal verdict of 'Extraordinary Simplicity': I said it was a tribute to character etc.

The Monday lunches are resumed tomorrow.

Now dearest goodbye, I must write a lot of letters.

Yours

Sidney

763 PP SIDNEY TO BEATRICE

By the beginning of October 1924 it was clear that the government could not survive much longer: the combination of internal stresses, incapacity, frustration of its policies and the growing opposition of both Conservatives and Liberals would bring it down. At the first Cabinet after the summer recess MacDonald asked his colleagues if they would welcome another electoral victory. Though a majority hoped for such a result, according to Beatrice, MacDonald then said he thought it would be a grave misfortune as the party (by which he meant his rebellious critics, not the Cabinet) was 'not fit to govern'. (BWD 24 September 1924) The proposed loan to Russia provided the context for defeat, a proposal to prosecute a Communist the occasion. On 25 July J. R. Campbell, the acting editor, published an allegedly seditious article in the *Workers' Weekly* and a prosecution was begun, then dropped, apparently as a result of left-wing protest. The whole affair was mishandled badly by MacDonald and his colleagues; for good reasons they created the worst of impressions. The affair had dragged on all summer, and under pressure it degenerated from an embarrassment into a crisis. Though the Law Officers insisted that there was no political motive behind the decision to drop the case, on 1 October the Conservatives put down a motion of censure. On the next day the Liberals tabled an amendment calling for a select committee to investigate the matter. MacDonald then announced that both motions would be treated as a vote of confidence. When the Conservatives voted for the Liberal amendment the government was defeated by 364 to 198. On 8 October MacDonald resigned: even if the government had not mishandled the Campbell case it could not have survived an attempt to push through the general treaty and loan to Russia.

Harrison was a candidate for the post of odd-job man and gardener who was not employed by the Webbs.

41 Grosvenor Road
Westminster
2/10/24

Dear One

I have no inside news to tell you; but it is generally assumed that 'our number is up': I am inclined to doubt whether we shall be defeated next Tuesday or Wednesday on the Communist prosecution motion, as the

Liberals have an excuse for not supporting the Unionist motion, because it blames the Government exclusively, and not the Attorney-General [Sir Patrick Hastings], who is the man the Liberals wished to go for; and having an excuse they may not see why they should be deprived of their own chance of turning out the Government on the Russian Treaty. Moreover, it would be unsatisfactory to defeat the Government before the Irish Bill is disposed of; and also unsatisfactory to them not to negative the Russian Treaty, which would be simply left hanging, duly signed, and merely *not* negatived (as there is nothing that the H. of C. *need* do). On the whole I expect the defeat to take place on Thursday 30 October, the dissolution and writs about Friday 7 November, and polling day about 25 November. I suppose the House could meet about 9 December; dismiss on 11 December: resignation 12 December. If I am wrong, it might all happen three or four weeks earlier.

The former hypothesis leaves our several visits to Seaham unaffected. If however the dissolution comes about 14 October I shall simply be already down there (I go on Saturday 11 October) and shall simply remain until the polling day. Your meetings in that case will have to be merged with the election campaign.

I have written to Harrison as suggested. You should, I think, tell Moss what work he should do for the few days he is alone before you come down (e.g. not only pumping etc., but he might cut a store of wood, continue the digging up of kitchen garden in specified places etc.).

I return Betty Russell's letter. I have not written to her, as I really know nothing of these preparatory schools, or their merits: and nothing about the Minchinhampton one. I should hesitate to advise. But if you have told her that I would write to her, I will do so.

MacDonald and Thomas both made most excellent speeches on Tuesday and Wednesday on the Irish Bill – eloquent, high toned, conciliatory: the Ulsterites cut a poor figure, though they mustered 124 against second reading, the Front Opposition Bench not voting at all.

I may be able to put in something more this afternoon, but I doubt it. Snowden and Thomas are by no means so pessimistic. They think we shall probably ride over both threats. Ben Turner is betting freely 2 to 1 in cigars that there will be no election this year!

The members of the Party are eager for the fight, and believe we shall gain many seats.

SW

## 764 PP SIDNEY TO BEATRICE

Clifford Sharp wrote what Beatrice called 'a furiously malignant attack on MacDonald in the interests of Asquith . . . So ends our relationship'. (BWD 10 October 1924) Sidney then resigned as director of the *New Statesman*. At the personal level the Webbs were also disturbed by Sharp's heavy drinking, which eventually made him incapable of editing the paper.

Sidney had drafted Labour's election manifesto before leaving for Seaham. The party had been rallied at its annual conference and by the attack on MacDonald as pro-Russian. The conference, nevertheless, again rejected a Communist bid for affiliation by 3,185,000 to 193,000.

G. W. Bloomfield was a miners' union official at Easington, and J. H. Blackwell was vice-president of the Seaham Labour Party; Atkins was presumably another party worker. Herron had left the area and Sidney acted as his own election agent: he was officially sponsored as a Fabian candidate.

32 Maureen Terrace
Seaham Harbour
12/10/24

Dear One

I am sorry the telephone was so imperfect and indistinct: it is often so at long distance. Do not be troubled about Sharp's article: it will soon blow over and be forgotten. Meanwhile my letter of resignation is quite formal enough. I put it that way deliberately, so as to make my resignation *date back* to last January. Courteous phraseology is never wrong; and the letter is 'cold' enough in its very reticence. (You will remember that I wrote also to Glynne Williams and Whitley, saying I held my Management shares at their service, for any action they might choose to take.)

I found all well here. Both Bloomfield and Blackwell were here on arrival, very cordial and helpful. Bloomfield had engaged a Committee Room at the bottom of Marlborough Street; ordered envelopes; and *tried* to get the Register (which may not be out until 17 October! I have therefore written Galton to start addressing from the old one at once). The local Association has £100 and also £50 to get from Durham and they *say* the Lodges will subscribe as before.

I did not actually tell them what I would do as to Agent, but said I must do myself what Herron did, and *greatly use* Atkins; and that I proposed to divide up the other work, and give each man a definite job: Bloomfield mainly speaking: and so on – making it clear to them both that they should get leave from work for the whole period, which would be paid for out of Election Fund.

Your train on Wednesday is not as I wrote down from old timetable. At Newcastle you must jump round, quickly, if your train arrives punctually at 3.32 (as it usually does); so as to catch the train to Sunderland leaving 3.47 p.m. This brings you to Sunderland 4.19; and there is no train to Seaham for half an hour. I fear I can't send a car for you to Sunderland; but I will see what can be done – I will write again tomorrow about it.

Great meeting at Murton, all things shaping well.

Yours

Sidney

765 PP SIDNEY WEBB TO SUSAN LAWRENCE [*unsigned copy*]

Susan Lawrence (1871–1947) came from a prosperous family. She sat on the London School Board and then, after 1910, on the L.C.C. as a Moderate, changing to Labour in 1912. She was a borough councillor in Poplar and elected M.P. for East Ham North in 1923. She and Sidney liked and respected each other but Beatrice found her irritatingly emotional: the diary comments on her over the years became tart and unsympathetic.

The Webbs had planned to give up the lease of Grosvenor Road and make their home at Passfield, with Sidney finding some 'comfortable diggings' for so long as he remained in the House of Commons. (BWD 1 October 1924) Susan Lawrence, however, agreed to share the house on the terms set out in Sidney's letter. She remained for several years, taking over the whole house when the Webbs vacated their share.

10 December 1924

Dear Miss Lawrence

My wife tells me that you are in agreement as to a sort of partnership in occupation of this house for about three months. Without legal formalities, I put down what I understand to be the agreement.

1. That your occupation would begin on or about 9th January 1925, and continue until Easter (the exact dates being as may be convenient to you).

2. That you should pay at the rate of four pounds per week by way of rental, with extra payment of two-thirds of the actual cost during the three months of coal, gas and electricity. I think we must leave ourselves each to contribute for telephone calls roughly according to relative usage.

3. That I should, of course, pay rent, rates and taxes, water rate, telephone rental, and any casual repairs.

4. I think we had better regard the two servants as being each at our separate costs. Our Emily Wordley would take charge; and Mrs Webb has secured Emily's niece as temporary cook for the period. We can share the wages equally, and as to board, they can either both be on board wages to be shared equally; or you can maintain both, I paying to you board wages for Emily. I shall simply get her to buy for me my very small food requirements.

5. You will have for your exclusive use the first floor drawing room and the second floor (two bedrooms); with use in common of bath room, study and (except on the mornings when I or my wife are staying here, when we should be using it exclusively up to one p.m.) also the dining room.

We should have the exclusive use of the two top bedrooms (and a box-room).

I hope we shall not quarrel!

Yours sincerely,

# 6. The grind of opposition

## December 1924 – March 1929

At the general election the Tories came back with 413 seats. Labour, taking many votes from the Liberals and increasing its poll by over a million, dropped to 151 seats. The Liberals, who had badly miscalculated the consequences of bringing down the government, were reduced to a rump of 40 in Parliament. They never recovered from this setback. The Labour losses were due in part to a sharp decline in the number of Liberal candidates, which increased the number of straight fights and may have cost Labour 30 of the 40 seats lost. The main feature of the election, however, was the anti-Communist hysteria generated by the 'Zinoviev' or 'Red Letter' scare.

Five days before the poll the press published a letter purporting to have been sent by Zinoviev, president of the Communist International, to an official of the Communist Party of Great Britain instructing the party to prepare for a military insurrection and to subvert the armed forces. MacDonald knew by 16 October that the alleged letter was in the hands of the Foreign Office which had prepared a draft note of protest. Exhausted by the campaign and lacking proper staff support he mishandled the matter; and his error was compounded by the haste with which Sir Eyre Crowe, at the Foreign Office, forced the issue into the open. The *Daily Mail* had a copy and the Foreign Office gave the text to other newspapers on 25 October. Beatrice commented that MacDonald 'has lost his balance and floundered about badly'. (BWD 29 October 1924) The anti-Labour newspapers and speakers wildly exaggerated the affair and abused MacDonald. The stunt threw the Labour Party into confusion. (It is now believed that the letter was concocted by White Russian refugees, and 'placed' in Britain with the connivance of some officials of the Conservative Party and members of the Intelligence Service.) At the time Labour denounced the letter as a crude forgery but such denials could not stop the scare at this late point in the election. Beatrice noted at the time that the Cabinet was told that the War Office and Admiralty intelligence considered the letter a fake.

After the election the incoming Conservative government set up a committee to enquire into the matter. Austen Chamberlain told the House of Commons that the committee was satisfied that the letter was genuine and exonerated the Foreign Office officials on the grounds that they had misunderstood MacDonald's wishes in releasing the note and the letter.

In the postal vote for the executive of the Parliamentary Labour Party after the election Sidney was defeated. He and Beatrice seem not to have been greatly upset by the party's defeat: 'So long as the Liberals are progressively eliminated and Labour betters its position, however slightly, we prefer that the Conservatives should take office'. (BWD n.d. October 1924)

Sidney now settled down to the grind of opposition. Never a successful House of Commons man, and beginning to feel his age (he suffered from occasional fainting fits), he took his parliamentary duties seriously over the next four years but made no significant contribution to the party leadership. With Beatrice settled at Passfield, working away at *My Apprenticeship*, he went down for long weekends and began again to pick up the work on the local government books on which the Webbs had worked so long and which were still incomplete.

### 766 PP SIDNEY TO BEATRICE

Almost fifty letters from Sidney to Beatrice in the first months of 1925 deal with the day-to-day business of Parliament, with travel times to Passfield, domestic business about water supplies and servants at the cottage, and occasional comments on casual meetings and conversations. Very few of Beatrice's replies have survived.

After the election MacDonald was exhausted, depressed and in poor health. He still had to spend much time speaking about the country and in leading the party in Parliament, and adding to his salary of £400 p.a. by freelance journalism. In 1925 a legacy from a wealthy supporter eased his situation. He bought a large house in Hampstead and could afford long foreign holidays when Parliament was in recess.

41 Grosvenor Road
Westminster Embankment
16.12.24

Dear One

I found London drenched in rain, and in cold wind, but I walked here, changed my shirt and read my letters, and then went to the House in time to hear Austen Chamberlain's very long and ponderous *empty* speech. It contained an apparently generous testimony that MacDonald had done nothing wrong about the Red Letter (which J. R. M. said afterwards at dinner had been forced on them by the F.O. Staff); and a most important 'climbdown' about the Nile water, in which he apologised for the wording ('unlimited') of the ultimatum, and proffered a joint Water Board with impartial chairman. But all was wrapped up in unnecessarily elaborate verbiage, slowly delivered and actually boresome.

MacDonald was again rather below par in reply, and, whilst decent, not very effective. Thomas at 10 p.m. was the success of the day, purely on the Red Letter, indicting the Government for winning the Election under false pretences, most effectively delivered; and (whilst not convincing to those acquainted with the whole case) very plausible to our back benches! (The Government theory, it appears, is now that the Letter *was* received by the British Communist Party, which destroyed it – this contradicts what Scotland Yard asserted five weeks ago. I distrust especially secret evidence *subsequently* formulated.)

I gather that Trevelyan spoke to the general motion, and that Ponsonby was allowed actually to move the amendment, but I did not hear him. (I gave him the invitation for Xmas Eve lunch (1.30), which he thought would suit admirably, but will write.)

I have spent a busy morning clearing up arrears, and putting things away. I do not find the current bank passbook. (It is not put away, as I thought, with the old cheques and counterfoils. But there were also *old passbooks*, and these were probably put away somewhere. Ask Miss Piercy where.)

Today it is dull and dark, but probably you are having a fine day; and I hope getting steadily more rested. I am coming more and more to the conclusion that *less* than 4 days a week will suffice for Parliament next year. As I am not on the Party Executive, I have no meetings to attend constantly; and though there will be some later, at Eccleston Square; and subject committees at the House, I think these will not amount to much *per week*. I expect we shall have comparatively few divisions after the outset; and relatively few calls to speak. I think probably a couple of days weekly may often suffice for me. It is too glaring a waste of time to be there unnecessarily. But we shall see. I shall be glad to be able to settle down to the Poor Law book, but this will not be until after Christmas.

Now goodbye dear one, with the utmost love – and gratitude.

Sidney

767 PP SIDNEY TO BEATRICE

The debate was on the Safeguarding of Industries Bill, a modest instalment of the Protection to which the Conservatives were now firmly committed. The Labour Party opposed on its customary anti-tariff grounds. The Government won the vote on 16 February by 335 to 146.

41 Grosvenor Road
Westminster Embankment
17.2.25

Dear One

Here is the best I can do for the enlightenment of the Seaham women. It is not a subject out of which I can make very much. I am told J.R.M. was involved and lifeless. Snowden whom I heard was impressive but marred by his usual apparent vindictiveness. Hugh Dalton made an excellent maiden speech, well delivered, full of argument and securing the ear of the House. I only heard the beginning of it, as I was called out – Haden Guest made a foolish speech, abjuring Free Trade, and welcoming the Government proposals. The Clyde men rather ostentatiously stayed away most of the time, and I think a few of them abstained. The nett effect of the debate was undoubtedly to demonstrate the practical ineptitude of the Government proposals: and to make it clear that they are quite unlikely to result in any but a very few cases in which protective duties will be put on; and these probably in small matters like fabric gloves etc.

Spoor appeared just before the division, *looking* quite well. I had no chance of speaking to him, as I went off as soon as I had voted. I had broken sleep for some reason that I don't understand, but I feel none the worse this morning. I have not yet got into the habit of starting the day alone, without the sweet companionship to which I have become habituated. I am glad you have probably fine weather, which will allow you to stride over the moors elaborating further improvements, sometimes to your chapter, sometimes to your house – perhaps varying these with expeditions for moss and ferns, of which we cannot ever have too many.

I enclose the Division List, which has just come. I make out that only about 120 Labour Party voted, out of 150 odd; with some 25 Liberals out of 45 (!); and I think one (or two) Unionists of sorts (Cowan, Scot Universities). Certainly some Unionists abstained (Atkinson of Altrincham spoke in the debate critically, and did not vote), whilst some 75 or so were absent. I am not sure that any Liberal voted with the Government.

Thus the chief feature is the failure of the Liberal Party to put its whole strength even on Free Trade.

The only letter for you is enclosed with the money order for your letter.

I have spent the whole morning over correspondence etc. and now I must go off to lunch at the House. Dear One, goodbye for the day.

Sidney

### 768 PP SIDNEY WEBB TO WILLIAM ROBSON

On 6 March a Conservative backbencher introduced a Bill to reverse the practice whereby trade unionists could individually 'contract out' of the political levy to support the Labour Party: this practice had been reasserted after the Osborne Judgement by the Trade Union Amendment Act of 1913. The measure was not carried, but the change was made after the general strike of 1926 by the Trades Disputes Act of 1927, thus producing a marked fall in Labour's income. The situation was again reversed by the post-war Labour government in 1947. In 1925 Winston Churchill made the interesting suggestion to Baldwin that, in place of financing by trade unions and business interests, the costs of elections should be borne by the state, each candidate receiving a minimum number of votes being paid £300.

House of Commons
18.2.25

Dear Robson

I got your card at the same moment as your letter, i.e. 7.15 p.m. but found you were not then in the Outer Lobby. There is no reason at all why you should not accept the Radical Group invitation, and every reason why you should instruct them. Note that the T.U. Act of 1913, brought in and passed by Asquith's Government was itself a compromise and only agreed to by those in the Cabinet who objected to Trade Unionism by including the protection of dissentient minorities; and this was only accepted by the T.U. (insofar as they accepted at all) as the price of getting the Act. I believe the Unionist Opposition of that day did not divide against the Third Reading, certainly Bonar Law did not. How has it worked? I believe the Chief Registrar says 'quite well': he had had hardly any complaints. In fact, the claims for exemption, duly allowed, have been (and still are) very numerous, to be numbered in *tens of thousands*. The T.U. only affiliate to the Labour Party for 4 million members, whereas their total membership is over 6 millions. The balance is, of course, not by any means all exemptions from political levy, as many *small* T.U. do not join at all, (though hardly any large ones beyond the National Seamen and Firemen's Union, and the Musicians Union). The Irish Unions account for one hundred thousand more. But the magnitude of those left outside the Labour Party shows how easy it is to be outside.

Note that no Employers Association has such a limitation imposed on it. It may and does take political action, if it makes rules allowing it, without restriction.

Note also that a T.U. is not allowed the legal rights of an ordinary corporate body in suing its members for their contributions. It cannot enforce payment.

There are nearly two wage earners outside the T.U. for every one inside it. The six million Trade Unionists are little more than a third of the total wage earners of the U.K. The non-unionists at any rate far outnumber the unionists.

As a matter of practice, hardly any T.U. knows its members' *addresses*. Consider the seamen and others on board ship, as the extreme case. They are not like limited companies, or any middle class body, having registers of shareholders. Their members shift about, and cannot easily be communicated with. Even if they had the addresses, to send a circular to a 6 million membership would cost *in postage alone* £12,500.

Of course, if the T.U. are attacked in the way proposed by the foolish Tories, it will be the best possible thing for the Labour Party, which was *made* by the Taff Vale Case, and only fortified by the Osborne Judgement.

In fact, I don't believe that Baldwin (or Steel-Maitland) will allow the Cabinet to be stampeded into giving 'facilities' though I dare say McQuisten will get a Second Reading. But all this will doubtless be known to you.

Yours

Sidney Webb

### 769 PP SIDNEY TO BEATRICE

C. Isler and Co. was a firm of artesian well engineers providing Passfield Corner with a new water supply.

Sir George Young (1872–1952) was a Foreign Office official who had lost his post during the war and not been reinstated. He became associated with the I.L.P. and worked as a journalist: he ran three times as a Labour candidate. Though the author of the pamphlet, *The Diplomacy of Ramsay MacDonald*, is still unknown it was definitely not Young.

*The Life and Letters of George Wyndham*, edited by J. W. Mackail and Guy Wyndham (1926) contained a number of references to the Webbs during the Edwardian period. George Wyndham (1863–1913) was an enlightened Conservative and one of the Balfour set who was Chief Secretary for Ireland 1900–05.

On 12 February left-wing Labour M.P.s sought to reduce the vote for the expenses of the Prince of Wales, about to tour South Africa. Sidney and a number of Labour Members voted with the Liberals and Tories against the left-wing move.

41 Grosvenor Road
Westminster Embankment
19.2.25

Dear One

You did not enclose Isler and Co.'s letter; but I rang them up, and settled for Easter week for the house, wiring only.

It is satisfactory about Blackhall Rocks Hotel. I will *try* to go over to see it on Monday, but it may not be possible for me to get there in daylight.

You may be right about influenza; but I am all right now, and feeling merely the effect of late hours and shall go to bed early tomorrow and Saturday: and travel by the 11.30 a.m. on Sunday to Sunderland.

I enclose a virulent pamphlet against J.R.M. which has been sent out broadcast by the Editor of the *Labour Monthly*. I am not quite satisfied that it may not be by George Young; from the F.O. atmosphere that it exhales! What a pity all this is, whoever is author. As to my vote on the expenses for the official journeys of the Prince of Wales, this will afford quite a convenient subject to speak on, whenever I get an opportunity. My line will be that we ought to use the King and Prince, and it is all to their credit that they are zealous in seeking work.

I spent most of yesterday morning in weeding out and destroying my election papers. I have now reduced those to be kept to a small lot (now in the study on a shelf, and marked to be kept). The large tin box thus emptied might be used to replace the smaller one on the landing (now broken): and filled with those old property papers, and sent with the furniture to Passfield (being first locked).

Wyndham's *Life and Letters* Vol. II has come; and I will finish it here.

I lunched with Galton at Parliamentary Labour Club. He said that the disaffection of the I.L.P. was wide and deep, but he thought it would not immediately result in action, though it would come later. He could not imagine either Snowden or Thomas, Wheatley or Trevelyan coming to the top, and he was inclined to think that Clynes might be taken *faute de mieux*.

He said the F.S. was in a difficulty for a place for a Summer School – no suitable school had yet been found, and time was running on. He also wants suggestions for a subject for the Kingsway Hall Lectures, which must get settled soon.

He told me that a certain Fabian – Meredith Roberts – who is now an English teacher in Russia, and temporarily in London, declares that the Soviet Government has been making the most wonderful strides in Education (of course, by no means all over the country) in some respects ahead of this country. The popular demand for education is enormous. Also the demand for books of every kind. He said there were more bookshops in a single street in Moscow than in whole cities in England. He said also the heaviest direct tax was *called* the tax for Foreign Propaganda: his salary was £14 per month and he had to pay £3 per month for *this tax*. He found that its proceeds were very largely devoted, not to Foreign Propaganda, but to educating the Red Army! It seems to me interesting that this Soviet Government should find the *name* of Foreign Propaganda a popular one for a heavy tax. This Fabian thinks he will return to Russia, or at least to Riga.

Alexander (the Co-ops) wants an assistant for research and statistics under himself at £250 a year. I told him to ask Greenwood and also Dalton for a man, I could not suggest anyone.

Now goodnight dearest

Sidney

770 PP SIDNEY TO BEATRICE

George Ammon (1873–1960) was a Labour member of the L.C.C. and chairman in 1919. He was M.P. for North Camberwell 1922–31, and 1935–44.

41 Grosvenor Road
Westminster Embankment
20.2.25

Dear One

I don't need the H. of C. papers here: it saves trouble to have them addressed to Passfield. I enclose a few books that I should like from London Library – *add yours*.

I propose to travel on Sunday, by 11.30 a.m. to the *Roker Hotel*, Sunderland, where you can post to me from London up to Wednesday afternoon. I shall go by train to Seaham Harbour on Monday and Tuesday afternoons; and then take a car to my meetings and back to Sunderland. I have ordered car from Meek.

The two letters objecting to my vote on Prince of Wales to me are neither typical nor important. I am answering them softly and at length; and enclosing a copy of our *Constitution of a Socialist Commonwealth*.

I fancy the attack on J.R.M. that I sent you was only one of *two* chapters (I thought they were duplicates). I now enclose the other one. J.R.M. agrees that they must be by George Young, whom J.R.M. failed to reinstate in the F.O. service. He says he tried his hardest to find it possible: and in despair referred it to Ponsonby, who, after seeking every possible explanation and excuse from Young, could not avoid agreeing that it was impossible – constant and reiterated failure to work at his job, in one place after another; flat disobedience to orders: actual desertion of his post, and so on. But certainly J.R.M. is not bothering to take any trouble to 'mend his fences'.

The Women's Suffrage debate was, of course, lively – so far as I heard it – but as usual, hollow. The Government amendment, which puts the decision off for several years, will of course be carried; but there will be some advantage in getting votes against the Bill recorded. There is a threat of making the age 25 for men or women alike – which no government will venture on!

I was talking to Ammon, who was on the Jamaica trip, and returned in the same ship with J.R.M. who, he says, shut himself up and practically refused to talk to anybody, as a rule except when he was dragged out by force and compelled to associate in games etc. Yet on the other hand, he would occasionally talk to a group, some Tories, other strangers, *when he could command the conversation*, and be the leading figure; and then he would be extremely indiscreet!

Thomas, by contrast, lived perpetually in a continuous flood of conversation and romping with everyone, down to the children. Thomas, he says, was 'immense' in Jamaica: he made thirty speeches at dinners and other functions – always fresh and lively, and full of good humoured stuff, yet never saying anything in particular. He, in London, always leaves his house for his office at 8.15 a.m., however late he has stayed up the night before; and is said to have accumulated for his T.U. nearly two millions sterling.

Now, dear one, goodnight, I don't like this separation, which is intensified by the thought that it is to last nearly another week. I shall certainly return by Thursday night, though it is possible that I may not reach Kings Cross until 10 p.m. But I don't expect it will happen again for some time.

Sidney

771 PP SIDNEY TO BEATRICE

Beatrice had decided to publish the first volume of her autobiography instead of delaying until the planned successor was finished: she was feeling tired and depressed.

Sir Drummond Shiels (d. 1953) was a doctor who became Labour M.P. for Edinburgh East in 1924; he was Under-Secretary to Webb when he was Colonial Secretary in the 1929 Labour government.

41 Grosvenor Road
Westminster Embankment
21.2.25

Dear One

Here is all I can find of Octavia Hill in *both* the 1882 Select Committee and the 1885 Royal Commission. It seems that in 1881 or 1882 she had an article in the *Nineteenth Century* which I have not seen, and which perhaps contains the quotation you have.

There is no news. The dry cold weather is very pleasant here, and doubtless even more so with you. I think you might encourage Moss to start digging the well as soon as he thinks it possible.

Wyndham's letters are extraordinarily charming in the second volume, which I am finishing tonight. He stands out as a vivid personality, very much alive; but of course, very much the product of wealth and its characteristic 'culture' – quite unaware of economic issues. He mentions us several times, at Stanway, Whittinghame etc; and his view of us (in connection with Minority Report) is largely that of his associates, Belloc and Chesterton. There is an impression, to my mind, of 'polite futility' about his feverish activities, reminding me of 18th century French aristocracy, but, of course, with English sportsman virility. But as he wrote such charming, lively letters, their publication is fully justified. Not much of permanent political interest is included; and there are not enough editorial notes, as to the facts, to make the book of lasting value. In a very short time, as memories fade, much of his correspondence will be only barely intelligible.

I go off tomorrow by 11.30 a.m. train to the Roker Hotel. I have two meetings on Monday night; two on Tuesday night – all in the Southern half of the Division – and one at Seaham (I don't know where) on Wednesday. I shall probably not be able to go to Blackhall Rocks Hotel, as I shall not be near there until 8 p.m. but if I can do so somehow, I will.

I find it *very* lonely without you today, and I shall be glad when this week is over. We must try to keep together, except when duty actually compels separation. One day one of us will be alone; but we need not multiply separations before then. We might hope for another ten years – this is the 'expectation of life' of each of us from the printed tables. On the one hand, longevity has increased since then, and we ought to be good livers; on the other hand, I suppose the chance of both living so long is less than that of each of us.

I was speaking to Drummond Sheils, the Edinburgh M.P. who was asking after you: he said no one could have any adequate idea of the extent to which you and I together had promoted the acceptance of Socialist ideas among educated people in Scotland, as elsewhere. All they said now was, please let it be done step by step, and with consideration!

Goodnight, dearest. You need not forward the things not plainly urgent;

and nothing after Wednesday afternoon. I shall be home at 10.30 p.m. on Thursday at latest.

Yours

Sidney

772 PP BEATRICE TO SIDNEY

At the end of 1924 Beatrice had decided that the public life of the partnership was nearly over. She and Sidney, she remarked, were 'at the beginning of the last lap together . . . with wage slaves digging, planting, building and path-making . . . Shocking sight – the aged Webbs – adding acres to acre . . . laying out these acres to park-like avenues, cutting down trees to make vistas . . . we see pictures of two old folk living in comfort, and amid some charm, writing endless works, and receiving the respectful attention of an even larger public'. (BWD 2 December 1924) One of her new pleasures in this retreat was the discovery, through wireless, of music – though she constantly complained about defects in the radio set.

Passfield Corner
Liphook
Hants
[? early Spring 1925]

Dearest

In discussing with Moss and Oliver about the well and engine house Oliver started a new idea which I think we ought to consider though there may be nothing in it.

He said why not run the water pumping by a dynamo instead of direct from the engine? The reason he gave is that, if it is some distance from the cottage, it means starting the engine every day which means a considerable extra work. If the pumping were done by a dynamo like the electricity the engine need only be run *twice a week*, saving time and cleaning. The only disadvantage he knows of is that you will need a larger *storage* of electricity.

And this suggestion opens up the question of using the other well. Oliver suggests that a dynamo over the other well (he says it could be fixed inside the well) would be a very small affair and could be hidden by a shrub and that a dynamo can be run anywhere from an engine house and that [*sic*] the pumping of the well in this house.

Is it worth ringing up Islers before you leave London and asking them about this? Of course Oliver admits he is not an expert. But Moss says that at various houses the dynamo is used from the well which is charged from the engine house way off.

I may meet you if it is a fine evening at the *Liphook Corner* of the field path.

BW

P.S. I have just had another talk with Moss and Oliver over the plan of engine house. I note that, as drawn, the engine house with cable on one side and exhaust pipe on the other is adapted to the *other side of the hedge, the doorway being on the same side as the cable to house* – over the present well – that stupid young man! Moss agrees that so far as he knows there is no reason against building in under surface of ground a dynamo to present well and connecting it by cable with battery rack exactly as the electricity is. I think it would be probably wise before deciding what to do to ask them to send a proper expert down to consult – whatever we decide to do because the present drawing is not right and there might be some misunderstanding.

773 PP SIDNEY TO BEATRICE

The county and borough council elections were under way. In 1921, in protest against unemployment and falling living standards, the Labour-controlled Poplar council – of which Susan Lawrence was a member – had refused to levy the 'precept' on its rates required by the L.C.C. and other authorities such as the Metropolitan Water Board. George Lansbury and other members of the council were imprisoned for defying a court order to meet this demand. What was known as 'Poplarism', however, continued. In March 1922 a complaint that Poplar was not enforcing the Poor Law policy of deterrence and was giving workhouse inmates too much food led to the councillors being 'surcharged' by the District Auditor for excessive expenditure. This surcharge was not enforced for three years while the argument went on. When the matter came to the High Court, Poplar was upheld against the Auditor though he continued to send surcharge notices (one to Lansbury asked for £43,000) which were disregarded.

In an effort to satisfy Beatrice about the defective wireless Sidney sought help from Earl Russell (1865–1931), the elder brother of Bertrand Russell, who was a Fabian, a neighbour and had contacts with electrical engineering firms. James Fitzalan Hope (1870–1949), the Deputy Speaker, became Lord Rankeillour.

[41 Grosvenor Road]
5.3.25

Dear One

I am glad you have a fine day for the delivery of the furniture. Emily said it went off all right yesterday, except the fender stool, which seems to have been in your list, but as you had not labelled it, and as you had put it in the diningroom, she did *not* send it.

I saw Miss Lawrence this morning, who said she was dead tired of the *standing* and canvassing. By the way (though I did not tell her) Slesser told me that Sir John Simon (Poplar's counsel) told him that he was afraid the case was going against them (by 3 to 2). This is the surcharge of £5,000 on the Borough Councillors for paying excessive wages. If judgement is given against them, for the £5,000 and all the enormous costs up to the House of Lords, it will be very serious for Susan and Lansbury, as there is no further appeal or possibility of remission.

Henderson told me this morning (and W. Graham confirmed it) that there is a growing feeling among trade unionists in Scotland against I.L.P. candidates, with a feeling that the trade unionists in the Clyde area are elbowed out of seats. It is impossible to gauge how much there is in this, but of course it represents something.

So far the news of the Durham County Council elections is very good. Labour has won 8 seats and lost 3 (two of the latter being accidental and illegitimate gains three years ago). Of the Seaham results only 2 are yet to hand. Peter Lee in by a large majority at Thornley and Wheatley Hills; but the Labour man unsuccessful at Hasell and S. Heaton – no change.

I will remember to speak to Russell next time I meet him but I do not do so often. I quite believe that the delivery is not quite right: and I will see what I can do on Saturday (though I am not a wireless expert!). I see a lady in Manchester paid £64 for a set, and found it quite useless, a law case.

We have just heard by a telegram that Labour in Durham County has already got 38 seats out of a total Council of 74 – thus a clear majority – with 7 more results to come. The Durham M.P.s are overjoyed. We have as yet no further particulars as to the Seaham divisions. Later news, final. There are 40 Labour to 34 Moderates, giving a majority of 6, which will be increased by the Labour Aldermen. Six years ago the majority was only 4.

There has just been a row. Austen Chamberlain was speaking portentously and verbosely; and Kirkwood was interjecting, not at all seriously. Suddenly Hope (the Chairman) got up, and sharply ordered him not to interrupt; and before anything more, ordered him to leave the House. Kirkwood did not refuse to go, or say anything, and did not even delay, because within a few seconds Hope 'named' him, and sent for the Speaker. When the latter came, J.R.M. tried quite cleverly to intervene, but the Speaker explained that he could not under the standing orders allow any debate; and so we divided in the Suspension which Chamberlain moved; and it was carried by 200 to 110 (or thereabouts).

Runciman voted with us, and said Hope's conduct was quite wrong. Thereupon J.R.M. got up and we all followed him, leaving the House! The Parliamentary Executive then met; and we were told to hang about. Soon we were summoned to a Party Meeting, when J.R.M. said he would (1) put down a vote of censure on Hope; (2) send a statement to the press; (3) ask for an early day (Monday) to discuss it. Meanwhile we are not to go back for the evening; and most of the London M.P.s are going off to help in the L.C.C. elections.

We did this quite with dignity; and I think it is all right. The worst thing is that it will glorify Kirkwood, and make him more obstreperous than ever. But the good thing is that J.R.M. *led*, and was unanimously followed. Goodnight dear one. I shall be glad to be with you on Saturday morning.

Sidney

774 PP SIDNEY TO BEATRICE

Max Beer's *A History of British Socialism* was a standard work, first published in 1919. Bartlett was the nurseryman who supplied the trees and plants when the Webbs laid out the garden at Passfield Corner. C. R. Fay (1884–1961), who had been a research student at L.S.E., was professor of economic history at Toronto until 1930, and then returned to a post at Cambridge. Sir Richard Rees (1900–1970), editor and critic, was treasurer and a lecturer for the Workers Educational Association in London, 1925–27.

41 Grosvenor Road
Westminster
19.3.25

Dear One

I have drawn £20, and will bring it tomorrow. I have looked for Beer's *History of British Socialism*; but I cannot see either Vol. I or Vol. II. I have no recollection of getting the latter from London Library. When was it? Perhaps the easiest thing is to *give* our copy of Vol. II in replacement.

We are to adjourn on Thursday, 9 April, and to resume on Tuesday, 28 April (and take the Budget that day).

I don't understand what Bartlett has been at. You have presumably written enough to him. Probably we have had all we can get from him.

I enclose a pretty little account of Professor [Alfred] Marshall, by Fay, from a Canadian weekly that the Private Secretary at the Board of Trade has sent me. You will see his reference to yourself, to Schloss etc. He was a curiously delicate 'hothouse' sort of person, whose 'sheltered' life exaggerated a very one-sided personality, in which even the sense of public duty and public service was exaggerated to the point of becoming abnormally fanciful and even fantastic. His conscience, like his intellect, lacked a healthy robustness; with the result that his influence on the coarser people who had the job of government and legislation must have been greatly impaired.

I enclose the Report of Standing Committee A when I failed utterly to get Neville Chamberlain to make clear his very obscure Bill. He is acting not at all in a conciliatory manner – in fact, he seems always to want to crush his adversary, even when there is no need for such a procedure. This episode is typical of his usual behaviour as a Minister. In this particular case, there is nothing in the matter, as, *probably*, the Government scheme is the best possible. But it will be absolutely obscure to the little property owners; it will, I feel, involve litigation; and I am inclined to think it may lead to many unfair small increases in assessment. There were half-a-dozen other Labour Members present – I think no Liberals – and I got no help from any of them. If I had not been there, there would have been no discussion or criticism at all.

It is *said* that Lord Curzon is dying, with complications arising from gastric ulcer. If so, it may even strengthen the Government, by enabling someone else to be taken in.

I have just seen Sir Richard Rees, who is quite pleased with his L.C.C. fight; and is now inclined to take on a parliamentary constituency. He is going to make an enquiry into the way that Social Insurance is working in 1,000 cases, taken as they come, with the help of Mallon at Toynbee Hall, and a friend who runs a boys' club.

The Durham County Council has started askew. At the first meeting, the Labour men failed to carry the chairmanship. By the help of the outgoing Aldermen, and owing to some failure to attend, the votes for Chairman were a tie (41 each); and the Moderate Chairman gave his casting vote for the Moderate candidate. Peter Lee was then elected Vice-Chairman; and the Labour members then found justification for refusing to re-elect any expiring Moderate Aldermen, and carried a full list of Labour men (including A. Purvis, the defeated of Blackhall and Trimdon). They have thus a substantial majority, and the failure to get the Chairman does not really matter; but they start in a bad atmosphere.

Goodnight, dear one. I shall [be] with you in 24 hours.

Sidney

775 BL SIDNEY WEBB TO GEORGE BERNARD SHAW

Beatrice had recently visited the Shaws, and noted that the 'great man' now had an income of over £30,000 a year. (BWD 19 March 1925)

41 Grosvenor Road
Westminster
25.4.25

Dear Shaw

It occurs to me to add two things. If you want the *best* security, the right thing to buy (at our age!) is the *3½* per cent British '*War Loan*', repayable in *1928* at latest. It is 96¼, and yields, taking the redemption into account, £5.1.8 per cent. You only pay Income Tax and Supertax on £3.10.0 per annum which is all you get annually; and thus (assuming that you pay 4/6+2/6 = 7/- in the £) it yields to you eventually the same *net* as a perpetual stock paying an annual dividend of 5¾ per cent – which is not bad for a British Government security, secured against depreciation in value.

The other thing is that I am rather tempted with the idea of buying sound industrial *ordinary* shares (not preferences or debentures) in British companies – out of sentimental preference I should myself avoid breweries and distilleries, armament firms and patent medicines! Also avoid gas-works, and any others with dividends limited by statute. My idea is that trade is going to improve; and that there might be a bare possibility of currency inflation (which I think wicked and disastrous); and in such a contingency the ordinary shares would go up whilst the fixed-interest securities would go down.

But this is a very speculative opinion of mine; and I have not myself yet acted upon it, partly because I don't care much to trouble about it. Expert advice is needed as to what *is* a sound industrial Ordinary Share!

Yours

Sidney Webb

776 PRO SIDNEY WEBB TO RAMSAY MACDONALD

Rose Rosenberg was MacDonald's secretary. MacDonald, still smarting under defeat and angry both with the I.L.P. in general and in particular with the carping attacks of its weekly *New Leader*, considered seeking control of the *New Statesman*. He and a group of friends were acquiring shares through Sir Hedley Le Bas. He first wrote to Webb on 7 April 1925 to inform him of the plan. The matter dragged on all summer. On 14 September MacDonald was still anxious to take over the paper: 'unless we can get some platform our press will ruin the whole spirit of our movement and turn it into a mere wordy, unpractical combination of sentimentality and fecklessness'. (PP)

H. B. Lees-Smith (1878–1941) was a lecturer in public administration at L.S.E. Elected as a Liberal M.P. in 1910 he joined the I.L.P. after the war and became Labour M.P. for Keighley in 1922. He was Postmaster-General and then President of the Board of Education in the 1929 Labour government. R. Richards was Under-Secretary for India and M.P. Major A. C. Church, elected for East Leyton in 1923, became a perennial candidate, contesting seven constituencies. He supported MacDonald in 1931. John Stocks (1882–1937), was fellow of St John's College, Oxford, and professor of philosophy at Manchester 1924–36.

41 Grosvenor Road
Westminster Embankment
28.4.25

Dear MacDonald

I was shocked, *late this afternoon*, to be handed Miss Rosenberg's letter of the 7th April and yours of the same date. They were not given to me before the adjournment; and unstamped letters are apparently not forwarded. (I don't know how many letters thus addressed to M.P.s have lain there for the last three weeks.)

As to the *New Statesman*, I had, of course, heard nothing of the idea, I had not seen Clifford Sharp for many months, nor heard from him, or any one concerned in the paper. As you may imagine, relations between us have been quite broken off; and I have nothing whatever to do with the concern. The shares have never paid any dividend whatsoever, and no one who has put money in the paper since its start in 1913 has ever received a penny piece. On the other hand, it ought to be very near the paying point now; and I was told a year ago that it could be sold for something like the £30,000 or more that it has cost to establish it.

I should entirely approve of its passing into the hands of our own people, if that should be practicable. Glynne Williams is now the predominant shareholder; and he is a non-party man, a 'Progressive' in sympathy, but not definitely 'Labour'. He is a wealthy Argentine ranch-owner, and not concerned to make money out of it. He refused, for instance, to sell out to Keynes and Layton, who wanted to merge the *N.S.* with the *Nation*, under their own control. I imagine he would not be unwilling to part with half the shares to people he approved of, or even the whole, at a fair valuation.

But the difficulty would be the fate of the present Editor, who has made the paper what it is. (I am wholly out of sympathy with his product; which, besides being utterly unappreciative of the Labour Party, is now hard and wooden, and sterile.)

I am not by way of seeing or meeting Glynne Williams; with whom, however, I have remained on cordial terms. I should be willing to do anything in the matter that you desired.

As to the Cape Government desire for a chairman of a Wages Commission, I assume he would be paid a handsome fee, besides expenses. I gather you wished me to suggest possible names, which is not easy. In many ways Tawney could be a suitable man, and not too much politically 'labelled'. Other names that occur to me, who *might* go for a fee, are *Olivier*, Dalton or Lees-Smith – if they can be spared. One available person, much inferior to the above, is Gilbert Slater, now retired from an Indian Professorship; or there is Richards, the late Under-Secretary for India, who was a Welsh professor of economics. Major Church, ex-M.P., did well on the Kenya trip, but is not an economist. I wonder whether Stocks of Oxford would care to go: if so, he might be acceptable.

These are all the names I can think of tonight. I return the telegram. Perhaps we might be able to have a talk about it tomorrow.

I am sorry for the delay, but it was not my fault. It would be better not to rely on H. of C. messengers to deliver unstamped letters.

Yours

Sidney Webb

777 PP SIDNEY WEBB TO LORD LONDONDERRY [*retained copy*]

The Marquess of Londonderry, the largest coalowner in the north-east, complained to Sidney on 8 April 1925 about a statement during the county council elections that, during a strike, the colliery owners 'were not going to have the county money spent on feeding the children'. Londonderry claimed that the Durham County Council had three years earlier implemented the Feeding of

Children Act without dissent. In his own colliery villages, he added, he paid for meals to schoolchildren not covered by the Act. He tartly observed that Sidney had given neither money nor help to the families affected by the long coal strike.

[41 Grosvenor Road]
[29 April 1925]

Dear Lord Londonderry

I was distressed to find, on returning to the House of Commons when the session was resumed yesterday, that a letter from you dated 8 April had remained unanswered during the recess. It had apparently been sent by hand just before the adjournment, and had not been delivered to me. The practice appears to be that unstamped letters are not forwarded. I apologise for what must have seemed my discourtesy.

I regret that the sentence which you quote from the much abbreviated report of my speech of two months ago should have given cause for complaint. But may I point out, with reference to some expressions in your letter, that I made no 'mis-statement of facts', still less any 'distortion of fact' or 'untruth'? Indeed, the offending sentence plainly refers one to arguments current at the County Council election of two months ago.

I am aware that the action of the Durham Education Authority during the disastrous stoppage of the pits in 1921, in supplying meals to school children evoked widespread admiration for its promptitude, completeness and efficiency, in which I believe it surpassed all other Local Education Authorities. I have repeatedly referred to this action with warm appreciation; and, as far as I remember, without ever attributing blame for opposition to any members of the County Council, or any Party thereon. I am glad of your assurance that not one member in 1921 opposed the decision. But, to my own knowledge, it did not escape animadversion; and naturally so, because whether, in a great industrial dispute, meals should be supplied to hungry children at the expense of the Education Rate rather than by private charity, is an important issue of policy on which there may well be a legitimate difference of opinion. I should indeed be sorry to think that the not inconsiderable number of persons who still honestly deprecate the feeding of school children at the cost of the Education Rate means that they wished the children to go unfed. If any sentence that I uttered or that I am reported to have uttered gave such an impression, I regret it; and I gladly take this opportunity of correcting such a misapprehension.

I hope, moreover, that nothing that I have said has been open to the misconstruction that I ignored or criticised the extensive charities dispensed in connection with the great Londonderry enterprises at Seaham and elsewhere. As for the help that I have been in a position to render, I prefer to say nothing, except only that I have always made it clear that I hold it to be improper, as setting up an invidious relationship, for any elected person to give money, even for the most deserving objects within the particular constituency in which he has to solicit votes. He has scope enough elsewhere.

Let me add, in conclusion, with my sincere regret that anything that I have said should have given offence, that I have always striven to avoid any denunciation, abuse and even personal criticism (as distinguished from policy on public issues) of my electoral opponent, or of any other person; and that to this practice I intend to adhere.

[Sidney Webb]

778 PRO SIDNEY WEBB TO RAMSAY MACDONALD

Passfield Corner
Liphook
Hants
19.9.25

Dear MacDonald

We hope to come to your party on Friday; and I want a word with you about the *New Statesman*. Glynne Williams, the largest shareholder, has now had a definite offer from Le Bas to buy *half* his holding, *including* the corresponding management shares, for cash. He wishes to accept, and he insists, anyhow, on retiring from the Board. I have told him that I cannot object or demur to *his* accepting this offer; and he will probably have done so.

Le Bas is seeking apparently to purchase other shares, including the management shares, and he may approach other (non-Labour Party) holders. He says he has no wish to alter the paper from its present political attitude, which he calls the 'Labour Right'. But this, of course, affords no security that, at any future time, he might not receive and accept an advantageous offer from the Liberals, or others – it would pay them to buy up the paper at far more than its commercial value – and I have no reason to be sure that this may not be already in view (equally, none to the contrary).

You suggested a sort of trust holding of enough of the management shares to prevent this (analogous to the present arrangement for *The Times*). I should be glad to promote this. But the difficulty is to find people to 'hold the fort'.

Personally, I should be glad to be bought out at once, and relieved of any trusteeship. I do not wish to 'abandon' any fort I hold; and I say this in order that, in considering the formation of such a trust, someone should be found, if possible, to relieve me.

Part of the uncertainty is that I do not know whether Le Bas is acting for you or with your cognizance and approval; or whether, on the other hand, you share my feeling of insecurity for the future of the paper in his hands.

Yours truly

Sidney Webb

### 779 PP BEATRICE TO SIDNEY

Arthur Ponsonby was a neighbour to the Webbs at Shulbrede Priory. While the Shaws were visiting Passfield Corner Beatrice hoped they would show some interest in the manuscript of *My Apprenticeship*. Shaw did ask 'somewhat perfunctorily how it was getting on but showed not the remotest desire to see any more of it; Charlotte has not even mentioned it'. (BWD 9 June 1925) Shaw showed Beatrice the draft of *The Intelligent Woman's Guide*. 'It will be a marvel if it is not a bad book and I think he knows it is', Beatrice noted. He liked startling people with an idea: 'To him it is irrelevant whether it turns out to be in accordance with fact . . . He is a magnificent critic of life and a consummate literary craftsman . . . he is absolutely futile as a constructive thinker'.

Passfield Corner
Liphook
Hants
[early June 1925]

Dearest

The P.M.'s statement is a thin business looked at as the result of the raid; but not quite so ineffective as an indictment of the idiotic conduct of the Soviet Government. The notion that Negro and Hindu shiphands would influence the British seamen is curiously comic. I wonder when they will learn how mentally defective they seem to us. However they are a thorn in the flesh, not to Capitalism, but to Labour. It is very like the French Revolution and the Corresponding Societies of the end of the 18th century – except that the members had not the Vote!

We motored over to call on Mrs Ponsonby – she was very pleased to see us. Their romantic abode struck us as gloomy and dark even in this warm weather – Charlotte said it smelt of death and decay! The lady of the Priory certainly looks ill and depressed.

It is very pleasant having the Shaws here and I am glad they are coming back for the weekend. But it means that my very slight capacity for reading and dictating is altogether swept away – what with the obligation to talk and the added thought about their comfort. However, it is [worth] while. It is clear that [I do] not need a resident secretary – if it were not for Diary I could not keep her occupied. If by the end of June I am not better I am almost inclined to go [to] Switzerland in July.

Ever yours

Beatrice

### 780 PP SIDNEY TO BEATRICE

J. Wignall was M.P. for the Forest of Dean 1918–24. Albert Arthur Purcell (1872–1935) of the Furnishing Trades Association and a member of the General Council of the T.U.C. was strongly pro-Russian. He held the Forest of Dean with an increased majority at the bye-election in August, despite MacDonald's refusal either to speak for him or send a letter of support.

Beatrice's diary contains many comments on the tension between MacDonald and the Labour left. On 22 June she noted that 'he has no body of ardent friends and is getting more and more isolated'. She commented on the contrast between the 'revolutionary' speeches of the I.L.P. and 'the vision of J. H. Thomas in frock coat and top hat at Ascot and J.R.M. taking tea with their Majesties at the Air Force pageant'. Though MacDonald had great gifts of charm and energy 'he is an egotist, a poseur, and a snob, and worst of all he does not believe in the creed we have always preached – he is not a socialist and has not been one for twenty years; he is a mild radical with individualist leanings and aristocratic tastes'.

Austen Chamberlain's speech was on the Locarno Peace Pact.

The Webbs were about to pay their first visit to Parmoor for eleven years. Though they had enjoyed good relations with Alfred and Theresa Cripps until 1912, they had drifted apart and there had been little warmth even when Lord Parmoor was a colleague of Sidney's in the government. Despite Theresa's death and Parmoor's second marriage, however, the relations became much closer from this time.

41 Grosvenor Road
Westminster
24.6.25

Dear One

It is raining here this morning, cold and dreary. By the way, I don't see Fenner Brockway's cheque anywhere, and Emily has not seen it. Perhaps you have found it by now.

Last night I stayed till midnight and then paired: the House sat till 1.30 a.m. Tonight I shall probably get home earlier. We are in a bad hole about Forest of Dean. Mosley, after accepting, has refused, as Birmingham will not let him go. Miss Bondfield has refused; and it appears that at the last contest, Wignall (who had a woman as Liberal opponent) declared everywhere that a woman could not represent the Miners – which is now brought up against her. The next preference is Purcell, the Communist! Henderson is going to try to get Miss Bondfield to fight though we may very likely lose the seat anyhow. MacDonald says that he finds the 'flirtations' with Communism, preference, Birth Control, Chinese insurrection, and general 'wildness' is doing serious harm. It can't be helped! But it all makes (a) for an early general election if the Unionists choose; (b) against any *early* Labour majority; and (c) against J.R.M.'s 'staying the course'. Also he is not well in health, has recurrent neuritis, and can't sleep.

I have just heard Austen Chamberlain on the Pact for three-quarters of an hour, when I could stand no more – he said just nothing, in sepulchral tones!

We move a Vote of Censure on Monday on Unemployment: the worsening in the statistics is almost entirely the new unemployment in coal mining.

I hope you will get this tomorrow before starting, as you will drive down. Dear One good night until tomorrow.

Sidney

781 BMJL SIDNEY WEBB TO HAROLD J. LASKI

Laski had recently published *A Grammar of Politics* as a restatement of radical pluralism. It was dedicated to the Webbs. In designing their model socialist constitution, the Webbs had been attracted by the idea of separate legislatures for social and foreign policy. Laski did not find a country cottage near the Webbs; his country home was at Little Bardfield in Essex.

Passfield Corner
Liphook
Hants
13.7.25

Dear Laski

This is my birthday which I am celebrating by another read at your great book, in preparation for journeying to an evening of successive divisions in the House on details of the Widows Pension Bill.

I am not familiar with all the previous books along similar lines, but I think yours has at least the great merit of superseding them. I always regard it as one of the (usually unfulfilled) duties of 'scientific' authors to make each book inclusive and supersessory of all that has gone before! You must have come near doing that. It is a great gain to get it done on *our* assumptions instead of on our opponents' assumptions.

I was told that the book was (unlike your conversation) dull. But I have not found it so. On the contrary I think you have been very successful in overcoming the inherent dullness of the subject.

I see you think very little of our 'Social Parliament' idea. I see all the shortcomings of it, but I still think there is something to come out of the idea. We shall be driven to unimaginable devices when we have really to grapple with the necessary enlargement of the work of the controlling legislature nor do you seem to smile on the 'shifting kaleidoscope' of wards that we suggest for Local Government. Well, you will have to find other devices for solving the problem. I don't mind tossing into the air suggestions that seem absurd. Some of them 'come off' after the necessary time lag.

Have you found your house in these parts yet? We shall be very glad to see you.

Yours

Sidney Webb

On 21 July Beatrice had noted in her diary: 'I am inclined to think that we are not so far off a very nasty upheaval – the worst we have ever had'. The miners had prepared a wage claim: conversely, the owners wanted reductions in wages and longer hours. The negotiations broke down in June. On 3 July the miners appealed to the T.U.C. for help. On 14 July the government set up a court of enquiry. On 26 July the rail and transport unions offered support to the miners and on 30 July a special T.U.C. conference empowered the General Council to call a large-scale strike. The government, playing for time, offered a temporary subsidy to the coal industry and appointed a Coal Commission under Herbert Samuel; it thus postponed the crisis for nine months, during which secret preparations were made for dealing with a general strike. On 17 August, known as 'Red Friday', Beatrice noted the 'headiness' of the left at Baldwin's apparent surrender to the threat of direct action. She felt that there was a drift towards a general strike, which would be 'a catastrophe for the Labour movement as the price of a return ticket to sanity'. She thought such a defeat would be followed by a 'period of quiescence which will last until 1940 or thereabouts'. (BWD 22 August 1925)

Sidney, bent on leaving Parliament at the end of its term, had asked MacDonald if he would like the reversion of the safe seat at Seaham. When MacDonald replied that he was content for the present to remain in Aberavon, Sidney made an abortive attempt to secure the nomination for his old agent, R. J. Herron, now somewhat unhappy as a minister in Somerset.

41 Grosvenor Road
Westminster
30.7.25

Dear One

I was very glad to get your letter, and to learn that you were going on all right. Because, last evening I broke out in a heavy cold in the head, running at the nose and tickling of the throat. I got home at 11.30 p.m., and went straight to bed, but could not go to sleep at all all night! I am better now, but of course I shan't stay late tonight, as I intended; and I hold myself free to go home at any time. I think I am getting over it all right. It is annoying, as I feel I must go up for Monday and Tuesday nights.

The coal crisis is still unsettled; and even my optimism begins to be shaken even about tiding over tomorrow's notices. J.R.M. last evening thought the position of the gravest. I took the opportunity to tell him about the Seaham seat, about which he was, of course, very gracious. He said, however, the present Parliament would last 4 years (its full term!). If it does, *I* may not last so long!

I propose to dispose of two engagements, and then go home at 4.30 p.m. to nurse my cold: it is going on all right, but I am clearly unfit to sit up into the small hours casting futile votes.

Until tomorrow

Sidney

The Labour Party conference was being held in Liverpool. Howard Kingsley Wood (1881–1943) was Conservative M.P. for Woolwich West 1918–43; he was Parliamentary Secretary to the Ministry of Health 1924–29 and held a number of senior posts in subsequent Conservative governments. Hollesley Bay was a Labour colony which Beatrice had visited in 1907 during her membership of the Poor Law Commission.

Herbert Morrison (1888–1965) was a rising Labour politician in London. He was mayor of Hackney and then leader of the first Labour-controlled L.C.C. in 1934. He held office in the 1929 Labour government, the wartime coalition and the post-1945 Labour government, his last post being an unhappy spell as Foreign Secretary. In his early career he was an expert on municipal transport and electricity supply, and he took up Webb's old role as the leading authority on London government. His wife's name was Rose. Annie Somers was the woman organiser of the London Labour Party.

MacDonald had recently acquired a fine Georgian house in Frognal, Hampstead.

This letter is wrongly dated: it should be 26 September 1925.

North Western Hotel
Liverpool
27.9.25

Dear One

Here I am safely settled in this great hotel, where most of the Executive are staying.

I travelled down in a crowded train, swollen by Atlantic boat passengers: lunched along with Lansbury and Morrison, who are just the same as ever. Lansbury said the West Ham Poor Law trouble was due, not to Neville Chamberlain but to Kingsley Wood, the Parliamentary Secretary to whom it had been left. Lansbury thought the Government action quite illegal, and imagined it would be settled by both parties giving way a little; really by the West Ham people winning. He said the root of the matter lay in the Government doing nothing for the unemployed; and when I said that 'Hollesley Bay' was requisite for the bottom layer, he warmly acquiesced. Miss Lawrence, by the way, to whom I sent to talk last night, said that the local enthusiasm was tremendous, and more than she had ever seen. As to the Surcharge on Poplar Borough Council, about which Miss Lawrence had been a little nervous about her own fortune, Lansbury volunteered the suggestion that *she* would be safe he thought, as the Government had offered to let them all off, if they would agree to be good for the future. Now as Miss L. is no longer on the Council, *she* has no opportunity of accepting this offer, or otherwise; and Lansbury suggested that under these circumstances it would be difficult to proceed against her for the past! I will put this point to her, so that she has it in mind, if proceedings *are* taken – which Lansbury thinks unlikely even in his own case.

MacDonald is here, looking ill, and continually in pain with arthritis. He says that Kennard, the ex-boilermaker-bonesetter who insisted on operating on him, did it solely for advertisement, and that he did him no good at all; but merely broke some adhesions, with only transient effect.

Mrs Henderson is here, with Will. Uncle Arthur has gone off to a football match. Greenwood is here (alone): Middleton, of course, who seems very well. They expect a good deal of row; but believe that it will be much less formidable than is anticipated; and that 'the platform' will carry its will, so far as rebellion is concerned.

Sunday

Last night I went out and dined at a restaurant with Lansbury, Mr and Mrs Morrison and Miss Somers; very pleasant intercourse, but of no importance. They finished up at a Cinema, but I went home and chatted with the Hendersons, MacDonald, Clynes etc. and early to bed.

This morning I breakfasted (heavily) with MacDonald, who talked about Hampstead etc., but never on anything interesting!

We have spent over 3 hours with Standing Orders Committee, and going through the whole agenda, [Arthur] Cook is to support the Executive on the Communist question; and very little doubt is felt about our getting through our resolutions. The agenda is beyond all precedent colossal and we contemplate holding two evening sessions, and sitting all Friday. Even so, I don't see how we can get through, without a great slaughter of the innocents on Friday, which will probably allow me to catch the 2 p.m. train arriving Euston at 6 p.m. We have adjourned until 2.30, and I am just going out for a breath of fresh air and to get a cup of coffee and a roll and an apple – preparatory to a hotel dinner tonight!

I will finish this letter when I come back as the post leaves at 4 p.m.

As the sun was shining, I walked up to the new Cathedral, which is half way up towards Sefton Park, on a fine site; a great red sandstone colossal building – only choir and transept finished and open – to be the very largest in Britain – a wonderful exhibition for a decaying (?) Established Church.

Now I must close otherwise I shall miss the post. Dearest I miss you badly. There is no news to send. This will be a noisy and disjointed Conference but the Executive expects to win hands down.

Sidney

784 PP BEATRICE TO SIDNEY

The Webbs published through Longman, Green: Beatrice was now concerned with the practical details of producing *My Apprenticeship*. The Wallas book was *The Art of Thought*, published in 1926. Baron Erik Palmstierna was the Swedish ambassador to Britain 1920–37 and on friendly terms with the Webbs.

Passfield Corner
Liphook
Hants
[?26 September 1925]

Dearest One

Here is a letter from Longman which is satisfactory. So we might notify Clark that we shall need that amount of paper – if the U.S.A. is included we shall require more. I wonder when we shall hear from U.S.A. The Wallases are very enthusiastic about the book – it is much more interesting than they expected – and they think it 'a work of art'. Graham read us his last chapter last night – or a large part of it – on public education giving his own experience – it was interesting and suggestive but it [?left] no definite significance in my mind; [?except] a 'doubting Thomas' about Compulsion and the working of democracy without giving any [?alternative toleration]. On our walk home I asked him what had made him turn towards the psychological aspect instead of the study of institutions and he said it was his growing doubt beginning about 1899 of the validity of democracy! as an abstract proposition. 'I never believed in abstract democracy so doubts have never troubled me' I answered him. He probably held his democratic faith in the same way that his father had the divinity of Christ. But of course there is something to be said for beginning a study of society by a study of man as a unit – it is our method of approach.

Here is an enigmatic note from Palmstierna – is it our view of the condition of British Trade he refers to? What is the Report he mentions? I can't read the name.

Do write me all the gossip – you will hear a good deal.

Ever yours

Beatrice

785 PP BEATRICE TO SIDNEY

The reference is probably to Sam Watson (1898–1967), leader of the Durham miners, who became one of the powerful trade unionists in the Labour Party. It may, however, be to Stephen Watson, delegate from the Sedgefield Labour Party in Durham.

Bertha Newcombe was an artist who was much attracted to Shaw in 1895–96, painting a noteworthy portrait of him at this time.

Passfield Corner
Liphook
Hants
Sunday morning [27 Sept 1925]

Dearest One

I can imagine you chatting after breakfast with Henderson and Watson – possibly Hodges? and I shall be intensely interested in anything new you send me. Do write me nice long letters. Suppose I forget will you ask Susan [Lawrence] whether she will go with me to *Mrs Warren's Profession* at Regent Theatre *Monday 12th*? *I am writing for 2 tickets* tomorrow.

I took the Wallases on a drive to Sherborne and we looked up Bertha Newcombe, lodging in a small bungalow on the Portsmouth Rd but she was out. They are leaving Palmers and have bought a house at Steepe. Then Graham and I got out about 1½ [miles] before Liphook and walked, by little paths in the heather, toward Woolmer Forest down home by Conford through the pretty grounds of Forest Mere – a charming walk of about 3 miles – Graham talking all the while chiefly about his young days and a good deal about the impression *you* made in his mind of overwhelming energy and determination to get reform.

He is a dear good fellow and deserves his happy and successful life – and Audrey is a good soul. There is a certain soreness in her mind about Charlotte, who has resolutely refused to endorse G.B.S.'s casual invitations to stay at Ayot – and Audrey has never seen the Shaws in any of their country homes. Charlotte has been unnecessarily exclusive, and only made an exception for us – because she owed her marriage to me – but she has not been keen about the Wallases and other old friends of G.B.S. However, she has the right to choose her own friends – and I think that is only fair – one does not bargain to 'take on' the partner of the old friend or one's own partner's friends! though I did so!

I am taking Graham out for a last walk this morning and he goes this afternoon.

Now goodbye dear one; take care of yourself and make yourself pleasant and helpful to everyone. I wonder what the miners will do – they have sometime to think about it and possibly the mineowners may persuade each other *not* to cut rates before the report of the R.C.?

Ever yours

Beatrice

### 786 PP SIDNEY TO BEATRICE

The Labour Party had still not disposed of the problem of the Communists. It had rejected the repeated demand for affiliation; it had banned Communists from being individual members of the Labour Party; but it had not yet been able to exclude Communists who attended local Labour Party meetings and national conferences as delegates from affiliated trade unions.

Sidney Arnold (1878–1945) had been a Liberal pacifist M.P. 1912–22. He joined the Labour Party in 1922 and was elevated to the peerage when he became Under-Secretary at the Colonial Office in 1924. He was a close friend and travelling companion of MacDonald. Mary Agnes Hamilton (d. 1966) was a journalist and author who supported MacDonald against the left: in 1933 she wrote the first biography of the Webbs. She was an active member of the L.C.C. and a Labour M.P. 1929–31.

North Western Hotel
Liverpool
28.9.25

Dear One

Your letter this morning, which is dull and rainy, was very welcome. It is good that Longmans think we should print 2,000 straightaway for a guinea book. We will write for the paper on Saturday. Palmstierna refers to our talk about the condition of British trade; and the 'Balfour' Report, which is an interim report of the Committee the Labour Government set up under Sir Arthur Balfour: it describes one after another the state of the foreign markets, and the condition of our export trade. The Wallas' approval of your book as a work of art is satisfactory, but they are enthusiastic people about their friends! However, what strikes them will strike other people. It *will* be a great book: my only doubt is as to how *quickly* it will sell, and this will depend much on the circumstances of the moment, and the kind of reviews.

Last night our Executive Committee sat until 5 p.m. I walked out again to the Cathedral, partly for the sake of companionship, with J.R.M. and Morrison (so I walked at least 5 miles that day!). I dined alone with J.R.M. and discussed with him and Miss Bondfield (who had been all day at the N.A.C. [National Administrative Committee] of the I.L.P.) until 9 p.m. (My own regimen these two days is no *lunch*: but probably for the rest of the week it will be no *late dinner*!) J.R.M. is full of anxiety about the state of mind of the Party; but is confident that this Conference will support the Executive against Communism very definitely. He complains of the intellectual anarchy, and of the lack of any willingness to work out constructive proposals, which he says he has no time to do himself – he has to earn his living, and he said he had, whether wisely or not, 'added £300 a year to its cost' (query, 5% on £6,000 house purchase, for which I infer he has borrowed the capital cost, probably from some friend).

He said he had asked Lord Arnold to go through the whole list of Labour M.P.s and peers, and of candidates at all likely to get in, in order to see whether it was possible to make a Government within view – not with regard to *allocation* of offices, but as to sufficiency of total *number* of possible Ministers. Arnold reported that there was a shortage of half-a-dozen or so! to say nothing of total failure to fill a few posts, such as the Scottish Law Officers. But J.R.M. naturally said it was not a problem for the near future, and one could not say what the next five or seven years might produce.

He was evidently worried about the state of the I.L.P. Clifford Allen relinquishes the Chairmanship shortly, which has considerably exhausted him physically; and there seems nobody to dispute Maxton's claim to succeed him. Miss Bondfield, when she came, agreed; and both regarded the prospect with anxiety. Both said the N.A.C. was now made up mainly of people practically unknown to them, who talked perpetually from first principles, and were incapable of grappling with the business, or of taking any statesmanlike views. Allen had been invaluable, but would cease to exercise control. They were furiously angry with Brailsford, with whom they (the above-mentioned) had almost broken; and were quite unable to control him. He was mentally an 'Anarchist Communist', and incapable of comprehending parliamentary government. The N.A.C. was full of 'winds of doctrine', – currency, workers control, disarmament, non-resistance, 'direct action', proletarianism etc., etc. They said that Brailsford had behaved disgracefully about Mrs Hamilton; getting her dismissed as assistant editor on the plea of economy, and saying he could do without her; and thus dealing a blow at her livelihood from which she had never recovered (Arnold found £200 to pay her for a time to 'devil' for J.R.M.) and then within a week or two Brailsford insisted on appointing a new assistant.

Miss Bondfield seemed as attractive and efficient as ever: an extremely competent instrument within a limited range.

I post this early, hoping you may get it by first post. Perhaps I will write again.

Sidney

787 PP SIDNEY TO BEATRICE

The Webbs were planning a winter holiday in the Mediterranean. Dudley Leigh Amon (1884–1954), later Lord Marley, was a neighbour of the Webbs. He gave up a naval career for Labour politics. He was Under-Secretary at the War Office in 1930–31; he subsequently became very sympathetic to the Soviet Union. C. T. Cramp (1876–1933) was general secretary of the National Union of Railwaymen.

North Western Hotel
Liverpool
28.9.25

Dear One

This is merely supplemental to my long letter of this morning, and I have nothing to report! I send it, notwithstanding, as it may come by the afternoon post; and it will anyhow serve as a greeting. I breakfasted with the Leigh Amons, who have been living in Paris for seven months: they say that Sicily in January will be warm and sunny, and advise railway to Naples. We are, of course, having difficulty with the Communists in the preliminary proceedings; and proceedings promise to be stormy tomorrow in Conference, as they want to move to suspend all standing orders, and so on, and generally to make their issue dominate the whole week, reviewing all the resolutions of last year. We decided today that the chairman (Cramp) should take a firm stand.

J.R.M. is very friendly, but uncommunicative. At lunch time today, he suggested I should sit by him, and when I said I was having none, and that he had better also have none, he was urgent that I should come with him to take a glass of milk and a biscuit, really seeming unwilling to be alone. Of course I went with him, but conversation came to nothing intimate.

In the afternoon I walked down to the ferryboat station on the river, and passed along the docks, making a round of an hour, to satisfy you that I was taking *some* exercise.

Hodges, by the way, does not seem, as yet, to be here; and I doubt his coming, as he is not a delegate.

J.R.M., by the way, is going to the meeting of the I.L.P. delegates tonight, in order to answer attacks, and strengthen his position with them.

I have written a long letter to Herron, putting to him the idea of his succeeding me, *if and when* etc.; and telling him that, if they *are* coming to Seaham, they might usefully come when I was there, and you.

Now, dear one, goodbye for today, I am glad to think you will still have Audrey Wallas, and will not be so long alone. This separation is a mistake: we can do everything better together – Love!

Sidney

788 PP SIDNEY TO BEATRICE

Thomas Samuel Beauchamp Williams (1877–1927) had been a lieutenant-colonel in the Indian Medical Service: he joined the Labour Party and became M.P. for Kennington in 1923. Ernest Bevin (1881–1951) was secretary of the Transport Workers 1921–40. He was Minister of Labour in the wartime coalition and Foreign Secretary in the 1945 Labour government. William Gallacher (1881–1965) from Paisley, who was one of the wartime shop-stewards on the Clyde, moved the reference back of the section of the executive report which dealt with the exclusion of Communists. He later became M.P. for West Fife and Communist Party chairman. Harry Pollitt (1890–1960) became its general secretary; he attended the Liverpool conference of the Labour Party as a delegate of the United Society of Boilermakers. Mrs Clara Rackham was the delegate from the Cambridge Labour Party.

North Western Hotel
Liverpool
29.9.25

Dear One

Here we are, in the great St George's Hall, completely filled by the thousand delegates, the galleries full of visitors, a temporary rostrum projected in front of the platform, into the middle of the hall. The Chairman (Cramp) is reading his address, excellent in tone and temper and substance, *explicitly* repudiating violence etc., but of course not very stirring.

There was no letter for me this morning: perhaps there will be one this afternoon. I only mention this by way of explanation if *my* letters to Passfield do not arrive as soon as may be desired!

I dinned last night with Col. Williams as others were away at Group Meetings, etc. He thought Lloyd George's Land speech important and significant, first of all as adopting Nationalisation but chiefly as being an attempt to engineer a break with the quasi-Unionist Liberals, and perhaps with Runciman; so as to become himself the sole leader of a Radical Party, small but united on a forward policy; eventually leading (so Williams thought) to an almost inevitable project of union or alliance with the Labour Party. I told him that the latter was impossible, and unlikely to be proposed; but that his first interpretation might be true.

We are expecting a great row presently; but all the news from the great groups is that they intend to vote solidly in support of the executive. But of this later.

I hear that Bevin, of Transport Workers (with whom is Tillett), has expressed the view in private meeting that he thought the time had come for an independent Trade Union Political Party, to which the Unions should divert their money, and make their own policy and their own M.P.s. His personal ambition is said to be illimitable!

The decisive vote has just been taken.

| | |
|---|---|
| For reference back | 321,000 |
| Against – ditto – | 2,954,000 |

Contrary to expectation there was no 'row' at all! We shall, however, have it over again presently.

Pollitt takes the rostrum, and moves reference back of the Executive recommendation as to individual membership of Communists, much abler and more adroit than Gallagher. But we adjourn at 12 noon for photography and lunch; so it breaks off.

I gather that the leaders in the Unions (miners, railway, textiles, general workers, transport etc.) have been concerned at the prospect of the Labour Party being weakened in Parliament by the Communist agitation; and after their failure to lead at the T.U. Congress at Scarborough, resolved to 'put their foot down'; and hence this satisfactory attitude of supporting the Executive. MacDonald's reception by the bulk of the thousand delegates was markedly enthusiastic. I think the impression of disaffection, which it is hard to resist, is due wholly to intercourse with the lieutenants and non-commissioned officers. The real 'rank and file' are still quite solidly behind the 'Front Bench'.

I sat down for lunch with Miss Lawrence and Mrs Rackham, the former eagerly voluble about her Russian experiences – *Hamlet* at the theatre with a wonderful actor: excellence of the police when her trunk was stolen on a midnight arrival at a railway station; bathing in the sea in the sun at Yalta, many of the ladies with nothing at all on etc., etc. She will be delighted to go with you to the theatre on Monday, 12 October.

I enclose 2 Communist appeals to the Conference – one signed by Brailsford, a dozen 'Clyde' M.P.s, the Coles, and others, on the sentimental tack. Send these to the School.

The Conference may possibly be held next year at Margate!

I see that Isler's bill is reduced by £9. I am still not satisfied that all these things are 'extras', and shall write them later.

I wrote to Conalt Electrical Co pointing out that £8 charged for line between engine and well was included in Isler's specification, and was chargeable to Isler. However, it is satisfactory to know the *maximum* that we are asked to pay!

You will have noted that you are (1) to accompany me to New Seaham on Monday 5 October: (2) to go yourself to Murton Miners Hall for a *Women's* meeting on Tuesday 6 October (when I lecture at Horden). This is good, as you omitted Murton last time.

Now dear one, I must close this, in order to go back to Conference; and I must post it now to avoid risk of not being able to catch the regular post this afternoon – we *may* go on late. Only three more days, and we shall be together again. I shall certainly catch the 2 p.m. train on Friday, arriving Euston 6 p.m., and come at once to Grosvenor Rd to accompany you to Kate's. I have felt this Liverpool visit a bore, without you; but it had to be – and you would have failed to get any sleep, after the excitement, in this noisy hotel.

Goodbye dearest

Sidney

789 PP SIDNEY TO BEATRICE

Lloyd George's home was at Churt, in Surrey. Mrs Anderson Fenn was the women's organiser of the Labour Party in the North-East. J. H. Blackwell was the delegate of the Seaham Labour Party and G. W. Bloomfield was now the local party secretary.

North Western Hotel
Liverpool
29.9.25

Dear One

Your card reached me this evening. I posted *Forward* to you in my budget on Sunday, with some other things; you you will doubtless have seen it by now. I will try to get the Sunday Worker tomorrow.

The first day of the Conference went off magnificently, as the figures of the divisions show. We did not get through quite as much business in the day, as we had hoped; because by 6 p.m. the Conference 'struck', and would not take, at that hour, when half had faded away, the report of the Parliamentary Party (with the Zinoviev Letter, and other 'misdeeds' of the Labour Government). But I think the business is well in hand, as many resolutions have been dealt with in connection with paragraphs in the

Report; and many others have been got rid of in the little committees on 'grouping' competing resolutions and amendments.

There is great satisfaction among the 'candidates' here (e.g. Col. Williams and others) at the conclusive defeat of the Communists, which they think will help greatly with the ordinary man in the electorate. By the way, Col. Williams drew my attention to a notice in the *Morning Post* saying that Runciman had summoned a meeting at Oxford of Liberals discontented with Lloyd George's land scheme (which is derisively called 'Magna Ch*u*rta'!). Col. Williams insists that Lloyd George *meant* this; meant to have a decisive *break* with Runciman (and any other rival!), and the half-hearted Liberals, so as to have a party, however small, completely under his own control. Col. Williams thinks it significant that L.G. chooses as the point to break on (Land Nationalisation) one in which he counts on the sympathy of 'Labour', which he does not clearly understand, with a view to some ulterior conjunction.

Wed. 30 Sept.

Last night, at the private session on finance of the Party, was somewhat dramatic. Henderson expounded the Executive scheme of a gradual stopping of the party grants to local Labour parties towards Agents' salaries, now costing £4,000 a year, and increasing; for the purpose of raising a friendly loan of £40,000 (really from half-a-dozen wealthy Unions), so as to enable the Party to clear off existing debts and liabilities, and ensure maintaining the present activities unimpaired during the present depression. Great objection was made by and on behalf of the Agents, who felt that this endangered their salaries. Suddenly W. P. Richardson, (of the Durham Miners Association) got up and said he objected to any borrowing; £40,000 was a paltry sum; it only meant doubling for one year ('a sort of Capital Levy') the annual fee of 3d. per head; any man could pay another threepence in a year; they must 'pay for the politics' as the miners did – he could answer that the Miners Federation *would agree* (this meant £10,000), if others did. The representatives of the Railwaymen, the Gas workers, Transport and other big Unions said they would do their best and on this understanding the Executive withdrew their scheme. A general 'push' of this sort throughout the Movement will do good in itself, and bring in 20 or 30 thousand pounds.

As I must post this during the forenoon, in a (possibly vain) hope, dear one, that it may reach you at breakfast. [*original syntax*] In a couple of days now I shall be with you again. I am afraid I am a bad gossip-gatherer, but with sessions from 9.30 a.m. to 10 p.m., there is really little time and opportunity for conversation. I have just seen Mrs Anderson Fenn, who will come over from Newcastle on Wednesday morning and stay with us Wednesday night. I have also seen for a few minutes Bloomfield and Blackwell.

Dear One, goodbye for the present.

Sidney

Shaw's play *Mrs Warren's Profession* had finally passed the censor into production, thirty years after it was written. Fred Bramley (1874–1925), formerly secretary of the Furnishing Trades Association and general secretary of the T.U.C. from 1923, had just died. C. G. Rakovsky, a Bulgarian by origin, was the Soviet representative in London 1923–25 and then Soviet ambassador in Paris.

Beatrice had completed *My Apprenticeship*. On 29 October she noted that she was 'utterly and painfully uncertain of its value . . . selling your personality as well as your professional skill' was always problematic. After their joint work on the history of the Poor Law was finished, she thought, she and Sidney would write *Methods of Social Study* and then, if she survived with sufficient energy, she would tackle *Our Partnership*.

41 Grosvenor Road
Westminster Embankment
[? 13 Oct 1925]

My own dearest

One line before I leave by the 9.50 train.

Reynolds is disappointing – of course we had better decline Harper's offer – I think their representative has rather let us down as he led us to expect something better than £100! I should not be disposed to accept £200 – I think we shall get more out of Longmans! in the long run – our sales are slow but they are sure. And there is evidently no fear of a [?pirate] edition if Longmans does not sell to [*illegible*]. It might be quite worth while to place one chapter in some U.S.A. periodical in order to be able to print Copyright in the U.S.A.? But we will talk of this on Friday when we meet.

*Mrs W. Profession* was slightly disappointing. The emphasis on poverty – desperate poverty, leading to prostitution – does not sound quite so plausible as it did in the last century. But the last scene with Mrs Warren and her daughter is very fine and she (Mrs W) is a first-rate actress. Otherwise the acting is not up to the mark and the play is not very well 'produced'. But it was throughout interesting. Susan's [Lawrence] dinner at the Rakovsky's did not come off – they put it off on the grounds of Bramley's death! but the message did not reach her and she went to the Soviet mansion and met some other guests on the doorstep! She was rather put out about it. Send you the *Nation*: there is an interesting article by Keynes on Soviet Russia. He went to Moscow on some deputation to Russian convention and gave them a lecture on birth control for Russia which was greeted with laughter, so Susan said! Goodbye dear one. Keep well.

Ever yours

Beatrice

791 PP BEATRICE TO SIDNEY

On pages 321–26 of *My Apprenticeship* Beatrice described how she unintentionally misled the House of Lords Committee on Sweating about her experiences in the East End. On page 354 she discussed her support of the anti-suffrage manifesto: the replies of Mrs Fawcett and Mrs Ashton Dilke appeared in the *Nineteenth Century* for July 1889.

Passfield Corner
Liphook
Hants
[22 Nov 1925]

My own darling

Here are a few letters. The Shaws go immediately after lunch. They seem to have liked their stay here and today is brilliant sunshine. They are both of them quite enthusiastic over the last two chapters: G. B. S. says I write in his style and he finds nothing to correct. Also he says that I alone among socialists entered the Socialist creed by the right gate! Charlotte was especially struck with the H. of L. episode!

By the way will you find the dates of the manifesto against the Suffrage 1889 and of Mrs Fawcett and Mrs Ashton Dilke's replies? *XIX Century*? I should like to finish up the galley proof this week end.

Now dear one goodbye. Write me [?nicer letters than last time].

Ever yours

Beatrice Webb

Bank balance is £545

792 PP SIDNEY TO BEATRICE

In *My Apprenticeship* Beatrice had included an appendix on techniques of social investigation, written earlier in her life, on which Shaw had commented favourably. H. T. Muggeridge, a senior and active Fabian, was the Labour candidate at Romford. The volumes published by the Caxton Publishing Co. were known as *The Book of the Labour Party*. Sir Robert Donald (1860–1930) was the editor of the *Daily Chronicle* 1902–18 and resigned when the newspaper came under Lloyd George's political control.

41 Grosvenor Road
Westminster Embankment
25.11.25

Dear One

I stayed pretty late again last night, and consequently feel rather 'washed out' this morning. For today I have paired, as I have to be at the School of Economics in the afternoon; and then go to speak at Upminster (Romford) for Muggeridge; returning by 11 p.m.

Your letter was cheering to me at my lonely breakfast. As to the bank balance, it is of course quite satisfactory; but there are probably some 'cheques not presented' to be deducted from the apparent balance.

I enclose a letter from Longmans, which we must answer on Friday, when we had better send *him* in London (for him to forward to his New York house) (i) the photographs; (ii) all the paged proofs that we can correct on that day; (iii) the best idea we can give of *when* we will forward the balance. (Any loss of time by our sending to Longmans here, will be balanced by the otherwise delay of Reynolds transmitting to Longmans in New York.) I am glad the Shaws approve the last chapters: which will make them advertise the book!

As to the *N.S.* [*New Statesman*], Lees-Smith told me that Hedley Le Bas, on rejoining the Board, evinced considerable criticism of the conduct of the paper: he wishing it more definitely and consistently Labour, believing a new clientèle can be thus obtained. The three-guinea book on the Labour Party, which he insisted on the Caxton Publishing Co. organising and publishing, against the advice of his partners and office, has proved a great success already; some ten or fifteen *thousand* copies being already sold (on the instalment plan) by their agents. Lord Arnold prefers *not* to become a director; so we must be content with Lees-Smith (with Whitley and Le Bas). I gather that E. D. Simon's shares (or part of Glynne Williams') are now in the name of *J. R. M.*, the others being in that of Le Bas – this is due to the fact that objection was taken (by Sharp, as a shareholder) to Sir Robert Donald acquiring an interest. It appears that the Articles of Association contain some clause (which I had quite forgotten) enabling *some such* opposition being raised by any holder of a Management Share.

In haste Dear One

Sidney Webb

793 PP SIDNEY TO BEATRICE

The photograph of Beatrice taken by Shaw in 1908 was eventually published in *The Webbs and Their Work*, edited by Margaret Cole (London 1949).

41 Grosvenor Road
Westminster Embankment
10.12.25

Dear One

I will come tomorrow by the 9.50 train: perhaps if it is fine, I shall find you at the station?

I found the Shaw photo-block after a long hunt. The practice of doing up things in brown paper, and fastening up tightly with string – *without writing on the outside what are the contents* – causes bad language! I have sent the block to Longmans, for their use if desired: but I am not sure whether they will send it to America.

How about the use of it on the dustcover?

Last night (when we finished with a rousing and extremely adroit speech by Winston Churchill) I did not get to bed until midnight, with the usual result that I am fit for nothing this morning, except routine jobs, which are a burden. But this is better than your 'worry' in the night, which is a pity, as it is useless and distressing.

The Poor Law Bill is postponed for a year, as we all along anticipated. Kingsley Wood said privately that they would have very great difficulty with their own Party, the rural members not at all liking the abolition of the Guardians and the overwork of the County Councils.

So our P.L. History may get out in time! The Guardians are not dead yet.

I spoke to MacDonald about a weekend in the early summer, for a garden party of the two constituencies. He was very approving, and practically agreed to come (by car, for the Saturday afternoon), but said he had to make £20 every weekend, and much doubted whether he could stay over Sunday. He said the doctor had given a bad account of his daughter Sheila, and that was why he was taking her (and the other girls) for a sea voyage to Ceylon and back. He said that an old supporter left him a few hundred pounds for holiday purposes; and it was this that determined him to spend it, for his own sake as well as Sheila's on this holiday. He said he would have gone to Sicily, if it had not been for the need for sea voyage.

He said that things were appalling bad in South Wales; but he entirely agreed with my view that *on the whole*, and barring the bad spots, the wage-earners were not doing so badly.

MacDonald, by the way, said that he had asked the Government Whip whether the House might not resume on 9 February, instead of 2 February as is provisionally arranged; and this was being considered, as he cannot be back, even overland from Marseilles, until Sunday, 7 February. This of course is strictly private, as any such attempt at 'arrangement' would make Lansbury blaspheme!

Now, I must close, to ensure your getting this by first post tomorrow. Goodbye, dear one. I don't like being separated, even for a few days; and it is not nice for you either!

Sidney

794 KCC BEATRICE TO J. M. KEYNES

The Webbs had just returned from a long holiday in Sicily: on their way back they had stayed in Rome to get some impression of the Mussolini regime. On their return Beatrice began to work seriously on the Poor Law history. The Keynes article in the *Nation* of 20 February was 'Liberalism and Labour'; it was based on a speech at the Manchester Reform Club on 9 February.

Passfield Corner
Liphook
Hants
22nd Feb. 1926

Dear Mr Keynes

I feel some hesitation in writing to you as I am afraid I have only once had the pleasure of meeting you, and that a long time ago at Sydney Olivier's. But your article in the *Nation* of this week on Liberalism and Labour has interested both my husband and myself immensely, more especially coming after your very astute study of Russian Communism. If it is not an impertinence, may I say that I think you are very wise to remain detached from the two larger parties, as I doubt whether discoveries and the broadcasting of discoveries can be done efficiently by anyone engaged in Parliamentary politics. Inevitably the professional politician must and should consider his constituency and his colleagues, and cannot be intellectually disinterested. It seems to me that you are quite right in saying that the Liberal Party cannot serve the State in any better way than by supplying Conservative Government with Cabinets and – and this seems to me the most important – Labour Governments with ideas. But the special point in your article that I wish to mention is your statement that 'The republic of my imagination lies on the extreme left of celestial space and is not within the present philosophies of, let us say, Mr Sidney Webb, etc., etc., etc.' For a long time I have felt that the particular line of research which we in the Fabian Society started in the nineties – the working out of a national minimum of civilised life, so far as regulation and public services can secure it – is now exhausted as a discovery though not yet applied, and that the new inventiveness must necessarily concern itself with the control of capitalist enterprise and landlordism at the top in its highest activities. But I have felt that whilst *we* are too old to undertake this entirely new task, there did not seem to be in the Labour Movement any young men and women at once sufficiently detached from party politics and sufficiently able and experienced to discover ways and means. Some of the currency heresies which are being elaborated with so little knowledge and so much fervour are rather deplorable proofs of this condemnation. It would certainly be an immense service, not only to the Labour Movement but to the world, if you and your friends could discover how national finance and international trade could be controlled in the interests of the whole community.

I wonder whether you would come and lunch with us in London and meet Bernard Shaw who is at work on a book on socialism and is, I think, finding it rather more difficult than he expected. We share 41 Grosvenor Road now with Miss Susan Lawrence, but I think you know her, and she certainly would be very glad to see you. The best day of the week for the

Shaws is Thursday or Friday, and perhaps if you are willing to come you could suggest a date towards the middle or end of March.

With kind regards from my husband
Yours very truly
Beatrice Webb

795 PP SIDNEY TO BEATRICE

At the end of December 1925 Beatrice estimated that, including the cost of research assistants, secretaries and travel, the Webb books had just broken even over the years – on the assumption that the Webbs themselves received nothing for their work. This, she added, 'is about what we hoped to do. We have used our income from property as a fellowship for research and unpaid administration. And we have had a jolly good time of it, always doing exactly what we had a mind to!' (BWD 31 December 1925)

The reviews of *My Apprenticeship* were good: 'my self-esteem ought to be more than satisfied'. (BWD 11 March 1926)

41 Grosvenor Road
Westminster Embankment
9.3.26

Dear One

Here is Clark's Bill – only £402, which is less than I feared. (Cost of stereos is still to come.) This makes the total cost of production as under:

| | £ |
|---|---|
| Clark – printing and paper | 402 |
| Emery Walker – illustrations | 83? |
| Garden City Press – circular | 6 |
| Postage of Circulars etc., telegrams to New York, etc. | 10? |
| Paul Reynolds commission | 24? |
| Ship Binding Works – binding | 130 |
| Advertising in Longman's account – say | 30 |
| | £685 |

or say £700, including items that we forget.

Towards this you will have received, gross

| | £ |
|---|---|
| From *The Survey* | 30 |
| From Advance on royalties | 205 |
| | 235 |

leaving £550 as your necessary Capital outlay. The sale of 800 copies in England will repay that – and you may quite possibly do it by 1 June!

Coming, now, to 'Ways and Means', there remains to be paid within the next few weeks, Clark (402), Emery Walker (83) and Ship Binding Works (30?) – say £515. Towards that I have got £250 on deposit; and we may be able to spare £200 out of current account immediately *after* 31 March: so that very little need stand over until 14 May, when Longmans will pay us something.

There will, further, be £100, or thereabouts to pay for printing 1,000 copies, and binding 500, of *Industrial Democracy* – which may be taken as quite exhausting Longmans May cheque!

I talked with Miss Lawrence about Grants in Aid; and I came to see (and admit) that for practical purposes she had devised an improvement on my proposals of 15 years ago. I don't think that what she is actually going to propose is open to the objection of giving undue freedom to the Local Authorities; and it is more precisely applicable to present circumstances than the particular plan that I suggested in 1911 – a long time ago!

I do hope you have been sleeping better at Passfield. But don't worry about not being in good form for work. There is lots of time! We need not hurry!

Sidney

796 PP BEATRICE TO SIDNEY [*unsigned*]

Now a regular listener, Beatrice thoroughly approved of the B.B.C. as 'always on the side of the angels!' (BWD 23 December 1925)

Haldane wrote a long review of *My Apprenticeship* in the *Observer* on 28 March. In her diary Beatrice remarked how he differed from the Webbs: he liked power, good society and, as a metaphysical Hegelian, abstract argument. Though less talented than many of his associates, and not a great lawyer, she felt that their old friend was kindly, loyal and public-spirited.

Mrs Murray was a neighbour at Passfield.

Passfield Corner
Liphook
Hants
[30 March 1926]

Dearest one

Here are a few letters. I gather that the War Savings Certificates are not due until November – I do not know whether this will upset your calculations. A. J. [?Balfour] accepts; I have written to ask them to come June 5th.

I felt quite sad coming back to our empty study without my boy. But I had a pleasant evening listening-in part of the time and reading the remainder and a decent night. This morning I amused myself by writing in the diary an appreciation of Haldane arising out of the review – describing our difference of outlook with regard to London society, Hegelian and

University education which I will read you some-day, and summing up with the conclusion that he is a big *Personality* without being either a great intellect or a Saint. How difficult it is to discover what constitutes Personality as apart from specific intellectual gifts and saintlike character. Leonard Courtney had it. Baldwin has it. But neither John Simon nor MacDonald have big personalities, and Arthur Balfour doubtfully!? [?Trevelyan and Isaacs are retired.] I met Mrs Murray going to Liphook as I went to the bank this morning and had a chat with her. Tell Emily I will bring 8 eggs, and some butter with me on Thursday. Why not ask Galton to meet us at lunch P.L.C. [Parliamentary Labour Club] on Thursday? The U.S.A. edition of the book has come: quite pleasant print and get up though not so good as ours. Now dear one goodbye. I shall bring the luggage to Grosvenor Rd about 11 o'c on Thursday.

797 PP BEATRICE WEBB TO WILLIAM ROBSON

W. R. Inge, Dean of St Paul's, published *The Platonic Tradition in English Religious Thought* in 1926.

Passfield Corner
Liphook
Hants
21st April 1926

My dear Mr Robson

You need never apologise for writing to an author about his book, so long as your criticism is appreciative. Certainly you have succeeded with me.

I was also very much interested in your letter, alike from the controversial and the personal point of view. I quite agree with you about the difficulty of defining what exactly we mean by the spirit of religion, and I think you are right in suggesting that intuition is the best term and that instinct ought to be reserved for almost the direct contrary to intuition. In the entries in the diary I am slovenly in my use of words, and I left all terms as they appeared in the diary without attempting to make them correct or consistent with each other. I do not think we have got much further, however, even if we stick to one term like intuition. I note that in Inge's last book on the Platonic Tradition in English Religious Thought he talks about divine sagacity – I think it is a quotation. Of course, the root difficulty is an uncertainty in our own minds whether this intuition is a separate and distinct faculty – possibly undeveloped – for apprehending forces in our environment which are not open to observation and reasoning. At this point we come perilously near to occultism! And when one thinks of all the experiences of Eastern religions in this direction, and of their imitators in Europe, it is difficult to dissociate occultism from obvious quackery and self-deception. However, that does not deter me from accepting the hypothesis of a spiritual faculty.

About the more practical question raised in your letter; it is extraordinarily difficult to devise any social institutions which will adequately provide a secure maintenance for research in sociology. I suppose universities are, on the whole, the best way out. I do not altogether object to combining the subsidy for research with some positive obligations to teach or to administer. Throughout our own career as researchers, Sidney has always had other work, sometimes taking up the larger part of his time and energy – for instance, the eighteen years on the London County Council. The fact that it was unpaid does not affect the question. And even I have always taken part in committee and propaganda activities. I think it is better for researchers to be compelled to carry on other forms of activity, especially teaching and administration – the former clearing the mind, and the latter providing a sort of laboratory for sociological experiment. The American sociologists seem to me to suffer very seriously from having had no experience in administration and politics, drawing their material from books, and not from observation of men and affairs. But of course there must be some sort of security if the research is to be of long duration, as well as considerable assistance if it is to be complicated and extensive. The London School of Economics appears to be slowly developing such opportunities for research.

Certainly I do not think it is worth while keeping the present inequalities of income on the chance of one or more men and women who happen to have private means devoting themselves to unremunerative drudgery. I shall always remember the case of D. F. Schloss – a very clever, and, as it happens, a very wealthy man, with a genius for investigation. He started off, doing work of his own, and contributed to Charles Booth's first volume. But he afterwards accepted a minor position in the Board of Trade at a salary of a few hundred a year because, as he told me confidentially, he could not trust himself to go to work every morning at ten o'clock and stick to it until five!

You must come down for a walk some Saturday.

Always yours

Beatrice Webb

### 798 PP SIDNEY TO BEATRICE

The Webbs were organising a large garden party on 31 July for the Labour parties of the two local constituencies, at which MacDonald was to be the main speaker. Harold Croft was the Labour Party organiser to the Home and Southern Counties. Sir William Joynson-Hicks (1865–1932), the Home Secretary notorious for his puritanical attitude, was popularly known as 'Jix'.

The anticipated general strike had at last come. On 10 March the Samuel Commission reported that costs in the mining industry must be reduced by wage cuts and/or longer working hours. The miners responded with the slogan 'Not a penny off the pay: Not a second on the day!'. When the government refused to renew the subsidy and the miners made it clear that they would not accept cuts, the mineowners locked them out on 1 May. The T.U.C. had attempted to negotiate with the government, but the Cabinet was obdurate: it was ready for a showdown. On 3 May the T.U.C. called out the transport, steel, building and printing workers; the engineers were not called on until 11 May, the day before the strike ended in defeat. There was no agreed settlement; the embittered and now isolated miners remained on strike for another six months.

On 3 May, as the strike began, Beatrice anticipated that the T.U.C. leaders would 'funk it' and that the strike would quickly collapse. The Webbs had for years believed that a general strike was doomed because they felt that any government would be forced to resist an attempt to coerce the whole community.

*Statutory Authorities* was the fourth volume of the Webb series on local government, published in 1922.

41 Grosvenor Road
S.W.1
4/5/26

Dear One

I saw [Egerton] Wake at 3 p.m. (he could not come to lunch). He said he was afraid you would be overwhelmed with work, and your Garden Party with an excessive crowd! He strongly urged you to use Croft, the organiser, who lives at Croydon but is (normally) at 33 Eccleston Square several days a week, and could undertake all details or any part of the job that you chose. He should, at any rate, be asked to come to you from time to time to see how things were going on, and to do anything required.

Wake was clear that persons under 10 should be excluded; and that you could not expect to get money before issuing batches of tickets. These should be sent out as soon as possible, with the detailed circular, saying that they must be either definitely taken or returned before say 24 July; asking for the money to be remitted before that date (though in fact some secretaries will bring it!); and saying that there would be no tea available for any who had not taken tickets.

He approved of charging others for admission if we could get competent stewards, especially if we chose to entrust them with discretion to admit labourers and by giving them free tickets. A band *would* entail Entertainment Tax on such gate receipts. But not if the band came gratuitously. (He approved of a suggestion that this *might* be managed by means of a private donation from us beforehand!) He was satisfied by my saying we contemplated getting 57 stewards, half from Petersfield and Guildford, and the rest from the parties. I have supplied him with the letter for the laggards of which he is to send you 110 copies tomorrow night.

As to the General Strike, the response is *said* to have been magnificent, universal, surpassing all expectation. This morning a very few 'independent' omnibuses were running, but none of the combine, no trams, no underground railway, and (it is said) no trains on the other lines. This is *said* to be universal everywhere. You will have had *The Times* and *Herald.* Other morning papers appeared today (not all); but there are to be no more! The scene in Grosvenor Road this morning at 10 a.m. was extraordinary. A dense block of every kind of motor car packed with people, a few loaded charabancs, heaps of pedal and motor-cycles covered with people: and crowds walking. At Ministry of Health nearly everyone was very late, and apparently many did not arrive. Slesser said that juries were suspended, as they could not be got; and he had to get a case adjourned for lack of witnesses.

Thomas said that in the incessant negotiations Birkenhead was always with Baldwin, for peace; but Churchill, Neville Chamberlain and Jix were always for war.

It is rumoured that a private omnibus was overturned in the East End today, deliberately.

That is all the news or gossip I have. The House rushed through necessary business today, and adjourned by 5.30 p.m. Tomorrow we spend discussing the Emergency Regulations.

I enclose Longman's account: only £55 (but there are only two books). *Statutory Authorities* has virtually stopped selling.

Also 2 reviews in *Fabian News* (by Sanders) and the *Sociological Review.* Letter from Ada, and other oddments.

To catch post, Dear One Goodnight

Sidney

799 PP BEATRICE TO SIDNEY

On 4 May Beatrice noted how, for her, a strike which closed the newspapers 'centres round the headphone of the wireless set'. She thought the strike would 'turn out not to be a revolution of any sort or kind but a batch of compulsory Bank Holidays without any opportunities for recreation and a lot of dreary walking to and fro . . . no one will be any the better and many will be a great deal poorer and everybody will be cross'. The anticipated defeat would lead, she thought, to 'terrible disillusionment. The failure of the general strike of 1926 will be one of the most significant landmarks in the history of the British working class'. The 'blacklegging' message was the reiterated government statement that those who continued to work would be 'protected and secured'.

Passfield Corner
Liphook
Hants
Tuesday [4 May 1926]

The announcer told us the date was *May 4th*; he seemed to think we could not know it!

Dearest One

Here are my engagements for Friday which I think ought all to be put off tomorrow. Unless strike is settled at once travelling will be a good deal disturbed on Friday. But use your own discretion. I will phone to-morrow morning 8.30 and repeat the addresses as Charles says that there are rumours that the postal workers are coming out if strike continues. No letters today, as yet, though I understand that local letters have been delivered in Bordon district but not London though railway service to Guildford from London was running according to wireless. We get news 10 to 4, 7 to 9.30. This morning it consisted of reports of district Commissioners – all quiet but [stoppage] complete – with long lists of [?recruiting offices, especially for Comps and others of printing trades] and a Paris telegram about French press and strike but no other news.

About Friday, if [Lord] Russell offers to take you to and from London next week I should accept – I think you ought to be in Parliament if it is possible to get there next week, even if you cannot do anything and it will be interesting; remember you will have to describe the G.S. [general strike] in our next edition of T.U.! We are taking down the wireless messages re strike. I decided to do so after the blacklegging message and I was interested that B.B.C. in the one o'clock delivery said that they had been requested by phone and wire to speak slowly so that messages could be taken down [in] shorthand. They remarked that news was copyright but all government messages could be reproduced. It will be interesting to watch their intervention. The Labor Party ought to insist on being permitted to broadcast and if not they ought to publish D.H. [*Daily Herald*] or some news bulletin. It is a remarkable episode. I had a long argument with the Cleaves, they are indignant about the general strike, but Cleave said this business will go against the government, but apparently not in favour of Labor Party.

I am feeling better and I dictated all the references to P.L. in Parish chapters.

Now dear one goodbye; don't keep too 'steady'; Peace is for those who know how to fight to win! Ever yours

Beatrice Webb

Will you give this address to Emily – Jessie thought she might go and see her sister on Wednesday afternoon. If she cannot go she might telephone on Thursday to know how she is and that you might bring down the news on Friday. The post may stop but I can hardly think so.

## 800 BL SIDNEY WEBB TO GEORGE BERNARD SHAW

Sidney had not played any significant part in the strike; throughout the previous years he had been remarkably detached from the struggle of the miners, though he owed his seat to the miners' union and represented a mining constituency. He spent much of the strike period working through the Poor Law archives at the Ministry of Health and Public Record Office, telling Beatrice that it was 'difficult to do anything else amid all this excitement'. (PP 5 May 1926)

Arthur Pugh (1870–1955), general secretary of the Iron, Steel and Kindred Trades Association, had been much involved in the pre-strike negotiations as the current chairman of the T.U.C. Edward Poulton was the secretary of the Boot and Shoe Operatives and a member of the T.U.C. General Council. Walter Citrine (b. 1887), had been an official of the Electrical Trades Union before becoming General Secretary of the T.U.C. in 1926 – a post he held for twenty years, when he was appointed chairman of the Electricity Authority. Herbert Smith (1863–1938) was a Yorkshire miner who had become president of the M.F.G.B. in 1921. George Sorel (1847–1922), engineer and social theorist, published *Reflections on Violence* in 1908; this book, which became the text for revolutionary syndicalism, argued that moral commitment to social change might be based upon non-rational feelings – an idea exemplified by Sorel's 'myth of the general strike'.

41 Grosvenor Road
Westminster
13.5.26

Private – not for publication on any account
Dear Shaw

I have been trying to write you a letter of news, but the times have been so exciting and distracting, and I have been so much at the beck and call of sudden committees, and such like, that I have been always prevented. And now the crisis is practically over!

The whole thing has been extraordinary and abnormal. You must understand that the Labour Party and its Parliamentary leaders or representatives *had nothing to do with it*. First came the miners' dispute, which (as usual) the Miners Federation Executive insisted on managing by themselves, refusing all offers of help, and fiercely resenting any interference. Then the General Council of the Trades Congress forced itself in, on the ground that the miners expected the active and prompt support of all other industries very shortly. Even then the Labour Party was defiantly kept at arm's length. Thomas, who is on the General Council this year, warned them against any 'General Strike' as bound to fail against any government with modern organisation and powers. Clynes (who is not on the General Council) said he could have no part in it – MacDonald and Henderson repeated the same warnings. The General Council does not seem *explicitly* to have decided on a General Strike until the *Thursday* before the Friday night (30 April) when the Mineowners notices expired, and the subsidy ceased. But all their actions, and trade union conferences *tended* to it, and (so far as I can learn) the decision on the General Council was taken as an inevitable and so to speak spontaneous outburst of feeling. I cannot learn that anyone in particular was responsible. The comic thing is that Arthur Pugh (Steel smelters) who is this year the Chairman of the General Council, and E. Poulton (Boot and Shoe) another leading member, are both extremely old-fashioned T.U. officials, not at all politically 'advanced', and in fact are often chosen as Government nominees on

Commissions etc. as 'safe' men! I am assured that they were as heartily and cordially in the decision as anyone – one cause is that they, and the General Council generally, and Citrine the new secretary thereof, are *anti-political*, jealous of the Labour Party, which has outstripped the General Council and old-fashioned trade unionism, especially as regards 'getting the limelight'.

Of course, once the thing was done we had all to make the best of it, and we started, individually, straightaway to contrive some way of resuming negotiations (as to the Miners' dispute). I ought to say that, in the final week of such negotiations with the Government anterior to the General Strike, the Parliamentary Labour Party Executive had pressed both the Miners Executive and the General Council at least to keep us informed of every stage in these negotiations; and in the last week they had both, very reluctantly, consented to let MacDonald and Henderson *be present*. They thus *saw* the tragedy happening, but could not interfere with it.

Herbert Samuel, very wisely and courageously, came posting back from Italy to see what he could do – *not* at the Government's request, and even, I believe, against their advice(!). Gradually, in consultation with various of our friends, he drafted a memo, which (after repeated revisions) the General Council was induced to adopt as a reasonable basis of settlement of the mining trouble. That memo (which is published in today's *Times*) puts the necessary clarity and precision into his Commission's recommendations (in which they had been somewhat lacking); and if it is really carried out, represents an immense stage onwards to nationalisation, and certainly all that is practicable under this Government. Of course this has not happened without secret consultations, and *implicitly* the Government is committed to it – with the result that Churchill in the Cabinet, and the Tory M.P.s generally, are said to be raging furiously. But there may be a hitch – there might, of course, be one more betrayal, (as after the Sankey Commission) owing to a Tory revolt. Anyhow, *we* know that the General Strike was showing signs of collapse; men were beginning to go back; in another day or two there might easily have been a debacle; and hardly any one doubts that the General Council did the right thing in calling the General Strike off, *whilst there was still something to call off*! *In form*, it had to be an unconditional calling-off. In reality, the General Council had secured very good assurances that the Government terms for the miners would be, not only enormously better than anything previously offered, but probably the best terms at the moment practicable.

Then came a hitch with the Miners' Federation Executive under the madman Cook, and the stubborn and somewhat dense hero Herbert Smith. Although they had explicitly put their case in the hands of the General Council when they merged (as they said) their own dispute in the General Strike, they now refused to acquiesce in the decision to 'call off', and would budge no inch from their declaration of *July last*, and would make no alternative suggestion. The General Council had the courage to be unmoved by this, and to reaffirm their decision to 'call off' the General Strike (in the early hours of yesterday morning, Wednesday 12 May) which they accordingly did by interview with the P.M. (at noon that day). The Miners Executive then summoned a delegate conference (of miners) for Friday tomorrow, which will decide whether or not to go back to work, *at the old wages* pending the carrying out of Samuel's Memorandum.

We *think* the delegate meeting will decide to resume work. But we very much doubt whether the Miners Federation Executive will have the courage to recommend this course (practically all the Miners' M.P.s tell us both that the Federation Executive ought to do so, and that it will not!). And then what will 160 delegates do, fresh from excited public meetings, and with no new *district* instructions?

The other possible hitch may be with the Mineowners who find themselves landed into a reorganisation of their industry and with a large measure of public control, based on actual Government ownership of the freehold of their leasehold interests – driven instantly to withdraw their notices and admit the men to work *at the old wages*. We believe that the Mineowners collectively *must* agree.

Then there is the Government, and the defiant Chancellor of the Exchequer, who will have to pay out millions, without having got more than a spectacular triumph. With these rebels the Prime Minister is now struggling.

On the whole I think it will go through, and be, bit by bit, and with many apparent checks and hitches, actually put in operation. (The 'inevitability of gradualness'!) Anyhow I am entirely convinced that we have done the right thing. MacDonald and Henderson (with Thomas), who have been all the week almost continuously at work, from early morn to past midnight, trying one proposal after another, wrestling with stupidity, and obstinacy and jealousy, seeking fresh avenues of negotiation, and bringing to bear all possible influences, deserve the greatest possible credit – of course, they will be denounced by the firebrands, but they have saved the whole Labour Movement from the most disastrous smash, and the most fatal setback of all our lifetime.

This is the dullest of summaries of what I know of the inside position, which is not very much more than could be inferred by any competent observer. *There is nothing more to it*. There never was any idea in the General Council of 'the General Strike' of the Socialists of 40 years ago, or of the more recent Syndicalists (e.g. Sorel), or of their feeble modern imitators, the Communist Party (which has had *nothing whatever* to do with the matter, but has, of course, seized every opportunity of getting arrested for 'creating disaffection'). Incidentally John Strachey has got arrested also (for publishing a silly rumour as to the troops mutinying); and the Oswald Mosleys are reported to have been making the wildest and most foolish speeches in the Midlands.

But Beatrice will have sent you a graphic account of what it looks like. This morning the armoured cars, steel helmets and khaki-clad troops in lorries seem to have disappeared; and this incomprehensible and illogical nation, with its strange commonsense, is acting as if nothing whatever had happened.

We were delighted to hear from Charlotte of your progress to complete recovery. Don't strive to get back to business or work.

We go to Passfield Corner tomorrow (14 May) for a fortnight's holiday.

Yours

Sidney Webb

### 801 PP SIDNEY TO BEATRICE

Lal Lajpat Rai (1865–1928), known as 'The Lion of the Punjab', was a leading member of the Arya Samaj movement. The Webbs had met him in 1911 when they crossed India. He was active in the nationalist movement from 1888, wrote a number of books on Indian politics and did much for Indian education. He was in London on his way back from an International Labour Office conference in Geneva. John Scurr was M.P. for Stepney; he had succeeded George Lansbury as mayor of Poplar and had been one of the councillors sent to prison for contempt. W. Wedgwood Benn, formerly a Liberal M.P., joined the Labour Party in 1927. He was Secretary of State for India, 1929–31. Sir Frank Nelson was Conservative M.P. for Stroud 1924–31. John Beckett, M.P. for Gateshead in 1924 and for Peckham in 1929, was a leading member of the I.L.P. who subsequently defected to Mosley's 'New Party' in 1931. Neil MacLean was also an I.L.P. member, sitting for Govan from 1918.

14 Grosvenor Road
Westminster
1.7.26

Dear One

I enclose 2 tickets for Ladies Gallery next Monday. Also a carefully written article by W. T. Layton on the economic position, which may convince you that my 'optimism' is not without some foundation (keep this). Also a letter showing that Thomas Wall (of sausage fame), who helped the Minority Report campaign, and the Labour Party candidate at Epsom, has given £20,000 to the Playing Fields fund! It is such obscure and humble people who are the best mark for donations. But how can one discover them?

Last night's dinner to Lajpat Rai (and another member of the Indian Legislative Assembly) included Mr and Mrs Snowden, Scurr, Benn, and one Unionist, Sir Frank Nelson. Mrs Snowden went off at 10 p.m. to the Royal Academy party. It would have been rather a dreary proceeding if we

M.P.s had not got on to election and other stories about other Members which carried us on till 10.50, when the first of a series of divisions took place.

Thomas is much troubled about his N.U.R. delegate meeting, which begins on Sunday at Weymouth. He says he advised his executive definitely on the Friday *against* joining in the General Strike but they overruled him. This ought to clear him but he does not feel free to say this; and the executive will have no opportunity to say it, even if they were willing. There are motions for his dismissal (a) for not letting them strike six months ago, (b) for making the General Strike and (c) for calling off the Strike from different groups of branches and the Communists are organised and active.

We are rather expecting that some of our extremists (such as Buchanan, Beckett, Neil MacLean and perhaps some of the miners) will make a brawl *in the House of Lords*, when the Royal Assent is given to the Eight Hours Bill, probably next Wednesday. There is not much scope for such a brawl in those surroundings and I don't know that it much matters if such a brawl does take place! MacDonald is convinced that the Party now commands greater and wider support than ever in the country, especially among the quiet people; but that such brawls annoy them.

Goodnight dear one, I have just time to catch post.

Sidney

802 PP BEATRICE TO SIDNEY

Beatrice had ordered a large marquee for the Labour fete at Passfield Corner in case it rained: in the event it was fine and over 2,000 Labour supporters turned up to hear MacDonald, Margaret Bondfield, Arthur Ponsonby, Lord Russell and Lord de la Warr (1900–1976), an aristocratic convert to Labour who was Labour whip in the House of Lords and a close friend of MacDonald.

On 26 July, before the garden party, Beatrice went up to the dinner given at the House of Commons to celebrate Shaw's 70th birthday. He spoke, she noted, with 'uncommon' depth of feeling like 'a seer dictating his last testament'. She felt that the dinner was 'the last assemblage of the men and women who had been mainly responsible for the birth and education of the Labour and socialist movement'. All the pioneers were there, save Hyndman and Hardie, who were dead. 'The greatest of all, whether among the dead or the living, was the guest of the evening – wit and mystic, preacher and dramatist.' (BWD 28 July 1926)

Beatrice had been mulling over 'a certain personal discomfort' about the miners, prompted by the controversy over the donation of £600,000 sent by the Soviet trade unions to relieve distress. 'Ought we or ought we not to give and ask others to give to the fund for the miners' wives and children? Neither Sidney nor I would have given a penny to it if no one would have been the wiser.' The Webbs had in fact sent £10 for the sake of appearances but they strongly disagreed with the continuing strike. (BWD 12 June 1926) Beatrice noted with some relief a letter from Durham which asserted that the families were 'amply provided for': when she later visited Sidney's constituency she was at pains to point out that the women and children seemed well-fed and not obviously in want. She was more concerned about the long-term consequences of the dispute; it had begun, she thought, 'a slow decline in population, trade and wealth *relatively to other countries*. . . . Both parties will be mildly collectivist and Great Britain will slither on to a state of relative quiescence and powerlessness in the world's affairs'.

Passfield Corner
Liphook
Hants
[end July 1926]

Dearest one

All goes well! [?Darrants] men come tomorrow and begin putting up the marquee. One little contretemps: Burgess – the Liphook grocer and confectioner – returned the order for 2,000 cakes as he had a large order for the flower show and could not do both. Miss Mason discovered that he is a strong Conservative and that his customers did not approve – more likely that we don't deal with him but with A.N. [Army and Navy Stores] for groceries. So rang up [?Darrants] and gave them the order at same price – it was too risky to go to another small man at bank holiday time and D. are large bakers. Mrs Blackwood really is bringing us flowers and her gardener's wife to help me for our big garden party. The weather is dull but dry and there is an anticylone approaching the S.W. Coast which ought to be here by Saturday! I am putting you in the small bedroom – we must build that other room when we can afford it. The B.B. [bank balance] is £237, but that includes some money paid in on account of Party – about £40 or £50 including subs and expenses. I suppose we shall have about £120 to pay for marquee and food – I think [?Darrants] estimate comes to about £90 if not £100 for marquee and services. So you will be rather short until our November cheque from Longmans. However this gathering will not occur again and it is more useful than sending it to the Miners' fund – which I believe is simple waste in their present mood.

I will expect you about 10 o'c.

BW

803 BOD BEATRICE WEBB TO J. L. HAMMOND

The Webbs spent two days at the T.U.C. in Bournemouth and noted the bitterness and divisions that followed defeat. MacDonald, Beatrice complained, was clearly 'not working at his job'. (BWD 10 September 1926) Indeed, 'he is not thinking about it; he is not associating with those whom . . . he has to guide and from whom he could get enlightenment . . . he is becoming impatient with the troublesomeness of the working class'. At Bournemouth he did not mix with the delegates but went motoring with members of the Rotary Club; instead of talking politics he rambled on about antique furniture and his social connections.

Passfield Corner
Liphook
Hants
Sept 21 1926

Dear Mr Hammond

How delightful of you and Mrs Hammond to write us such letters: old people, I am afraid, are too much pleased by such testimony from those still in their prime of life. In a sense we have always regarded you too as colleagues who equal us in literary skill whilst we have had the advantage of more subordinate brain-work. I was also glad to find that you take the same view of the present state of the T.U. movement. This year is going to be a turning-point in working-class history. The trade unions are, I think, at the zenith of their power and at the nadir of their capacity for leadership – a state of things usually meaning the decadence of the particular type of organisation under consideration. (German Empire for instance!) What will be its successor; or how will it be transformed to be better fitted for its task? At the present time trade unionism is a tragic case of maladjustment that may also be true of profitmaking enterprises. Whither goes civilisation? Moscow, Rome or Washington? These three governments are alone cocksure they are right.

However, I did not mean to say more than how much we enjoyed our little [*word omitted:* ?chat] with you both.

Yours sincerely

Beatrice Webb

### 804 KCC BEATRICE WEBB TO J. M. KEYNES

The I.L.P. put forward a set of proposals to the Labour Party conference in October which became known as the 'Living Wage' policy, on which the I.L.P. campaigned for the next three years. The members of the committee were J. A. Hobson, H. N. Brailsford, E. F. Wise, a wartime civil servant and later a Labour M.P., and Arthur Creech Jones (1891–1964), then research officer of the Transport Workers Union, and later Colonial Secretary 1946–50. It suggested a national minimum wage enforced by law, with expanded social services and family allowances. Though soliciting the opinion of Keynes Beatrice was privately caustic: 'There must be a scarcity of politically constructive minds if J. M. Keynes seems such a treasure', she noted. For all his great talents she thought him indifferent to common men or common tastes – 'all the common or garden thoughts and emotions that bind men together in bundles'. (BWD 9 August 1926)

At the Margate conference Sidney, as he half-expected, was defeated in the poll for the Labour executive. At Seaham Beatrice thought the miners looked healthier for fresh air and enforced abstention from tobacco and alcohol during the strike.

Passfield Corner
Liphook
Hants
3rd Oct. 1926

My dear Mr Keynes

I wonder whether it would interest you to see this revised report of the I.L.P. Committee. I send it partly because I think I showed you the unrevised version, and my rather stringent criticism of it. As it stands at present, it seems to me a useful propagandist document, though quite unfit to be the programme of the Labour Party, seeing that all its separate and complicated proposals are not adequately worked out, even if they were individually practicable and expedient. I do not of course ask for your written opinion about it; I only want to submit it for your consideration, as I think the lines on which it proceeds are far more hopeful than the old slogan of the Labour Party – the nationalisation of the means of production, distribution and control. It accepts what we have always considered the next step – the control of capitalist enterprise from the standpoint of public advantage through such devices as costing (though, by the way, it does not mention this). Personally, I feel that this control of capitalism will want a far more expert treatment than is open to anyone in the Labour Party owing to their ignorance of international finance and the control of marketing, etc.

Do not trouble to return these proofs as the pamphlet will presently be published.

We are leaving tomorrow for three or four weeks – the Labour Party Conference at Margate, and then to Seaham where I am afraid we shall find a very gloomy situation. The setback to trade union organisation by the events of this last nine months is, I think, almost as catastrophic as that of 1834, though there is far more chance of remedying the disaster. And there is the indirect advantage that I think the very catastrophic character of the collapse will explode the inflation of the trade union ideal characteristic of the last few years. We shall be in London the end of October, and up and down during the autumn session, and perhaps we may have the pleasure of seeing you and Mrs Keynes.

Yours sincerely
Beatrice Webb
(Mrs Sidney Webb)

805 NLS BEATRICE WEBB TO LORD HALDANE

Haldane's *Human Experience* was published in the summer of 1926. He had been miffed by Beatrice's failure to write of their early friendship in her autobiography although, she confessed, the omission 'was due to absentmindedness in the hurry-scurry of a fagged brain to finish the damned thing'. (BWD 12 August 1926) She thought Haldane likely to be ignored in other memoirs because 'his brand of political thought and his capacity for intrigue are not liked or admired by Englishmen' and he was too subtle and 'contemptuous of the common man'.

The Webbs had dined with Haldane and his sister on 7 November.

Professor John Dewey (1859–1952) was at Columbia University 1904–1951: a noted theorist of education, his *Experience and Nature* was published in 1925.

Passfield Corner
Liphook
Hants
11th Nov. 1926

My dear Lord Haldane

I have just finished your book – I have read it with great interest and I hope with some understanding though its subject matter is mostly out of my depth. I think your exposition and criticism of Dewey's Behaviourism is a model of conciseness and lucidity, and I am glad that at the very end you leave room for the Act of Faith for those who have not made philosophy the study of a lifetime. I am afraid this will continue to include the great mass of humanity. So we come back to the need of a creed with its attendant code of morals. It is a favourite hypothesis of mine that the rise of a new type of creed autocracy – Russian Communism and Italian Fascism – is a direct result of the absence in the pre-War Russia and the pre-War Italy of any satisfactory creed commonly held by the intellectuals and the masses of the people, with its consequences of a dissolution of all codes of morality. So Lenin and Mussolini come along with their rigid dogmatism and their clear-cut code of conduct and impose it on their people in order that there shall be some homogeneity of thought and feeling and some definite purpose for the national life. I doubt whether the mass of men can live without a common metaphysic and a common scale of values; though it is all-important that there should be freedom for other metaphysics and other codes to rise up as modifications and even substitutes of the common one. But the period during which substutution is going on will necessarily be chaotic; and chaos is apt to have its reaction in militant minorities getting control of the nation's life and undermining liberty.

We so much enjoyed our evening with you.

Always yours sincerely
Beatrice Webb

Passfield Corner
Liphook
Hants
15.11.26

My dear Halévy

It was very kind of you to send us your handsome new volume, so full of interest for those who have lived through the series of events of which you have given so detailed and so painstaking an account. I have, so far, only cut the pages at many points, and read stretches of the narrative here and there. But I am amazed at the extent and accuracy of your knowledge of all the details; and at the success with which you have woven the story into an interesting and so brilliant a history. The terrible difficulty in all recent history (just because we know the details better than we know the general *trend* of events) is that of 'not being able to see the wood for the trees'. This I am sure you have surmounted even better than an Englishman could do.

I have noticed hardly any real 'errors' (as appears to me). Of course, I don't always agree with your estimate of 'values' – but on this point we shall all differ from each other! *I* think you make too much of 'the Webbs', who are only small and very partial influences among a mass of others; and much more 'effects and manifestations' than 'causes'.

Your remarks in the 'Avant-Propos' seem to me full of 'sagesse'! I admit the national 'malaise', but I wonder whether this has not been, for several centuries, a permanent national characteristic. My wife has the 'malaise', but I do not think that I have felt it: this is because I am less sensitive, less introspective, and perhaps more characteristically English in my illogical empiricism – I should put otherwise the change in religion, which does not seem to me any approach to Catholicism; but rather a widespread abandonment of *any* theological doctrine for a vague and general sentiment of 'mysticism' – *not* a real Atheism but little more than a superstitious remnant colouring an effective 'agnosticism'. The important thing is that the people in general, *in all classes*, seem to have lost practically all their 'taboos' in such matters as sex relations; and to be bound only by 'the law', for which they have no effective respect except as a sanction to be feared, so as to avoid punishment and calamity. I don't know whether this change is more marked in England than in various other countries, but it may well prove to be more 'revolutionary' in its results than any other change of thought.

I hope your volume will get published in English – though the book trade with us seems to be unusually bad! When this happens – or when you reprint in French – I should like to be allowed to look through the proofs. I have no important mistakes to tell you about; but the frequent repetition of *John* Ramsay MacDonald jars on an Englishman. He is James! Such slips are of no consequence, and practically inevitable; but you should allow your friends to try to save you from them.

With kindest regards from my wife, and to Madame.

Yours truly

Sidney Webb

By the time you come to England again, we shall have really read the book; and we hope that you will come here to let us talk about the thoughts it raises.

807 PP SIDNEY TO BEATRICE

The miners held on desperately and in October sought an intensification of their strike; the mineowners were equally obdurate; and all attempts to find a settlement foundered between the embittered antagonists. Beatrice thought that Labour and the Conservatives had become agents of 'two exasperated and exasperating combatants'. (BWD 19 October 1926) On 14 November the Mineworkers Federation voted to accept terms that were little better than unconditional surrender but referred the decision to each district – leaving the men to drift back in a catastrophic and demoralising defeat. Beatrice drafted a candid letter to the Seaham women and told Sidney (PP n.d. November): 'I am afraid it may not be quite what the miners' wives will like but it is no use humbugging them about the possibility of winning through mass strikes – leave alone sabotage and guerilla warfare'.

The Fabians, with a subsidy from E. D. Simon, had set up a Local Government Information Bureau to assist Labour councillors on local authorities: William Robson, as an expert on public administration, ran this advice service and edited its monthly *Local Government News*.

Beatrice had discharged her housekeeper because of a scandal with a man in the village and for petty pilfering of drinks and money. She advertised in the *Daily Herald* for two new servants and two Wesleyan deaconesses of Labour sympathy went down to Passfield. They were too genteel and temperamentally difficult: Beatrice got rid of them with the reflection that 'there are some disadvantages in "comrades"'.

A. J. Bowley, L. T. Hobhouse and T. Gregory were all professors at L.S.E.; their colleague, the economic historian Lilian Knowles, had recently died.

41 Grosvenor Road
Westminster Embankment
17.11.26

Dear One

Here are a few unimportant things for you – E. D. Simon sent me this morning, entirely spontaneously, £100 for *Local Government News*; see his letter herewith as to Robson. I have gratefully replied – and I have offered him the paper as a gift(!), if he will accept it. (We cannot continue it indefinitely.)

People are very doubtful whether there will be any national majority for acceptance of the coal terms. It is thought that the Government will renew the Emergency Powers Act regulations next Monday: this may further postpone the Merchandise Marks Bill, but I *fear* I shall have to come up on Monday afternoon anyhow. Wallas will come to tea at the House to-morrow. I have to go to the School this afternoon to the Meeting for the Beveridge portrait, as a (feeble) opposition is threatened. It *must* go through now, as Steel-Maitland has circulated a letter to the *Governors*, asking them to subscribe.

I hope the Wesleyan deaconesses will arrive today; and will start satisfactorily and happily: you will doubtless, with your usual efficiency, put them on the right footing of 'co-operation'.

It is not raining at present, but the whole sky is the melancholy grey and sad, which increases my own dissatisfaction at being separated! But, at least, you will be here the day after tomorrow (don't forget to draw from Miss Piercy the 10/- I left with her for you).

Easington, Dawdon, New Seaham and Horden, also Ryhope, have voted to *reject* the terms. (On the other hand, Monk Wearmouth (Sunderland) has voted for acceptance.) Several Durham members feel convinced that the County decision will be for rejection on balance, by a large majority; and that the County will continue to stand out for some time! We are in hopes that London University Bill may come on in the next two or three days: but the Bishop of Gloucester (Headlam) has a long letter in *The Times* today apprehensive for the theological colleges, which is a new line of opposition!

At the School meeting of the Staff, as to the Beveridge portrait, we got it through all right, but only after a struggle against Bowley, Hobhouse and Gregory, who did not utter any objection to the proposal, but wanted to delay all proceedings for three months, lest the memorial to Mrs Knowles should be interfered with. Meanwhile Steel-Maitland has already himself circularised all the Governors and many of them have sent in cheques. Finally we got assent by agreeing not to send out any appeal to the *students* past and present, for 3 months. The Knowles committee has never yet met, but will meet next Monday and at once appeal to the students. I regard these as almost immaterial to the Portrait Fund, which will evidently be done mainly by the Governors and some only of the Professors. Sir John Cockburn was in the chair. He said afterwards that there was a nasty, disagreeable spirit abroad which be attributed to Bowley.

But I am more than ever persuaded of the shortcomings of any body of professors!

Goodnight, dearest

Sidney Webb

The Swedish Government agent sent his respects to you – thirty years ago he had read your book, and had started Co-op stores there.

## 808 PP SIDNEY WEBB TO LUJO BRENTANO

The Webbs had been awarded honorary degrees at the University of Munich.

Passfield Corner
Liphook
Hants
27.11.26

Dear Professor Brentano

We had already received the letters from Dr Strieder, informing us of the gracious act of the Faculty, and University of Munich. We had suspected that it was *your* kind appreciation that was at the bottom of this honour; and we tender to you our warmest thanks. We have already replied formally, accepting with gratitude.

We think it very nice of you, and of the University of Munich, to have included *both* of us in their honour! It is in Germany only that we are 'das Ehepaar Webb'. Here, in England, people insist on quoting our books as if they were by me only – not choosing to believe that they are really joint products.

We still keep rooms at 41 Grosvenor Road, Westminster, in which I sleep on the nights when I have to be late at the House of Commons. But our home is now our cottage in the country (as on the head of this paper), where my wife lives almost continuously; and where we expect to remain for the rest of our lives. I think the diplomat had better be addressed to this place.

We rejoice to hear from you, and to learn of your activity, which we trust may long continue. With all good wishes from both of us, I am

Yours very truly
Sidney Webb

P.S. We are just finishing vol 1 of a history of the English Poor Law, reaching down *to* 1834: our second volume will continue the story *from* 1834 to 1927. We are struck by the similarity of the position in 1926 to that in 1834, but on another plane.

## 809 HRCUT SIDNEY WEBB TO EDWARD PEASE

Passfield Corner
Liphook
Hants
5.12.26

Dear Pease

Galton showed me your excellent draft for Bye-Election Fund circular.

On the whole – good as it is – I am inclined to doubt whether it is wise to express so trenchantly our desire to exterminate the Liberal Party! In the first place, I doubt whether it is quite the best way to get the money. The wish to get rid of the Tory Government, anyhow, is strong and widespread, more especially among middle-class people of means. I am afraid that it will not be congenial *to them* to put this point so strongly. We may well scare off half-a-dozen relatively substantial donors in the country, who do not realise how *impossible* it would be – even if any Labour Party leaders wished it – to prevent the local Labour Parties from running candidates everywhere.

I entirely share your view on the matter, and have done so consistently for the ten years that I have been 'inside' the Labour Party. I have always pressed Egerton Wake to run the largest possible number of Labour candidates; and I wholly believe it still, and more than ever. It is, in fact, vital to the Labour Party to do so. Nevertheless, I don't think *this* Circular is the place to express it so strongly.

In the second place, I have a feeling that we are in a *fiduciary* capacity in issuing this Circular; in the sense that we hardly ought to put in anything which the whole Society does not agree with. It seems to me not quite the place to 'force the pace'. I don't know whether you will feel this on reflection, but I have a 'stop in my mind' about it – which *you* will respect!

Your draft is so good and so telling that it is only with the greatest reluctance that I have brought myself to urge you to leave out its most trenchant sentences.

The trade union calamitous action this year has, I think, produced a certain amount of reaction in certain strata of society, where timidity and apprehension now prevail. This is represented among the F.S. membership.

Yours

Sidney Webb

810 BEAV BEATRICE WEBB TO JOHN ST LOE STRACHEY

Passfield Corner
Liphook
Hants
10th Dec. 1926

My dear Mr St Loe Strachey

How very kind of you to write to me about 'My Apprenticeship' – of course your letter is most welcome – such a testimony from such an authority makes me very proud. I well remember descending upon you and Mrs St Loe Strachey with Bernard Shaw, and I think Graham Wallas, and the delightful evening we had with you all. I remember so well that charming little boy and his amazing intelligence – we said he was an intellectual Redmond. I have often thought with deep regret of his early death which must have been a great sorrow to you and Mrs St Loe Strachey. However, your other son is going to make his mark among the rising generation, who have of course reacted in politics against the opinions of their parents. What will happen to their children is an interesting question; probably a reaction against all forms of democracy.

When you return from South Africa, do come and spent a night in our cottage and have a long talk about the past and the future. What I fear is another sixteenth century, with the rise of creed wars, only the rival creeds will be economic and political, and not theological. The world has got into a state of creedlessness, and I am afraid the reaction will be fanaticism. However, we can discuss this when we meet.

With kind regards from my husband

Yours very sincerely

Beatrice Webb

(Mrs Sidney Webb)

## 811 SU BEATRICE WEBB TO KINGSLEY MARTIN

Basil Kingsley Martin (1897–1969) was then a lecturer at L.S.E. From 1927 to 1930 he was a leader-writer on the *Manchester Guardian*; from 1930 to 1960 he was editor of the *New Statesman*. He had married Olga Walters in 1926. Beatrice described him in her diary on 7 February 1926: 'Umkempt and with the appearance of being unwashed, with jerky ugly manners . . . a fluent and striking conversationalist . . . with a certain religous fervour for reconstruction'. Martin became one of the most influential of his generation of Fabians. Several of his contemporaries, including Robson, Laski, Woolf and Tawney, were involved in the discussions about starting a new quarterly magazine which eventually emerged, with financial help from Shaw, as the *Political Quarterly*.

Passfield Corner
Liphook
Hants
7th Jan. 1927

Dear Mr Kingsley Martin

I was just thinking of writing to you to suggest that you and Mrs Kingsley Martin should come down here some Friday early in February and stay a night. The first Friday in February would suit us very well; and if you could come down to lunch we could have a walk that afternoon as well as a talk. Mr Laski, who has been here this week, tells me that you are generally free on Friday. But if you and Mr Robson and Mr Tawney want to see us before that time, it would be very pleasant if you could all come down to lunch and return by the 5.12. There is a very good train from Waterloo either at 9.50, reaching Liphook at 11.29, or at 10.17, reaching

Liphook at 12.7; Mr Robson and Mr Tawney both know the way up here; and then we could have lunch and a talk, and perhaps a walk.

About a quarterly review, my husband and I think – without having heard the argument in favour of it – that this particular form of publication is not likely to be a success, as it has been cut into by the pamphlet or booklet on the one hand, and the weekly paper – leaving alone the daily paper – on the other. I was turning over a lot of volumes of the *Edinburgh* and the *Quarterly Review* the other day, and the articles seemed to me to be quite inoperative owing to the form in which they appeared. I do not believe that anyone wants to read a set of articles, some of which do not exactly fit his requirements: he prefers to buy the pamphlet or the booklet on the question. However, that is only our impression without having discussed it. Then again, there is the question of funds. I am quite sure, for instance, that Bernard Shaw would not advance any money for the purpose, and I do not know of anyone else who is likely to do so. But of course if you know of a reserve of money it might be worth trying the experiment, and we would gladly give you any suggestions that we are capable of. I wonder how the *Round Table* is doing today? The other notion of booklets seems to work satisfactorily in the publications of that society for pure English – I forget the exact title. I wonder whether you could combine the two ideas and publish the articles in pamphlet form and also to subscribers in a bound form?

If you cannot arrange to come down here, we shall be in London the last week in January and we might lunch together at the School of Economics on Tuesday or Wednesday the 25th or 26th if we could get a quiet place where we could have a talk. But it would be very jolly to see you all down here, and we could fix it up over the phone if you would prepare a list of dates when you are always engaged. Any Saturday would do for us except the 29th January: or any other day would suit us.

Yours sincerely

Beatrice Webb

(Mrs Sidney Webb)

812 SU BEATRICE WEBB TO LEONARD WOOLF

Abraham Wolf, a member of the L.S.E. staff from 1905 and professor of logic from 1922, published 'The Oldest Biography of Spinoza' as a pamphlet in 1927.

Leonard and Virginia Woolf spent the weekend of 29–30 January 1927 at Passfield Corner. Beatrice remarked that they were an 'exceptionally gifted pair'. Of Virginia she added: 'I do not find her work interesting outside its craftsmanship which is excellent but *precieuse*. Her men and women do not interest me . . . no predominant aims . . . one state of mind follows another without any particular reason'. (BWD 5 February 1927)

George Henry Lewes (1817–1878), the common-law husband of George Eliot, wrote widely on philosophy: the reference is probably to his *Problems of Life and Mind* (1873–79).

Passfield Corner
Liphook
Hants
31st Jan. 1927

Dear Mr Woolf

It so happened I got this pamphlet from your namesake, which I venture to send you. Do not trouble to return it unless quite convenient. I send it because it expresses exactly what I was muddling over yesterday afternoon, i.e., the ascending grades of knowledge (I do not bind myself to the adjective 'ascending') – perceptual, rational and intuitive. You will notice that in Wolf's explanation of Spinoza's metaphysic it is clear that verification comes into the second grade of knowledge, and that the third grade is incapable of what we call verification – that is, testing the correspondence of the order of thought with the order of things. Whether this third grade of 'thoughtfulness matured to inspiration' is anything but a delusion (*vide* G. H. Lewes) is of course open to assertion and counter-assertion. But it so happens that a large number of human beings – and perhaps some of the most eminent in character and intelligence – do recognise the validity of this third grade of mentality, and think, with Spinoza, that this 'brings peace and inspires effort'. What I was trying to explain was that this 'thoughtfulness matured to inspiration', being quite incapable of expression in words which carry to all alike, may take many forms according to the grade of mentality or conviction of the thinker or the person incapable of what *we* call thought. To thousands and millions of the human race it is only represented by what is called a myth or a symbol, or even a ritual; to others, the whole of this religious materialisation is intensely repulsive. But I believe in freedom; and I think the majority of men have a right to insist on the sort of mental atmosphere for their children which 'brings to them peace and inspires effort'. That religion in the ordinary meaning of the term does bring peace and inspire effort to many human beings is, I think, historically proved. Hence my belief in denominational schools for those who desire them; for all schools will be denominational – agnosticism is a denominational form of metaphysic as well as Christianity.

May I add that I think it is quite conceivable that those minds who can find 'peace and inspiration' in absolute agnosticism have as much right to their state of mind as we have to ours; and if they wish that their children shall have the agnostic atmosphere they have a right to demand it if it is administratively possible; but they have no right to impose it on sections of the population which have a different mentality.

We so much enjoyed your and Mrs Woolf's visit and all our talk together.

Yours sincerely

Beatrice Webb

Sidney had written on 8 February (PP) describing the Labour Party reception at the beginning of the new parliamentary session: meeting Lady Warwick there he had invited her to Passfield Corner. Her latest scheme for the use of Easton Lodge had been to turn it into a Labour college with T.U.C. support and with G. D. H. Cole as its principal. After the general strike the trade unions were short of funds and in no mood for such an innovation: a proposal to spend £50,000 on converting the building was defeated at the T.U.C. meeting in Bournemouth in 1926.

Beatrice was discussing the arrangement of material in the book on the history of the Poor Law on which both partners were now working steadily.

Passfield Corner
Liphook
Hants
[c. 10 February 1927]

My own dear one

I am glad I did not come up for the party – it sounds very exhausting. I have written to Lady Warwick and asked her either to come to lunch during a week-end when she will see you or to stay the night with me in the middle of the week – it would be rather amusing to have her here for a gossip. It looks as if the session would end early and begin in October – also that the general election will be postponed till 1929 – so we need not hurry on with our building.

I have an aperçu about the chapter on the R.C. 1905–9. It must be a description of the emergence of the two new [?criteria]: (1) the abandonment of the principles of 1834; (2) the growth of the new preventive service. That will mean that we shall not have a preceding chapter on the new preventive service; the chapter I am now writing will follow that on the *Sphere of charity and the abolition of outdoor relief* which leads up very well to the Commission of 1905–9; because it was the failure of this crusade which led the L.G.B. to ask for a Commission of Enquiry. Then we might have a chapter immediately following the R.C. on the Prevention of Destitution which would include the past developments and those which come after the R.C. of 1905–9, to lead to the chapter on overlap and duplication 1909–1928. The Book would be better balanced in that way and we should not be giving the discovery away before it was made. However we will discuss it when you return. I am at last working at the Guardians and shall be for some time.

Ever yours

Beatrice Webb

I am sorry to say the Engine has proved intractable – the self-lubricator has gone wrong and it cannot be worked without damage – Islers are sending down a man I hope today but we may be without electric light for a day or so.

BW

The two mining accidents were at Marine Colliery, Cwm, and Bilsthorpe Colliery, Mansfield; a Mansion House Relief Fund was set up and closed within a few days.

The complex situation in China, where there was a danger of foreign military intervention, led the Labour movement to protest against British policy. Haden Guest, onetime Fabian rebel and now the ambitious Labour M.P. for Southwark North, resigned from the Labour Party in disagreement with its stand, precipitating a bye-election which cost Labour a seat. He eventually rejoined the party and became a Labour peer.

Kingsley Martin had published *The British Public and the General Strike*. He had already fallen out with what Beatrice called 'the Beveridge–Mair dictatorship' at L.S.E. and the booklet further jeopardised his position at the School. (BWD 7 February 1927)

William Robson had become a lecturer at L.S.E. and found that he could no longer spare time to edit *Local Government News*. Neep was a young barrister.

41 Grosvenor Road
Westminster
3.3.27

Dear One

A fine day here, and also with you I hope. I went off to the British Museum, but found the Reading Room shut for annual cleaning. So I went on to the Record Office, which does not open until 10 a.m., and got through five more volumes of minutes which is all I shall do, as they yielded practically nothing. Neville Chamberlain, in reply to my question as to the Salford Poor Relief experiment, which includes education for the younger men, instead of work, said he *had* sanctioned it for six months as an experiment; and would consider favorably applications from other Boards. I think this is an important step.

MacDonald has just made a first-rate speech on Russia, extremely well-delivered and cogent, not at all 'playing to the Left', yet strongly anti-Tory. He certainly is head and shoulders above all the rest of us in this kind of thing.

But our internal difficulties multiply. An instance is this double mining disaster. We wanted to get a fund started for the widows and orphans; we deliberately abstained from any overt move, so that the fund might not be prejudiced by being called a party move; we wanted the Lord Mayor of Cardiff or the Lord Lieutenant of the County or the Lord Mayor of London to start the fund. Now *Cook* has publicly appealed for subscriptions to such a fund, and asked that the money may be sent to the Miners Federation! This will close the pockets of every donor outside the wage-earning class; and probably prevent any other fund being started.

It seems probable that Haden Guest will *not* resign his seat, and continue in the House as an Independent. This would be convenient.

I think Galton's point as to proposed joint Fabian Tract on the General Strike is a good one; and I don't think it had better be published under such five names. We will see what Laski says. There is no need for Kingsley Martin, and the others, to annoy Beveridge further. Keep the letter for me.

The appended scheme for the *Local Government News* appeals to me, if there is a change in Robson's position. We are paying rather too high a price for editing, and answering the enquiries (which Galton says are incessant and numerous). I should be inclined to try Neep (Edward Whitley's nephew).

Emily went to the Lost Property Office yesterday, but your umbrella was not there; she was told it had not yet come in; and she looked for herself and could not see it. It may yet arrive (I think they will communicate if it does).

Now, dear one, I must post this. Goodnight

Sidney

## 815 PP SIDNEY TO BEATRICE

There were rumours of an early general election. Beatrice hoped that there would be a dissolution as she wished to get Sidney out of Parliament, close down Grosvenor Road and settle finally at Passfield Corner. Sidney, she said frankly, 'is merely walking through the part of M.P. and he could be writing books that would count far more than any speeches he is likely to make in or out of Parliament'. She was particularly anxious to see the Poor Law history finished before the government could carry its intended Bill to reform the system. Her health, moreover, was poor: she had another nervous breakdown and recurrent dizziness and insomnia.

41 Grosvenor Road
Westminster
10.3.27

Dear One

Pray take it easy – there is no hurry; and you ought to do all you can to recover your health and energy. Moreover, it will not be wasted time, as you will be brooding!

I have quite recovered today, after a long night. I went to bed at 9.30, and went to sleep promptly, not waking until about 7 a.m. I thought I would go to the B.M. to clear up a few points that I wanted for my current chapter; and I found a few things.

I am pretty well convinced that there will be no premature dissolution. Trevelyan told me he took the same view. Any other course would greatly annoy the new women voters, who are unlikely to be able to vote until October 1928 and now it seems that the Government is going to concede a common franchise at 21: this seems to me to involve enabling these millions of new electors to vote at the general election, which means that they must be on the register. They can, *by expedition*, be put on the register coming into force in October 1927 – hence the election cannot be *before* this coming autumn.

I enclose an official invitation *for you* to give, next autumn, the Sidney Ball Lecture at Oxford. Note, the lecture must be written, and the copyright is to be given to the University. There *is* a fee, but I don't know how much. (I think it is rather 'cheek' of them to ask for the copyright, which might prevent you using it up in some other way.)

Did you notice, in today's *Times* (p. 11, col. 3) in the report of the Philip Stott College meeting a statement by a Conservative Party office representative, that at the London School of Economics, Socialism was taught: and the reply that this was a matter for its Governing Body? I have not done anything, as Beveridge or Steel-Maitland, or both, may have seen it; and it is 'up to' the latter, in any case, to take action if he thinks fit.

I must stay until 4.50 tomorrow, and return on Monday, as there is an important party vote; moreover I must be there early on Tuesday.

I see that Neville Chamberlain has been meeting the agricultural Conservative members as to his P.L. proposals; and said he would 'consider' the relation between the County Council and the local councils. He therefore persists – at present – in his intention to produce the Bill.

The Speaker's Secretary has complained formally to the Labour Party that no fewer than 82 of our members neither attended any of his Levees, *nor* wrote to excuse themselves. We are asking them to write now: and next session we propose to tell them, at the outset, that they really ought *either* to attend or to write. (Friday is an inconvenient evening for the provincials, but this does not excuse their not writing.)

Now, dear one, goodbye for today: tomorrow I shall be with you by 7 p.m., and we shall have a quiet weekend together alone, which in many ways is best.

Sidney

816 PP SIDNEY TO BEATRICE

The Liberals had done unexpectedly well in bye-elections at Leith and Southwark. The Labour Party, moreover, was in difficulties: the trade unions were nearly bankrupt and badly demoralised; and the Labour Front Bench, Beatrice pointed out, 'held different views from the most active propagandists and *dare not say so*'. (BWD 5 April 1927) She thought it a miracle that, so deficient in brains and starved of money, the Labour Party should be attracting more and more votes. 'The impression left on the observer's mind is of a slow underground social upheaval, moving independently of leaders or organisation – propelling a lower stratum of society into a more dominant position.'

H. Baillie Weaver was a well-to-do Fabian and I.L.P. member.

41 Grosvenor Road
S.W.
30/3/27

Dear One

Henderson was at the House, and they will come on Friday – he is to let me know today at what hour. The doctors say he is to be taken care of, but he seems as usual.

There is a definite feeling that the Liberals have 'turned the corner', and started to improve. Galton said that a change is already visible as to candidates. They asked endless people to stand for Leith, in vain; now, he says, men are ringing up their office, and offering to stand! But apart from *their* terrible previous slump, and our undue expectations, I think the Labour feeling is that neither place portends any slackening of the Labour advance. At Leith the Labour candidate, on his fourth attempt, continued his numerical increase at an entirely satisfactory rate. (Besides his confiscatory utterances, he insisted on Birth Control, and thereby antagonised the Irish Catholics.) At Southwark, it was inevitable that Haden Guest should draw off *some* personal following, to which, in fact, had been due his election in 1924. The Liberals, in both cases, had the luck; and the Unionists the ill luck – only one-seventh of the electorate supported the Government by their votes, though *a few* doubtless voted for the Liberal at both places. But the upshot is that we must revise our prophecies as to the Liberal total.

Enclosed from Charles Buxton as to Clifford Allen. I had a chat with him about it, and explained that we *could* do nothing. Allen's standard of life is £700 a year, and he has less than £300; his wife is just *beginning* to make a little. He can't live anywhere except in the country, and not in an office. He has been living on sums supplied by Baillie-Weaver, who is now dead. A few people have offered £50 each donation. I explained that nothing short of an endowment was worth troubling about: and I knew of no chance of this. I don't know that you need reply; unless you like.

I gave Emily your note; and got £10 from the bank.

My afternoon has been entirely cut up by having to attend to the Pacific Cable Bill, on which I am supposed to have made a 'brilliant' little speech. But it deprived me of any tea, and now compels me to cut this short to catch the post. Tomorrow I shall be with you about 6.30, I hope.

Sidney

817 PP SIDNEY TO BEATRICE

The police had raided Arcos, the Soviet trading agency, on the excuse of possible espionage but also looking for evidence of Russian support for the Communist Party. Soon afterwards Britain broke off diplomatic relations with the Soviet Union. Beatrice, commenting on the raid in her July letter to Seaham women, thought it a 'silly business' but added a strong criticism of the revolutionary rhetoric of the Communist Party: 'the Russian revolution, and especially the propaganda of it in Great Britain, has been the greatest disaster in the history of the British Labour movement'. She suggested that, just as the French Revolution held back political democracy in Britain for two generations, so the Russian Revolution might delay economic democracy in Britain for half a century. She thought the Labour Party the best bulwark against the polarisation of British politics between reactionaries and revolutionists. She cited as evidence of increasing class hatreds the Trades Disputes Bill recently introduced by the government. It created a class of illegal strikes – extending beyond one industry and intended to be politically coercive – restricted the right of picketing, prohibited civil servants from joining trade unions and made 'contracting-in' necessary for the political levy.

41 Grosvenor Road
S.W.1
19.5.27

Dear One

Another brilliant day; which I hope you will be able to enjoy! Don't trouble to do more than a little intellectual work: if you get on ever so little each day, that will suffice.

Emily found a small article of dress, in a draper's envelope, in the wastepaper basket, which I will bring tomorrow. (I omitted to take it out to discover exactly what it is!)

We are awaiting Joynson-Hicks's statement as to the results of the raid. Henderson thinks they may have found (a) payments to Labour men: (b) employees who are relatives of Labour men – R. J. Davies hears that the most important document is a list of the *real* addresses of Communist Party offices, the nominal offices being merely a blind. Neither of these discoveries justifies the raid as such. But we shall know at 4 p.m. Anyhow, it will be 'worked up' for horror.

Thomas and Henderson discussed who would be chosen as Prime Minister if Baldwin suddenly resigned. I said Austen. But Henderson said that Joynson-Hicks would be chosen, as representing the Die-Hards, who cannot forgive Chamberlain for not dealing drastically with Russia and China: they have barely tolerated Baldwin, and would now insist on a 'strong man'. I can hardly believe in such a choice, which would hardly appeal to the mass of citizens, or make for unity on their side of the House.

After all, an anti-climax! About 2.15 p.m. a note was handed in from Joynson-Hicks regretting that he could not make his statement today, but would do so on Tuesday! (There has been a long Cabinet this morning; and we infer differences between the Foreign Secretary and 'Jix' – they were seen in heated altercation at the great function at the Guildhall.) We are to have a day on Thursday for a full discussion: but Baldwin shuffled, telling us we could put down the Home Office vote on that day, (thus using up one of the twenty days allotted to Supply); or else move a Vote of Censure. Henderson and Clynes claimed freedom to frame their own resolution; and at last Baldwin conceded this – thus seriously snubbing his Chief Whip, who was prompting him to fob us off with a Supply day. (We have been contemplating to move for a Select Committee to enquire into the whole proceeding, in which 'Jix' seems to have blundered badly.)

Now the House is going quietly on with Second Reading of Finance Bill, on which Lees-Smith is to make the attack.

Please tell Miss Piercy to complete, without fail, typing my article for America *tomorrow*, as I must post it early on Saturday.

Now, dear one, Goodnight. I do hope you will decide to rest quietly at Passfield; and not be so eager to undertake social and other enterprises away from there. You really ought to concentrate on getting better nights – you don't realise how precious you are!

Sidney

818 PP SIDNEY TO BEATRICE

During a visit to the United States MacDonald suffered from a severe throat infection. He nearly died in hospital in Philadelphia in April and was not fit to sail home until late May. Sir G. Croydon Marks had been Liberal M.P. for North Cornwall until his defeat in 1924.

Borodin was the Soviet representative with the Kuomintang; Rosengolz was the Soviet ambassador in London. H. B. Usher was a civil servant who stood as Labour candidate at Leicester South in 1924 and 1929 and became MacDonald's personal secretary from 1929 to 1935.

41 Grosvenor Road
Westminster Embankment
24.5.27

Dear One

Another brilliant day – to aid your convalescence!

Liberty's van called 'for the hat' – Emily said. She did not hand it over, not having instructions. The man asked when he should call again. This morning I opened the box (which was delivered last week) to see if it contained anything beyond one hat. I found only the invoice (enclosed). Is this merely a belief that the hat was sent only on approval? Or is it merely a reminder that you had not paid for it on delivery? Perhaps you will send a cheque.

We still know nothing (this morning) of the Government intention as to Arcos etc. There are rumours of asserted *bribes* to particular Labour leaders, by the Soviet authorities; coupled, however, with asserted Russian complaints that the said persons did not act in accordance with what they had been paid for! Probably there is nothing in this, or other wild rumours.

A wireless message has been received from a known friendly person on J.R.M.'s steamer (one Croydon Marks, ex-M.P.), saying that J.R.M. is by no means fit to resume work, and urging that he be pressed to rest quietly for some time. We shall see this evening what he can (and will consent to) do.

Emily has just come to tell me to clear out by 11 a.m., as she has to prepare the dining room for today's lunch – there are to be 11 of us – and my writing table must be moved etc., etc. – so I must resume this letter this afternoon.

In the excitement I failed to get this off in time, and you will get it only by second post. The P.M.'s statement seemed to us unimpressive, and even trivial, for such a tremendous conclusion, and this alone evoked the Unionist cheers. The main thing, the telegram incriminating the Soviet Government from Borodin, of November last, was not got from the Arcos raid at all, but was evidently obtained at Peking. We thought that Austen Chamberlain looked unhappy, but Churchill triumphant. It may be that the revelations implicating Labour leaders, in trivial matters, were deliberately withheld, as beneath the dignity of an international quarrel, to be produced later (if there are any). We decided to move for a Select Committee (if our Party agrees to it tomorrow).

MacDonald arrived just before 6 p.m., after a splendid and sunny voyage, which made him bronzed. But we thought him ill. He then presided over Executive but seemed much exhausted by it. We ordered him not to speak on Thursday, and only to appear in the House tomorrow for a few minutes, at 7 p.m., when he had a great reception. He has to come to Party Executive tomorrow at 10 a.m., and will then see his doctor; and doubtless go away for some weeks, probably for the rest of the session. All that can be seen at present is that he is seriously shaken.

Susan's lunch went off admirably. Mr and Mrs Rosengolz, Mr and Mrs Usher, Mr and Mrs Laski, and Geo. Young. She gave sparkling Moselle, cold salmon, cucumber, and cold chicken and salad; many flowers.

Opinion is against there being an early general election.

Lord Arnold begged to come down for lunch and walk on Thursday 9 June.

Goodnight

Sidney

## 819 NLW BEATRICE WEBB TO THOMAS JONES

Stanley Baldwin's son Oliver had become a member of the Labour Party. In 1931 he resigned with Oswald Mosley, John Strachey and others to form the brief-lived New Party.

Passfield Corner
Liphook
Hants
4th July 1927

My dear Mr Jones

I wonder whether it would interest you to see my letter to the organised women of Seaham – there are about 1,000 – on the work of the session, ending up with a warning against revolutionary talk? It is of course very difficult to explain elaborate measures in a short letter, but the letter certainly represents the views of what may be termed the 'Right' of the Labour Party. I hope that the section on the proposals to reform the House of Lords will be obsolete after Wednesday's announcement. But what a strange miscalculation to have introduced them as a scheme of the Cabinet! However, we put our trust in the Monarchy to prevent a new aristocratic autocracy arising to foment a real civil war.

We are getting on with our second volume of the History of the Poor Law and find it much more interesting than we expected. The question is – How did the Poor Law Division of the L.G.B. and Ministry of Health give up so completely the principles of 1834 – even where these principles were valid for the present day? Of course we are inclined to blame the Poor Law Commission of 1905–9 for having destroyed one set of principles without establishing any other set of principles. But we of the Minority, at any rate, did our level best to stem the tide by proposing that money payments should be virtually handed over to a stipendiary who would have a complete register of the inhabitants, with all the information about their earnings and their other sources of income. I do not envy Mr Chamberlain. To operate on the Poor Law when it is in such a swollen and inflamed condition is indeed a risky business.

By the way, we had Oliver Baldwin staying here for a week-end. What an attractive youth he is – quite different from what I expected, as I had heard that he was a bit erratic. But he seems singularly unselfconscious, and did not emit, in our company, any hot air – perhaps he is learning wisdom – certainly we noticed a very wholesome depreciation of the I.L.P. propaganda of 'socialism in our time'. I should have thought he and his father would have had a good deal in common – I imagine that he is really sympathetic to Mr Baldwin's general outlook, if only that could be disentangled from the Diehard section of the Conservative Party.

Yours very sincerely
Beatrice Webb
(Mrs Sidney Webb)

### 820 BOD BEATRICE WEBB TO J. L. HAMMOND

Beatrice was becoming increasingly dependent upon weekend visitors to keep contact with politics and social life. Her diary records a steady stream of visitors over the next ten years, though Beatrice often complained that such entertainment was a strain. 'One of the disadvantages of a small country home is that if you happen to combine a hospitable temperament with old age or other forms of delicacy you find yourself continually overtaxing your strength. I am no longer fit for the friction of visitors staying in the house – the most I can bear is two nights.' (BWD 3 June 1927)

Passfield Corner
Liphook
Hants
15th July 1927

Dear Mr Hammond

I am delighted to send you my letter to Seaham though the *Manchester Guardian* picked out the best part of it. Of course the effect of the Russian Revolution has been particularly pernicious in the mining areas owing to the long lock-out and the Russian money during the Strike. From what I gathered on our Easter visit to Seaham, and from what we hear from other mining areas, the Miners Federation is in danger of disintegration, largely through Communist propaganda, always citing the Russian Revolution and the Soviet system as the new model which must be followed in Great Britain. With regard to the vast majority of the miners and their wives, the impossibilism of the Left Wing makes them apathetic and fatalistic, and they are almost inclined to accept any conditions of employment rather than have another dispute, and even to leave the Union sometimes to join the non-political Union – which, by the way, is fairly strong in Northumberland and Durham – whilst a smaller section enjoys the revivalism of A. J. Cook's speeches and becomes fanatical and embittered. What fools the Conservative Government are, from their own standpoint, not to leave the Communists alone in their attempt to wreck the trade union movement and, to a lesser extent, the Labour Party. I have not the remotest fear of revolution in Great Britain. What I fear is the reaction, even among the workers, against any organisation which seems in the slightest degree to be revolutionary in its objects and methods.

We are hard at work on our second volume, which I am afraid will be even longer than the first. But the condition of the Poor Law is so desperately serious at the present time that one has to bring heavy guns to make any impression.

When you return to England it would be very pleasant if you and Mrs Hammond would come and spend a couple of nights with us for a long talk.

Pray remember me to Mr Gilbert Murray.

Yours very sincerely
Beatrice Webb
(Mrs Sidney Webb)

## 821 PP SIDNEY TO BEATRICE

The central building for the University of London was erected in Malet Street, behind the British Museum. Beatrice went to visit Beatrice Ross, now living in a cottage on the Longfords property. The Fabian summer school was at Cirencester: one of the themes was the perennial issue of Poor Law reform, again topical with the prospect of government legislation at long last.

41 Grosvenor Road
S.W.1
27.7.27

Dear One

Here is the Summer School programme. It *is* 11 a.m. on Friday. Some 60 are going down on Thursday, largely by the 3.15 p.m. train. At least six cars will be there; and no doubt one or other will take us to Reading, from which we have the trains.

What a queer person is J.R.M. Today, at the Executive he burst out about the wickedness of London University securing the Bloomsbury site; of Beveridge going off to America of his own initiative, and securing money from Rockefeller for the site; that the University ought not to beg from America; that the Labour Party ought to oppose the vote for the Government contribution, and so on. We of the University (myself, Dalton and Lees-Smith) lay low (knowing that the vote would be voted under the guillotine tonight without any chance of opposition). At Dalton's suggestion, I said a few soothing words, and Lees-Smith said that there was another side to the question, but it could not be gone into; and the matter passed over. It appears that J.R.M. spoke as a British Museum Trustee; and resented the erection of the University building in juxtaposition to the Museum. But *I* realised that it was a flaring up of his old opposition to the University on the L.C.C. a quarter of a century ago, *then* largely motived by hostility to me! The episode is interesting only as a psychological study.

Noel Buxton will apparently do something (£100 or £200) possibly renewable annually for the *Local Government News*, as to which I have seen Galton and Robson. He is really a *most* excellent person.

Now dear one, I have no time for more, if I am to catch the post. We shall be together again on Friday. Say all nice things from me to Miss Ross, and to the others that you will be meeting.

Sidney

By the way I enclose the report of my speech, which does not read so badly.

## 822 BEV SIDNEY WEBB TO SIR WILLIAM BEVERIDGE

Webb had recently passed his sixty-eighth birthday.

Passfield Corner
Liphook
Hants
8 August 1927

Dear Beveridge

I do not know whether it is to the Vice-Chancellor or to the Director that I should address this letter, or to both personages; but you will probably be good enough to make it serve. I have come to realise that I ought to take the initiative in *tendering both to the University and to the School of Economics, my resignation of the Chair of Public Administration,* or rather of the title of Professor of Public Administration, which the Senate was good enough to confer on me during my absence in the Far East in 1911–12. For one or other reason I soon ceased to justify that honour by any systematic lecturing, even if I ever did so; and I cannot hope now to be able to resume such courses as I formerly gave. I have done something to help advanced or specialist students and researchers but this I can do, from time to time, without the title of Professor, which it is unseemly that I should continue to hold at my age.

It is with real gratitude that I recall how much I have been privileged by the opportunities afforded to me, ever since the reorganisation of the University in 1900, of taking a part in its work, and of giving to it such services as were within my power.

I hope that I may still be able to do some little for the University in one way or another.

Yours very truly

Sidney Webb

823 PP SIDNEY TO BEATRICE

Mrs Bygott was the wife of Dr A. Bygott, one of the discoverers of the cause of typhus, who was an adviser to the Labour Party on public health policy. Colonel F. E. Fremantle (1872–1943) was Conservative M.P. for St Albans from 1919 until his death. He had a distinguished medical career in the Army and in local government; and was a leading Conservative spokesman on public health and housing.

41 Grosvenor Road
S.W.1
15.11.27

Dear One

Here is a letter from Mrs Bygott. Among the members are Mrs Bernard Shaw and Miss McTaggart.

Also an advertisement from Constables as to 'Limited Editions', which please *keep*, as we may take hints.

I have been reviewing the financial position, and have decided *not* to send Clark any money in advance. The gain is doubtful, as Income Tax will eventually have to be paid anyhow. If we are very successful over the Private Edition we shall anyhow be landed in Supertax on the 1928 figures. On the other hand if it is not successful we may just escape; and in that event the £200 payment would be more profitable if it fell in 1928, as it *might* keep us under the limit.

I have therefore reckoned that we might safely invest £500 this month. This might all be put in Building Societies, £200 in the Abbey Road (making £1,000 there), and £300 more in the Co-operative Building Society (making £700 there); we have also £1,000 in the Halifax Building Society – these three are reputed the best; and they all pay 5% free of tax (equal to 6¼ per cent).

On the other hand I should rather like to patronise Emil Davies's Investment Trust, to the extent of £100 or £150 from each of us. It pays 7 per cent subject to Income Tax, mostly gained in 'unpopular' securities.

Halévy fixes 10.45 train on Friday, which will suit me very well.

I spoke to Col. Fremantle today, who says he is keen on reform of Poor Law, and he was impressed by my explanation as to the collapse of the L.G.B., the abandonment of the 'offer of the House', and the virtual recommendation of Outdoor Relief without any Labor Test. Of course, what he is most interested in is the provision for the sick; but we may as well go on talking about all the other things – not that *he* will take any action!

What I gather from the M.P.s who have been speaking in the country is that (1) the provincial meetings are splendid; (2) those in London have been small and flat, through bad organisation; but that (3) some report that the people are dispirited, 'fed up', made hopeless at failure, and not much disposed to struggle, either politically or otherwise.

Now goodnight, dear one. I am sure you will be recuperating in the quiet and sunshine – 'every day a little' must be the motto.

Sidney

## 824 PP SIDNEY TO BEATRICE

Beatrice was to make her first broadcast – a talk on Herbert Spencer – on 27 February 1928. Mrs Surrey Dane was a Fabian and the wife of a well-known journalist. Leonard and Dorothy Elmhirst founded Dartington Hall as a coeducational progressive school. Lloyd George's 'war chest' was a private fund derived in part from the sale of honours during his premiership.

MacDonald's health showed increasing signs of strain; his diary records many occasions when he complained of his head and his inability to concentrate. He had been unwell and out of effective politics from April until September.

41 Grosvenor Road
S.W.1
30/11/27

Dear One

Here is your B.B.C. agreement to be signed. Also letter from Mrs Surrey Dane: query ask her and her son to lunch on 13 December when you come up; or, alternatively, on Monday, 5 December when you return from Ayot?

MacDonald is dealing with the question of Haldane's Memo, which the latter has stated to have been a *legal* opinion given at the request of the F.O. when he was Lord Chancellor; and that Chamberlain was not warranted in quoting it *as* he did. The incident has not, however, been terminated.

I enclose a P.S. to a letter from Bloomfield, as to the rumours of future vacancy at Seaham; which *looks* as if he were not going to be an aspirant. As regards Ben Porter of Murton, I am inclined to believe Herron. But it is odd. (*Keep* Bloomfield's P.S.)

J.R.M. turned 'queer' today in Parliamentary Executive and left the Chair – said it was one of his bad days, and that his head was queer; he had an awkward cough! We have at last got agreement with Snowden as to Surtax, and he is to make a speech in ten days time. But he is still angry with Arnold and others, I think because the whole matter was not left to him from the start. Curiously enough, I think I am in favor with both sides!

Laski has seen Mrs Elmhirst (Willard Straight), and hopes for a donation from her to the F.S. I am to write to her presently; she says her husband is running a foolish scheme of a school at Totnes, where they live; but that she has still 12 million dollars!

It is said that L.G. has vested his whole fund in about four Trustees, all Liberals, on trusts not stated publicly. If it is for the Liberal Party, it would be inconvenient if it ceased to exist as such, or if it sank down to the size of the 'Wee Free' Scottish Church! But this may be provided for.

Now dear one, I have to catch the post, and have no time for more than my love.

Sidney

825 UI BEATRICE WEBB TO H. G. WELLS

Catherine Wells died of cancer on 6 October 1927. Charlotte Shaw wrote to T. E. Lawrence a sardonic account of the 'dreadful' cremation ceremony at which Wells delivered a lachrymose panegyric to the wife to whom he had been notoriously unfaithful. Wells afterwards published a private memoir, *The Book of Catherine Wells*, to which Beatrice refers.

Shaw had caused a sensation by praising Mussolini's dictatorship and spending six weeks in Italy, where he was lionised by Fascist officials. Beatrice commented in her diary on 1 October: 'Imagine the hot indignation and withering wit with which the meagrely-fed Irish journalist of the Eighties, writing in his dark lodging, would have chastised the rich world-famous dramatist of 1927 defending the pitiless cruelties and bombastic militancy of the melodramatic Mussolini!'. When Shaw delivered a Fabian autumn lecture criticising democracy it was a depressing failure – as he confessed when the Webbs spent the weekend with him at Ayot. Beatrice disliked his utopias of compulsory equality and compulsory work to produce a new race of supermen. 'There has set in some sort of mutual contempt between G.B.S. and the Labour movement', she noted on 5 December. 'The sooner he gets back to his plays the better for all concerned . . . he has lost his pity for suffering . . . He has become complacent with the world of wealth and leisure he lives in . . . Alas! poor Shaw, you have succumbed to Charlotte!'

Passfield Corner
Liphook
Hants
Dec 6th 1927

My dear Mr Wells

Some thoughtful friend has sent me the exquisitely felt and expressed memory of your wife, delivered at Golder's Green; which will be remembered in my diary as a reminder of an old friendship with you and with her. When I saw her last during a ten days visit to Easton Lodge – some three years ago – I was immensely interested in the development of a beautiful soul – and felt drawn to her as I had never done before. But she was very reserved – partly no doubt from a lack of egotism, partly because her experience of life had been peculiar and far-reaching. I did not like to write to you when first I heard of her illness and afterwards of her death because I knew you had a host of more intimate friends and would find it difficult to answer or leave unanswered so many letters about her. But now that the immediate strain and stress have passed, let me say how deeply Sidney and I sympathised with the sorrow entailed in this break – this final break – in an inspiring partnership, in a way so like our own.

Perhaps, someday when you are motoring to your brother's – you will stay a night here and talk about these troublesome times and what will come out of them. I have read some of your current articles on G.B.S. and Labour leadership etc. Are you not a *little* hard on poor mortals? Oh! where oh where is the Superman? I don't believe he exists or ever will exist. We are all miserable sinners and mental defectives in one way or another. With every rise in human values the Superman will recede further – further off from existing human nature. However, every genius has his own method of presentment – and certainly yours is effective.

We spent the weekend with the Shaws: he is not quite at ease in his new role of finding the Superman in Mussolini – a strange phantasy!

Yours very sincerely
Beatrice Webb

Please be patient with my scrawl; but it is not a letter I could dictate.

Beatrice, who had just passed her seventieth birthday, felt that her strength was failing: before her broadcast – 'I was in a devil of a funk' she wrote on 29 February – she went to Hastings for a few days with her sister Catherine Courtney.

A new social enquiry to complement the pioneer survey of the East End by Charles Booth was being launched by the L.S.E. Llewellyn Smith had been associated with Booth's work, as had Beatrice. Sydney F. Markham, author, museum official and M.P., was the secretary to the London Survey, 1928–9.

The drafts mentioned were for the new Labour programme, *Labour and the Nation*, to be submitted to the 1928 party conference. Both R. H. Tawney and Arthur Greenwood contributed much to the final version. It was essentially a restatement of Webb's earlier *Labour and the New Social Order*: since it was more a set of principles than a legislative programme it was attacked by the left of the party for its imprecision and lack of commitment.

41 Grosvenor Road
S.W.1
24.2.28

Dear One

Why be nervous about Monday? You will do it admirably, and the less you think about it the better! (I have given to Emily your message about food.)

We have had a meeting of the Booth Enquiry Committee this morning, and appointed Llewellyn Smith at £500, and Markham as Secretary at £400. Smith and Bowley seem to be going to put themselves strongly into it. It is to begin on 16 May. Besides an Advisory Committee, there is to be an inner Finance Committee of Smith, Beveridge *and myself*, which will become a sort of executive. The first difficulty that has arisen is the discovery that many of the *areas* inside and outside London, have been changed, so that the official statistics do not always fit (as between 1891 and 1921).

The Ilford result confirms our worst forecast. The only thing to be said is that the drop in the Unionist vote (when the 5 per cent *increase* in the vote is taken into account) represents a drop of some *23* per cent. But the Liberal candidate has reaped nearly all this harvest. St Ives will almost certainly show a like result.[1]

Snell showed me in confidence drafts sent in for the party programme. J.R.M. has himself done a lengthy one, but Mosley [*word omitted:* ? and] Miss Wilkinson have submitted rather shorter drafts – all of them too long for practical use. I presume these drafts have emerged from some meeting as they all agree substantially. Of course, J.R.M.'s is by far the best and will no doubt be made the basis. It is literary and well phrased, and properly vague and comprehensive, without anything new to you and me.

I infer that the programme *will be* constructed and adopted without undue strife. But *I* don't think it will be any improvement on *Labour and the New Social Order*!

Now goodbye Dear One until 11.39 a.m. tomorrow.

Yours

Sidney Webb

827 BEV BEATRICE WEBB TO SIR WILLIAM BEVERIDGE

The copies of the Haldane and Mandell Creighton portraits are hung in the senior common room of the L.S.E. The School proposed to commission a portrait of the Webbs, as its main founders. Though flattered by the suggestion, Beatrice was far from sure that she wanted it to be done by 'the fashionable portrait painter' Sir William Nicholson. (BWD 5 March 1928) Charlotte Shaw had refused a similar request, saying that the painting 'would not be me but my shell'. Beatrice thought it ungracious to decline, though she complained that the sittings 'wasted time and dissipated strength' when she and Sidney were trying to complete the last chapter of the Poor Law history. (BWD 15 June 1928) In the event the Webbs liked the painting, which hangs in the Founders' Room at L.S.E.

Werner Sombart (1863–1941), a post-Marxist and conservative social theorist, wrote mainly upon class structures and the development of capitalism.

Sidney had decided definitely to retire at the next election and again suggested that MacDonald should have the reversion of the Seaham seat. This time MacDonald agreed. 'Who would have thought that the embittered vendetta of former years would terminate in such a model manner', Beatrice reflected. (BWD Whit Sunday 1928)

Passfield Corner
Liphook
Hants
March 19th 1928

Dear Sir William

Here is a note from Miss Haldane about the portrait. I think that a copy would be practicable and that we might find a copyist who would do it well enough for a modest sum. We should be prepared to contribute £50 towards a copy.

I should also like to have a copy of a portrait of Mandell Creighton but that would not be possible for us just at present unless you could get money for the Haldane copy elsewhere. If so we would get a copy of Creighton's portrait. I am pretty certain there is a good one. As to a copyist, you might consult Mr Nicholson, which I have not liked to do.

He has made a very good study of us and is coming down with his big canvas next week end. He is a very pleasant house-mate.

We were so sorry to see so little of Professor Sombart; I suppose he is going back to Germany almost at once.

Yours sincerely

Beatrice Webb

(Mrs Sidney Webb)

The Webbs had almost finished their history of the Poor Law: its publication was to coincide with the end of the ninety-year-old system against which they had campaigned all their public lives. They were already beginning to think of a journey to Russia at the end of Sidney's parliamentary career. They were also planning to move out of Grosvenor Road, which had been damaged by floods from the river: relations with Susan Lawrence had become strained and the Webbs decided that they would merely retain part of the house as a *pied-à-terre* until Sidney retired from the House of Commons. For their summer holiday they were considering a hotel that Elie Halévy had recommended in the Savoy Alps.

41 Grosvenor Road
Westminster Embankment
25.4.28

Dear One

The Budget affects our book! The Poor Law Bill will be introduced early in November; and Churchill said it would be passed by Christmas, or at any rate by Easter! This means that it will certainly be *passed*, before the Dissolution in May, as the whole Budget structure is involved. I don't think we must let it change our plans; unless, indeed, to make us keep the proofs open even a little longer. Unless we could actually publish in November there is no great advantage in publication whilst the Bill is before Parliament. There is something to be said for just noticing the *virtual* passage of the Bill into Law (which we could do at Christmas) – as the end of the Guardians – and making the suggestion that *it leaves all the problems of policy unsolved*; that the new administration should take care not to repeat the series of mistakes of their predecessors, and hence should read our book! – to be published in March.

Churchill very definitely negatived any transfer of the able-bodied to the national government, or the transfer to it of anything else.

Our Circular should go to County and County Borough Councils quite as much as to Guardians, even more so. We must take a good holiday in June–July, and come back prepared for another six months work.

Miss Lawrence very decidedly says no one can travel in Russia in March or April. No Russian does so. I thought this was the case. We may have either (1) to go elsewhere, or (2) put off our trip until May, so as to get to Odessa in June. There would be some advantage in avoiding the general election! (She is quite agreeable to our paying by the day after July: in fact, prefers it. She suggests our distempering the basement in July, roughly, and she will furnish it as a sitting room for Emily, in bright colours, which she wants to do.)

Here are two tickets for the Ladies' Gallery for next Tuesday afternoon – in case you care to telephone to Mrs Travers Rawson for her friend, if she can use them.

I walked up to Piccadilly to the P.L.M. [Paris–Lyons–Mediterranée] railway office to enquire as to the P.L.M. Autocars etc. I think the Halévy's place (Val d'Isère) is more inaccessible than Lautaret; and I think we should find the latter journey more convenient, and the place offers more excursions. The motorcars carry *enough* luggage.

Dear One – goodbye until tomorrow at 8.30. What splendid weather!

Yours

Sidney Webb

829 UI BEATRICE WEBB TO H. G. WELLS

*The Open Conspiracy*, published in May 1928, was a Wellsian manifesto for building 'the new human community' to serve 'the common ends of the race'. Shaw told Wells that it was written with the muddled rhetoric of a leader-writer.

Passfield Corner
Liphook
Hants
May 25th 1928

My dear Mr Wells

How very kind of you to have sent me your inspiring essay which I have read with deepest interest. I especially like your chapter I because I think it goes to the root of the new type of government, the creed autocracy of Italy and Russia. Nature abhors a vacuum and if there is no creed with regard to man's relation to the Universe and to man, existing in a community some sort of rule of conduct has to be imposed and enforced. Fortunately in Great Britain we have a great measure of common consent as to what is desirable as an authoritative outlook on life. Also your analysis of the forces of resistance, external and internal, is admirable. What I do not like is the title. Why 'A Conspiracy' open or otherwise? 'Open Conspiracy' seems to me an arresting catchword which has very little real meaning in it. However what's in a name! Of course you leave off where we are wont to begin: but then you and we each have our own sphere and it is very difficult to combine the two. I fear you will think it a gross impertinence, but after I had read the book I said to myself 'What a magnificent introduction to the works of the Webbs'!

In a few days time we are going for three weeks' holiday in the Savoy mountains before we tackle the last chapter of our big work on English Poor Law.

When are you motoring past our cottage and spending a day and a night with us on your way to your old haunts? We shall be here throughout August and September and probably the first two weeks in October.

Always yours sincerely

Beatrice Webb

(Mrs Sidney Webb)

The Shaws had become increasingly friendly with Waldorf and Nancy Astor. The first woman to be elected to the House of Commons, Lady Astor sat for the Sutton division of Plymouth 1919–45. It was an intimacy which the Webbs watched 'with a wry smile'. (BWD 13 April 1928) Beatrice noted Shaw's response to the flattery of Society: 'so far as G.B.S.'s mind is concerned, the game is up; we evade serious discussion and must acquiesce in his pleasantries and paradoxes'.

When *The Intelligent Woman's Guide to Socialism and Capitalism* appeared in June Beatrice was surprised that it 'paralysed his critics and opened the hearts of fellow socialists', as she thought the book an abstract bore. (BWD 9 June 1928) It was, she remarked, 'a patchwork of observation, personal experience and hearsay . . . he lacks the necessary equipment in the knowledge of facts and the power of thought'. (BWD 5 July 1928)

Miss Burr was Beatrice's part-time secretary. She typed a substantial part of the diary.

Passfield Corner
Liphook
Hants
[mid-June 1928]

Dearest one

I have asked Miss Burr to come tomorrow to copy the suffrage report and help me generally to clear up. What about Scurr coming to lunch on Thursday 1 o'c? I asked him to do so in my note – would you find out whether he is coming or not. Of course the M.O.H. report raises the question of immediate outdoor relief to doubtful cases without test as in [?other] unions – but the administration is evidently *respectable*.

The Shaws seem very happy here. G.B.S. said my superior artisan cooking was preferable to the dishes served up by 'Chefs'. He is evidently very touched by Nancy's personal devotion and Charlotte and Waldorf [*word omitted:* ? seem] to be devoted to her! But he told me that he went among these people because Charlotte enjoyed it so. He believes his book will have a great effect on the results of the general election – for good among the Have-nots and for bad among the Haves. He is contemplating a cheap edition for the multitude, 5/-. He won't consider any shortened version. He is busy all day writing letters in answer to criticisms.

He is certainly a great charmer – in his good nature and freedom from every kind of humbug or insincerity, in his wit, and wisdom of a sort. The two are very devoted to one another.

Ever yours

Beatrice

## 831 NLS BEATRICE WEBB TO LORD HALDANE

When the Webbs returned from their French holiday they dined with Haldane and his sister Elizabeth. After Sharp had visited Passfield Corner Beatrice commented that he was drinking himself out of a job and out of life. Ishbel MacDonald was Ramsay MacDonald's daughter and hostess. Philip Laszlo de Lombos (1869–1937) was a successful and fashionable portrait painter. Charles S. Peirce (1839–1914) was the author of a number of important philosophical works.

Passfield Corner
Liphook
Hants
14th August 1928

Dear Lord Haldane

I wonder whether this letter will get through the barrier of a complete rest cure? Sidney and I frequently talk and think about you and our long years of common effort (some would call it common intrigue!) for the public good. Your sister tells me that you are ordered to give up all sustained public work alike in the judicial and political sphere. That will be a great loss for those particular worlds, but from the point of view of advanced movements I think you are very much more needed as the 'great consultant', and we hope that if you are a really good invalid for the next two or threee months we may see you back at Queen Anne's Gate in the autumn and winter. Otherwise we shall have to come all the way to Cloan to get your advice.

We have been seeing a good deal of Beveridge lately. What an abnormally energetic and adventurous administrator he is. It certainly does credit to the environment of the civil service that there should have come out of it a man with so much initiative and such amazing persistence in the pursuit of his objects. He is going over to U.S.A. at the end of this month to attend a conference of American political economists and sociologists on the organisation of research. Apparently the Rockefeller Trust is very keen on what they call *co-ordinated research* as distinguished from the research carried out by one principal researcher with mere assistants, and what puzzles Beveridge is their requirement that psychology should come into economics; because, as he says, there are not any psychologists who can provide the requisite data for economics – they are all too vague and general in their conclusions; however Beveridge is an Oxford man and Oxford apparently detests psychology.

Clifford Sharp came down to spend the week-end with us – we have not seen him of late years as Sidney was displeased with his attitude to the Labour Party. He still professes confidence in the prospect of the Liberal Party surviving and even regaining a position of equality with the Labour Party which would entail a Coalition Government – assuming as he does that Baldwin will be heavily defeated. He told us that Ll.G. told him that he, Ll.G., would not accept office but would insist on representation according to numbers between the two parties. However Sidney still believes that Baldwin will maintain his majority. Anyway you and we will be out of the business, for which I am devoutly thankful as we want to devote all our life to finishing up our research. For the moment I think research into the various problems which confront the Government is more important than participation in politics.

You will have seen that we have settled MacDonald comfortably at Seaham and we are going up in October and I am introducing Ishbel to my Women's Section, which has about 800–1,000 members. If he behaves at all wisely in the constituency it is an absolutely safe seat for life and a very pleasant and cheap constituency.

Will you give my love to Miss Haldane and tell her that I should immensely appreciate a photograph of the Laszlo portrait whenever it is available?

By the way I have been very much impressed with a book by Charles S. Peirce *Chance, Love and Logic*. Apparently he is considered by the Harvard authorities as the founder of pragmatism. I wonder what you would think about it or whether you have read it? There is a lot that I do not agree with and a great deal I do not understand. But some of his ideas seem to me extraordinary illuminating and throw light on the modern developments in thought.

Always affectionately yours
Beatrice Webb
(Mrs Sidney Webb)

832 NLS BEATRICE WEBB TO ELIZABETH HALDANE

'It was Haldane', Beatrice noted on 21 August, 'who created and fostered the "Webb myth" that flowered so agreeably and advantageously for us and our schemes in the first decade of the XXth century . . . What bound us together as associates was our common faith in a deliberately organised society – our belief in the application of science to human relations with a view of betterment. Where we clashed was that *he* believed more than we did in the existing governing class – in big personages whether of Cabinet, City or Court, whilst we held by the common people, served by an elite of unassuming experts, who would appear to be no different in status from the common man.'

Passfield Corner
Liphook
Hants
21/8/28

My very dear friend

Your sad little note reached me after I had heard of the passing of your beloved brother and *our* oldest and most constant friend. It is indeed a comfort to all who knew him that the end came swiftly and painlessly. When we saw him last time we felt that active life was over – though we hoped that he might still be there for months or years to comfort and advise us in the few more years we may still be here. What a noble and creative spirit has been his – that spirit cannot pass away – his words and actions will still go on moulding future generations. He had a great personality – in some ways the greatest I have known – with an all-embracing beneficence, lit up by humour, and based on a broad understanding of men and affairs. It was inevitable that shallow natures with a coarse outlook on life should misunderstand him: but he took this mean depreciation with such splendid serenity and absence of malice – it was no doubt his sense of perspective that enabled him to do so – a sense of relative values arising out of the faith that was in him. What always attracted me was the rare combination of noble purpose with an almost fanatical faith in research as the one and only way of discovering how this noble purpose could be best fulfilled. It is so seldom you find a man or woman who feels deeply the sorrows and miseries of human beings and can yet think out, clearly and decisively, what can be done to make matters better for all concerned.

For you I fear the blow will be as heavy as if I were to lose Sidney or he me – but you will feel that you have been a perfect mate – far more sympathetic and understanding than most wives are to their husbands. A real *kinship* in character and intellect is not easily attained in married life: and it is sad to see how many of one's married friends get separated when they grow old, and cease to share each other's thoughts and feelings.

Perhaps when you come south you will come and stay with us down here – we shall so much enjoy a talk about the past and also about the future.

I go to South Wales on Thursday for ten days in the distressed areas to see for myself what really is happening to the unemployed miners and their families.

Don't think of answering this until you have settled your plans for the future.

With love from Sidney

Ever yours affectionately

Beatrice Webb

P.S. My sister Kate Courtney, who is with us here, sends her warmest sympathy: she remembers so vividly Lord Haldane's courage during the war with regard to his work about the Aliens.

Passfield Corner
Liphook
Hants
25th August 1928

My Dear Friends

I daresay that some of you have wondered why I did not before this send you my usual letter. Well, I thought it better to wait until the vital question was settled, of who was to be the Labour Candidate for the Seaham Division of Durham (and therefore its future Member) in succession to my husband. The Seaham Labour Party has made a splendid choice and I congratulate you most heartily. It will be an honour as well as an advantage to Seaham to have as its Member the Leader of the Labour Party; one who has been Prime Minister, and who, we believe, will at no distant date, by the Nation's decision, again be Prime Minister.

But in advancing your own interests you have also done your level best to further the cause of Labour throughout Great Britain and the British Empire. To be a Member of Parliament at all involves, in these days, no small amount of work. To be a Party Leader is a still greater strain. On the Leader of the Opposition in the House of Commons falls a burden of duty which is severe and continuous. Upon one who has been both Prime Minister and Foreign Secretary even holidays bring constant claims in having to confer with other statesmen, and in never getting free from the responsibility of speeches. When to all this is added the obligation to earn by writing the daily bread of a family, we must all realise that the burden becomes almost too much for continued health.

What the Seaham Labour Party has done in providing Mr MacDonald with a safe seat and, as I can testify, with a most loyal and intelligent body of supporters, may well mean years of added service from him to the State. If a devoted wife may be excused in saying so, I think you did precious well when you got Sidney Webb to represent you in Parliament. But in persuading Ramsay MacDonald to take on the task you have made one big jump to the very top of the political ladder.

But for me there is another and more personal reason for satisfaction; a reason which will appeal to the members of the Womens' Sections of the Seaham Labour Party. For I also, as a helpmate of the Member for Seaham, have found an admirable successor in Miss Ishbel MacDonald, Mr MacDonald's eldest daughter. This young lady is not only attractive and accomplished, but also keenly interested in all the questions which you and I have so often discussed together. From the time she finished her education, only a few years ago, she has worked on Childrens' Care Committees and Maternity Centres, and she is now an elected member of the most important Local Authority in the world – the London County Council. I am glad to tell you that Miss MacDonald will come with me to

Seaham in October, in order to make acquaintance with the members of the Women's Sections. I am now asking Mrs Peacock, as Federation Secretary, to arrange for a Meeting of all the Women's Sections. I hope that we shall have a record attendance on Thursday, the 25th of October.

I wish I could feel equal satisfaction with the industrial position, on which the life of the thousands of households of the Seaham Division depends. The terrible reductions in wages, the frequent loss of shifts, and the disastrous unemployment from which so many are suffering unfortunately continue their baleful influence. The Government seems to be doing nothing to restore prosperity: nothing, even, to protect the Mining population from increasing destitution. The projected changes in the rating system seem to me to promise scarcely any relief in the crushing burdens on the Easington and Seaham Harbour Councils, which compel them to levy such heavy rates, alike on the Colliery Companies (which still further lower Miners' wages), and on the local shopkeepers and Co-operative Societies (which prevent retail prices from falling). Even the promised reduction in railway charges on Coal will bring little help to the Seaham Collieries, which usually need only short hauls by rail. The Ministry of Labour will not even provide training for more than a handful of Seaham youths: and although the proposals of the Transference Board with regard to migration and emigration may assist a few hundred or a few thousand families in the whole Kingdom, the share of the Seaham Division can be but trifling. I wish I could give you a more favourable report. I can see nothing for it, so long as this Government lasts, but grim endurance of what is, in many cases, almost unendurable; such mutual help in the most necessitous cases as the local Lodge and the local Women's Section can organise: and that steadfast loyalty to the Union and its leaders as the Durham men and women have always given. There is a grim irony in giving the only advice that can be given to the miners and the miners' wives. Try to send your young sons away from the mining villages into other occupations, so that they may not compete with their fathers and elder brothers.

As for such service as my husband and I may be able to render, I will only say that, though resigning his seat in Parliament, my husband is not giving up work. Both he and I hope to be able to continue to serve the Labour Party, and the Miners in particular, in whatever opportunities may be afforded to us. We hope that the friendships we have made in the Seaham Division may long endure. We can only repay the confidence and the consideration that have been extended to us by placing such time and strength as may remain to us at the service of those to whom we owe so much.

With best wishes

Yours very sincerely

Beatrice Webb

Collecting material for the concluding chapter of the Poor Law book, Beatrice went on a visit to South Wales to study the distress in the mining valleys and the adequacy of relief measures. She stayed in Cardiff with J. D. Morgan, 'one of the least known but most distinguished local Labour leaders'. (BWD 24 August 1928) William Noble and his wife Emma were Quakers who had just founded the settlement of Maes-yr-haf in the Rhondda Valley as a cultural and educational centre in a derelict area.

Cardiff
[26 Aug 1928]

Dearest one

Here I am after my after-lunch sleep and cup of tea preparing to write out my notes of all the interviews of the last 48 hours. But before doing so I must have a word or two with my dear very dear boy.

I have been most comfortable here and Morgan has done everything possible to take me in his motorcar from one person to another. He is a dear little man, the soul of goodness and very intelligent, an intimate friend of MacDonald and Snowden and knowing everyone who counts in the Labour movement past and present – his wife is as good but not so intelligent as himself, and busies herself about the house with one servant who has her meals with us, to help her – it is a very small house – smaller than our cottage. This morning we motored to Rhondda to arrange for my visits – the Nobles were away until Tuesday, so I arranged to go there to lunch on Wednesday and stay there until Friday morning, spending Thursday in the Aberdare valley with one Proud who seems to be the most active Labour Guardian in the district. Then we went to Pontypridd to interview Evans, a wealthy multiple tradesman who has the administration of the Lord Mayor's Fund, and saw also the Clerk and R.O. of the Pontypridd Union, who are at their wits end to meet their bills with huge loans outstanding. These valleys are desolate – and the men and women standing about in the streets in a listless fashion seem very much on the borderline of starvation. The U.D.C. Council houses, built under the Aberdare scheme and costing nearly £1,000 each, are either crowded by lodgers or empty, and it is difficult to collect either rates or rent. The L.E.A. refuses to fund the children and the Guardians are cutting down their relief, not from policy but because they have not the money to pay their tradesmen bills. I don't know that I have discovered anything new; but I realise the chaos better than I did. The P.L.A. seem to me absolutely chaotic. At Newport the Guardians give or think they give, only to the wife and children of men out of work and therefore say they don't submit the list to the M. of H.!

They ask for no loans and are paying off those they have. They have had no enquiry by the M. of H. Inspector. Nor have they had any at Pontypridd – the M. of H. mainly restricting their borrowing and leaving them to restrict relief. At Pontypridd the S.R.O. said they only sent the numbers up not the particulars – they had not enough help to make out the census. What comes out clearly is that the children and infants would be much better under the L.E.A. and L.H.A. than under the P.L.A. But the chaos is so great and the local administration so incompetent that the transfer of powers from one authority to another will bring about immediately a most untidy mess unless the debt is cancelled. How derating is going to affect them heaven only knows, as it will diminish the revenue from agriculture and there are no productive industries to benefit by the subsidy except agriculture outside Cardiff and Newport. To unravel the state of things would need a good month's investigation with you to get the statistical facts and I to get the psychology of the various parties concerned.

Give my love to Kate and read her any part of this letter that interests her, and tell her that if she liked to send me a contribution towards the relief of distress in the Rhondda valley I would pass it on to the Nobles who are said by everyone to be the wisest persons in the neighbourhood. A Mr Gillett – an idealistic Quaker – was in command at the school during the absence of the Nobles.

Now dear one goodbye – I shall soon be back again and then we will settle down to finish the book.

Ever yours

B. Webb

835 PP BEATRICE TO SIDNEY

Dr Edward Colston Williams was Medical Officer of Health for Glamorgan 1926–43. Erskine Pollock was the husband of the Playnes' adopted daughter. Arthur Jenkins, vice-president of the South Wales Miners Federation and later M.P. for Pontypool, was the father of the Labour politician Roy Jenkins.

Cardiff

[? 27 Aug 1928]

Dearest one

Here I am at the M.O.H. – a villa, with 2 servants and a pleasant genteel wife. Colston Williams himself is an elderly and impressing person – rather like Erskine Pollock to look at but of course considerably better in character and intellect. He is slow on the uptake, says that except in a few patches (how big he cannot tell me) there is no abnormal child or infant malnutrition. The bad patches are places where the coal has been going out of cultivation for some time. The Glamorgan C.C. and the L.E.A.'s are dead against school feeding – partly because of high rates, partly because the Labour element wants money and not food. All there is in the way of feeding is medical feeding to selected children – milk etc. at 11 o'c. I am trying to get the amount but I doubt whether I shall do so. My general impression is that all the local authorites have got into a panic about the debts and the rates and are cutting down expenditure automatically. The evidence about malnutrition is most conflicting: George Newman, who came down here to [?report] is quoted on both sides and I must write and ask him what he did report. There is also the cleavage between the Communist and 'sane' Labour – the one asking for more money for the poor at all times and for all cases – the other getting alarmed at local bankruptcy and tending to cut down every other expenditure, *but* outdoor relief, and even that also.

Of course I have done comparatively little owing to lack of strength.

Yesterday, Sunday, I rested at the Morgans, coming here for tea. Today I shall see Jenkins at Cardiff and I hope Labor Exchange officials and perhaps others. Tomorrow Dr Williams is going to take me about – where to I don't know. On Wednesday I go to Nobles to lunch and I hope to return on Friday – unless something useful intervenes. What strikes me about S.W. is that the advent of Labour representatives of a very inferior sort has [?smashed] up, not only the Poor Law, but the present local government machine. I doubt whether the minor authorities will be able to go on – they are thoroughly incompetent – extravagant and penurious in turn – equally unintelligent.

I am sending this to Grosvenor Road.

Ever yours

Beatrice

## 836 PP SIDNEY TO BEATRICE

Sidney had made a long speech in the House of Commons on the previous day on the Local Government Bill, attacking the proposal to abolish the Boards of Guardians without breaking up the Poor Law system as a whole. Beatrice had worried about the speech as she knew he was an ineffective parliamentary speaker. Sir Josiah Stamp (1880–1941), later Lord Stamp, was a statistician and financial administrator who was a governor and later Chairman of L.S.E.

The Marchioness of Londonderry was a prominent hostess whose friendship with Ramsay MacDonald was too cordial for the susceptibilities of the Labour movement.

[41 Grosvenor Road]
29.11.28

Dear One

I can manage to get off this line of greeting before post time.

I need not tell of congratulations from all and sundry – Sir J. Stamp at the School meeting and so on. The *Daily News* and *Daily Mail* quite cordial and friendly. At the Parliamentary Executive Henderson raised the question of reprinting, which he said many had asked for; but he said such reprints of speeches were not good reading, and he wants a pamphlet signed by me and Miss Lawrence. I said I could not spare the time; but ultimately agreed to dictate 'answers to questions', on the several points of the Bill; Miss L. to do the same; and then Greenwood and W. Henderson to edit, complete and dispose of without further troubling us.

J. R. M. *very* cordial and congratulatory. He told me privately that Lady Londonderry, who was an old friend of his, on Christian name terms, had just written him apologising for not having invited him to a Seaham Harbour Centenary function, and now pressing him to come – what did I think? I said decidedly he must *not*, for reasons that are obvious; and he decided to write very civilly saying they must not shadow each other at Seaham, not in those words but in effect!

The School very flourishing. The building alone has to be insured for £255,000, and the books for £100,000 – not a bad accumulation within 33 years.

Goodnight dear one

Sidney

The trains on Saturday are 2 p.m. and (very bad ones) 2.24 and 3.24 p.m. I am informing [? C. M.] Lloyd, I shall catch the 2 p.m.

## 837 PP SIDNEY WEBB TO WILLIAM ROBSON

Catherine Courtney had just died. In January, 20 years after the Minority Report, the Webbs had finally finished their history of the Poor Law, now plainly on the point of drastic reform. 'To be able to *make* history as well as to write it – or to be modest – to have foreseen, twenty years ago, the exact stream of tendencies which would bring your proposal to fruition, is a pleasurable thought! So the old Webbs are chuckling over their chickens!'

Before taking a long rest Sidney helped to prepare a possible legislative programme for a Labour government. The portrait of the Webbs was hung at a ceremony at L.S.E. which Beatrice enjoyed. 'Altogether our stock is up – or rather we have, through old age, ceased to have detractors – no one troubles about aged folk except those who respect and like them.' (BWD 16 January 1929)

41 Grosvenor Road
Westminster Embankment
27.2.29

The *only* address until 30 June 1929

My dear Robson

I am afraid that owing to many affairs, complicated now by Lady Courtney's death, my wife and I are quite unable to give any useful counsel about the proposed quarterly review. I am sorry, but it is a matter which must be undertaken by younger people!

I can think of no ideal Editor, who is available, and recognisable as ideal. I see no objection, under such circumstances, to an Editorial Board, on which even half-a-dozen persons might find places, including Woolf, Lowes Dickinson, Hammond, Laski, Tawney, Hobson and Cole. But there should be someone, perhaps as Chairman, who would lead, act and when necessary throw a decisive weight into the scales, when opinions were evenly divided. And the idea of such a Board seems to me feasible *only* if all the members were not only enthusiastic but also sympathetic to each other – a somewhat difficult thing to ensure.

I fear that J. A. Hobson would seem, to the world, too much associated with what is considered 'crankiness' to make him a suitable sole editor. I should think Delisle Burns would be a better figure to present to the world. You must avoid the septuagenarians!

But, as I said at the beginning of this letter, you really must 'leave us out', at any rate until we return – if we can get away at all – in June next.

Yours very truly

Sidney Webb

# 7. The second Labour government

## June 1929 – July 1931

As the general election of 1929 approached the Labour Party was still sharply divided. The I.L.P., effectively a party within a party, was the spokesman of the non-Communist left, arguing that even if the policy set out in *Labour and the Nation* were to be implemented it would make no real impact on the class structure and economic organisation of Britain. MacDonald and other party leaders, who at the height of the 1929 boom had no inkling of the crippling collapse which lay ahead, were not willing to put a timetable on the programme or to make any definite commitments before taking office. In fact they doubted whether Labour would come back strong enough to form another government; and even if it were the largest party, it would have to depend on the votes of the much-divided Liberals. The only problem which was clearly a priority, despite the improvement in the economy, was the continuing high level of unemployment. And MacDonald's own interest in the continuing diplomatic consequences of the Versailles treaty – reparation and disarmament – made it certain that Labour would pay much attention to foreign policy.

The election was the first to be fought on a full adult franchise, women having at last been given the vote on the same terms as men: the 'flapper' vote enlarged the electorate from 21 to 29 million. Labour, with bye-election gains, was defending 162 seats; and the party was contesting virtually all the seats in the country for the first time. Its popular vote rose from 5.5 million to 8.3 million and it came back with 287 seats, as against 261 for the Conservatives and 59 for the Liberals, who thus held the balance in the House of Commons.

On 30 May, before the poll, Beatrice anticipated that a Labour success 'would probably send Sidney into the House of Lords and another Cabinet post'. She thought that 'Sidney would rather like to be in office again, and that I should dislike it . . . But I doubt whether the remainder of our lives would be much affected'.

Baldwin resigned three days after the result and MacDonald, now backed by the largest group in Parliament, had no hesitation about forming another minority government. It was not at first certain that MacDonald would offer Sidney a post: the first offer was of a peerage without an appointment. When, on 6 June, Sidney was offered a peerage and the Colonial Office he was delighted: he had begun his career as a civil servant in that department. Beatrice noted a further coincidence. Joseph Chamberlain, whom she might have married, and Sidney, whom she did marry, had both been at the Board of Trade and the Colonial Office. Sidney became Lord Passfield.

The main issues which Sidney had immediately to confront as Colonial Secretary were Kenya, where there was concern with the pressure of the white settlers on the native reserves; Egypt, where Britain's pro-consular regime was running into problems of nationalism; India, where the Indian National Congress led by Gandhi, was moving towards a civil disobedience campaign; and

Palestine, ruled by Britain under a League of Nations mandate and in the shadow of a wartime commitment to a National Home for the Jews, where anti-Zionist rioting by the indigenous Arabs had raised the question of Jewish immigration and land settlement.

MacDonald was again Prime Minister, but Henderson had become Foreign Secretary – a post in which he was to perform with credit. Beatrice's brother-in-law, Parmoor, was Lord President and leader of the House of Lords. Philip Snowden was Chancellor of the Exchequer, J. H. Thomas was Lord Privy Seal and Clynes was Home Secretary. Sydney Olivier was not offered an appointment. There were important newcomers in the government. Hugh Dalton was Under-Secretary for Foreign Affairs, Sir Oswald Mosley was Chancellor of the Duchy of Lancaster, sharing responsibility for unemployment with Thomas; Arthur Greenwood was Minister of Health; the left-wing was represented by George Lansbury as First Commissioner of Works; Sankey became Lord Chancellor; Margaret Bondfield was Minister of Labour; and Sir William Jowitt, elected as a Liberal, crossed the floor to become Attorney-General.

Beatrice summed up her reactions after the government settled in. 'In home affairs I doubt the zeal of the P.M. and Snowden and the capacity and courage of Thomas, Greenwood and Margaret Bondfield. In foreign affairs it may be that this Cabinet is vastly superior to the last.' (BWD 26 July 1929)

## 838 HL SIDNEY WEBB TO SIR HERBERT SAMUEL

Samuel had been out of the House of Commons for ten years, though he had been chairman of the Liberal Party 1927–29, and returned to Parliament in 1929 as M.P. for Darwen. Two years later he became the Leader of the Liberal Parliamentary Party.

[41 Grosvenor Road]
12.6.29

My dear Samuel

Many thanks for your kind expressions of appreciation, and cordial offer of co-operation. (With regard to the peerage our feelings are, to say the least, very 'mixed', but we decided that I could not refuse to *serve* if asked – and that anything necessarily incident to serving had got to be accepted!)

Of course, there is an almost endless succession of things on which we ought to be able to join forces. But I wonder what you meant by the phrase in your last speech as to applications of the Socialist theory being outside the sphere of possible agreement. I should have thought that you (and I) had been supporting 'applications of the Socialist theory' for the last twenty years – in collective ownership (e.g. municipal housing; B.B.C. wireless; the electric grid etc. etc.); in collective regulation (e.g. Factory Acts); in collective provision (£350 millions a year for Social Welfare schemes); and finally, Collective Taxation deliberately for the purpose of equalising, *pro tanto*, wealth distribution (e.g. progressive Death Duties,

Supertax etc.). But these constitute, as was said 40 years ago, the 'Fourfold Path'. Every one of them would have horrified Mr Gladstone.

However, this is only my way of 'poking fun' at the very necessary attempt to draw some line! It may be nonetheless practically useful if we none of us can tell exactly *where* the line is drawn because we can then deal with each case on its merits!

I hope you will come to Passfield Corner again, when we could talk it over. My wife sends her kindest regards.

Yours very truly

Sidney Webb

839 BOD BEATRICE WEBB TO J. L. HAMMOND

When the Webbs discussed the question of Sidney's peerage Beatrice was uneasy. 'My instinct was against the use of a title and Sidney, tho' feeling less strongly, acquiesced. But breaking a convention which all accept needs something more than mere dislike, which may arise from distorted pride, unconscious superiority, self-advertisement or other forms of egotism.' (BWD 20 June 1929) She persuaded herself that it was 'a question of manners and not of morals; and a question which was different for the peer and the wife of the peer'. Sidney was bound to use the title for official purposes; she was not required to use it privately. 'By merely passing over my right to use a title I help to undermine the foundations of British snobbishness . . . An honour ignored is an honour deflated.' Her decision to remain Mrs Sidney Webb had the additional advantage, she felt, that she would not be drawn into the whirlpool of Court and Society receptions: 'I *want* to be dropped out of the Buckingham Palace list'. When her decision was published it was in fact taken more as a feminist gesture than a protest against snobbery.

She was not, however, to escape so easily. On 31 July Ramsay MacDonald wrote a personal note to Sidney. (PP)

> You are getting me into hot water. Stamfordham [Lord Stamfordham (1849–1931) was private secretary to Queen Victoria and George V] drew my attention this evening to an H.M. Govt. invitation to Dominion teachers 'with the Royal Arms' upon it, which says that Lord Passfield and Mrs Webb will receive. They object most strongly to this and have referred the matter to me. It is rather awkward as it does set a precedent which needs the consent of the King, who is the boss of the Peerage, and without consultation with me who am the channel of communication. Cannot you meet us on the matter? There is really no principle involved. In this matter poor Mrs W. is pinned on to you and you drag her up automatically. I promised to put these views before you and the King wants to know your reply.

After this letter Sidney instructed his office to omit Beatrice's name from all future invitations; she decided not to appear at official functions. 'Let me be considered your morganatic wife, living in a country cottage', Beatrice suggested to Sidney. (BWD 4 August 1929) In the event she was not wholly able to avoid some official occasions or evade the formal curtsey to royalty which she found most distasteful.

41 Grosvenor Road
Westminster Embankment
June 18th 1929

My dear Mr Hammond

How nice of you to write that little note of congratulation. You must have been amused to hear of my husband's appointment after our talk about it that morning you came to Cheyne Walk. He did not in the least expect to be in J.R.M.'s Cabinet and was very unwilling to go to the Lords. But I think he is enjoying his work – certainly the Colonial Office is ever so much more interesting than the Board of Trade. Also he has a romantic feeling about it as those ten years in the Colonial Office constituted a sort of university training for him.

You and your wife must come and stay with us at Passfield Corner in the autumn and talk over things.

Always yours sincerely
Beatrice Webb
(Mrs Sidney Webb)

*Private.* By the way *I* am going to remain Mrs Sidney Webb!; and Sidney will resume the old name on the termination of office. His new name will be, for public purposes, 'Passfield'.

840 PP BEATRICE TO SIDNEY

41 Grosvenor Road
Westminster Embankment
[? early summer 1929]

Dearest one

Here are a few communications. Also Robson's criticism (please keep or return) – a good debating point similar to Laski's. But the judiciary already interprets laws (T.U. judgements) and its possible intervention in declaring Acts *ultra vires* is more than set off by the existence of a second chamber. How many of the legislative assemblies of the world are based on written constitutions and therefore subject to *ultra vires*? What about the Scandinavian legislature? However, it is a useful criticism and we should have to meet it.

The two ladies arrived in excellent form – very jolly. They brought me some cowslips from Standish fields. They are enthusiastic about the house and the new sitting-room. I read *Lady Chatterley* yesterday afternoon and sent it back to Dick [? Meinertzhagen]. What strikes me most is the inanity of all the people in it, *on every other subject except sex*. The sex episodes are the only part of the book which are worth reading – all the more so, as they are purely physical, without any other human faculty, intellectual or emotional – in fact – subhuman. What a craze this subhuman business is? We listened to some modern music last night – a regular zoological gardens. It is a quaint reaction from the supernatural being, and the superman. When shall we reach the robot – not even an animal, as the hero of romance?

Ever yours

Beatrice

841 WI SIDNEY WEBB TO CHAIM WEIZMANN

Chaim Weizmann (1874–1952) was born in Russia but became a teacher of chemistry at the University of Manchester in 1913. He became an active Zionist and played a leading role in the events leading to the Balfour Declaration of 1917 in favour of a Jewish National home in Palestine. In 1920 he became secretary of the World Zionist Organisation. In 1929 the British government agreed to a Jewish Agency in Palestine; this provoked fierce reactions among the indigenous Arab population. The British White Paper of 1931, for which Webb was responsible, was considered to be adverse to the Jews and Weizmann was forced to resign at the ensuing Zionist Congress. He later became the first president of Israel.

'I admire Jews and dislike Arabs', Beatrice noted on 2 September 1929, but she was strongly anti-Zionist. She thought the Zionist case 'hypocritical nonsense' which could as easily justify white settlers in Kenya as Russian Jews in Jerusalem. 'Shall we come, in the last resort, to a scientifically planned distribution of this planet's surface among different races according to relative fitness standardised by a controlled birth-rate and a national minimum of civilised life for each race – coupled with anaesthesia for all unwanted infants?'

Sidney, apparently, had no strong feelings. He had, Beatrice observed, 'lost all his old irritability and aggressiveness; he is a most pleasant person to live and work with; he has become complacent towards the world, minimising all present trouble, optimistic about the future'.

The Marquess of Reading had been Viceroy of India 1921–26, then president of Imperial Chemical Industries. He became Foreign Secretary in 1931. He was a leading figure in British Jewry.

[Colonial Office]
20th August 1929

Dear Dr Weizmann

Thank you for your letter of the 19th instant regarding the situation in Palestine, which, I need hardly assure you, continues to engage my earnest attention.

I will now take the points which you raise in the order in which they appear in your letter.

(1) I fully agree that as complete a settlement as possible of the Wailing Wall question is urgently necessary. I had indeed already taken steps which would, I hoped, have enabled a definite settlement to be effected in the near future had it not been for the dislocation caused by the outbreak of

disorder and it may be necessary in present circumstances to reconsider the position. As soon as conditions are more settled I expect to receive definite recommendations from the High Commissioner. In the meantime I await with interest any suggestions which Lord Reading may be good enough to offer towards a solution of this difficult and urgent problem.

(2) Your second point concerns the disarming of Jewish special constables and others. The unofficial reports which have appeared in the press, and which seem to correspond to some extent with the information on which you base your remarks, are shown by a report which I have received from the Acting High Commissioner to be both misleading and inaccurate. As you will see from this morning's newspapers steps were taken to correct misapprehensions by the issue of a communiqué from the Colonial Office last night. As you may wish to have a somewhat fuller statement I may tell you that the ascertained facts are as follows:

On the 23rd and 24th of August the Government put into force the emergency provisions of the Police Ordinance under which, *inter alia*, any persons found in any public place in possession of a weapon which might be used in a disturbance is liable to arrest without warrant and to certain penalties. This provision is of course applicable to all sections of the population.

At an early stage of the disturbances special constables were enrolled, and armed by the police, and of these a number were Jewish. On the 17th of August, following on representations from a Moslem deputation to the effect that in this respect the assurance of the Government that it had not armed the Jews was inaccurate, the Officer Administering the Government gave orders for the Jewish special constables to be disarmed. This action was taken with the concurrence of his civil and military advisers. The Officer Administering the Government reports that the decision was an unpalatable one to take in view of its apparent harshness to the individuals whom it affected but there can be no doubt that it was taken on an unassailable principle and was in the best interests of the Jews as a whole since it removed an important irritant of the whole Arab population, both in Palestine and Trans-Jordan.

It is of course natural that the Jews in Palestine, many of whom have been subjected during the last few days to bloodthirsty and ruthless attacks, should be anxious to be armed by the Government. It is, however, the considered opinion of the Officer Administering the Government that the Jewish Leaders seem to have failed to appreciate the greater danger to the Jewish population and the possibility of a general rising throughout the country if their request had been granted.

(3) You next raise the question of compensating the Jewish victims of the outbreak. It is primarily for the Palestine administration to consider what steps should be taken for the immediate relief of sufferers, and I expect to receive a full report on the position from the High Commissioner

at as early a date as possible. I will satisfy myself that all that can properly be done by the Government of Palestine for the relief of distress will be done without delay. I wish to make it quite clear that I cannot as at present advised accept the suggestion that His Majesty's Government should make themselves responsible for paying compensation for damage arising out of the present disorder.

(4) Your fourth point is a request that His Majesty's Government may consider the propriety of relieving Mr Luke and Mr Cust of their duties. While making every allowance for the depth of your feelings at the recent tragic occurrences in Palestine, I cannot but express surprise that you should have made such a suggestion. It is surely obvious that the first step must be to get at the facts by searching investigation of all the circumstances leading up to the disorders, and the action taken by the local administration in connection with them.

(5) Your fifth point concerns the issue by His Majesty's Government of a statement as to the execution of their obligations under the Mandate in regard to the establishment of the Jewish national home. This is a point upon which I have also received representations from Lord Melchett, and I can only repeat what I have already said to him, namely, that in my opinion it would be premature at the present moment to publish a statement of future policy. The moment is inappropriate and publication might give rise to misunderstandings which would only be an embarrassment to those who have the welfare of Palestine at heart. It is, however, not too soon to consider the terms of such a statement which will not be long delayed, and I will carefully weigh any suggestions with regard to its terms which you may wish to offer.

Later on in your letter you ask if the Zionist Organisation may have an opportunity of offering observations on the proposed terms of any statement on the situation in Palestine to be made on behalf of His Majesty's Government, at Geneva within the next few days. Such a statement had already been prepared for immediate transmission to Geneva. This was based on official reports from the Palestine Government and even had time permitted it would not in my opinion have been fitting that its terms should have been discussed beforehand with the Zionist Organisation, whose version of the events could obviously not be accepted without full enquiry where it conflicted with official information.

(6) *Immigration Certificates.* As you are aware the Palestine Government agreed shortly before the outbreak of disorder to the issue of an increased number of certificates. The question of any further issue in the immediate future might, however, raise the whole question of the Government's immigration policy, and it is clearly not possible to deal with it adequately at the moment. It is open to you to raise this question as soon as conditions become more normal and every effort will be made to give it sympathetic consideration if you do so, but I think that I should say that

if you have in mind immigration on a scale so large as to be incompatible with existing policy, I cannot, as at present advised, hold out any hope that it will be possible to meet your wishes.

Yours very truly

Passfield

842 NLS BEATRICE WEBB TO ELIZABETH HALDANE

Sir Sydney Cockerell (1867–1962) had been secretary to William Morris; he was the literary executor of Morris, Thomas Hardy and W. S. Blunt. From 1908 to 1937 he was Director of the Fitzwilliam Museum, Cambridge.

At the end of August the Webbs made their first aeroplane flights, from Brooklands airfield, in the private plane of their old friend Sir Horace Plunkett, who had taken to flying late in life. They moved out of Grosvenor Road on 30 September, temporarily taking a furnished flat as neighbours to the Shaws in Whitehall Court.

Snowden had just returned from The Hague where, at an international meeting on reparations, he had made a strong defence of British interests and reached a popular agreement.

Passfield Corner
Liphook
Hants
August 30th 1929

My dear Elizabeth

I wonder when you are coming back to London? I assume that you have been in Scotland all the summer and will be during the early autumn. Do let us know when you would be free to come down and stay with us here for a weekend. What about the weekend towards the end of October or beginning of November? It is so much easier to fix up distant than near dates.

Sidney is thoroughly enjoying his job, in spite of the anxiety about Palestine and the far more difficult question of Kenya. About Palestine; he thinks there must have been some very bad staff work in the Palestinian government not to have been aware of what seems to be an organised movement. But it is easy to be wise after the event, and there will have to be a very careful enquiry. What a gorgeous success Snowden has made; and Henderson also in a quieter way. It seems that the Labour Party has a particular talent for foreign affairs; which is not altogether to be wondered at, seeing that the principal men in the Labour movement have probably travelled far more widely and in a far more effective way than the members of the Conservative government. It is one thing to go touring about the two continents, and another thing going as a delegate to important international assemblies, as these men are constantly doing. Whether Thomas will be as successful in dealing with unemployment as Snowden has been in securing an extra two millions for Great Britain I have my doubts. It is a far more complicated problem, and I am not sure that Jim's rough and ready ways are best suited for any success. However, Oswald Mosley is said to be doing very well as a subordinate colleague.

When we meet I want to talk to you about Lord Haldane's portrait for the School. We have arranged to have the portrait of Bishop Creighton which Mrs Creighton prefers, and of which she is in present possession, copied by a lady strongly recommended by Cockerell of the Fitzwilliam Museum, and constantly employed by the leading picture dealers for copying. We should like to employ her to copy some portrait of Lord Haldane, if Creighton's portrait proves successful. Personally, I do not like Laszlo's portrait and I should very much like to see any other portrait which you think would be suitable and available. Is there not one at the Inns of Court that is really characteristic? Of course if Beveridge and you prefer Laszlo's, we would accept the choice. We very much want to have portraits of him and of Creighton hanging on each side of the fireplace.

'The Inevitability of Gradualness' in the application of the Socialist creed supported by the Law on the one hand and the Church on the other, seems very characteristic of British development?

We shall be mainly here until the end of September and then mainly at 2 Whitehall Court, where we have taken a small furnished flat for six months; but we shall spend our weekends here.

Always affectionately yours
Beatrice Webb
(Mrs Sidney Webb)

843 WI SIDNEY WEBB TO CHAIM WEIZMANN

Colonial Office
Downing Street, S.W.1
4th September 1929

*Private*

Dear Dr Weizmann

In reply to your telegram to the High Commissioner, Sir John Chancellor asks me to transmit to you his reply as under:

'Your telegram 30th August I deeply regret loss of life at Safed where there is now adequate military force to protect the town, and neighbouring colonies. Secretary of State will doubtless make clear to you reasons which have compelled the Government not to arm Jews. I believe military forces now sufficiently strong to afford protection to colonies.'

I am sending you this personal letter, rather than make it an official matter, because it is not quite in order for you to telegraph to the High Commissioner, and yet I did not like to leave you without a reply. It would be kind of you not to do this again.

Yours very truly
Passfield

## 844 PP SIDNEY TO BEATRICE

The Webbs had met Lord Lugard (1858–1943) when he was Governor of Hong Kong 1907–12 and they were on their way home from Japan. They then 'singled him out as the wisest and most humane Governor we had known'. (BWD 13 August 1929) He was currently pressing Webb to curb the 'barbaric capitalism' of the white settlers in Kenya. Joseph Oldham, a former missionary, was on the Advisory Committee on Education in the Colonies 1925–36.

[2 Whitehall Court]
24.9.29

Dear One

I am sorry I failed to write yesterday, but I was very fully occupied. In the evening I went to my official dinner (of 'mycologists' = plant disease investigators from all parts of the Empire). Sydney Buxton was there on my right, to respond (as Chairman of the Committee directing the above) to the toast which I had to propose. He was very friendly and of wish to be helpful: asking kindly after you. I had a whole hour's friendly talk with the P.M. yesterday, when he received Lugard and Oldham, with me present (which was, I think, not what Oldham had intended!). We spoke them fair, but non-committal. I stayed on when they left, for various items, and then we talked at large. He was criticising Clynes and Greenwood for some, as he thought, imperfect documents and decisions. I am afraid this is merely a trick of the mind; a very natural one, as things must inevitably be done not 'just so', as one would prefer. It is, I suppose an almost invariable weakness of Supreme Chiefs, who cannot, in the nature of things, do everything themselves – nor yet learn to be *quite* free from a 'superiority complex'. My own attitude, I think, in these inter-ministerial relations is to be prompt and outspoken in praise of others where I can, and to be silent where I cannot!

But then, they are not my subordinates, nor I in any sense a Supreme Chief!

I have been too much pressed to finish this letter properly – spending an hour with P.M. and Lord Reading as to difficulties of Palestine Commission, and then asked to stay to tea with the P.M. alone – he is rather too conscious of gathering clouds!

I met Albert Ball, who asked after 'Mrs Sidney Webb – I believe that is right?'

Goodnight dear one

Sidney

## 845 PP SIDNEY TO BEATRICE

Sir Leslie Scott (1869–1950) was a Conservative M.P. who was Solicitor-General in 1922, later a lord justice of appeal. The autobiography of W. A. S. Hewins, first Director of L.S.E., was *The Apologia of an Imperialist* published in 1929. During the first phase of the government's life Sidney also acted as Dominion Secretary.

2 Whitehall Court
S.W.1
14/10/29

Dear One

I have had the busiest day! Stamfordham's business concerned only the succession to the Governor-Generalship (complicated enough). I attended the Lord Chancellor's reception at 1 p.m., in the Royal Gallery of the H. of L. Many of the lawyers asked after you, notably Sir Leslie Scott who was most effusive – he said he thought it ought to have been Lady Passfield and Mr Sidney Webb! Sir Nathan Row, now a Visitor in Lunacy, was also enthusiastic about you, and particularly the dinner he came to when A.J.B. [Balfour] and some other magnate was there.

I have now to rush off to a Cabinet Committee about our Dominion Constitutional difficulties, but I seize a few minutes to send you a greeting of love.

I read Hewins' book in the train – very good about us and the School, but intensely egotistical and really devoted throughout to proving that *he* has been the author and inspirer of all the Conservative politics of the past 25 years, except the Conservative leaders were stupid, ignorant and blundering. It is a monumental exhibition – an inside record of all his intrigues.

Now dear one Goodnight

Sidney

846 PP SIDNEY TO BEATRICE [*incomplete*]

Dennison Ross was a Labour candidate in St Pancras at a bye-election in 1928 and again in 1929.

Sir James Arthur Salter (1881–1975) later Lord Salter, was a civil servant who made his reputation in the wartime shipping control, becoming subsequently a member of many public bodies and Gladstone Professor of Politics at Oxford 1934–44. After 1945 he entered Parliament and held office in the 1951 Conservative government.

2 Whitehall Court
S.W.1
24.10.29

Dear One

I had my little meeting with half-a-dozen I.L.P. members plus [Leonard] Woolf and Dennison Ross (the latter a very able, but very fanatical person). Really, their only effective point was the maintenance of the Official Majority in Kenya – to which I think they attach undue importance. At any rate that is the existing position which has admittedly proved very unsatisfactory. All the same, the clamour is so great that it is possible the Cabinet will refuse to take my recommendation on this point. The only effect would be that any Governor of Kenya would have to face a storm of opposition from the Settlers. Meanwhile all the other constitutional improvements that I am elaborating would come into operation, but would have to work in a very hostile atmosphere.

I met at lunch Sir Arthur Salter, who was enthusiastic about *My Apprenticeship*, which he said was in the very first rank of autobiographies. It was *the* description of Victorian Society. I thought him able but not necessarily a Superman – insignificant in appearance.

### 847 PP BEATRICE TO SIDNEY

For all her feeling of exhaustion with entertainment Beatrice did more than her duty as a private hostess. By 1930 she had given lunch to over 200 Labour M.P.s and a number of dinners to other political personalities; the weekend round at Passfield Corner also continued. Lord Amulree (1860–1942), a lawyer and industrial arbitrator, became Secretary of State for Air in 1930.

Passfield Corner
Liphook
Hants

No letters for you to answer 5/12/29

Dearest one

One line of greeting. Our luncheon party went on till 2.45 or 3 o'clock – talking in little groups. Amulree said that your speech the previous night was perfect, 'you caught the atmosphere of the House'; Poor old Parmoor a fumbler. Laski, by the way, volunteered that he would accept a peerage – he thought that Cole and Tawney ought to be also there. So that's that. Laski would be useful in the House and can probably afford to go there. Everything is right here except that Mrs Oliver had a bad fainting fit yesterday – but she has had them before. The Connaught Co. sent the [*word illegible*] house and offer to supply extra parts. The gale and rain raged all night and is as bad this morning – the floods will be awful presently – as the ground is soaked. I am glad to be here, rather than in London, though it is lonely without you and I don't feel strong enough to start work. I shan't do more than keep up the Home fires and entertain while you are in office and when you return I shall be too aged to work, even as your assistant. However, I can always write in my diary – I have written about 24,000 words since we came home – think how you will enjoy reading it when I am gone. To edit and annotate your wife's diary will be better than the B.M. subject catalogue – as a light job for your *real* old age – say between 90–100.

Ever your darling

Beatrice Webb

Malcolm John MacDonald (b. 1901), the son of the Prime Minister, fought Bassetlaw twice before winning the seat in 1929: he was also a Labour member of the L.C.C. He left the Labour Party in 1931 with his father and held both Cabinet and diplomatic offices until 1966. His primary interest was in Dominion and colonial policy.

The Webbs had met and liked Sir John Hope Simpson, during their visit to India: Sidney was shortly to appoint him as chairman of a special mission to Palestine. In India they had also met the famous cricketer, the Maharajah of Nawanagar (1872–1933), known as 'Ranjitsinji', who had become the political leader of the Indian princes.

At the end of the year Beatrice reviewed the state of the government. Unemployment had risen by a million in the past twelve months and she thought that social and industrial problems had been left to ministers of inferior quality, especially J. H. Thomas whom she dismissed as a boozer who had lost his nerve and found refuge with the rich racing set.

In February Beatrice entertained the Soviet ambassador and his wife, who were to have a significant influence on her political views. Gregori Sokolnikov, subsequently lost in the purges, was a Ukrainian who had been Commissar for Finance in 1921–26, and was ambassador in London 1929–32.

[2 Whitehall Court]
8.1.30

Dear One

I was glad to get your greeting just before I went off to a Cabinet at *9.30 a.m.* (!) – about South Wales Coal, which, we think, is being temporarily settled, by great exertions of Graham and Shinwell.

We then had consultation with Henderson etc. about Palestine, quite satisfactory, but putting off further, owing to his going away to Geneva etc. until end of month. I am to continue with Dr W. [Weizmann] alone (with Malcolm) on some points.

Then I spent the afternoon seeing one person after another, and arranging a variety of matters.

It is very cold here, and foggy in parts. Tonight I have Hope Simpson dining with me at U.S. Club at 8 p.m.

I have declined an invitation from 'Ranji', the cricketer-Maharajah, for next Monday night. I don't particularly want to go; and you may be coming that afternoon – we may as well have the evening together! I have never known him, and I don't feel inclined to meet the Hindoos or Moslems on India in the present critical phase.

Now dear one Goodnight

Sidney

849 HRCUT SIDNEY WEBB TO EDWARD PEASE

The Webbs gave up the flat in Whitehall Court and moved to a less expensive flatlet in Victoria Street at the beginning of April.

Before the Baldwin government resigned it had put through the Local Government Act of 1929 which abolished Boards of Guardians and transferred responsibility for poor relief – with the exception of the able-bodied unemployed – to county and county borough authorities who were to establish public assistance committees to deal with money relief and take charge of institutions for the destitute. Though the Poor Law System still applied to the able-bodied, the persistence of mass unemployment through the depression years made it necessary to establish an Unemployment Assistance Board in 1934. The principles of the Minority Report and the policy of social insurance, which had seemed so opposed in 1909, were gradually fusing into what became after 1945 a national system of social security. In an epilogue to their Poor Law history the Webbs concluded that the 1929 Act 'finally disposes of the "Principles of 1834"'.

Passfield Corner
Liphook
Hants
6.4.30

Dear Pease

Thanks for writing and for remembering. It is a coincidence that it is just 21 years since Minority Report; this being sufficiently near the expiration of the mythical 'Time Lag' which, we say, exists in England between the idea and its adoption!

I am afraid that many useful Guardians like Mrs Pease are being dropped out but most of these will, I believe, soon get back in some capacity, because the present Councillors can't cope with all the work, or don't want to.

I happen to be exceptionally pressed with official work, but shall manage to stay here for the Easter week. Could you and Mrs Pease come here to lunch in that week (*not* Easter Tuesday)? Let us know in advance which day is likely (you can always telephone in the morning if you are not coming).

We have given up finally 41 Grosvenor Road; and also moved from 2 Whitehall Court – to P.6 Artillery Mansions, Victoria St S.W.1. Tel. 2834 Vic (please note this). But Passfield Corner is our permanent address.

With kindest regards from my wife and myself to you both – we shall soon be in the 50th year of acquaintance!

Yours

Sidney Webb

## 850 PP SIDNEY TO BEATRICE

Webb was caught between the conflicting pressures of the white settlers in Kenya, who sought wider powers for the Legislative Council which they controlled, and the defenders of African rights in the Labour Party who argued for a common electoral roll for blacks and whites based on a 'civilisation' test. Webb's Kenya proposals were published as a White Paper in June 1930: they emphasised the principle of 'trusteeship' for British colonies and emphasised that 'the interests of the African Natives must be paramount': where these interests conflicted with those of immigrants they should prevail. As the argument continued Sidney set up a joint committee of both houses of Parliament which sat until June 1931. This committee looked towards an eventual East African federation but the Labour government fell soon after its report was published.

In March 1930 the Indian National Congress launched its campaign of passive resistance to British rule: Labour policy had not moved beyond the hope of an agreement that India might sometime achieve Dominion status.

A special commission led by Sir Walter Shaw (1863–1937), a well-known colonial judge, had reported on the recent disturbances in Palestine. It had gone beyond its immediate brief to declare that a national home for the Jews was inconsistent with the Mandate. MacDonald, upset by this, suggested that the leader of the South African opposition, Jan Christian Smuts (1870–1950), should be asked to review the Mandate; on second thoughts, Smuts was considered too sympathetic to Zionism and Hope Simpson was asked to study the problems of land settlement, immigration and development.

P.6 Artillery Mansions
Victoria St
30/4/30

Dear One

1) Here is the schedule of Colonial Office Conference engagements so far.

2) The Cabinet agreed today to my Kenya proposals, but still subject to my seeing C. R. Buxton and Snell privately, so as to get them to persuade the malcontents on that side!

3) Prospects in India are very bad – serious trouble is feared, much worse than the present.

4) Hope Simpson has arrived, but asks to be excused coming to us. He starts, via Geneva, on Tuesday next, and must go to Liverpool for weekend to see his daughter. His wife is only today leaving Athens for Geneva, and then for England. Hope Simpson has to return to Greece for the rest of this year, after the Palestine trip. He is full of life and eagerness for his Palestine job, for which I am sure we are lucky to get him.

Goodnight dear one

Sidney

## 851 BOD BEATRICE WEBB TO LORD PONSONBY

Arthur Ponsonby was now a Labour peer. Beatrice was preparing a broadcast for delivery on 24 July. She proposed to call it 'How to Make the British Parliamentary Constitution Equal to its Task', but it was transmitted as 'Taking the Strain Off Parliament'. She drafted an outline and submitted it for comment to Ponsonby, Harold Laski and C. M. Lloyd. She thought the talk might be developed into an autumn lecture for the Fabians and, when Sidney retired, a book.

Her mind was setting towards two main ideas. First, to create different organs of government for internal and foreign affairs; secondly, to create national agencies to take over most public services from smaller local authorities.

[Passfield Corner]
May 14th 1930

Dear Lord Ponsonby

I waited until I had my secretary, to answer your letter about the scheme.

Have you considered how very revolutionary your proposals would be compared to mine? In my scheme the supreme sovereignty is vested, *as at present*, in the King, Lords and Commons, and is concentrated, *as at present*, by statute and custom, in the House of Commons. With regard to the powers of the new Assembly, my proposal follows the precedent of all the devolution from Parliament which has yet happened in Great Britain. Within the United Kingdom the administration of social services has already been largely devolved by Act of Parliament on local Assemblies and their Executives. In Northern Ireland the control of the local administration has been given over to the North Ireland Parliament together with new legislation. [Irish affairs: *written in margin*] The new national Assembly for the United Kingdom would approximate in its activities to the North of Ireland Assembly and be somewhat similar in its constitution to the London County Council. There is, therefore, no revolutionary change at all but merely a further development of devolution of home services to subordinate bodies according to well established principles alike in structure and function.

On the other hand you propose to abolish the House of Lords, and to create another Assembly representing the United Kingdom and, I assume, Northern Ireland, with jurisdiction over all internal and foreign affairs including defence, Colonies and Dominions. Meanwhile your House of Commons, which I assume has created this Assembly, is degraded by being left with jurisdiction over a smaller area? (Northern Ireland excluded and the whole of the Colonies, not to mention the Dominions.) It is also debarred from dealing with national defence and therefore from declaring war or making peace. But this is not all. You propose that the new Assembly shall supply the House of Commons with an Executive after its own heart. That is to say, the joint set of Ministers will all be selected by the new Assembly which will therefore control the two Cabinets; its own and that of the House of Commons?

The supreme sovereignty, so far as I understand your scheme, will be vested in a joint meeting of the new Assembly and the old House of Commons? (the latter having no control over its Executive). This is a very revolutionary proposal. So far as experience goes of sovereignty vested in *two separately elected assemblies* the outlook is not promising – even when these assemblies are concerned with exactly the same business. But your own criticism of the scheme seems to be conclusive. There is no likelihood of the two Assemblies being exactly of the same political complexion. Even if one party dominated both Assemblies, it would certainly have a different proportion of members in each Assembly. But if we are to judge from experience, there is a distinct tendency for such Assemblies and Executives as the London County Council to be of the opposite party to that dominating the House of Commons. For instance, in the first eighteen years the Cabinets were mainly Conservative, but the dominant party on the L.C.C. was progressive. In the next eighteen years the Cabinet was predominantly Liberal or Coalition Liberal, whereas the London County Council was throughout Conservative. And seeing that the two national Assemblies will have to specialise on external affairs on the one hand, and domestic administration on the other, there would be no kind of reason why the same party should dominate both Assemblies?

Excuse this very rambling criticism which may arise from my misunderstanding of your scheme. But you gave me a shorthand version of it. Why not elaborate it?

What I want to start is not an agitation in favour of my own particular plan, but a detailed study of all the possible ways of remedying the evils of the present state of things. What I fear is that through apathy and failure to take thought, the British people will drift into inefficiency and chaos and that we shall then either become decadent or have to submit to some form of dictatorship.

Always yours sincerely
Beatrice Webb

852 BEV SIDNEY WEBB TO SIR WILLIAM BEVERIDGE

The tone of this letter contrasts sharply with the favourable comments on Soviet Communism by Beatrice in her diary entries on 22 June, 30 June and 3 August. The Soviet system, she wrote, was an achievement unique in the world's history and 'a wonder which unnerves observers accustomed to the slow and halting social reform characteristic of the western political democracies'.

Passfield Corner
Liphook
Hants

*Very Confidential* 18.5.30

Dear Beveridge

It is unlikely that I can manage to attend your meetings next Thursday. I agree with your proposals.

Without suggesting any action on your part, I think you should know that I learn that, at a meeting of the Executive of the Communist Party, it was reported that organisation was proceeding among the 'native' students of the School of Economics, some 30 members having been enrolled in the 'League against Imperialism', by 'comrades H—— and K——'. One 'M——', who is otherwise 'Mrs B——' was mentioned as also active. [*names omitted*]

(I don't suppose that these three named persons are themselves students though they may be.)

As I say, I don't suggest any action. But the League against Imperialism is a mere alias for a Communism which is almost a criminal offence; and the Colonial Office and India Office very much resent such attempts to seduce 'native' students in London. (It does not suit the police to take proceedings, which would give the League the advertisement of a 'political' trial.)

I need hardly say that this is very secret information (and open to the usual scepticism as to its accuracy!). But I think you ought to be aware of it.

Yours

Sidney Webb

853 PP SIDNEY TO BEATRICE

Lt. Col. Henry de Satze was head of protocol at the Colonial Office. Beatrice had managed to avoid attending a reception for colonial governors on 23 June but it was impossible to decline a dinner invitation to meet the Prince of Wales. At this dinner early in July at York House Beatrice had 'an oddly intimate talk' with the Prince about his religious difficulties. She thought him neurotic, given to drinking too much – 'a horrid dissipated look, as if he had no settled home either for his intellect or his emotions'. She was disturbed by his reactionary opinions, 'the odd combination of unbelief and hankering after sacerdotal religion . . . As I talked to him he seemed like the hero of one of Shaw's plays . . . the Dauphin of *St Joan* or King Magnus in The Apple Cart'. Her decision to go (as 'Lady Passfield') was a concession which she felt obliged to follow up by accepting invitations to Buckingham Palace.

Lord Strickland (1861–1940) was a former colonial governor who had become the dominant figure in Maltese politics. Rt Rev. William F. Brown, Vicar-General of the Diocese of Southwark and Bishop of Pella, had been a member of the old London School Board and a Catholic spokesman on education. Sir Fabian Ware (1869–1949) was the former editor of the *Morning Post* and was the active vice-chairman of the Imperial War Graves Commission. Geoffrey Dawson (1874–1944), one of Milner's protégés in South Africa, was editor of *The Times* 1912–19 and 1923–41. He was a diehard Conservative and became an outstanding spokesman for 'appeasement' of Nazi Germany. Julian Huxley (1887–1975) was currently professor of physiology at the Royal Institution; from 1935 to 1942 he was secretary of the Zoological Society. In 1946–48 he was the Director-General of Unesco. He was a notable author as well as a distinguished scientist and took an active part in public life.

[P.6 Artillery Mansions]
26.6.30

Dear One

I am afraid we must go to the P. of W., and De Satze has sent a proper acceptance. He has ascertained that it is merely 'evening dress' (for me that is, not kneebreeches).

You will see that I had a lively time in the H. of L., with general approval. When I went to a Privy Council this morning, the King made me stay behind to talk about Malta, cursing both Strickland and the Vatican – very civil to me.

This afternoon Bishop Brown came to ask how the quarrel could be made up; saying he had no mission and no authority, but he would do what he could. He deplored the hotheadedness of his R.C. people over this, and over English education, and was all for his own smooth diplomatic way of compromise and instalments.

I went in the evening to preside over a Government dinner to the Empire's entomologists (insect destroyers); and spoke a clever and witty speech drafted for me in the office, with great acceptance. Then to bed by midnight, and to sleep soundly for at least 5 hours on end!

I enclose various things. I have invited Fabian Ware, Geoffrey Dawson and Julian Huxley as directed. Now I must rush off to see our Party Committee about Palestine to answer a Jewish complaint.

Yours

Sidney

854 PP BEATRICE TO SIDNEY

Passfield Corner
Liphook
Hants
[? 16 July 1930]

Dearest One

I have already written to S.W. Lost Property Office telling them the train we went by and giving a sufficient description of the brooch. I am afraid it is a 'gonner' – I was so tired that morning that I hardly knew what I was doing. It may have been left in [the] flat and 'nipped' or I may have accidentally tumbled it out of the case.

However it is no use worrying over it: in our future life there will be few occasions to sport it, and I can do quite well with the brooches I have left.

I hope to finish my B.B.C. talk today and then read it tonight to test the length and you shall revise it before I send the copy to the B.B.C. on Sunday.

The conference seems to have been a great success. But what a state of affairs in India, I don't believe if passive resistance goes on we can hold out indefinitely – and yet the alternative of Chinese chaos is tragic – perhaps the best way would be to let the representatives of all the Indian interests try to agree on some constitution and then Great Britain might come in to negotiate between them. Laski's article in *P.S.Q.* is very pessimistic – he has become curiously enamoured with equality of [? life] – oddly so because I don't think he would appreciate equality if it came about. He is a very 'viewy' person – always flirting with new charmers.

Ever yours

Beatrice

855 PP SIDNEY TO BEATRICE

The policy statement on Palestine was published as a White Paper in October. It proposed to set land aside for landless Arabs and to provide money for irrigation. Beyond that initial policy it suggested land should be equally divided between Arabs and Jews.

Sir John Campbell (1874–1944), formerly a civil servant in India, was economic adviser to the Colonial Office 1930–42. Sir John Chancellor (1870–1952), formerly governor of Southern Rhodesia, was High Commissioner and Commander-in-Chief in Palestine 1928–31. Lord Thomson (1875–1930), a regular soldier who became a Labour politician, was Secretary of State for Air in the 1924 and 1929 Labour governments and a close friend of MacDonald: he was killed in the crash of the airship R 101 in France. Basil Williams (1867–1950), professor of history at Edinburgh, wrote several biographies. Harry Gosling (1861–1930), a former docker, had been Minister of Transport in the 1924 Labour government. H. C. Charleton was Labour M.P. for South Leeds 1922–31, and 1935–45.

[P.6 Artillery Mansions]
10.9.30

Dear One

Your letter duly received this morning – my only post at Artillery Mansions – but without the enclosure of letter from someone of unintelligible name! Also the two books at C.O.

By order, I have telegraphed to Hope Simpson to come to London for consultation some time during the ensuing fortnight. So we *might* possibly ask him down for the day and night of 22 September (Monday), when I might not have to be in London. But I shall doubtless learn by telegraph when he is coming.

I got my great draft declaration of policy on Palestine through the Cabinet Committee today easily enough. Snowden, Thomson and Thomas expressed admiration for it. It is really the work of the office, in consultation with Sir J. Campbell, Sir J. Chancellor and Sir J. Hope Simpson, on my instructions. It will come before the Cabinet next week.

I saw Basil Williams today at the Athenaeum. He said they hoped to get down to Petersfield soon, but had to stay in London for some troublesome business.

Fabian Ware wants suggestions for a T.U. successor to Gosling on his Committee. He demurred to Citrine as having avoided service in the war, and suggested Charleton M.P. (a very sensible N.R.U. man). Apart from Poulton, who is old, I know no one better for his purpose.

Fabian Ware said that Miss Haldane had told him tales of our courtship at Box derived from her brother!

But I must close to catch the post. Goodnight dear one

Sidney

856 PP SIDNEY TO BEATRICE

Graham and Audrey Wallas had just spent a weekend at Passfield Corner.

[P.6 Artillery Mansions]
15.9.30

Dear One

A brilliant day, and I hope also with you. I have nothing to report or to send you – except my lover's greetings!

I thought the Wallas's visit very satisfactory, she so much more 'amiable' than heretofore. Graham is to me enigmatical. He seems always to be resisting and protesting – subconsciously at least on the defensive – against every kind of Progressive action (except any secularist aggression against Christianity). I think his Secularism is the only part of Progressivism, as he would estimate it, with which he is completely in agreement. He is not, of course, willingly a Tory reactionary; but he does not really *like* any Radical or Collectivist proposals; partly because he feels that all such are put forward by people who do not sufficiently consider all of what he regards as fundamental principles of social philosophy (from Aristotle or others); and partly because he is sceptical about any Democratic reform working out free from corruption, perversion, or other evil (such as tyrannical interference with individual liberty). He estimates every proposal from the standpoint of the ideal; never as merely the best practicable alternative to the existing order. The result is that he is 'unhappy' in his politics; a particular kind of 'mugwump', finding no party with which he can scrupulously agree. I imagine, too, that he is subconsciously far more concerned to discover unthought-of refinements and distinctions that he can put into his book, than with the topic itself. This foible is not without its uses to us when we put projects before him, because something may be gained from his refinements and distinctions; but it affects and (as I think) enfeebles his judgement for practical action. In fact, he has ceased to be competent *for action*. His will is 'sicklied over by the pale cast of thought'. I can't imagine what he would do in my place, where I have to authorise daily, by initialling, innumerable decisions one after another, one endless matters on which I can form only the roughest kind of judgement on the advice of others. But there *have to be* decisions, irrespective of what the philosophers might say about them. These people have their uses, but their usefulness is conditional on their *producing* books, as to which he has always been rather slow! Over 70, of course, we must all need (and make) excuses for such slowness.

Goodnight dearest

Sidney

857 WI SIDNEY WEBB TO CHAIM WEIZMANN

Webb's letters to Weizmann show that, despite the tension between the Zionists and the British administration of Palestine, Webb was keeping open an informal and personal line of communication.

[Colonial Office]
24.9.30

Dear Dr Weizmann

I was pleased to hear from you by your letter of 19 September – in fact, I was thinking of writing to you – and I shall, of course, be very glad to see you immediately you return to London. I want to put before you some of the important points arising out of Hope Simpson's Report, (which is not yet completely printed); and also to consult you as to matters which the Cabinet has under consideration.

I hope that you have been fully restored by your holiday, although I fear that you will not have managed to keep free from troublesome business.

Yours very truly

Passfield

P.S. In case this may miss you, I am sending a copy to 77 Gt Russell St.

858 PP SIDNEY TO BEATRICE

[P.6 Artillery Mansions]
24.9.30

Dear One

The whole Palestine proposals were approved today; and I am to have the troublesome task of imparting them confidentially to Lord Reading (at once), and to Dr Weizmann when he returns here next week. Whether we can anyhow avoid a shriek of anguish from all Jewry I don't know!

Here are various letters (including your own interesting letter from Worcester 27 years ago). Note the very clear assessment to Supertax – £512 – which is rather more than I expected. If we enjoy a full year's salary from 1 April 1931 to 31 March 1932, it will be over £600 payable 1 January 1932. But we are not likely to be so enriched! You will see that the income apart from salary is £2,091, from which Income Tax to the extent of £434 has been paid, making a net income, apart from salary but including the value of the house, of £1,657 or, from dividends alone, (excluding earnings and the value of the house), £1,391. (The receipts as 'Author' of £211 are after deducting Secretary, Typing etc.) For the current year it may be more, as recent investments will yield a full year, instead of part, to the extent of £130 or so addition. On the other hand Railway Signal Co. may not repeat its high dividend. But you will probably find a clear £1,500 a year coming in, *after* payment of Income Tax, and with a house rent free.

Alfred [Cripps, Lord Parmoor] said Marion was much better. Goodnight dearest

Sidney

The keys arrived safely

859 WI SIDNEY WEBB TO CHAIM WEIZMANN

[Colonial Office]
17.10.30

*Private and Confidential*

Dear Dr Weizmann

I hasten, as promised, to send you proof of Hope Simpson's Report – still, unfortunately, without its maps and other appendices – together with proof of the Statement of Policy which will be published next week.

I am sure I need not assure you that very great consideration has been given by the Government to this Statement – latterly, in the light of the representations that you have made, which have all been carefully weighed, and certain adjustments have been made in consequence of those representations.

I do not hide from myself that the position is grave in some respects; but I am not without hope that you may find, on careful reading, that I have in my talks with you, concentrated rather unduly on what seem the adverse elements. We can, at least, try to make the best of the situation.

Yours very truly

Passfield

P.S. I need not say that the documents must be scrupulously kept secret until Tuesday.

860 PP SIDNEY TO BEATRICE

The Zionist reaction to the White Paper on Palestine was quick and fierce, with strong protests coming from the United States as well as from Palestine and the Jewish community in Britain. Beatrice remarked on the absence of any recognition that Palestine was the Holy Land of Christendom as well as Jewry: 'a touch of irony to this ill-advised episode lies in the fact that the Jewish immigrants are Slavs or Mongols and not Semites, and the vast majority are not followers of Moses and the prophets, but of Karl Marx and the Soviet Republic'. (BWD 26 October 1930) She thought the protection of the Arab cultivator against the loss of land to immigrant Jews was justified on grounds of justice and expediency. Unless Britain kept a permanent army in Palestine it could not 'prevent the old and new Jewish settlements from being continually raided by neighbouring Arab states as well as by the resident Arabs . . . The responsibility for this debacle lies with the fatuous promise of a Palestinian Jewish Home, which if it meant anything worth having for the Jews meant a Jewish Palestine from which the Arabs could be gradually excluded by economic pressure. Meanwhile Sidney remains unperturbed. He has done his best to hold an even balance'.

James McNeil (1869–1938) was Governor-General of the Irish Free State 1928–1932. Ethel Brilliana Tweedie was a prolific writer of travel books. O. F. Morshead was assistant keeper of the Royal Archives 1926–58

Felix M. Warburg (1871–1937), a member of the Warburg banking family, was much interested in adult and Jewish education.

[P.6 Artillery Mansions]
22.10.30

Dear One

1) I received your two sweet letters together this morning, as the earlier one came after 10 p.m. when I had gone to bed!

2) The School Refectory telephones that Stamp *has* engaged the private dining room for lunch on 31 October but has not yet given any particulars. We shall hear in due time.

3) The Jewish hurricane continues. I see Felix Warburg (in U.S.) has resigned his Zionist posts. They seem to go wild with excitement and rage, on mere partisan telegraphic summaries and interpretations of a lengthy document. We are (i) putting *no* limitations on continued colonisation, (ii) making no change as regards the previous limit on non-rural immigration and (iii) expressly and defiantly declaring we will carry out the Mandate, whatever the Arabs say or do. The Jews have therefore no *ground* of complaint against us. But we *do* negative the idea of a Jewish State, which the British Government has consistently done – and this (rather than a National Home *in* Palestine) is what so many of them want.

I am telegraphing today to Hope Simpson offering him the place.

4) McNeil telephoned my Secretary today offering to take me down tomorrow by car, at 2 p.m. I sent word thanking him, and asking him to go at that hour; but explaining that I must come by rail at 5.22. Tell Cleave to meet that train.

5) I went to lunch with the Siamese Minister at Claridges. He is leaving

England for Siam this week, so it is a farewell. Guests – Belgian Minister and his American wife; Morshead (young Librarian at Windsor Castle) and his wife; Mrs Alec Tweedie(!) whom I have persistently refused to have anything to do with; other minor diplomats etc. Then I hurried back, to meet at 3 p.m. (along with Thomas) a great deputation of the 'Tobacco growers of the Empire', who want to increase their sales in U.K. Tonight I might go to the great Geographical Society's Reception, but have no wish whatever to do so!

6) There seems to be a distinct chance that Lloyd George will seek to turn us out on the King's Speech, unless we promise *P.R.* which we are determined not to do. Whether (1) he will persist, and (2) he can get enough Liberals to follow him – perhaps on a Tory motion on Unemployment – is obscure. (Notice the formation of a new 'Socialist' group, largely trade unionist, which Mosley may head.) The Indian Round Table does not begin until 20 November and this makes such a challenge in the first week of November unlikely.

Dear One – goodnight until tomorrow evening

Sidney

861 PP BEATRICE TO SIDNEY

'Why is it that everyone who has dealings with Jewry ends by being prejudiced against the Jews?', Beatrice asked. (BWD 30 October 1930) 'Sidney started with a great admiration for the Jew and a contempt for the Arab – but he reports that all the officials, at home and in Palestine, find the Jews, even many accomplished and cultivated Jews, intolerable as negotiators and colleagues.' She noted that Sidney thought Weizmann 'a clever devil'. The fact that Hope Simpson's evidence was against Weizmann put him 'in the difficult position of a company promoter, confronted with an adverse expert's report, damaging to his prospective enterprise'. Weizmann, Sidney felt, had tried to shift the argument from the facts of the Palestine situation to the terms of the Mandate, 'to excite the *indignation* of the Jews and make them forget the adverse report'. Hope Simpson set such difficult terms for the post of supervising future land development that he could not be offered it.

E. S. Montagu's *An Indian Diary* was published in 1930.

Passfield Corner
Liphook
Hants
[end Oct 1930]

Dearest one

The hurricane is unpleasant for you and for the P.M. but I think the worst is over and reaction will set in. Here are two newspapers – *Manchester Guardian* article which is moderating its tone and a casual reference from Bevin which is interesting as I gather it is pro-Arab.

The Jewish outburst is so hysterical that I think it will work itself out all the sooner. Did you notice the extract from Montagu's Indian diary cursing the Balfour declaration as a 'blow to the London Jews' and suggesting that it might cause a break in his political life! I have ordered the book for your Library. But the fact remains that the promise cannot be kept *in reality* and that is always annoying to the promisee. So one must be patient with the Jews.

I shall look forward to seeing you about 3 tomorrow.

Ever yours

Beatrice

862 WI SIDNEY WEBB TO CHAIM WEIZMANN

[Colonial Office]
25th October 1930

Dear Dr Weizmann

In replying to your letter of the 20th of October. I must begin by expressing my sincere regret that after so many years of devoted toil you have thought it necessary to resign your position as President of the Zionist Organisation and the Jewish Agency. I regret it the more as I feel that, in spite of our past conversations, your action can only be based on an imperfect appreciation of the Government's attitude and intentions. On various occasions His Majesty's Government have not failed to express their admiration of the work done under your auspices for the building up of the Jewish National Home and the fact that they have felt bound, in the recent White Paper, to make certain important criticisms, must not be taken as a general censure on your past work as a whole. Nor do I think it fair to describe the decisions now taken as placing most serious obstacles on your work in the future, or as intended to crystallize the development of the Jewish National Home at the present stage of development. For instance, it is expressly pointed out in the White Paper that the operations of the Jewish organisations can continue without break, while more general steps of development, in the benefits of which Jews and Arabs can both share, are being worked out.

His Majesty's Government have not acted without consulting you in advance. Your representations including those made verbally to myself, were duly considered by them, and, so far as they related to the Statement of Policy, have led to certain changes in the wording of that document. So far as they related to the scheme of development and other matters, they will be carefully borne in mind, though I cannot, of course, give any assurance that His Majesty's Government will find it possible to give effect to them.

You are at liberty to publish this letter if you wish to do so.

Yours very truly

Passfield

863 ISH SIDNEY WEBB TO HAROLD J. LASKI

Passfield Corner
Liphook
Hants
1.11.30

Dear Laski

I am very grateful for your efforts towards dispelling the extraordinary Jewish misconceptions of our Statement of Policy. (I have my own suspicions that the misconstruction is deliberate and intentional on the part of the original disseminators.) But of this I will talk to you when we meet.

I enclose a copy of the telegram which I authorised you to send, as from yourself, to your American friends. The Prime Minister has offered to see Dr Weizmann himself in the course of the coming week; and the Government may then decide to issue a statement, which would be in the sense of what I have given you.

My wife hopes to hear your Kingsway Hall lecture. I, alas, cannot hope to be able to do so, what with Imperial Conference and other commitments.

Yours

Passfield

864 BL BEATRICE WEBB TO GEORGE BERNARD SHAW [*unsigned copy*]

Shaw wrote on 30 November that Sidney, 'though an extraordinary and exceptional man, conceives himself a commonplace sensible Englishman living in a world of just such commonplace sensible Englishmen and refuses to attach any importance to anything because everything must yield to common sense in such a world'. (PP) Shaw proposed a new set of Fabian essays on 'The Political Machinery of Socialism'. The essays, he suggested, might first be published in the *Political Quarterly*. Beatrice's article was a reworked version of her July broadcast.

Writing to Sidney at the same time and enclosing Shaw's letter Beatrice commented that it might be a good idea to prepare a new set of Fabian essays as it was forty years since the original volume. She added that 'the difficulty is that there is a chasm between the Aged and the Young, which is not easily bridged ... we are living in a period of dissolution of an old order and, as yet, the direction of the new order is very difficult to decipher'. (BWD 2 December 1930)

Stafford Cripps, the son of Beatrice's sister Theresa and Alfred Cripps, was making a reputation as an outstanding barrister and he was about to be appointed Solicitor-General. Sir Robert Vansittart (1881–1957), later Lord Vansittart, after a career in the foreign service, became Chief Diplomatic Adviser to the government 1931–41: he was a notable opponent of the appeasement policy towards Nazi Germany. 15 Sheffield Terrace was the home of Beatrice's niece Barbara Drake and her husband Bernard, a solicitor. The Drakes occasionally entertained for the Webbs after they gave up their London house. Barbara

Drake was close to the Webbs in their last years and was the joint editor of Beatrice's posthumous *Our Partnership*.

[Passfield Corner]
December 2nd 1930

My dear G. B. S.

I agree substantially with all you say in your little note.

I have already consulted Galton about a new set of Fabian Essays on the re-organisation of our Machinery of Government, central and local, and he is very keen about it. It would not be in the least necessary that these essays should appear in the *Political Quarterly*, and as to my article, it will appear in January so no time will be lost. The difficulty is to get the little group together who would write these Essays in such a form as would present a practicable programme.

Until he is out of office, Sidney cannot contribute either in counsel or in authorship. (By the way the 'placidly aggravating manner' is a sort of cloak to his mental fatigue, due to his official work. This week, for instance, besides all his departmental interviews and routine decisions, he has to defend the Government handling of the Dominion Conference from an attack by Lord Hailsham; the Palestine policy, from a double attack by a Zionist and an Arab-loving Peer, as well as to guide the work of the Joint Committee of Lords and Commons about Kenya and the relation between the White Settlers and the Natives. And then there is the Cabinet with the whole question of India in the melting pot. It is quite impracticable for him to think either of unemployment or of political machinery.)

Then there is the difficulty with the young men, such as Laski and Robson. Able young men are completely taken up with their own work as there is an extraordinary shortage of capable men between thirty and forty years of age, owing to the slaughter of the War; everybody is complaining about it, whether in the civil service or in private enterprise or in local government.

But in spite of these difficulties, I think we could, in the course of the spring, arrange for a series of Essays such as you suggest; if we can get agreement on the lines of my scheme. Ponsonby would need to be paid, as he is a poor man, with a great many responsibilities.

We will expect you on Wednesday the 17th, 8 o'clock at 15 Sheffield Terrace. Besides the Stafford Crippses, I have asked the Mosleys and the Soviet Ambassador and his wife, and the head of the Foreign Office, Vansittart – a very able and distinctly attractive man. But I do not know whether he will care to meet the Soviet Ambassador. Barbara Drake might contribute one of the Essays. If the Mosleys and the Soviet Ambassador cannot come I will ask the Laskis and Robson, so that we might make the dinner an opportunity to discuss the Essays.

We shall be alone for the week-end of the 13th and would be delighted to see you down here for the week-end either from Friday or Saturday as best suited you. You could work in the sitting room with the door open on to the loggia.

Affectionately yours

865 KCC SIDNEY WEBB TO J. M. KEYNES

Madame Lopokova, the distinguished dancer, was married to J. M. Keynes.

Passfield Corner
Liphook
6.12.30

My dear Keynes

My wife asks me to be her scribe, and to send you and Mrs Keynes our most cordial invitation to come to a little family dinner on Wednesday, 17 December, at 8 p.m., at 15 Sheffield Terrace, Campden Hill.

My wife will be staying there with Mr and Mrs Bernard Drake, (nephew and niece); and we have coming the Soviet Ambassador and Madame Sokolnikov, and Sir Stafford and Lady Cripps (the new Solicitor-General), and Bernard Shaw.

Among other things, my wife hopes to engage you in talk (as a relief after completing *Money*) about her scheme for making Parliamentary Government equal to its task. I am not sure that, as we shall have seen Madame Lopokova the evening before, that we shall not talk about extending the B.B.C. subvention from the Opera to the Ballet. What Shaw will talk about, not even he knows. We want to make the Sokolnikovs acquainted with the Drakes (Barbara Drake is on the London Education Committee).

So there you are! We much hope that you can both come. Kindly reply to Mrs Sidney Webb at Passfield Corner, Liphook. The Secretary of State for the Colonies does not presume to manage these things.

I have handled your book, and skimmed the first volume; but had no more time!

Yours very truly

Passfield

866 PP SIDNEY TO BEATRICE

Early in 1930, as one of the ministers tackling the problem of unemployment, Oswald Mosley produced an ambitious scheme for 'insulating' the British economy and reflating it. The Labour leaders, as well as the Liberals on whose support they depended, were emotionally and conceptually wedded to Free Trade, suspecting anything that smacked of the Tory policy of Tariff Reform. They were similarly committed to the gold standard and the parity of Sterling. They were bound to react against Mosley's proposal. When it was rejected by the Cabinet in May he resigned from the government. The contents of the memorandum were leaked and they evoked considerable support from the Left: there was a debate on the issue at the Labour Party conference in October. Mosley continued to receive the backing of the party Left; in December 17 M.P.s signed a Mosley manifesto. Among them were W. J. Brown, John Strachey and Aneurin Bevan (1897–1960), a young Welsh miner who became the outstanding leader of the Labour Left during and after the Second World War. Richard Meinertzhagen, Beatrice's nephew, was a professional soldier who had served in Palestine and was a strong Zionist.

[P.6 Artillery Mansions]
8.12.30

Dear One

Just a morning greeting to my dearest! I have no news to send you.

I think the Mosley document is going to prove a very damp squib. It is rather a revelation of Mosley's failure in leadership. The document is characteristically 'woolly' in language; and gives an impression of being only 'words'. It paints no picture of a remedy against Unemployment.

I forgot to say, after reflection, that I don't object to your inviting the Malcolm Muggeridges to occupy the flat for the Christmas days if you think fit. (I think I should advise them to give their tip to the maids *on arrival*, rather than on departure.)

I have seen no one outside the office and have spent the day over the usual succession of administrative decisions, meeting one difficulty after another.

Here is a violent (and biblical!) speech by Dick Meinertzhagen against me!

Goodnight dear one

Sidney

867 PP SIDNEY TO BEATRICE

Clifford Sharp had become incapable of editing the *New Statesman* and for a year C. M. Lloyd had been acting editor: Lloyd and G. D. H. Cole were the two obvious candidates to succeed Sharp. After a long period of indecision the directors appointed Kingsley Martin as editor of what became the combined *New Statesman and Nation*: the first issue of the new regime appeared on 28 February 1931. The Webbs had no part in this decision. Alister was the eldest son of Ramsay MacDonald. Stanley Adshead (1868–1946) was professor of town planning at London University 1914–35.

C.O.
11.12.30

Dear One

1) I asked Ponsonby for 17 December, and he will come. So that finishes it!

2) I return Cole's letter, which is very satisfactory.

I wonder what the Directors of the *New Statesman* are doing. As between Cole and Kingsley Martin I don't feel inclined to intervene, or even to advise.

3) We had our first public meeting today of the Joint Committee on E. Africa, which will evidently be a long affair. Not only do many witnesses want to be heard, but so many members of the Committee want to ask questions that progress is slow. However, I am philosophical about it. Someone else will have to settle it next year!

4) Tonight I have to dine Alister MacDonald and Prof. Adshead (Town Planning), as to North Rhodesia, where the latter has been.

5) Tomorrow (Friday) is still uncertain. *Perhaps* I can catch the 5.22 p.m., but *don't* order Cleave.

Now I must rush off to H. of L. where Alfred [Cripps] may want me.

Yours

Sidney

868 BOD SIDNEY WEBB TO LORD PONSONBY

There were rumours that MacDonald and other ministers were dissatisfied with Sidney's performance at the Colonial Office; MacDonald, particularly, blamed him for the odium incurred by the Palestine White Paper. It was also said, with some reason, that he was too dependent upon his officials and insufficiently assertive. In May 1931, Sidney wrote to MacDonald to say he would wish to be released from his post as soon as convenient and not later than the end of October; his declared motive was that Beatrice was ill and depressed and needed him at home. For these and other reasons, when MacDonald shuffled his Cabinet on 5 June, Thomas was made Dominions Secretary: though Sidney was thus superseded in one half of his responsibilities, he remained Colonial Secretary.

Colonial Office
Downing Street
S.W.1
14.1.31

*Private*

My dear Ponsonby

I am sorry we did not meet in the train on Monday. (I always get into a front carriage.) I looked out for you, but missed you.

Let me say to begin with that I am not consulted, nor at all 'in the know'. I have not been able to have a word with the personage [J.R.M.] for months and months – I don't know for how long! But I had to press for an interview on 5 January, because he was annoyed about a little lapse, as much his fault as mine, and he vented his annoyance on his own staff, which led to their transmitting it to mine. When, at last, I got to him, he was most unexpectedly cordial, and we presently talked at large about the situation. I seized the opportunity to make him realise that, *if* he wanted any *reconstruction*, I should not only expect, but also desire to be dropped. He then broke out into admissions that we were 'too old a lot', and that he had looked round *the House of Commons* for younger men to replace the elders, but who was there? He named one or two of the obvious, but said he could not find others. It was entirely of the H. of C. that he was speaking and thinking; and I made neither suggestions nor criticisms, but took leave! The fact is that I am not on sufficiently intimate terms. I, too, have my grievances, but do not care to raise the question.

The 'shot in the air' that my wife made (which perhaps I mentioned to you) that *he* might himself become an S/S [? Secretary of State] in the H. of L., did not, of course, arise in the above talk with him – I never dreamt of mentioning it. It is quite unlikely to happen, I think; and even if thought of, there would be procrastination; and the defeat and dissolution would come suddenly. Now as to your case. I entirely sympathise; but these things do happen! There is nothing to be done. Of course, I would put in a word, *if I got a chance*. But I have not had a chance, nor do I anticipate I shall have any. [Lord] Arnold, likewise, has his own case, which he came to me on Tuesday evening to talk about. But I could do nothing there.

I wonder whether anyone's character can stand up against the difficulties, the temptations and the chances of such a position. You and I probably cannot adequately allow for the obstacles and difficulties that – apparently inevitably – lead to seeming unfairness, disloyalties, breaches of faith etc. etc.

I begged Arnold to withhold his resignation (don't let him know that I have mentioned it to you), at any rate, for a few weeks. These weeks may easily be decisive: anyhow I don't believe we can outlive April (or May). *Any* resignation is a blow, and would be magnified. *You* must not think of leaving the ship. Anything may happen anyday, and we must await events.

Yours

Passfield

869 PP SIDNEY TO BEATRICE

Beatrice was taking a gloomy view of the government and of the deterioration of the economic situation at home and abroad. Much more critical of MacDonald than Sidney, who showed no energy and little appetite for radical policies, she confessed that she now doubted 'the inevitability of gradualness or even the practicability of gradualism in the transition from a capitalist to an equalitarian civilisation . . . we shall just drift into some sort of disaster'. As a distraction she had begun to draft *Our Partnership*: 'When in doubt about the future', she remarked, 'describe the past.' (BWD 4 February 1931)

Sandy was Beatrice's dog.

[P.6 Artillery Mansions]
2.2.31

Dear One

What a brilliant day! I like to think of you walking with Sandy across the moor; turning over in your mind the phrases of the 'artist in words'; and perhaps thinking of the companion and colleague on whom you will try them first!

I am struggling with official complications one after the other, with a very full day. But I feel quite well, and am not disturbed.

I should like to ask Malcolm MacDonald for a weekend when you have a place to spare, and can give him at least a week's notice. He is very promising, and quite friendly to us. He is a friend of Weizmann, but has become very tired of Zionist encroachments and essential duplicity. My interview with Weizmann was very friendly. He professes admiration for Hope Simpson, but wants first to talk to him!

I have no political or other news. There is nothing new bearing on the welcome possibility of my being 'discharged' at any early date, and thus enabled to resume 'Our Partnership' that has been so charming as well as so profitable.

Goodnight

Sidney

870 PP BEATRICE TO SIDNEY

Graham, then President of the Board of Trade, followed the fiscal conservatism of the Chancellor, Philip Snowden. The unemployment figures had now risen to over 2.7 million.

Marley Corner, near Haslemere, was the country home of Lord Arnold.

Passfield Corner
Liphook
Hants
9/2/31

Dearest One

Arnold rang me up this afternoon and came to tea and stayed one hour or so – he wanted to consult me about making his home at Marley with a *pied-à-terre* in Hampstead, rather than, as now, vice versa. Would he be able to stand the country? We discussed the pros and cons indefinitely. Incidentally he asked me whether his impression that the Ponsonbys did not care to see much of their Labour colleagues was my own – to which I said yes; that Lady Ponsonby has a neurotic aversion to anyone outside her own little circle of intimates (she hates *Henderson* he said) and that she expected Ponsonby to protect her from seeing too much of them. The other motive was whether he should resign or not in a friendly way from the government. He had had a long talk with P.M., quite friendly but not satisfactory. MacDonald always excused himself from doing what he ought to do behind the back of someone or other – [William] Graham had refused to allow him to appoint Arnold in Chair of the Cabinet enquiry and Graham had neglected it shamefully himself. He, Arnold, could not support the Government on Unemployment – he did not believe that either Snowden or MacDonald meant business from the working-class standpoint – and the Labour Party was disintegrating very fast. He (Arnold) would like to retire and devote himself to free trade and economic sanction in time of war. But he thought, on the whole, he would hold on until July when it would be clear whether or not the Labour Government was going on indefinitely – when there *might* be reconstruction and he would drop out. The P.M. does not like the idea of reconstruction, because he does not know whom to promote: he does not care for Lees-Smith and detests Dalton – Morrison is the only one he favours – he won't have Ponsonby in the Cabinet. But he may be compelled to reconstruct. But the only member of the Cabinet who would be *willing to resign*, MacDonald thinks, is you – Parmoor will stick to his position until death removes him – so that's that. My own impression is that there will be some reconstruction which will enable you to slip out before the session is over. I am not in the least in a hurry to see you out – the money is always useful – but I think you are right to make it quite clear that you will be ready and even glad to retire if it is better for the party. I think it is probable we could do more valuable work outside than inside the Government, and should be happier together for the few remaining years of our life. I think we are going to see a very rapid disintegration of the Labour movement partly because of its lack of common conviction or given direction, with regard to social organisation; but more because of world movements which are going to bring about a far deeper cleavage between the *Haves* and *Have-nots* throughout the world than we have as yet experienced. The burden of rent and interest plus [? new] debt will become too great a handicap to enable a steady rise in the standard of livelihood and security for the common people to be achieved throughout; the policy of *gradualness as it has been practised in Great Britain during the last two or three decades* – you cannot do it without control of the natural resources and a drastic cutting down of rent and interest. However, I may be wrong. I incline to exaggerate, and I think, you to minimise the likelihood of changes – another instance of our complementary faculties!

You will get this letter tomorrow evening to welcome you when you return to the flat after dining at the Club as you probably will do.

I got on this morning with the chapter and shall dictate it tomorrow.

Ever your always enduring partner in love and work.

Beatrice

## 871 BOD SIDNEY WEBB TO LORD AMULREE

Colonial Office
Downing St
S.W.1
10.2.31

*Strictly Private*

My dear Amulree

I am very much obliged for your suggestions as to the wording of the letter to Dr Weizmann. They contain much with which I am inclined to agree.

Unfortunately it is now *too late* to reopen the question, even as to re-wording. You can have no idea of the amount of time and wrangling that has gone to every line of the letter. The Jews quibbled and fought over every sentence. Henderson (as Chairman of the Cabinet Committee) did his job about as well as it could have been done; but the position was very ticklish politically, and he *had* to get a statement which the Jews would accept, whilst not ignoring the High Commissioner with whom we were in telegraphic communication – and not doing anything to incense the Arabs. As you will have realised, the whole conduct of the proceedings was taken out of my hands. Some Ministers would have resigned rather than stand what I have had to stand since last October. But my resignation would have aggravated the Government's troubles; and I don't do that sort of thing. So I have put up with everything, and allowed the direction to be taken out of my hands.

I ought to say that, when the Cabinet Committee stuck at any point, it was handed over to the Lord Advocate (with Malcolm MacDonald) to see the Jews separately; and 'settle' disputed phrases etc. They have both been most helpful.

Now the letter has been telegraphed to the American Jewish leaders by Dr Weizmann, and to the High Commissioner for private communication to the Arab leaders this week (to placate them if possible). So that we really cannot alter a word of it. It will be published (in the newspapers only, I hope) this week, but possibly not until Saturday, because it had better not be published in Palestine until after the Moslem and Jewish Sabbaths.

It has been a bad three months; and all the more vexatious because there was really nothing in the White Paper of October (which the Cabinet itself passed), to which the Jews can honestly object. The present letter to Dr Weizmann really takes nothing back, and contradicts nothing in the White Paper. But Dr Weizmann saw fit in October to use it as a means of stirring the emotions of World Jewry, in order to revive the flow of donations – he has to raise £400,000 a year to keep the work in Palestine going – and the flow had very seriously fallen off owing to the American slump. Well, his scheme has had a partial and temporary success. He has got some more money; how much we don't know, but certainly not enough to relieve him from anxiety. He is going to Palestine in a fortnight. and then to America, as he declares, in order to make peace!

Yours very truly

Passfield

872 PP SIDNEY TO BEATRICE

Malcolm Muggeridge's play, *The Three Flats*, had been given a performance by the Stage Society. Charles Dawes (1865–1951), the author of the Dawes Plan for financing German reparations, was the Vice-President of the United States 1925–29, and then U.S. Ambassador to London. Dwight Morrow (1873–1931), a U.S. Senator and a partner in J. P. Morgan and Co., had stayed the weekend with the Webbs in February, while attending the London naval conference.

P.6 Artillery Mansions
Victoria St
17.2.31

Dear One

In case you don't notice it in *The Times*, I enclose the review of Malcolm's play performance – very favorable – and not shocked at all (!), which shows how aged we are – it will be very encouraging to him, though I do not suppose [that] this particular play will get publicly performed in a commercial way.

Last night I sat next to Dawes, the American Ambassador, who was very civil. I talked to him first about Zionism and the stoppage of American subscriptions, as to which he agreed. And then I put into his mind the idea that 'Capitalism was not now delivering the goods', and this might lead to revolution even if it were true that no alternative is practicable. He admitted that some of the American business men were losing faith in themselves but his only admission was that there would have to be, in the U.S., much more collective provision. He said that Dwight Morrow had spoken of his stay with us. He was 'lying low', and doing nothing for the moment, but was merely biding his time. The speeches were interminable, and both Dawes and I slunk off at 11 p.m.

Today is perfectly dreadful in the way of weather, continual slight snow, making the pavements cold slush. I am quite well, but finding the cold wet uncomfortable.

We have ascertained by telephone that the Refreshment Room at the Persian Exhibition will be definitely completely closed after 5 p.m. on the particular day that we propose to go there! It appears that on that day (Thursday next week) there is a Government Soirée at Lancaster House, to which all those who have done anything for the Exhibition will be invited – and the entire staff of the Refreshment Room at Burlington House will be drafted to Lancaster House to feed the guests there! This is unlucky for us. But I don't think you need put off Miss [Bice] Ross. Why not have a simple meal at Artillery Mansions at 6.30, and go on to Burlington House at 7.30 p.m.? This will give us a clear hour there – and you can't stand more than an hour's gazing!

By the way there came up to me at the Guildhall a prosperous-looking business man who was respectfully admiring; on the strength of having been associated with the Fabian Society 40 years ago, when he was a clerk trying to live on 27/- a week. His name proved to be Cunningham – quite unknown to me.

The Estonian Minister of course asked after you, and said that Madame Kallar was looking forward to coming.

The weather has improved and my spirits! – Alfred [Cripps], however, though at Wilton Crescent, is not to appear *this week*.

Goodnight dearest

Sidney

### 873 PP BEATRICE TO SIDNEY

Mosley, in what Beatrice called 'an amazing act of arrogance', had resigned from the Labour Party. Together with his wife, John Strachey and three other M.P.s he formed the brief-lived New Party. Strachey soon left the group; other Labour M.P.s who had previously supported Mosley, such as Aneurin Bevan, did not defect at all. Beatrice thought the New Party's manifesto 'falls dead in the No Man's Land between those who wish to keep and those who wish to change the existing order . . . another instance of a little knot of clever and inexperienced young men talking themselves into an impossible project – exactly like Mellor, Cole and Co. did about Guild Socialism'. (BWD 25 February 1931)

Passfield Corner
Liphook
Hants
[end Feb 1931]

Dearest One

I went for my slow walk in Ludshott woods and common and listened to talks and music – and read scraps of work in between – I am bored and rather depressed and shall be better for ten days at Margate in ten days time. Perhaps it will do me good to go to London and a change of ideas. I spent the morning clearing up all my papers – I am not going to do anything more of *Our Partnership* until I am rested.

Extraordinary arrangements on the part of Mosley and his four followers to get up on their own. Unless they continue with the Press Lords they will have little chance of political survival at the next election. But what a state of disintegration all the three political parties are in and on every subject! And it seems the same in U.S.A. and in Germany. Only

Soviet Russia is sure of itself – and that by suppressing all other opinions. What a world!

Until tomorrow 1.15 or thereabouts at C.O.

Ever yours

Beatrice Webb

P.S. I am driving over to bring back Bertha Newcombe to lunch here – I have not seen her for a long time and they have no motor car – and I am sending her back after lunch. I thought the two old women might enjoy a talk together.

## 874 MMLMU SIDNEY WEBB TO EARL RUSSELL

On the death of Earl Russell his brother Bertrand succeeded to the title. 'Poor Bertie', Beatrice remarked, 'he has made a miserable mess of his life and he knows it.' (BWD 21 April 1931) She was referring both to his marital difficulties and to the fact that he seemed unable to make an academic career worthy of his remarkable early work. Lord Marley (1884–1952) lived at Marley Edge, near Haslemere.

[Hastings]
14.3.31

Dear Bertie

When may we hope to welcome you to the House of Lords! The Party happens to be relatively rich in Earls – we are destitute of Dukes, Marquises and Viscounts – so that we can arrange for you to be inducted in due form – as their Lordships' phrase is 'in the usual manner'. Marley, as our Whip, would willingly make the necessary arrangements when you are ready.

It is a deadly dull assembly with no rules, but habits; and these are dilatory in the extreme. I never saw a place in which so little was done in so much time. But it may give us more opportunities of meeting.

Beatrice is spending a week at Hastings, for change and sunshine; and I write from there where I am only for the weekend.

Yours

Sidney Webb

If an Earl can make shift with the robe of a mere Baron, I could *lend* you mine (which I bought).

## 875 PP SIDNEY TO BEATRICE

The I.L.P. group led by Maxton was becoming increasingly restless and critical of MacDonald. Its formal relationship with the Parliamentary Labour Party and its amenability to party discipline were becoming open questions. The I.L.P.

rightly suspected that the government, in the face of worsening conditions, was preparing to sacrifice social services to solvency.

Snowden had been ill: he told Sidney that he was unwilling to fight another election and wished to go to the Lords if the government was reconstructed in the summer. His wife wrote to MacDonald two days before the visit that he was to say nothing 'that will either cloud his spirits or irritate his nervous system'. Snowden then, and again on 13 April, refused to reveal his Budget intentions on the grounds that telling the Cabinet was 'as good as a full page advertisement in the *Daily Mail*'. He had in fact made up his mind to a policy of financial retrenchment and a balanced budget. Rather than play his hand during the Budget in April, he set up a committee to consider economies under Sir George May (1871–1940), the retiring chairman of the Prudential Insurance Co.

P.6 Artillery Mansions
S.W.1
31.3.31

Dear One

I will come down tomorrow (Wednesday) probably by the 4.50 p.m. train, to stay I think, until Monday week (13th).

We heard a little of the visit of the P.M. and three others to Snowden. They were followed by a newspaper car, which got information, not from them, but 'from the house'! I don't gather that they discussed Ministerial changes at all, but only Snowden's own anticipation as to giving his Budget in person, and when he can appear at the Cabinet, where some urgent matters have to be postponed in his absence. I gather that he is showing himself very obstinate in respect of his Budget proposals, which he almost refuses to discuss in advance.

I have packed a box for the School, and directed Carter Paterson and Co. to call for it. Did you send the key back by post? If not, this should be done (to B. M. Headicar, or in enclosed envelope).

It seems that it is quite possible for the Government to be defeated tomorrow (Wednesday) night, on Maxton's amendment to the Army Annual Bill, when our 'Left' will vote against the Government, and the Conservatives may go away or abstain. But I doubt whether such a defeat would 'count'.

I shall be glad to spend 10 days with you at Passfield, as I am rather tired of the perpetual struggling with one administrative difficulty after another. I fear we must not expect my immediate release: it may not come before July – but one never knows!

Goodnight

Sidney

Colonial Office
Downing Street
S.W.1
1st June 1931

Dear Dr Weizmann

I am obliged to you for your letter of the 27th May about the Protection of Cultivators Ordinance.

I am sorry that you should regard the procedure adopted in the matter as not altogether fair to you. I can find nothing in the minutes of the Cabinet Sub-Committee that records an 'understanding' in the form mentioned in your letter. But I do not want to go into that. No one disputes that the terms of the proposed Ordinance were to be a matter for discussion with the Jewish Agency; nor can it be denied that such discussion did in fact take place, and that the Agency had the fullest opportunity of expressing its views on the subject both orally and in writing.

In agreeing to discuss the Ordinance with the Agency, we could not discount in advance the criticisms which the High Commissioner might wish to offer on the outcome of such discussions; nor (I need hardly add) did we bind ourselves not to authorise promulgation of the Ordinance without first obtaining the Agency's express concurrence in its final terms. As you were informed in our official letter of the 25th May, the whole question was referred to the High Commissioner by dispatch and was subsequently discussed orally with Sir J. Chancellor during his recent visit to London. He fully satisfied me on two points; first, that the draft Ordinance as framed in March last required amendment: and secondly, that, in view of local conditions, there was urgent need for the promulgation of the Ordinance. In the circumstances I felt bound to send the necessary instructions to Palestine without delay; and I had the less hesitation in doing so because I did not (and do not) find anything in the amendments introduced into the draft that could be held to prejudice Jewish interests or to run counter to the general trend of the views expressed by the Agency.

Further discussion would not, in my view, have served any useful purpose; and it must have meant that the disposal of this question, already long overdue, would have been further delayed. I could not take the responsibility of letting matters drag on any longer.

Turning to practical points, I see that your one criticism of substance relates to Section 4 of the amended ordinance (Compensation). The language of this section may be 'vague', but I cannot agree with you that it is 'ambiguous', whether in land, in money or in any other form, is to be regarded as 'equivalent' for the purposes in view. I can see no grounds for your apprehension that the section might be read as ruling out the alternative of money compensation.

In conclusion – let me say it again – I should be very sorry to think that you had cause to feel aggrieved at the action that has been taken. But I consider that the Ordinance, in its amended form, enables the Administration to meet, temporarily and with a minimum of inconvenience, a situation which calls urgently for remedy, and I regret that I do not see my way to modifying the instructions which I have sent to the Palestine Government for its immediate enactment.

May I say how much I regret to hear that the state of your health is not good, and express the hope that you will soon be restored to complete fitness again.

Yours very truly

Passfield

877 PP SIDNEY TO BEATRICE

F. O. Roberts (1876–1941), a former printer, was Minister of Pensions in the 1924 and 1929 governments. He was chairman of the National Labour Club, which was always struggling with financial difficulties.

During a weekend visit Shaw had read the Webbs the first act of *Too True to be Good*: 'Amazing, suggestive, brilliant, but leading nowhere . . . restless disgust with human nature', Beatrice remarked. (BWD 18 June 1931)

[P.6 Artillery Mansions]
17.6.31

Dear One

I have arranged to see F. O. Roberts tonight, and will see *how best* to give the £50 to N.L.C. I agree that it must not be allowed to fall down.

I have just been told by a man at the Athenaeum that the Senate this afternoon will decide to give *me* an honorary doctorate! He said nothing about you sharing it! It may not be exactly true or at least not finally settled, so let us wait before talking, or even thinking about it.

The danger of a Government defeat, entailing dissolution, is not yet *quite* passed. We continue to live from week to week, with one alarm after another. The P.M. warns us that the session may have to extend into August; and even that Parliament may have to be called together again early in October to complete the present session, before beginning a new session early in November. But we can only 'wait and see'.

I am very glad you have the Shaws with you for company. What an extraordinary 'fantasy' of a play! But the extreme cleverness seems to me wasted on what is practically no thesis.

Goodnight

Sidney

In July the May Committee, with its two Labour members dissenting, produced a sensational report which, by running all the public deficits together, forecast a disastrous total deficit of £120 million. It suggested cuts totalling £96 million in public expenditure, to be met in part by a large reduction in unemployment benefit, in part by cutting the pay of teachers, the police and the armed services, and in part by reducing public works. Confidence in sterling had already been undermined by the growing depression, the swelling cost of unemployment benefit and the likelihood of a Budget deficit; matters became worse after the failure of the Kreditanstalt bank in Vienna in May, which set off a collapse of German credit. Foreign holders of sterling, their German assets frozen, wanted their money. British banks, whose liquidity was equally affected, found themselves under pressure. What began as a problem of liquidity became a crisis of confidence. The run on sterling was accelerated by the gloomy conclusions of the May report. It soon became clear that its demand for trenchant economies would be echoed by the City, by the Liberal and Conservative parties, and by foreign financiers; the MacDonald government would not be propped up in Parliament and on the exchanges without such cuts.

The wife of the Soviet ambassador had written a book on the women of the French Revolution, for which Charlotte Shaw was seeking an English publisher, and for which Beatrice was writing a preface.

Beatrice was becoming forgetful and fretful about domestic trivialities; several diary entries show that she was inclined to blame her servants for pilfering if anything was mislaid. In an attempt to improve her states of mind and health she had taken holidays at Margate and Hastings; in July she went to her old favourite hotel at Beachy Head.

Passfield Corner
Liphook
Hants
[? mid-July 1931]

Dearest one

It is a lovely warm day this morning. I have been sitting in the verandah and reading the Insurance Evidence. I see the Committee on Economies is proposing large cuts in social services – carrying out our pessimistic forecast that Labour Government would extend doles and Conservative Government would reduce service! There is certainly some ground for concluding that profitmaking enterprise is *not consistent* with a steady rise in security and sufficiency of livelihood – and one or the other will have to go or be done without.

I sent the Preface off to Cape, Sokolnikova and Charlotte Shaw – I thought G. B. S. might perhaps improve the ending – I added the draft suggestion of an Institute of Socialisation.

About the handkerchiefs, I have a distinct remembrance of a square box coming from A. & N. and putting it, I think, on one of your drawers – which chest of drawers I don't remember. I have it not in the bedroom chest I see. It might be elsewhere – in wardrobe? But I am afraid not. I ought to have given you notice of it – but probably it was not there. It is not here – Annie says – and I am sure I ordered it to go in our flat, thinking you would want it there. Look again. If not I can write order for some more – a loss of about 30/-. I shall hope to see you tomorrow evening by 8.30 arr. train.

Ever your devoted

Beatrice

879 PP SIDNEY TO BEATRICE

P.6 Artillery Mansions
Victoria Street
S.W.1
15.7.31

Dear One

I hope you arrived not unduly tired; and that the rain has exhausted itself for the present (!). The Financial situation was reported yesterday as very black indeed; but we can't see at the moment whether the next few days *may not, after all, avert a collapse.* Yesterday I received a *very* friendly letter from J.R.M. to let me know that he was studying the H. of L. position assiduously, and was working towards a solution, which might surprise us all. I will bring the letter with me.

I was so tired yesterday that I came home by 6 p.m. and had only coffee and toast, doing nothing until 10 p.m. when I went to bed (and slept until 4 p.m.!). But I am still tired this morning, and it is clear that I need a rest (!), perhaps as much as you do. But July is half over; and Passfield is as good a place to rest in as any other.

It now seems likely that the present session (with perhaps *10 weeks* adjournment on 31 July) will continue until near Christmas – a new session beginning in February. This is convenient for my Joint Committee, which will have time to settle its report in October and November, even supposing that I am no longer S/S [Secretary of State] after September – which I fully intend and expect. However, it is certain that I shall be quite free before Christmas, as the Joint Committee will have ceased to exist.

There are no letters for you. Perhaps you did not see *The Times* today with you in an F.B.D. [? Full Ball Dress]. I enclose it.

Goodnight dear one until tomorrow night

Sidney

880 PP BEATRICE TO SIDNEY

Beachy Head
[20 July 1931]

Dearest one

As I shall not be able to post a letter today I will post one for the early post tomorrow so that you will get it in the evening when you return.

After you left I wrote in my diary and then went for a short walk and came back and read *The Times* – a good sleep and a cup of tea and then this letter to you before I go for another little walk. My head is very muzzy: perhaps I walked too much yesterday – also away from home I never get really the food that suits me – which looks bad for travels in Russia etc. I am afraid in our old age we shall have to live mostly in our own dear little home upon which I have lavished your salary during these two years. However if its charms keep us in it it is an indirect economy as we shall not take expensive holidays or be otherwise restless. I think we can write some useful books together when once you are free from Office. But it has been a good life for you these last two years, and if Henderson becomes P.M. we shall still be connected with the Labour Party, in office and out. The next few years will be an anxious time – we are living on a rotten crust and I doubt whether we shall ever get back to the Peace and Prosperity of the rentier class of pre-war days. I wonder whether the Capitalist leaders will be able to devise a safe transition to another form of civilisation – it could be done but I doubt whether it will be done; there is too much greed and the stupidity brought by greed, in the individual and in each nation, to make a safe transition possible in U.S.A., Europe and Asia. The Industrial Revolution of the 18th and 19th Centuries was made safe for men of property but disastrous for the wage-earners; the I.R. of the 20th century may be made safe for the masses of poor but disastrous for the propertied classes! The result of political democracy and the education of the proletariat?

Write me a letter tomorrow which I shall get before I start on Wednesday. Now dear one goodbye and think of your old woman.

Ever your devoted

Beatrice

# 8. Crisis and collapse

## July 1931 – September 1939

The few letters referring to the crisis in August 1931, which led to the collapse of the Labour government, add little to the published accounts. Read together with the contemporary entries in Beatrice's diary, however, they suggest that Sidney had no idea of the scale and urgency of the difficulties that the government faced at the end of July. His subsequent reconstruction of events (in an article in the *Political Quarterly*, January–March 1932, republished as Fabian Tract 237) indicates that it was affected by discussions with his former colleagues: the article differs significantly from the impression given by the letters and diary entries, not least in attributing greater deviousness to MacDonald.

After the May Committee had reported the Cabinet set up an 'Economies Committee', consisting of MacDonald, Henderson, Snowden, Thomas and Graham, to devise cuts in public spending which, by going some way towards the swingeing proposals of the May Committee, might reassure foreign investors and ease the strain on sterling. Each cut proposed, however, was resisted by a minority in the Cabinet; and there was bitter opposition within the Labour Party and the trade unions to the imposition of sacrifices on the working class at the apparent behest of British financial interests and foreign bankers. When Snowden visited the Webbs in mid-August Beatrice noted that 'all the Front Bench including ourselves find our sympathies with the unemployed smothered under our own comfort and personal freedom. We just don't think about them, except when we have to prepare official memoranda on the subject'. (BWD 18 August 1931) This cynical comment was in line with her growing distaste for what she considered the moral collapse of the leading members of the Cabinet – MacDonald succumbing to the flattery of Society hostesses, Snowden to the Court and Thomas to the City. She was, moreover, anxious for Sidney's retirement and – like Sidney – thought that MacDonald might be on the point of resigning in favour of Henderson, and then retreating to the House of Lords. This assumption was strengthened by MacDonald's repeated complaints about the inadequate Labour representation in the Upper House, and by a letter which MacDonald wrote to Webb on his birthday. 'You may think I have been doing nothing but as a matter of fact I have been working at it for weekend after weekend, and am at a completely dead end. We have not the material in our own party that we ought to have. The solution will have to come, I am afraid, by moves which will surprise all of you. I am still working at it however.' (PP) The ambiguous wording of this letter has been interpreted in various ways. The Webbs originally inferred that MacDonald planned to go to the Lords; they decided, after the event, that in fact MacDonald was hinting at the formation of an emergency coalition, and the phrases have been quoted by others to the same effect.

The series of Cabinet meetings which led to the fall of the government began on 20 August, with an all-day session to discuss possible economies. At the same time Macdonald was in close touch with the Tory and Liberal leaders in an attempt to find some all-party agreement on a package of emergency measures which might restore confidence. By the morning of Saturday 22 August it was clear that such an agreement could not be reached. Snowden suggested raising £90 million by new taxes and saving £99 million by cuts in spending – some £67 million was to come from a cut of 20 per cent in unemployment benefit, and an increase in contributions. The Tories and the Liberals stood out for a balance achieved by a 75 per cent cut and only 25 per cent new taxes. The Cabinet opponents of further cuts had been strengthened by MacDonald's consultations with the Labour Party executive and the General Council of the T.U.C., which showed that the movement outside Parliament was even more strongly opposed than the recalcitrant Parliamentary party to reductions in wages and benefits. The question on Saturday was whether the Cabinet could devise any formula which would persuade U.S. bankers to save the pound with a substantial loan; without such a loan Britain would have to go off the gold standard – in effect suspending the convertibility of the pound – and declare a moratorium on foreign debts. The Cabinet was apparently agreed on the whole range of cuts except the slashing of unemployment benefit. On that it remained divided; though that was rapidly becoming the touchstone for support from the opposition parties and foreign banks. MacDonald was plainly uncertain what to do. He could try to save the pound, at the cost of splitting his party; or he could preserve party unity by resigning, running the risk of financial collapse before the Tories and Liberals could form a succeeding government. In fact, MacDonald had seen Neville Chamberlain (Baldwin was on holiday) and Samuel on the previous evening: they had offered to serve under him in an emergency administration. It was that conversation that he reported to the Cabinet on Saturday morning.

Up to this point, Sidney told Beatrice, he thought that MacDonald had 'behaved in good faith over the whole business'. (BWD 22 August 1931: the dating and timing of Beatrice's entries over this weekend are obscure.) Sidney also reported that there had been some cursory discussion about a coalition and MacDonald allegedly said that this 'was what the King desired and might propose'. (George V returned overnight from Balmoral and was in London by Sunday morning.) Henderson and other Cabinet members opposed the notion of a coalition, but the discussion left Sidney with the impression that MacDonald, Snowden and Thomas '*might consider* it'. Alternatively, he thought MacDonald would resign, leaving the decision about his successor to the King.

On Sunday morning MacDonald saw the King, telling him that he could not carry all his Cabinet on the economies and that he proposed to resign. The King implied that it would be better for him to remain prime minister of a coalition government – an act MacDonald considered 'political suicide' for himself. When Samuel and Baldwin called at Buckingham Palace they each assured the King that they would, if asked, serve in an emergency administration with MacDonald at its head.

MacDonald made one more attempt to carry his colleagues: he still seemed bent on resignation if he failed. When the Cabinet met at 7 p.m. on the Sunday evening it was pathetically awaiting a cable from the American Federal Reserve Bank stating the conditions for a loan to save the pound. A little after nine the cable arrived and MacDonald read it aloud – it offered nothing more than a short-term credit, provided the bankers and opposition parties endorsed the economy measures. MacDonald made it clear that these must include, as a minimum, a 10 per cent cut in unemployment benefit, and polled the Cabinet on that issue. Beatrice noted that eight members (Alexander, Addison, Clynes, Graham, Greenwood, Henderson, Johnston and Lansbury) voted against the cut. Sidney Webb voted with the majority of eleven to accept the terms.

MacDonald knew that the government was finished; so many senior ministers were prepared to resign that he could not carry on. He then left to see the King at Buckingham Palace. The Cabinet waited. When MacDonald saw the King he was again asked to consider leading a coalition. He returned to Downing Street at a little before 11 p.m. and told his colleagues that the King would see himself, Baldwin and Herbert Samuel the next morning. The Cabinet would meet at noon after his visit to the Palace. His colleagues assumed that, when they met, MacDonald would tell them that he was no longer prime minister; before they separated, shortly after ten, MacDonald had asked for authority to place all their resignations in the hands of the King. After his colleagues had left, MacDonald received Baldwin, Chamberlain, Samuel and three bankers at Downing Street. Chamberlain noted in his diary that MacDonald offered to help pass the economy measures through the House of Commons but was unwilling to join a coalition government; Chamberlain and Samuel both pressed him to form or at least participate in an emergency administration.

He was still uncertain when he went to the Palace meeting next day; when he offered his resignation, George V appealed to him to remain in office, and Baldwin and Samuel agreed to serve with him until the legislation necessary to restore British credit and regain the confidence of foreigners had been carried through Parliament. MacDonald, believing he was sacrificing himself for the good of the country, assumed that he was forming a stop-gap and non-party government, and that it would be followed by an election in which all three parties would compete. It seemed to him to be an administration of co-operating individuals, rather than a coalition of parties – with the exception of the ten per cent cut in unemployment benefit, indeed, its immediate programme was that approved by the outgoing Labour Cabinet.

The confusion in his mind – and the constitutional novelty of the situation – helped to confuse his former colleagues when the Cabinet reconvened. He announced that some 'individuals' would carry on the government for the time being. He gave the impression that he had not yet accepted office, only that he would 'assist' the new government at the King's specific request. The Cabinet assumed that the details of MacDonald's resignation and reappointment had yet to be settled. (He actually resigned and kissed hands on reappointment at 4.10 that afternoon, and the main posts were agreed in 24 hours.) The members of the Cabinet were so shocked and depressed that they clearly came away with differing impressions: the one point on which there was agreement was that the government had in fact collapsed and very few of its members either wished – or would be invited – to follow MacDonald into an association with the Tories and Liberals. MacDonald, indeed, urged some of the promising young Labour men not to follow him for their own and the party's good. In the event he was joined by Snowden, Thomas, Sankey and some junior ministers. Of his other colleagues he noted bitterly in his diary that night: 'They chose the easy path of irresponsibility and leave the burdens to others'.

For personal as well as political reasons Sidney had no doubts about his own resignation. His parliamentary career was over and he could resume the partnership whose balance and productiveness had been upset by his ten years in Parliament.

881 PP SIDNEY TO BEATRICE

P.6 Artillery Mansions
Victoria St
S.W.1
29/7/31

Dear One

I am quite well, with nothing at all wrong. The Government dinner last night went off very happily.

L. G. [Lloyd George] (as you will doubtless hear) has undergone a serious operation, but is reported to be satisfactory.

I have no news about the matter we are concerned about; and I don't know whether to expect immediate reconstruction or a postponement for a couple of months. I believe things are very much 'touch and go' as regards the attitude of the Chancellor of the Exchequer to the hourly changing financial proposals. I expect there is a lot of friction among the three or four Ministers at the top of things. Whether that makes for immediate action, or for procrastination, I don't know.

I am quite uncertain whether I can catch the 7 p.m. train tomorrow, and I shall not be able to let you know. So don't order Cleave, and don't be anxious if I do not appear. I should then come by the 9.50 a.m. on Friday.

Now Goodnight dear one

Sidney

882 PP SIDNEY TO BEATRICE

A. V. Alexander (1885–1965) was the leading Co-operator in Parliament; first elected for Hillsborough in 1922, he was First Lord of the Admiralty in the 1924 and 1929 Labour governments, the wartime coalition and the 1945 Labour government; then being elevated to the peerage.

P.6 Artillery Mansions
Victoria St
24.8.31

Dear One

I did not get away until 11 p.m. last night; and after consideration, I thought it best to telephone you, though at the risk of waking you up – lest you should be expecting in vain. I am sorry for breaking in on your sleep, but it was a choice of risks! The purport of my message was that no conclusion had been definitely reached, but that it was to be expected today, in the sense that you and I wish. (The reply we awaited did not reach us until after 9 p.m., and was then rather inconclusive!) We meet again at 12 noon today, when I assume all will be settled; and we may hand in our seals this afternoon! or at latest tomorrow. I think that all that is now doubtful is the *character* of the Government that succeeds us (as *we* have all along speculated).

I spoke to [A. V.] Alexander, but soon found that he did not want our flat, or any other. He proposes to go off for a short holiday whilst his new house is being papered and painted (nothing else is required); and then to make that do. In fact, he said he must, as he could not afford a flat. (When we speculated on his wanting one, we thought of his simply moving to B. of T.)

Miss Bondfield will come on Saturday next, 29 August, by 4.15 p.m. train, which I said we would send to meet; and return Sunday afternoon by 4.29 p.m.

I shall probably return to you tomorrow, Tuesday, by 4.50 p.m. train, but I may reopen this to put in a sheet of later news! I am clearing out my office drawers and tables, directing the Cabinet papers etc. to be moved to Artillery Mansions in locked tin boxes!

Later. J.R.M. announced at noon that he had been asked, and had agreed, to head a non-party Emergency Government of about a dozen ministers, personally selected from all parties, for duration of crisis only, perhaps only five or six weeks. He announced this very well, with great feeling, saying he knew the cost, but could not refuse the King's request; that he would doubtless be denounced and ostracised, but could do no other. We uttered polite things, but accepted silently the accomplished fact.

I am going to lunch with a scratch dozen or so of my colleagues to talk it over.

At lunch (8 present) we agreed to make no statement today, and none tomorrow unless we were attacked, and then only to say we reserved ourselves for the meeting of Parliament and the Parliamentary Labour Party. Half-a-dozen others who were not present are expected to agree. But bitter attacks and controversy were expected.

It is believed that J.R.M. will take with him Thomas, perhaps Snowden, perhaps Sankey, and if asked also Amulree – Henderson thinks L.G. will be there nominally, for the sake of his name, along with Herbert Samuel and perhaps Reading, for the Liberals.

J.R.M. had a meeting of the Under-Secretaries today, and made it clear that he wanted some of them. Shiels reports a very bitter feeling among them, even Pethick-Lawrence (who had not been consulted by Snowden).

I must stay here tonight, as I expect to have to go to Buckingham Palace tomorrow *morning* 'to give up the seals'. Then I will come down by the 4.50. As Thomas will probably take over the Colonies, no explanations will be required from me. Goodnight.

Sidney

883 PP SIDNEY TO BEATRICE

[P.6 Artillery Mansions]
25.8.31

Dear One

It is now nearly 3 p.m., and there is still no summons to Buckingham Palace to give up the seals. It looks as if it may be put off until tomorrow morning, which would be a nuisance, involving my staying in London again tonight, merely for this formality. (On the other hand, I should get one day's pay the more, which is some £10!) It might still happen today, but I cannot now catch the 4.50 p.m. I will in that case telephone to you saying whether or not I am coming by the 7 p.m. If not, it must be some time tomorrow.

Parliament is evidently going to meet on 8 September, so I can spend that week mostly in London attending my East Africa Committee; and you can go happily to Malvern feeling that I am fully engaged and provided for!

I left word in the Estate Office that we wanted the flat taken off our hands furnished or unfurnished, if a new tenant could be found; and I wrote in the same sense to Robins, Snell and Terry, the agents.

I have written suitably to the United Services Club, and asked Longmans to send them the 9 vols. *English Local Government.*

I still know nothing about the filling of the offices – the newspaper reports are mere invention – but a few hours will show. I hope that Thomas succeeds me. (J. R. M. is evidently going to the H. of L. promptly as Baldwin is to lead the H. of C. apparently.)

Dear One Goodnight.

Sidney

884 FP SIDNEY WEBB TO F. W. GALTON

In fact Sidney continued to use both signatures until Beatrice's death when he reverted to 'Passfield'.

Passfield Corner
Liphook
Hants
29.8.31

Dear Galton

1) Enclosed person may call, but I doubt if he should be shown the *Minute Books*, from which I have dissuaded him.

2) I find that I am now 'running down' fast, after the hectic 10 days; and I propose to be very tired indeed for a week or so!

3) Meanwhile I take the opportunity of asking you to revert, in *Fabian News*, and all such references, to my 'accustomed name' of

Sidney Webb

This is serious, and I mean it!

885 FP SIDNEY WEBB TO EDWARD PEASE

Passfield Corner
Liphook
Hants
1.9.31

*Very Confidential*

Dear Pease

I have not enough time to explain. But the 'drain' was a reality of some months standing steadily increasing in magnitude. The publication of the May Report at end of July made the drain suddenly larger. The Bank itself borrowed 50 millions, but even this failed to keep up its gold. The last few days saw terrible withdrawals of the 200 to 400 millions of 'short' term deposits and balances. A moratorium was said to be only two days off.

Some of us doubted whether things would have come to a smash.

But there was also actual difficulty in the Exchequer Bill borrowing that the Government had to make for indefinite time ahead for the weekly deficiency in Unemployment Fund etc. This was quite apart from the drain.

Further there was the Parliamentary difficulty arising from the fact that the Government would have been defeated on meeting Parliament if we could not announce a balanced Budget.

For these three separate reasons we *had* to try to (a) make economies, and (b) increase taxes.

The Opposition Leaders *and* 'the City', and also the American and French finance magnates insisted on both; and whilst we were discussing they made it clear that nothing would gain their support unless it included large and manifest reductions from the Unemployed! This led to an openly expressed determination to resign rather than agree to such dictation. Whereupon the P.M., without any sanction from his colleagues, and in concert with the Opposition Leaders, without our knowledge advised the King to form the present Government; and came to us to *announce* that it was *done*!

Yours

Sidney Webb

886 KCC BEATRICE WEBB TO J. M. KEYNES

Though members of the MacDonald government disliked the economies they were asked to make they had no alternative policy to offer; for the most part they accepted the economic orthodoxy which insisted on the gold standard and a balanced Budget – though few of them accepted these views as dogmatically as Snowden. When the government fell, however, the former ministers and the trade union leadership rejected the policies actually agreed in the last days of office and claimed that retrenchment was wrong and that excessive deflation would make conditions worse. The only advice to this effect given to MacDonald before the crisis came from Keynes. He asked Keynes for his views on the May report. Keynes replied on 5 August that his views were not fit for publication. In a long memorandum he told MacDonald frankly that Britain must devalue by going off the gold standard (as it did on 21 September, after a general election fought ostensibly to maintain the value of the pound); that disaster might be converted into success by a reform of international currency exchange; and that 'we should then proceed to organise activity and prosperity at home and abroad along the boldest possible lines'. MacDonald may not have understood this novel advice; he certainly did not take it.

Passfield Corner
Liphook
Hants
3/9/31

My dear Mr Keynes

We should very much like to come to you for a night – would Monday September 21st suit you? Sidney may have to go up to London on Tuesday 22, and if you will send me back home, (or better still come for lunch here with me), that would be very kind. Unfortunately we have no motor car, so we will accept your suggestion to send for us with gratitude.

What frightens me about the future is the emergence, through the crisis of the last weeks, of class war in its most insidious form; the sabotage of the standard of living – education, health, security of livelihood – by an organised Capitalist Party, and, on the other hand, an unintentional sabotage of Capitalist enterprise by a trade union labour party – neither party having a constructive policy and neither party being prepared to sacrifice their assumed interests to the public [welfare].

But what is the moral of this sorrowful tale? It points to agreed Dictatorship? Better a bad future than no future at all except the policy of 'Ca Canny' adopted by Capital and by Labour.

However, we can talk over this troublesome time when we meet. If Monday 21 does not suit you we could fix up some other date after October 8 – we shall be at the Labour Party conference from October 5 to October 8.

With love to Mrs Keynes
Beatrice Webb

P.S. Thanks for your compliment sent to Miss Bolton. [?I imagine I owe the honour to your interests.]

BW

887 PP SIDNEY TO BEATRICE

The statement attributed by Lansbury to Stafford Cripps, though often quoted as evidence that MacDonald planned a coalition earlier in the year, is of doubtful value. It is probable that the Webbs told Cripps about the ambiguous remarks

MacDonald made in his birthday letter to Sidney: if this were the case, Lansbury's remark might be no more than a garbled and gossipy version of a remark that in fact originated with the Webbs. The belief that MacDonald had long planned to defect and become an ally of the Conservatives was essential to the widespread belief that Labour was the victim of a capitalist conspiracy; and it was almost as necessary to the argument that he had been seduced by the aristocratic embrace. Apart from such dubious speculation as the Lansbury–Cripps anecdote it rested upon some facts, and some facets of MacDonald's ambiguous personality. The facts were that he had talked vaguely about a coalition at a dinner with Churchill, Lloyd George, Lord Reading and Sir Robert Horne in October 1930; and that the proposal was put to him several times and in a variety of forms in the days immediately before the collapse. The ambiguity lay in the way he toyed with the idea, seeing both its attractions and its risks, and in the clear impression he gave that he preferred the company of the well-to-do to that of his comrades in the party and the Cabinet. There is, however, no evidence of any conspiracy on his part. Whether he was manipulated by an intrigue to bring down the 'socialist' government and impose harsh cuts in living standards on the working class is another matter. The behaviour of the Conservatives after their 1924 victory, and MacDonald's own evidence after 1931, suggest that there was no intrigue but simply tough, self-interested political tactics on their part – backed up by bankers at home and abroad who shared their assumptions about economic policy.

William Adamson was Secretary of State for Scotland in the 1924 and 1929 governments.

P.6 Artillery Mansions
Victoria St
S.W.1
7.9.31

Dear One

I met Snell at Waterloo, returning from a weekend. He said he had been invited to start in 10 days to attend at Shanghai the Pacific Relations Conference, expenses paid. He was going to ask Henderson whether he might go. When I saw Henderson, I found he was counting on Snell as one of Labour's representatives at Indian Round Table Conference, so I silently advised him of Snell's intention. I fear I have deprived him of a pleasant trip!

I found the Ex-Cabinet sitting (as they have been repeatedly these past days: apparently thinking to spare my aged brain they had not invited me; though I was made welcome without explanation). Henderson is high busy making all sorts of preparations. The others are at work revising a confidential statement of what actually happened during the hectic week (I shall get revised copy in due course).

I lunched at National Labour Club with Alexander, Lees-Smith, Benn, Lansbury and Adamson, full of life and excitement, but unable yet to realise what form the fight will take. They all expect early election, which it is said Rothermere and all fighting Conservatives are pressing for, whilst the City and the Court are supposed to be against it, and to be contented with the present Government.

Lansbury told me that *Stafford Cripps* told him that he had definite knowledge that J.R.M. contemplated a National Government two months ago.

Dr [Marion] Phillips had been lately at Seaham; said the women were weeping at losing J.R.M., and that many of the miners felt the same. She thought there would be a widespread feeling for him.

Hope you have arrived not too tired. Pray do not get excited arguing with G.B.S. or anyone else, so as not to sleep. The music is enough by itself!

Now dear one goodnight

Sidney

Love to the Shaws.

888 PP BEATRICE TO SIDNEY

Beatrice was staying at Malvern with the Shaws to attend the Gloucester music festival. Shaw had recently made a much-publicised visit to Russia with Lady Astor and his reports increased Beatrice's desire to go to the Soviet Union.

Frank Harris wrote an 'unauthorised' life of Bernard Shaw, substantially redrafted by Shaw himself as an act of old friendship: it was published in 1931. Sir Edward Elgar (1857–1934) was Britain's foremost composer: born locally, he took a close interest in the festivals at Worcester and Gloucester.

Tage Erlander, the Swedish social-democrat, became prime minister in 1946.

[Malvern]
[? 7–10 September 1931]

Dearest one

We are not going in till lunch time – for the Shaws to lunch at the Deanery and I at the New Inn which is quiet and comfortable and then for the afternoon performance. Tomorrow (*The Messiah*) we go for the morning and I meet Bice [Ross] at the New Inn for lunch and motor back to Box Cottage directly afterwards. I went to the expense of a motor because I thought I should like to drive over the old country and far nicer for Bice than going home in a crowded train and then motoring from Stroud. Of course the Shaws are paying for my tickets, etc.

G.B.S. is very tired and the constant company that Charlotte insists on keeping exhausts him. She is here happy enough when motoring out to lunch or tea – he gets tired on no exercise. Also he is at work on a horrid job. Frank Harris left a rather libellous MS Life of G.B.S. – which G.B.S. threatened to injunct as publishers would like. Whereupon the widow, who is devoted to Shaw, represented that it was her sole asset – would G.B.S. correct it?

So he is doing this and the result will be a queer jumble! Otherwise he is just as usual: but what an unhealthy life to be so run after. I do *not* wish that we had half his complaint. By the way Elgar told Shaws that he would very much like to be introduced to *me* – 'as he had a great admiration for Mrs Webb'! There now. However the occasion has not arisen.

Here is an able article by Erlander – keep it as it sums up the position. I send this to Passfield, your speech reads excellently.

BW

889 PP BEATRICE WEBB TO WILLIAM ROBSON

Robson had asked for an article for the *Political Quarterly* on the crisis: this was eventually written by Sidney.

[Malvern]
Sept 11 [1931]

Dear Mr Robson

S. is too busy and I am too perplexed to write on the political crisis so soon after the event. It is a far-reaching declaration of war by the financiers of U.S.A. and Great Britain on the standard of life of the workers, and how it ought to be countered is a question to answer, and what I do not yet know. Of course the issue will not be decided by [? dialectic] – the Beveridge–Stamp–Keynes–Gregory discussion about credit, currency, and wage level might go on till domesday without adding one jot to the solution. It will be decided, over our heads, by the relative advantages enjoyed by the manual workers under U.S.A. capitalism, on the one hand, and on the other under Soviet communism. I plump for the latter! But I have not the equipment to carry the controversy further today – perhaps I shall never have it. You younger folk ought to do it!

I am with Shaw at Malvern enjoying the music at Gloucester. I was carried away by Holst's Choral Fantasia – but G.B.S. says it is the work of an amateur, so I feel very small.

With remembrances to your wife

Yours

Beatrice Webb

890 PP BEATRICE WEBB TO RACHEL CLAY

Rachel (b. 1883), the eldest daughter of Margaret and Henry Hobhouse, was married to Sir Felix Clay (1871–1941). Eleanor, Rachel Clay's unmarried sister, lived mainly abroad, as did Beatrice's sister Rosie Dobbs, still travelling energetically.

Passfield Corner
Liphook
Hants
28/9/31

My dear Rachel

I am delighted to hear you are so much better. You have had a bad time which is hard on you at your time of life. We are getting old – and I am particularly so. Sidney though weary, is never ill and still enjoys his life – especially his new freedom from daily grind at his late office. However, it has been a good and profitable experience for him. It is a terribly difficult time in politics and will become worse in our own country, I think; whilst the issue is being decided, over our heads, by the relative worth of American Capitalism and Russian Communism in those two vast continents with their rival philosophies of life. I am inclined to back Communism. I am afraid I cannot help you with your propaganda, the Co-operative Movement, of course, is quite alive to the financial situation and has its own propaganda by its own leaders. I have far too much to do with our own Labour Party programme, alike financially and in brains. We are of course wholeheartedly with the Labour Party and we are going to the Scarborough Conference. Between ourselves, we are delighted to be rid of J.R.M. and Thomas, and that Snowden is retiring into the Lords.

I am afraid poor Eleanor will be most hit by the exchange if it goes down seriously – and also Rosie Dobbs will not find it so comfortable to be abroad!

Ever yours affectionately
Beatrice Webb

891 PP BEATRICE WEBB TO FRIENDS OF SEAHAM

This was the last letter written by Beatrice to the Seaham women: she was in a difficult position, since Sidney had been responsible for MacDonald's move to the constituency at the last election and she now had to appeal for support for William Coxon, the official Labour candidate against MacDonald. Coxon, who had been MacDonald's agent, did well. He pulled MacDonald's majority down from 28,000 in 1929 to 5,900 in 1931. Four years later Emmanuel Shinwell defeated MacDonald and regained the seat for Labour with a majority of over 20,000.

Passfield Corner
Liphook
Hants
14th October 1931

Dear Friends

I have been asked by several members of the Women's Sections of the Seaham Divisional Labour Party whether I would not come to Seaham for a talk with you, so that we might take counsel together as to what to do in these tragic days. There is no holiday that I should enjoy so much as to be once more among you in one or other of the Miners' Halls, watching your kind eyes and eager faces, and hearing your news about the earnings of your husbands and sons, and the prospects of your own young ones at school and work. Above all I should like to hear your views of how to make life better and brighter for yourselves and your children, and for all workers by hand or by brain.

But alas! I am well on in the seventies; and though I keep my hearing and my eyesight, and also, as I tell my husband, a remnant of my wits, I am no longer equal to long railway journeys and public meetings. I must content myself with writing a letter about the world of politics, just as I used to do, during the years that my husband and I were bound up with the work and welfare of the Miners of Seaham.

I think I hear your first question. What about the 'Great National Crisis' which has led to all sorts of disasters to the wage earners of Great Britain, from cuts in the Unemployment Benefit and cuts in the pay of the teachers and the policemen, the soldiers and the sailors, the doctors and the chemists, to economies – which mean worsenings – in the education of our children, and in the Public Health Services on which we depend to keep off illness and to lessen the unnecessary mortality now accompanying childbirth? Most tragic and surprising of all, this crisis has led to our own Labour Prime Minister becoming the Prime Minister of a Coalition Government pledged, as *The Times* newspaper proudly declared the other day, not only to defeat, but actually to smash the Labour Party at the hurried election at which you will have to cast your vote on the 27th of October. No wonder you are bewildered. Are we living in a madhouse, you will ask?

Now the first thing to notice about the 'Great National Crisis', which ended so dramatically in the resignation of the Labour Government, and in the formation of a Coalition Government of Liberals and Conservatives, with Mr MacDonald at its head, supported by a handful of former Labour Members, is that this so-called 'crisis' had nothing whatever to do with the daily work of the Labour Ministers, or with the government of the country. It happened altogether outside politics in the sphere of profit-making finance, in which no interference by the Government has been tolerated by the Capitalists concerned, whose devious ways have been hidden from the eyes of the public.

The crisis was, in reality, a very simple matter. A few dozen financial firms in the City of London have long done a profitable business by taking care of the money of foreign bankers and traders, and paying them interest on these temporary current balances – just as the Post Office Savings Bank does with your own savings. These financial firms, however, unlike the Post Office Savings Bank, had been tempted by their eagerness for profit to lend the money entrusted to them to various bankers and manufacturers in Germany and Austria at high rates of interest. All these transactions were kept secret, so that neither the Government nor the Bank of England, nor even any one of these financial firms themselves knew HOW MUCH was the total for which the City of London had made itself responsible. When the owners of this money asked for its return, the financial firms who had undertaken to repay it on demand, found that they could not get back from Germany and Austria the sums they had lent and therefore they were driven to draw gold from the Bank of England in order to meet their obligations. This caused what was called the 'drain' of gold. In order to keep a sufficient stock of gold the Bank of England itself borrowed no less than fifty million pounds from American bankers; but even this did not stop the drain. Then these Capitalists appealed for help to the Labour Government, which had known practically nothing about the matter. (You will notice, by the way, that our great financiers are always willing to 'share their losses' with the Government and the people, but not their profits!) It was said that unless help could be given immediately, and the Gold Standard maintained, the whole City of London would be bankrupt, and that all sorts of calamities would fall on the wage earners. Some of you may have listened to alarming accounts of these calamities broadcasted by Mr MacDonald and Mr Snowden. Meanwhile the American Bankers refused to come again to our help unless the Labour Cabinet did two things, namely 'balance the Budget' (that is, impose new taxes sufficient to enable the Government to pay its way without further borrowing); and also effect great economies in the Government expenditure, including a drastic 'cut' in Unemployment Insurance. I see that the Prime Minister publicly stated in the House of Commons that this 'cut' was 'a condition of borrowing'. Why did the American Bankers impose this condition? Because the capitalists of the United States are to-day confronted with something like ten millions of Unemployed workers, to whom they are sternly refusing any State maintenance; and they were desperately anxious to discredit, among their own people, the British system of Unemployment Insurance. The Labour Cabinet refused to accept the dictation of the American Bankers; and (realising that they would be defeated by the united Conservative and Liberal Parties as soon as Parliament met) on Sunday evening, 23rd August, unanimously authorised the Prime Minister to tender their resignation to the King.

We do not know what happened that night and early the next morning. But at noon on Monday, 24th August, the Prime Minister informed his astonished colleagues that he had been asked by the King, and had agreed, to remain Prime Minister, with a new set of Ministers drawn mainly from the Conservative and Liberal Parties. He had taken this step without any consultation with the Labour Cabinet, still less with the Parliamentary Labour Party. Unlike Mr Baldwin and Sir Herbert Samuel, who immediately consulted the Conservative and Liberal Parties, Mr MacDonald never came near the Parliamentary Labour Party, which passed a resolution repudiating any connection with the so-called 'National Government' and its policy. Mr MacDonald with his new set of Ministers, proceeded promptly to accept the American Bankers' terms (including the cut at Unemployment Insurance) and borrowed no less than eighty millions sterling at a heavy cost to the British taxpayer, merely to 'save the pound'. The irony of the situation is that it all proved in vain, as the 'drain' went on unabated; and within a week Mr MacDonald and his new Ministry had 'taken the Country off the Gold Standard' – which only means that the Bank of England is no longer legally obliged to pay in gold.

At this point I wish to make clear that I have no desire to denounce Mr MacDonald. He is a man of charming personality; good to look at and delightful to listen to, with a rare gift of emotional oratory. For all these reasons his joining the enemy is a calamity for the Labour Movement. But as to the result of his action there can be no dispute. The so-called 'National Government' which he has created is acclaimed by the whole of the Conservative Party and its newspapers as the one and only bulwark against the spread of Socialism, and against the coming into power of the representatives of the Trade Union and Co-operative Movements. All over the country (as in the Seaham Division) the Liberals and Conservatives are eagerly uniting to vote for this new 'National Government'. Is it not significant that the 'Management' of every colliery in the Seaham Division (who used always to oppose my husband) are now publicly supporting Mr MacDonald on his new platform? Within the new Ministry that Mr MacDonald has formed are the most prominent enemies of the Labour Movement, such as Mr Baldwin and Mr Neville Chamberlain. Why should the late Labour Member for Seaham have superseded George Lansbury, as First Commissioner of Works, by the Marquis of Londonderry? I can only observe that, as the Bible says, 'Evil communications corrupt good manners'.

And now, dear friends, I must ask you a question. What are you going to do about it? You must remember that every vote given for Mr MacDonald is a vote, not only for him but for his Government, with its avowed policy of drastically reducing the Social Services, cutting down all Unemployment Benefit. sending those who have been longest out of work to the Public Assistance Committee to be put on the pauper standard, and generally 'economising' at the expense of the wage earners for the advantage of the wealthy payers of income and supertax. So much for the action of this new Government during the past seven weeks. The future offers us an even darker prospect. Besides the cuts off the money income of millions of families we have now an inflation of the currency, with its consequence in a gradual rise in the prices of food and clothing that you have to buy – an inflation that as you will remember, Mr MacDonald and

Mr Snowden had described, only a few weeks ago, in alarming terms. But such a rise in prices and such a reduction of money incomes, already put in operation, is not enough for this essentially capitalist Government. It is not concealed by Mr MacDonald, and it is eagerly proclaimed on every platform by his supporters, that after the Election, if they get a majority, one of the earliest tasks of the Government will be to impose new Customs Duties on the commodities (including foodstuffs) that come to us from the foreign countries to which we sell our coal and our manufactures. Every woman knows that the sure and certain effect of putting taxes on commodities is to make them dearer, even at the Co-operative Stores. Thus the wage earner, employed or unemployed, will be made to suffer in three separate ways – by the cut in his money, by the lessening of the value of the pound due to inflation, and by the new dearness of imported articles caused by Custom Duties – in order to save those who own the land and the mines, the factories and the banks, the railways and the Government bonds, from having to pay as Income Tax, an additional sixpence in the pound of their dividends.

In conclusion, I repeat my question: What are you going to do about it? I cannot believe that any working woman in the Seaham Division will be so misguided as not to work and to vote for the election of the candidate chosen by the united delegate meeting, representing all the Miners' Lodges, all the Women's Sections and all the Trade Union Branches in the Division. That Candidate, Mr William Coxon, the schoolmaster of South Hetton, is living and working in your midst. He has been teaching the children of many of you. He knows, from personal experience, the dismal conditions of life in the mining village of today; and he realises even better than most of us how necessary it is to open up new opportunities for employment for the boys and girls of the Division. In character as well as in brains he would be an admirable representative in Parliament of the working men and women of Seaham. I shall listen eagerly to the wireless on Wednesday the 28th October, and hope to hear that Mr Coxon heads the poll with an even greater majority than that you gave my husband in 1922, 1923 and 1924.

Beatrice Webb
(Mrs Sidney Webb)

### 892 NLS BEATRICE WEBB TO ELIZABETH HALDANE

The National Government went off the gold standard on 21 September; on 7 October Parliament was dissolved. 'What an election J.R.M. has imposed on us! What malice and anger are being shown! We shall know in a few days how nearly the Labour Party has escaped being smashed at the hands of one or two of those who contributed so much to its upbuilding', Sidney wrote to Pease. (FP 21 October 1931) Henderson had to lead a demoralised Labour Party into a campaign against a coalition of its former leaders and their Tory and Liberal allies: the situation was even more difficult and the atmosphere more hysterical than that which it had faced in Lloyd George's snap 'coupon' election after the war. Labour had to face straight fights against coalition candidates in 445 seats. Its poll dropped by two million – the panic was intensified by a scare that Post Office savings would be endangered by a Labour victory – and the Labour representation in Parliament fell from 289 (after the 'National Labour' defections of MacDonald and his followers) to 46. Five I.L.P. members were elected independently. The Liberals supporting the coalition polled much less overall than Labour, but, thanks to the electoral arrangement which gave them straight fights, they won 72 seats. The Labour leadership was smashed. Lansbury was the only member of the former Cabinet to hold his seat; his main lieutenants were Stafford Cripps and Clement Attlee (1883–1967). In 1935 Attlee succeeded Lansbury as leader of the Parliamentary Labour Party and, after serving as deputy prime minister 1940–45, became prime minister of the first majority Labour government, 1945–51.

Passfield Corner
Liphook
Hants
Nov. 18th 1931

My dear Elizabeth

I was so glad to get your little note. It was certainly a catastrophic landslide but I think it was quite accounted for by the scare about the Savings Bank and the sudden going over to the enemies of the Commander-in-Chief and two of his leading generals. A political transformation scene which bewildered everyone. I do not regret it; I am heartily glad to get rid of those three men. The Labour Party came into office prematurely through Lloyd George smashing the Liberal Party in 1918. They have now had a taste of office and I think ten years in the wilderness will enable them to find their own soul. Also I think that the future organisation of industry will be settled over our heads by the relative success of American Capitalism and Russian Communism in giving a good life to their peoples.

I am very seldom in London but I shall be there on December 4th. Shall I come and lunch with you?

Always affectionately yours
Beatrice Webb
(Mrs Sidney Webb)

## 893 PP SIDNEY WEBB TO MALCOLM MACDONALD [*copy of draft*]

When Sidney's article on the crisis appeared in the *Political Quarterly*, MacDonald's son Malcolm wrote (PP 6 January 1932) complaining that it was an unfair attack on his father and challenging some statements as factually wrong. There was, he said, no truth in the allegation that his father was treacherously planning a coalition government before the final crisis. He claimed that he telephoned his father daily during the critical period and kept a diary record of the conversations which, he asserted, 'make it quite clear that the Prmie Minister was fighting as hard as he could to keep the Labour government in office'; that MacDonald expected to resign in favour of Baldwin; and that he anticipated his own retirement from politics on resignation. 'There was', Malcolm MacDonald added, 'no suggestion of any other alternative until within the last few hours.' The most recent review of the evidence, in David Marquand's biography *Ramsay MacDonald* (1977), favours Malcolm MacDonald's case rather than Webb's. MacDonald's own diary entry for 8 January sarcastically commented on Webb's article. 'Interesting point is that I alone am blamed and reason for my downfall is flattery. Whole Webbs diplomacy has consisted in flattery and so they have come to see no other influence in life. Article itself is contemptible, but for some time evidence that Webb has been going "gagga".'

Sidney drafted the letter which follows but on second thoughts decided not to send it, despatching the subsequent and shorter version instead.

My dear Malcolm

Thanks for writing to me so frankly. I always regard criticism addressed to the truth of any statement as an act of genuine friendship. You may probably by this time have read the article itself. I only hope that, as a whole, you may not think it so untrue a presentation as you thought the extract.

Let me say that the P.M.'s behaviour at the final Cabinet Meetings seems to me – as I recollect it – to have corresponded exactly with what you report of his contemporary communications to you. He gave me the impression at the time (so fully that I thought of no other) that he was trying his utmost, with great patience and ingenuity, to get general agreement among his colleagues on anything that would, in his judgement, sufficiently meet the needs of the situation. This is why he succeeded to a great extent – as it appeared at the moment – in inducing his colleagues to agree provisionally, and with many reserves, to a large part of what seemed to be requisite. He himself repeatedly said, on point after point, 'this is not a decision'; 'we are taking no decision; I ask only for indications of opinion', and so on. As you know, our view is that the Cabinet came to no *decision*, except to resign. But I certainly thought that the Prime Minister was doing his best to bring about some agreement. Thus, I quite accept your account of your father's communications to you whilst the Cabinets were being held.

Then during the Sunday night and at the Palace on the Monday morning, things happened of which I could, of course, give only an avowedly hypothetical account.

I cannot easily believe that the apparent initiative of the King that morning arose without previous consultation, then – or weeks before, with the P.M. It was the duty of the King to discuss such a matter with the P.M. before plunging it upon him and the Opposition Leaders.

But when did the idea first arise? Gradually various previous utterances by the P.M. were recalled by sundry persons as well as by myself, which gave me the impression that the idea of a National Government, had been in the P.M.'s mind for at least two months.

Notice, by the way, that there had been several different National Governments projected during the year, by Garvin, by Winston Churchill, by Beaverbrook and so on, having different objectives. I am not connecting the P.M. with any of these. My interpretation of what I know is merely that the idea of a National Government as a way out of the actual difficulties was 'played with' in the mind of the P.M. as one of several possible alternatives.

I do not know whether you see any difficulty in reconciling such a state of mind with the action (as to which we agree) taken during the last week of the Cabinet. To me the two seem quite compatible. Psychologically it is a case of a complicated mind, habitually running together all possible alternative courses, within the range, of course, of what is for the country's welfare, tentatively following out one, and then another; and not coming to any decision between them, as to what to do when the actual crisis comes – meanwhile taking wholeheartedly the action necessary from day to day – so as to have ready at the final moment, with rival courses still open, a fairly well-informed and mature decision, according to the hypothesis ultimately chosen.

I can quite understand the necessity of considering possible alternative courses of action, long before the moment arrives when a choice becomes imperative. It is important gradually to accumulate information as to all conceivable courses, in order to be ready with a decision at short notice. It is awkward that secrecy should be involved, but the conditions make it imperative. And I do not mean to imply that entirely wrong courses should be admitted as possible alternatives. But whatever seems to be for the welfare of the Nation must be the decision.

I do not feel able to discuss with you – and you cannot discuss with me – the propriety of your father's conduct. We must all have our own views.

894 PP SIDNEY WEBB TO MALCOLM MACDONALD [*retained copy*]

This more formal letter was the one actually sent to Malcolm MacDonald.

Passfield Corner
Liphook
Hants
9.1.32

*Private and Personal*

My dear Malcolm

Thanks for writing to me so frankly. I always regard such criticism addressed to the truth of any statement as an act of genuine friendship.

You may probably by this time have read the article itself. I only hope that, as a whole, you may not think it so untrue as an historical presentation as you thought the extract to be.

What you report as to your father's communications to you about the final Cabinet meetings is most interesting, and, needless to say, I entirely accept your statement. And of course there were various projects for a National Government during the first six months of 1931, by Garvin, Churchill, Beaverbrook etc., having different objectives, with which nobody can suppose that your father had any connection, if indeed he ever heard of some of them.

But you will realise that I cannot discuss with you – and you cannot discuss with me – the rights and wrongs of your father's action in July and August last, about which people will continue to differ. We may all have in view a common end, the country's welfare, whilst we can honestly differ about policy and methods.

I am grateful for your impulse to write to me.

Yours very truly

Sidney Webb

895 SP BEATRICE WEBB TO SIR ARTHUR SALTER

After the government fell the Webbs settled down to completing *Methods of Social Study*. They were also preparing for their Russian journey. Beatrice noted sardonically their hope that a 'pilgrimage to the Mecca of the equalitarian state led by a few Fabians, all well over seventy years of age, will bring about the world's salvation! Well, well, it is an exhilarating, even an amusing prospect, if only it were not so damnably expensive . . . What attracts us is Soviet Russia, and it is useless to deny that we are prejudiced in its favour, in that its constitution, on the one hand, bears out our *Constitution of a Socialist Commonwealth*, and, on the other, supplies a soul to that conception of government which our paper constitution lacked'. This 'soul', Beatrice remarked, was essentially Comte's Religion of Humanity, expressed in the 'puritanical religious order' of the Russian Communist Party. (BWD 4 January 1932)

Beatrice described Salter as 'the admirable Crichton' of the civil service, hard-working and public-spirited. He had recently visited Passfield Corner and discussed his new book, *Recovery*, which attacked the perversity of government and business and argued for international economic agreements and a managed world order. (BWD 9 April 1932)

Passfield Corner
Liphook
Hants
April 12th 1932

Dear Sir Arthur

Oddly enough my husband and I, in discussing our talks with you, came to exactly the same conclusion as you did in your very kind letter received this morning. We realise that it is of the utmost importance to see whether the present organisation of industry and commerce cannot be amended in the direction that you suggest – the partial control of profit making enterprise in the interests of the community. Of course there are two questions to be answered: first, whether it is possible to adjust production to consumption under a profit making system, and secondly, whether you can persuade the profitmakers to submit to the necessary control. We are inclined to be pessimistic on both these points and therefore we are inclined to examine alternative methods of organising industry to that by the profitmaker. For instance, to produce for consumption, entailing reciprocal imports instead of a profit making export trade. It is only fair to add that from an ethical standpoint and in the interests of the mass of the people we prefer public administration to profit making enterprise. That is to say it accords with our personal scale of values – so to speak our creed. That means, I am afraid, that we are inevitably biased in our investigation into the practicability of an alternative organisation of industry. However, I think, in the present circumstances, bias is not so detrimental as it would be if there were not the two experiments on a large scale actually going on in the world of today – American Capitalism and Russian Communism. I wish there could be a really competent enquiry into the working of American Capitalism from the standpoint of its reliance on pecuniary self-interest as the motive underlying all American activities.

I hope we shall have an opportunity of talking it all over with you after our return from Russia.

By the way, did I foist on you a volume of *Annals of Collective Economy* containing four descriptions of the Soviet Plan? If so, would you let us have it back at your convenience as we rather wanted to take it with us to Russia? If not, do not trouble to answer; we shall probably discover it underneath all our papers or in one of our pamphlet boxes – a search we are always making for mislaid documents! Or perchance we have lent it to someone else.

Always yours sincerely
Beatrice Webb
(Mrs Sidney Webb)

### 896 PP SIDNEY TO BEATRICE

'All I know is that I *wish* Russian Communism to succeed', Beatrice noted on 5 April 1932, 'a wish which tends to distort one's judgement'. In fact, before the Webbs left for Russia they had drafted a set of 'hypothetical conclusions' which were amplified but not significantly modified during their visit. (BWD 17 May 1932) These conclusions were based upon their preparatory reading of novels, memoirs and travellers' tales, upon Soviet propaganda material and conversations with the Soviet ambassador, and upon translations of Soviet documents. They saw the Soviet Union as a tripartite system, its components being three separate structures for Political Democracy, Vocational Democracy and Consumers' Democracy – or the state, the trade unions and the Co-operatives. They believed that these components were knitted together by a dedicated elite organised in the Communist Party.

They left for Leningrad by boat on 21 May 1932, and on arrival were greeted like 'a new type of royalty'. (BWD n.d. May 1932) They attributed this in part to the fact that Lenin had spent part of his exile in Siberia translating their *History of Trade Unionism* into Russian. Their eight-week stay, in fact, revealed that the Soviet government spared no effort to make a good impression, providing comfortable facilities for travel, shepherding them closely and supplying them with much material on the nominal machinery of administration which the Webbs apparently took at face value. They were conducted on the usual round of visits to schools, factories and official institutions. Within a few days of their arrival Beatrice had already used the key phrase 'a new civilisation' with which they were to characterise the Soviet system. They went to Moscow, down the Volga to Stalingrad and on to Rostov. Here Beatrice collapsed with chronic colitis and was taken to recover at a spa in the Caucasus while Sidney continued the planned tour of the Ukraine.

Several letters from Sidney similar to those printed below have been omitted. Rachov was Sidney's official interpreter: he was a former German prisoner-of-war who had fought in the Red Army, become an official in the Communist International and then was an employee of the Soviet Foreign Office. He was efficient, but the Webbs did not like him. Mrs Tobinson, attached to Beatrice, was a Pole who had emigrated to America after the 1905 revolution, returning to Russia after 1917 with her husband, who became a commander in the Red Army: her domestic misfortunes are described in Beatrice's diary: Beatrice thought her 'a charming little person', though sad.

Narzan is a Soviet mineral water.

Kharkov
Monday 20 June 1932

Dear One

Here I am, safe and sound, in a splendid 'suite' of an apparently good hotel where I propose to stay three days. But we had misadventure. At the very last moment, on the platform, just as the train was about to start, Intourist and Rachov discovered that the dining car, with the through coach to Moscow, had been *taken off* – it was said that the axles had become hot. There we were, with a 14 hours journey, without even a biscuit between us. What was done was to telephone to the Co-op Society at the first stop to bring luncheon to us in the train. This was then imparted to me; and I thought it would be pleasanter than the dining car. But at 1.30, first stop, nothing arrived for us. (It was suggested by Rachov that as it was only a little place, probably no one was at home.) But we had no food!

Perhaps you had heard all this from Mrs Tobinson although that discreet lady may have thought it better not to alarm you. However Rachov was resourceful. He said that all Russians were mutually helpful and presently borrowed a loaf of black bread and a pot of excellent butter from a neighbour. He had his invariable teapot for which he got boiling water at the station. So we lunched off bread and butter. At the succeeding stations he foraged among the peasants, buying successively lumps of fried fish (which I refused) hardboiled eggs and eventually half a chicken fried and cold. So (with the Narzan that we had with us) we did not do so badly. Rachov also found two acquaintances on the train – one a woman whom he had met as a staff typist in the Civil War; and the other, whom he brought in to talk to me, an elderly German technician in Mining and Chemistry who he said was second-in-command of one of the big non-ferrous metal enterprises; the latter had been 11 years in Soviet service, to which he had become attached. Rachov said he got £1,500 or £1,800 a year, besides extras. He had married a woman doctor who still practised, and had a son who had qualified as a mining engineer. (Incidentally he said a train of boxcars full of people, like what we had seen, was '*ganz schrecklich*', and suggested to Rachov to conceal this from me. But the latter told me he had replied that I ought to see everything, and that they had no 'inferiority complex' leading them to hide imperfections. (He explained that these were poor peasants who were offered the chance of very cheap transportation to districts of the Ukraine where the sowing was in arrear, and that they gladly took the chance of earning something in the nature of Harvest Money.)

In the evening it grew very cold, and it rained: and Rachov spontaneously suggested that I must not take cold, and that the window ought to be partly – and eventually wholly closed, and even put on my overcoat. So what with eating and sleeping and discussion the long hours passed, and we got to Kharkov before 2 a.m. The train was almost the same sort as the one we travelled in to Rostov – crowded, indiscriminate and slow. At Kharkov at 2 a.m. we were met by Intourist agent, and a young woman who is apparently to be our local guide, with two cars, which took us to (apparently) a swagger hotel prepared for our reception. Supper was laid for us (!): but I refused to eat; and just washed and tumbled into bed, not even getting out my sheet-bag, (which proved needless).

I could not help feeling thankful that you had not been with us! This morning I got (from an intelligent but entirely monoglot chambermaid) a warm bath, not as hot as you like it, but enough for me, and the bath *full* of water in which I could lie down. I ordered breakfast at 9 a.m. of coffee and toast, but they brought at 9.20 also steak and potatoes, and delicious compote of stewed pears and cherries to which I succumbed (only a little!).

Then whilst writing this love letter (!) Rachov appeared with the Intourist Agent. They had already arranged a lunch today for 1.30 p.m., at which the local Government Commissars, the Co-ops, the T.U. and the *local agent of the Moscow Foreign Office* are to be present, at which interviews are to be arranged. I propose, also, to stop a night here on my way back from Dnieperstrog; and shall reach Moscow *on the morning* of 30 June – hoping then to meet you sometime that day thoroughly restored and reinvigorated.

This morning I am doing nothing, being (though quite well) still tired. This seems a more 'European' city than any we have seen so far: it might easily be Leipzig. My suite has six windows, at a corner, looking from my first floor down several broad streets, but you would find it with the tramways as noisy as Athens!

I hope you are, as I write, preparing for a pleasant night journey to the mountains. Dear one, take care of yourself as life would be a dreary waste for me without you. I shall look for a letter from you at Kieff, where I shall stay two and a half days.

I hear no news, except that a big American bank has failed (Lee Higginson and Co.) which does not touch us.

I forgot to say that all yesterday afternoon we were travelling between mines, cement works, chemical factories and so on (the Donetz Basin), much equivalent to our own Black Country. I think this was where Miss Clark (Mrs Whitley) began her revolutionary adventures.

Yours

Sidney

## 897 PP SIDNEY TO BEATRICE

V. K. Korostovetz (1888–1953) was a Ukrainian-born Russian diplomat before the revolution. As an emigré in London he edited *The Investigator*, a bulletin published by Ukrainian political refugees.

'Our first conclusion is that the Soviet government is perhaps the most firmly established government in the world and the least likely to be radically altered in the next few decades', Beatrice wrote on their return. (BWD n.d. August 1932) Secondly, the Webbs decided that they had seen 'a new civilisation and new culture – all of which I believed is destined to spread, owing to its superior intellectual and ethical fitness'. Thirdly, the backwardness of Soviet society made it 'repulsive to more developed races': Beatrice cited 'repression of heresy, not to mention the sudden disappearance of unwanted persons'. She confessed that she and Sidney had 'little opportunity' of observing 'the dark side' of the system, though she noted an 'atmosphere of fear and suspicion'. They had returned wondering how to disentangle the good in Russian Communism from the bad, the fervour of the Communist Party from its fanaticism, the economic organisation from the dictatorship of 'a creed or caste'. There is no written evidence that their journey changed their prior opinions in any important respect or that the stage-management of their tour made them doubtful about information supplied by the Soviet authorities. The tone of Beatrice's diary entries suggest a strong emotional desire to have her wish to like the system confirmed.

Krasnaya Hotel
Kharkov
7.15 a.m. 23 June/32

Dear One

It is a beautiful morning – the fifth day of my exile from you (and without even hearing that you have safely arrived – probably you have written to me at Kieff). We are starting at 12.25 for Dnieperstroy, and I have packed up; I am ready to write out some notes, but I must first talk to my dear one.

Yesterday I had long interviews morning and afternoon with the Minister for Planning and the Minister of Labor (with the T.U. there) and in the evening I went for an hour's talk alone with the agent of the Moscow Government here, in his official house (a large and comfortable villa residence of an ex-wealthy man, with extensive garden, only now being hemmed in by high buildings). He occupies a curious position. He is described as the representative of the Narkomindel (Foreign Office), and might be deemed a sort of ambassador to the local Republic. He is clearly not the Governor. Yet he told me he has a seat on the local Sovnarkom, or Cabinet of Ukrainian Ministers, and takes a full part there in all matters as a member: It seems a good combination for what we should almost call a Self-governing Dominion.

He was an old revolutionary, and became Counsellor and virtually Ambassador at Berlin, where he was for 11 years on end (1921–31). Then appointed here in January last. He resembled a little Harold and J. A. Spender.

He knew all about Korogevetz [Korostovetz], and thought there was nothing in the movement for independence. He said 'independent of what? What they mean is simply independence from the Bolsheviks'.

The Planning Minister was also an ex-diplomat, Minister to Poland, a charming, modest, learned man – also an old revolutionary – of the Krassin type. I had 2 hours with him, and his able woman assistant, and they asked us to stay to lunch which we did. But I failed to get the precise details I wanted on some points.

The T.U. and Minister for Labor were interesting as usual. I surprised them at the end by asking them to tell me what they individually felt short of, and got some interesting replies. Their desires were singularly few and trivial.

By the way the Moscow Agent told me that the new dwellings here (3 rooms etc.) are not *allowed* to occupy more than a single family, apparently by local law or regulation.

I have written lengthy notes of all this, and must now write up the latest, as I am being taken for a drive round the outskirts this morning before going to the train. Dear One goodbye for the present. We must resume at Moscow on 30 June.

Sidney

Your telegram of 22 June just received – good! Also letters herewith sent on from Moscow.

S.W.

898 UI BEATRICE WEBB TO H. G. WELLS

Wells was also to make a pilgrimage to Russia and, after an interview with Stalin, to have a notable exchange with Shaw on their respective conclusions about Russia.

Maurice Dobb (1900–76), fellow of Trinity College, Cambridge, was a Marxist economist and author of a number of works on political economy and socialist planning.

Moura Budberg (d. 1975) was a Russian aristocrat, successively the mistress of R. Bruce-Lockhart, the British representative in Petrograd after the Russian Revolution, the Soviet writer Maxim Gorki and, from 1931 until his death, of H. G. Wells. Her first husband had been a Russian diplomat in London before 1914.

Beatrice broadcast 'What I have learnt about Russia' on 28 September 1932.

Passfield Corner
Liphook
Hants
October 21st 1932

Dear Mr Wells

Ever so many thanks for sending me so promptly your book which we shall both read with great interest and find much no doubt both to agree with and to disagree with. By the way, pray do not address me outwardly as 'Lady Passfield', as the postman might fail to deliver it as my postbag is entirely Mrs Sidney Webb. Also, why an 'antagonist'! even an affectionate one! Are we not, generally speaking, on the same line of intellectual development, compared relatively to the rest of the world?

I send you herewith my broadcast on Russia. What especially interested us was the amazing unity of purpose manifested in four or five different types of organisation which go to make up the Soviet Constitution. It seemed to us the most highly stabilised constitution in the world as well as the most elastic, as it is a constitution which can creep over frontiers almost unseen and unrecognised. Sometimes it is the Soviet democracy which appears in Mongolia and China; sometimes it is the Consumers Co-operative Movement or the Red Trade Union; or the Association of Self-governing workships; or the Communist Party. But when one of these organisations gets hold of a village the other four appear after a time – and this without any legal enactment or conquering army. The other impression one gains in travelling about Russia is the amazing activity of mind and body and the rapid growth of personal responsibility and personal initiative on the part of the youth of Russia. Of course the execution of the Plan is sometimes hideously imperfect: but they are always overcoming their difficulties. I notice that in your chapter on Russia you imply that Stalingrad is a great failure. Today the Stalingrad Tractor Factory which we had an opportunity of studying, is a great success; the big failure is the Autostroy at Nijni-Novgorod (changed to 'Gorky' recently); when we were there it seemed an absolutely hopeless failure, but they assured us that it would become a success as Stalingrad has become. Anyway, they know their difficulties and are moving heaven and earth by persistent education from the infant to the young men and women in their twenties and thirties, to remedy these defects. Someday you ought to go there yourself because it is the spirit of the place which is impressive.

I send you under separate cover our little book on *Methods of Social Study* which is to be published on the 27th, and which may or may not interest you. Anyway, the entries from my diary will remind you of the Webbs as investigators – an activity with which I think you always sympathised.

Do come and spend a night with us for a long talk. Our spare bedroom is seldom engaged except at weekends. If by any chance you were disengaged for the weekend of the 19th we should be delighted if you could come as Maurice Dobb, the clever Cambridge Don, who is a very accomplished Communist economist, will be with us, and his wife who I believe manages some theatre at Westminster, but whom I do not know.

By the way, what has happened to your attractive Baroness? I learnt afterwards that she was the widow of Nicholas Benkendorf who was killed in the War. Has she gone back to Russia like Prince Mirsky?

Always yours

Mrs Sidney Webb

## 899 NH BEATRICE WEBB TO ÉLIE HALÉVY

On page 229 of *Methods of Social Study* the Webbs suggested that foreign observers, such as Lawrence Lowell and Halévy, had difficulty in verifying and evaluating oral statements made by the inhabitants of the country visited.

Passfield Corner
Liphook
Hants
Nov. 15th 1932

My dear Professor Halévy

By all means give the second copy of our book to an inquisitive student or to some library, as best it seems to you.

We were both very much interested in your letter. The right use of hypothesis is a very controversial point: owing to the different temperaments of investigators. Speaking for myself, I have done the best research when I have started either with no hypothesis at all or with the ordinary current views on the subject, and have had to drop these views and search about for all other hypotheses, some of which I have regarded at first as absurd, but found afterwards useful. I remember very well that this was the case with our *Industrial Democracy*. Even after we had done all our investigation for the *History of Trade Unionism* and published it, we had no theory of Trade Unionism, except the false one which was then current and we certainly could not have foreseen our conclusions after 2 years more research. A still more striking instance was with regard to the Poor Law policy carried on by the L.G.B. between 1834 [*mistyped*: 1832] and 1906. Neither we nor any of my colleagues had the remotest conception of what that policy was until Sidney and I, with the aid of our research secretaries, began to shuffle about the extracts from the general circulars, special circulars, and private letters, of the L.G.B. to the Boards of Guardians. That is why the employment of research secretaries with a different bias from your own is always so useful: they select points to emphasise or illustrate, which you would never select yourself. What I think does really bias your conclusions are not the hypotheses which you start with, as to what the facts are, but your social ideal – your emotional preference for one social order over another social order. For instance no investigator of Soviet Communism who is at heart an anarchist could be fair in his investigation of the General Plan: whilst those who at heart believe in a planned society will certainly take an over-favourable view of what is happening in Soviet Russia. The experiment is so vast and so complicated and the conditions are so extraordinarily diversified in different parts of that vast continent that it is quite impracticable not to be biased in selecting one set of facts rather than another. Therefore any book we write on Russia would be submitted not as a result of research but as a succession of hypotheses as to what was actually happening which would be proved or disproved 'by the event'.

About the reference to you, in your and Lowell's work on British History, you will note that we imply that your questions were quite as likely to get correctly answered by interested parties as those of a British investigator, and of course it is useful to start with a knowledge of some other country as a foreigner does, as it enables you to distinguish what is common to all countries from what is peculiar to the country you are studying. Even when your research is as superficial as our vision of Soviet Russia, it is an advantage to understand the working of trade unionism and Consumers Co-operation in the land of its birth, Great Britain, and your estimate of these same institutions under Communism.

But I will not run on. We shall hope to see you both sometime in the Spring.

Always yours

Beatrice Webb

(Mrs Sidney Webb)

900 FP SIDNEY WEBB TO EDWARD PEASE

Passfield Corner
Liphook
Hants
22.12.32

Dear Pease

The Oxford Dictionary apparently wants to have some early quotations giving 'State Socialism', (see enclosed). Can you by using your unique recollections of half-a-century supply (e.g. from early Fabian literature, or writings of members) some uses of the phrase? If we did invent it, the F.S. may as well get the credit of it.

With all the season's greetings.

Sidney Webb

901 ISH SIDNEY WEBB TO KARL KAUTSKY

The London School of Economics, like other academic institutions, sought to find posts for academic refugees from Nazi Germany. Karl Kautsky (1854–1938) was the foremost theoretician of Marxism and of the German Social-Democratic Party: he died in exile in Amsterdam. Rudolph Hilferding (1877–1943) was a Marxist economist whose most notable work was *Finanzkapital*, 1910. He died in the Buchenwald concentration camp.

Passfield Corner
Liphook
Hants
19.9.33

Dear Dr Kautsky

I hasten to reply to your friendly letter; though, unfortunately, not because I have any useful proposal to make relating to Dr Hilferding. I do not think he would be wrong to apply for any suitable vacancy in this country. But, alas, such vacancies occur *most seldom*. We have so few posts of the kind, and they are not being increased in number. Our academic institutions are suffering like everybody else, from shrinking incomes. We are glad enough to be able to avoid actual reductions of staff.

But, as you doubtless know, we are trying to do what we can for those academic persons, whether professors or writers or mere students, who have been so cruelly treated in Germany, various funds have been raised for actual relief; and we are trying in particular to get all 'our' academic institutions to *add*, temporarily, to their staffs, extra or research posts. (We cannot injure the prospects of our own junior teachers by giving away the few permanent professorships to which they look forward.) In this way, we hope that some, at least, of the exiled Germans, whatever their subjects, may get a footing here for a year or two. The Jews have their own fund which will, we hope, enable the needs to be met of such as manage to get admitted to Great Britain at all.

Now, the only thing I can say usefully to Dr Hilferding is that he should, if he has not already done so, *write* to Sir William Beveridge K.C.B. at the London School of Economics, Houghton St, Aldwych, London W.C.2.

Beveridge is joint secretary of the Committee for dealing with academic people; and will know what is likely to be available. Naturally, these things are not made public.

My wife and I (who will be 150 next month!) are well but ageing. We are working on a book analysing Soviet Communism. With best wishes

Yours sincerely

Sidney Webb

902 PP SIDNEY TO BEATRICE

After their return the Webbs toiled to sort their material on Russia: spending most of their time at Passfield Corner together meant that they wrote few letters to each other in 1933. (Of the few surviving letters from this year, three deal with the death of their old friend Graham Wallas in August.) By the end of 1933 they had reached a point where they had an agreed outline for the book on the Soviet Union. Beatrice was tired and unwell. But for her concern for Sidney, she noted on 25 April 1933, 'I would gladly sleep and rise no more'.

Beatrice occasionally wondered whether they had taken too much at face value during their Russian visit. When her nephew Malcolm Muggeridge, stationed in Moscow for the *Manchester Guardian*, began to report the great famine, Beatrice confessed: 'What makes me uncomfortable is that we have no evidence to the contrary'. (BWD 29 March 1933) Her exhaustion meant that much of the book was written by Sidney, with her 'perfunctory help' – a fact which made her fear with some justice that it would turn out to be 'a mere mechanical and inaccurate recital or summary of the bare formal facts of the Soviet, trade union and Co-operative organisations of the U.S.S.R., together with a misunderstanding of the C.P., its metaphysics and ethics'. (BWD 4 July 1933) Such doubts were offset by the encouragement of the new Soviet ambassador, Ivan Maisky (d. 1975) who, Beatrice said, 'comforted us about the food shortage'. (BWD 11 April 1933) Sidney, always cooler in his reactions, told Dr Meyendorff, an emigré Latvian landowner who was a lecturer at L.S.E. from 1920, that 'we are always striving to read "the other side" and not to allow our bias to lead us to error or exaggeration . . . we can do something to make the course of events *understandable* to the British public'. (PP 26 March 1934)

At the Labour Party conference at Hastings at the beginning of October Beatrice collapsed with a serious kidney condition and was operated on at the local hospital. She was soon doing what she could as a semi-invalid to complete 'our last will and testament' but noted that 'I have a sense of working against time'. (BWD 24 November 1933) She and Sidney now listened regularly to the broadcasts in English from Moscow. By the end of December it was clear that the kidney complaint persisted. In January Beatrice went into a Westminster nursing home where she had another operation and remained until 9 February.

Jean Smith was one of the maids at Passfield Corner, who herself was suffering from a kidney complaint. Charles Webb was Sidney's elder brother.

Passfield Corner
Liphook
Hants
7.1.34

Dear One

You were scarcely awake when I kissed you at 4.15 p.m. and stayed by you for a few minutes. I was glad to get the Matron's telephone at 8 p.m. and ventured to hope that you would have a good time.

Both doctors spoke to me by telephone on Saturday morning about 11 a.m. They said they had found nothing but '*a bleeding kidney*', which caused the haemorrhage. They said they thought they could treat it by some injections which they proposed to do on Monday. They asked me whether they should tell you about it, and consult you. I said I put implicit confidence in them, and they were to apply what treatment they thought best; *but* that they should certainly explain fully to you, and consult you beforehand, as I was sure you would much prefer this. They said that the treatment would *not* require an anaesthetic; and was in no way dangerous.

So I expect that one or both of them will see you on Sunday; or early on Monday. Naturally, I cannot avoid being anxious; but we must have patience and confidence in taking the best advice and using the utmost skill – the rest is beyond us!

Lloyd and Snell travelled down with me, both very well and kind: We are just going for a walk round Wolmer Lodge (it is wet and rainy).

Sandy has been sick for two days, having perhaps swallowed something bad for him. Jean has asked the veterinary to come, but he has not yet appeared.

Everything else is in good order – Jean had already ordered 6 new laid eggs for Monday, which I will bring on Tuesday about 11.30 a.m. I propose *not* to go to the Athenaeum that day at all, but to the School (as I have to be at Beveridge's tea party at 4 and then catch a train to Eltham (Charley) about 5 p.m. or a little later) – I will come to you on Wednesday morning when I arrive from Eltham – and then go to the Athenaeum until Friday (or perhaps Saturday).

Dear, dear, dear One, goodbye.

Sidney

903 PP SIDNEY TO BEATRICE

The slump and the German default had reduced the income of the Webbs and they were, in any case, over-spending on travel and research. They now used the

Soviet Bank in London. With this gift Shaw wrote that the function of the cheque was purely therapeutic for no one could resist the 'bucking effect' of a thousand pounds. (PP 30 January 1934)

Passfield Corner
Liphook
Hants
29.1.34

Dear One

The enclosed note from the bank shows that Shaw has paid to our credit *£1,000* (!) one thousand pounds. I have written him a letter of warm thanks. We need, I think, have no scruple in accepting this most generous gift from my oldest friend. It will just pay for all the cost of illness during the past four months, plus our bill for printing *Soviet Communism* next Autumn; and thus relieve us of any financial worry. I shall give the Moscow Narodny Bank £1,000 tomorrow to invest out of the proceeds of *our* sale of our remaining Japanese securities.

I tried to tell you over the telephone that Annie got *no information* as to Jean on Sunday. She was better, but still had a pain in her lower back (which is *not* where appendicitis gives pain, I believe). The hospital doctor was going to consult on Tuesday (tomorrow) with Jean's doctor (who is named Johnson). So we have still no news of whether she is coming back – would it not be well to *secure* Barbara's jobbing house-parlour maid for a week, anyhow? You might tell me tomorrow.

Otherwise all is well here. I have written Moss that the temporary electric bell *must* be fixed up by 7 February – I shall bring tomorrow eggs, scones, jelly, writing pad, envelopes, postcards, and the aluminium hotwater tin in readiness for your car. I may not get to you before 5 or 5.30 p.m.

But the main thing is that you are getting better every day. Dear One, it has been dreadful without you, and feeling that you were in discomfort and pain. Now we will have a restful spring and summer in our comfortable home, with you lying on the sofa and giving me directions and criticisms for the rest of the book, which goes very slowly in my inability to concentrate my thoughts on it. We could go to the seaside if you felt like it, in the late summer or early autumn.

Goodnight dearest.

Sidney Webb

### 904 PP BEATRICE WEBB TO CAREY THOMAS

This retained copy is undated. Carey Thomas was president of Bryn Mawr College, Pennsylvania, 1894–1922; the Webbs had visited her during their American visit in 1899. She was a fervent advocate of a constitutional amendment in favour of women's rights.

[? Passfield Corner]
[? March 1934]

My dear Miss Thomas

I am afraid I was unduly unsympathetic yesterday afternoon in my answers to your cross-examination. But you did not give me notice of the question you were going to discuss, so I had not prepared my mind to discuss it!

What I feel is that my opinion about legislation for women is of no value to the United States of America. I am afraid that you will not realise the reason of – shall I call it my modesty – unless I explain to you my general attitude towards political or economic principles and their application.

The American and English mind seems to differ radically in this respect. The Americans regard certain principles as having a pre-eminent, almost an absolute value. We in England regard all principles as having strictly limited and constantly varying values; values determined by the circumstances or conditions under which they are to be applied. I remember an English lawyer, who sat on the same Government Committee as I did, remarking that every principle has its 'margin of utility': that is to say, the point at which it comes into conflict with other principles which may become, relatively to given circumstances, more important than the principle advocated.

Now with regard to Great Britain, there seem to be two principles which, for the last century, have competed for public approval. There is the principle of sex equality; a principle which is good in itself and results, under certain circumstances, in bettering the conditions of a woman's life. But there is another principle: the principle of legislative regulation. Under the capitalist system we now perceive that it is imperative to regulate competitive wage-earning, and that without this regulation the physical and moral state of the workers suffers indefinite deterioration. Without this protection of the standard of life of the workers, no personal freedom or personal comfort is practicable. This principle of a legal minimum standard of life is of even greater value to women that it is to men because of their weaker bargaining power. Right through the nineteenth and twentieth century, the experience of the British workers proves that such regulation not only increases the material comfort and income of the workers, whether men or women, but also gives them that personal freedom and independence which enables them to combine to their own advantage on matters which cannot conveniently be regulated by law. We had no trade-unionism among women until we regulated their hours and other conditions of employment; it might almost be said that legislative regulation was the main cause of trade unionism among the women workers in our country, and that without it trade unionism would not have been practicable.

Let me explain by the light of these remarks the seeming inconsistency of some of my own pronouncements on Women's Labour. During the seventies and eighties there was, in Great Britain, an embittered controversy about the regulation of women's labour, and in this controversy I took a leading part. At that time a little group of distinguished professional and propertied women were intent on obtaining 'equal rights' for women, whether in the professional or the political sphere. These women opposed through thick and thin any regulation of the conditions of women's employment, even of the manual workers, which did not apply equally to men. On the other hand, the women who were striving to improve the conditions of women's work in the factories and workshops, and who knew what these conditions were, strove might and main to secure this legislative regulation in spite of the fact that it was, at that time, impracticable to get identical legislation for men. I found myself fighting on the side of those who were in favour of regulating women's work, and I am still convinced that events have proved that we were right and the anti-regulators were wrong.

The position of affairs has now changed. Partly owing to the great success of legislative regulation as applied to women, more especially in increasing personal freedom, the male trade unionists became converted to its application to their own conditions of employment. Today men are as keen as women to obtain legal enactments; the only exception being the regulation of the rate of wages in those industries in which the men's union happens to be in a position of vantage through a practical monopoly of the craft. Men who are in a weak position – agricultural labourers and distributive workers, for instance, clamour for Wages Boards fixing rates of wages. Hence today, having secured the adoption of the principle of a legal minimum standard of life for men as well as for women, we can afford to consider the other principle of sex equality. Hence the Minority Report of the War Cabinet Committee which you quote quite correctly.

I think you will see from this explanation that anyone living in England is quite incapable of judging what is the relative 'margin of utility' today in the United States of America for each of the two main principles affecting women's labour: the principle of legislative regulation and the principle of sex equality. With regard to Great Britain my opinion is that if regulation be impracticable with sex equality, I prefer to get regulation and do without the sex equality. There comes a time, however, when it is desirable to risk the complete application of the principle of regulation in order to get the principle of sex equality accepted as the policy of the community. But I should be very doubtful how far I would proceed in the way of incurring this risk, not only because I think the absence of regulation undermines personal freedom, but because I am certain that, whatever the law was, you would not get sex equality, if public opinion among employers and workpeople was not sufficiently ripe for the reform. We English always hesitate to promote legislation which we do not believe will be carried out because we believe in the sanctity of the law as perhaps the most vital of all principles. As a matter of fact, the principle which I laid down in the Minority Report of the War Cabinet Committee is so elastic that sex inequality may reappear by a back door. And I am not sure that I did not do this deliberately. For it is desirable that there should be a legalised outlet for the working of a principle which is really believed in by the majority of the persons concerned. Let me explain this. You will note that I say in the report that every job ought to have its particular standard rate, and that that rate ought to be given to men and women alike. But will women, under the circumstances, be employed *if the job is highly rated*? Supposing, for instance, that whilst the principle of sex equality was accepted, the job of teaching boys were to be rated higher than the job of teaching girls. There is a great deal to be said for this suggestion. Boys seem to require a greater expenditure of energy, or at any rate the employers of teachers think so. Nominally, the position of teaching boys might be open to women as well as to men: as a matter of fact it *is* at present open to women; but very few women get the job, even though, under present circumstances, the women are paid at a lower rate than the men for doing the same work. The medical world has accepted the principle of identical rates, and, owing to the B.M.A., no distinction is made between men and women in the salaries paid by public authorities. But men are, in fact, appointed to be medical officers of health; and women are appointed to be assistant-medical-officers of health and therefore, as assistants, get a lower rate of pay. Doubtless if the rate fixed for the superior officer was a low rate the women would sometimes get the job. The same would be true in engineering establishments. At present, by the custom of the trade and the trade union regulations, women are definitely excluded from certain forms of engineering work. But I do not believe it would make much difference if those regulations and customs were abrogated and women accepted nominally as competitors in employment, so long as the men's rate was insisted on. One or two women might get jobs, and that in itself would be valuable. The London Society of Compositors, for instance, opens its ranks to women, and I believe there are always one or two women in the United Kingdom getting the compositors rate. But if the man's rate were to be insisted on for all compositors there would be precious few of the thousands of women now employed who would remain employed. Thus, though the principle of one job one rate and no exclusion of women, carries out the *principle* of sex equality, it does not, in practice, restrict sex discrimination.

I am still puzzled at what you said about a civil service act securing equality between men and women in Great Britain. I asked my husband whether there was anything of the sort which you could have mistaken for such an Act of Parliament. He tells me there is no such change of policy and that the position of women with regard to the civil service has been in no way legally changed during the last few years. There was a clause which I got in to the Report of the *Machinery of Government Committee* presided over by Lord Haldane of which I was a member, advocating the opening to women of Class I and II of the civil service, but the clause was never put into practice either legislatively or administratively. What has happened is that one or two women have been given the rank and salary of first division civil servants; but they did not pass through the recognised examination and they are not technically belonging to Class I though they may have, in the way of security of tenure, salary and power, an equivalent status to that of Assistant Secretaries in the Government Departments. But these women come in under the rule that Ministers may introduce into the civil service specially qualified persons who have not passed through the civil service examination. It is needless to say that the customary exclusion of University women from the University Professoriate is not legislative at all, it is merely that the University authorities seldom choose to appoint them.

I wonder whether if you get your amendment to the constitution of the United States of America there would be much difference made in the practice pursued by the state, the municipality, and private enterprise in the employment of women? Of course the very notion of a written constitution is abhorrent to the English mind. We think that a written constitution throws far too much power into the hands of the Judiciary as compared to the supreme representative assembly and its Cabinet. Further, we value the principle of local autonomy, we prefer it to efficiency. In particular, any attempt on the part of Parliament or the Central Department concerned to interfere with the right of local authorities to select their own employees would be deeply resented unless such interference were necessary for the safety of the Community, as for instance the appointment of the duly qualified medical men and sanitary inspectors. The present tendency is of course, as you know, in favour of increased local autonomy. In both these controversies we watch the ups and downs of the margin of utility of particular principles according to day-to-day circumstances: and what is good for Great Britain may easily be bad for the United States of America.

I hope I have made my meaning clear without being too longwinded.

Yours sincerely

Beatrice Webb

## 905 SU BEATRICE WEBB TO KINGSLEY MARTIN

Martin was collecting material for an issue of the *New Statesman* to celebrate the paper's twentieth anniversary. The Shaw article in 1914 was his provocative 'Commonsense About The War'. Sharp's 'malady' was heavy drinking.

Muggeridge's previous novel, a satire on the *Manchester Guardian*, had been withdrawn on the threat of a libel action.

Anna Louise Strong, an American Communist, was a Soviet propagandist for many years before she switched her allegiance to the Chinese Communists and moved to Peking. Naomi Mitchison (b. 1897), author and wife of the Labour M.P. George Mitchison, had visited Russia with a party of Fabians in 1931.

Passfield Corner
Liphook
Hants
April 3rd 1934

Dear Mr Kingsley Martin

Here are one or two entries, which you might like to use in your editorial about the starting of the *New Statesman*. The other material I send you relates to Bernard Shaw's contributions and his letters about them, which I should not like published or referred to, but which you might like to see, especially the description of Sharp, December 22nd 1917, and his later deterioration; also the account of the negotiations with the *Nation*. Pray return them.

There are one or two episodes in the first years of the *New Statesman* which I think you ought to notice. First the supplements, of which we were the first contributors but which were afterwards carried on in the form of careful analyses of current blue-books by Fred [Ben] Keeling and I think Arthur Greenwood, but I do not quite remember what part Greenwood played in it; it was mainly Keeling's adventure, and you certainly ought to mention Shaw's brilliant supplement at the opening of the War. It was a misfortune that these had to be dropped. You might mention also Bernard Shaw's generous help at the beginning of the venture. You will see in the entries from Bernard Shaw and also a letter from Sharp about the impossibility of working with him. The plain truth was that he desired to make the paper his organ without taking any responsibility for it by affixing his signature to his own articles, and of course his articles without his signature were worth very little to the common garden reader who took him as a celebrity and did not otherwise understand him. But there remains the fact that he was extremely generous about the whole business.

Then of course there was Arnold Bennett's contribution which was very considerable in capital and in articles. I think at a much lower rate than he could have got from other press organs. Sidney, I may say, was never paid for his articles: they were only credited to his capital account in the way of shares which of course have proved to be valueless. But Clifford Sharp made the *Statesman* and ought to have the credit of it. I am delighted to hear that you think he has recovered from his distressing malady. I wonder what line he will take if he really pulls himself together.

I am making a good recovery and am able to walk two or three miles and am back again at work on the book. If all goes well Sidney is going to Moscow at the beginning of September with Barbara Drake to look after him and John Cripps in attendance – Stafford's son. He wants to see some of the leading personalities and get explanations about certain things which we cannot fathom from reading the documents. I am afraid our book is assuming big dimensions – about the same as *Industrial Democracy.* But I think it will be interesting to students, if only as a series of hypotheses as to what is happening in the U.S.S.R.! I wonder what is happening in the U.S.A.: The world seems to have become a most explosive laboratory of experiments in social institutions. I hope we shan't be all blown up before we know where we are!

When the weather is warmer you must come down for a walk and a talk about things.

Always yours

Beatrice Webb

(Mrs. Sidney Webb)

Have you seen Muggeridge's hysterical tirade about the U.S.S.R. and the journalists and tourists – Fabian and otherwise – *A Winter in Moscow*? He has an incurable impulse to libel persons he meets: the caricatures of Anna Louise Strong of the *M.D.N.* [*Moscow Daily News*] and Naomi Mitchison – F.R. [Fabian Research] Group – are actionable – I should imagine?

### 906 KCC BEATRICE WEBB TO E. M. FORSTER

Edward Morgan Forster (1879–1970), novelist and critic, had just published his memoir of his friend G. Lowes Dickinson. Forster had visited the Webbs in May 1933 when collecting material for this book: Beatrice asked herself 'aesthete or social reformer, which is uppermost' in him? (BWD 11 May 1933)

Pearl S. Buck's best-selling book on China, *The Good Earth*, was published in 1933. Lancelot Hogben (1895–1975), professor of social biology at the University of London 1930–37, was the author of the notable *Science for the Citizen* (1938).

Passfield Corner
Liphook
Hants
April 24th 1934

Dear Mr Forster

It was ever so kind of you to send us a copy of your delightful study of Lowes Dickinson which, as I said to my husband, is 'the description of one rare spirit by another'. I have read it with very great interest as I have always wanted to understand exactly what Lowes Dickinson meant by his vision of an ideal culture. Your account of his life and analysis of his writings has revealed to me why I was never able to appreciate him as a thinker, though I admired one or two of his books – *John Chinaman* and the *Modern Symposium* for instance. The truth is that our scales of value were mutually exclusive – perhaps they ought to have been complementary! This is brought out vividly by his impressions of India and China.

It so happens that we were in those parts in 1911 and 12: for instance I note his liking for the Maharajah of Chhattarpur. We also stayed with that 'tiny and fantastic figure': we thought him the last word of Hindu decadence and especially repulsive when he asked my husband to help him to save his soul. I may add that we sent him the *Art of Creation* by Carpenter, whereupon he implored us to send Carpenter to stay with him at his expense as he was sure that he was exactly the person to solve his difficulties. It is needless to say that we did not hand on the invitation – as we doubted the fulfilment of the condition even if that eminent prophet had been willing to leave England. Then again about China and the Chinese: we were in Peking, Tsientsin and Shanghai during the revolution in the autumn of 1911 and we saw many officials and revolutionaries who had been my husband's students at the London School of Economics and who introduced us to their friends: every one of them was betraying either the republic or the emperor and usually both alternately. We saw very little beauty in modern China and its furniture or in the modern temples; and when I cross-examined the German expert at his Embassy, who had lived there twenty years buying museum pieces, he told me that there had been no art in China for many hundreds of years, the last sign of it being some pottery about 250 years ago. One thousand years ago they seem to have had 100 musical instruments but all of them had been dropped except two which emitted horrid noises. We went to one or two Chinese theatres and the Chinese plays seemed to us the last word of vulgarity and senseless noise. Perhaps we were prejudiced but I gather from Pearl Buck's wonderful novel, *Good Earth*, that the home life is very ugly in its relationships, whether between husband and wife or parents and children. What puzzles me is the cause of this fundamental difference in judgement between us and Lowes Dickinson, because I readily admit that he had an exquisite sense of beauty and that we have very little artistic faculty. Moreover his conception of the good is so completely different from ours, which I am afraid is always based on the social value of an institution or law – that is, the way in which it will raise or lower the culture and development of what are called the common people. I imagine that Lowes Dickinson would loathe Soviet Communism which we think has discovered the root of the matter in its aims and methods. Then again Lowes Dickinson seems to have ignored science and its application to social organisations.

Why don't you write another great novel (analogous to the *Passage to India*) giving the essence of the current conflict all over the world between those who aim at exquisite relationships within the closed circle of the 'elect' and those who aim at hygienic and scientific improvement of the whole of the race? I think the exact antithesis of Lowes Dickinson and his immediate followers may be found in Professor Hogben and his wife; and I am afraid I am instinctively on their side.

But forgive the lengthiness and combativeness of this letter of thanks. If you are ever in this neighbourhood it will be so pleasant to see you.

Sincerely yours

Beatrice Webb

(Mrs Sidney Webb)

907 FP SIDNEY WEBB TO F. W. GALTON

The Fabian Society was in such low water that in January 1934 its jubilee was celebrated only by a modest reception with sandwiches. Beatrice remarked that its fiftieth anniversary might be a good occasion to wind it up. It did little, she wrote, but run the autumn lectures, circulate a few book boxes and promote the summer school, which became 'every year more respectable and seedy', appealing to ageing females and stray foreigners. The Society could not even meet the payments on the loan from Shaw with which it had bought its premises. (BWD 24 August 1934)

In January 1934 Harold Laski had persuaded the Fabian executive to set up a committee to review 'the future organisation and activities of the Society'. Its lame report concluded that the Society should 'restate principles' rather than compete with Cole's New Fabian Research Bureau and the Labour Party: no further action was taken. The Society just scraped along until it merged with the N.F.R.B.

Passfield Corner
Liphook
24/6/34

Dear Galton

I think the suggestions of the Special Sub-Committee admirable; and I hope that they may become a new start for the Society. Most of the other suggestions, not at present brought forward by the Committee, seem to me also useful; and I hope they will be kept in mind. I need not say that I should be glad to be of any use to the Special Committee if they have anything to ask me about. But I cannot undertake any work of any kind, being already burdened to the very limit of my strength. I can only rarely come to London.

That last consideration brings forcibly to my mind the greatest difficulty that the Society and the Committee has to face. *It is the difficulty of getting members to do things*! The Committee has in mind new subjects, more lectures, more pamphlets, more agitation, possibly weekend schools, and so on. I think the Committee is quite right. But I fear the trouble is that it will be hard to find members able and willing to undertake these things gratuitously; or to produce the income necessary to pay for them. We have in the past occasionally paid members small sums to remunerate them for time spent in such services. But the Society cannot well incur more expense at the moment that many members are reducing their individual subscriptions year after year.

Would it be possible to get those members who are specially interested in particular lines of work, if they cannot do them themselves, to increase their subscriptions, or to make donations of sums specially earmarked to whatever plan of work they particularly desire?

Another way of ultimately getting things done might be to form study groups to put in some serious study of particular problems. Sometimes members propose new Tracts, or suggest new subjects for lectures, largely *because they themselves desire to learn something on these subjects.* If special committees were formed on particular subjects, and the necessary study was undertaken, a detailed syllabus for the desired new Tract might emerge from the discussions, or even a draft. At worst, those members who attended the committee might at any rate learn what they want to know about; and incidentally fulfil that part of the Society's programme which is organised investigation and study.

May I make another suggestion? *All* the matters suggested are useful additions to the work hitherto done by the Society. They do not involve abandoning any of our present activities, or scrapping any of our publications, or disclaiming any of our objects. Would it not be well for those who have suggestions or proposals to make to realise that these are *projects for additions* – most desirable additions – not projects for destruction or elimination. Let each member throw his or her energies into whatever part of the Society's activities that he or she is specially interested in, without opposing or discouraging the work of other members in other directions in which they are specially interested. We cannot hope – we ought not to desire – to control our members' individual work. There is, in the aggregate, none too much activity among members. We had better not discourage anyone who is, or may be, doing anything. Rather let us see that we are doing our own little bit!

Yours

Sidney Webb

## 908 PP BEATRICE TO SIDNEY

In September 1934 Sidney returned from a five-week visit to the Soviet Union – the longest period in which the Webbs were separated during the whole of their married lives. He was accompanied by Bernard and Barbara Drake, and Stafford Cripps's son John. The purpose of the visit was to fill in gaps in the material and to submit drafts of several chapters to the Russians for comment and revision.

Alfred Cripps was the grandson of Willie and Blanche Cripps. The young

Cornishes were the children of Laurencina, wife of Hubert Warre Cornish and daughter of Georgina Meinertzhagen. Ralph Fox published his *Lenin* in 1933. The 'new French book' may have been *England's Crisis*, by André Siegfried. William Bullit, an American official who had been on the first U.S. mission to Russia in 1919, played a significant part as a senior member of the State Department in the normalisation of U.S.–Soviet relations in 1934.

It is not clear whether Beatrice is referring to all the volumes of Charles Seignobos (*Ancient Civilisation* 1907, *Mediaeval Civilisation* 1908, *Contemporary Civilisation* 1909) or only to the last of these.

Edmondo Rossoni, who had set up a trade union for Italian workers in the U.S., returned to Italy and in 1918 began to organise the Fascist Confederation of Trade Unions. He was Mussolini's Under-Secretary 1932–35; in 1934 he made an abortive attempt at rapprochement between the regime and some Italian Socialists.

Passfield Corner
Tuesday morning: 11th [Sept 1934]

Dearest one

I am hoping to get your first letter from Leningrad today – it has been a long wait for news since the Kiel letters and the arrival wireless. The Cripps trio have been very pleasant guests; Alfred is rather a charmer – a perfect public schoolboy – he is now immersed in Fox's Life of Lenin and is sampling the other vols – wants some book *against* the Bolsheviks – I am giving him Kerensky. They all went off to Faringdon where they found 3 or four young Booths and Cornishes and evidently liked each other. They leave this month. The Blanco Whites and Birches come to tea on Thursday and I am motoring over to see Lady Murray tomorrow trying to feel not too lonely! I was rung up this morning by the Editor of *London Mercury* who wanted an article by you – and then by me – but I could not make out what it was to be about and rang off.

With the Cripps in the house and with my Soviet party on Sunday afternoon I have done very little work: but this morning I shall go on clearing up. I meander through the vols on Civilisation – Seignobos is the best that I have hitherto looked at – but his optimism about the character of Western Civilisation and the inevitability of political democracy and capitalist prosperity and ever widening culture – reads rather queer today. Mosley's parade in Hyde Park – only 3,000 – was a farcical failure, owing to the perfect police organisation – a low-flying police aeroplane making all speaking inaudible except the booing of the crowd. The Blackshirts have, I think, been killed by Hitler. Eden wirelessed an address from Germany – dully conventional but very complimentary to the U.S.S.R. – whose prestige seems steadily growing. I am sending you the *New Statesman*. I note that neither the English nor the American *Economic Journals* have a single article on Soviet Communism except, in the American, a complimentary review of a White Russian attack on Planning. The wilful blindness of the economists – especially the English – to the *existence* of

Soviet Communism (no mention of it at the British Ass.) is certainly amazing. When will they wake up: will our book make them? A new French book on England – much reviewed – concludes 'nothing happens in England'; universal and well-mannered apathy; neither revolution nor reaction – outstanding comfort in the upper class and a decline in health and birth rate among the poor, but apparently no resentment owing to the dole which is an anaesthetic. Is Mussolini contemplating a change over? He is making overtures to the Italian socialists, and [our friend Rossoni] is *acting Deputy* to the Dictator! I shall be intensely interested to hear all your news; especially Bullit's reaction to his stay in the U.S.S.R. Ask him to come and see [me] when he comes to England.

There is no letter this morning perhaps it may come this afternoon – in any case tomorrow. The Cripps are just gone – so I start on my renewed 'clearing up'.

Best love dear one – write me often. I shall be at the Royal Bath Hotel unless anything untoward happens from the 20th to the 27th. Otherwise address here. It takes about 5 days to get to country address in England.

Ever your devoted

Beatrice

Love to Barbara and John. The balance at bank £671.

### 909 PP SIDNEY TO BEATRICE

Louis Fischer (b. 1896), for many years a correspondent in the U.S.S.R., wrote biographies of Lenin and Gandhi. Ernst Toller (1893–1939), the expressionist writer, was a member of the Communist Party and emigrated on Hitler's seizure of power. He committed suicide. Sokolnikov was arrested in the mass purges, which began at the time of Sidney's visit. Ivan Maisky, the new Soviet ambassador in London, became a close friend of the Webbs in their last years. Regrettably, promised copies of their letters to him could not be obtained before his death in 1975.

Hotel Metropol Room 387
Moscow
12/9/34

Dear One

You will be at Bournemouth before this is delivered, so I send it to Passfield. I hope you are having our weather – another day of bright sunshine and blue sky, almost cloudless, but distinctly colder. Today is a 'free day', when the offices are closed, so we are driving out this morning to a Collective Farm, an hour or more away, returning to a late luncheon about 2 p.m. and going later to the Park of Culture and Rest.

Yesterday we went to the Ministry of Agriculture where we were received by some eight heads of departments under the Assistant Commissar (the Commissar being on vacation). (It is said that they tend to wait until Stalin goes for *his* vacation when they take theirs!) Incidentally, the refreshments were absurdly lavish, dishes of cold meat, great caviare sandwiches, masses of cakes and biscuits, several dishes of sweets of sorts, and a profusion of beautiful pears, grapes, peaches etc. [*sidenote*: N.B. I ate none of them!] A deputation of a dozen cotton-growing men (and one woman with a baby in arms) from Uzbekistan, bearing specimens of their products, was filing out as we entered, all in native costume – all the departmental heads were anxious to tell of their agricultural successes and new devices, so that I found some difficulty in getting *organisation* details. They laughed at the idea of 6 million deaths from famine and minimised the extent of failure of crops. But they willingly undertook to read our draft chapter on Collective Farms, which was handed to the one responsible for the Ministry's journal to correct etc.; and they *promised* statistics and documents etc. After lunch, a long talk with Louis Fischer, and his beautiful Persian wife. He described, with American diffuseness, what he declared he *knew* to be the truth as to the famine (he had repeatedly visited the various districts in those years); which (to my pleasure) *coincides remarkably with what we have written.* He said the expropriation of the recalcitrant peasant had undoubtedly involved great sufferings, but said he did not see what else the Government could have done without making things worse. In the evening, *at 9 p.m.*, we went to see the Vice-Chairman of the Moscow City Soviet (the only hour he could manage) in his office. He came out of a committee to see us, and was going back to it when we left at 10.15 p.m. – a man of charm, ability and modesty, who promised to send a memo amplifying his oral answers, with statistics etc. He said they would do everything for me, whom they knew to be a friend of the Soviet Union! He wanted to see us again; saying he would like to ask *us*, and especially Barbara, some questions; so we asked him to dinner at our hotel, which he accepted, subject to date being arranged. John and I had a few minutes with Ernst Toller (whose book *I was a German* you read). He said we were not only his teachers: he had constructed his play 'The Machine Wreckers' entirely from the facts in our books (query the Luddites?). Barbara had another long morning in the schools with great appreciation. Both she and John write out copious notes, in books that we can borrow. I do it also, but I find it rather a grind! I find I prefer to write to you! I am really quite well; inside all right; no nasal catarrh; sleeping as well as I do at home; getting out of bed at 6.30 or 6.45, and breakfast is brought *punctually* at 8 (by Mrs Tobinson's repeated commands!).

Sokolnikov telephoned yesterday asking us to fix a day for us three to dine with him – we proposed 16 September, which he is going to confirm in writing – he named the hour of 6 p.m., I imagine out of consideration for the Webb's known desire to go to bed at 10 p.m.! I gather that the fact that Madame's baby is only four weeks old does not interfere with such things. I said casually to Mrs Tobinson that I gathered that Sokolnikov was 'waiting for an appointment', to which she assented. I then casually observed that we thought he would do well for the Paris Embassy, to which she (with admirable discretion) *avoided replying*.

There is no doubt that we are being 'petted' by everybody here, in all sorts of ways. Many people ask after you with affectionate concern: whom I reassure by saying you are quite well, and really not incapable of the *journey*; but doubting your strength to stand the constant *talking* and interviewing – already one-third of my exile is over!

Sidney

[*Note in margin*]
Maisky telegraphed yesterday (through Narkomindel) their greetings from Kirlovolsk, but they do not expect to be in Moscow until after we have left.

910 PP SIDNEY TO BEATRICE

Professor S. N. Harper (1882–1943) wrote a standard work, *The Government of the Soviet Union*, which appeared in 1938. Nikolai Shvernik (b. 1888) was secretary of the All-Union Trade Union Council 1930–44, and the leading figure in Soviet trade union organisation throughout the Stalin era. Mollie Holt was the seventh child of Robert and Lawrencina Holt.

Hotel Metropol Room 387
Moscow
13.9.34

Dear One

It is (was) nice to get yesterday your letter of the 5th. (It takes practically 7 days from Liphook to delivery by transfer to the hotel.) Today it is again bright sunshine and a cloudless blue sky, autumnly chilly in the early morning, but *hot* in the afternoon sun. The farm Mrs Tobinson took us to proved to be two hours drive, partly over bad roads, and across the River Moskwa by a bridge which opened to allow ships to pass; and involved a long wait each way. The farm turned out to be, not a *Kolkhos* but a small commune, started in 1929 by 30 families whose total capital was 3,000 roubles, mainly 5 cows and 7 horses. The Government gave them the land and also credit for loan, which they have already nearly paid off. They lived very hard for the first year, allowing themselves only 70 copecks per day for food and necessaries each – now they share over 7 roubles per day each.

It was a strange place – very primitive and 'handmade' as if by amateurs, but very practical and efficient. They produced wheat and other grains; milk; pigs and all sorts of vegetables and fruit, which they sold at their own stand in the Free Market at Moscow. The living arrangements were much as we saw at Seattle but much more primitive – the same simple room for sleeping and common dining room etc. But the whole arrangements for the babies were most perfect (so Barbara said) – though again hand-made. The babies asleep in the sunshine, perfect cleanliness, medically-approved dietary etc., under the management of a qualified woman – the whole thing was started and is still run, by an evident 'leader of men', a humble, unsophisticated young man of peasant upbringing, obsessed with the commune idea. Being a free day, the farm was visited by *two* groups of its 'patrons', a lorry full of Red Army men, and another of young women from some physical culture institution, who came to work in the fields to get in the harvest, as their 'social work' – we were so tired by our $5\frac{1}{2}$ hours excursion, whence we got back only at 4 p.m., that we gave up the Park of Culture and Rest, and rested indoors. From 7 to 8.15 p.m. we talked with Professor Harper, or rather he talked to us. He has innumerable 'contacts' with Russians as well as Americans and newspaper men here, from whom he gathers impressions, without wholly believing any one of them, which he gradually sorts out into some sort of residuum. He is a big, fat, clumsy figure of a man, not at all like a professor or a scholar. It is hard to believe that he could produce good books. His present idea is that the authorities are pushing the workmen *too hard*; 'labour discipline' is too sternly enforced; the Triangle has become an empty form because the Party man always sides with the management; and so on. This seems merely a matter of *impression*. I see no *evidence*. It is admitted that the workers show no signs of discontent, but it is suggested that they will presently do so! I place no value on this loose talk *about the workmen* – those whom Harper sees cannot know what the mass of workers are thinking. We have not yet managed to see Shvernik (the plenum of the A.U.C.C.T.U. ended the day before we reached here). We have his speech in *Moscow Daily News* – the 47 trade unions are to become over 150 and greatly reorganised.

Today we are driving to Bolshevo (reformatory): to utilise the fine weather whilst it lasts, and whilst so many people are still on vacation. I write this to my dearest at 7.30 a.m., whilst waiting for the others to emerge for 8 a.m. breakfast. You will be now at Bournemouth before this reaches you, I hope with Molly Holt and in good weather. Take care of your dear self.

Sidney

911 PP BEATRICE TO SIDNEY

Goodfellows was the home of Stafford Cripps in Gloucestershire. Tobias Weaver (b. 1911) married the daughter of Sir Charles Trevelyan: his brother Lawrence Purcell Weaver married Diana Cripps in 1939.

In reaction to MacDonald's defection, the economic crisis and the rise of fascism in Europe, some of the Labour left drifted away to Marxism or to fellow-travelling with the Communist Party; the I.L.P., which had now broken its old ties with the Labour Party, was a melange of pacifism and Trotskyism; and another group, led by Stafford Cripps, had formed the Socialist League within the Labour Party as a means of pushing it towards more radical politics.

Walter Citrine (b. 1887) was a leader of the Electrical Trades Union, who became general secretary of the T.U.C. 1926–46; later elevated to the peerage he held many public appointments. He was considered to be on the moderate wing of Labour politics.

Konradin Hobhouse was the wife of Beatrice's nephew Sir Arthur Lawrence Hobhouse.

Goodfellows 5.30 a.m.
Sunday 16th [Sept 1934]

Dearest one

I had a lovely drive here and found Biche Ross, two young men – one a Weaver and all the young ones – including Diana, whom I have not seen, just back from Germany with Biche. Also George Lansbury. He looks rather a wreck and is very depressed about the T.U. Congress – which is completely dominated by Citrine. Can the Miners put up no kind of opposition to his vitriolic reaction? He and Stafford expect defeat at the L.P. Conference – and feel a split of the younger men away from the Party. They are both certainly bitter against [Arthur] *Henderson* – more so than against Citrine, whom they acknowledge to be a convinced reactionary and to fight them overtly. I pressed our point: go ahead with your own propaganda and don't break with the party or abuse its leaders – your time will come if your policies prove practicable. Stafford thinks that the present government [and the governing class] generally is doing the best for Capitalism and is in a sense on the right track – as compared with the U.S. Young Weaver who has returned from Canada and has been in the U.S.A. says that the state of U.S.A. is unutterably bad and that Canada is becoming infected with racketeering – kidnapping has already begun though it is believed by American agents. Stafford agrees that Great Britain is gaining by the collapse of Germany and the U.S.A. as exporting powers and the general discredit of their type of Capitalism. He had seen the Swedish Finance Minister who gave a depressed view of Scandinavia – owing to Germany's disorder.

I read some of John's letters. Very long and descriptive – he must be a nice lad. He says you are travelling as royalties in the new Civilisation and that *you* are looking very well. I am sure this trip will do you good, give you a fillip. And certainly a book on the realities of Soviet Communism is needed today more than any other work. Now I will leave off until Hadspen this afternoon. We had a terrific thunderstorm yesterday afternoon but it seems likely to be fine today for our 70 mile drive.

Hadspen
[16 Sept 1934]

A lovely drive, through the countryside on Sunday morning brought me here. Certainly one gets the impression of an accumulation of [? old] charm and comfort of South England and orderly well-mannered life. Hadspen was looking its best: and all the Hobhouses are very flourishing and the last baby a great success, with lovely blue eyes and golden red hair – always laughing. There are odds and ends of people here – but a very different atmosphere from Goodfellows – a life of leisure and small talk. I shall find the three days I've had quite restful – one thinks of nothing and Konradin is very bright and pleasant to look at – and talks great nonsense about all and sundry. It is rather cold here and they don't have fires.

I shan't get another letter until Tuesday. So far as I can see we shall stay at the Royal Bath Hotel for ten days and drive back to Passfield on Sunday, 30th September.

Goodbye for the present.

from your Bee

912 PP SIDNEY TO BEATRICE

Sidney returned, Beatrice wrote to Leonard Woolf, 'full of confidence in the eventual success of *Planned Production for Community Consumption*, as practised in the U.S.S.R. – a delightful prospect for two aged socialists before they depart!' (SU 17 October 1934) Lazar Kaganovitch (b. 1893) was in charge of the construction of the Moscow Metro; later Commissar for Heavy Industry, he was expelled from his leading posts in 1957 as a member of the 'anti-party' group. *Kustarni* is the Russian for 'merchants'.

Hotel Metropol Room 387
Moscow
23.9.34

Dear One

I send this so that you may find a letter waiting for you at Passfield, so that you may not be disappointed! We continue quite well, the weather still fine, warm in the sun, but chilly in the evening – Kaganovitch did not appear: Narkomindel is trying to fix him, but he is very much occupied and on the move. We had a valuable interview at Moscow City Soviet to which Narkomindel sent a competent official fearing that Mrs Tobinson's vocabulary would not suffice! In the afternoon I rested until 4.30, when we went to a factory meeting to meet Comsomols, which satisfied John. To dinner at the British Embassy, given by Charles, the Counsellor, in his own room for us to meet Dr Schiller, the Agricultural attache to the German Embassy. (The Chilstons did not appear.) I was put next to him at dinner, and at once plunged into talk. On the whole he merely confirms what we have already written. He says the peasants are this year working well, even in the villages formerly the most recalcitrant. But he feels that this zeal is induced only by the fear of starvation. If the Russian peasant ever comes near to being 'well-to-do', his overwhelming preference for sloth will inevitably lead him to lessen his work! When I spoke of awaking new wants, he was unconvinced. It is his *idée fixe*. The Counsellor of the German Embassy, who was also at the dinner, said the reason why the peasant was now demanding boots was merely that it was no longer easy to buy lapti, the straw foot covering, because the Kustarni had been so reduced that they no longer made them! The peasants, he said, much preferred the lapti to the leather boots! This obstinate refusal to believe that the peasants, even the younger ones, are ordinary human beings, is characteristic of nearly all the English residents that we have seen. Coupled with this, is the equally obstinate belief that every good thing here is 'only on paper'; meaning, when they are pressed, that the good hospitals, schools and social services are enjoyed only by a few ('growth of a favored class'), and denied to the great mass – whereas they are being, *as quickly as possible*, extended to all. But they nearly all admit, when pressed, that the progress in the past seven years, has been extraordinarily great. Dr Schiller agreed that the Government was quite stable, and the Kolkhosi certain to endure. Goodbye dear one; in another fortnight we shall be together.

Sidney

913 PP BEATRICE WEBB TO WILLIAM ROBSON

Passfield Corner
Liphook
Hants
26th October 1934

Sidney wishes me to remind you of Fabian Tracts
*Facts for London* and *Facts for Bristol* published in the 80s
Dear Mr Robson

I am afraid I cannot refer you to any contemporary source of information about 'gas-and-water Socialism' which, as you justly remark, was a term of abuse. The only justification for it was, that the public supply of water and gas was, in the late eighties and early nineties, a vital question: partly owing to the high price charged by the Companies, and more especially – in the case of water – to the free use of it for the wealthy quarters – parks, fashionable streets, etc., – and the very mean use of it in the slums and other working-class quarters. As a matter of fact, the movement for municipalization became, during the last years of the nineteenth century and ever since, far more closely connected with education, public health, recreation, higher wages, and provision for unemployment, than with gas, water and electric light. This movement I think may be said to have culminated in the Fabian Crusade in favour of a national minimum of civilized life. This Crusade, as you will probably remember, arose out of the Minority Report of the Poor Law Commission – which I venture to think was the high-water mark of Reformist Socialism.

Our little book on *The Prevention of Destitution* was the final statement of this policy of 'Compensation' for the capitalist system. I see, by the way, that Walter Lippman in his recently published booklet on *The Method of Freedom* adopts the principle of a national minimum of civilized life, in a vague sort of way, under the term 'compensated economy' as distinguished from *laissez-faire*. The compensated economy is the solution of all our troubles!

Sidney has come back very well and full of energy. We hope to send part I. of our work on Soviet Communism [the Introduction] to the printers before Christmas: we have four out of six chapters of the second part on Social Trends in Soviet Communism finished, but it has of course to be corrected with up-to-date information. I am afraid that the work is too consecutive and detailed for publication, by way of extracts, in the *Political Quarterly*.

It would be a great pleasure to see you and Mrs Robson down here some day. If you could come down to lunch for a walk in the afternoon you could get back to London by 7.30 by the 6 o'clock train from Liphook.

Always yours sincerely

Beatrice Webb

(Mrs Sidney Webb)

## 914 UI BEATRICE WEBB TO H. G. WELLS

Wells had just published *Experiment in Autobiography*, a lively and frank account of his early life and the first part of his career. Wells used the term 'Samurai' to describe the scientific elite which ruled in *A Modern Utopia* (1905).

Passfield Corner
Liphook
Hants
1st November 1934

Dear Mr Wells

How delightfully kind of you to send us the two volumes of your autobiography. We had meanly got volume I. from the Times Book Club – with the intention of buying the whole work second-hand! It is, by the way, one of the vagaries of book selling that, owing to the multitudinous output of lending libraries, the works of popular and distinguished authors appear on the second-hand list after the immediate demand has been fulfilled.

But to return to your book. We have both been most interested and also enlightened by reading it. You certainly have a marvellous gift for disinterested analysis of your own career, which makes the reading of your autobiography extraordinarily stimulating. I was particularly charmed with the portrait, always present in the background, of 'Jane' which brought back to my memory her fastidious refinement and real wisdom about life.

Of course, what interested us most was your forecast of a *vocation of leadership* in the Samurai. I admired it at the time – but now it appears all the more remarkable because it has been fulfilled by the U.S.S.R. Communist Party. There remains the question whether you can have such a disciplined order or companionship without a definite metaphysic behind the projects which are advocated. It is in fact a revival of a social institution which has always been called a Religious Order – the Salvation Army was also a revival of that social relationship – but with a very poor metaphysic behind it. The C.P. of the U.S.S.R. gets its creed in Marx–Leninist economics, which by the way I think you undervalue. As for a planned society, I doubt your preference for Roosevelt's controlled capitalism over the planned production for communal consumption inaugurated by the U.S.S.R. However, time will show which project is successful.

If you should ever be in this neighbourhood, do come and see us again; we are nearly always here, as we are completely absorbed in getting on with our book on Soviet Communism. When it appears, as I hope it will, next autumn, you shall certainly have a copy – though I rather doubt whether you will be able to read through these two solid volumes?

With greetings from both of us

Always yours sincerely

Beatrice Webb

(Mrs Sidney Webb)

## 915 PP BEATRICE WEBB TO ARNOLD TOYNBEE [*incomplete*]

Arnold Toynbee had become Director of Studies at the Royal Institute of International Affairs. He began to publish his impressive survey, *A Study of History*, in 1934. Sir James Jeans and Sir Arthur Eddington (1882–1944), were distinguished astonomers whose speculations about the universe had a religious cast. Professor J. B. S. Haldane (1892–1964), the geneticist, was for many years a prominent member of the Communist Party.

Julius Hecker (b. 1881) wrote several books popularising Soviet philosophy, including *Religion and Communism* (1933) and *Russian Sociology* (1934), to which Sidney Webb provided a foreword.

The Albany
Hastings
May 20/35

Dear Mr Toynbee

Ever so many thanks for your most interesting and suggestive letter. Certainly keep the proofs: we can presently send you the proof of the chapter on the Social Services. The one on Science in the U.S.S.R. is written but not printed, and the last on 'A New Civilisation' is in process of being written. We will let you have the typescript of these in the course of the next month. Perhaps in July you and Mrs Toynbee could come to spend a couple of nights with us for a talk over our somewhat divergent views about the main contribution of the U.S.S.R., in her new type of social institution.

We have read with great interest and a large measure of agreement your description of the 'contradictory trends' in Soviet foreign policy – which we have dealt with very cursorily in our XI chapter. Where I think we differ, is in the relative importance of the new society – Soviet Communism – and that of the contradictory trends in her foreign policy. This is an inevitable difference owing to the fact that you are interested in foreign affairs and we are interested in social institutions.

Perhaps we can learn from each other? I quite see your point – which has also been made, in a less informed way by H. G. Wells, that Stalin has given up the messianic faith in the immediacy and inevitability of a world revolution, fomented and perhaps actually helped by the Soviet Communist Party and its allies in other countries. He has banked all his hopes and resources on making a new social order within the U.S.S.R.; on holding it out, in the course of the next decade, as an *Examplar* which other communities will accept, or not, according to the upshot of the class struggle within their respective countries. Whether this decision will lead to the suppression of the Third International (we hope it will) depends on Stalin's power over the C.P. – which I think – is not so great as some people imagine.

The other point you raise as to the character of the C. faith – whether it is a religion – depends on how you define the word? If 'religion' means faith in the *supernatural* – as it is expressed in the great religions of the world – then the answer is in the negative. If you mean an ideology in a definite purpose – with a code of conduct fulfilling that purpose – then the C.P. has certainly a religion – the religion of humanity – not altogether dissimilar from that of August Comte. Where Communism differs from all the former religions is first, the substitution of the service of man for the service or worship of God or Gods, and secondly, in their insistence that their purpose must be carried out, not by any form of magic but exclusively by the scientific method of making the order of thought correspond with the order of things.

How they have arrived at their purpose of improving the human race and how they decide on a scale of values, they do not know. All they do is to deny that this *purpose* arises from any communication with an outside spiritual force; even when they take the form adumbrated by Jeans and Eddington or even by J. B. Haldane in a mathematical formula. But this denial is, I think, not necessarily permanent: it is due to Lenin's hatred of the great church and the evil part it played in the Tsarist regime. I doubt whether this dogmatic atheism will survive. Have you read Hecker's *Religion and Communism*? He is an American-Russian philosopher, living in Moscow and though not himself a member of the Party, very sympathetic to its activities – his books are well worth reading. He was and I think is still a Christian of the Quaker type.

## 916 BL BEATRICE WEBB TO GEORGE BERNARD SHAW

Shaw's play, *The Millionairess*, was based in part on Beatrice's experiences in the East End of London fifty years before, when she had worked briefly in a tailor's sweat-shop. After a visit from Shaw, when he read her the first act, Beatrice noted that she disliked the play – yet another instance of Shaw's admiration of 'the *forceful*' – and contrasted the young idealist who had supported rebels with the old man who idealised dictators. (BWD 1 July 1935) Just before this visit Shaw had written glowingly about the proofs of *Soviet Communism* as the culmination of the partnership's skill. (BWD letter inserted 9 May 1935)

Passfield Corner
30th July 1935

My dear GBS

In my brightest moment – after the early cup of tea, I have amused myself by reading and pondering over *The Millionairess*. Here are observations and reflections.

*The Sweater's Den* (in some ways the best scene in the book). A workshop is a workplace *where no power is used*: if power be introduced the workplace becomes a factory, subject to all the restrictions and penalties of the Factory Acts, many of which do not apply to workshops. The Clothing industry is subject to a Wages Board, which fixes minimum wages, and any employer, whether in a workshop or a factory, paying less, is not only fined, but has to pay his workers arrears of wages.

About your 'man's' workplace. I doubt this introduction of a gas engine into such a workshop: with only six machines it would be far too costly and the older the engine the worse it would be. When I knew the ready-made clothing industry, that part of its conducted in workshops – even large workshops employing 50 workers, survived, just because no power was used: they lived on cheap labour. What has happened to the clothing industry in particular I do not know. But generally speaking throughout industry, chronic under-employment and low wages alike have been altogether superseded, as causes of destitution, by unemployment. Not because wages have risen – as they undoubtedly have, but because increased productivity depends on the perfecting of machinery and the use of power – with fewer and fewer human beings working it. That is why the person with an *effective demand* is today the all-important factor in promoting the wealth of nations. Hence the success of Soviet Communism, which provides this *effective demand* continuously and permanently – by planning production for community consumption. Under this system it is the machine that becomes the slave of humanity: all that is needed is skilled workers who can control more and more machines, and who are provided with more and more commodities and services, or, alternatively, with more and more leisure in which to enjoy life and develop their personalities. Hence the drive among the youth in the U.S.S.R. for 'improving their qualifications'; and the T.U. delight in piecework, and socialist competition and voluntary work, so that the total national product may be larger and larger – to meet the *effective demand* on the part of all the inhabitants, ablebodied and non-ablebodied, for more and more commodities and services, and longer and longer holidays. Forgive this return to the subject matter of our own book!

Now about the play itself. Frankly, I don't like it – perhaps I am too obsessed with our highly specialised work, or too lacking in sense of humour, or both. My complaint is, its intolerable ugliness. In the *Unexpected Island* and in *Too True to be Good* there is a strain of beauty, which compensates for, or balances, the burlesque situation and lampooned personalities. But in *The Millionairess*, every character is detestable, and every scene an ugly farce – which seems to lead nowhere. Of course the dialogue is often witty and illuminating – but even here you are not at your best. I hope the distinguished actress will not accept the part and that you will not stage it. Anyway it is too short to be more than a curtain-raiser? Leave it to be discovered after your death, as a neglected spark from the genius of Bernard Shaw!

Always your loving and admiring friend

Beatrice Webb

I have tried to write legibly sitting up in bed.

917 PP SIDNEY WEBB TO WILLIAM ROBSON

Passfield Corner
Liphook
Hants
27.11.35

Dear Robson

I forgot to comment on your *ferocious* denunciation of the Soviet architects! This is quite certainly *indecently* unmeasured. I have no pretension to 'taste' in any art. But we all of us have had *experience* as to the receptions of every kind of *l'art nouveau* by both the contemporary public and many, if not most of the contemporary practitioners! The sane reader would say of your ferocity (so unlike all the rest of your document) 'who is he that he should so dogmatically pronounce sentence on all contemporary Soviet "architects"'. As for my own impression, I thought some of the new steel and concrete buildings hideous, and some quite pleasing to look at. The government buildings at Kharkov struck me as 'successful'. (The Lenin Mausoleum seemed to me just *perfect*!)

Yours

Sidney Webb

918 NLW SIDNEY WEBB TO THOMAS JONES

Tristan Jones, the son of Thomas Jones, became a journalist.

Passfield Corner
Liphook
Hants
5.12.35

Dear Jones

We hope the leg is better. But pray give it horizontally *long* enough!

We hope that Tristan did not find the old people boresome. We liked his candid ingenuousness and intellectual independence. I hope he will soon get a definite job. If (as seems probable) it is executive, he should certainly be pressed to go on studying in his spare time, even if it is no more than studying the U.S.S.R. There are so many parents in respectable positions who now have sons or daughters with Communist leanings that I am tempted to issue a leaflet pointing out the advantage, in such cases of prescribing and insisting on an exhaustive study of the Webbs' book, in order that the young people may at least know the truth about what is attracting them! Don't forget what I construe as a promise to let us know as soon as you can visit us.

Yours

Sidney Webb

919 UI BEATRICE WEBB TO H. G. WELLS

'It's a great piece of work', Wells wrote to the Webbs about *Soviet Communism*. 'You keep your feet on the ground and yet you seem to have everything within your reach . . . You're great people. Sometimes in the past, in the heat of our mutual education, I may have seemed a trifle "detractive" of you. I am glad to have this occasion to render you a phrase or so of unqualified respect.' (UI mid-January 1936) His main criticism, repreated in substance in another letter of 27 July 1937, was that the Webbs had underestimated the extent of 'personal autocracy' and suppression of controversy.

Wells had become closely involved with the filming of his book, *The Shape of Things to Come*, by Alexander Korda.

Passfield Corner
Liphook
Hants
17th January 1936

My dear H. G.

We were delighted with your most kind and appreciative letter. There is no one whose approval of our monstrous performance we so much relish as your own. We are off to Majorca in a few weeks time, and do not expect to be back until about Easter, but do remember to come down and spend a night with us some day after that, when you are through with your big job.

We were most interested in hearing about your new departure. I am sure that elderly geniuses ought to take to new subjects, and new techniques, like G.B.S. did with *St. Joan*, and we have done to some extent with *Soviet Communism*; so we shall look for great things from you. Film making is certainly a new technique which has not yet been properly exploited.

With affectionate regards from both of us

Always yours sincerely
Beatrice Webb
(Mrs Sidney Webb)

920 PP BEATRICE WEBB TO A. C. PIGOU [*unsigned copy*]

Sir Esmond Ovey (1879–1963) was British ambassador in Moscow 1929–33. The anecdote, based on Moscow gossip, cannot be verified. W. B. Reddaway, who became professor of political economy at Cambridge, published *The Russian Financial System* in 1935.

*Soviet Communism – A New Civilisation?* proved to be a massive and turgid tome: like Marx's *Capital* it was more quoted than read, its main impact deriving from the public endorsement of the Soviet Union by the two eminent Fabians and labour historians. It was not, however, so adulatory of Soviet society as some critics have suggested: its main weakness lies in its normative description of the Soviet system – the Webbs had neither the knowledge, the time nor the opportunity critically to assess the information given to them – just as it was about to be transformed by collectivisation, the second Five Year Plan, and the succession of draconic purges which followed the 17th congress of the Communist Party in 1934. All through the late thirties it was cited as a primary text on Soviet reality when in fact much of the material was provided in draft by Soviet officials and the situation it purported to describe had been overtaken by events at the time it was published. The Webbs, however, made no serious attempt to revise it: their conviction that they were right was underlined when they dropped the query after 'A New Civilisation' in later editions; and

Beatrice wrote a preface to a wartime edition which went further than the text of the book in praising Soviet institutions.

Writing to Mrs S. P. Turin, personal secretary to Beveridge at the L.S.E. and the wife of a lecturer at the School of Slavonic Studies who had translated much Russian material for the Webbs, Beatrice said that it did not matter whether Beveridge or other critics objected to the book or disliked the Soviet system. 'Today the published results point to its success – it is exactly this that makes B. [Beveridge] so angry. We who believe in Soviet Communism must just smile and smile again. The winners in a game can always afford to be polite to the losers.' (PP 18 March 1935)

A. C. Pigou's review in the *Economic Journal* of March 1936 was called 'The Webbs on Soviet Communism'.

[? Passfield Corner]
February 11th 1936

Dear Professor Pigou

We were of course delighted with your review of *Soviet Communism* – all the more because your very warm and, I am afraid, rather over-appreciative account, was accompanied by a delightful sense of humour! It is certainly one of the most 'selling' reviews we have had because it gives a description as well as a criticism of our book. We quite agree with your own one or two demurrers. Whether we have over-estimated the success of the U.S.S.R. the event will prove.

About currency, we were in a difficult position. Currency and the price system generally are mere tools in the hand of Gosplan; they are mere machines and used in this way or that as it suits the immediate exigencies of the Gosplan. To give one amusing instance:

When we were in Moscow in 1932 the Soviet Government was very anxious to conciliate the diplomatic circle; so they opened a rouble shop where all diplomatists could buy at a very low price the rationed articles. Knowing this privilege the British Ambassador brought an extra motor car over the frontier and sold it for 30,000 roubles to another diplomat. Suddenly, and without any notice, the rouble shop was swept away and the diplomatic circle had to buy all its commodities at the Torgsin shop where valuta alone was taken; or buy them at an extravagant price in the open market. This step was taken because certain inferior diplomatists had been buying huge quantities – it was said one bought a ton of sugar – at their rouble shop in order to sell at a higher price to the Moscow citizens. Ovey was furious, and one of the reasons why he made himself so unpleasant about the British Engineers was said to be this unfortunate adventure. Today the Torgsin shops have been swept away, and an attempt has been made to established a fixed rate of exchange for the rouble. When we were there in '32 the official exchange was $5\frac{1}{2}$ roubles for the pound; it is now 25 roubles for the pound. Whether this will or will not sweep away the black exchange we do not know.

Another change which has recently taken place is the sweeping away (described by Reddaway) of the closed co-operatives with their differential rates for commodities according to the character of the plants or the factory. So far as state or municipal manufactured commodities are concerned there is assumed to be a single price; I say *assumed*, because, as you will see, in our chapter 'In Place of Profit', the Trusts will open shops to compete with collective farmers if they think these are trying to get higher prices than is reasonable, even if they have to sell the commodities at a loss.

Another distinction between currency in the U.S.S.R. and in capitalist countries is that it has no kind of influence on the activities of the foreign trade department. They are not interested in international rates of exchange. All they do is to produce articles for export for which they can get the highest price. Today they are concentrating on gold. Foreign trade is, in fact, a question of barter, hitherto modified by their desire for long-term loans, a desire which is diminishing year by year.

I wish that some currency expert would go over to the U.S.S.R. and discover the way in which money has been used by Gosplan for all sorts of purposes mainly psychological and not economic in the profit-making meaning of that term. For instance, if the Soviet Government thinks it is desirable to raise money wages they start a crusade for a government loan to build socialism in the U.S.S.R.; in that way *de*flating the currency which they had *in*flated. This loan is subscribed largely for patriotic motives, but incidentally it serves as deferred wages which can be drawn on when commodities are more plentiful. Today they are advertising commodities and not raising loans and they advertise those commodities which they think it is best that the people shall buy, not those which realise the biggest surplus on cost of production. For instance, they are pressing the collective farms not to buy gramophones and wireless sets but to use steel and concrete for building theatres, schools and creches. And of course their enormous expenditure on newspapers and books is deliberate policy on the part of the Communist Party. Capitalist economics have nothing whatever to do [with], and are hopelessly irrelevant to, the work of Soviet Communism.

Pray forgive this long answer to your kindly criticism of our omission to deal with currency.

My husband and I are going to Majorca the end of this month for a complete rest. If you should ever be in this neighbourhood after Easter we should be so glad if you would spend a night here and have a talk about things.

With kind regards from my husband

Yours sincerely

## 921 PP BEATRICE WEBB TO MADAME HALÉVY [*unsigned copy*]

Denis Nowell Pritt (1887–1973) was a prominent barrister, Labour M.P. for Hammersmith 1935–50, and briefly a member of the Labour Party executive. His pro-Soviet views, already evident in his reaction to the purge trials in 1937–39, were expressed in a number of books and recognised by the award of the Lenin Peace Prize in 1954. Lord Edward Cavendish was one of the victims of the Phoenix Park murders in Dublin. Leon Trotsky was already in exile when the Webbs met him in 1929. Maxim Litvinov (1876–1951) was Soviet Foreign Minister 1930–39 and 1941–46.

The trial in the summer of 1936 of the old Bolsheviks, Gregori Zinoviev (1883–1936) and Lev Kamenev (1883–1936) for 'Trotskyism' and 'Terrorism', was the first of a series of 'Show' trials which heralded the next phase of great purges. Beatrice noted: 'For the defender of Communism in foreign parts the sensational trial in Moscow . . . is a nasty shock'. (BWD 28 August 1936)

[? Passfield Corner]
September 1st 1936

My dear Madame Halévy

We were very much interested to get your letter, though I am afraid I have not the material for a satisfactory answer to your enquiry about the Moscow Trial.

I understand that Pritt K.C., a very distinguished English lawyer, has attended the trial, and is convinced that it has been conducted fairly. My own impression is, that with a governing class recently come into power whilst sections of the community are still unreconciled to its authority, it is extremely unlikely any political trial will be carried out in the same manner as it would be in an absolutely stabilised country like Great Britain or France. For instance, it would be contrary, I think, to the principles of English jurisprudence to accept as conclusive evidence the testimony of the criminals concerned about themselves and other people. We do so, of course, in political trials in those parts of our dominions in which the government is not recognized by any considerable section of the community as a rightful and constitutional government. For instance, the murderers of Lord Edward Cavendish and his companion in 1883 were convicted solely on the evidence of the criminal who turned *Kings* Evidence: that is to say, he was given a free pardon in return for his evidence. You will remember that he was afterwards smuggled away to South Africa in order to avoid the vengeance of the Irish people, and was there murdered by one of the Irish Nationalists. The same procedure is followed in India where murderers are not only convicted on the evidence of associates, but if there is no evidence at all they are kept in prison without trial. There are said to be a hundred thousand political prisoners in India at the present moment.

To return to the Moscow Trial: how far all the defendants were intimidated or falsely reassured as to their destiny before the trial, we do not know.

Whether apart from the evidence in the trial, it is likely that Trotsky and the prisoners were guilty of a plan to murder leading Soviet officials, I really have no opinion. We saw Trotsky in 1929 and we thought that he was in a state of megalomania, ready to do anything against Stalin and his associates, partly for personal reasons, but perhaps mainly because in giving up promoting revolutions in other countries, Stalin and his friends were betraying the revolution in Russia. He flatly refused to admit that socialism could be brought about in one country unless you had a proletarian rising in all countries. Kamenev, and by the way, Litvinov, assured us in 1918, when we saw them in London, that it would be impossible to build up socialism in Russia unless there was a revolution in the rest of the world. And that was, undoubtedly, the dominant faith of the Bolshevik party up to 1928, when Stalin and his friends adopted the policy of socialism in one country and turned their attention to collectivising farms and thus completing the process of planned production for community consumption.

We are convinced that it is only by this means that you can solve the problem of maximising plenty so that every individual in the country can enjoy full development, whatever his race, or whatever his capacity. About this part of Soviet Communism we feel quite convinced. The problem seems to be how can you combine this planning of the mental and physical environment without to some extent, limiting the freedom of exceptional personalities. That problem has not been solved in the U.S.S.R.

There is also the problem of creating a moral code which will be accepted by all parties; and which will, once for all, prohibit terrorism or duplicity as a means of obtaining your ends. This is not likely to happen in a revolutionary world.

I don't know whether this statement of our point of view will help you and Professor Halévy to come to any conclusion about the rightfulness or wrongfulness of the Moscow Trial. Civil war is a hateful business because both parties have to remain on the battlefield after one of them has been beaten. It seems to me to necessitate certain forms of injustice. For instance, the Spanish Government which came into power through the will of the people expressed at the polls last spring ought, being wise after the event, to have arrested and interned all the generals and most of the officers in the Spanish army! After that they could have put their secret police to unearth the conspiracy which undoubtedly had taken place to upset the duly elected government by force and terrorism; then they could have shot the conspirators and have done with it. What is the moral?

In *The Anatomy of Frustration* Wells produced another of his homilies on the fate of mankind and the frustrations of mortality. Beatrice, noting that he thought he could save the world if he were dictator, commented that 'his vision of the future turns out to be a series of bombastic sentences, big emotional phrases, without intellectual content'. (BWD 2 November 1936) She had a similar reaction to the film of *Things to Come*, feeling that it reduced human beings to scurrying ants. 'Restless, intolerably restless, is this new society of men: ugly and depressing in its sum total . . . As an attempt to depict *a new civilisation* the film is a disastrous failure.'

Passfield Corner
Liphook
Hants
20th October 1936

My dear H. G.

Ever so many thanks for your most kind thought in sending us your book. As a pathological study of frustration it is of first-rate interest. But as an assumed essay in autobiography I venture to think it is surprisingly unwarranted. You have romped through the world, living the life you liked, and doing the work you intended to do, amid a multitudinous applause. If you feel frustration instead of being grateful for over-fulfilment, I think you exceed all bounds of expectation. Perhaps it is that you wanted to combine quite incompatible ambitions. You chose to fly in the air and survey the world, bombing what you did not like, and recording what you approved of. That pursuit is quite inconsistent with leading an army of occupation. For that purpose you must lead the pedestrians – and you loathe pedestrians, or at any rate you suffer them with benevolent contempt.

We, on the other hand, who are mere pedestrians, have no feeling of frustration, for the simple reason that we knew we could not fly in the air and survey the world, and destroy the barriers we objected to. But we also have lived the life we liked, and done the work we intended to do, and we are supremely grateful for the good time we have had.

However, you are a genius, and on the whole on the side of the angels. Mind, I say 'on the whole'! – in some ways you have combined the incompatibles.

I have not yet seen your wonderful film but I am arranging to go next week to Farnham, where I understand it will be on. Why don't you come down and see us someday? I should have liked to have been at the dinner to add my congratulations on your seventieth birthday – but alas!, on the eve of my 80th year I am no longer fit for these celebrations.

Always yours

Beatrice Webb
(Mrs Sidney Webb)

923 PP BEATRICE WEBB TO A. C. PIGOU [*retained copy*]

Sidney's article on 'Soviet Currency' appeared in the *Political Quarterly* No. 1 1937: Beatrice sometimes confused this journal with the American *Political Science Quarterly*.

Passfield Corner
Liphook
Hants
19th January 1937

Dear Professor Pigou

Very many thanks for your most concise and witty answer to my question.

One reason for my interest in these technical terms used by the opponents of socialist planning is, that we are thinking of a little book entitled *The Unexpected in the Economics of Socialism as Applied in the U.S.S.R.* Certainly to us the use of currency (perhaps you have read my husband's article in the *Political Science Quarterly*?) and its relation to saving and pricing, and the absence of any relation to foreign trade, was quite unexpected; also the success of the self-governing workshop, the collective farm, and the consequent appearance of a free market and free contract always supervised by Gosplan. Moreover, who would have imagined that in the first socialist state you would have had this mass movement in favour of increased productivity by the lowering of labour costs, and the frantic effort to increase mechanisation. Poor Citrine, (the General Secretary of the Trade Union Congress) was terribly distressed to discover that the trade unions who administer the artificial wage fund are insisting on piece work, costing, shock workers' brigades, and every other device which can be invented to increase productivity relatively to the number of persons employed! Also the trade unions encourage production by prisoners and the Red Army – it all adds to the wage fund by diminishing expenses. Such is the effect of the absence of the landlord and the capitalist!

It is this socialist competition, accompanied by the obligation to bring all your defeated rivals, whether individuals or factories, *up to your own level of productivity*, which is now ensuring the success of Gosplan. Then again, we socialists have always considered that the nationalisation of the means of production, distribution, and exchange was the main principle of socialism. Now we discover that it is the exclusion of the *profitmaker*, whether employer, trader, or financier, which is the fundamental principle of collectivism. Indeed, so far as one can see, there will be a far larger distribution of the instruments of production among individuals and groups of individuals than in any capitalist country in the world. All that is needed is the nationalisation of land and the key industries, whilst penalising all forms of profit-making by individuals or groups of individuals, and the requirement from every able bodied man and woman of their contribution towards the national income to be used for national defence, social services, cultural development, scientific research, an artificial wage fund and governmental expenses.

Forgive this lengthy reply. It needs no answer.

We should very much like to see any report of your popular lectures about Socialist Central Planning, and I do hope you will print them. I think there would be a large demand for the book.

Always yours

Mrs Sidney Webb

924 BEV BEATRICE WEBB TO SIR WILLIAM BEVERIDGE [*retained copy*]

In *Planning Under Socialism* (1936), Beveridge referred to an article by the anti-socialist economist George Halm called 'The Possibility of Adequate Calculation in a Socialist Community' published as Chapter IV of *Collectivist Economic Planning*.

Passfield Corner
Liphook
Hants
19th January 1937

My dear Sir William

I venture to think you will be interested in the enclosed correspondence with Professor Pigou. I do not know whether you would endorse his very contemptuous dismissal of the term 'economic calculus'. I looked in your *Planning under Socialism* and I do not see that you have used that term. But if you have used it I would very much like your definition of its meaning.

I note that you refer to an article (page 7) of George Halm 'On the Possibility of Adequate Calculation in a Socialist Community'. Does 'adequate calculation' take the place of the 'economic calculus'? I looked up the article, but as he has no knowledge of any socialist community, neither of the U.S.S.R. nor the modified socialism of Scandinavia, New Zealand, and other countries who had adopted part of socialist planning, his opinion is, in my mind, quite worthless. It is amazing that with the U.S.S.R. there to study as well as the middle way of Scandinavia, these economists refuse to look at the facts. But before we can discuss the facts we must clear the way by settling what is the meaning of the terms we use. What exactly do we mean by *the price system*? Does this term involve the environment of profit-making? Of course all countries have a price system of one sort or another: the U.S.S.R. has a very decided price system which they are constantly changing according to the exact point they have reached in the development of a socialist economy. What is so confusing are the assumptions which seem to lie at the base of all these terms. It is this underground meaning that I think accounts for Keynes's inability to stick to one meaning of a term that he is using. At some places he accepts the current assumption of profit-making as part of the meaning of the term, and at other times he seems to reject these assumptions, therefore altering the meaning of his term.

All this means that I do hope that you will have the time and opportunity, some day, to study the present experiments in altering the capitalist basis of society. There are so few people who are really capable of doing that job.

Always yours sincerely
(Mrs Sidney Webb)

925 PP SIDNEY WEBB TO J. WALTON NEWBOLD

J. Walton Newbold (1888–1943), journalist and lecturer, was successively a member of the Fabian Society, the I.L.P., the Communist Party, the Labour Research Department and the Labour Party. He was briefly Communist M.P. for Motherwell 1922–23. Max Eastman, the American journalist who was a prominent early member of the Communist Party, became a supporter of the exiled Trotsky and a fierce critic of the U.S.S.R.

Passfield Corner
Liphook
Hants
10.2.37

Dear Mr Newbold

I fear I cannot answer your letter of 7 February at the length which its subject deserves! I have not seen Max Eastman's article. But he has for the last decade been constantly calumniating the Soviet Union, in the interest of Trotsky. I don't think he has any recent knowledge about the subject.

*Equality* of wages (or of incomes) has never been either a tenet of Communism or a precept of Socialism, or of the U.S.S.R. in its progress towards either of them. Why should inequality of incomes be made a matter of reproach to the Soviet Government? (As a matter of fact, the inequality in U.S.S.R. is far *less* than in any other great country – and much less extreme than Eastman suggests. A typical industrial Director gets about *10* times the wage of his least skilled day laborer; whereas in England it would be nearer 50 times, and in America 100 times. In the U.S.S.R. the author is the best paid person(!), because he is paid roughly according to the number of copies of his books that are printed.)

As to Democracy, it is all a question of definition. The new constitution is plainly a great advance in that direction. (It is very characteristic of Eastman to argue *as if* Democracy, Socialism, Communism etc were fixed, tangible entities, which you *were* or *were not*!)

May I say that the question whether Soviet Communism amounts to a 'New Civilisation' should not be confused by enquiry whether it is a *Good* Civilisation. Naturally it is not all good, or throughout good. It has, according to my judgement, or to yours, good features and bad ones – exactly as our own civilisation has! The important question is what can we learn from it.

Yours very truly

Sidney Webb

P.S. The death sentence on children of 12 is a characteristic slander started, I believe, by the Roman Catholics here. Like most slanders, it has an apparent basis of truth. I feel pretty sure that there has been *no* death sentence on any child of 12, or even 15 or 16. What happened was that, an it was found that boys and girls were being used as *tools*, in executing crimes devised by elder criminals, the age above which criminality was made judiciable was lowered to 12. Theoretically this made a child of 12 liable to *any* of the penalties of the criminal law. In fact, not even for murder is there the death penalty. Ten years imprisonment is the highest sentence; except when, *in cases of High Treason* (as we should call it) the Procurator specially asks for the 'supreme' penalty of death (a rare occurrence among 170 million). It is, therefore, a slander to talk as if children were actually liable to be executed. It is inconceivable that a child of 12 should be even charged with High Treason, let alone convicted of it.

## 926 UI BEATRICE WEBB TO H. G. WELLS

Stanway was the country home of Lady Wemyss, formerly Lady Elcho, one of the 'Souls' and a close friend of Arthur Balfour, where both the Webbs and Wells had visited in the early years of the century. The Wemyss family had become so impoverished that the house had been let to the author, Sir James Barrie, who allowed Lady Wemyss to be hostess in her own house for a few weeks each summer.

On 12 June 1937 the Webbs gave a party at Passfield Corner for over a hundred Potter descendants and a few old friends, such as Shaw and other Fabian survivors. It was their way of withdrawing at last from a public life which had continued for nearly twenty years beyond the date when Beatrice had anticipated a comfortable retirement and a leisurely old age.

Passfield Corner
Liphook
Hants
[May 1937]

My dear H.G.

What horrible epithets you use in addressing me. I return a soft answer in calling you H.G.

In response to your question about the Moscow Trials I enclose a long answer embodied in the first 18 pages of the postscript to our second edition of *Soviet Communism*, to be published this autumn. You might return it when read? If you have the patience to read it you will have our view of the Moscow trials. The question which remains to be answered is: 'Will a counter-revolution be avoided? and how long will it take to wear out the particular pattern of behaviour which has hitherto, in all the revolutions known to history, resulted in counter-revolution, and counter-counter-revolution, for a generation or two?' I think on the whole the Soviet Government has acted with wise restraint – with a population of 170 millions the number of trials and executions is comparatively small, as compared with those of the British Government in the Irish Free State civil war fifteen years ago! Violent revolutions are horrid episodes, but could anything have been done to destroy the Tsarist system without a violent revolution? Could we have upset feudal catholicism without a revolution? Or the French have got rid of their corrupt autocratic king? All we know is that *they did not do it*, and had to go through this terrible ordeal.

What is happening to Stanway? The death of the owners and the distinguished occupier was very sudden, almost a family tragedy. I think you remain friends with the group. The dear old lady came down to see me some time ago, and I thought she was more charming in her old age even than she was when she was a beautiful young woman. I understand the family has become poor, like other great families.

It would be so pleasant to see you if you would come down and spend a night with us some time in the autumn?

Always yours

Beatrice Webb
(Mrs Sidney Webb)

P.S. We should be delighted to see the charming Russian lady, we met 5 years ago with you at the Shaws. What does *she* think of Stalin? I am glad you have an [? instructor living over here].

### 927 HL BEATRICE WEBB TO SIR HERBERT SAMUEL

The anniversary was not $\frac{140}{2}$ but $\frac{160}{2}$, as the Webbs approached their eightieth birthdays.

Passfield Corner
Liphook
Hants
23/1/38

My dear Sir Herbert

Sidney and I were delighted to get your charming letter – we often think of those old days when you and C.P.T. [Sir Charles Trevelyan] used to carry on long discussions either with me, or between us. In those days I should have prophesied that *you* could have been more on the side of labour than Trevelyan. But where exactly any progressive finds himself in the present aftermath of the war seems more chance than intention. You certainly have had an extraordinarily interesting career – and it is not half finished yet. It has been very pleasant to watch it from afar off.

Your suggestion that Sidney and I should be guests at a public dinner in honour of our $\frac{140}{2}$ birthday, rouses gratitude for the kindness of the thought, but non-acquiescence. We are not the sort for such public testimonies of respect. Indeed I am not sure that anyone however famous and ornamental except the singled-out – it is invidious for all the other equally directed and able workers who don't get noticed – and if you were to dine them all, the custom becomes burdensome. But I hope we may see you and Lady Samuel someday – we so much enjoyed your visit here more than a year ago. After the general election, when we have been all told our places in the world, we must have another visit from you – I wonder how our forecasts (confidential forecasts) would agree to differ!

Ever yours sincerely

Beatrice Webb

## 928 FP BEATRICE WEBB TO F. W. GALTON

'The inevitable has come – one of the partners has fallen on the way – we shall never march together again in work and recreation', Beatrice wrote when Sidney was afflicted by a stroke. (BWD 25 January 1938). He never fully recovered from it; he was partially paralysed, his speech impaired and he was confined to Passfield Corner. He was able to read, but he could never write easily again. From this time until her death Beatrice had to assume the management of their finances, the maintenance of their vestigial contacts with the outside world, and cope with Sidney's semi-invalid condition. These difficulties were compounded by the shortages and difficulties of wartime life in the country.

Passfield Corner
Liphook
Hants
26th January 1938

Dear Mr Galton

I very much regret that I am not coming up to London tomorrow. The truth is that Sidney has had rather a serious breakdown and I shall have to keep him quiet here for two or three weeks. I have even been obliged to give up my broadcast – or rather, I hope to deliver my statement to another speaker, as I dread the strain added to my looking after him. Our medical adviser gives us every hope of a recovery, but it will be a long business.

Please do not mention this to anyone, as we do not want enquiries, but I thought you should know.

Yours very sincerely
Beatrice Webb
(Mrs Sidney Webb)

929 SU BEATRICE WEBB TO KINGSLEY MARTIN

H. G. Wells had written the article 'Mrs Webb's Birthday' in the *New Statesman*; Shaw had contributed one to the *Spectator*. Wells described Beatrice as 'the animating soul of Fabianism; flushed, bright-eyed, incessant, with an aquiline pounce on a fresh idea'. On 28 February 1938 Beatrice sketched out chapter headings for the second volume of *Our Partnership* 'for someone else to complete?'. She hoped to finish the two remaining chapters of the first volume.

W. Somerset Maugham published *The Summing Up* in 1938; J. B. Priestley's *Midnight in the Desert*, and Aldous Huxley's *Ends and Means* appeared in 1937. The American journalist, Eugene Lyons, described his disillusionment with the Soviet Union in *Assignment in Utopia*, reviewed by Kingsley Martin in the *New Statesman* on 22 January 1938.

Passfield Corner
Liphook
Hants
[Jan 1938]

My dear Kingsley Martin

I am overwhelmed by the recognition of the aged Mrs Webb, and the *New Statesman* – I have not seen the *Spectator*. Why not get G.B.S. to write about something else – later on – something about 'The Faith he holds' – why not have a series on *Living Philosophies*? I have been reading the autobiographies of Somerset Maugham, Priestley and Aldous Huxley – an odd absence of any vision of a new social order, national or international – but a return to mysticism in the two last, and, in the case of S.M., a pessimistic materialism or agnosticism – with the idolisation of *loving kindness* – without any indication that knowledge and its application are needed as well as good intentions, whether in the treatment of disease or the organisation of a public Health Service.

I thought your review of Eugene Lyons book excellent. He, like Malcolm Muggeridge and Aldous Huxley, suffers from the neurotic joy in libelling persons and institutions; they ought all [of] them, to join the R.C. Church and confess and be absolved every few months – to rid themselves of hatred of everyone else, as a way of manifesting their own superiority to men as they see them. It is strange this delight in debunking everything and everybody.

About *Our Partnership* I have settled not to publish any part of [it] during my life time. I am tired of publicity and don't want to hurt anyone's feelings – even *by leaving them out of my picture.* Also there is my own family to consult – 170 of them!

Do come and see us some weekend or weekday in March?

Ever yours

B. Webb

930 BL SIDNEY WEBB TO GEORGE BERNARD SHAW

Passfield Corner
Liphook
Hants
2.6.38

Dear Shaw

I wrote to you one of my first letters! I am sorry Beatrice Webb is put off. I was thinking of writing by her, wishing you both a long life, and lots of rest. Doubtless it is wise for you to get away. I am well but unable to write, and even to speak; but I am reading lot of novels, one a day almost! What a long life you and I have had, and done so much in it, with the aid of wifes! With all possible blessing I send this

Yours

Sidney Webb

931 LSE BEATRICE WEBB TO ALEXANDER CARR-SAUNDERS

Alexander Carr-Saunders (1886–1966), a distinguished social scientist, had succeeded Beveridge as Director of L.S.E. The purpose of the lunch was to decide which room at L.S.E. should be named after the Webbs: the place finally selected was part of the law library.

The Munich Agreement on 29 September 1938 depressed Beatrice despite her sense of relief: 'It seems to my poor senile brain that evil triumphs everywhere'. (BWD 29 October 1938)

The Albany Hotel
Hastings
Sussex
Oct. 8. 38

My dear Director

I hope to be in London on Wednesday November 2nd and I should so like to come and lunch with you and Mrs Carr-Saunders, if she happens to be in town – at the L.S. of E. We are here for a fortnight's change – my husband is much stronger and is enjoying the change of scene – in spite of the stormy weather.

I am sure that you are thinking about the nightmare in which we have been living?

My *feeling* (I have no knowledge on which to base an opinion) is cowardly relief of being saved from war, shame at having let down a heroic little democratic state; regret at increasing the power of the Hitler regime – but a sort of instinctive conviction that the creation of Czecho-Slovakia, with 3 million Germans – was one of the big mistakes of the Versailles treaty? The other big mistake was the National Jewish home – Palestine? Poor Jews! They are having a tragic time of it?

Ever yours

Beatrice Webb

932 BEV BEATRICE WEBB TO SIR WILLIAM BEVERIDGE

The new secretary of L.S.E. was Walter Adams (1906–1975), who himself later became Director of the School. He was, Beatrice noted, 'remarkably able, pleasant and attractive'. (BWD 10 November 1938)

Passfield Corner
Liphook
Hants
17th November 1938

My dear Sir William

We were so grieved to hear from the Bowleys that you had been seriously ill, and that you were still in a nursing home. I console myself with the thought that ever since I have known you, you have had bouts of serious illness, and always returned to the scene with increased health, and a capacity for work. So I hope there will be a repetition of the same experience. In fact I know there will be, having witnessed your extraordinary recoveries from what seemed to be dangerous experiences in the way of health.

I wonder what you are thinking about the present state of things, and on which side are your sympathies? I gather from various signatures to manifestoes, that you are, on the whole, dead against the Munich friendship with Germany. The last move of the Nazi government, its outrageous persecution of the Jews, seems to have brought a reaction, especially in the U.S.A., and I was glad to hear over the wireless yesterday that both Great Britain and France had definitely decided not to transfer any of their colonies or those of Portugal to the German Reich. I assume that Holland and Belgium will be equally determined. It would be a cruel business to transfer the natives to such an unrelenting government in its national hatreds.

When you are recovered and feel inclined to come and see us for a night, it would be delightful to have you here.

I was up in London the other day, and lunched with Carr-Saunders and met the new secretary, who seems a very pleasant and energetic young man. The ostensible reason for my visit was to decide which room should be dedicated to Sidney and Beatrice Webb, and at the Director's suggestion we fixed on the Law Room – which is certainly sufficiently dignified – I should have been content with a smaller room. They also took me over the new building, which owes its existence to you, and I thought it very admirable – especially the theatre.

Always affectionately yours
Beatrice Webb
(Mrs Sidney Webb)

933 PP SIDNEY WEBB TO A. EMIL DAVIES

For some time it had been clear that the Fabian Society and the New Fabian Research Bureau must come together: after the Munich agreement a number of prominent Fabians, believing war inevitable, felt that the parent Society would be unable to survive as an independent body. The stresses between the Coles and their colleagues, on the one hand, and the older Fabians on the other, had long since eased. Beatrice Webb had by now accepted Douglas and Margaret Cole as the obvious heirs to her own partnership with Sidney.

The purpose of Rule 3 of the proposed new constitution – what became known as 'the self-denying ordinance' – was, as Sidney points out in this letter, to ensure that the Society should not be manipulated by snap votes into accepting factional policies. It also left the Society free to publish contentious proposals over the signature of individuals or groups without committing the Society to them. As Beatrice remarked in a message welcoming the new organisation (*Fabian News* February 1939) this rule left the Society free for open-minded research; if members wished to influence Labour Party policy they should do so as individuals belonging to a local Labour party or affiliated trade union.

Cole became Chairman, Margaret Cole Hon. Secretary, John Parker (b. 1906), who was elected as Labour M.P. for Romford in 1935, became the General Secretary (a position he held until 1945), and Beatrice Webb assumed the new honorary post of President of the Society.

Passfield Corner
Liphook
Hants
6th December 1938

My dear Davies

I have followed the proceedings of the Fabian Society with regard to its amalgamation, though I have not been able to visit London for twelve months. I feel that I am attached to the Fabian Society, after more than 50 years' membership, and more than ever do I feel that the needs of the time commend the amalgamation. I have sought to follow the proceedings of the two committees, and without going into details I must say that I am convinced that the terms of amalgamation now arrived at seem to me fair and reasonable. It must go hard with those old stagers such as myself, but I am convinced that the Society cannot do better than accept the conditions so well described in the report.

There seems to have been some mistake as to the terms in the last paragraph of Paragraph 3, which says that no resolution of a political character shall be put forward in the name of the Society. The intention is that such resolution ought to take the form of pamphlets, such as most of those to which the Society is committed, giving reasons for such propositions, and supplying arguments in support of them. Such pamphlets are clearly intended. What is aimed at as to be avoided is the expression, in a resolution, of something or other which might be passed at a meeting attended by fewer than a hundred members – such as a resolution in favor of the refugees, or against war with Italy – which ought to have been put into a pamphlet. I am against such resolutions which have, indeed, very rarely been voted. It is not [at] all consistent with the character of a Society having several thousand members, to commit all the members to a resolution of this sort. After all, if there is a majority for such a resolution, it can surely be left to a subsequent meeting.

Yours sincerely

Sidney Webb

934 FP SIDNEY WEBB TO EDWARD PEASE

On 12 February Beatrice wrote to Harold Laski (BMJL) that 'there will be no more Webb treatises – a good riddance with so many new men coming along'.

Passfield Corner
Liphook
Hants
12th January 1939

Dear Pease

I was very pleased to receive your letter, and glad to hear that you are well enough to enjoy life sitting by the fire, instead of doing twelve hours gardening!

My fate has been a somewhat serious one. A year ago I was attacked by what was called a seizure. This has destroyed all my capacity for inventing anything, and also my power of writing. My life is now a happy contentment in reading books of every kind, and in remembering other things, but without any capacity for using either invention or discovery in any new enterprise.

My wife, who is fully seized with the desire to enable the husband to live, takes it out in innumerable letters and memoranda, which she proposes to transform into books. She is now doing something for *Fabian News*, in connection with the amalgamation of the two societies.

We were both very glad to see the proposal to give you a dinner, which is the very least that could be done for someone who was the beginning of the Fabian Society, and did so much to build it up. I shall not be able to be present, indeed I have not been to London during the past twelve months; but my wife may possibly be able to be present, so long as the date does not fall between Easter and Whitsuntide, when we shall probably be away from here.

Give our love to your wife. We should be delighted if you would motor over here, as you did on one occasion.

Yours sincerely

Sidney Webb

935 PP BEATRICE WEBB TO HERBERT MORRISON [*retained copy*]

With the rise of fascism abroad and growing opposition to the appeasement policies of the Chamberlain government at home, the Left in Britain was attracted by the idea of a Popular Front, promoted by the Communist Party but also having a self-evident appeal. For some time Stafford Cripps and Aneurin Bevan had been seeking to persuade the moderate Labour leadership to seek an alliance of anti-fascist political groups in Britain. When they circularised local Labour parties in January with a memorandum drafted by Cripps, the party executive expelled Cripps for disruption: the formal argument was that the Labour Party should not associate itself with groups or individuals to which it was electorally opposed. Before long Bevan and George Strauss, the wealthy Labour M.P. for Lambeth, had also been expelled for supporting Cripps, together with the Webbs' old friend C. P. Trevelyan. 'My own impression', Beatrice wrote on learning that Cripps was defiant, 'is that the *more done and the less said* about a United Front, the better the result. But Stafford inclines to assert his own leadership . . . The tact which is needed to unravel the tangled skeins of the British Labour Movement – which was Arthur Henderson's special gift – is not one of Stafford's characteristics . . . he takes up a cause and then drops it.' (BWD 21 January 1939)

Passfield Corner
Liphook
3rd March 1939

My dear Mr Morrison

I hope you will not be annoyed by a few words from old friends, on the issue of expelling members of the Labour Party on the ground of their activities.

First a word about Stafford Cripps, whose activities I assume are the beginning of the trouble. Though he is my nephew I am quite aware of his defects. Moreover, so far as we have an opinion Sidney and I are against a proclaimed and publicly announced united front with the Liberals, or with anyone else outside the Labour Party, which would involve modifying the programme and necessarily admitting non-members into a future government. What we and many other old members of the Labour Party object to in the recent action of the National Executive, is the much advertised expulsion of members because they differ as to tactics or even as to policy.

This objection is not based on any moral principle, but merely on expediency, and the experience of other political parties. I recall the period between 1885 and 1906 when the Liberal Party was distracted by splits on one or two important questions of policy. First there was the split about Ireland. Mr Gladstone introduced his bill for Home Rule suddenly, and without, I think, due consultation with his colleagues. This led to some of his Cabinet, and many members of the Liberal Party becoming Liberal Unionists. Some of these subsequently re-joined the Liberal Party. George Trevelyan returned to the party within a few months; my two brothers-in-law, Leonard Courtney and Henry Hobhouse, broke away for some years, and then returned to the Liberal Party, prior to the great election of 1906. None of them were expelled from the party. Other Liberal Unionists joined the Conservatives and eventually the Conservative Cabinet. But even they were not expelled from the Liberal Party – they simply left it.

Another split, and in a sense more serious, was the split over the Boer War. Here again the Liberal Party, even in its highest ranks, was completely disrupted. The Asquith–Haldane–Grey clique supported the South African War, whilst John Morley, Lloyd George and a lot of others were fervent Pro-Boers. Rosebery, of course, retired to his citadel and issued furious manifestoes against the Pro-Boers, but no one was expelled from the Liberal Party. The consequence was that when the Boer War was over the new issues arose, like fiscal Protection, Chinese Labour, the Education Act 1902/3, and new projects of social reform, the Liberal Party came back with a huge majority and became the government of the country for eight years. No such victory could have been gained if there had been a series of expulsions from the Liberal Party over the Home Rule and Boer episodes.

Then again, it would surely have been unwise for the Labour Party to have expelled Oswald Mosley and the dozen or so Labour Members who followed him for a few weeks? By ignoring him and his followers, he wandered into the wilderness, and has been lost from public view, whilst the others resumed their places as Labour Members.

It seems to me that if once you begin expelling, with pomp and circumstance, members of the Labour Party who disagree with the tactics or even with the policy of the Executive, there may be endless disruption, and an irretrievable loss of credit among the general body of electors who may be interested when the time comes in quite a different set of questions. Surely it would be better for the National Executive to quietly reject policies which it does not approve of, and merely ignore the promoters of those policies. Certainly our own experience is that you get more done by ignoring your opponents within your own movement, than by denouncing them. People always forget that denouncing and punishing by expulsion advertises a cause, and even gains it adherents. What you want to achieve is that the opposition should cease to be talked about.

Do forgive me for jotting down our reflections – Sidney agrees with my statement, I may add.

(Mrs Sidney Webb)

936 UI BEATRICE WEBB TO H. G. WELLS

Wells had just published *The Outlook For Homo Sapiens*. 'It is the work of genius in its indictment of western civilisation but of obsessed old age in its outworn suggestion of a World Brain implemented by an Encyclopaedia of all knowledge'. (BWD 5 August 1939) The volume of 'creeds', *I Believe*, to which both Beatrice and Wells contributed, was published in 1939. On 30 March Beatrice had lunched with Wells at his home in Regent's Park. 'I was sorry for him', she wrote: 'a physical wreck . . . obsessed with his own vague vision of a world order.' (BWD 31 March 1939)

Passfield Corner
Liphook
Hants
10th August 1939

My dear H.G.

Now that I have read your book let me express my unlimited admiration for the extraordinarily vivid description of what is going on today in the various regions of the world. But I was especially touched with your chapter on 'Estimating Hopes' with its introduction of the personal factor. The first paragraph on page 106, and that on page 108, exactly expresses my own feelings. The plain truth is that the 'over-seventies' tend to be either obsessed or scatter-brained. G.B.S. is scatter-brained – but his brains are so brilliant that it yields a good return. I once asked him to tell me frankly and seriously what he thought was going to happen in the world, and what he wished to happen. He answered: 'That is your business, not mine'. Whether you are obsessed with your brain trust and encyclopaedia I am incapable of judging; but I am certain that we are obsessed with Soviet Communism.

I am amused, by the way, to see the postscripts which you and I have contributed to the new volume of *I Believe*, as they are both concentrated on our obsessions, and not on the way we have arrived at them. You may be interested to hear that Sidney has been absorbed in your big book *The Work, Wealth and Happiness of Mankind* – he has read it from first to last and says it is, perhaps, the best of your big books. As you say in your last book, the title was not a good one – not sufficiently provocative. However, it will get read by students.

With best wishes for your future products – the more (I will not say the merrier) but the wiser and therefore the better.

Always sincerely yours
Beatrice Webb
(Mrs Sidney Webb)

Charlotte Shaw, who died in 1943, was ailing and crippled with arthritis for the last years of her life. The Maiskys did make 'a flurried visit' on 23 September: the Soviet ambassador, Beatrice noted, was 'grim and defiant'. (BWD 24 September 1939) Maisky, Shaw replied on a postcard, 'should realise that Stalin has trumped the Franco-Soviet project and left him cock of the walk in London'. (PP) Shaw argued in the *New Statesman* and elsewhere that with the collapse of Poland the war was over and that peace should be made at once. The Oliviers had settled in retirement near Bognor.

Passfield Corner
Liphook
Hants
19/9/39

My dear G. B. S.

We were so glad to get your letter as we were getting anxious about Charlotte. Poor Bernard Drake has been held up at Harrogate with a violent attack of lumbago, which is also attributed to nerves accentuating a constitutional ailment; while I have been suffering from chronic bladder trouble made worse by old age plus nerves! You are a marvel – do send us any duplicated copy of your new act to *Geneva*, to distract our minds from the tragedy of the stalemate war.

The Maiskys telephoned last Friday that they were coming down on Sunday afternoon; but on that afternoon, just after we had heard of the Red Army's advance into Poland, they phoned that he could not leave London, but they hoped to come later on. Last time they were here about three weeks ago, he still believed that there would be an Anglo–French–Soviet pact – he was and is in favor of it. They are great friends of Litvinoff's – who appears, by the way to be still a member of the Superior Council, but evidently disapproves of Stalin–Molotov policy of making themselves safe by annexing some of the lost territory of old Russia inhabited by Russian minorities.

All Foreign Offices have become gangsters – in the way of ignoring past treaties with other small powers to protect themselves against another great power. How shall we get out of this guarantee to Poland? I don't know. Unless Germany breaks up I don't see how we can reconquer and reconstitute the old Poland – and on what principle we can set up again the old Poland we erected at Versailles? We can't fight the U.S.S.R. to reconquer White Russia and Ukraine minorities, even if Germany breaks into revolution. Eventually she will go Communist: she will never return to Capitalist political democracy. It is a tragic look out for Great Britain and France.

Sidney remains calm and happy – he reads incessantly and goes for a walk with his maid–valet every morning. The maid–valet – a stalwart

Scottish woman – insists on going to Scotland for her holiday next week; she says she is coming back and I have got a substitute for the time – so we are fairly comfortable and delightfully quiet. London, I am told, is almost impossible in its gloomy darkness – your flat will, I suppose, be uninhabitable if aerial war breaks out? Meanwhile love to you both – as you say 'we are too old to love' in such tragic times – but we should miss each other!

Beatrice Webb

The Oliviers called here the other day, he is exhilarated – she is depressed.

# 9. The end of the partnership

## September 1939 – September 1947

Beatrice sensed the coming war as an apocalypse after which the world she had known would be utterly changed. The one question in her mind was whether the Soviet Union would be the harbinger of a new civilisation beyond the sufferings of war and revolution which she foresaw. The hope, if not a firm conviction, that Communism was the wave of the future was the one sustaining theme of the last years of ill-health and semi-isolation in the country.

In 1938, drafting a concluding passage for the planned volume of *Our Partnership*, Beatrice declared that she and Sidney had been 'hopelessly wrong' in 'ignoring Karl Marx's forecast of the eventual breakdown of the capitalist system'. Step by step, from their return from the Far East in 1912, they had abandoned their old Fabian idea of a 'modified capitalism' and come to the conclusion that Marx was right and that the Soviet Union was in fact the new social order within which their lifelong aims of planned production, efficiency and social equality would be achieved. The demonstration of this belief in *Soviet Communism*, she wrote, was 'the final and certainly the most ambitious task of "Our Partnership"'.

This ultimate conversion was less of a paradox than it seemed. The Webbs had always believed in government *by* a dedicated elite *for* the prople: the 'average sensual man', to whom Beatrice so often condescendingly referred, needed guidance and control in his own interests and in the interests of society at large. That notion had always run through the work of the Webbs; it had been implicit in much of Fabian policy and had shaped the Webbian tactic of permeation. It was partly rational. The Webbs assumed that men of power could be persuaded to do what was useful and sensible; hence their emphasis on persuasion and education. But it was also emotional, especially in Beatrice's case. All her life she had hankered after a sense of purpose, of mystical fulfilment, and dreamed of some kind of 'religious order' which might embody it: the influence of Comte's enlightened 'priests of humanity' lingered long and strongly in her mind. The attitude of the Webbs to democracy, moreover, was ambiguous. Beatrice undoubtedly had a streak of high-minded ruthlessness, which made her wish to sweep away the stupid, the wasteful and the incompetent: the object was not to help the 'undeserving poor' but to abolish them, 'cleaning up' the terrifying morass of ignorance and pauperdom which troubled the conscience and impeded the emergence of an efficient and morally acceptable society. Though both the Webbs had devoted much of their lives to the study of trade unions, Co-operatives and public administration, they never displayed much enthusiasm for working-class politicians or much confidence in the vagaries and frustrations of Labour politics. Such institutions, they felt, could only work effectively as instruments of social change if they were amenable to the advice of disinterested experts guided by the science of society which they had attempted to define and exemplify.

For Beatrice – and, to a lesser extent, for Sidney – the Soviet system fitted into that framework of attitudes: its shortcomings, for them, were not a matter of principle or false assumptions, but simply of the backwardness of Russian society. Even with its shortcomings it had come to seem preferable for them to the moral disintegration, economic failure and political frustration of western capitalism. In the final phase of the partnership, the need to believe was very strong.

It was reinforced by the little company that the Webbs now saw at Passfield Corner. They were glad to see Soviet representatives, maintaining a close relationship with Ivan Maisky, or Soviet sympathisers; to hear good news of the Soviet Union, whether by regularly listening to Soviet broadcasts or reading Soviet and Communist publications; and in the last three years of her life Beatrice displayed little interest in the course of politics and the progress of the war except in so far as the news bore on Soviet defeats and victories. She had taken to calling herself a Communist and to corresponding warmly with Communist journalists and party officials, though she never took the final step of applying for membership.

During the final phase of her life, apart from this consuming interest, she had only one concern. Aware that her health was failing she realised that Sidney, himself an invalid, might soon be left alone. It was a fear that had haunted her since she had first accepted the partnership, fifty years earlier. As she had told him then, she had never been able to feel for him the passion she had felt for Joseph Chamberlain. But in its place there had grown a deep trust, affection and respect which had preserved her sanity and made life bearable for her. She had brought great gifts of intellect and will-power to the partnership; she recognised, however, that it was Sidney's undemonstrative but unfailing devotion that had been the cornerstone of all its achievements.

### 938 WSL BEATRICE WEBB TO RUTH CAVENDISH-BENTINCK

Passfield Corner
Liphook
Hants
28th September 1939

My dear Ruth

I was very glad to get your letter, all the more so that I have a consciousness that I did not answer your last most entertaining letter. The simple truth is that I have been in rather a feeble condition, suffering like many other aged persons from bladder trouble, which cannot be cured. Also I have had a lot of foreign visitors of one sort or another, who come and ask me what I think about the present outlook.

Frankly, I do not know what to think. Foreign affairs and military tactics have never been our subject of study. We have concentrated entirely on the internal organisation of different countries, more especially of those Christian capitalist political democracies which we call western civilisation. I am sure that civilisation is on the down grade, and I think it will gradually, or violently, disappear in the course of the next fifty years. As for the aims of this war to destroy Hitlerism and reconstitute the old Poland of the Versailles Treaty, I am certain we shall not accomplish them. But we may create revolution in Germany and incidentally Hitler may be murdered, or thrown out. But marching through Germany in revolution, to reconstitute the old Poland, with half of it transformed under the direction of the U.S.S.R. into a multiform democracy with a planned production for community consumption, I think will be impossible, and I doubt whether we shall attempt it. Sooner or later there will be a patched up peace, some sort of compromise between the old civilisation and the new. Which will get the best of the bargain remains to be seen. Certainly the U.S.S.R. has got the best of the bargain with Germany.

Sidney, I am glad to say, is very happy, and considering his breakdown 18 months ago, very well. He reads incessantly. I struggle on, trying to write a book for publication sometime before I die, but I doubt whether I shall succeed in doing it. With my large family connection, and the stream of people who insist on coming to see us, I have not much strength left for really good work.

Always affectionately yours
Beatrice Webb
(Mrs Sidney Webb)

939 SU BEATRICE WEBB TO LEONARD WOOLF

Woolf's book, *After the Deluge*, was part of a trilogy; the second and third parts were called *Principia Politica*. His books on Co-operation were *Co-operation and the Future of Industry* (1919) and *Socialism and Co-operation* (1921). His review of Toynbee was entitled 'Moribund Civilisations' and it appeared in the *New Statesman* for 23 September 1939. Beatrice, who had been up to London to meet the Woolfs at their request, added a further comment on the Woolfs in her diary entry for 27 October 1939.

Sir Thomas Potter (1773–1845) and his brother Richard Potter (1778–1842), who was Beatrice's grandfather, were co-founders of the *Manchester Guardian*: both were prominent reformers.

Passfield Corner
Liphook
Hants
19th October 1939

Dear Mr Woolf

I so much enjoyed meeting you and your wife. We live so completely retired from the world, that it is delightful to meet those who are more actively engaged in the writing of books, and seeing other intellectuals. As your wife said, we are all at sixes and sevens, and it is difficult to have any clear understanding of what is likely to happen after the war is over.

In connection with our talk about your book, it occurs to me that if you will be writing your third volume dealing with the period of 1832–95, you might like to read the last chapter of our *Statutory Authorities for Special Purposes*. So I have asked Messrs Longmans to send you a copy, which pray keep for your library. This last chapter gives the transformation of municipal government from the out-worn basis of Manor and Guild under the supervision of His Majesty's Justices of the Peace, to a compulsory association of consumers. As you probably know, all the innumerable statutory authorities which started up in the 18th and 19th centuries, were originally voluntary associations of consumers, who found it necessary to get compulsory powers, so as to supply themselves with lighting, cleansing, water and gas. The Municipal Corporations Act of 1834 abolished the old form of local government (of course with the exception of the County Borough Magistrates) and practically accepted the pattern of the statutory authorities, thus transforming them into municipal corporations. My great-uncle, Sir Thomas Potter, started municipal gas works in 1815 without any local act, but eventually got that and other public services under local acts embodied in the Manchester Municipal Corporation established in 1837 of which he was the first mayor.

I have been reading with great interest your two little books on the Consumers' Co-operative Movement, and should some day very much like to discuss the whole question of the limitations of voluntary associations of consumers with you: I think, of course, that you under-rate them, perhaps you will think we over-rate them!

If we do come to Eastbourne in the spring, we will certainly come and see you.

With kind regards to your wife

Always yours sincerely

Beatrice Webb

(Mrs Sidney Webb)

P.S. By the way I thought your review of Toynbee VI volume, a masterpiece of courtesy, with slightly sarcastic observation on his conclusions – that strange form of verbal analogies, inspired by mysticism?

940 PP BEATRICE WEBB TO GEORGE BERNARD SHAW [*unsigned copy*]

Stephen Spender's review was called 'Honey-Bubblings of the Boiler' (*New Statesman*, 11 November 1939). The phrase which worried Beatrice was: 'A distinguished octogenarian recently, I hear, divided the aged into those who are scatter-brained and those who have obsessions. One great living Irishman provides the outstanding example of the scatter-brained . . .'. Beatrice feared that the Shaws had been offended by her reported flippancy. Shaw replied (PP 15/6 November 1939) that he had not connected her with Spender's remark. He urged her to read Gerald Heard's *Pain, Sex and Time* which was published in 1939.

Passfield Corner
Liphook
Hants
14/11/39

Dear G. B. S.

I have been worrying over the absence of any answer to two letters to Charlotte during the last three weeks. The reason for this is a consciousness of sin and the desire for forgiveness. This consciousness was brought home to me by Stephen Spender's review of Yeats book in the *N.S.* of this week. He cites the reporter saying it was Octagenerian who divided the Aged into those who were *obsessed* and those who were *scatter-brained* and suggested that G.B.S. was among the scatter-brained, whilst the Webbs were among the obsessed. I am aware, that during a casual conversation I did say something of the sort. But there was not on my part the slightest intention of denigrating your work – indeed I remember remarking that if you had a brilliant intellect the more you scattered it over to all creatures the better it was for the world. What was in my mind was an old classification made years ago: those who concentrated their mind on one discovery or ideology – like Milton and Luther, Marx; and those who took the whole world as their province – [? science and industry and art and music] – like Shakespeare and Voltaire and Erasmus. I always thought of you as the Shakespeare of the 19 and 20 century; and ourselves, not like Milton because we are not poets, nor like Luther, who was religious, but like the modern scientific specialist, who never goes beyond his own researches.

However, I won't trouble you with the thoughts of a tired woman. The cost of getting old is that one does and says things without realising what effect they may have on other people or oneself.

Sidney says this letter is unnecessary – too self-conscious – that if this silly saying has been reported to you you will merely laugh at it and that you may be unaware of it.

Don't bother to answer this letter unless you feel inclined to send me a postcard.

'I am unaware of your sin but I give you my absolution.'

941 BL BEATRICE WEBB TO GEORGE BERNARD SHAW

Shaw's letter in the *New Statesman* of 7 October 1939 was called 'Uncommon Sense about the War'; it echoes his similar debunking article published after the outbreak of war in 1914.

Passfield Corner
Liphook
Hants
19/11/39

My dear G. B. S.

Ever so many thanks for your letter which has cleared up my sin-complex of careless disregard for all your kindness to the Webbs, and of our one-ness with you on most life values – though not in the way of explaining things.

We read Gerald Heard; but his style did not attract us – there is a certain shoddyness in his easy going generalisations – but I have forgotten what exactly were his hypotheses. I agree with your letter in the *N.S.* about War aims. It is absurd to state what they *ought* to be – and leads to wishful thinking about what is going to happen as a result of the war. So far as I have seen such statements, by Cole and Laski, they amount to imposing our own Social order in all other countries – a magnificent absurdity.

Germany will eventually go Communist. The alternative is returning to the *First* Reich – with an Emperor. What Labour seems to demand is that she should go back to the Second Reich, i.e. a feeble attempt at parliamentary democracy with Monopoly Capitalism and control. The truth is that the English people are at sixes and sevens, as to what sort of social order they themselves intend to have in the British Empire or even in Great Britain; how can they impose a social order on Europe, still less on Asia and Africa? It is depressing to think how many centuries it may take to create a decent world order. I agree that the U.S.S.R. and the U.S.A. will be the leading Powers after the War. I am still inclined to back the U.S.S.R. But I wish they would get rid of their disease of orthodoxy – of the human parrot, and the human herd.

We are so sorry that Charlotte has had so much pain – it is far worse than my continual tiredness, or Sidney's regrets that he cannot *think* and express his thoughts. Except for that, he is very comfortable and happy and finds plenty of interest in endless reading of old books and new. He sends his love to you both.

Give my love to Charlotte.

Always yours affectionately
Beatrice Webb

### 942 UI BEATRICE WEBB TO H. G. WELLS

Wells sent a copy of *The New World Order*. He had been involved in the effort to draft war aims in 1918, and he took up the same idea on the outbreak of war in 1939, announcing in a letter to *The Times* on 23 October 1939 that he was drafting a new statement of human rights. This was published as *The Rights of*

*Man, or What Are We Fighting For?* at the beginning of 1940; it was followed by variations on the same theme in other books published during the war years.

Beatrice refers to the revision of her contribution to *I Believe*. Her desire for a stalemate repeated the position she took on the outbreak of war in 1914.

Passfield Corner
Liphook
Hants
4th January 1940

My dear H.G.

I was so grateful to you for sending me that inscribed copy of your new book. Sidney read it straight away. He said it was very clever, but would express no opinion as to your suggestions. He is well and happy, but says that he cannot think though he reads incessantly.

I was delighted with all your chapters describing the past and present state of things. My difficulty about your suggestion of a coming together of the intellectuals to think out the problems arising out of this terrible state of things, is that all the younger intellectuals are being caught up for war service of one kind or another. I shall have a dozen or so of great-nephews actually serving as privates, and from what I hear of them their state of mind is one of complete perplexity about what they are fighting for. The middle-aged and elderly intellectuals are so busy trying to make up for extra taxation that I doubt whether they would be willing to sit down seriously with other intellectuals and discuss international affairs. I think all the points you raise are of the utmost importance. Personally I do not feel I know enough about international relations to have any opinion.

Then, as to drafting a new declaration of human rights: I have read yours again with a great deal of interest, but without being able to formulate a criticism. Also the history of these declarations of rights is not promising. The very simple and truistic declaration of rights by the newly-formed American Republic – the right to life, liberty and the pursuit of happiness – did not prevent slavery on an intensive scale in the southern states for three-quarters of a century, and when the northern states waged war to enfranchise the slaves they certainly did not endow them with the right to life, liberty and the pursuit of happiness. President Wilson's fourteen points, and his declaration that it was a war to end war and to make the world safe for democracy, was wholly ignored by Versailles and the subsequent treaties, and the League of Nations. Of course you could answer: What do you propose? To which I can only reply I do not know.

It so happens that I have been engaged on a task of contributing an interposition, 1940, between my 'Living Philosophy' of 1928 and the 'Postscript' of 1938. I wonder whether you would care to read it? I should be so glad of any observations you may make about it, as it does give, in a way, my view of international relations – I fear a very negative one. Have you also written an interposition? I have re-read both your contributions. It seems to me that the first chapters of your new book would be an admirable interposition between your two essays, as war has now arrived and the indifference of the thirties to all international problems, which you describe so vividly in your last essay, has certainly been blown to pieces.

You need not trouble to return the typescript as I have another copy. I am glad to say that Stanley Unwin has accepted it: I had my doubts whether he would!

When spring comes I should like to come and lunch with you and have a talk about things. My nephew, who is a director of the Bank of England, tells me that the war will be over before Easter. What I really want is a stalemate on all fronts: in China, in Finland, and in France and Germany. Then when all parties are convinced that they are going to be ruined by another year of stalemate war, there may be a chance of peace on the right lines.

With affectionate remembrances from both of us

Always yours sincerely

Beatrice Webb

(Mrs Sidney Webb)

943 NUL BEATRICE WEBB TO SIR CHARLES TREVELYAN

Trevelyan had visited the Webbs in the autumn of 1939. 'It is queer that he and we should be in the same boat – Soviet Communism – in the last years of our ourney through life?' (BWD 30 October 1939) On 1 February 1940 she noted that Trevelyan 'is even more confident than we that capitalist civilisation will not survive'.

Passfield Corner

Liphook

Hants

24th January 1940

Dear Charles

It so happens that during Christmas I had to answer, in a roundabout way, what I was thinking about the U.S.S.R., as a link between two essays – one written in 1928 and the other in 1938 published in two American volumes. The interposition with the essay of 1938 has been accepted by Allen and Unwin for an English edition of the English essays, with some foreigners such as Einstein I assume. The American volumes were almost exclusively by Americans. The first had a huge sale, and my 8,000 words brought me in over £100 in royalties; I doubt whether there will be any such sale in Great Britain.

Briefly put, I think the Kremlin statesmen were quite justified in making the Soviet–German pact and sending the Red Army into the Russian part of Poland, where it was accepted by the inhabitants, as against the Polish landlords. But, on the other hand, I think that they have made a mistake about Finland, as the Finnish race is entirely different from the Russians, and they have their own particular type of civilisation. As you will see I had to explain my own outlook on international affairs.

I am very pessimistic about the result of this war: even if we win, which I think is probable, I do not see how we are to re-organise Germany according to our own views of what is desirable in social organisations. Also I think France has made up her mind to dismember Germany and that will be worse than Versailles from the standpoint of permanent peace.

If, later on, you are in London, do come down for the day, I should so much enjoy a talk with you.

Always yours

Beatrice Webb

(Mrs Sidney Webb)

944 PP BEATRICE TO SIDNEY

Beatrice had gone to London for the annual general meeting of the Fabian Society on 17 June and then to see her brother-in-law at Parmoor. Ellen Wilkinson (1891–1947) was a trade-union organiser, on the left of the Labour Party, who became Minister of Education 1945–47; in 1929–31 she had been parliamentary private secretary to Susan Lawrence. Francis Noel-Baker (b. 1920), the son of the Labour leader and specialist on foreign affairs, Philip Noel-Baker, was a Labour M.P. 1945–50, and 1955–69, when he retired from British politics. Geoffrey Wilson (b. 1910) served in the Foreign Office 1940–45, and subsequently in the Treasury and the Cabinet Office. In 1971 he was appointed Chairman of the Race Relations Board. The government had been reorganised under Churchill to include Labour and Liberal ministers. Stafford Cripps was sent as special envoy to Moscow in late May 1940, then became British ambassador to the Soviet Union. The evacuation from Dunkirk had been completed two days earlier; on 10 June Italy declared war.

Passfield Corner
Liphook
Hants

I doubt whether I shall write another letter

18/6/40 7 a.m.

Dearest one

By the time I got to London the news of France's appeal for peace had come over the wireless – and the question everyone raised was what was going to happen to the French navy and would it be surrendered intact to Germany? Poor Bernard looks wretched – Barbara takes it, as you and I do, more philosophically as the proof that 'Western civilisation' is going, going – gone. So did [Annie NcNaughton] who was here to lunch and is a fervent Communist, much engaged today in preaching Communism to the Women's Co-operative Guild.

There were some thirty persons at the sherry meeting at the F.O. [Fabian Office] among them Ellen Wilkinson, Leonard Woolf, Susan Lawrence and an attractive son of Noel Baker: and other young men and women. The Coles were very glad to see me, so were the others and I made a good little speech – beginning with greetings from you, which were very much appreciated. Everyone was dazed – no one was hopeful – a bewildered horror was on some faces and humiliation at being so completely let down by the [? Baldwin] Chamberlain government. The England governing class is suffering from *sleeping sickness* [? my quote's from] Lloyd George. 'Will Russia help' was the question asked me, to which I answered that they would consider their own interests – and I doubted whether that would lead them into the war except in defence of their own territory.

There is no news about Stafford – Isobel may go out later on – Geoffrey Wilson is with him. [*Eighteen words deleted: inaccurate comment on a living man*] Andreas [Mayor], is to be an officer in the Royal Rifles (?) – Henry Cripps reports, and also Dick Meinertzhagen. The latter is put in charge of the safety of Downing Street, and the House of Commons. He believes we shall hold out successfully. He reports gross incompetence among the generals – and an absurd under-estimate of the German equipment and numbers. Altogether my impression is that for the time, public confidence in our governing class is shattered and will take some time to recover. Barbara is coming with me to lunch with the Maiskys, and I go to Parmoor this afternoon (Tuesday) and shall be back with my dear one about 5.0 on Thursday. I shall be glad to get back to my dear one: we must hobble along to the end of the road.

I confess to wishing that end not to be too long delayed – but so long as I have my dear one I shall 'carry on'.

B.W.

## 945 PP BEATRICE TO SIDNEY

Maurice Eden Paul had been a friend of Beatrice and Ella Pycroft when they ran St Katharine's Buildings in the East End sixty years earlier. Beatrice had recently had letters from him; in March 1939 she and Sidney had seen Ella Pycroft for the last time in Exeter on their way to a Cornish holiday. He and his second wife Cedar Paul had been Communists and translated Russian and other works. Rosa Luxemburg (1870–1919), Marxist theoretician, was murdered after the Spartacist revolt in Berlin in 1919. Clara Zetkin (1857–1933) was a prominent German feminist and Communist politician. A. J. Cummings (d. 1957) was political editor of the *News Chronicle* 1932–55. Beatrice was not introduced to him at this lunch and, thinking he was Lord Beaverbrook, 'talked accordingly'. (BWD 19 June 1940) Lord Halifax (1881–1959) was Foreign Secretary 1938–40 and subsequently British ambassador to Washington. Seddon Cripps was the eldest son of Lord Parmoor.

Parmoor
[? 20 June 1940]

Dearest one

I was so glad to get your little note. Also thank Annie for sending me my sponges and toothbrush which I had forgotten to pack.

I had a busy yesterday. In the morning Maurice Paul came to see me: an attractive intellectual old man – and we talked about the U.S.S.R. and old times. He had joined the first C.P. in the early twenties, but had resigned when the Moscow Comintern had insisted on it taking its orders from the Central Committee – but he had maintained friendly relations. His wife had been quite friendly with Rosa Luxemburg and Clara Zetkin. She was still in France in a small farmhouse with some German and Austrian refugees and he had with great difficulty got £50 over to her. He was anxious as to what was going to happen to her. Then Barbara and I went to lunch with the Maiskys – and met Cummings, the journalist – an interesting person. He was certain that there would be a revolution in France and might be an upheaval here after the war against the present governing class who had made such a d--d mess of it. But he was despondent about the Labor Party and the absence of any big man. Maisky was *non-committal* – still angry with Halifax and all his absurd obstructions to Stafford's mission – and doubtful about the outcome of the war. And then I came on here. Poor old Parmoor has become very feeble, in mind and body, and as usual is rather an egotist with regard to the devoted Marion. She is an angel in her devotion to her dear one. Seddon appeared in the late evening – he is very busy about the 'protected areas' between here and Portsmouth. The garden and country are looking beautiful and Marion and I will go for a walk. It is very restful down here after all the talking in London. I have to send the F.S. a report of my little speech for the next issue of the *Fabian News*.

I shall be with you about 5 o'c the day you get this and then we shall be together again. I thought of you listening to Churchill's long-winded speech, which was not well done. Chamberlain is said to be going to resign on grounds of old age. Till 5 o'c.

Ever yours

Beatrice

### 946 BOD BEATRICE WEBB TO J. L. HAMMOND

On 17 July 1940 the Webbs visited the nearby Ponsonbys, still pacifist and believing Hitler had won the war. At the end of the month their daughter died tragically.

By this time there were regular air fights and scattered bombing around Liphook. 'Sidney and I are little disturbed by it.' (BWD 9 September 1940)

Professor Eileen Power (1889–1940) was professor of economic history at L.S.E. Ray Strachey was the daughter of Frank and Mary Costelloe.

Passfield Corner
Liphook
Hants
August 15th 1940

Dear Mr Hammond

I was delighted to get your most kind little note and was glad that you and the Simons approved of my presidential address. I really do believe that there is a future for the reconstructed Fabian Society, with its inclusive membership and its devotion to research. I think so many people who were formerly convinced that capital profit-making was an inevitable economic system for Great Britain and France now turn to planned production for community consumption. Sir William Beveridge, who was here the other day, is very depressed and sad as he had thought (see his pamphlet on Federal Union) that we should be able to dictate disarmament and reconstruction by an overwhelming victory over Germany. Now I think he realises not only that we shall not have that overwhelming victory but that we shall be so exhausted with the war that we shall need a reconstructed social order which will do away with unemployment and arrest a decline of the birth rate.

I wonder whether the Simons are thinking in that direction. It would be so pleasant to see them and you again. Meanwhile you will be interested to hear that I have been re-reading your four great volumes on the Industrial Revolution with great appreciation. I am trying to write a book on the three stages of our pilgrimage: Fabian Socialism, the Decay of Capitalist Civilization and Soviet Communism. I am now attempting to summarize our researches into the Trade Union movement and I have found your books most helpful in their analysis of the Industrial Revolution.

It is very sad about the Ponsonbys; also the sudden death of Eileen Power, who was a great friend of ours, and of Ray Strachey, a beloved niece of Alys Russell.

With affectionate remembrances to your wife and the Simons

Yours very sincerely

Beatrice Webb

(Mrs Sidney Webb)

947 WSL BEATRICE WEBB TO RUTH CAVENDISH-BENTINCK

R. A. Butler (b. 1902), later Lord Butler and Master of Trinity College, Cambridge, was Under-Secretary for Foreign Affairs, 1938–41, and Minister of Education in the wartime coalition government, and then Foreign Secretary and a leading figure in the Conservative administration after 1951.

Ruth Cavendish-Bentinck's brother-in-law, Major Ferdinand Cavendish-Bentinck, was prominent in East African business and politics. Her son, N. F. W

Cavendish-Bentinck, had returned to the Foreign Office in 1937 from a succession of diplomatic posts.

Passfield Corner
Liphook
Hants
September 19th 1940

My dear Ruth

I have been wondering how you and your husband are faring? I thought you had probably gone into the country to stay with that sister-in-law or in some other palatial residence. It is brave of you to stay put in London. I quite agree with you about the scandal of the big unoccupied houses: their basements should be used for the refugees from East London; but we have no access to ministerial authority.

Since the London raids have diverted German planes from camps and aerodromes, which surround us, we live a peaceful life with air alarms which turn out to be merely Germans hurrying overhead to get to the London area. At first we had battles in the air above us, gun fire and bombs a mile away; the countryside is far safer than the town, the chance of being hit living in a small house among woods, fields, hills and valleys is very remote. Sidney and I are not in the least affected; we remain in our bedrooms at night and I walk out whether or not an air raid warning is off or on. But Sidney's stalwart maid valet gets into a wild panic and my two girls were sleepless and my little group seemed likely to break up through mutual irritation. However that is all gone, and as my two servants, who have been with me for 11 years, have found a nephew from Canada, as a soldier here, they [are] able to welcome him when off duty.

I believe we shall win the war so far as resistance to Germany is concerned and probably a successful stripping of Italy of her African colonies; but to reconquer France and the other subject countries and occupy Germany – I don't think is possible.

The Maiskys come here every few weeks and they brought the Swedish Minister and his young wife. Do get to know him. Herr Pritz is a remarkable man, tall good-looking, and very able; not a diplomatist by profession but belonging to the wealthiest financial family in Sweden. He has been here two years. I gather that in a cold and cynical way, he is anti-German and anti-British and inclined to be pro-Soviet. But he is enigmatical and does not intend to give himself away. He asked to come here as he was reading *Soviet Communism*, and wanted to take stock of the authors. Maisky is still contemptuous of that 'pious old fool' Halifax and has many amusing anecdotes about his rooted antipathy to the U.S.S.R. He prefers Butler! What does your foreign office son think? and what about the Boss of Tanganyika?

Sidney is very well and happy, reads incessantly and believes that all will be well *eventually* when the human race has recovered from its fit of Nazi madness.

When raids have ceased to stop transport to and from London do come and spend a day here.

Here are extracts from a letter to me from [S.K.] Ratcliffe which may interest you and your husband. Would you return it? I don't suppose your F.O. son would care to see it – if so do show it to him.

Ever yours affectionately

Beatrice Webb

948 PP BEATRICE WEBB TO WILLIAM ROBSON

The enclosed book cannot be identified. The Robsons had visited Passfield Corner earlier in November.

Passfield Corner
Liphook
Hants
November 21st 1940

Dear Mr Robson

Very many thanks for sending me that little book. As you know Sidney and I are not orthodox Marxists; neither do we think that he invented the political and economic constitution of the Soviet Union. I remember at a dinner given to us by some official organisation in Moscow after Sidney had made a most appropriate speech I was asked to say something. I began by saying that it was strange that the Fabian Society alone among the socialistic organisations of western civilisation had been very sympathetic to Soviet Communism; I thought it was due to the fact that Fabians had never read Karl Marx, that if they had read him they would not have understood him and if they had understood him they would not have agreed with him. There was a dead silence then a few began to laugh. I went on to explain that what we admired was not Marxist dialectics, but the working out by Lenin and Stalin of a multiform democracy – Man as a citizen, man as a producer and man as a consumer led by a vocation of leadership and eventually to planned production for community consumption and the supersession of the profit-making motive by the motive of social services. However I am interested in Karl Marx and did in fact start on *Das Kapital.*

Give my love to your wife. I think things look more promising today than that day you were here, a visit which we enjoyed very much. Come and see The Institution of the aged Webbs again.

Always yours

Beatrice Webb
(Mrs Sidney Webb)

Martin, 'genial,' intellectually scatter-brained, clever', visited Passfield Corner at the end of May: the Webbs had not seen him for several years. (BWD 31 May 1941) Edgar Snow's book, *Red Star Over China*, was the first widely-read report on the Chinese Communist movement. Dorothy Woodman, the companion of Kingsley Martin from the mid-thirties until his death, took a close interest in Asian politics. The reference is to the assets of the Baltic republics which were frozen when they were occupied by the U.S.S.R.

Virginia Woolf drowned herself on 28 March 1941. Writing to her niece Beatrice Mayor ('Bobo') at the end of April 1941 (n.d. PP) Beatrice said that 'a tragic end to the beautiful and brilliant Virginia was almost certain; and a voluntary withdrawal from life is better than a long-awaited mental illness'. Beatrice commented that the Webbs and Woolfs had never been 'sympathetic friends . . . In a way which I never understood, I offended Virginia. I had none of her sensitiveness, her understanding of the inner life of the subjective man, expressed in the birth, life and death of social institutions. Also we clashed with Leonard Woolf in our conception of what constitutes human freedom'. (BWD 7 April 1941)

Passfield Corner
Liphook
Hants
April 10th 1941

Dear Mr Kingsley Martin

Sidney would very much like to know whether you are paying any dividend on the *New Statesman* – and if so how much? – this year. The circulation seems most satisfactory, but I suppose the expenses have gone up and you may not have a good balance. I think of the variety of opinions which are expressed in it and ably expressed.

I expect you are very busy and not likely to be in our neighbourhood? But I need hardly say it would be a great pleasure to see you and talk over the terrible state of things.

I had an application from the Anglo-Chinese Development Society to subscribe to the Company known as the Anglo-China Development Society Limited and I felt obliged at the time to refuse as we are rather short of income and have a good many commitments; but I am so impressed with Edgar Snow's book on China and the desirability of starting these industrial co-operatives that I have sent a subscription of £1 to Miss Dorothy Woodman. We lost seven thousand books in the great fire of December 29th, so we shall have to bring out a new edition of all those books which seem to have a continuous sale and bring us in a little income. One of these is *Soviet Communism* and I am arranging for the cheap edition to be made up into a Longmans edition of two volumes with a long introduction which I have been writing during the last couple of months.

We are living in terrible times and I doubt whether this war will be ended for another two years, especially if we carry out the policy of Vansittart of calling all the Germans 'butcher birds' and add to that abuse, lack of friendliness to the U.S.S.R. If we fail to get the whole-hearted participation of the U.S.S.R. in the peace conference, however much we may be able to beat Germany and even occupy her territory, we cannot prevent her re-arming if the U.S.S.R. remains merely a detached neutral. It is strange that our statesmen do not see that eventuality, and that our government goes on refusing to recognise the incorporation of the three Baltic States within the U.S.S.R. Without that recognition and the liberation of the gold and the ships we shall not get the participation of the U.S.S.R. in the peace conference.

However I do not think my opinion is of much consequence. I wonder what yours is?

Sidney is very well and happy and reads incessantly. I am always tired but I carry on.

What a tragedy Virginia's suicide! Have you heard anything about the reason of it?

Yours sincerely

Beatrice Webb
(Mrs Sidney Webb)

950 BMJL BEATRICE WEBB TO HAROLD J. LASKI

J. B. Priestley broadcast a series of 'postscripts' on the B.B.C. on Sunday evenings. The 1941 Committee was formed to support his radical ideas for post-war Britain. Edward Hulton, publisher of *Picture Post*, and Sir Richard Acland, M.P., were active members. A successor group, Common Wealth, began to run progressive candidates in violation of the party truce, and some were elected as precursors of the 1945 Labour election victory. The Socialist Clarity Group was founded in April 1939 to foster objective study of Labour policy and provide a critical but 'loyal' opposition within the Labour Party. It was disbanded at the end of the war. C. E. M. Joad (1891–1953) was reader in philosophy; he was a regular member of the 'Brains Trust' which was a notable feature of wartime radio. In May Beatrice resigned as president of the Fabian Society. Her letter of resignation appeared in *Fabian News* for June 1941.

Passfield Corner
Liphook, Hants
31st May 1941

My dear Harold

I am engaged in writing a thirty-page introduction to a third edition of *Soviet Communism*. We lost all the Longman edition of about 1,500 copies in the great fire of December 29th, and Longman suggests that as the book is still selling we should try to issue a third edition. This is fortunately possible, as we have about 2,000 copies of the cheap edition still at our printers, Clarks of Edinburgh, and Longman suggests that they could be made up into two volumes, exactly similar to the former editions, and published at a cheaper price, perhaps 18/- or 22/-s. and would keep the book going.

When I get the proof of the introduction I will ask you to look at it and give me your criticism. Meanwhile, could you tell me the most authoritative works on the legal constitution of Nazi Germany as dictated by Hitler and accepted by the Reich when he first came into power; and also the Italian constitution, giving exactly what is the legal status of Mussolini within that constitution? I want it because I am discussing the status of Stalin, first as decided by the 1936 Constitution of the U.S.S.R., and secondly owing to his power as a predominant influence in the Communist Party, the constitution of which I also describe. I have a section analysing the working of the one-party system characteristic of the U.S.S.R. and the Republic of Turkey; and the so-called two-party system of the U.K. and U.S.A., and the many-party system of the German Second Reich, established at Weimar, and of the Republic of France and of most of the political democracies existing in Europe prior to Hitler's conquest.

Sidney and I read with great interest your articles in the *Nation* and the *New Statesman*, and the *Daily Herald*, which we thoroughly agree with. Of course, where we differ from the present government, including the Labour Ministers, is in their overt and continuous hostility not only to the Third International, which I partly agree with, but the internal organisation of the Soviet Union. I think this continued hostility will prevent any permanent peace, as without the co-operation of the Soviet Union we shall not be able to prevent the rearmament of Germany.

What do you think about the activities of the Fabian Society? Their researches seem to me very valuable, but the questions dealt with are very limited and no agreement, so far as I can see, has been come to as to what shall happen after the war. I wonder what you think of the other Socialist groups: the 1941 Committee of which Priestley seems the founder, and the Socialist Clarity Group? I suggested in my letter to the Fabians resigning the Presidency, that the Fabian Society, as the Doyen of the Socialist movement in Great Britain, should have an annual conference of all the socialist groups, just as the trade unions and the labour party and the consumers co-operative movement have annual conferences. We do not want the Socialist movement to split up into endless groups which are proposing different peace aims, and different types of reconstruction after the war.

Kingsley Martin and his friend Dorothy Woodman were here yesterday. Kingsley Martin was very interesting with all his gossip, but I gather he varies from day to day as to what he wants to happen after the war. I feel rather like a ghost from the past wandering in my ruined home. All

I can foresee is what the Canadian soldiers tell me, who come and visit my two girls – one of them being their nephew. They expect that Great Britain will be a nice little green island, fortified as an outpost of the English-speaking federation. The Court, they tell me, will obviously move to Montreal. In return the English-speaking America and the Dominions will permit a wholesale emigration from England into their countries.

However, *we* shall not be alive to see it, but I wonder what you middle-aged leaders will think of it, and whether all your children will emigrate to the western hemisphere and Australia and New Zealand.

Sidney is very well and happy; reads unceasingly – 15 books from the London Library every fortnight, and two books from the Times Book Club every week. I struggle on with my dwindling powers of body and mind to do these small literary jobs.

Remember me to your wife. I need hardly say that it would be a great pleasure to see you down here for tea some day. There is a train arriving at 4.2 and one leaving 6.43. But I expect you are desperately busy.

What a brilliant broadcaster Joad is, but why do they exclude political and economic issues from their questions, where you would have a chance of replying to them? I thought what explanations you have given were extremely good, but the questions refer nearly always to mechanical science or vague metaphysics and give no opportunity to those interested in social reconstruction. Are they excluded deliberately or are there no such questions coming from the forces?

Always yours

Beatrice Webb
(Mrs Sidney Webb)

951 BOD BEATRICE WEBB TO J. L. HAMMOND

Stafford Cripps was given reports from British Intelligence to communicate to Stalin warning of a German attack in late June. Beatrice went to London to meet him on 13 June; their discussion is summarised at greater length in her diary entry for 14 June 1941.

Passfield Corner
Liphook
Hants
June 24th 1941

My dear Mr Hammond

How kind of you to write to me. Unfortunately we do not see the *Manchester Guardian* now because owing to the absence of the second post during the war we cannot get it until the next morning when it is rather late to read it; otherwise it is undoubtedly the best paper in Great Britain and I have always had a great admiration for the editorship even though I am quite aware that the present editor is, for some reason which I do not understand, very hostile to the Webbs. But what does it matter; I never object, indeed I am rather amused, when we get abused.

It would be very nice to see you and Mrs Hammond again. Are you ever in London? Some of our friends come down to tea with us; there is a train arriving at 4.2 from Waterloo and one returning at 6.43. Unfortunately we have no spare room now that my husband's maid valet has to have a bed-sitting room.

I wonder what you and the Simons are thinking about the present state of affairs. The U.S.S.R. coming into the war is a great piece of luck for the British Empire. It is possible of course that the Germans, with their far greater military efficiency and experience will succeed in occupying the Ukraine and then getting the Baku oilfields; but I think they will find themselves bogged there and subject to constant threats by the other eastern army of the south-east in Siberia. I don't think that the Bolshevik government will now surrender to the German demands, which seem to be preposterous and to have been presented to the Soviet government in a monstrously unfair way.

I went up to London to see Stafford and his wife ten days ago; he thought that the war would break out the following Sunday – just a week before it did. I assume that he has gone back. His wife of course will remain in England and his two daughters who were in Moscow have already flown to the British Embassy in Persia. I see the Finns are hesitating before they are ranked as the overt supporter of Nazi Germany.

I have now just about finished my 30-page Introduction to the 3rd Edition and I hope to get back to my permanent job of writing a continuation of *My Apprenticeship* in an account of Our Pilgrimage. I should like to send you the last chapter I have written on *The History of Trade Unionism*, if you would be kind enough to read it. The next chapter is on Industrial Democracy and will give our impression of the more recent development in the trade union movement viewed by our conclusions in *Industrial Democracy*; which were, as perhaps you will remember the dominance of trade unionists as trade unionists over any possible Labour Party. The worst of it is, as I daresay you do too, find the extraordinary excitement of the present state of affairs makes it very difficult to concentrate on historical work. What are you writing now or are you devoting yourself to journalism?

With affectionate remembrances to your wife and also to the Simons whom I should very much like to see.

Yours very sincerely

Beatrice Webb

(Mrs Sidney Webb)

## 952 BL BEATRICE WEBB TO GEORGE BERNARD SHAW

William Maxwell, of the Edinburgh printing firm of R. and R. Clark, had handled the arrangements for the Webb books from *The History of Trade Unionism* onwards. The news that Beatrice had written a new 'Introduction' to *Soviet Communism* coincided with the surge of interest in the U.S.S.R. after the Nazi attack. Shaw wrote an article to accompany a photograph of the Webbs in *Picture Post*. The new edition of the book appeared in October.

Passfield Corner
Liphook
Hants
Aug 2/1941 4 a.m.

My dear G. B. S.

Ever so many thanks for your corrections. I have incorporated many of them, adapted others, and left out some, as not in keeping with my prosaic and factual mind and work-a-day style. I hope to get the corrected proof off on Thursday and shall be greatly relieved to get rid of this d—d task – if not completely exhausted by decrepit brain and tired body. Maxwell, by the way, is probably coming down to spend the day. You, with your brilliant intellect and literary talent, and we with our painstaking scientific examination of endless detailed facts, have come to much the same conclusions about the present embodiment and future destiny of man. I am rather depressed about the future of poor dear England – shall we change our social and economic organisation *sufficiently swiftly* to survive as a great people? Stafford Cripps seems the one outstanding personality who has the new outlook on life – the Labour leaders have been embraced by Churchill who is a reactionary, they can't rid themselves of this one object – to make the best of the Capitalist system, for the aristocracy of labour – and leave the mass of the workers as they were between 1918–1939, underpaid, undereducated, and subject to unemployment and with a rapidly declining birth rate.

However this is the pessimism of an exhausted brain. How is Charlotte? I should so like to see you both again. Sidney is happy and content and reads incessantly – and enjoys seeing the stream of nephews and nieces and old friends who come to tea here every day or two. Ask Miss Patch to write to me?

Ever your devoted
Beatrice Webb

953 ISH BEATRICE WEBB TO HAROLD J. LASKI

Passfield Corner
Liphook
Hants
Nov. 18 [1941]

My dear Harold

Many thanks for your very affectionate note. We were so grieved to read of the accident to your father, with its fatal consequence. The one consolation is that for a man of his age, it is fortunate to slip out of this troubled and depressing world, without the pain and discomforts of a long illness. But you [? will grieve] for your mother.

I am glad you recognise the heroic 'epic' of the magnificent resistance of the Soviet people, with its unity of purpose and personal initiative, due to its *living philosophy* of scientific humanism. I [? would wish] that the Labour leaders, now taking part in the Government, were less prejudiced against the internal organisation of the U.S.S.R., which is also prevalent among some of the prominent members of the Fabian Society. However, it is a hopeful sign that Walter Citrine that arch reactionary is seeing the light from Moscow and is arranging a giant organisation with the Red Trade Unions. Also Cole's book is very good and I am sending copies of it to various friends. What is going to happen to the official Labour Party after we have won the war with the help of the Soviet Union; what will be its declared policy at the next general election? What will Stafford do? He will, I think, not rejoin the Labour Party – nor will he accept office for the Conservative Government. I fear we are in for a period of internal discord and so, I think, is the U.S.A. I wonder what you think of all these questions? We are too old and tired to be of any use – our last contribution is in the reissue of *Soviet Communism: A New Civilisation* and in my introduction to it (I have had four requests from different departments of the B.B.C. to broadcast on the subject but have had to refuse them all – I am too [*illegible* ?tired]). But you will be a deciding factor in the future of the Labour Party. You are on its Executive, and yet you belong, I trust, to its Left Wing? So your responsibility is great! May you live up to it!

Ever yours affectionately
Beatrice Webb

954 UI BEATRICE WEBB TO H. G. WELLS [*unsigned copy*]

Beatrice described *You Can't Be Too Careful* as a 'great' novel by 'a disheartened and angry man'. Wells replied to this letter on 6 January 1942 (PP) saying that in the past 'we wasted too much energy upon mere differences (of method and so on) *in* the Fabian movement that would have been better spent perhaps in aggressive attacks on the fundamental enemy. I and the Blands and G. B. S. were incurable coat-trailers'.

[? Passfield Corner]
Jan. 5th 1942

My dear H.G.

It was very kind of you to send us your amusing indictment of decadent Great Britain with its appropriate inscription '*Preposterous but true*'. That is exactly the inscription which I ought to have inserted in any gift of *Soviet Communism: A New Civilisation* a bare year ago. Today the tide has turned and I am bombarded with requests for talks or messages in favor of the heroic Soviet people: even the Colonel of a neighbouring regiment has offered to send his military car to enable me to address his officers and men on the courage and initiative shown by the Red Army in beating back Hitler's German hordes of ruthless invaders. You will say that this only points the moral and adorns the tale of the decadent state of British public opinion. And in a sense I agree with you.

But what interests me most is your last chapter in which while denouncing the social system you seem to agree with its fundamental basis: of planned production for community consumption, together with its declaration of the Rights and Obligations of Man, its multiform democracy of man as a citizen, man as a producer and man as a consumer, the existence of an elite, and its elaborate popular education. Even with regard to faith in the supernatural embodied in religious creeds you propose the same policy. The practice of religious ceremonies, and the provision of churches of different denominations – whether christian or mohammedan is permitted and in no way discouraged in the U.S.S.R. What is prohibited – and you propose the same policy – is propaganda hostile to the *political and economic* system of the country concerned. That is, of course, characteristic of the little democratic Republic of Switzerland where no Swiss citizen may be a member of the Society of Jesus or the Communist party. As a matter of fact there are 40,000 priests of the Greek Church on the voting register in the U.S.S.R. There are many who are members of the local soviets. This liberality towards vital differences of opinion in the U.S.S.R. accounts for the unity of the Soviet people in the present war.

However, whether you or the Webbs are right or wrong about the desirability of Soviet Communism, as a step forward in the progress of the human race to higher levels of the Good, the Beautiful and the True – will be proved by the events of the next hundred years. Probably by that time *quite different issues* will be the subject matter of research and discussion. Meanwhile I greet you as one whose ideals do not substantially differ from my own – as well as an old friend of 40 years standing. How are your two clever sons? What is the scientist thinking and film artist producing?

Beatrice had produced a pamphlet, *The Truth About Russia*, based on her new introduction to *Soviet Communism*, to which Shaw provided a preface. She found visitors exhausting and confusing. Early in the war she had mistaken the pro-Soviet Dean of Canterbury for the Archbishop, and she sometimes muddled up relatives. The strain of running the household – two ageing maids, Sidney's nurse, a gardener and housekeeper – under wartime conditions was telling on her. She also was anxious about their financial position.

Passfield Corner
Liphook
Hants
March 19th 1942

My dear G. B. S.

Do read Aldous Huxley's *His Eminence Grise*. It is an historical biography of a remarkable father of the church who was at one and the same time a deeply devotional saint and an unscrupulous politician who was trying to secure the utter defeat and annihilation of Protestant Germany. If you were thinking of writing a play dealing with the present situation I think you would find it useful information as it is very documental.

Did you get my letter and the novel by the Irish lady and the periodical with an article about you? If so would you ask Miss Patch to write to me and give me your news and perhaps send me back the book and the periodical.

I wish we could meet again but with the petrol ration and the unpleasant weather it is difficult for us to get to London; but later on if you would let me know when you or Charlotte are in London I would come and lunch with you or meet you at lunch, as I would dearly love a talk with you. I suppose it would be impossible for *you* to come for a night, (we have a small bedroom) and see *Sidney* once again as he would love to see you.

I am just correcting the final proofs of Longman's booklet – *The Truth about Russia*, with your preface – which is most flattering and useful – and with the translation of the New Constitution of 1936 as an Appendix. We have only got paper for 10,000 copies and it is unlikely whether we shall get any more. It is to be published at 2/6. That and the reissue of *Soviet Communism* with my Introduction will bring in quite a nice little sum of money and enable us to go on living here in comfort for the duration of the war. If you are not coming up to London I might, when the days get longer and weather warmer, come to lunch with you at Ayot St Lawrence as Lady Snowden did; if you would send for me at Hatfield and back again.

I wonder what these new restrictions on light and heating are going to be. Do you have difficulty about food? I suppose you, as a vegetarian, get the extra allowance of milk etc. and a plentiful supply of new-laid eggs from home producers at Ayot St Lawrence. I don't claim to be a vegetarian as I want my meat ration for Sidney and my fat rations for the household though I never eat either, but then I consume more of the eggs and more of the milk than other members of our little group. I am glad to say that Annie is too old and Jean too delicate to be called up and as my gardener is 60 and engaged to grow vegetables I think he will be exempt from the Home Guard.

But do tell Miss Patch to write me a gossiping letter. I heard the other day from Katherine Sladen and I hope to see her some time this summer as she is a great friend of a medical man who lives nearby – and is my servants' panel doctor.

We have a continuous stream of nephews and nieces, and persons wanting information about the U.S.S.R. – mostly young – down here for talks – the difficulty is providing tea, or lunch for them – my two girls also have two nephews in the Canadian army here, who come on Saturdays and Sundays for the weekend, sleeping in the girls' sitting room. They are the sons of a well-to-do farmer, and very respectable and intelligent.

Sincerely yours

Beatrice Webb

956 BMJL BEATRICE WEBB TO HAROLD J. LASKI

Laski's article 'The Future of Political Parties in Great Britain' was published in the *New Statesman* of 21 March. Frida was Harold Laski's wife. Stafford Cripps had joined Churchill's Cabinet as Leader of the House of Commons. In March 1941, before Russia's enforced entry into the war the *Daily Worker* had been suppressed by Morrison as Home Secretary for anti-war propaganda: the ban was not lifted for a long time after the British and Russians became allies.

Passfield Corner
Liphook
Hants
March 26th 1942

My dear Harold

I was very much interested in your article on Political Parties in the *New Statesman* of last week. In your very complimentary reference to me you mistake my analysis of the Party system as *a defence of the one-party system.* I expressly state on page XXIII that I do not defend the one-party system and I suggest that when a country has one dominant living philosophy, political parties covering the whole field of foreign and home affairs will be out of date as on the whole they are an unsatisfactory way of ascertaining public opinion still more of leading it. In fact it seems to me that you and I agree on this point as you assume in your article that there will be a unity of opinion against the survival of capitalist profit-making – just as there came to be a unity of feeling in the 20th century in favour of political democracy. There was a time in the 19th century when the Conservative party was dead against political democracy. No one outside the Fascist countries suggests that we should go back to an oligarchy. Perhaps leading members of the ruling class will become advocates of planned production for community consumption and the elimination of the profit-making motive.

I think it is a great misfortune to the present Labour Party that its official representatives in the government and the Labour party executive are so very unsympathetic to the internal organisation of the Soviet Union. For instance this last decision refusing to condemn the suppression of the *Daily Worker* by Herbert Morrison. Also in all their projects of reform they never mention the experience in constructing the socialist state of the Soviet Union. G. D. H. Cole distinguished himself by recognising that the U.S.S.R. was a social-democratic country whatever might be its failure in permitting free thought and free speech. As a matter of fact we ourselves do not permit it and in times of war with the danger of Fifth Column activities I fail to see how it is possible to allow criticism which would injure the chance of the government of the country winning the war. Anyhow I wish you could somehow or other persuade the leaders of the present Labour Party to be more sympathetic towards Soviet Communism. Otherwise I fear that after the war there will arise another party which will be more representative of the feelings and desires of progressive-minded working men and women than the present Labour Party Executive. On the whole I think Stafford is very wise not to join any political party until he sees what is going to happen after the war.

Give my affectionate remembrances to Frida – it will be very pleasant to see you down here some day but I am afraid you are too busy to spare the time. Perhaps we may meet in London later on in the year.

Always yours sincerely
Beatrice Webb
(Mrs Sidney Webb)

957 SU BEATRICE WEBB TO LEONARD WOOLF

Sir John Maynard reviewed the new edition of *Soviet Communism* in the *Political Quarterly*, No. 1, 1942.

Passfield Corner
Liphook
Hants
[1942]

Dear Mr Woolf

Very many thanks for the *Political Quarterly* which I have received after some delay. The review of my Introduction is certainly most encouraging to its author.

Sidney and I agreed with your admirable summary of our relations to the U.S.S.R. in the former number of *Political Quarterly*. It is quite clear that if the U.S.S.R. succeeds in beating back and demoralising the German army and also in providing us with the Siberian airfields to bomb Tokyo out of existence and to invade Manchuria, she will be the paramount power to decide on the terms of peace.

I wonder what you think of that extraordinary agreement made the other day by the representatives of the conquered countries to bring all Germans guilty of atrocity to trial and to punish them accordingly. My reaction was that as we had no international law – having failed completely to create one by the League of Nations – there could be no legal trial of anybody belonging to other countries. There could of course be court martials during the war but after the war they could hardly court martial hundreds and thousands of persons. I note that *The Times*, in a very wise article, made substantially the same criticism. This world war is so much more terrible than the last that I am afraid it will be very difficult to get into the right state of mind especially as to a new international order. I hope you will be somehow or other connected with the group of people who have the job to do.

We should very much enjoy seeing you if you could spare the time when the days get longer and warmer and you are staying in London to come down either in the morning and stay to lunch or for tea at 4 o'clock and return by the 6.43 train to London. We have no spare bedroom now – Sidney has to have a maid valet. But he is always delighted to see old friends and he remembers with great pleasure his co-operation with you in deciding the policy of the Labour Party in international affairs. I am afraid I am not very hopeful about the official Labour Party as it is at present constituted, but then the aged are apt to be pessimistic about the future in which they will not be concerned.

Always yours sincerely
Beatrice Webb
(Mrs Sidney Webb)

958 RPD BEATRICE WEBB TO R. PALME DUTT

Ranji Palme Dutt (1896–1974), one of the leading Communists in Britain, founded and edited the *Labour Monthly*. He had been associated with the Webbs in the Labour Research Department before the founding of the C.P.G.B. Beatrice exchanged a number of letters with him about articles and reviews on Soviet policy. In another detached fragment of about the same date she made the same point again to Dutt. 'It seems to me that you would be more powerful as propagandists of Soviet Communism, as a living philosophy, as *individuals* within the Labour Movement . . . that is a matter for all of you to decide – and not for those, like ourselves, who have thought it wise to be in the inner circles of the British Labour Movement . . . best wishes for our common cause.'

Passfield Corner
Liphook
Hants
May 28th 1942

Dear Mr Dutt

I am sorry a mistake was made in the letter as I certainly only intended to subscribe to your periodical. So please forget about the 10/- and cash the cheque for 7/-. As a set off to this mistake I enclose a copy of the booklet which Messrs Longman is on the point of publishing as you might find it interesting to read and perhaps to review it in the *Labour Monthly*.

I should greatly like to hear what you think of my suggestion at the end of the essay that the Third and Second International should be merged and there should arise a real International Federation of Labour and Socialist parties in which the Russian Communist Party would be represented by Russians and not by Englishmen who are pledged to follow the instructions of an organisation which is centred at Moscow. As I point out the reason for this unfortunate antagonism was the refusal of the International Federation of Labour and Socialist parties to accept Russian representatives of the Communist Party – which was also the case with the International Federation of Trade Unions.

Yours sincerely
Beatrice Webb
(Mrs Sidney Webb)

P.S. If there ceased to be a British branch for the Third International – there would be no reason why the present members of the C.P. of Great Britain should not belong to the British Labour Party, exactly as Bernard Shaw and the Webbs do inspite of being non-party Communists.

BW

959 UI BEATRICE WEBB TO H. G. WELLS

The new book by Webb was *Phoenix: A Summary of the Inescapable Conditions of World Organisation.*

Passfield Corner
Liphook
7/6/42

My dear H.G.

I was so glad to get your new book; I have read it once or twice; I will not bore you with a statement of where I agree, or disagree with its conclusions. You and G. B. S. have the satisfaction of realising that you are read and listened to, not only in the Capitalist Democracies, but also in the Soviet Union, where you are especially appreciated as the most powerful and significant of authors and dramatists of the 19th and 20th Centuries.

I sympathise with your vivid description (on pages 92–96) of your *tiredness* of body and mind; as I feel exactly as you do of living on, though over seventy and over eighty, in this tragic world. But you and we have at least the satisfaction of having lived the life we liked, and done the work we intended to do. What more can a mortal want – except to die a sudden and painless death? I sometimes long for a German to bomb the aged Webbs out of existence – so long as we were both disposed of, without feeling the loss of the other.

Sidney sends his greetings – he is happy and well, except that he cannot go on writing, writing, writing, as I do. He reads endlessly – 15 books from the London Library in a fortnight, and two from the Times Book Club in a week. We have a succession of visitors for tea in the afternoon – Lloyd George turned up the other day – he is *very* pro-Soviet – but gloomy about the state of Great Britain after the war. The Maiskys have been here last week – convinced of ultimate victories, but anxious that we should start a Second Front this year – so as to stop this destructive war in the U.S.S.R. I have only been up to London twice for a year – and then to meet Stafford Cripps and see my other 160 nephews and nieces – 3 generations of them. Altogether I am kept busy – I am not bored, but desperately tired – uncomfortable by day, and sleepless by night – a sorry plight!

Ever yours sincerely

Beatrice Webb

960 BMJL BEATRICE WEBB TO HAROLD J. LASKI

Laski had written saying that the 1936 Soviet constitution was meaningless, and asserting that the U.S. and Britain were effective political democracies. Joseph Davies, U.S. ambassador to Moscow, published an account of his impressions as *My Mission to Moscow*.

Passfield Corner
Liphook
Hants

[*Ten illegible words as headnote*] July 13th/42

My dear Harold

I was very much interested in your letter. We agree substantially in our outlook during this greatest tragedy in the history of the human race. Where we differ (in degree, rather than in substance) is in our estimate of the importance and validity of the New Constitution of 1936 – compared to the old-established political democracies of the U.K. and the U.S.A. Are the Anglo-Saxon Countries political democracies, *in the actual working* of this constitution? I doubt it. In some ways they are more down to earth than the U.S.S.R. and other ways less democratic – even in this *political* constitution. *Political democracy without industrial and social democracy* is a farce. It is only well-to-do people like you and we who enjoy the four freedoms. The mass of unemployed and poverty-stricken people in the U.S.A. as well as in the U.K. are not 'free and equal in the pursuit of happiness'. Also there is the all-important question of *racial equality*, which does not exist in separate states of the U.S.A. or in the British Empire. New Zealand is the one and only exception to this denial of racial equality.

About Stafford – I think he is an enigma. He is a great lawyer and a good man. But he is ignorant about political social and economic institutions. *And he does not know he is ignorant.* That is his great defect.

We like him and Isobel. But we will never become intimate with them. About Americans, I am much impressed with and I wish [? to read] Roosevelt. How intensely interesting is Ambassador Davies' *Mission to Moscow*? A great book. Hoping to see you someday at Barbara's.

Ever yours

BW

961 PP BEATRICE WEBB TO REGINALD POTT

Pott was a longtime member of the Fabian Society. The 'Beveridge Report' – the popular name for the report of the Inter-Departmental Committee on Social Insurance and Allied Services – had created a great impression with its concept of a social security system 'from the cradle to the grave'. The report seemed the one specific contribution to the debate on the post-war condition of Britain and became a touchstone of the willingness of the government to plan far reaching reforms.

Passfield Corner
Liphook
Hants
14/12/42

Dear Mr Pott

We were so glad to get your letter. Sidney is well and happy: he reads incessantly – 15 books go to London Library every fortnight, and 2 for the Times Book Club every week!

I 'carry on'; looking after my dear lifetime partner, and am writing for publication. *I send you our last booklet* – if you have not read it, it will interest you: especially Bernard Shaw's preface about the Webbs?

I have had a good deal of correspondence about the Beveridge Report. I have just sent off a long review of it to the *Co-operative News* – which has a large circulation among 8 million co-operators. I will send you a copy of it if it is accepted. It is both an appreciation of the state and Municipal Health Service, and a criticism of the *Unemployment Insurance* – which if *carried out* (which I think *unlikely*) – will increase the catastrophic mass unemployment, which will happen here and in the U.S.A. The better you treat the unemployed in the way of income, without service, the worse the evil becomes; because it is pleasanter to do nothing, than to work on low wages and in bad conditions, which are provided by Capitalist profit-making in times of bad trade for the millions of low paid, who are not included in the trade union movement. As Beveridge is an old friend of ours – criticism is an unpleasant matter. But physically, I am a wreck and suffer from sleeplessness and intestinal troubles. There is no cure for old age – and Sidney and I are well on in our ninth decade.

The one thing I *long* for, *is a hot water-bottle, which is unobtainable in retail* shops. If *you* could get one from some wholesaler – or other agency in the City, I should be eternally grateful – the stone bottles, of which I have one, do not serve my purpose as it is difficult to refill them in the night from an electric kettle.

How do you find the Fabian Society? It seems to be doing good work. And what do you think of my nephew Stafford Cripps? He seems to have broken with the Fabian Society and also with Shinwell.

Regards from Sidney

Sincerely

Beatrice Webb

962 PP BEATRICE WEBB TO R. H. TAWNEY

On 15 December Beveridge married Janet Mair after her husband's death: he was made a peer in 1946. W. J. Brown, who had defected from the Labour Party with Oswald Mosley, had returned as independent M.P. for Rugby during the wartime political truce between the main parties. Hesketh Pearson's biography *Bernard Shaw: His Life and Personality* was published in 1942.

Passfield Corner
Liphook
Hants
29 December 1942

My dear Professor Tawney

I am so glad to hear from Mostyn Lloyd that you have had a successful operation for your old complaint. I see that Mrs Tawney signed the register of Beveridge's marriage to that remarkable woman – his life-long companion for twenty years. I had the most friendly letter from him inviting me to the wedding – and I replied with sincere congratulations – it is good that that episode is closed. I think he will, like Keynes, be made a peer – so she will be The Lady Beveridge and will appear at Court in a scarlet velvet robe?

About the Beveridge Report: I think it will be an incendiary bomb thrown into the Capitalist system here and in the U.S.A. It will either be, overtly or covertly, extinguished by the great capitalist agencies, or it will produce something like civil war in the U.S.A., France and Germany. Public opinion in the U.S.A. is hostile to the U.S.S.R. and its new civilisation of planned production for community consumption, and the elimination of the profit-making motive. But as the peace will bring in its train, mass unemployment and the decline of the birth rate – far worse than after the last war, the workers by hand and by brain will revolt and refuse to go on working or having children for whom no [?salary] is in sight.

Have you read that interesting *I meet America*: by W. J. Brown M.P.? He is very pessimistic about the Labour Movement in the U.S.A. He had long talks with two old friends of ours – Bertrand Russell and Granville Barker. I wonder whether you met Russell? He has ceased to be pacifist and is all out to win the war. He had an interesting article in the New York *Nation* – suggesting a Committee to be set up by our government and given full power to come to some arrangement with all Parties in India to grant complete self-government to India as a Federation of more or less independent states. The committee is to consist of representatives of the U.S.A., U.S.S.R., Kai-Shek China and the U.K. I wonder whether that is feasible?

Have you read the *Life of Bernard Shaw* by Hesketh Pearson? I could lend you a copy if you cared to read it while in Hospital? I appear to the author as 'cold, commanding and often too right to be pleasant!' There are some excellent portraits of G. B. S. and his friends – the last being a charming portrait of Lady Astor – who is an intimate friend of Charlotte Shaw.

With affectionate greetings to your wife

Ever sincerely yours

Beatrice Webb

(Mrs Sidney Webb)

### 963 PP BEATRICE WEBB TO WILLIAM ROBSON

The 'balloon' was the remains of a parachute flare dropped during a raid in the early hours of 9 March 1943: it had enough material, Beatrice noted, 'to furnish all the household with silk nightgowns'. (BWD 10 March 1943)

Passfield Corner
Liphook
Hants
March 19th/43

Dear Professor Robson

I think you will probably know which is the authority which is *charged with the duty of collecting all the German* balloons which come down in particular districts. We have had one in our garden which we are keeping as a souvenir of the Second Great War. Ought we to notify the authority that collects these yards of German silk and cord? We should very much like to keep it, as a 'souvenir', if this would not make possible a heavy fine? The notice has not been notified to us and we have not heard it broadcast or seen it in the papers.

How are you and your charming wife?

Ever

Beatrice Webb

964 SU SIDNEY WEBB TO LEONARD WOOLF

Beatrice's health deteriorated in the autumn of 1942. She wished for release, but for her sense of obligation to Sidney; in the last months, as her kidney disease worsened she was able to do little more than take a short walk in the garden and spend most of the day resting, listening to one news bulletin after another. She still kept up her diary, as if the habit of writing prevailed to the last though the content was little more than an attempt to catch her wandering thoughts; the last confused entry, on 19 April, gave a vivid impression of the onset of extinction. She died on 30 April 1943.

Sidney sent similar letters in reply to the condolences of other friends.

Passfield Corner
Liphook
Hants
May 4th 1943

Dear Woolf

Very many thanks for your most kind and appreciative letter. I am much touched by all the messages of sympathy I have received.

About all the letters that I have to write, none comes so welcome as your own! Now that I cannot write, I am glad to think that you can.

Yours

Passfield

965 UI SIDNEY WEBB TO H. G. WELLS

Passfield Corner
Liphook
Hants
July 22nd 1943

Dear H.G.

Thanks for your report of the memorial meeting.

Your suggestion of reprinting our book on the U.S.S.R., which is already ten years old, falls to the ground owing to the refusal of the government to ALLOW ANY PAPER. The future will depend on how much money there may be collected and will be determined according to the Committee which the meeting appointed.

Your document as to the Rights of Man is interesting as ever. I put the present constitution of the U.S.S.R. into the nearest form that I could devise. Have you seen *The Truth about the U.S.S.R.* which my wife published last year? I send a copy to you.

The trouble about freedom arises from the fact that all the way from Calais to Vladivostock the power remains in the hands of the policeman. You will find the same sort of irresistible coercive power in a Paris policeman, a German policeman, a Polish policeman and a Russian policeman, whatever the Constitution prescribes. I don't see how we are to avoid this except by some drastic supervision.

Yours truly

Passfield

966 BEAV SIDNEY WEBB TO DAVID LLOYD GEORGE

In 1944, when Sidney was awarded the Order of Merit 'for eminent services to social and political science', he wrote similar letters to a number of correspondents who had congratulated him. To C. P. Trevelyan, on 19 June, he added that Beatrice had left her diary unfinished: 'my effort will be to prepare for the Authorised Edition years hence!' For fifty years he had respected the privacy of what Beatrice had once called her 'Other Self'.

Passfield Corner
Liphook
Hants
15 June 1944

Dear Lloyd George

Many thanks for your congratulations.

My one impression is one of vexation at my wife not being included in the Presentation.

Will you please say that the award has no political significance; 'services to social and political science'.

Passfield

967 PP SIDNEY WEBB TO RUTH CAVENDISH-BENTINCK

It had always been the desire of both Webbs to leave their home either to the L.S.E. or the Fabian Society. In the event, with Sidney still living, Beatrice's wish was carried out by the purchase of what was named Beatrice Webb House, at Pasture Wood near Dorking, as a centre for meetings and conferences. It was opened by the Labour Prime Minister, Clement Attlee, on 13 September 1947.

Sidney himself died on 13 October 1947. After his death Shaw wrote to *The Times* urging that the remains of the Webbs should not lie, as they had directed, in the garden at Passfield Corner, but in Westminster Abbey, to 'commemorate an unparalleled partnership'. On 12 December 1947 the ashes of the Webbs were re-interred together, the first husband and wife so to be honoured. The Prime Minister, one of the ten Fabians in the Cabinet, delivered the address.

Passfield Corner
Liphook
Hants
September 11th 1947

Dear Mrs Bentinck

I am afraid that the difficulty about permits will continue. I agree that the requirements are silly.

The whole world is full of permits and control of people; I am afraid the old ones such as I fall to have to put up with much.

I see you are back at Marley House. I fear you will not be able to hear the Prime Minister opening on Saturday the Memorial for Beatrice. I shall not manage to go the small distance from here to Pasture Wood, as I should have wished to do.

Yours truly

Passfield

# List of recipients

The figures refer to the Letter numbers

# Index

Users should also consult the indexes of Volumes I and II for biographical references to individuals first mentioned in those volumes.

Webb
923.242
W368zl
v. 3
The letters of Sidney and
Beatrice Webb

Box House,
Minchinhampton,
Gloucestershire.

My [illegible] dear Darwin,

Walter [illegible] and I [illegible] rather a gruesome evening at the Playhouse last night — a set of stiff [illegible] of [illegible] & servants dance & sing afterwards. The supper [illegible] & rather [illegible] & there were [illegible]